Legal Theory and the Social Sciences
Volume II

The Library of Essays in Contemporary Legal Theory

Titles in the Series:

The Methodology of Legal Theory
Volume I
Michael Giudice, Wil Waluchow and
Maksymilian Del Mar

Legal Theory and the Social Sciences
Volume II
Maksymilian Del Mar and Michael Giudice

Legal Theory and the Legal Academy
Volume III
Maksymilian Del Mar, William Twining and
Michael Giudice

Legal Theory and the Social Sciences Volume II

Edited by

Maksymilian Del Mar
University of Lausanne, Switzerland

and

Michael Giudice
York University, Canada

ASHGATE

© Maksymilian Del Mar and Michael Giudice 2010. For copyright of individual articles please refer to the Acknowledgements.

All rights reserved. No part of this publication may be reproduced, stored in a retrieval system or transmitted in any form or by any means, electronic, mechanical, photocopying, recording or otherwise without the prior permission of the publisher.

Wherever possible, these reprints are made from a copy of the original printing, but these can themselves be of very variable quality. Whilst the publisher has made every effort to ensure the quality of the reprint, some variability may inevitably remain.

Published by
Ashgate Publishing Limited
Wey Court East
Union Road
Farnham
Surrey GU9 7PT
England

Ashgate Publishing Company
Suite 420
101 Cherry Street
Burlington
VT 05401-4405
USA

www.ashgate.com

British Library Cataloguing in Publication Data:
Legal theory and the social sciences. – (The library of
  essays in contemporary legal theory)
  1. Law and the social sciences. 2. Sociological
  jurisprudence.
  I. Series II. Del Mar, Maksymilian, 1979– III. Giudice,
  Michael.
  340.1'15–dc22

Library of Congress Control Number: 2010926164

ISBN 9780754628897

Printed and bound in Great Britain by
TJ International Ltd, Padstow, Cornwall

Contents

Acknowledgements vii
Series Preface ix
Introduction xi

PART I METHODOLOGY: COLLABORATIONS AND DISPUTES

1 Martin Krygier (1982), '*The Concept of Law* and Social Theory', *Oxford Journal of Legal Studies*, **2**, pp. 155–80. 3
2 Kim Lane Scheppele (1994), 'Legal Theory and Social Theory', *Annual Review of Sociology*, **20**, pp. 383–406. 29
3 Brian Z. Tamanaha (1995), 'An Analytical Map of Social Scientific Approaches to the Concept of Law', *Oxford Journal of Legal Studies*, **15**, pp. 501–35. 53
4 Roger Cotterrell (1998), 'Why Must Legal Ideas be Interpreted Sociologically?', *Journal of Law and Society*, **25**, pp. 171–92. 89
5 Nicola Lacey (2006), 'Analytical Jurisprudence Versus Descriptive Sociology Revisited', *Texas Law Review*, **89**, pp. 945–82. 111
6 Christopher McCrudden (2006), 'Legal Research and the Social Sciences', *Law Quarterly Review*, **122**, pp. 632–50. 149
7 Geoffrey Samuel (2008), 'Is Law Really a Social Science? A View from Comparative Law', *Cambridge Law Journal*, **67**, pp. 288–321. 169

PART II COMMON PROBLEMS: MODES OF EXPLANATION OF BEHAVIOUR

8 Gunther Teubner (1989), 'How the Law Thinks: Toward a Constructivist Epistemology of Law', *Law & Society Review*, **23**, pp. 727–58. 205
9 A.I. Ogus (1989), 'Law and Spontaneous Order: Hayek's Contribution to Legal Theory', *Journal of Law and Society*, **16**, pp. 393–409. 237
10 Lewis A. Kornhauser (1999), 'The Normativity of Law', *American Law and Economics Review*, **1**, pp. 3–25. 255
11 David Nelken (2004), 'Using the Concept of Legal Culture', *Australian Journal of Legal Philosophy*, **29**, pp. 1–26. 279
12 Matthew Noah Smith (2006), 'The Law as a Social Practice: Are Shared Activities at the Foundations of Law?', *Legal Theory*, **12**, pp. 265–92. 305

PART III COMMON OBJECTS: MODES OF EXPLANATION OF LEGAL PHENOMENA

13 Martin Krygier (1986), 'Law as Tradition', *Law and Philosophy*, **5**, pp. 237–62.   335
14 Elizabeth Mertz (1992), 'Language, Law, and Social Meanings: Linguistic/Anthropological Contributions to the Study of Law', *Law & Society Review*, **26**, pp. 413–45.   361
15 Rodolfo Sacco (1995), 'Mute Law', *American Journal of Comparative Law*, **43**, pp. 455–67.   395
16 William Twining (2005), 'Social Science and Diffusion of Law', *Journal of Law and Society*, **32**, pp. 203–40.   409
17 Brian Z. Tamanaha (2008), 'Understanding Legal Pluralism: Past to Present, Local to Global', *Sydney Law Review*, **30**, pp. 375–411.   447

Name Index   *485*

Acknowledgements

The editor and publishers wish to thank the following for permission to use copyright material.

Annual Reviews for the essay: Kim Lane Scheppele (1994), 'Legal Theory and Social Theory', *Annual Review of Sociology*, **20**, pp. 383–406. Copyright © 1994 Annual Reviews, Inc.

Australian Journal of Legal Philosophy for the essay: David Nelken (2004), 'Using the Concept of Legal Culture', *Australian Journal of Legal Philosophy*, **29**, pp. 1–26. Copyright © 2004 David Nelken.

Cambridge Law Journal for the essay: Geoffrey Samuel (2008), 'Is Law Really a Social Science? A View from Comparative Law', *Cambridge Law Journal*, **67**, pp. 288–321. Copyright © 2008 Cambridge Law Journal.

Cambridge University Press for the essay: Matthew Noah Smith (2006), 'The Law as a Social Practice: Are Shared Activities at the Foundations of Law?', *Legal Theory*, **12**, pp. 265–92. Copyright © 2006 Cambridge University Press.

Oxford University Press for the essays: Martin Krygier (1982), '*The Concept of Law* and Social Theory', *Oxford Journal of Legal Studies*, **2**, pp. 155–80. Copyright © 1982 Oxford University Press; Brian Z. Tamanaha (1995), 'An Analytical Map of Social Scientific Approaches to the Concept of Law', *Oxford Journal of Legal Studies*, **15**, pp. 501–35. Copyright © 1995 Oxford University Press; Lewis A. Kornhauser (1999), 'The Normativity of Law', *American Law and Economics Review*, **1**, pp. 3–25. Copyright © 1999 American Law and Economics Association.

Rodolfo Sacco for the essay: Rodolfo Sacco (1995), 'Mute Law', *American Journal of Comparative Law*, **43**, pp. 455–67. Copyrighty © 1995 Rodolfo Sacco.

Springer for the essay: Martin Krygier (1986), 'Law as Tradition', *Law and Philosophy*, **5**, pp. 237–62. Copyright © D. Reidel Publishing Company.

Sweet and Maxwell for the essay: Christopher McCrudden (2006), 'Legal Research and the Social Sciences', *Law Quarterly Review*, **122**, pp. 632–50. Copyright © 2006 Sweet & Maxwell and Contributors.

Sydney Law Review for the essay: Brian Z. Tamanaha (2008), 'Understanding Legal Pluralism: Past to Present, Local to Global', *Sydney Law Review*, **30**, pp. 375–411. Copyright © 2008 Sydney Law Review.

Texas Law Review Association for the essay: Nicola Lacey (2006), 'Analytical Jurisprudence Versus Descriptive Sociology Revisited', *Texas Law Review*, **89**, pp. 945–82. Copyright © 2006 Texas Law Review.

John Wiley and Sons for the essays: Roger Cotterrell (1998), 'Why Must Legal Ideas be Interpreted Sociologically?', *Journal of Law and Society*, **25**, pp. 171–92. Copyright © 1998 Blackwell Publishers Ltd; Gunther Teubner (1989), 'How the Law Thinks: Toward a Constructivist Epistemology of Law', *Law & Society Review*, **23**, pp. 727–58; A.I. Ogus (1989), 'Law and Spontaneous Order: Hayek's Contribution to Legal Theory', *Journal of Law and Society*, **16**, pp. 393–409; Elizabeth Mertz (1992), 'Language, Law, and Social Meanings: Linguistic/Anthropological Contributions to the Study of Law', *Law & Society Review*, **26**, pp. 413–45; William Twining (2005), 'Social Science and Diffusion of Law', *Journal of Law and Society*, **32**, pp. 203–40. Copyright © 2005 Cardiff University Law School.

Every effort has been made to trace all the copyright holders, but if any have been inadvertently overlooked the publishers will be pleased to make the necessary arrangement at the first opportunity.

Series Preface

Contemporary Legal Theory

The last thirty years have witnessed a proliferation of theorising about law, as well as reflection on the very practice of that theorising. As the discipline of legal theory has flourished, so have methodological debates and controversies. These debates are not only relevant to how legal theory understands its own enterprise: its problems and aims, and issues of scope. They are also relevant to many other aspects of the practice of legal theory, and its role vis-à-vis the practice of law and the practice of other related activities, such as legal scholarship and legal education. Further, as the ambitions of legal theory grow, so do questions concerning its relations with other disciplines, such as comparative law, but also, much more broadly, the social sciences.

This three volume series on Contemporary Legal Theory aims to track and project the relations between legal theory and related disciplines. Accordingly, the first volume is devoted to preparing the way, by assembling recent work on the methodology of legal theory. It examines the problems and aims of legal theory, issues of semantics and epistemology, perspectives on morality in the theory of law and issues of scope.

The second volume follows naturally from where the first volume ends, and takes up issues to do with mapping the intersections between legal theory and the social sciences. It is divided into three parts: first, it looks at methodological disputes and collaboration; second, it considers how both legal theory and the social sciences employ a variety of different modes of explanation of behaviour, and the role that these modes play in the construction of theories about law; and third, it surveys how both legal theory and the social sciences might work together to portray legal phenomena, especially insofar as one sets out to study the language of law in its social context as well as the place of laws within a broader context of normative phenomena.

The third volume completes the series by considering four further aspects of relevance to the practice of legal theory: first, its role in the common law curriculum; second, how legal theory has been and may be taught; third, the relationship between legal theory and legal scholarship; and fourth, the relationship between legal theory and comparative law.

Although this series looks back, offering a panorama of the most important contributions made to legal theory in the last thirty years, it does so with one eye to the future. Given the richness of contributions, any selective project such as this one is bound to be a risky business. In that respect, we should stress that we have not aimed for comprehensiveness. Certainly, our selections have been informed partly by the acknowledged importance of certain contributions to the field, and the continued popularity of certain debates, but they have also been informed by the directions we think legal theory may develop in decades to come. This future-oriented aspect of the three volumes can be seen particularly well in its discussion of the scope of legal theory and its relations with other disciplines.

Each volume in the series contains seventeen papers, and is supported by a substantial introduction that summarises and contextualises the chosen articles. Where it was thought to be necessary, we have developed the context in some detail (for instance, as in the case of the role of legal theory in the common law curriculum in Volume III); at other times, we have used our selection to offer highlights of the relevant debates. These introductions are supplemented by selective bibliographies.

If the past thirty years provides any indication, the future for legal theory looks bright. Of course, at least when compared to certain other debates in philosophy, many of the issues that have emerged in contemporary legal theory are but newborns: the great majority of the work lies ahead us. We hope that with this series we are able to provide the future generation of legal theorists with the necessary tools for success over the next thirty years.

We would like to acknowledge the support and professionalism of the Ashgate team. We owe particular thanks to Professor Tom Campbell.

We dedicate this series to the memory of Sir Neil MacCormick, who was to be involved as a co-editor before falling ill. Contemporary legal theory is so much the richer for having had the privilege of both his work and his intellectual generosity and openness of spirit.

MAKSYMILIAN DEL MAR
University of Lausanne, Switzerland

MICHAEL GIUDICE
York University, Canada

Introduction

There are many ways of mapping the intersections between legal theory and the social sciences. Here, we have decided to cut the cake in the following way: first, to focus on methodological collaborations and disputes; second, to consider the affinities between problems in legal theory and the social sciences, especially as they concern different modes of explanation of behaviour; and third, to examine the common objects of legal theory and the social sciences, including, most prominently, the study of language in its social context and normative pluralism. There is, of course, an even bigger literature of the treatment of these topics outside the discipline of legal theory; in this volume, as in the entire series of *Contemporary Legal Theory*, our focus is on the view from within and the prospects for legal theory.

Methodological Collaborations and Disputes

The focus of Volume I in this series is on the methodology of legal theory. Some of the debates from that volume, then, will also be pertinent here. Nevertheless, although some overlap is inevitable, the methodological issues raised in this first part of Volume II are somewhat peculiar to, and also of particular importance for, the relationship between legal theory and the social sciences. The overlap, but also specificity, of these issues is exemplified in Chapter 1, Martin Krygier's '*The Concept of Law* and Social Theory'. The overlap is largely explained by the enormous influence, at least within the recent tradition of Anglo-American legal theory, of H.L.A. Hart's *The Concept of Law* (1961). What this means, in practice, is that the focus of debates tends to be on the advantages and limitations of adopting a Hartian explanatory framework; the question that then arises is whether the social sciences can assist in the advantages and supplement the limitations.

Some of the controversy concerning the relationship between a Hartian approach and the social sciences was caused by Hart's own comments. Famously, or perhaps by now infamously, Hart claimed that his book could be regarded 'as an essay in descriptive sociology' (1961, p. vii). At the same time, as Krygier points out, in other writings Hart distanced himself from the discipline of sociology – for example he said, by way of advice to teachers and students of jurisprudence, that 'the limited time which the student can spend on jurisprudence is better devoted to analytical inquiries than to sociological jurisprudence' (quoted by Krygier, p. 5). Hart, it seems, thought that sociology and other social sciences were not yet sufficiently developed to be of use to jurisprudence: 'Both psychology and sociology', he said, 'are relatively young sciences with an unstable framework of concepts and a correspondingly uncertain and fluctuating terminology.' 'If they are to be used', he continued, 'to illuminate us as to the nature of law, these sciences must be handled with care and with a sensitivity to the types of ambiguity and vagueness, and also other linguistic anomalies, which the student will best learn to appreciate in handling the leading concepts of the law in an analytical spirit' (quoted by Krygier, p. 5). As Krygier notes, most if not all of the traffic here is one way: from analytical jurisprudence to the sociology and psychology of law; there is little, if anything, that 'Hart believes analytical jurists have to learn in the conduct of their *own* enterprise, from theoretical or empirical social science' (p. 6; emphasis in original).

Krygier certainly recognizes, and endorses, the value of conceptual rigour and nuance in analytical jurisprudence, but he also believes that much is to be gained by travelling in the opposite direction – that is, from the theoretical or empirical social sciences to legal theory. For one, Krygier argues that Hart himself could have benefited from a consideration of the discussion of 'social control' in the social sciences. According to Krygier, a key element of Hartian jurisprudence is that law is a means to social control. However, how are we to understand this notion – for example 'what or who controls or what or who is controlled' (p. 10)? It is important to note here that Krygier has the same criticism to make of the sociology and anthropology of law; they too, he argues, have worked with too narrow a range of the social function(s) of law. For much-needed sophistication on this front, then, we need to turn to the social sciences. We need to turn to them not to bolster our arguments but in order to learn from how they imagine social life in a different way. Further, says Krygier, Hart could also have considered how sociological and anthropological research and theory might support, or question, his account of the differing social functions of primary and secondary rules. Indeed, more generally, Hart might have done well to have considered the long-standing debate within the social sciences over the very idea of a social function. With respect to this last point, Krygier notes that out of the multiple functions that law can be said to serve, there may be some that are more significant or universal than others but the selection of such functions among others is a task that requires serious sociological research, which goes beyond ascertaining what people in general perceive (his example is that people who marry do not necessarily 'know (or care) much about the social functions of the institution whose rules they enlist'; p. 15). It is not that Hart's insights about the social functions of law are outright mistaken: it is just that, given their reliance on general ideas as to the nature of social life, they ought to be both informed, and tested, by research and theory in the social sciences.

Krygier also mentions a number of other such intersections between the interests of Hartian legal theory and the social sciences. For instance, Hart's distinction between internal and external points of view sometimes vacillates, says Krygier, between a theory of two different kinds of attitudes and a methodological position as to which perspective it is best to adopt when attempting to understand the social life of law. Understood methodologically, Hart's contribution – indeed, his injection of the hermeneutic perspective into legal theory – is, and has remained, of profound significance for the discipline of legal theory. However, seen as a substantive theory about the attitudes that persons can, and do, take to law in social life, it remains somewhat reductive – for example, according to Krygier, there may be many distinguishable attitudes within both the internal and the external points of view (pp. 18–19; see also Postema, 1998, which is included in Volume I of this series). One might want to distinguish, for example, between the 'bad man', the utilitarian and the foreign visitor within the external point of view or, within the internal point of view, one might think that there are important differences of attitude among the judiciary, the police force, prosecutors, administrative officials and so on. And, of course, one might also add that such differences in attitudes cannot be gleaned merely from the statements made by such persons but from the ways such attitudes are expressed in the practices of these officials. In all these cases, one can profitably draw on the social sciences.

Another intersection – the final one to be mentioned here with respect to Krygier's discussion – can be found in Hart's contrast between pre-legal and legal systems. Only those systems, said Hart, that have secondary rules, and where their officials adopt the internal point of view towards them, have legal systems: all others, including (or especially) primitive (though also, again infamously, international law) systems, are not legal. Krygier is careful to point out that some sociologists and anthropologists have found Hart's account useful in accounting for pre-modern societies. On the whole, however, this aspect of Hart's argument has been happy hunting ground for sociologists and anthropologists. As Krygier points out, much of the viability of Hart's account here lies in the explanatory power of the concept of a rule (as Hart understands it). However, many sociologists and anthropologists have provided at least equally powerful explanations of social life – especially in pre-modern communities – that have not relied on the concept of a rule (or norm). They have done so not merely for the reason that in many cases members of the communities being studied do not speak of their own communities in this way (that is, they do not use the language and concepts of rules, standards and norms). Rather, they have done so more on the basis of a careful observation of the unique interpersonal dynamics at play, especially in small-scale and closely knit communities, where, Krygier says, 'there are many ways of knowing, and being reminded, what is expected, other than by a reliance on rules' (p. 23). In other words, it may be (as Max Weber (1954) pointed out in great detail) precisely in largely impersonal, heavily institutionalized and bureaucratized communities – such as, arguably, the modern, Western world – that an emphasis on rules is more pertinent. If that is so, then to argue on the basis of a distinction between primary and secondary rules that pre-modern communities did not have legal systems is, at the very least, to beg the question.

We have already encountered – simply on the basis of our single, opening essay – a number of intersections between legal theory and the social sciences. The key themes are threefold: first, the benefits for legal theory to be gained by being informed by the rich variety of conceptions of the nature of social life in the social sciences; second, the need for conceptions of social life relied on by legal theorists to be tested by social scientific research methods and findings; and third, the utility for legal theory of the methodological discussions in the social sciences, which are characterized by their high degree of reflexivity in terms of the role of the social theorist as an observer/participant. These themes arise again and again in the essays selected in this volume. It will be useful to briefly point out how these themes are addressed in the six remaining essays in Part I of this volume.

Chapters 2 and 3 – the first by Kim Scheppele, the second by Brian Tamanaha – both offer maps, though of very different sorts, of intersections between legal theory and the social sciences. Where Scheppele's map is largely disciplinary, Tamanaha's is analytical – that is, instead of grouping together insights about law based on divisions between legal theory, sociology and the anthropology of law, and the social sciences more generally, Tamanaha offers 'two fundamental categories of the concept of law', or two paradigmatic 'social scientific concepts of law', and gathers the various contributions under that categorization. Our focus here will be on Tamanaha's essay, but it is worth pointing out just how different (apart from certain classics such as Weber, Marx, Durkheim and so on) are the literatures drawn on by Tamanaha and Scheppele. Perhaps the most striking difference is Scheppele's sensitivity to the political undertones (or overtones) of legal theories and ways of framing the nature of social life (Tamanaha, as we shall see, groups theories more on the basis of explanatory tendencies than on political orientations or reform agendas). Indeed, in being so sensitive, Scheppele reminds us of the many contributions made to politically informed, and politically charged, social theory under the guise of theories of law and legal institutions. Scheppele's essay is not a Cook's tour of contemporary legal theory; rather, it is a masterly survey, managing an incredible range of literature, of the contributions made to social scientific issues by law and rationality studies, critical jurisprudence (including feminist jurisprudence and critical legal theory), the literary turn in legal theory (including postmodern legal theory), various forms of structuralist legal theory (which we shall return to later, in Chapter 8 of this volume) and various forms of legal pragmatism. Her impressive bibliography is almost reason alone for inclusion in this volume.

As noted above, Tamanaha's essay is quite different in scope and spirit. Tamanaha identifies two categories under which he groups social scientific concepts of law: first, law as actual patterns of behaviour; and second, law as a state law model of rules and institutions. This mapping work is already original and helpful, but Tamanaha also has his own theoretical agenda. Although he has developed it in much more detail in subsequent work (see, for example, Tamanaha, 2001), Tamanaha's perspective is already visible here. The central idea of this perspective is that the concept of law is itself a construct, that law has no universal or essential nature but that, rather, whatever it is that people, in any community at a certain time, call law simply is law; 'Law', says Tamanaha, '*is* whatever we attach the label *law* to' (p. 87; emphases in original; for a critical view of this claim, see, for example, Himma, 2004). This debate over the universal or contingent status of any concept of law has already been discussed in Volume I of this series. The key point from the perspective of the scope of this volume is that it is often those who argue that the status of any concept of law is a contingent construction who are also more likely to call on, and be generally more sympathetic to, the insights and research methods of the social sciences.

Of course, one may also say that any construction of the categories of concepts of law – such as Tamanaha's – is itself contingent (that is, that it is itself a construction that can be done differently) and that it is precisely the contingency of this mapping work that leads to Tamanaha's own contingent concept of law. Indeed, it is common in both legal theory and the social sciences for theorists to present two extreme views, as a summary of the literature, and then situate their own view in between them or as a synthesis of them. In this sense, any mapping work (whether synchronic and/or diachronic) of theories of law is itself a theoretical contribution, with important theoretical implications (especially if any one way of mapping the literature becomes established and influential).

But let us return to Tamanaha's categories. In the first – to recall, of law as actual patterns of behaviour – Tamanaha places figures such as Eugen Ehrlich and Bronislaw Malinowski. The key for both, according to Tamanaha, is the focus on actual, concrete usages; they both study social life, he asserts, on the basis of direct observation of customs and habits, and although some of their explanations would make use of the concept of a rule, that concept is not one anchored to any account of formalization or institutionalization; rather, it is but a way of expressing what is stable, regular and familiar in social life. These accounts – and their close kin, such as Marc Galanter's influential account of law as 'concrete patterns of social ordering' (1981, p. 14) – all suffer, says Tamanaha, from the same problem: given their generous interest in 'actual, regularized behaviour within groups', 'all of them are plagued by an ability to identify the distinctively legal' (p. 58). The second category – represented, according to Tamanaha, by figures such as Max Weber – conceives of law as consisting of 'institutionalized norm enforcement' (p. 58). Although Tamanaha does not seem to notice it, it is interesting to observe that the theorists in the second category begin with the very problem that is said to plague the first category; or, differently put, what is a problem for those theorists in the first category is but a beginning for those theorists in the second. Thus, for example, Tamanaha quotes Adamson Hoebel as having said: 'A social norm is legal if its neglect or infraction is regularly met, in threat or in fact, by the application of physical force by an individual or group possessing the socially recognized privilege of so acting' (p. 59). In other words, theorists in this second category begin with a delineation of the concept of law, which then immediately sets the ambit of their inquiry (whereas theorists in the first category prefer to keep the concept of law suspended, perhaps on the back of a belief that law cannot be separated too quickly from social life). Tamanaha associates the above definition by Hoebel – and others in this second category – with the state law model – that is, Tamanaha argues that on such a conception, 'Norm enforcement is the presumed function of state legal institutions' (p. 59). The problem with this concept, Tamanaha says, is that it grates against the intuitions of many scholars that communities without the state law model of political organization – or, even more broadly, without institutions whose specific task it was to enforce norms – nevertheless had/have law.

We will return to the departures within legal theory from the state law model in Part III of this volume. For now, it is important to see how Tamanaha differentiates social scientific concepts of law. As Tamanaha notes, despite the above-mentioned differences between the two approaches, they have a lot in common. For example, both approaches seek 'to distinguish the *real* law from that which merely was claimed to be law' (p. 64; emphasis in original). It is just that one approach thought that 'real law' was to be found in the behaviour of people within the community or social group, whereas the other approach thought it appropriate to focus on the behaviour of legal actors or legal institutions. Helpfully, Tamanaha observes that there are, in this respect, two versions of the 'gap problem':

> One version is the gap between state legal rules (or the rules cited as binding by non-state 'legal' institutions) and *what people in the community actually do*, the rules they actually follow in the course of social life. Many of the concepts of law in the first category highlighted this first gap. A second version is the gap between state legal rules (or the rules cited as binding by non-state 'legal' institutions) and *what the legal institutions actually do*, which norms they in fact enforce and how they do so, regardless of what they claim. Many of the concepts of law in the second category highlighted this second gap. (p. 64; emphasis in original)

Tamanaha's point here is useful, for, as he notes, the 'gap problem' has been a constant companion of legal theory; its influence is visible in such distinctions as 'law on the books' versus 'law in action' or, arguably, in the very research programmes of various forms of realism and various forms of positivism. But Tamanaha's purpose is not merely clarificatory: he traces both of these categories and their specific versions of the gap problem to the 'same fundamental belief' – that is, that '*law maintains social order*' (pp. 65–66; emphasis in original). Whether one focuses on the patterns of behaviour in communities or groups (in the 'social relations themselves'), or on the state-centred forms of institutional norm enforcement or dispute processing, the common element to both approaches is the idea that the function of law is the maintenance of social order. We have already witnessed Krygier's comments concerning both the concept of 'social order' and functional analysis. Krygier called for more reflection on that concept and that form of analysis – a form of reflection, furthermore, that he thought could glean a great deal from the social sciences. And that is precisely the kind of reflection that Tamanaha provides in his essay. We shall not retrace his steps here. Neither will it be desirable, given space restrictions, to summarize Tamanaha's many points concerning other links (empirical as well as conceptual) between the two categories. What is, however, of particular importance for present purposes is how integral Tamanaha sees the role of the social sciences in our grappling with legal phenomena. Perhaps his clearest statement in this respect is the following: 'What needs to be investigated is the complex mix of interrelations among the expansion of law as a mode of cultural discourse, the increasing rationalization of transactions through legal means, and the scope and nature of the coercive activities of legal institutions, and this will require contributions from both interpretivist and behaviourist social science' (p. 85).

An equally powerful argument for the importance of the social sciences for legal theory was made by Roger Cotterrell in an influential essay included here as Chapter 4. Of course, Cotterrell has since developed his approach in much more detail (see Cotterrell, 2006), but the essay selected here continues to be influential and is likely to continue to occupy a central place with respect to the issues being discussed here (for a critical review of Cotterrell, 2006, see Roberts, 2008). Cotterrell's essay tackles a commonly witnessed claim concerning the division of labour between legal theory and the sociology of law. This claim is one in which it is said that whereas 'lawyers and jurists analysed law as doctrine – norms, rules, principles, concepts and the modes of their interpretation and validation ... sociologists were concerned with a fundamentally different study: that of behaviour, its causes and consequences' (p. 89). As a result, sociology of law is thought to be irrelevant to 'the understanding of legal ideas, abstracted from their effects on specific actions' (p. 90). The task of Cotterrell's essay is to undermine that claim, and thus to show the relevance of the sociology of law for legal theory.

Indeed, Cotterrell's argument can be stated even more strongly. Cotterrell does not believe that the relation between legal theory and the social sciences is one where 'social science should be "on tap rather than on top"' (p. 90), by which he means that there is no reason to think that social science can only ever play a subordinate role that never challenges the '*meaning* of law (as doctrine, interpretation, reasoning, and argument)' (p. 91; emphasis in original). This hierarchical division has, he says, been detrimental to both disciplines. On the back of it, Cotterrell notes, both disciplines have caricatured each other: jurists have 'often ignored scholarship expressing well established sociological positions', and social science has 'sometimes treated lawyer's legal understanding as entirely positivistic', neglecting to make room for such experiences central to the legal process as 'interpretation, argument, negotiation, presentation, influence, decision-making and rule-formulating' (p. 91). Making a case for a role for the social sciences, then, requires that one distance oneself from this division, as well as from these mutually detrimental caricatures. But it also requires one to be ambitious about what the social sciences can achieve. In other words, it is not enough simply to suggest that social science can explain aspects of legal doctrine; rather, it is necessary to consider what 'specially powerful' insights social science can provide. It is necessary, in short, to demonstrate the unique benefits to be gained from employing the insights of the social sciences.

It is useful to step aside for a moment here to consider the arguments of those who do attempt to make room for 'law's truth' (the phrase is David Nelken's; see Nelken, 1994). Law, it is said by some, 'interprets social life in its own terms'; it tends towards self-closure and is self-referential (and resourcefully so); it produces its own specifically legal point of view and has 'no need, and no possibility, of doing more than creating its own normative understanding of its social environment' (pp. 93–4; the last quotation refers to the work of Niklas Luhmann; see, for example, Luhmann, 2004). It is important to raise these points as they touch directly upon the very possibility of methodological collaboration between legal theory and the social sciences. Indeed, they have been interpreted by some to suggest that the sociologist of law ought not to focus too much on substantive law but more on forms of legal professional competence. Thus, Reza Banakar suggests that:

> Law is *how* to get things done legally, that is, about tasks which require institutional facts, thus opening up the law to meaningful *exchanges* with sociology. Focusing on law as a practice-based activity places social sciences in a privileged position to describe and analyse legal practice, without reducing it to legally irrelevant observations. Sociology can, for example, provide law with systematic empirical knowledge of the limits of institutional action, while learning from the law about society, and its own paradigmatic limitations. (2000, pp. 283–84; emphasis in original)

Cotterrell, however, is not content to maintain such a constrained role for sociology. His answer to the above arguments is twofold. First, he says, the very idea of law's truth is false. The falsity of the idea, however, does not render false, or any less important, the fact that the claim to law's truth is often made. Indeed, that is the rub of Cotterrell's critique, namely, that it is not to be doubted that 'law is presented professionally as a more or less unified, specialized discourse' (p. 99); it does not follow, however, that this self-presentation also constitutes or guarantees its status. Second, sociology is vital for the understanding of legal ideas, for 'the *only* way to grasp these ideas imaginatively as ideas about the organization of the social world is through some form of sociological interpretation' (p. 95; emphasis in original). The balance that needs to be struck, then, is between attention (and sociology can assist with this) to law's claim to unique self-sustaining existence (including placing this claim properly in its social context) and recognition (and, here, sociology is not only useful, but necessary) that 'Theorizing legal ideas is not a separate enterprise from theorizing the nature of social life' (p. 103). Certainly, there are specific aspects to legal ideas, and to the legal process more generally – but we should not think these aspects are so specific as to divorce law from its character 'as a social phenomenon, a phenomenon of *collective human life*: an expression and regulation of communal relationships; a means of codifying, being systematically aware of, working out, planning, and co-ordinating the relationships of individuals who co-exist in social groups' (p. 103; emphasis in original). All this has a profound methodological implication: there is no distinction, Cotterrell argues, to be made between internal and external points of view; the attempt to make and impose such a distinction is better understood as part of the self-presentation of the legal world. Such a distinction is better replaced 'by a conception of partial, relatively narrow or specialized participant perspectives on (and in) law, confronting and being confronted by, penetrating, illuminating, and being penetrated and illuminated by, broader, more inclusive perspective on (and in) law as a social phenomenon' (p. 106).[1]

A different, but related, attempt to re-imagine the relationship between legal theory and the social sciences is evident in Chapter 5, Nicola Lacey's 'Analytical Jurisprudence Versus Descriptive Sociology Revisited'. Lacey's essay is helpful not only because she articulates 'the mutual dependence of analytic-conceptual and social-institutional aspects of legal theory' (p. 113) but also because she offers a unique perspective of the disjunction between the way Hart practised legal theory (and the repercussions this has had) and Hart's own claims concerning his work being an essay in descriptive sociology. We shall leave the reader to consider Lacey's sympathetically critical account of Hart's approach to legal theory and its legacy (for an equally sympathetically critical review of Lacey's reading of Hart, see Schauer, 2005–2006). What requires some attention here, though, is her specific proposal for a rapprochement between legal theory and the social sciences.

Lacey develops her proposal in the context of three specific case studies: causation, responsibility and corporate criminal responsibility. In all these cases, she distances herself from what she sees as methodological limitations of Hart's approach. In the case of causation, for example, she argues that we need to go beyond an analysis of linguistic data gleaned almost exclusively from appellate case law (this being what Hart and Tony Honoré are said to have done in *Causation in the Law*, 1959). What Lacey would have preferred to see is 'a systematic analysis of the institutional, practical, professional, or social context in which that legal language was used' (p. 133). For example, it would be important, she says, to consider 'the institutional factors that restrict the extent to which judges will appeal to pragmatic or policy arguments' (p. 134) (which itself may differ depending on the matter at hand, for example whether it is contractual, criminal or tort-based). In the case of responsibility, Lacey goes further. Here, she extends the scope of investigation to encompass a historical dimension. Thus, for example, she argues that certain kinds of approaches to criminal responsibility only became possible on the back of other cultural shifts (responsibility based on character rather than on capacity was much more prevalent in the eighteenth century than now and this can only be understood in the context of the spread of liberal, democratic and humanist sentiments). Of course, there were other important 'minimum institutional conditions' involved in the rise of capacity responsibility, which included '1) a systematic law of evidence; 2) regular representation by lawyers…; 3) law reporting…; and 4) a system of appeals' (p. 138). Against that background, then, it becomes inadequate to claim that there is a general, universal structure or content to the idea of criminal responsibility, or to claim to have found such a structure or content in the justifications of decisions offered by appellate courts. And it is precisely in the need for the study of such historicized institutional conditions that we meet the happy marriage of legal theory and the social sciences. In the context of her third case study, corporate criminal responsibility, Lacey makes the following representative statement:

---

[1] For criticism, see Nelken (1998) and Roberts (2008), the latter of whom argues that the distinction is important, as is the very 'aspiration to distanced commentary in accordance with some "analytical scheme" that attempts to remain distinct from folk perspectives' (p. 140). See also Kahn (1999), who argues for the infusion of legal scholarship with the social sciences but at the same time advocates a radical separation between legal theory and legal practice.

If we are interested in the philosophical foundations of law and of other social institutions, we must be concerned with the structure and dynamics of how these social institutions operate and hence (potentially) with literature in political science, sociology, and economics, as well as with the more obviously relevant interdisciplinary literature on corporate governance. And if we agree with Hart that attributions of criminal liability are a legal or political matter and not a matter of logic, we should not follow him in holding that practices or conceptions of attribution can be analyzed without adverting either to the circumstances in which questions about holding collectivities socially responsible are raised or to details about the actual workings of the relevant collectivities. This is because it is a mistake to think that law can afford to ignore insights into the operation of the institutions whose practices it seeks to shape, or that the structure of those practices places no constraints on the development of adequate legal policy. Both policy and theory are, in short, answerable to context. A radical separation between the analytic and the contextual will, therefore, occlude our understanding of law. (pp. 144–45)

Where Lacey makes a specific case for collaboration between legal theory and the social sciences, Christopher McCrudden, in Chapter 6, surveys much of the work that has already been done in this spirit. McCrudden usefully organizes the issues taken up by legal scholars (he includes legal theory as part of legal scholarship) into four research agendas: first, *'the understanding and internal coherence of legal concepts and legal reasoning'*; second, *'the meaning and validity of law'*; third, *'the ethical and political acceptability of public policy delivered through legal instruments'*; and fourth, *the effect of law* ... on human behaviour, attitudes and actions' (p. 149; emphasis in original). What is of great benefit for the present volume is that he goes on to examine whether, and if so how, the treatment of these agendas has been informed by social scientific research.

McCrudden's contribution is valuable also because he reminds us that there have been different models of science – models that have had their own distinct life in legal scholarship. Thus, in one model of science, one 'acquires knowledge on the basis of constructing logically coherent conclusions from elementary principles' (p. 150) – and this is a model that certainly flourished in legal academies during the last few centuries. The second model is based on 'the generation of knowledge by *empirical investigation* of natural phenomena, often using laboratory investigation' (p. 150; emphasis in original), and over the course of the last few decades, and increasingly so now, this model has become more popular in legal academies. Of course, to say it is becoming more popular is not to say that it dominates the methodology of scholarship in legal academies, but a certain shift is discernable. McCrudden's point, in any event, following on from the survey of previous and current efforts, is to argue that contemporary legal academies have embraced 'methodological pluralism'.

It is also important to note that the traffic has not all been one way. While legal scholars have reached out to other disciplines, other disciplines have also become more sympathetic to legal scholarship. Thus, for example, 'rational choice theory', as developed in economics and political science, 'is now more open to the role that institutions and organisations play in individual decision-making' (p. 159), and this has made its insights more readily applicable to legal institutions and organizations. Further, and as we shall see more in Part III of this volume, the emergence of certain objects – such as non-state forms of regulation – has meant that more theorists, from different disciplines, are becoming interested in the same phenomena, also making the research less grounded in specific cultures and legal systems, and thus increasing dialogue between theorists and intersections between bodies of research. A form of multi- or trans-culturalism, then, accompanies methodological pluralism.

McCrudden is not opposed to such a paradigm shift in legal academies, but he is careful to stress that taking legal research seriously can be beneficial for the social sciences. He argues that legal research can make a contribution to the social sciences in four ways: first, 'doctrinal and philosophical consideration of law can help provide conceptual clarity and specificity about particular sets of social norms and social concepts that occur in both the legal and social contexts'; second, careful attention to legal research can indicate that 'Law is not a datum; it is in constant evolution, developing in ways that are sometimes startling and endlessly inventive'; third, without attention to legal research, 'social scientists who are not lawyers are perhaps less likely to recognise when law is playing an important role in the social and economic phenomena they are attempting to analyse'; and fourth, legal research may have something specific to offer when it comes to 'navigating practical decision-making, normative principles, and institutional considerations' in the context of offering specific policy recommendations (pp. 164–66). If one is persuaded by McCrudden, the future appears to be bright for methodological collaboration between legal theory and the social sciences.

To close Part I, we offer an example of a legal theorist who has, for some time, sought to show the relevance and significance of the social sciences for legal theory and legal practice (for more on the use of social science in legal practice, see Feeley, 2001; Nelken, 2001; Mertz, 2008). Already in his *Epistemology and Method in Law*, Geoffrey Samuel had argued that we can learn a lot about legal epistemology, primarily in the form of historical framing and structuring of facts, if we look to the 'schemes of intelligibility' developed in the social sciences (2003, pp. 302–18). These schemes include the causal scheme, the functional scheme, the structural scheme, the hermeneutical scheme, the actional scheme and the dialectical scheme (Samuel drew on Berthelot (2001) for the schemes). In that work, he also drew on other traditional debates in the philosophy of the social sciences – such as the debate between those who favour holistic and those who favour individualistic (or atomistic) accounts of society – and used them to illustrate the law's social ontology (how law cuts the cake of social life; see Samuel, 2003, pp. 320–29). In Chapter 7, Samuel returns to the question of the similarities and differences between law and social science, and in doing so once again places on the agenda the question of legal method. His essay is a response to Berthelot's claim (2001) that the object of law, and legal scholarship, is a body of norms and not an interacting social reality, and that for this reason we can exclude law from an investigation into the epistemology of the social sciences. Samuel's riposte is that if we understand legal method as we should understand it we will find much more in common with the social sciences than first meets the eye.

The key, for Samuel, is not to look at the law as a system of propositions but rather to consider law as a history of changing methods. Here, Samuel leans again on the idea that the very same schemes of intelligibility that exist in the social sciences also exist in legal method – for example 'the dialectical scheme finds expression … in a whole range of conceptual and category dichotomies such as the distinctions between public and private law, real and personal rights, corporeal and incorporeal property and so on' (p. 179). Indeed, in some cases it may even be in the law itself that these schemes originated. Thus, for example, Samuel traces the notion of an interest (a key concept in economic theory), which he associates with the structural scheme, to the jurist Paul telling 'us that it is not just the owner of stolen property who has the *actio furti* but anyone who has an "interest" in the thing, such as a hirer' (p. 181). The point, in any event, is not to argue for the historical priority of legal concepts vis-à-vis social scientific concepts but to show how if one thinks about legal method in a certain way, then drawing on the social sciences will not only be useful but perhaps inevitable.

Samuel places great emphasis on the diachronic dimension of legal method: he constantly reaches back to the Roman jurists and in so doing traces the genealogy of modern legal concepts and models. Samuel's point is that it is only when we extend our understanding of law and legal method in this historical way that we will avoid making of modern law a caricature (as we do when we present it simply as a system of propositions). Much of legal theory, however, according to Samuel, does not go that way. The emphasis in contemporary times is on 'a static or synchronic view', on law as a momentary system (p. 190; for an argument for the vital importance of historical jurisprudence, see also Berman, 1988). All too often, Samuel notes, the contemporary law student is not invited 'to examine a statute or a judgement as a signifier for a deep cultural mentality; what the student is invited primarily to do is to read a legal text in such a way that she will know what the law "is" and be able to apply it to relevant factual situations' (p. 191). Samuel calls this approach to law and legal education one that operates under 'an authority paradigm', where hermeneutics gives way to 'conceptual causality' (p. 193). He argues that even much of legal philosophy 'has largely devoted itself to identifying, and thus implicitly supporting the authority of, the "valid" source of the normative propositions expressed in' legal texts (p. 194). To avoid drowning in the authority paradigm – and thereby also divorcing the study of law from the social sciences – one needs to develop both a diachronic (historical) and a synchronic (comparative) sensitivity to law and legal method.

It can be seen, then, that there are at least two ways of proceeding here to make social sciences relevant to legal theory. One can either transform one's understanding of legal rules, principles and concepts – that is, come to see them (perhaps from a historical/comparative perspective) as ways of imagining, or constructing, the social world – or one can see legal rules, principles and concepts – let us say, the body of positive law – as sitting within a larger realm of social reality and cultural life, which includes 'master trends and dominant features of the social landscape' (such as, in contemporary times, the increasing legal significance of civil society, NGOs and the like; Selznick, 2003, pp. 179–80). Of course, ways of imagining, or constructing, the social world, as well as certain forms of institutionalization of legal phenomena, are not themselves without moral and political significance. For Selznick, for example, one 'cannot separate positive law from debatable principles of fairness, truth-finding and morality. The more attention we give', he says (and he develops this in detail in Selznick, 1992), 'to basic legal principles such as due process of law, contractual obligation, or fiduciary duty, the harder it is to draw a bright line between distinctively legal norms and other social, intellectual, or even theological standards, such as moral equality, social mores, or parental authority and responsibility' (2003, p. 179). Selznick himself is hopeful that legal institutions can become more responsive, as long as we, scholars and theorists of the law, exhibit 'fidelity to context' – that is, if we look not, for example, at rights in the abstract but consider certain rights with respect to the special needs of families, business enterprises or democratic institutions (2003, p. 184; of course, more than that is required for responsive law, see Nonet and Selznick, 2001). Others place more hope in creating a critical space. Scott Veitch (2007), for example, has drawn on sociology and social theory to make an argument that certain macro-forces, such as the division of labour, the rise of individualism and the separation of the political and economic spheres – all of which lead to the compartmentalization of responsibility (in the form of role responsibility) – have the effect that rather than organizing responsibility, the law becomes ever better at instituting (while also making us feel good about or at least blind to) irresponsibility. In Veitch's case, then, the social sciences can assist in distancing ourselves from some of the self-serving self-presentations of the legal system. The opportunities here for matching and mixing legal, moral and political theory and the theoretical and empirical social sciences are rich indeed.

Common Problems: Modes of Explanation of Behaviour

We have introduced some of the major issues that either make possible or make difficult collaboration between legal theory and the social sciences. It is time now, in this part and the next, to show how, with respect to two domains (the explanation of behaviour and the explanation of legal phenomena), legal theorists have looked towards the social sciences for assistance. In Part II we consider how both legal theory and the social sciences deal with the problem of what kinds of explanations of behaviour may be suited to what ends – and, in particular, what kinds of explanation of behaviour may be of particular use in making sense of, including evaluating, the behaviour of peoples in legal systems, including both citizens and officials.

The first point to make is to observe the sheer diversity of approaches to modes of explanation of behaviour. Although certain modes of explanation of behaviour have been particularly robust in legal theory – for example the approach of practical reason, as in the work of Hart and as developed by Joseph Raz – more and more legal theorists are now drawing on approaches developed in the social sciences. Indeed, the social sciences themselves are undergoing many radical changes, with an increasing number of links being made with the cognitive neurosciences and the affective sciences. One example is the growing field of social cognition, which has drawn on the embodied, embedded strands in cognitive neuroscience or on externalist and enactive strands in the philosophy of mind and perception (see, for example, Di Paolo, 2009, which is part of a special issue on enactive social cognition in *Phenomenology and the Cognitive Sciences*). Although these approaches have only resulted in small ripples in the legal academy, one can safely predict that this will soon change (see, for example, Lane *et al.*, 2007, who extend the model of implicit social cognition to law). More and more legal scholars, and others interested in legal policy, then, are drawing on models of explanation of behaviour that develop somewhere in between the social and the natural sciences: for example, models such as that of situationism (see, for example, Benforado and Hanson, 2008) or, as noted above, the affective sciences (for an account of criminal punishment and the social emotions, see, for example, Rodogno, 2009; and for legal education, see, for example, Lerner, 2004).

Much remains to be done in the context of legal theory specifically (rather than, in a broader sense, legal scholarship). Theories of legal reasoning – especially of judicial behaviour – are the obvious forums in which the above-mentioned models can be (and to some extent have been) applied but, as we shall see below, they can also be of relevance and importance in tackling such standard legal theoretical problems as the normativity of law or the authority or legitimacy of legal institutions. In other words, models of explanation of behaviour are relevant not simply in a direct way, where they inform our understanding of the way legal officials and citizens behave, but also in an indirect way, in the sense in which we arguably always and already have a model of behaviour in mind when tackling virtually any legal theoretical problem.

This last point is worth dwelling on for a moment. If it is, for example, an important part of our theory of law that the law functions to provide exclusionary reasons (as in the work of Raz – for example Raz, 1990), then we need to be mindful that this may already narrow down the models of behaviour we have either assumed or posited. Of course, even within a model of behaviour where persons are conceived of as responsive to reasons, there is still a great deal of room for different approaches (depending, for example, on how large a role one wants to leave for the emotions, for institutional path dependence, for interpersonal dynamics and so on). But being mindful of the fact that each treatment of any legal theoretical problem is likely to be supported by and to promote some mode of the explanation of behaviour is useful, even if only to realize there are alternatives (and perhaps thereby to avoid overstating the case for one's own preferred mode). Thus, in some instances, we may wish to appeal to other kinds of capacities in persons (that is, capacities other than the responsiveness to reasons) – for example we may wish to appeal to the capacities of persons to act spontaneously and unreflectively (yet intentionally), or we may wish to appeal to the capacities of persons to imitate others or to empathize with others and so on (for a detailed discussion of this notion of appealing to different capacities as part of efforts to reform institutional culture, see Del Mar and Onazi, 2008). Or we may want to say that only a small but vitally important part of the experience of legal life – whether in legal institutions or in legal systems more generally – is a matter of responsiveness to reasons (perhaps precisely when things go wrong or expectations are frustrated in some way). Of course, even such divisions as the ones mentioned above between reason and emotion or reflection and spontaneity are already part of a certain manner of understanding behaviour.

Being aware, then, of the variety of modes of explanation of behaviour can help make one's legal theory more nuanced, more modest and thereby also, arguably, more persuasive. It can also make one more careful about proposing policies based on certain 'solutions' to legal theoretical problems. If that is so, then the question may be asked just where legal theorists can look for a sense of the well-developed, well-articulated diversity of approaches on offer. And it is here that one can answer with some confidence: to the social sciences. In an earlier work Maksymilian Del Mar (2008) has offered an initial map of such modes of explanation of behaviour in the social sciences based on 'spatio-temporal objectification'. The map provides nine different modes of explanation of behaviour: first, a mode that focuses on short-term internal explanations, such as those that appeal to reasons, deliberation and decision-making; second, a mode that focuses on long-term internal explanations, such as habits, dispositions and skills; third, a mode that emphasizes ongoing internal phenomena, such as the notions of personality and character; fourth, a mode that looks at short-term external factors, such as certain institutional spaces and procedures within those spaces; fifth, a mode that points to long-term external conditions, such as systems, structures and institutions; sixth, a mode that considers ongoing external factors, such as institutional ways of life or organizational culture; seventh, a mode that emphasizes short-term intersubjective phenomena, such as communication, discourse and argumentation; eight, a long-term intersubjective mode that focuses on paradigms and epistemes; and ninth, an ongoing intersubjective mode that looks at traditions, practices and social imaginaries (a diagram is available in Del Mar, 2008, p. 140). In all these cases one can add references to the social sciences – for example, in the case of paradigms and epistemes one can look to the work of Michel Foucault; in the case of communication, to the work of Jurgen Habermas; in the case of traditions, to Edward Shils; in the case of dispositions, to Pierre Bourdieu and so on. On the basis of this map alone one can see just how diverse, nuanced and rich modes of explanation of behaviour can be (certainly more rich than, say, a simple divide between reflective and unreflective action or between agency and structure – though to say this is not to deny that these divisions can still themselves be very useful for certain purposes).

The essays we have selected here all reflect this diversity and thus also indicate points of intersection, with respect to the need for an explanation of behaviour, between legal theory and the social sciences. Chapter 8, by Gunther Teubner, is directly informed by a string of social theorists: Habermas, Foucault and Luhmann. What they all have in common, says Teubner, is that they seek 'to replace the autonomous individual, not with supra-individual entities, but with communicative processes'; however, he says, 'They differ ... in their identification of the new cognitive unit' (p. 210). In the case of Habermas, it is consensus and intersubjectivity; in the case of Foucault, it is historically contingent power/discourse constellations; and in the case of Luhmann, individuals are conceptualized as communicative artefacts, which are 'a product of self-observation of social autopoiesis' (p. 210). Teubner draws on these theorists in the name of sketching a 'constructivist legal epistemology', though it is important to recall here that both Habermas and Luhmann (Foucault only ever in patches) themselves develop their own theory of law based on their distinct modes of the explanation of behaviour (Luhmann, 2004; Habermas, 1996).

Drawing on these theorists, Teubner asserts that 'law is communication and nothing but communication' (p. 217) – that is, put differently, the 'basic elements' of a legal system 'are communications, not rules'; or yet differently again, 'Law as an autopoietic social system is made up neither of rules nor of legal decisionmakers, but of legal communications, defined as the synthesis of three meaning selections: utterance, information, and understanding' (pp. 217–18). The legal world is not a world of individuals (and what they had for breakfast), nor is it a world of bodies of propositions; rather, it is a world of discourse (one of many such discourses in the social world). Teubner's (as indeed Luhmann's) account has been influential, even if somewhat marginal, with a whole new generation of legal theorists conceiving of 'law as communication' (see, for example, the papers collected in Hoecke, 2002). Arguably, this conception could not have been achieved without serious collaboration with the social sciences; indeed, a theory of law as communication is also a significant contribution to social science.

A very different legacy is the subject of our second selection. In Chapter 9, A.I. Ogus offers a helpful exposition, but also a moral critique, of a legal theory based on Friedrich von Hayek's theory of society. As Ogus notes, Hayek's remit was wide-ranging: he made contributions to political and economic philosophy, as well as epistemology. Of course, he also developed a theory of law, most especially in his three-volume *Law, Legislation and Liberty* (1973, 1976 and 1979), though Ogus believes that an evolutionary theory of law can and should also draw on Hayek's general theory of society.

We will not rehearse Ogus's step-by-step articulation of Hayek's contribution and its relevance for law, but it is worth pointing out that at the heart of Hayek's corpus is a mode of explanation of behaviour that urges us to acknowledge the limitations of explicit human knowledge and reason. For Hayek, individuals who make decisions do so on the basis of limited information; it is not possible, nor indeed desirable, for persons to attempt to exhaustively plan the creation and maintenance of social order. The human mind, for Hayek, does not stand above the rest of nature and social life, as if lord and master of all beneath it; rather, it is very much part of a spontaneously emerging and exogenous order. One obvious example of such a spontaneous order was the market; another, equally if not more powerful for Hayek, was the common law. For it is within the common law that one gets the clearest sense of law-making, and thus the growth and development of law as 'a continuous, adaptive process dealing with unforeseen consequences' (p. 240). Ogus is in favour of Hayek's 'explanatory model of the development of political and legal institutions' (p. 250), though he is much less keen – indeed, he is forcefully critical of – what he sees as Hayek's excessive insistence on the value of liberty. The argument has many more elements to it but what is important to highlight here is that Hayek's ideas, even if not explicitly drawn on in legal theory (two other exceptions are Amstutz (2008) and Ratnapala (1993)), have remained important, not only in the continually dominant strand of liberalism but also in the focus on common-law decision-making in the great majority of Anglo-American legal theory (as, for example, in the cases of Ronald Dworkin or Gerald Postema, the latter of whom writes directly on, and draws a legal theory from the virtues of, the common law; see, for example, Postema, 1986).

Chapter 10 is offered here as a representative example of the intersection between the enormously influential (especially in the US) law and economics approach and legal theory. The specific problem that Lewis Kornhauser turns to is the normativity of law, and his essay offers a neat contrast of traditional jurisprudential answers to this problem and an answer that can be gleaned from the law and economics approach. The problem of legal normativity, as Kornhauser proposes to understand it, is 'What role should legal rules play in an agent's practical deliberations?' (p. 256). As Kornhauser notes, the problem of legal normativity is, in fact, many different problems and is understood differently, even within those quarters of legal theory that take a predominantly practical reason approach to many traditional legal theoretical problems. Thus, it can mean: 'What reason does an agent have to obey the law?' or 'When is an agent justified in obeying the law?' (p. 256, fn. 2). Indeed, it may be thought that in some cases the problem of the normativity of law is more like a litmus test for the evaluation of the practical and moral guidance that any one rule or principle can provide. (For practical guidance, see Endicott's attempt (2005) to argue that the vagueness of certain rules or principles does not necessarily impede, and may even enhance, their practical operation; and for moral guidance, see, for example, Finnis, 2007 and Gur, 2007.) For others still, the very problem of the normativity of law can help us see how different subjects experience the law in different ways (for example, consider the distinction made by Giudice (2005) between norm-subjects and norm-subjecteds). However one sees it, the problem of legal normativity is certainly a fertile ground for discussion of the relevance of social scientific modes of explanation of behaviour for legal theory.

Kornhauser's essay is also helpful for its reminder of the social norms literature, which has often been influenced by an economics-driven approach and which has also become important for legal theorists (and legal scholars generally). Again, the use made by legal theorists of (and also their contributions to) the social norms literature has been particularly popular in the US, with prominent figures being Cass Sunstein, Eric Posner, Dan Kahan, Richard McAdams, Robert Cooter, Robert Ellickson and Lawrence Lessig (for a neat overview with references to these legal scholars, see Etzioni, 2000). Of course, to list them all in one breath is not for a moment to suggest that their views are even remotely similar – for example, consider Ellickson's plea (1989) for 'bringing culture and human frailty to rational actors'. Of course, the reception within the legal academy of the social norms literature can itself be seen as part of the 'law and society' movement, of which there are too many different strands to address here (a recent overview is provided by Friedman (2005); we do not address it specifically here for that would fall more within the scope of a volume on legal scholarship and the social sciences).

Chapter 11 is David Nelken's account of how the concept of legal culture can be used in understanding (as well as comparing) legal systems (Nelken has for a long time been known as an advocate of the comparative sociology of law). The concept of legal culture can, of course, be interpreted in a great many different ways, but it does tend to point to a certain kind of sensitivity when it comes to the mode of explanation of behaviour. That sensitivity is one that manifests itself by looking for robust patterns of social behaviour, rather than, for example, isolating and making much explanatory noise out of any one instance of rule-following. Of course, as Nelken says, legal culture is not confined to the external observations of conduct; it can be interested also, or even predominantly, in attitudes, mentalities, aspirations and so on. This sensitivity is also one that has certain important repercussions for how one conceives of the scope and ambitions of legal theory. As Nelken notes, 'The sort of investigations in which the idea of legal culture finds its place are those which set out to explore empirical variation in the way law is conceived and lived rather than to establish universal truths about the nature of law'; 'to map', he continues, 'the existence of different *concepts* of law rather than establish *the* concept of law' (p. 280; emphasis in original; Nelken here refers to Tamanaha, 2001).

This attention to everyday experience of living under and within a legal system has been picked up by many other legal theorists. Some, such as Marc Hertogh, have drawn on figures such as Eugen Ehrlich and sought to develop an account of 'legal consciousness', utilizing social scientific methods in doing so (see Hertogh, 2004; see also Hertogh, 2009 for a collection of essays inspired by Ehrlich; Nelken himself has a chapter in that collection). This focus on everyday experience overlaps with the literature on legal and normative pluralism (for example, see Jutras, 2001), which we will return to in Part III of this volume. Historically, within the tradition of legal theory, this approach also has close affinities with Lon Fuller's approach to law (even this legacy is only rarely acknowledged these days), which was always heavily insistent on seeing law as deeply part of human interaction (see, for example, Fuller, 1969; indeed, it is important to keep in mind, as is evident in the 1969 essay, just how much Fuller drew on the social sciences in developing his theory of law). The point, in any event, in this context is to notice how much of the divide in focus and interest in legal theory is dependent on what kind of mode of explanation of behaviour one will tend to favour. It is a further point to observe that much of the literature on legal culture – as Nelken surveys it – draws on social scientific insights rather than insights based in analytical philosophy.

Our final essay in this part switches gear somewhat, back to a central problem of analytical legal theory, namely that of the alleged conventionality of the Hartian rule of recognition (or secondary rules more generally). Chapter 12, by Matthew Noah Smith, is particularly relevant for our purposes here because it reminds us that as much as legal positivists may place emphasis on explicitly formulated legal propositions and their chains of validity, they also – once again, at the level of the function of secondary rules – confront the question of how to conceive of social life. In other words, it is misleading to criticize legal positivists for reifying rules and principles at the expense of less easily quantifiable or graspable features of social life, especially if one notices the incredibly fertile debate over the nature of social practices right at the heart of legal positivism. Typically, though, the attempts of legal positivists such as Gerald Postema, Jules Coleman, Scott Shapiro and Andrei Marmor to articulate the conventionality of secondary rules have drawn on philosophical sources, such as Robert Brandom, David Lewis and Michael Bratman, rather than social scientific ones. Even Marmor's latest book-length consideration of the topic (2009) has a very narrow range of references, limited largely to analytical social theorists (like Margaret Gilbert) and philosophers (such as John Searle).

As a result, what tends to happen – as Smith notices – is that the account of social practices presumed by legal positivists, and those they draw on in the analytical tradition, paints a picture of social life that is over-intellectualized, typically demanding a great deal of consensus as well as conscious and deliberative mind-reading. Put differently, Smith argues that the rich accounts of shared cooperative activity developed by Bratman simply do not exist at the foundations of law (although they may exist in other social contexts). Smith's account of Bratman's notion of shared agency (1999) reveals that participants in a Bratmanian shared activity must, among other things, be in conceptual and epistemic agreement, and be committed to that conceptual and epistemic agreement. As Smith notes, anyone who notices how rife disagreement is in legal institutions might get reasonably anxious about the applicability of Bratman's model to the conventionality of secondary rules (it should be noted here that Bratman himself does not attempt, nor does he even encourage, the extension). As Smith further notes, one has good reason to be sceptical about whether 'shared activity is possible only in cases of explicit deliberative agency in which the agent reflects on all her reasons and then, based upon a careful consideration of all of them, identifies what it is to which the reasons recommend she ought to be committed, and she so commits herself' (p. 331, fn. 76). The social sciences have been sensitive to the social fluency of unreflective action for a long time; what is interesting (perhaps even somewhat dispiriting) is that for certain legal theories, operating with certain modes of explanation of behaviour, reminders of the spontaneity and even automacy of action should come as such a surprise.

Common Objects: Modes of Explanation of Legal Phenomena

Part III focuses on modes of explanation of legal phenomena, canvassing approaches within legal theory that have drawn on the insights and methods of the social sciences.

We begin with an influential essay by Martin Krygier, whom we have already encountered in the first part of this volume. In Chapter 13, Krygier laments the lack of concepts in legal theory 'which address the *traditionality* of law and life' (p. 337; emphasis in original). He does not denigrate, but he does distinguish his own position from those strands in legal theory that have conceived of law 'as a species of ... commands, norms, rules, rules-and-principles, principles and policies' (p. 335). In its most general terms, his 'project' conceives of law as 'a profoundly traditional social practice' (p. 337). Krygier acknowledges that the project of conveying law's traditionality is a large one, and he confines himself in the essay to examining three of its elements: the pervasiveness of traditionality in legal systems, the presence of change within the very concept of traditionality, and the notion that 'tradition is inescapable in law' and that, although not always, this is 'frequently ... a good thing' (p. 338). In order to establish the first of these, Krygier posits three characteristics of tradition: 1) its pastness; 2) its authoritative presence; and 3) the fact that it is transmitted.

We will not elaborate on these points here – the essay speaks for itself – but it will be useful to indicate how, in some of his later work, Krygier has extended this general model, which is clearly informed by social theory and the social sciences, to specific aspects of legal systems. A good example of this extension is his 'Traditionality of Statutes' (1988). There, Krygier continues to press home the point that his thesis is not merely that 'law includes traditions' but that 'legal systems should be understood as traditions' (1988, p. 20). Further, Krygier is at pains to point out that his thesis is not to be geographically and historically delimited – that is, it applies equally to all legal systems, and it ought not to be thought that it is only capable of explaining the phenomena of custom, case law and precedents and not contemporary statutes. In this 1988 essay specifically, he tackles statutory law, which he sees both as an important contemporary phenomenon (he says that both common law and civil law systems are 'submerged' in statutory law) and as a challenge (that he believes he can meet) for his concept of traditionality. A brief summary will indicate how his general model for explaining legal phenomena applies to a specific instance of a popular legal form.

Krygier does not depart from a characterization of statutes as 'deliberately made ... at a particular time', possessing 'legal authority' that 'stems from formal sources not historical origins' (1988, p. 23). He does not disagree with views that suggest that statutes 'need not refer to what went before' or that they 'can change the legal landscape swiftly, radically and broadly' (Krygier, 1988, p. 24). The kernel of his argument for the traditionality of statutes lies in the idea that statutes are 'situated in and deeply affected by contexts which they presuppose, from which they cannot escape, and which make it possible for them to have such effects as they do' (Krygier, 1988, p. 27). For Krygier, the 'facts' that statutes are 'conceived and born into a world they did not make' and that 'they are designed to control the behaviour of large numbers of people, in a variety of circumstances, that they do not know' have important consequences (1988, p. 27).

What do statutes presuppose? First of all, and most obviously, they presuppose language – but it is important to see that language, for Krygier, is made up of activities: 'ways of speaking and writing, and ways of thinking about, reading, interpreting ... etc.' (1988, p. 27). Conceptualizing language in this manner also makes it inseparable from the 'particular community of speakers and readers' from which the statute emerges (Krygier, 1988, p. 27). In the case of statutes, which use 'legal language', their meaning is given life and dwells in the activities of the particular community of lawyers who, often and at least sometimes necessarily without any awareness or self-consciousness, use 'conventions' containing 'expectations' (for example about how some term or phrase is used; Krygier, 1988, pp. 28–29). Statutes also presuppose the entire panoply of 'substantive law, procedures, remedies, methods of interpretation', such that even if it may be correct to say that the 'Code' itself does not 'depend upon pre-existing law', nevertheless its 'content almost invariably does' (Krygier, 1988, pp. 30–31), meaning that without being able to 'be made to fit the existing canon' the statute will have a difficult time playing the role it is designed by the legislators to play. Here, then, we have a legal theorist developing a concept – traditionality – that draws heavily on the sensitivities and insights of the social sciences to the legal system generally but also to specific legal forms (in the above case, statutes). Krygier's concept has been taken up by other legal theorists such as John Bell (1994), who has also utilized other concepts, such as legal culture (Bell, 2001 and 2006), in re-imagining legal phenomena. Perhaps the most prominent recent exposition of the concept of legal tradition is Patrick Glenn's *Legal Traditions of the World* (2007).

Chapter 14, by Elizabeth Mertz, also asks legal theorists to place and study legal language in its social context. Like Krygier, Mertz draws on explanatory resources in the social sciences: in this case, anthropological linguistics. Mertz situates anthropological linguistics as going beyond, rather than between, what she refers to as the reflectionist and instrumentalist views of language. According to the reflectionist view, language itself is seen to be 'important only because it provides a window on social process; language is [here] understood to be a straightforward expression of its social context' (p. 365). According to the instrumentalist view, 'people use language transparently to achieve social goals ...[where by] "transparent," we mean that there is no distinctive effect imputed to language; linguistic forms operate as tools through which actors achieve certain social results' (p. 365). It is a distinction that, as Mertz recognizes, harks back to Ferdinand de Saussure's long-standing division between *langue*, that sense of language as an abstract system with its own dynamics, and *parole*, that sense of language 'as an instrument effecting social ends' (p. 362).

The kind of anthropological linguistics that Mertz has in mind is not a mere combination of these formal and functional or reflectionist and instrumentalist approaches to language. Rather, she says, there is a third way: an integrative approach that provides a picture of what she calls 'socially grounded linguistic creativity' (p. 367). Anthropological linguistics, she asserts, reverses 'the usual assumption in the philosophy of language and other traditions that the dominant function of language is conveying semantic information' (p. 367). 'As a result' of this assumption, she says, 'a great deal of work on language structure has proceeded with a blind eye to the social grounding of language' (p. 363). What we ought to recognize, she argues, is that for 'language to be actually used – for the abstract system of language to be translated into speech – there is a necessary move to the indexical or social contextual realm' (p. 368). 'Conveying semantic information is but one of the things it [language] does ... it can also express emotion, maintain social distance, etc.' (p. 368). Language functions indexically, she argues, and when it does, 'Semantics ... becomes a subset, a special case of pragmatics' (p. 368). Arguably, then, and precisely on the back of social scientific insights, Mertz is able to also go beyond much of what is commonly assumed or posited with respect to the nature of language in legal theory. In doing so, she also establishes (and illustrates in her essay) a novel research agenda for legal theory, namely one that studies socially grounded linguistic creativity at play in legal institutions. Indeed, she suggests that the legal world might be a particularly fertile ground for language conceived of in this fashion.

What both of these contributions show is just how much legal theorists often struggle to tame the distinctiveness of legal language. 'Submerged' as all legal scholars tend to be – using Krygier's term – in authoritative texts and schooled as they are to be sensitive to the undeniable richness of legal language, it is all too easy to believe that all the explanatory resources one needs can be found precisely in legal language itself. As both Krygier and Mertz show, however, and in different ways, all language, and perhaps even especially legal language, cannot and ought not to be divorced from its social context. (Naturally, we could include here many other legal theorists who have pressed this point and themselves developed distinct research agendas. To mention but one more, consider, for example, Bernard Jackson's situating of legal language in social narratives (2000).) But, of course, studying legal phenomena is not simply a matter of finding ways of re-imagining legal language; it is also a matter of studying other forms of non-verbal communication. This is the point made by Rodolfo Sacco in Chapter 15 (for a book-length treatment, available so far only in Italian, see Sacco, 2007).

One of the particularly useful features of Sacco's account of 'Mute Law' is that he connects the expression of law to the ways in which legal systems are organized or institutionalized. Thus, he traces the prioritization of the expression of law in the form of explicit propositions to the organization of legal systems in the form of a centralized law-giving or law-making power. In doing so, he reminds us that 'law may live' and, Sacco argues, 'lived, even without a lawgiver' (p. 396). The very notion of a 'law-giver', he says, is 'a recent innovation, in the actual meaning of a central authority entrusted with overall legislative powers' (p. 395). At other times, and in other places, the creation of law was left to other sources: in Chinese and Japanese law, for example, he says, 'the rules of social interaction were thought to mirror a cosmic order' (p. 395). In Roman law, at least in its origins, and in the customs of the common law, we find a law that precedes any individual design. Further, Sacco says, law can and has existed and evolved without lawyers. We do not find the more or less bureaucratized, centralized, professionalized structures of law that we are accustomed to everywhere, 'nor – more importantly – have they always existed everywhere. And even where they do exist, they can influence the life of society to greater or lesser extent' (p. 397). Looking back, Sacco argues that 'When the Homo Habilis produced the first pebble tools ... Ceremonies and acts constituted legal acts. Adherence to the rule implied its existence and validity (manifested by the spontaneous conduct of the members of the group).' 'The law', continues Sacco, 'was mute, except for the yelling accompanying ceremonies and self-help. Sources were mute. Acts were mute' (pp. 399–400).

Of course, Sacco does acknowledge that the emergence of articulated language was greatly important. Language, he says, introduces 'questions about the future, abstract questions about law not yet applied, principles unrelated, at least for the moment, to realities' (p. 400). But even now, when the expression of law via explicit propositions is so dominant, we must not confine ourselves to analysing such propositions but see, instead, legal systems as operating with both spoken and mute elements. In unspoken sources Sacco includes 'commercial uses, determination of standards of conduct, construction, by an interpreter, of concepts such as fault, reasonableness, bad faith' (p. 404). We are familiar, says Sacco, 'with acts carried out through words (contracts made by fax, deeds, wills)' but we ought also to recognize that there are 'acts carried out with words (deliveries, contracts made through devices that allow the buyer to pay and receive merchandise)' (pp. 404–405). There are categories with both spoken and mute elements: 'such are contracts that can be made by declarations, but also by material acts; such are confirmations; such are acceptances of inheritance, which can be express or implied' (p. 405). Those interested in making sense of the law, then, Sacco insists, must overcome their uneasiness with respect to mute sources and acts; further, they must seek to understand those mute sources and acts on their own terms, and not on 'analogy to spoken acts' (p. 405).

Our final two essays are concerned less with expressions of legal phenomena than with their diffusion and their place vis-à-vis other forms of normative regulation. Diffusion, on the one hand, is the specific topic of William Twining's essay. Pluralism, on the other hand, in the form of a recent and reasonably comprehensive historical review offered by Brian Tamanaha, is the topic of our final chapter.

In Part IV of Volume III of this series the relationship between comparative law and legal theory is considered in more detail. Both disciplines, it is said there, have a great deal to learn from each other. Indeed, comparative law deals precisely with, and thus contributes to even without realizing it, legal theoretical problems and models. The practice of comparative law, after all, requires that one either assumes or posits the nature of law in a certain way for the purpose of comparison. Does one, as some theorists do, consider law to be an autonomous body of norms or professional discourse that has little to do with everyday social life? Or does one consider law as a tradition, as a mentality or as a culture – which then necessitates a very different kind of comparison? The point to be made in this context is that comparative law, being already theoretical precisely in this way, is also a fertile ground for interaction between legal theory and the social sciences.

As Twining notes in Chapter 16, with respect to the issue of diffusion, which also requires understanding the nature of law in a certain way (in this case, for analysing how, and how well, it travels), the social sciences, and particularly anthropology and sociology, has a long-standing tradition rich in conceptual models. Examples include the study of the diffusion of cultural traits and the study of the diffusion of innovation. What is impressive, and exemplary, about Twining's essay is that he proceeds to carefully work through two social scientific studies in the diffusion of innovation and then considers, in detail, how well the concepts developed as part of that literature apply to understanding legal diffusion (he finds there are links between the two bodies of literature, and that they coalesce around the notion of 'the communication of ideas across space and time'; p. 446). The point, then, in including Twining's essay is not merely, or even especially, to do with the specific argument he makes. The point, instead, is to show the manner in which a legal theorist has drawn on social scientific literature in dealing with a legal theoretical problem.

Whereas the topic of diffusion is probably unlikely to become a popular, mainstream issue for the interaction between legal theory and the social sciences, pluralism has been, is and is likely to continue to grow in theoretical and empirical interest. This is especially so in the increasingly more intimate global environment, where all kinds of international, multinational, supranational, transnational and other regulatory networks flourish, often in greatly differing degrees of formality and influence. These kinds of normative phenomena challenge traditional understandings of law based predominantly on models of state sovereignty. The study of transnational law, for example, suffers perhaps less from this state-bias than other areas, such as international law, the foundations of which were constructed on state consent. There is much to do in international legal theory in coming to terms with the great paradigm shift away from states and towards the individual (and other non-state actors). Of course, the study of human rights is a central component of such work. Here, as elsewhere, the question of pluralism also has important political implications – as, say, in the argument that although, in their abstract form, human rights are universal, their democratic value lies in specific institutionalization at grassroots level (this argument is made, among many, by Seyla Benhabib; more radical voices prefer to speak only in terms of bottom-up governance and eschew the universal language altogether – for example, see Santos, 1995). Some defend the universalization of human rights – again, at the abstract, 'dogmatic' level – as the last bastion of defence against the mushrooming of rule by technology and scientific experts (see Supiot, 2007, who combines this defence of 'legal dogmatism' with a call for opening up 'the doors of interpretation'). Yet others have argued for a form of multicultural jurisprudence, which understands law to be a forum for the communication of a multiplicity of identities (see Cotterrell, 2009). For those who speak strongly in favour of multiculturalism and bottom-up governance, the state tends to have no special or privileged place or, if it does, that is a cause for concern – which is precisely the subject of criticism by some who argue that these emerging transnational (and other kinds of self-)regulatory networks are 'negotiated orders' rather than 'government' strictly speaking, and that we lose too much (also of political importance) if we forget about the specifics of government (especially state government; see Roberts, 2005).

Naturally, the above is not an attempt to provide an overview of the issues. But even from this brief sample of controversies one can see just how burgeoning this area of study already is. It is, of course, an area of study as much of interest to social scientists as to legal, political and moral theorists. For example, if one believes that, in this context, legal theory, in making sense of rights, must be sensitive to how those rights can be realized in the special spheres of education or economic or family life (Selznick, 2003), then one will have to develop an understanding of those special spheres (in distinct cultures or as overlapping cultures), which is arguably impossible (or at least is going to be much weaker) without the assistance of social scientific research. It is one thing to argue for the democratic value of grassroots institutionalization; it is another to be in a position, as a legal theorist, to evaluate any one instance of institutionalization or a string of such institutionalizations (by, say, a local court). If some legal theorists are right that the world is becoming a criss-crossing network of different kinds of communities (for example Cotterrell, 2008, included in Volume I of this series), then the question of how we can come to see and recognize such forms of social ordering becomes a matter of sensitivity to patterns of behaviour, which brings into play all the usual methodological difficulties (for example, how much emphasis should one place on actors' self-understandings and so on). All this is bread and butter for the social sciences.

But we should not think that the challenge of pluralism – or indeed contributions to the literature of pluralism – is either an exclusively or even a typically modern phenomenon. As Tamanaha shows in Chapter 17, pluralism and its literature have a long and rich pedigree. Perhaps pluralism and unity are two kinds of theoretical temperament: the moment one is sympathetic to one, one sees it everywhere. Of course, that temperament is not only a theoretical one: it is also moral and political. All these strands are intertwined in scholarship, as is visible in the research programmes of, say, constitutionalism in international law (see, for example, Klabbers *et al.*, 2009), global administrative law (see, for example, Kingsbury *et al.*, 2005), the push for *jus cogens* and other allegedly universal principles and procedures (all on the unity side) and in, say, self-governing networks or local community ownership of public resources (on the side of pluralism). All these are hot issues at the moment in legal theory and other disciplines, and so it helps, as Tamanaha's essay so helpfully enables us, to stand back and see these debates from the perspective of over two thousand years of history. Ultimately, it is important to remember that unity and pluralism are not only two modes of explaining legal phenomena: they are also two kinds of attitudes persons as theorists and human beings can adopt to the question of how we can best live together.

Conclusions

As with the other volumes in this series on *Contemporary Legal Theory*, our aim has not been to cover in any comprehensive fashion the nuances and subtleties involved in the interaction between legal theory and the social sciences. If anything, our aim has been to respect past achievements, while also revealing the great promise and potential for future work. We have, then, sought but to illustrate a number of points of intersection between legal theory and the social sciences. Whether it be at the level of methodological disputes and collaboration or at the level of modes of explanation of behaviour and legal (or normative) phenomena, the future for 'legal theory and the social sciences' looks bright. It is true that ten years from now a series such as this one will be unthinkable without a volume dedicated to legal theory and the natural sciences. Much is happening on that plane, with more and more legal theorists turning to cognitive neurosciences and the affective sciences, and with many brain and other scientists looking for applications of their models in the law. Be that as it may, however, legal theory will be all the poorer if it neglects the relevance of the social sciences. The imagination of social life may sometimes seem vaguer, more ambiguous, less palpable than, say, a logical system of propositions or some sequence of neurons firing, but then it is important to remember that vagueness and ambiguity are a part of who we are; a part we would be loathe to forget or neglect.

Select Bibliography

As with the other volumes in this series, this bibliography is select, targeting the specific ambit of the relevant volume. It refers to many sources not referred to above, and in this way hopes to supplement the introduction.

Amstutz, M. (2008), 'Global (Non-)Law: The Perspective of Evolutionary Jurisprudence', *German Law Journal*, **9**, 4, pp. 465–76.

Banakar, R. (2000), 'Reflections on the Methodological Issues of the Sociology of Law', *Journal of Law and Society*, **27**, 2, pp. 273–95.

Banakar, R. and Travers, M. (eds), (2002), *An Introduction to Law and Social Theory*, Oxford: Hart.

Bankowski, Z. (2001), *Living Lawfully: Love in Law and Law in Love*, Dordrecht: Kluwer.

Bankowski, Z. and Mungham, G. (1976), *Images of Law*, London: Routledge & Kegan Paul.

Bankowski, Z. and Mungham, G. (eds) (1980), *Essays in Law and Society*, London: Routledge.

Bell, J. (1994), 'Comparative Law and Legal Theory', in W. Krawietz, N. MacCormick and G.H. Von Wright (eds), *Prescriptive Formality and Normative Rationality in Modern Legal Systems*, Berlin: Duncker & Humboldt, pp. 19–31.

Bell, J. (2001), *French Legal Cultures*, Cambridge: Cambridge University Press.

Bell, J. (2006), *Judiciaries within Europe: A Comparative Review*, Cambridge: Cambridge University Press.

Benforado, A. and Hanson, J. (2008), 'The Great Attributional Divide: How Divergent Views of Human Behaviour are Shaping Legal Policy', *Emory Law Journal*, **57**, 2, pp. 311–408.

Berman, H.J. (1988), 'Toward an Integrative Jurisprudence: Politics, Morality, History', *California Law Review*, **76**, 4, pp. 779–801.

Berthelot, J.M. (2001), *Épistémologie des Sciences Sociales*, Paris: Presses Universitaires de France.

Black, D. (1976), *The Behaviour of Law*, New York: Academic Press.

Bourdieu, P. (1987), 'The Force of Law: Toward a Sociology of the Juridical Field', *Hastings Law Journal*, **38**, 5, pp. 805–53.

Bratman, M. (1999), *Faces of Intention: Selected Essays on Intention and Agency*, Cambridge: Cambridge University Press.

Chase, O. (2005), *Law, Culture and Ritual*, New York: New York University Press.

Chiba, M. (1998), 'Other Phases of Legal Pluralism in the Contemporary World', *Ratio Juris*, **11**, 3, pp. 228–45.
Coleman, J. (2001), *The Practice of Principle: In Defence of a Pragmatist Approach to Legal Theory*, Oxford: Clarendon Press.
Cotterrell, R. (1983), 'The Sociological Concept of Law', *Journal of Law and Society*, **10**, 2, pp. 241–55.
Cotterrell, R. (2004), 'Law in Culture', *Ratio Juris*, **17**, 1, pp. 1–14.
Cotterrell, R. (2006), *Law, Culture and Society: Legal Ideas in the Mirror of Social Theory*, Aldershot: Ashgate.
Cotterrell, R. (2008), 'Transnational Communities and the Concept of Law', *Ratio Juris*, **21**, 1, pp. 1–18.
Cotterrell, R. (2009), 'The Struggle for Law: Some Dilemmas of Cultural Legality', *International Journal of Law in Context*, **4**, 4, pp. 373–84.
Deflem, M. (2008), *Sociology of Law: Visions of a Scholarly Tradition*, Cambridge: Cambridge University Press.
Del Mar, M. (2008), 'The Spatio-Temporality of Objectification in Legal Theory: Concepts of Legality between Theory and Practice', *Problema*, **2**, pp. 127–55.
Del Mar, M. and Onazi, O. (2008), 'The Moral Quality of Work in International Economic Institutions: Resisting Complacency', *International Journal of Law in Context*, **4**, 4, pp. 337–72.
Di Paolo, E. (2009), 'Editorial: The Social and Enactive Mind', *Phenomenology and the Cognitive Sciences*, **8**, 4, pp. 409–15.
Dworkin, R. (1986), *Law's Empire*, Oxford: Hart.
Ehrlich, E. (2002), *Fundamental Principles of the Sociology of Law*, trans. K.A. Ziegert, London: Transaction.
Ellickson, R.C. (1989), 'Bringing Culture and Human Frailty to Rational Actors: A Critique of Classical Law and Economics', *Chicago Kent Law Review*, **65**, pp. 23–55.
Ellickson, R.C. (1991), *Order Without Law*, Cambridge, MA: Harvard University Press.
Endicott, T. (2005), 'The Value of Vagueness', in V.K. Bhatia, J. Engberg, M. Gotti and D. Heller (eds), *Vagueness in Normative Texts*, Bern: Peter Lang, pp. 27–48.
Etzioni, A. (2000), 'Social Norms: Internalisation, Persuasion and History', *Law & Society Review*, **34**, 1, pp. 157–78.
Ewick, P. and Silbey, S. (1998), *The Common Place of Law: Stories from Everyday Life*, Chicago: University of Chicago Press.
Falk-Moore, S. (1978), *Law as Process: An Anthropological Approach*, London: Routledge.
Feeley, M. (1976), 'The Concept of Laws in Social Science: A Critique and Notes on an Expanded View', *Law & Society Review*, **10**, 4, pp. 497–523.
Feeley, M. (2001), 'Three Voices of Socio-Legal Studies', *Israel Law Review*, **35**, pp. 175–204.
Finnis, J. (2007), 'On Hart's Ways: Law as Reason and as Fact', *American Journal of Jurisprudence*, **52**, pp. 25–53.
Freeman, M. (ed.) (2006), *Law and Sociology*, Oxford: Oxford University Press.
Freeman, M. (ed.) (2009), *Law and Anthropology*, Oxford: Oxford University Press.
Friedman, L. (1994), 'Is There a Modern Legal Culture?', *Ratio Juris*, **7**, 2, pp. 117–31.
Friedman, L. (2005), 'Coming of Age: Law and Society Enters an Exclusive Club', *Annual Review of Law and the Social Sciences*, **1**, pp. 1–16.
Fuller, L. (1969), 'Human Interaction and the Law', *American Journal of Jurisprudence*, **14**, pp. 1–36.
Fuller, L. (1981), *The Principles of Social Order*, Durham, NC: Duke University Press.
Galanter, M. (1981), 'Justice in Many Rooms: Courts, Private Ordering, and Indigenous Law', *Journal of Legal Pluralism*, **19**, pp. 1–25.
Galligan, D. (2007), *Law in Modern Society*, Oxford: Oxford University Press.

Garcia-Vellegas, M. (2006), 'Comparative Sociology of Law: Legal Fields, Legal Scholarships, and Social Sciences in Europe and the United States', *Law and Social Inquiry*, **31**, 2, pp. 343–82.
Garland, D. (1990), *Punishment and Modern Society*, Oxford: Clarendon.
Gessner, V. (1994), 'Global Legal Interaction and Legal Cultures', *Ratio Juris*, **7**, 2, pp. 132–45.
Gilbert, M. (1989), *On Social Facts*, Princeton: Princeton University Press.
Giudice, M. (2005), 'Normativity and Norm Subjects', *Australian Journal of Legal Philosophy*, **30**, pp. 102–21.
Glenn, P. (2007), *Legal Traditions of the World*, Oxford: Oxford University Press.
Griffiths, J. (1986), 'What is Legal Pluralism?', *Journal of Legal Pluralism*, **24**, pp. 1–55.
Gur, N. (2007), 'Legal Directives in the Realm of Practical Reason', *American Journal of Jurisprudence*, **52**, pp. 159–228.
Habermas, J. (1996), *Between Facts and Norms*, Cambridge, MA: MIT Press.
Hart, H.L.A. (1961), *The Concept of Law*, Oxford: Clarendon Press.
Hart, H.L.A. and Honoré, A.M. (1959), *Causation in the Law*, Oxford: Clarendon Press.
Hayek, F. von (1973, 1976, 1979), *Law, Legislation and Liberty*, Chicago: University of Chicago Press.
Hertogh, M. (2004), 'A "European" Conception of Legal Consciousness: Rediscovering Eugen Ehrlich', *Journal of Law and Society*, **31**, 4, pp. 457–81.
Hertogh, M. (ed.) (2009), *Living Law: Reconsidering Eugen Ehrlich*, Oxford: Hart.
Himma, K. (2004), 'Do Philosophy and Sociology Mix? A Non-Essentialist Socio-Legal Positivist Analysis of the Concept of Law', *Oxford Journal of Legal Studies*, **24**, 4, pp. 717–38.
Hoecke, M. van (ed.) (2002), *Law as Communication*, Oxford: Hart.
Hunt, A. (1993), *Explorations in Law and Society: Toward a Constitutive Theory of Law*, New York: Routledge.
Jackson, B. (2000), 'Literal Meaning: Semantics and Narrative in Biblical Law and Modern Jurisprudence', *International Journal for the Semiotics of Law*, **13**, 4, pp. 433–57.
Jutras, D. (2001), 'The Legal Dimensions of Everyday Life', *Canadian Journal of Law and Society*, **16**, pp. 45–65.
Kahn, P. (1999), *The Cultural Study of Law*, Chicago: University of Chicago Press.
Kerchove, M. van der and Ost, F. (1994), *Legal System between Order and Disorder*, Oxford: Oxford University Press.
Kingsbury, B., Krisch, N. and Stewart, R.B. (2005), 'The Emergence of Global Administrative Law', *Law and Contemporary Problems*, **68**, 3&4, pp. 15–61.
Klabbers, J., Peters, A. and Ulfstein, G. (2009), *The Constitutionalization of International Law*, Oxford: Oxford University Press.
Krygier, M. (1988), 'The Traditionality of Statutes', *Ratio Juris*, **1**, 1, pp. 20–39.
Lacey, N. (2000), 'Philosophical Foundations of the Common Law: Social not Metaphysical', in J. Horder (ed.), *Oxford Essays in Jurisprudence* (Fourth Series), Oxford: Oxford University Press, pp. 17–39.
Lacey, N. (2004), *A Life of H.L.A. Hart: The Nightmare and the Noble Dream*, Oxford: Oxford University Press.
Lane, K.A., Kang, J. and Banaji, M.R. (2007), 'Implicit Social Cognition and Law', *Annual Review of Law and the Social Sciences*, **3**, pp. 427–51.
Legrand, P. (1999), *Fragments on Law-as-Culture*, Deventer: WEJ Tjeenk Willink.
Lerner, A. (2004), 'Using Our Brains: What Cognitive Science Teaches About Teaching Our Students to be Ethical, Professional Lawyers', *Quinnipiac Law Review*, **23**, pp. 643–707.
Lewis, D. (2002), *Convention: A Philosophical Study*, Oxford: Blackwell.
Luhmann, N. (2004), *Law as a Social System*, Oxford: Oxford University Press.
Macdonald, R. and Kleinhans, M.M. (1997), 'What is a Critical Legal Pluralism?', *Canadian Journal of Law and Society*, **12**, pp. 25–46.

Marmor, A. (2009), *Social Conventions: From Language to Law*, Princeton: Princeton University Press.
Merry, S.E. (1988), 'Legal Pluralism', *Law & Society Review*, **22**, 5, pp. 869–96.
Merry, S.E. (1990), *Getting Justice and Getting Even: Legal Consciousness Among Working-Class Americans*, Chicago: University of Chicago Press.
Mertz, E. (ed.) (2008), *The Role of Social Science in Law*, Aldershot: Ashgate.
Nader, L. (1965), 'The Anthropological Study of Law', *American Anthropologist*, **67**, pp. 3–32.
Nader, L. (1984–85), 'A User Theory of Law', *Southwestern Law Journal*, **38**, pp. 951–63.
Nelken, D. (1984), 'Law in Action or Living Law? Back to the Beginning in Sociology of Law', *Legal Studies*, 4, pp. 157–74.
Nelken, D. (1994), 'The Truth about Law's Truth', in A. Febbrajo and David Nelken (eds), *European Yearbook in the Sociology of Law*, Milano: Giuffré, pp. 87–163.
Nelken, D. (1998), 'Blinding Insights? The Limits of a Reflexive Sociology of Law', *Journal of Law and Society*, **25**, pp. 407–26.
Nelken, D. (2001), 'Can Law Learn from Social Science?', *Israel Law Review*, **35**, pp. 205–24.
Nelken, D. (2008), 'Eugen Ehrlich, Living Law, and Plural Legalities', *Theoretical Inquiries in Law*, **9**, 2, pp. 443–71.
Nonet, P. and Selznick, P. (2001), *Law and Society in Transition: Toward Responsive Law*, New York: Transaction.
Perreau-Saussine, A. and Murphy, J. (eds) (2007), *The Nature of Customary Law: Legal, Historical and Philosophical Perspectives*, Cambridge: Cambridge University Press.
Podgorecki, A. and Whelan, C.J. (eds) (1981), *Sociological Approaches to Law*, New York: St. Martin's Press.
Postema, G. (1982), 'Coordination and Convention at the Foundations of Law', *Journal of Legal Studies*, **11**, pp. 165–203.
Postema, G. (1986), *Bentham and the Common Law Tradition*, Oxford: Clarendon Press.
Postema, G. (1998), 'Jurisprudence as Practical Philosophy', *Legal Theory*, **4**, pp. 329–57.
Ratnapala, S. (1993), 'The Trident Case and the Evolutionary Theory of F.A. Hayek', *Oxford Journal of Legal Studies*, **13**, 2, pp. 201–26.
Raz, J. (1990), *Practical Reasons and Norms*, Princeton: Princeton University Press.
Roberts, S. (2005), 'After Government? On Representing Law without the State', *Modern Law Review*, **68**, pp. 1–24.
Roberts, S. (2008), 'Domesticating the Sociology of Law', *Modern Law Review*, **71**, 1, pp. 132–44.
Rodogno, R. (2009), 'Shame, Guilt and Punishment', *Law and Philosophy*, **28**, 5, pp. 429–64.
Rokumoto, K. (ed.) (1994), *Sociological Theories of Law*, New York: New York University Press.
Rosen, L. (1989), *The Anthropology of Justice: Law as Culture in Islamic Society*, Cambridge: Cambridge University Press.
Rosen, L. (2006), *Law as Culture: An Invitation*, Princeton: Princeton University Press.
Rudden, B. (1974), 'Courts and Codes in England, France and Soviet Russia', *Tulane Law Review*, **48**, pp. 1010–28.
Rudzinski, A. (1976), 'Petrazycki's Significance for Contemporary Legal and Moral Theory', *American Journal of Jurisprudence*, **21**, pp. 107–30.
Sacco, R. (2007), *Legal Anthropology: A Contribution to the Macro-History of Law*, Bologna: Mulino.
Samuel, G. (2003), *Epistemology and Method in Law*, Aldershot: Ashgate.
Santos, B. de Sousa (1995), *Toward a New Common Sense: Law, Science and Politics in the Age of the Paradigmatic Transition*, New York: Routledge.
Sarat, A. (ed.) (2004), *Blackwell Companion to Law and Society*, Malden, MA: Blackwell.
Schauer, F. (2005), 'The Social Construction of the Concept of Law: A Reply to Julie Dickson', *Oxford Journal of Legal Studies*, **25**, 3, pp. 493–501.

Schauer, F. (2005–2006), '(Re)taking Hart', *Harvard Law Review*, **119**, pp. 852–83.
Searle, J. (1995), *The Construction of Social Reality*, London: Penguin.
Selznick, P. (1992), *The Moral Commonwealth: Social Theory and the Promise of Community*, Berkeley: University of California Press.
Selznick, P. (2003), '"Law in Context" Revisited', *Journal of Law and Society*, **30**, 2, pp. 177–86.
Shapiro, S. (2002), 'Laws, Plans and Practical Reason', *Legal Theory*, **8**, pp. 387–441.
Shils, E. (1981), *Tradition*, London: Faber.
Simon, R. and Lynch, J. (1989), 'The Sociology of Law: Where We Have Been and Where We Might be Going', *Law & Society Review*, **23**, 5, pp. 825–47.
Smith, M.N. (2006), 'The Law as a Social Practice: Are Shared Activities at the Foundations of Law?', *Legal Theory*, **12**, pp. 265–92.
Suchman, M. and Edelman, L. (1996), 'Legal-Rational Myths: Lessons for the New Institutionalism from the Law and Society Tradition', *Law and Social Inquiry*, **21**, 4, pp. 903–41.
Supiot, A. (2007), *Homo Juridicus: On the Anthropological Function of Law*, trans. S. Brown, London: Verso.
Sutton, J. (2001), *Law/Society: Origins, Interactions and Change*, Thousand Oaks, CA: Pine Forge Press.
Tamanaha, B. (1993), 'The Folly of a "Social Scientific" Concept of Legal Pluralism', *Journal of Law and Society*, **20**, 2, pp. 192–217.
Tamanaha, B. (2001), *General Jurisprudence in Law and Society*, Cambridge: Cambridge University Press.
Turkel, G. (1996), *Law and Society: Critical Approaches*, Boston: Allyn & Bacon.
Unger, R. (1976), *Law in Modern Society: Toward a Criticism of Social Theory*, New York: Free Press.
Veitch, S. (2007), *Law and Irresponsibility: On the Legitimation of Human Suffering*, London: Routledge Cavendish.
Wickman, G. and Pavlich, G. (eds) (2001), *Rethinking Law, Society and Governance: Foucault's Bequest*, Oxford: Hart.
Webber, J. (1995), 'Relations of Force and Relations of Justice: The Emergence of Normative Community between Colonists and Aboriginal Peoples', *Osgoode Hall Law Journal*, **33**, pp. 623–60.
Webber, J. (2004), 'Culture, Legal Culture, and Legal Reasoning: A Comment on Nelken', *Australian Journal of Legal Philosophy*, **29**, pp. 27–36.
Weber, M. (1954), *Law in Economy and Society*, ed. M. Rhenstein, trans. E. Shils, Cambridge, MA: Harvard University Press.
Ziegert, K. (1979), 'The Sociology Behind Eugen Ehrlich's Sociology of Law', *International Journal of the Sociology of Law*, **7**, pp. 225–73.

Part I
Methodology: Collaborations and Disputes

[1]

THE CONCEPT OF LAW AND SOCIAL THEORY†

MARTIN KRYGIER*

For the past twenty years, analytical jurisprudence particularly in Great Britain, but also in the United States and much of the rest of the world, has been profoundly influenced by one author and one book. The author is, of course, H. L. A. Hart; the book is *The Concept of Law*.[1] As one of the editors of the *Festschrift* to Hart has remarked, 'No serious writing upon the subjects with which Professor Hart dealt can afford to neglect his work, and the key concepts with which he was concerned will, for a long time, be discussed within the parameters he laid down'.[2]

Hart has, without doubt, had his greatest influence on legal philosophy. Through his masterly combination of conceptual analysis with deep knowledge of law, he has demonstrated both to philosophers and jurisprudentially inclined lawyers how much each can gain from an application of philosophical techniques to legal materials and of legal techniques to philosophical materials. However, while this might be its most obvious achievement, the importance of *The Concept of Law* does not end there. For it is a remarkably catholic work, whose relevance and insights do not fit neatly within one disciplinary pigeon-hole, or even two. A number of authors have noted, for example, that it also makes, or can be used to make, contributions to social theory, though few have tried to specify these in any detail,[3] and most have acknowledged, indeed emphasized, that the general influence of *The Concept of Law* on social theory generally and legal sociology in particular has been small. Conversely, the influence of these disciplines on analytical jurisprudence, except as an occasional source of apt, or in the case of Malinowski exotic, illustration, has not been remarkably conspicuous.

Several reasons might be adduced for this. For a long time, despite its Durkheimian and Weberian ancestry, sociology had little to say about law, treating it, as Talcott Parsons recently put it, as an 'intellectual step-child',

---

*Senior Lecturer, University of New South Wales.

†An earlier version of this paper was read to a seminar of the Australian Society of Legal Philosophy in April 1981. I am grateful to the participants in that seminar, particularly Lauchlan Chipman and Wojciech Sadurski, for their comments, which have now appeared, with a reply by me, in the *Bulletin of the Australian Society of Legal Philosophy*, no 19, August 1981.

1 Clarendon Press, Oxford, 1961. Future references to passages from *The Concept of Law* will be followed by their page numbers in brackets in the text.

2 P. M. S. Hacker, 'Hart's Philosophy of Law' in P. M. S. Hacker and J. Raz eds, *Law, Morality, and Society, Essays in Honour of H. L. A. Hart* (Clarendon Press, Oxford, 1977) 1.

3 However, see E. Colvin, 'The Sociology of Secondary Rules' 28 *U of Toronto LJ* 196–214 (1978); Lloyd Fallers, *Law Without Precedent* (University of Chicago Press 1969) esp 11–22; P. M. S. Hacker, op cit 8–11.

considered less important than the economy, polity, society or morality.[4] This is somewhat, though not altogether, less true today. Secondly, especially in English-speaking countries, many sociologists and philosophers do not read outside their own discipline, and the mere fact that *The Concept of Law* is so obviously a work of legal philosophy may well have determined whom it would influence.

A distant antipodean might also be forgiven for suspecting that there was an odd conspiracy between partisans of legal sociology and analytical jurisprudence, to minimize the relevance of one for the other, and more specifically to ignore the sociological elements, and their importance, in Hart's work and his kind of work. On the one hand, among those (relatively few) writers interested in sociological approaches to law who have noticed Hart's claim that *The Concept of Law* might be regarded as an 'essay in descriptive sociology', several have greeted it with surprise, others have rejected it, and very few appear to have treated it very seriously. Thus, in an article which seeks to persuade lawyers and sociologists to collaborate and take each other seriously, Professor Willock emphasizes that Austin and Kelsen, 'the two main modern suppliers of a definition and analysis of law, both see the need, once its nature has been established, to study its connection with other disciplines'. He adds in a surprised after-thought, 'Even H. L. A. Hart claims that *The Concept of Law* "may also be regarded as an essay in descriptive sociology".'[5] Again, two prominent British legal sociologists have identified as one of the reasons for the relatively late development of their discipline, the alleged fact that British courses in jurisprudence

> ... were of a character inimical to the development of interest in law in society research. Analytical jurisprudence and legal positivism (in particular the writings of Bentham, Austin, Kelsen and, more recently, Hart) have proved of intimidating endurance as archetypes for 19th and 20th century British legal theory. Neither sociological jurisprudence nor legal realism triumphed over positivism as they did in America.... Of course there have been exceptions to this.... But such incursions have been of tangential importance; the precepts of such writers have, almost uniformly, been 'translated' in terms acceptable to the general perspective of analytical jurisprudence.[6]

The language of this complaint does not suggest that these authors see much scope for enlightenment from any of the 'archetypes' they mention. Finally, in a more measured assessment of Hart's influence and contribution, Twining remarks that, although several contributors to Hart's *Festschrift* 'explicitly treat law as a social phenomenon, the overall impression created by the collection is that this type of work is proceeding in almost complete isolation from contemporary social theory and from work in socio-legal studies, with little overt concern with the law

---

4 Talcott Parsons, 'Law as Intellectual Stepchild' 47 *Sociological Inquiry* 11–58 (1977). Cf Klaus A. Ziegert, 'The Sociology Behind Eugen Ehrlich's Sociology of Law' 7 *Int'l J of the Sociology of L* 256 (1979).
5 I. D. Willock, 'Getting on with Sociologists' 1 *Brit J of L and Soc'y* 9 (1974).
6 C. M. Campbell and Paul Wiles, 'The Study of Law in Society in Britain' 10 *L and Soc'y Rev* 565 (1976).

in action'.⁷ Twining, too, mentions 'the tantalizing claim that *The Concept of Law* may be regarded "as an essay in descriptive sociology"', and he concludes:

> ...A sympathetic critic can be sceptical about the claim, not because it is wrong or misleading, but because the idea of a descriptive sociology of law is not developed in *The Concept of Law* nor in Hart's other writings. What, for example, is the scope of a 'descriptive sociology' and how does it relate to other kinds of sociological enquiry? Why 'descriptive' if the purpose is understanding? What within this field might be important concepts that might be usefully clarified by the kind of analysis of which Hart is an acknowledged master? Hart's individual concerns, and the intellectual tradition of academic law within which he has worked, have not led him to direct much attention to such questions. But it is important to recognise that while his focus of attention may have been relatively narrow, the philosophical techniques and approach which he has introduced into legal theory are capable of application to a much wider range of concepts and issues.⁸

If legal sociologists and sociological jurists have not been much influenced by the renaissance in analytical jurisprudence which Hart inaugurated, analytical jurists have frequently remained rather innocent of social theory and empirical social research, and have at times manifested an attitude of haughty, and not always benign, neglect towards work in these fields. Few now deny that there is a place for such inquiries, and some have insisted that it is an important place.⁹ However, they appear to have remained confident that it is a clearly different place from their own, and few show evidence of frequent visits. In this, they might be following Hart's lead, for some time ago he made it clear where he believed that at least a teacher's emphasis should be: 'the limited time which the student can spend on jurisprudence is better devoted to analytical inquiries than to sociological jurisprudence'.¹⁰ One reason for this, which Hart rightly says 'no candid student of sociology could deny', is that

> valuable as the insights have been which it has provided, the average book written in the sociological vein, whether on legal topics or otherwise, is full of unanalysed concepts and ambiguities of just that sort which a training in analysis might enable a student to confront successfully. Both psychology and sociology are relatively young sciences with an unstable framework of concepts and a correspondingly uncertain and fluctuating terminology. If they are to be used to illuminate us as to the nature of law, these sciences must be handled with care and with a sensitivity to the types of ambiguity and vagueness, and also other linguistic anomalies, which the student will best learn to appreciate in handling the leading concepts of the law in an analytic spirit.¹¹

---

7 W. L. Twining, 'Academic Law and Legal Philosophy: The Significance of Herbert Hart' 95 *LQ Rev* 561 (1979).
8 Ibid 579.
9 See Neil MacCormick, 'Law as Institutional Fact' 90 *LQ Rev* 102, 129 (1974) and MacCormick, 'Challenging Sociological Definitions' 4 *Brit J of L and Soc'y* 94 (1977).
10 H. L. A. Hart, 'Analytical Jurisprudence in Mid-Twentieth Century: A Reply to Professor Bodenheimer' 105 *U of Pa L Rev* 972 (1957).
11 Ibid 974.

And Hart has on at least one occasion shown us the benefit of such an application of analytic techniques to sociological theory, in his dissection of the views of Lord Devlin and of Durkheim on the sources of social solidarity.[12] Thus analytical inquiries should be distinguished from sociological ones, students should be taught the former and sociologists could, and need to, learn much from conceptual analysts. It is not clear, however, what, if anything, Hart believes analytical jurists have to learn in the conduct of their *own* enterprise, from theoretical or empirical social science.

Ronald Dworkin, Hart's successor at Oxford, has stressed that a 'general theory of law' relies on many branches of philosophy and must 'constantly take up one or another disputed position on problems of philosophy that are not distinctly legal',[13] but he shows no sign of believing that social theory has much to contribute. When he writes about legal sociology, he, like many lawyers, does not seem to have in mind its theoretical branches, but is thinking of empirical sociological research on legal institutions. Lawyers who attempted such research, he suggests, 'discovered that lawyers do not have the training or statistical equipment necessary to describe complex institutions in other than an introspective and limited way. Sociological jurisprudence therefore became the province of sociologists'.[14] In any event, it is not clear what Dworkin believes sociologists could offer jurisprudence, for he insists that 'jurisprudential issues are at their core issues of moral principle.... [I]f jurisprudence is to succeed, it must expose these issues and attack them as issues of moral theory',[15] and Dworkin criticizes 'the sociological approach' among others for obscuring these issues.

Finally, such confident boundary-drawing is epitomized in Joseph Raz's rather impoverished conception of the domain of legal sociology, and perhaps legal philosophy. According to Raz, the difference between legal philosophy, which he does, and legal sociology, which presumably is to be done by someone else, is that 'the latter is concerned with the contingent and with the particular, the former with the necessary and the universal. Sociology of law provides a wealth of detailed information and analysis of the functions of law in some particular societies. Legal philosophy has to be content with those few features which all legal systems necessarily possess'.[16]

My contention in this paper is that such delimitations of what analytical jurists such as Hart *have* been doing, let alone what they should do, are too modest, and that this modesty, while perhaps disarming is not altogether salutary. It obscures some important contributions to a social theoretical

---

12 H. L. A. Hart, 'Social Solidarity and the Enforcement of Morals' 35 *U of Chicago L Rev* 1–13 (1967).
13 Ronald Dworkin, 'Introduction' in *Taking Rights Seriously* (Duckworth, London 1978) ix.
14 Ronald Dworkin, 'Jurisprudence' op cit 4.
15 Ibid 7.
16 Joseph Raz, 'The Institutional Nature of Law' in *The Authority of Law* (Oxford University Press 1979) 105. See also his 'Legal Positivism and the Sources of Law' op cit 42 and 44.

understanding of law which a work such as *The Concept of Law* can make. It also allows some rather central social theoretical assumptions and presuppositions of analytical jurists to receive less attention than they otherwise might. I believe this to be generally true, but because of the stature, importance and breadth of Hart's analysis, I will concentrate my attention here on *The Concept of Law*.

1. 'DESCRIPTIVE SOCIOLOGY'

In the preface to *The Concept of Law*, Hart invites the attention of sociologists, among others, to his work. His aim, he explains,

has been to further the understanding of law, coercion, and morality as different but related social phenomena. Though it is primarily designed for the student of jurisprudence, I hope it may also be of use to those whose chief interests are in moral or political philosophy, or in sociology, rather than in law (p vii).

Moreover, several of the more programmatic statements in the work, such as Hart's commitment to 'the theoretical or scientific study of law as a social phenomenon' (p 205), have a distinctly sociological ring.

But if Hart believes his book will be of *use* to sociologists, this is not because he plans to *do* what they do, and certainly not because he sees himself as involved in explanatory social theory. Rather it is primarily because the conceptual distinctions, refinements and methods with which the book is concerned have sociological bearing and importance. By examining the different ways in which we use words, and the ways in which we use different words, according to the context in which they are appropriate, we stand, Hart believes, to gain much in our understanding both of words *and* context. As he explains in a footnote, there is

great need for a discrimination of the varieties of imperatives by reference to contextual social situations. To ask in what standard sorts of situation would the use of sentences in the grammatical imperative mood be normally classed as 'orders', 'pleas', 'requests', 'commands', 'directions', 'instructions', etc., is a method of discovering not merely facts about language, but the similarities and differences, recognized in language, between various social situations and relationships. The appreciation of these is of great importance for the study of law, morals, and sociology (p 235).

It is in this sense, I believe, that Hart's description of the book as 'an essay in descriptive sociology' is to be understood. Hart rightly insists that his analysis and his *mode* of analysis raise issues of interest to others besides lawyers, philosophers and lexicographers:

Notwithstanding its concern with analysis the book may also be regarded as an essay in descriptive sociology; for the suggestion that inquiries into the meanings of words merely throw light on words is false. Many important distinctions, which are not immediately obvious, between types of social situations or relationships may best be brought to light by an examination of the standard uses of the relevant expressions and of the way in which they depend on a social context, itself often left unstated. In this field of study it is particularly true that we may use, as Professor J. L. Austin said, 'a sharpened awareness of words to sharpen our perception of the phenomena' (p vii).

Hart's claim as to the virtues of what might be called 'linguistic sociology' is true, and, to anyone who reads *The Concept of Law,* obviously true. One merely needs to reflect on the sociological insights which abound in Hart's discussion of the differences between 'being obliged' and 'having an obligation' or between habits and social rules.

More generally, Hart's suggestion that sociologists would do well to pay attention to the conceptual issues with which analytical jurists are concerned, is clearly warranted. It is simply nonsense to suggest that sociology of law can replace, or do without, rigorous, philosophical, conceptual analysis. It must begin with it and return to it continually.[17] I take it that the importance of conceptual issues for a social *theory* of law is obvious, but an adequate conceptual base is scarcely less important for empirical work. Empirical sociologists are often impatient with conceptual debates, but to ignore such matters is not to insulate oneself from the problems with which they are concerned. Not only is there a constant danger of working with muddled and confused concepts, there is also the problem of misdirected research either because one's priorities are set by voguish and often still unexamined concepts or because one works with familiar concepts, often inherited from older conceptual analysts, without realizing their deficiencies. In another context, Lord Keynes nicely characterized this latter problem:

the ideas of economists and political philosophers, both when they are right and when they are wrong, are more powerful than is commonly understood. Indeed the world is ruled by little else. Practical men, who believe themselves to be quite exempt from any intellectual influences, are usually the slaves of some defunct economist.[18]

If we replace 'economist' by 'jurist' in this passage, we will better understand how the following complaint could have been made relatively recently:

Most contemporary research on law and society suffers from its unwillingness to even consider a definition of the concept of law and hence the boundaries of investigation. This reluctance is perhaps the most widely shared feature of social scientists interested in law ... the dominant Austinian conception of law pervading most of the social sciences is too narrow.... My point is merely to emphasize that social scientists have not drawn on a concept of law that adequately addresses forms of law other than commands, a conceptual failure that has led to improperly drawn boundaries of investigation. More importantly, empirical investigations premised upon this initial

---

17 See further Neil MacCormick, 'Challenging Sociological Definitions' op cit; Neil MacCormick, *H. L. A. Hart,* (Edward Arnold, London 1981) 78 and Philippe Nonet, 'For Jurisprudential Sociology' 10 *L and Soc'y Rev* 525–45 (1976).
18 John Maynard Keynes, *The General Theory of Employment Interest and Money* (Macmillan, London 1936) 383.

failure have led to generalizations about law and society that are of questionable usefulness.[19]

The author himself is well aware of Hart's illuminating contribution in this regard, and he draws heavily on Hart's distinctions between 'duty-imposing' and 'power-conferring' laws to make his point. Yet it is astounding that a complaint such as this can appear so long after Hart had made such distinctions central to his refutation of the Austinian 'gunman' concept of law.

Legal anthropologists have long been explicitly concerned with conceptual issues, because their problem is not the one Hart believes generally plagues most of us—'"I can recognize an elephant when I see one but I cannot define it"' (p 13)—but rather one of deciding whether societies with institutions quite different from the anthropologists' own, or with no differentiated institutions, have anything elephantine at all. However, though their materials raise conceptual issues in an acute form, much anthropological discussion has been marred by even more explicit borrowings, than one finds among sociologists, of outdated and inappropriate juristic definitions of law, with which the institutions of small-scale societies are compared.[20] Though this is controversial among legal anthropologists, I doubt that their enterprise would be harmed by a dose of Oxford legal philosophy.

II. THE SOCIAL FUNCTIONS OF LAW

Important as Hart's conceptual analyses are, however, they are not the only forms of sociology in which he indulges. One quickly discovers that he is prepared to use far more than 'a sharpened awareness of words' to enlighten us about phenomena. Unlike Kelsen, it is no part of Hart's ambition to develop a 'pure theory' of law. Indeed, he insists that no adequate account of such an important social institution can be given without reference to social facts, and he repeatedly refers to facts, or alleged facts, about people's behaviour, attitude to rules, resources, and so on. More important, though there are no references in *The Concept of Law*[21] to the major social theorists who have developed analyses of law and its functions in society, some of the central themes, distinctions and arguments of that work rest on important, if unsystematic and often unsubstantiated, sociological claims.

Thus, Hart lays great emphasis on the 'social functions' which law performs, and he frequently invokes these functions to criticize others', and to support his own, concept of law. At a general level, Hart appears to have no doubt about what law is for. Like many sociologists, he sees it as a means of social control. In an earlier article, replying to Professor Bodenheimer, he suggested that there is 'at

---

19 Malcolm M. Feeley, 'The Concept of Laws in Social Science: A Critique and Notes on an Expanded View' 10 *L and Soc'y Rev* 503, 508, 509 (1976).
20 I have discussed these issues at greater length in 'Anthropological Approaches' in E. Kamenka and A. E.-S. Tay eds, *Law and Social Control* (Edward Arnold, London 1980) 27–59, esp 28–39.
21 As in much of the work influenced by Hart. See W. L. Twining, op cit 567.

least one aim' which he and Bodenheimer must have in common, 'namely, the increase of our understanding of the character of law as a means of social control'.[22] Again, in *The Concept of Law*, Hart objects to views of law that obscure 'the specific character of law as a means of social control' and 'the principal functions of the law as a means of social control' (p 39), and he criticizes 'narrow' concepts of law which would exclude iniquitous laws, on the grounds that

> ...what really is at stake is the comparative merit of a wider and a narrower concept or way of classifying rules, which belong to a system of rules generally effective in social life... the use of the narrower concept here must inevitably split, in a confusing way, our effort to understand both the development and potentialities of the specific method of social control to be seen in a system of primary and secondary rules (pp 204–5).

Given Hart's extraordinary ability to probe and unravel concepts in common use, it is a pity that, like many sociologists, he does not tell us what he means by social control. For it is an extremely murky concept, whether used by sociologists, as it so often is, or by analytical jurists. If ever a concept stood in need of clarification and dissection, this one does: it does not make clear what or who controls or what or who is controlled, and it invites a host of ontological problems when any attempt to clarify it is made. It is in fact a heavily theory-laden concept, which means very different things to Marxists and to functionalists, and would be rejected as a characterization of the function of law by writers such as Fuller.[23] Hart never suggests, however, what theory his use of the concept is laden with. Moreover, to describe law as 'a means of social control' suggests that law has *one* pre-eminent or over-arching function, a claim which is either so general as to be vacuous, or, if made more precise, is likely to be false.

It seems to me no accident, given the ordinary connotations of 'control' in English, that many sociologists who have regarded law as a means of social control have been led to make precisely the mistake that Hart so often warns us against: to regard law primarily as a coercive instrument for the control of deviance. Thus, as one sociologist has recently remarked:

> ...the basic feature [of social control] is meant to be not the power of a particular social agency or a special social group (though this... can be modified), but the normatively guiding influence of the social environment of individuals. As such, social control is an indispensable condition for any human behaviour and sociologists accordingly focused their attention on this phenomenon at a very early stage. It is however remarkable that the emerging outline, after the massive scholarly interest taken by sociologists in the topic of social control in the early and mid-sixties, is that of a coercive mechanism to help keep social *deviance* down and conformism in society up. Deviance is indeed the key-word for sociological research in this field.... On the other hand, sociological studies and research

---

22 'Analytical Jurisprudence in Mid-Twentieth Century: A Reply to Professor Bodenheimer' op cit 953.
23 See Lon L. Fuller, *The Morality of Law* (Yale University Press 1969) 215. See also R. S. Summers, 'Naive Instrumentalism and the Law' in P. M. S. Hacker and J. Raz eds, op cit 123.

very drastically falsified the inadequate picture of law which sociologists had and still have, which many mistake to be the sociology of law: if social control is a check on social deviance, what else can law be than a state check on social deviance, what else can law be than a state check on possible criminal behaviour? Without doubt, the vast majority of the lay public would equate law with criminal law in this way.[24]

In legal anthropology, too, the loose association of law with control for a long time tended to narrow the dominant conceptions of the role and functions of law and, in particular to focus anthropologists' attention on disputes and dispute settlement at the expense of the many other legally affected domains of social life. Writing in 1951, David Riesman assured us that:

> the anthropologist is not likely to harbour the naive assumption that the law, or any other institution, serves only a single function—say, that of social control—and that any other functions which in fact it serves are excrescences or 'contradictions'. The concept of ambivalence is part of his equipment; he tends to search for latent functions, transcending the ostensible.[25]

In fact, the bulk of work in legal anthropology, as in many other areas of social science, has proceeded on the basis of just this 'naive assumption'. As Laura Nader has pointed out several times,

> ... the law does not function solely to control. It educates, it punishes, it harasses, it protects private and public interests, it provides entertainment, it serves as a fund-raising institution, it distributes scarce resources, it maintains the status quo, it maintains class systems and cuts across class systems, it integrates and disintegrates—all these things in different places, at different times, with different weightings. It may be a cause of crime; it plays, by virtue of its discretion, the important role of definer of crime. It may encourage respect or disrespect for the law, and so forth. We have assumed that there was probably a cross-cultural difference in the content and form of a legal system, and at the same time we have ignored the variety of functions (sometimes referred to as extralegal, latent, or unintended) that a legal system may or in fact does have.[26]

It is unfortunate that one of the few concepts which Hart explicitly shares with social scientists is such a vapid one.

However, if all that Hart had to say about the 'social functions' of law was that it is a 'means of social control' one could be pardoned for ignoring this element of his work. For Hart gives the concept virtually no work to do; a reader whose copy of *The Concept of Law* had all references to social control expurgated by some benevolent Bowdler would miss little of the argument of the book. Moreover, though Hart makes no attempt to clarify the concept, and though I believe that it has misled many sociologists and anthropologists, it is less clear that it misleads

---

24 Klaus A. Ziegert, 'A Sociologist's View' in E. Kamenka and A. E.-S. Tay eds, op cit 63.
25 'Toward an Anthropological Science of Law and the Legal Profession' reprinted in *Individualism Reconsidered* (The Free Press, New York 1954) 445.
26 Laura Nader and Barbara Yngvesson, 'On Studying the Ethnography of Law and its Consequences' in John J. Honigmann ed, *Handbook of Social and Cultural Anthropology* (Rand McNally, Chicago 1973) 909. See also Martin Krygier, 'Anthropological Approaches' op cit 38–9.

Hart. He is manifestly aware, indeed it is central to his account, that law performs more than one function, and he is very concerned to reject any narrow conception of the law as control which would focus our attention on means of law enforcement or mechanisms of dispute settlement. In this his motivation is explicitly sociological, and he is wiser than many social scientists. In one passage, for example, Hart considers the view that 'by recasting the law in a form of a direction to apply sanctions, an advance in clarity is made, since this form makes plain all that the "bad man" wants to know about the law'. Hart replies:

> This may be true but it seems an inadequate defence for the theory. Why should not law be equally if not more concerned with the 'puzzled man' or 'ignorant man' who is willing to do what is required, if only he can be told what it is? Or with the 'man who wishes to arrange his affairs' if only he can be told how to do it? It is of course very important, if we are to understand the law, to see how the courts administer it when they come to apply its sanctions. But this should not lead us to think that all there is to understand is what happens in courts. The principal functions of the law as a means of social control are not to be seen in private litigation or prosecutions, which represent vital but still ancillary provisions for the failures of the system. It is to be seen in the diverse ways in which the law is used to control, to guide, and to plan life out of court (p 39).

This point, that the social functions of law can only be appreciated if one attends to the behaviour of law and to law-affected behaviour outside official institutions, where the bulk of law-affected behaviour occurs, rather than merely inside them, has been made by a number of sociologists of law.[27] But legal sociology has too often combined a narrow view of the function of law with an image of law borrowed from lawyers, and focused excessively on what happens in courts or in response to court decisions.[28] Similarly legal anthropologists have in the last forty years given the bulk of their attention to what Llewellyn and Hoebel called 'trouble cases'. As a result they have, as I have argued elsewhere,[29] constantly run the risk of giving accounts systematically skewed by their reliance on manifest conflict and ways of resolving it rather than on the many other areas of life where Hart rightly suggests law is most characteristically at work. The significance of Hart's observation has also been lost, at times, on his philosophical colleagues. Thus Ronald Dworkin ventures the following extraordinary remark: 'What, in general, is a good reason for decision by a court of law? This is *the* question of jurisprudence; it has been asked in an amazing number of forms, of which the classic "What is law?" is only the briefest'.[30] The issue Dworkin identifies is, as his own work shows, of great importance to lawyers and to moral and legal

---

27 Among them Eugen Ehrlich and Leon Petrażycki. On Ehrlich see Klaus A. Ziegert, 'The Sociology Behind Eugen Ehrlich's Sociology of Law' op cit 242. On Petrażycki, see Adam Podgórecki, *Law and Society* (Routledge and Kegan Paul, London 1974) 67.
28 See Malcolm M. Feeley, op cit 513–16.
29 See 'Anthropological Approaches' op cit 39–50. See also Glynn Cochrane, 'Legal Decisions and Processual Models of Law' 7 *Man* 50–6 (1972).
30 Ronald Dworkin, 'Does Law Have a Function? A Comment on the Two-Level Theory of Decision' 74 *Yale LJ* 640 (1965).

philosophers seeking to give an adequate account of the features of those 'hard cases' which most trouble the best, if not most, lawyers. But Dworkin nowhere shows that this question constitutes '*the* issue of jurisprudence' or that the question 'what is law?' can be reduced to it. That he believes this and that he also chooses to base his criticism of Hart's concept of law solely on what judges do in hard cases, suggests he has overlooked the sociological point Hart is making in the above passage, and the importance of it. It is precisely Hart's concern to give greatest emphasis in his account to the socially most significant features of law that distinguishes the centre of gravity of his work from that of Dworkin, and that, in my opinion, makes his work far more important than is commonly acknowledged for social theory and for a sociological understanding of law.

Hart's concern to identify and account for the principal ways in which law affects social life pervades *The Concept of Law*. As is well known, the book develops an exhaustive critique of the Austinian, 'imperativist' definition of law, which occupies three of its chapters. A great deal of Hart's criticism, and much of the weight of his alternative account, rest firmly and explicitly on assertions as to the different social functions performed by two classes of rules: duty-imposing and power-conferring rules. Thus Hart argues that the Austinian analogy between law and orders backed by threats might to some degree fit *criminal* law, for:

The social function which a criminal statute performs is that of setting up and defining certain kinds of conduct as something to be avoided or done by those to whom it applies, irrespective of their wishes.... But there are important classes of law where this analogy ... altogether fails, since they perform a quite different social function (p 27).

Certain theories which seek to save the analogy 'purchase the pleasing uniformity of pattern to which they reduce all laws at too high a price: that of distorting the different social functions which different types of legal rule perform' (p 38). Finally, Hart runs together his observations about social functions with a related but distinct sociological claim (which it is not clear that he realizes *is* distinct) about differences between the way in which the two kinds of rules are *looked upon* by those whom they affect:

Rules conferring private powers must, if they are to be understood, be looked at from the point of view of those who exercise them. They appear then as an additional element introduced by the law into social life over and above that of coercive control. This is so because possession of these legal powers makes of the private citizen, who, if there were no such rules, would be a mere duty-bearer, a private legislator.... Why should rules which are used in this special way, and confer this huge and distinctive amenity, not be recognized as distinct from rules which impose duties, the incidence of which is indeed in part determined by the exercise of such powers? Such power-conferring rules are thought of, spoken of, and used in social life differently from rules which impose duties, and they are valued for different reasons. What other tests for difference in character could there be? (pp 40–41).

Hart's emphasis on the profoundly important role in law of rules which do not forbid, but channel, protect and enforce the public and private exercise of powers is of great significance for any analysis of the functions of law. But it is precisely at this point that his discussion begins to require more deliberate attention to problems of social theory and to the findings of empirical sociological research than he demonstrates. As we have seen, Hart's argument hinges on his distinction between two types of law, each performing a distinct and apparently readily identifiable social function. But it is no small matter to identify the social functions performed by *any* social institution, let alone law, which permeates so many areas of life and operates in so many different ways. Like all important institutions, law performs many functions, not all of them obvious, and it requires a considerable act of faith to believe that one has identified and distinguished the major functions of all laws, on the basis of the meagre evidence that Hart produces. One problem is that identified by Raz: Hart does not distinguish between what Raz calls the 'normative' functions of law, which 'are ascribed to laws by virtue of their normative nature, their mode of normativity' and its social functions, 'the social effects they have or are intended to have',[31] and he indiscriminately moves between both. The normative functions of laws can be identified relatively straightforwardly. They 'provide reasons for action... by determining that certain legal consequences follow on the performance of certain actions',[32] and one can classify the types of reasons they provide. But, as Raz points out, 'By stating that a reason for action exists a normative remark is made, not a psychological one. Similarly, stating that there is a reason for a certain course of behaviour does not mean that it is a conclusive or overriding reason. Other reasons may be there, some working for the same conclusion and others opposing it. Nothing can be said in general about the rational outcome of such deliberations, let alone their actual conclusion'.[33] There is, then, no reason to believe that the social functions of laws are reducible to their normative ones, nor is it a light undertaking satisfactorily to specify the former. And while Raz's speculations about the social functions of law are both wise and illuminating, he chooses not to argue for, and thus gives us no reason to agree with, his claim that 'all legal systems necessarily perform, at least to a minimal degree, which I am unable to specify, social functions of all the types to be mentioned [in his article], and that these are all the main types of social functions they perform'.[34] Nor is it clear how such a claim *could* be substantiated without a great deal of sociological and anthropological research and theory. The passage from Nader quoted above suggests something of the complexity involved in identifying the social functions of law, a complexity which can also be surmised from the following attempt to outline the functions of two social institutions, schools and hospitals, whose functions are considerably more specific than those of law:

31 J. Raz, 'On the Functions of Law' in A. W. B. Simpson ed, *Oxford Essays in Jurisprudence* (Second Series) (Clarendon Press, Oxford 1973) 280.
32 Ibid 282.
33 Ibid 284.
34 Ibid 289. Raz's choice is deliberate. After the sentence I have quoted, Raz continues: 'These claims will not, however, be argued for here. Instead the classification will be simply put forward and explained in general outline'.

What do structures actually do? Schools are established to educate pupils, and they perform that mission with varying degrees of proficiency. They also serve, for younger children, as baby-sitters and day-care centers, as the context for possibly deviant peer-group socialization, as preliminary sorting mechanisms for adult social placement, and possibly as a devious or at least indirect and not very effective device for palliating racial and ethnic discrimination in housing and employment. For younger teenagers, schools keep their pupils off the streets during school hours and serve as 'day reformatories' for juvenile delinquents not committed to official reformatories. For later teenagers and young adults the adult placement function becomes more precise; meanwhile staying in school delays entrance into the competitive and possibly overcrowded labor force, and in that sense at least represents a prolongation of infancy.

Hospitals provide another convenient example of multifunctionality. While at least nominally providing medical therapy for the sick or wounded, they must necessarily also provide custodial and hotel-and-restaurant services. They get the sick or dying persons out of the household and, especially for the moribund, provide a kind of emotionally sterile setting for death. Concentration of medical services in a separate establishment eases the problems of coordinating specialized services and has the more than incidental consequence of requiring the patient to get to the services rather than the physician or visiting nurse delivering the services to the patient's home ...

Like the various examples of the utility of derogated practices such as magic or corrupt urban government, the unadvertised and often unintended consequences of organized behavior go well beyond common sense or the unreflective experience of participants and lay observers.[35]

It is, then, a major task simply to identify the functions performed by law, particularly since similar institutions can perform different functions in different societies, and in the same societies at different times, and in developed Western societies law is continually called upon to perform new functions. It is another major task of social theory to analyse these purported functions and decide which are 'major' or 'universal'. Neither of these tasks can be satisfactorily performed simply on the basis of a lawyer's acquaintance, however sophisticated, with the normative functions of law. Nor can they be performed by calling in aid, as Hart does, the ways in which rules are 'thought of, spoken of and used in social life'. This is because, to use old-fashioned functionalist terminology, law, like any institution, performs at least both 'manifest' and 'latent' functions and the latter are not easily detectable on the basis of the sort of evidence Hart adduces. Few people who marry, for example, know (or care) much about the social functions of the institution whose rules they enlist. However, even if the evidence Hart relies upon were appropriate to his purposes, we run up against the fact, pointed out by MacCormick, that the truth of Hart's conclusions about the functions of rules 'depends upon a testable but untested sociological assertion. The truth is that we do not know nearly enough about the way in which people in general perceive, or the extent to which they understand, the law, to rest any theoretical account of the

---

35 Wilbert E. Moore, 'Functionalism' in Tom Bottomore and Robert Nisbet eds, *A History of Sociological Analysis* (Heinemann, London 1979) 339–40.

168   *THE CONCEPT OF LAW* AND SOCIAL THEORY

structure of the law upon such grounds'.[36] What we have from Hart are hypotheses serving the role of factual premises in an argument. As hypotheses they are fruitful, if only because Hart's guesses are likely to be more interesting than most. They cannot, however, bear the weight he seeks to load onto them.

III. INTERNAL AND EXTERNAL ATTITUDES TO LAW

Hart does not merely invoke people's attitudes to law in order to indicate its social functions. Throughout *The Concept of Law*, he lays great stress on the importance of understanding the attitudes to laws of those who are affected by them and use them. Hart's discussion is confused, however, and has confused others; so it must be unravelled. According to Hart, 'one of the central themes of the book is that neither law nor any other form of social structure can be understood without an appreciation of certain crucial distinctions between two different kinds of statement, which I have called "internal" and "external" and which can both be made whenever social rules are observed' (p vii). Later he claims that until the distinction is grasped between an 'external' predictive account of law, and his own account, which allows for the internal aspect of rules, 'we cannot properly understand the whole distinctive style of human thought, speech, and action which is involved in the existence of rules and which constitutes the normative structure of society' (p 86). Unfortunately, Hart's spatial metaphor is used in a number of different ways which he does not differentiate, but which for our purposes it is important to distinguish.[37] Hart first uses the metaphor to distinguish between habits and social rules:

When a habit is general in a social group, this generality is merely a fact about the observable behaviour of most of the group.... By contrast, if a social rule is to exist some at least must look upon the behaviour in question as a general standard to be followed by the group as a whole. A social rule has an 'internal' aspect, in addition to the external aspect which it shares with a social habit and which consists in the regular uniform behaviour which an observer could record (p 55).

Hart uses the same metaphor to make a second and different distinction, within a social group where one or more social rules exist, between those who voluntarily accept and use the rules, and those who reject them and only follow them to avoid punishment:

At any given moment the life of any society which lives by rules, legal or not, is likely to consist in a tension between those who, on the one hand, accept and voluntarily co-operate in maintaining the rules, and so see their own and other persons' behaviour in terms of the rules, and those who, on the other hand, reject the rules and attend to

---

36 Neil MacCormick, 'Law as Institutional Fact' op cit 116.
37 Distinctions similar to the ones made here can be found in Frederick Siegler, 'Hart on Rules of Obligation' 45 *Australasian J of Phil* 350 ff (1967), and, following Siegler's analysis, John D. Hodson, 'Hart on the Internal Aspect of Rules' 62 *Archiv für Rechts-und Sozialphilosophie* 381–99 (1976).

them only from the external point of view as a sign of possible punishment. One of the difficulties facing any legal theory anxious to do justice to the complexity of the facts is to remember the presence of both these points of view and not to define one of them out of existence (p 88).

Hart adds the cautionary final sentence quoted, because he is concerned to refute the predictive view of obligation which defines it 'in terms of the likelihood that threatened punishment or hostile reaction will follow deviation from certain lines of conduct' (p 86). That account pays no attention to the 'internal' attitude of voluntary rule-followers. Observers are led to such an account by their faulty methodological position, a position which Hart discusses again in terms of the internal/external distinction. He distinguishes three different 'points of view' from which one can make assertions about the rule-affected behaviour of members of a group. If one is 'a member of a group which accepts and uses them [its rules] as guides to conduct' (p 86), one makes assertions from an 'internal point of view'. In fact, to be consistent with the previous 'internal/external' distinction and with other passages in the book, this phrase will need to be limited: only a member of such a group who *himself* accepts and uses the rules can be said to have the internal point of view.

If one is an observer who does not accept the rules oneself, but acknowledges that the group does, one 'thus may from outside refer to the way in which *they* are concerned with them from the internal point of view' (p 87). Hart calls such a point of view an 'external' one, but he has little to say about it and nothing to say against it. This is fortunate since if *such* a point of view were illegitimate, all anthropology and most social science generally would also be illegitimate. We may call this a moderate external point of view to contrast it with what Hart calls the 'extreme external point of view' held by those who neither accept the rules nor give 'any account of the manner in which members of the group who accept the rules view their own regular behaviour' (p 87). Such an observer cannot describe the life of a group 'in terms of rules at all.... Instead, it will be in terms of observable regularities of conduct, predictions, probabilities, and signs. For such an observer, deviations by a member of the group from normal conduct will be a sign that hostile reaction is likely to follow, and nothing more' (p 87). It is *this* sort of observer who, Hart believes, will 'miss out a whole dimension of the social life of those whom he is watching' (p 87), for

The external point of view may very nearly reproduce the way in which the rules function in the lives of certain members of the group, namely those who reject its rules and are only concerned with them when and because they judge that unpleasant consequences are likely to follow violation.... What the external point of view, which limits itself to the observable regularities of behaviour, cannot reproduce is the way in which the rules function as rules in the lives of those who normally are the majority of society. These are the officials, lawyers, or private persons who use them, in one situation after another, as guides to the conduct of social life, as the basis for claims, demands, admissions, criticism, or punishment, viz, in all the familiar transactions of life according to rules. For them the violation of a rule is not merely a basis for the prediction that a hostile reaction will follow but a *reason* for hostility (p 88).

For anyone interested in examining social behaviour, the points Hart makes in these passages are of obvious and great importance. So, however, are the differences between them, which Hart obscures. In particular, while Hart has much the same thing in mind when he discusses the, for him more interesting 'internal' point of view, he obscures the differences which exist between 'external' points of view. The 'external aspect' of a habit is simply 'regular uniform behaviour' which lacks not only the 'internal aspect' but also any of the compulsion which drives someone to comply with a rule even though he rejects it. In other words, the external aspect of habits has as much and as little in common with the external aspect of rules as it has with their internal aspect, viz regular performance. 'External' rule-affected behaviour is still rule-affected; 'external' habitual behaviour is not. Even if you do not accept the rule, in following it you *obey* it, if only from fear of coercion. But you do not *obey* your habits. And the attitude of a criminal who 'reject[s] the rules and attend[s] to them only from the external point of view as a sign of possible punishment', has nothing at all in common with the attitude of someone with a habit; as we know many people are quite attached to their habits. When Hart contrasts rules with habits he is making a distinction similar to that which Durkheim made between custom and habit: 'Ce qui la distingue, ce n'est pas sa fréquence plus ou moins grande; c'est sa vertue impérative. Elle ne représente pas simplement ce qui se fait le plus souvent, mais ce qui doit se faire'.[38] On the other hand, Hart's second distinction is similar to, perhaps it influenced, that made by a Polish empirical sociologist of law, between 'outer' and 'inner' attitudes to law:

An outer-oriented individual obeys the law as a result of consideration of what might happen if he deviated from a legal norm. On the other hand, we say that a law-abiding individual is inner-oriented if he accepts a given norm as his own, as well as knowing that he will meet disapproval if he behaves unlawfully; deviant behaviour is for him not only grounds to expect some consequence or other but a sufficient reason or justification for such consequences.[39]

Both these distinctions—that between habits and rules and that between acceptance of and mere obedience of rules—need to be made, but little of use for social theory, or conceptual analysis, is gained by confusing them.

Moreover, apart from eliding what is 'external' about habits and a certain way of obeying rules, Hart also confuses *substantive* questions about the attitudes that might be expected from group-members with an 'external' interest in rules (such as criminals or, for that matter, act utilitarians), and

---

38 Emile Durkheim, 'Introduction à la sociologie de la famille' *Textes* vol 3 (Editions de Minuit, Paris 1975, first published 1888) 19.
39 J. Kwaśniewski, 'Z badań nad motywacją przestrzegania prawa' in *Prawnicy, socjologowie i psychologowie* (Warsaw 1970) quoted in Adam Podgórecki, op cit 28.

methodological questions about the proper point of view for an observer to adopt. Whether observers should merely record observable behaviour, seek via 'empathy' or *'Verstehen'* to understand its meaning to group-members, or 'go native' are not new issues in the social sciences, or, for readers of Weber, in the sociology of law. The issues are not simple, but I agree with Hart (and Weber) that to ignore the *meanings* of rule-affected behaviour to those involved *is* to 'miss out a whole dimension of social life'. Hart's arguments are a valuable hermeneutic corrective to a great deal of 'positivist' sociology.[40] But this methodological issue must be distinguished from the substantive one of what attitudes members of a society take to their rules. Because Hart does confuse these two issues, he claims that '[t]he external point of view may very nearly reproduce the way in which the rules function in the lives of certain members of the group, namely those who reject its rules...'. This is to ignore the complexity of attitudes usually involved in rejecting or not accepting a rule and indeed it is to sell short the importance of the hermeneutic method that Hart endorses. For a behaviourist observer will fail to understand the rule-affected behaviour, not merely of those who accept the rules but also of those who reject them or have some mixture of attitudes toward them. He will simply not be able to know what their behaviour means, though he might, nevertheless, be able to predict it.

IV. PRE-LEGAL AND LEGAL SYSTEMS

The different uses Hart makes of the internal/external metaphor do not all play the same role in his theory. In particular, the second use of it, to distinguish between those *members* of a society who manifest different attitudes to its rules, is central not only to Hart's account of fully developed legal systems but also to his discussion of the differences between 'pre-legal' and legal systems. This discussion mixes conceptual analysis, 'state of nature' thought experiments, and, of particular importance for our purposes, forays, sometimes deliberate sometimes inadvertent, into explanatory social theory.

Hart asks us to consider how society, and in particular 'social control', would be managed if our familiar legal institutions—in Malinowski's phrase 'central authority, codes, courts, and constables'—were absent. Though he believes, wrongly, that 'few societies have existed in which legislative and adjudicative organs were all entirely lacking' (p 244), he concedes that such a society is

---

40 According to Donald Black, 'It is crucial to be clear that from a sociological standpoint, law consists in observable acts, not in rules as the concept of rule or norm is employed in the literature of jurisprudence and in everyday legal language. From a sociological point of view, law is not what lawyers regard as binding or obligatory precepts, but rather, for example, the observable dispositions of judges, policemen, prosecutors, or administrative officials'. See his 'The Boundaries of Legal Sociology' in Donald Black and Maureen Mileski eds, *The Social Organisation of Law* (Seminar Press, New York) 41, 46 and the critique of his position, drawing partly on Hart, by Philippe Nonet, 'For Jurisprudential Sociology' op cit.

'possible to imagine' (p 89) and that many anthropologists 'claim that this possibility is realized' (p 89). Whether or not they exist, however, Hart, like the social contract theorists, considers it useful to think away familiar institutions, for by conceiving life without them, we might gain insight into their purposes and functions. In such a society, Hart believes, 'the only means of social control is that general attitude of the group towards its own standard modes of behaviour in terms of which we have characterized rules of obligation' (p 89), that is, primary rules. That sort of social control, moreover, could only be effective in stable, small-scale societies, for:

> It is plain that only a small community closely knit by ties of kinship, common sentiment, and belief, and placed in a stable environment, could live successfully by such a régime of unofficial rules. In any other conditions such a simple form of social control must prove defective and will require supplementation in different ways (pp 89–90).

The specific problems a society with only primary rules would face are the uncertainty of its rules, their static character, and 'the *inefficiency* of the diffuse social pressure by which the rules are maintained. Disputes as to whether an admitted rule has or has not been violated will always occur and will, in any but the smallest societies, continue interminably, if there is no agency specially empowered to ascertain finally, and authoritatively, the fact of violation' (p 91). The remedies for these defects are *secondary* rules of recognition, change and adjudication; rules about rules. The addition of such rules 'is a step forward as important to society as the invention of the wheel' (p 41); only with them do we have what can correctly be called a legal system:

> The introduction of the remedy for each defect might, in itself, be considered a step from the pre-legal into the legal world; since each remedy brings with it many elements that permeate law: certainly all three remedies together are enough to convert the régime of primary rules into what is indisputably a legal system (p 91).

According to Hart, once secondary rules of these three kinds are added to the primary ones, not only does law exist, but members of a society can manifest a more complex range of attitudes to their rules than was possible in the simple, pre-legal world. For one of the conditions for a society 'to live by primary rules alone', 'granted a few of the most obvious truisms about human nature and the world we live in' (p 89) is that most of the members of the society must have the *internal* attitude to its rules since:

> though such a society may exhibit the tension, already described, between those who accept the rules and those who reject the rules except where fear of social pressure induces them to conform, it is plain that the latter cannot be more than a minority, if so loosely organized a society of persons, approximately equal in physical strength, is to endure: for otherwise those who reject the rules would have too little social pressure to fear. This too is confirmed by what we know of primitive communities where, though there are dissidents and malefactors, the majority live by the rules seen from the internal point of view (p 89).

In this passage, as his appeal to 'what we know' about primitive societies indicates, Hart is seeking to explain the *empirically* necessary conditions for an undifferentiated society to endure. He also makes the conceptual point that in

> a simpler decentralized pre-legal form of social structure which consists only of primary rules ... since there are no officials, the rules must be widely accepted as setting critical standards for the behaviour of the group. If, there, the internal point of view is not widely disseminated there could not logically be any rules (pp 113–4).

In complex societies which have law and officials, however, there is no necessity, either logical or factual, for ordinary members of a society to take an internal attitude to the law, though in a 'healthy' society they commonly will. In such a society, private citizens need only generally *obey* the law. Officials, on the other hand, must have the internal attitude to the secondary rules of the legal system, in particular to its criteria of validity; 'they must regard these as common standards of official behaviour and appraise critically their own and each other's deviations as lapses' (p 113). These are the two conditions necessary and sufficient for the existence of a legal system: the law must be generally obeyed, and officials must have the 'internal attitude' to the secondary rules.

There is much of sociological value in this hypothetical evolutionary theory. As Colvin has demonstrated,[41] it can be used to shed light on a range of important issues in the sociology of law; among them the sources of legal development, its relationship to social complexity and change, the role and importance of a division of legal labour. Again, in his excellent study *Law without Precedent,* the anthropologist Lloyd Fallers adopted Hart's view of law as a combination of primary and secondary rules, in order to make useful distinctions between societies, including our own and the Basoga of Uganda which do, and those which do not, make use of 'the legal mode of social control'. In this usage the legal mode 'requires that values with respect to human conduct be reduced to normative statements which are sufficiently discrete and clear so that it may be authoritatively determined *whether or not* in a particular case a particular rule has been violated'.[42] Fallers contrasts this 'way of looking at social conflict—in terms of violation of rule' with two other ways: regarding and dealing with such conflicts simply as conflicts of *interest,* as political, or military conflicts might be regarded; and 'full moral evaluation' where 'community standards may exist, but an attempt is made to take account of the full moral complexity of conflict situations'.[43] Like Hart, Fallers believes that 'law' properly so called requires secondary rules.

Nonetheless, Hart's discussion is not without difficulties. On his account, the major differences between pre-legal and legal systems are that the former have primary rules alone whereas the latter have both primary and secondary rules; the only means of control in the former are 'the general attitude of the group' to its primary rules whereas the latter have laws and legal institutions; in the former,

---

41 Op cit, *supra* n 3.
42 Chicago University Press 1969, 11.
43 Ibid 11–12.

most people have and must have the 'internal' attitude to the society's primary rules whereas in the latter only officials need to have the internal attitude to the secondary rules of the legal system.

In all of this, the central concept is that of a rule. For a theorist concerned to understand law and rules as means of social control, Hart is surprisingly uncurious about alternatives to law or rules. Were he more curious, he might rely less on contrasts such as those outlined above. It is a real anthropological and ultimately philosophical problem whether the understandings of members of many small-scale societies should be described as rule-following behaviour. Often anthropologists have difficulty in *finding* rules at all, for, as Llewellyn and Hoebel point out,

> if one takes as his main road ... the road of felt or known 'norms', he meets in some cultures with bafflement on the part of the informant. A Comanche, or a Barama River Carib, does not like to think that way. He finds trouble in reducing such general 'norms' to expression or in stating a solution for an abstract or a hypothetical case.[44]

Conversely, in societies where general norms *can* be gleaned from informants, it can be misleading to interpret them as the norms which guide social life. This is not merely because one might be misinformed, or because one is hearing an idealized story. It is because, though the rules one gleans might really be endorsed by members of a society, these rules may not play the normative function in that society which outsiders expect. Thus it was common, after the pioneering work of Fortes and Evans-Pritchard,[45] to interpret the segmentary lineage systems of many African stateless societies as the basis for dispute resolution in such societies. As E. L. Peters has demonstrated, however,

> When a Bedouin kills another in Cyrenaica, one of a number of consequences ensues. According to the Bedouin, the particular consequence is determined by the genealogical positions of the persons or groups concerned ... [in fact] the lineage model neither covers several important areas of social relationships nor enables an accurate prediction of events to be made.... The argument advanced [by Peters] is that the lineage model is not a sociological one, but that it is a frame of reference used by a particular people to give them a common-sense kind of understanding of their social relationships. For sociological purposes this means that the lineage model, with its supporting theoretical presuppositions, must perforce be abandoned.[46]

These anthropological problems may not seem important for Hart, for people could still be said to be following rules without knowing it, or following rules other than the ones they say they follow. This is true, though it is difficult to see how people can have the 'internal' attitude to rules of which they are apparently unaware, and we should remember that Hart does consider important the way

---

44 *The Cheyenne Way* (University of Oklahoma Press) 22.
45 M. Fortes and E. E. Evans-Pritchard eds, *African Political Systems* (Oxford University Press 1940).
46 E. L. Peters, 'Some Structural Aspects of the Feud Among the Camel-herding Bedouin of Cyrenaica' 37 *Africa* 261 (1967).

that rules are 'thought of, spoken of, and used in social life'. In any event there are deeper problems with Hart's 'model of rules'. For in many undifferentiated societies, whose social structure is, as Hart notes, small in scale and closely-knit, rules do not play the same role and do not operate in the same way as they do among lawyers, and many of their clients, in differentiated societies. In small-scale societies, where one is in the constant company, and under the constant surveillance of one's peers, and the community has numerous cross-cutting and interdependent ties, there are many ways of knowing, and being reminded, what is expected, other than by a reliance on rules. And in such societies, as among contemporary families, friends and small communities, the *stakes* of social relationships are quite different from those of a contemporary litigant. As one of the foremost students of stateless societies has written (of the Tonga-speakers of Zambia),

The Tonga in particular have taught me something about what it means to live without the formal apparatus of courts, police, or public officials. Some of the devices they used, and still attempt to use, for organizing and regulating their affairs are recognizable as common to other small-scale communities that must depend upon persuasion and stalling tactics for social control. Indeed, some of these devices are not unknown to the academic world and the world of committees with which I sometimes deal, if survival and continuity come to be more important than individual interests or adherence to abstract principles.[47]

Though societies appear to differ greatly in the use they make of explicit norms, none of this is meant to suggest that small-scale societies have no norms. It is to suggest, however, that Hart's speculations about 'pre-legal' societies are excessively 'rule-bound'. Norms in small-scale societies, even where they are discernible and effective, are rarely clear-cut, almost never apply impersonally or across the board, and often cannot even in principle be stated in abstract terms. For the way in which a dispute over, say, theft or assault is handled will vary greatly with the status and general reputation of the specific parties involved, the relationships between them, between them and potential allies and opponents, between these potential allies and opponents themselves. Nor will these relationships necessarily *determine* the outcome of 'legal' disputes; they will, however, profoundly influence them and what is done about them.

These points serve to give specific confirmation to one of the major themes in MacCormick's recent work on Hart:

Despite its claimed and indeed its genuine superiority over prior theories, Hart's theory can itself be shown to be defective. First, it ties the relevant concepts solely to *rules;* but ... 'rule' is too restrictive a category to comprehend all that needs to be said about moral values, standards and principles; nor is there better reason to suppose that law is an affair of rules *only.*[48]

It is significant that MacCormick's point has force not only with regard to

47 E. Colson, *Tradition and Contract: The Problem of Order* (Aldine, Chicago 1974) 3–4.
48 *H. L. A. Hart*, 58. See also 41–2, and with specific reference to Hart's discussion of 'pre-legal' systems, 100–01.

'pre-legal' systems, but to 'legal' ones as well. For, though they are important, the differences between the way in which rules operate in differentiated societies and other forms of 'social control' in undifferentiated ones should not be overemphasized. Indeed contrasts such as Hart's, between 'pre-legal' and 'legal' systems can rarely be made with accuracy or more than notional precision. They also often involve false comparisons, where similarities between different societies are overlooked, and peculiarities of each are emphasized. However, given that the differences between the institutions, structures, and ways of life of small-scale and highly differentiated societies are so considerable, it would be surprising if the only important differences between their 'means of social control' were that the former had one type of rule of which there was general acceptance, and the latter had two types, and officials had to accept the second. However, this is all that Hart allows for. Since he does not conceive of social cohesion without rules, and since he believes that the only alternative to secondary rules is 'the general attitude of the group', he is led to contend that the majority in small-scale societies must have an internal attitude to their rules. But many small-scale, stateless societies do not conform to this account. Cohesion in these societies is not maintained by general rules which all accept, but by complicated balancing and cross-cutting group ties. Colson revealed the principles underlying order in such a society in her pioneering study on the Plateau Tonga of Northern Rhodesia, and the system she revealed has since been found in many other stateless societies, particularly in New Guinea. According to Colson,

> Tonga society, despite its lack of political organization and political unity, is a well-integrated entity, knit together by the spread of kinship ties from locality to locality, and the intertwining of kinship ties within any one locality. It obtains its integration and its power to control its members and the different groups in which they are aligned, by the integration of each individual into a number of different systems of relationships which overlap. When a man seeks to act in terms of his obligation to one set of relationships, he is faced by the counter-claims upon him of other groups with which he must also interact. This entanglement of claims leads to attempts to seek an equitable settlement in the interests of the public peace which alone enables the groups to perform their obligations one to another and a Tonga to live as a full member of his society.[49]

---

49 E. Colson, 'Social Control and Vengeance in Plateau Tonga Society' 23 *Africa*, 210 (1953). Galloway has made a similar criticism of Hart, drawing on Barnes' account of Colson's findings. He cites an apposite passage from Barnes: 'In Tonga society, order was maintained, more or less, neither through the operation of centralized authority mediated through a system of courts, nor through the operation of pressure to conform imposed by a homogeneous and undifferentiated community. Order was achieved through the potential opposition of each group to all other groups, so that no one group dominated the rest, and, more importantly, by the fact that every individual had a plurality of loyalties'. J. A. Barnes, 'Law as Politically Active' in G. Sawer ed, *Studies in the Sociology of Law* (ANU, Canberra 1961) 175, quoted in Donald C. Galloway, 'The Axiology of Analytical Jurisprudence: A Study of the Underlying Sociological Assumptions and Ideological Presuppositions' in Thomas W. Bechtler ed, *Law in a Social Context. Liber Amicorum Honouring Lon L. Fuller* (Kluves, The Netherlands 1977) 85–86.

For such a society, an explanation of social cohesion in terms of a generalized 'internal' attitude to 'rules' is inappropriate and misleading. It over-emphasizes rules, under-emphasizes the considerable amount of conflict in small-scale societies, and ignores the powerful role of what Hart would associate with an external attitude—simple fear—in the endurance of small societies. In such societies, without rules to limit the power of the powerful, the 'fear of violence that brings more violence'[50] plays an important role in preventing, or damping down, disputes. As Colson remarks,

> Anthropologists have a liking for paradoxes and it should therefore be no surprise to us if some people live in what appears to be a Rousseauian paradise because they take a Hobbesian view of their situation: they walk softly because they believe it necessary not to offend others whom they regard as dangerous.[51]

One reason for this situation is the absence of institutions with authority to adjudicate and power to enforce judgments. Though he has little to say about enforcement, Hart is therefore right in emphasizing the importance to a legal system of public secondary rules. But his speculations about what would occur without such rules—a society glued together by a generalized internal attitude to primary rules—are not very helpful either in understanding control in small societies or in the societies with which they are contrasted.

Moreover, even in regard to fully developed legal systems, Hart's emphasis on the need for officials to 'accept' the system's secondary rules is ambiguous and potentially misleading. Hart appears to believe that there is a specially close link between *voluntariness* and the official acceptance which is necessary for a legal system to exist, a link which does not necessarily exist between voluntariness and mere obedience. Obedience, which is all that is required from non-officials for a legal system to exist '*need* involve no thought on the part of the person obeying that what he does is the right thing for himself and for others to do: he need have no view of what he does as a fulfilment of a standard of behaviour for others of the social group. He need not think of his conforming behaviour as "right", "correct", or "obligatory".... But this merely personal concern with the rules, which is all the ordinary citizen *may* have in obeying them, cannot characterize the attitude of the courts to the rules with which they operate as courts.... Individual courts of the system though they may, on occasion, deviate from these rules must, in general, be critically concerned with such deviations as lapses from standards, which are essentially common or public. This is ... logically a necessary condition of our ability to speak of the existence of a single legal system' (pp 112–13). Now it does appear to be a conceptual truth that unless a system's valid rules were generally obeyed we would not say that a legal system exists, and perhaps like deciding when a man is bald, one cannot ask for more precision than that. It also appears necessarily true for the existence of a legal system, in Hart's sense, that its officials at least must recognize the secondary rules of the system *as rules* and

---

50 E. Colson, *Tradition and Contract* 40.
51 Ibid 37.

regard the rules as applicable to the behaviour of other officials. But, as Hodson,[52] from whom I have drawn these two conditions, has argued, Hart believes that acceptance on the part of officials includes far more than that. In particular, towards the end of the book, Hart recapitulates his argument. He recalls that

> In the earlier chapters of this book we stressed the fact that the existence of a legal system is a social phenomenon which *always* presents two aspects, to both of which we must attend if our view of it is to be realistic. It involves the attitudes and behaviour involved in the *voluntary* acceptance of rules and also the *simpler* attitudes and behaviour involved in mere obedience or acquiescence (p 197, my italics).

I see no reason to believe, however, that official 'acceptance' of rules need be any more 'voluntary' than masses' 'mere obedience'. Certainly, it is *possible* to imagine a society in which those who accepted and applied the rules *as rules,* did so purely out of fear. And in fact Stalin's *Ezhovshchina* was full, and frequently emptied, of bureaucrats to whom such a description appears more plausible than talk of voluntary acceptance. Paradoxically, much *popular* behaviour appeared much more voluntary than that of officials. But if Hart is making a point of social or political theory, about the need for legitimacy of every régime, or the need that someone should internalize its norms, then his analysis does not take us very far. For it is an interesting and complex question of theory and research *who* in a society needs to regard it and its rules as legitimate, how much, and for how long. The Shah of Iran could certainly have used some enlightenment in this regard. Analysis which considers 'mere obedience or acquiescence' as simple attitudes, or suggests that there is a necessary connection between voluntariness and the analytically central constituents of official legal behaviour, would not have helped him.

V. THE MINIMUM CONTENT OF NATURAL LAW

A similar insouciance about what is required to substantiate a statement of social theory pervades Hart's final and most explicit venture into this field; his account of what he calls 'the minimum content of natural law'. This is Hart's solution to 'the hoary perennial known as "Natural Law versus Legal Positivism"'.[53] By means of it, he seeks to avoid both the Scylla of an absolute distinction between law and morals and the Charybdis of traditional natural law theories. Hart derives the 'minimum content', or the 'empirical version' of natural law from the combination of 'a mere contingent fact which could be otherwise, that in general men do desire to live... survival has a special status in relation to human conduct and to our thought about it' (p 188), with five general characteristics of the human condition. These are that humans are physically vulnerable, approximately equal, and have only limited altruism, scarce resources, and limited understanding and strength of will. From these contingent but universal 'natural facts', Hart argues,

---

52 Op cit 392 ff.
53 H. L. A. Hart, 'Kelsen Visited' 10 *UCLA L Rev* 709 (1963).

we can derive 'a *reason* why, given survival as an aim, law and morals should include a specific content' (p 189), a reason for certain mutual forbearances, for example, on random killing, as well as for rules relating to promises that are '*dynamic* in the sense that they enable individuals to create obligations and to vary their incidence' (p 192) and for a system of organized sanctions, 'not as the normal motive for obedience, but as a *guarantee* that those who would voluntarily obey shall not be sacrificed to those who would not' (p 193). It is *this* which is the solution to the 'hoary perennial':

> The simple truisms we have discussed not only disclose the core of good sense in the doctrine of Natural Law. They are of vital importance for the understanding of law and morals, and they explain why the definition of the basic forms of these in purely formal terms, without reference to any specific content or social needs, has proved so inadequate... It is in this form that we should reply to the positivist thesis that 'law may have any content'. For it is a truth of some importance that for the adequate description not only of law but of many other social institutions, a place must be reserved besides definitions and ordinary statements of fact, for a third category of statements: those the truth of which is contingent on human beings and the world they live in retaining the salient characteristics which they have (pp 194–95).

No social scientist could disagree with the last sentence of this passage. However, since so much of Hart's account of the 'minimum content' hangs on statements in this third category, one might want to know their source. Typically, it is Hobbes and Hume rather than, say, Durkheim or the theories and findings of sociologists or anthropologists. This is a rather cavalier way to found 'the central indisputable element which gives empirical good sense to the terminology of Natural Law' (p 187). For when Hume gave his account of the origins of society and morals, he was, after all, something of a pioneer in what Hart has elsewhere referred to as the 'relatively young sciences' of psychology and sociology. Hume was, as Mackie has recently reminded us, attempting to explain the existence of morality 'in sociological and psychological terms... It is not for nothing that his work is entitled *A Treatise of Human Nature* and sub-titled *An attempt to introduce the experimental method of reasoning into moral subjects*'.[54] Hart's attempt to continue Hume's *enterprise* is important and valuable; what is wrong is that he rests with Hume as the source of his *data*. One might, for example, discover that men *universally* have goals and purposes other than survival, which would lead us at least to augment Hart's account. Hobbes after all, spoke of a desire, not merely to live but for 'commodious living'. Freud mentioned other concerns, and other apparently universal purposes could be suggested. Moreover, men may universally have goals and purposes which are incorporated generally into morality and law but which are inconsistent with individual survival. Conscription laws exist in many societies and are used for wars which often cannot be said to threaten the survival of a State, let alone its non-combatant population. They frequently, however, lead to the demise of individual

---

54 J. L. Mackie, *Hume's Moral Theory* (Routledge and Kegan Paul, London 1980) 6.

combatants. And in those (relatively few) societies which allow conscientious objection, an individual's fervent wish to survive is never taken to be adequate reason, either in morals or law, for exemption. One might, then, share Hart's aim, to derive the 'core of good sense' in natural law doctrine, without being persuaded that he has revealed it.

Furthermore, quite apart from the fact that Hart has chosen to rest with 'truisms' about the human condition, these are truisms of a specifically individualist, pre-sociological kind. Hart's 'natural facts' refer to the needs and characteristics of individuals and the nature of their environment, but, apart from relating the division of labour, found 'in all but the smallest groups', to power-conferring rules and 'the perennial need for co-operation' to rules about promises, he has nothing to say about other 'social facts' which might be relevant to his account. One does not need to indulge in Hegelian metaphysics to suggest that the forms of social organization in which individuals find themselves cannot simply be jettisoned or ignored either by their members or by observers. In this sense, one must account for what is required for *societies* to survive, and though Hart considers such issues elsewhere, he hardly does so in this context. Certainly, there are elements common to law and morality in all societies, such as incest taboos, rules regarding kinship, marriage and descent, the existence of which needs to be explained. A methodological individualist might explain such phenomena in terms of universal individual purposes other than survival; a functionalist sociologist might identify 'social functions' which are regularly performed in all societies, and which are necessary if certain forms of social organization are to persist despite the passing of individuals. In either case, the minimum content of natural law is unlikely to survive unscathed.

VI. CONCLUSION

Like members of craft unions, academics are rather fond of erecting and maintaining disciplinary boundaries. Such boundaries, of course, have legitimate purposes, particularly pedagogic ones, and as indications of special skills, approaches and areas of interest. Certainly, for example, there is a great deal of legal philosophy which does not raise issues of social theory, and much legal sociology which is of little interest to legal philosophers, among others. But not all such boundaries are worth preserving, and even those that are should allow free passage where appropriate. Sometimes, precisely because one has only a sketchy idea of what is happening on the other side of the fence, one caricatures it, the more easily to distinguish between what can be done over there and in one's own field. This appears to me to have happened in some of the contrasts between the domains of legal philosophy and sociology, which I quoted earlier. More generally, even where boundaries are accurately drawn, there are times, as I have sought to suggest here, when it might be fruitful, even necessary, to ignore them, or at least cross them deliberately and often.

[2]

LEGAL THEORY AND SOCIAL THEORY

Kim Lane Scheppele

Department of Political Science, Institute of Public Policy Studies and Law School, University of Michigan, Ann Arbor Michigan 48109

KEYWORDS: sociology of law, social theory, jurisprudence, feminist theory, race and ethnic relations, literary theory, critical theory, rational choice theory.

Abstract

While social theory and legal theory were once closely intertwined, contemporary American sociology pays scant attention to recent developments in legal theory. But the problems that legal theory currently wrestles with are very similar to those with which sociology is now centrally concerned. This essay reviews major schools of thought in contemporary legal theory to introduce sociologists to some potentially useful literatures on the meaning of rationality; on critical theory; on the importance of gender, race, and class in understanding social institutions; on the interpretive turn; on the relationship between structure and agency; and on the revival of pragmatism.

"[S]ociology [is] the ghost of jurisprudence past."
Donald R. Kelley, *The Human Measure* (1990: 275)

INTRODUCTION

Annual Review articles customarily begin with a statement about the current salience of the field under review for the discipline of sociology. I cannot make any such claim. Legal theory (jurisprudence) is a field that is today largely unrecognized by sociologists, even sociologists of law. Why then devote an *Annual Review* paper to a field that is not prominently on the intellectual map of the discipline?

One answer is that sociology as a distinct discipline grew out of jurisprudence and maintained a close alliance with jurisprudence for most of the nineteenth century. Many early European social theorists studied law at university because sociology did not exist as an independent field of study. "Indeed," as historian James Q. Whitman has noted, "it is a striking fact that when modern social science finally appeared, it appeared not among theologians or philosophers, but among lawyers." (1991: 205). Understanding sociology's past requires understanding jurisprudence.

Another answer might be that legal theory has the potential to be important to contemporary sociology because legal theorists and social theorists have relevantly similar agendas these days. The main object of legal theory is legal doctrine, the set of concepts and categories that law students learn in law schools: constitutional provisions, statutory enactments, administrative regulations, precedents. But sociology is itself increasingly focused on cultural products as well: representations, mentalités, texts, and images. The ways in which legal theorists think about legal doctrine may be of more than passing interest to sociologists who are thinking through cultural formations.

But there is something even deeper about the contemporary connection between legal theory and social theory. Both try to reconcile the same tensions—between the written word and social practices, between structure and agency, between the normative and the descriptive, between formal elegance and descriptive adequacy. Just as the nineteenth century social theorists turned to law to see how society was organized, late twentieth century social theorists may look to law to find fellow travellers who are also trying to understand the complexity of the social world.

That said, I should provide one note of caution to sociologists about to undertake extensive reading in jurisprudence. Legal theorists often find that the same questions sociologists ask need different sorts of answers. Legal theorists tend to go back and forth between descriptive and normative arguments more fluidly than most social theorists (though feminist social theorists are one notable exception to this). Many legal theorists also accept certain contingent features of legal systems as being more fixed than sociologists would be inclined to imagine, sometimes conveying the impression that courts are the only institutions in the universe or that American rules of civil procedure (for example) are as fixed as fortresses and as unremarkable as gravity. Nevertheless, as I hope to show in this essay, social theorists may well find that legal theory is quite relevant for answering pressing questions in contemporary sociology.

JURISPRUDENCE AND SOCIOLOGY: A BRIEF HISTORY

Marx, Durkheim, and Weber had strong and deep ties to the law; Marx and Weber received their university educations in law, and Weber spent seven years being miserable while practicing it. Durkheim wrote about law throughout his career. He believed that law was the preeminent example of a social fact and that the evolution of societies could be traced through the relative elaboration of civil and criminal law (Durkheim 1964, Lukes & Scull 1983, Hunt 1978, Grace & Wilkinson 1978). Marx thought that class was most importantly defined through the legally constituted relationship of ownership of property and that law could best be understood as an ideological formation (Cain & Hunt 1978, Collins 1984). For Weber, the modern age was characterized primarily by the triumph of rational-legal authority in which social institutions were progressively conquered by norms modelled on formal legal procedure (Weber 1978, Kronman 1983, Tronto 1984).

What law represented for Weber, Marx, and Durkheim was not just a set of institutions and professions (though these were important in their own right), but it was also a system of ideas: rational legality, ideology, doctrine. Law was important because it provided an intellectual framework within which bureaucrats, capitalists, and common people thought about and acted in the social world.

The idea that law was an important subject of academic study was common in nineteenth century Europe. The term "jurisprudence," both then and now, has at least two distinct meanings that are often intertwined: (i) the body of scholarship that theorizes about law (legal theory), and (ii) the set of rules, principles, and official pronouncements that constitute "the law" as a substantive field (legal doctrine). Nineteenth century social theory drew freely from both because jurisprudential writing at the time took for granted that legal doctrine should be the main object of legal theory. Legal scholars like Montesquieu (1748), Maine (1864), Savigny (1829), and Gierke (1913) traced broad patterns in the history of legal doctrine to illuminate equally broad conceptual categories of legal theory. Marx, Weber, and Durkheim also examined the historical development of law, believing that social theory should comprehend legal forms (Kelley 1990).

It is no wonder that European social theory had its origins in legal scholarship. The nineteenth century continental social theorists were writing in a time that was enthusiastic about general codes. Reading the French Civil Code of 1804 or the German Civil Code of 1900, one can see that legal doctrine is like a rough draft of social theory, comprising concepts, categories, rules and procedures for managing the vast array of human conduct in an orderly and systematic way. A comprehensive system of contract law reads like general social theory, for example. It specifies types of social actors, the ways they may interact with each other, what they may expect, what they may do when expectations are violated. Legal rules are the general principles for understanding and managing such interactions. The social theory that arose from familiarity with legal doctrine also engaged in systematic examination of social life, specifying the same sorts of things that nineteenth century legal codes did in a systematic and comprehensive way.

American sociology, however, never had such strong formal ties to jurisprudence. Concern with law as an intellectual enterprise, so prominently featured in continental social theory, gave way in the new American urban sociology to the empirical study of deviance, criminality, and social control. Not that these things weren't important; they were crucial in understanding the problem of social order that had become central to American sociology. But once the historical study of law was transformed into the contemporary empirical study of criminal behavior, doctrinal ideas and legal ideals became less prominent in social theory.

Within American legal scholarship, however, the new empirical sociology was influential. Oliver Wendell Holmes explicitly distanced himself from Continental abstract theorizing by urging his colleagues to focus on "our friend the bad man" for "we shall find that he does not care two straws for axioms or deductions, but that he does want to know what the Massachusetts or English courts are likely to do in fact" (Holmes 1920:172–73). Harvard Law School Dean Roscoe Pound launched a movement in sociological jurisprudence that concentrated on the relation between law and social interests, seeing the developing social sciences as crucial in the understanding of legal forms (Pound 1911–1912). The laissez-faire attitude of sociological jurisprudence eventually gave way to the New Deal theorizing of the Legal Realists, for whom theory took as its object the way law worked in practice, breaking down the intellectual walls between law, politics, society, and culture. While mainstream American legal thought had previously emphasized the pure logic of abstract legal concepts through legal formalism, the Realists and their precursors were at pains to demonstrate that law was a human product contingent on time and place (Hunt 1978, Harris 1980).

European social theory had an influence on the Legal Realists, but not through the mediation of American sociologists. Instead, Columbia law professor Karl Llewellyn, who discovered Weber's writings on a trip to Germany in 1927 (Ansaldi 1992), provided one link (Llewellyn 1930, 1962). Weber had noted that "order will be called ... law if it is externally guaranteed by the probability that physical or psychological coercion will be applied by a staff of people in order to bring about compliance or avenge violation" (1978: 34), and a similar view of law echoes eerily through the American Legal Realist movement (Rumble 1968, Frank 1930, 1949, Cohen 1935). Llewellyn's lectures to the entering class of the Columbia Law School in 1930 borrowed Weber's emphasis on the importance of legal professionals in defining the law: "What [legal] officials do about law is, to my mind, the law itself" (1930: 3). This emphasis remains in socio-legal scholarship to this day.

In the meantime, back in American sociology, European social thought reappeared through a different line of transmission. Through Parsons' *The Structure of Social Action* and later through strategic translations of the works of Durkheim, Weber, Marx, and Simmel, American sociologists adopted the newly defined classics, but without the background to see just how these ideas resonated in European jurisprudence. Sociology appeared as a free-standing field with law as one possible subject; law was not seen as an intellectual tradition that had contributed in important ways to the development of social theory in the first place.

Numerous attempts in this century to provide a theoretically ambitious general social theory based in jurisprudence have been largely ignored by the discipline (Ehrlich 1913, Timasheff 1939, Hall 1963, Gurvitch 1973, Aubert 1969). More successful were attempts to link the sociology of law more directly to the classic writers: Durkheim's legacy was kept alive and extended in different ways by Schwartz & Miller (1964), Black (1989), and Evan (1990); Philip Selznick's discussion of the pervasiveness of norms of legality (1968) followed strong themes in Weber; Pashukanis (1929), Balbus (1977), Chambliss & Seidman (1982), and Thompson (1975) followed Marx. A group of scholars working in the 1960s and interested in combining social science and legal scholarship laid the foundation for what became the law and society movement, in which empiricism became the rallying cry (Friedman 1986). Demonstrating that "law in action" was different from "law on the books," early law and society scholars rejected normative jurisprudence and the doctrinal scholarship prevalent in law schools at the time, further estranging sociology of law from legal theory.

From the 1970s on, however, theoretical ferment in law and in social science brought the agendas of jurisprudence and general social theory closer together again. Theorists like Coleman (1990), Bourdieu (1987), Foucault (1977), and Luhmann (1985, 1988–1989) explicitly turned their attention to legal forms. Sociolegal scholars like Lempert & Sanders (1986), Post (1988, 1989), Simon (1993), and members of the Amherst Seminar on Legal Process and Legal Ideology (Silbey 1985, Sarat & Felstiner 1986, Yngvesson 1989, Merry 1990) embraced social theory in the course of studying law. Recently, the *Northwestern Law Review* published a symposium issue on Law and Social Theory in which notable social theorists and legal scholars explored the connection (1988–1989, with overviews by Mertz 1988–1989, van Zandt 1988–1989 and Calhoun 1988–1989). Social theory is having an increasing effect in law review articles, and legal theory is increasingly seeping into sociological writing, particularly in law and rationality studies and feminist theory.

But the overlap of potential mutual interest is even larger than this. In this essay I track some of the connections, outlining the major lines of work in contemporary legal theory: law and rationality studies, critical jurisprudence, the literary turn, discursive structuralisms and pragmatism. My discussion proceeds roughly chronologically, both across sections and within sections.

LAW AND RATIONALITY STUDIES

"Law and rationality" includes various schools of law and economics as well as the new public choice theories. They share a focus on individual choice and human rationality as the building blocks of social theory. Launched in the early 1960s, this field has since become crucially important in American law, and during the Reagan years many prominent theoreticians in the law and economics movement were appointed to the federal bench.

The growth of law and economics has paralleled the growth in legally informed rational choice theories in sociology, particularly those of Coleman, Elster, and Buchanan & Tullock. Coleman's *The Foundations of Social Theory* (1990) envisions social action as a system of rational decisions that both operate within an institutional framework and form the institutional framework itself. Coleman analyzes the way social context is derived from and influences the aggregation of individual decisions, through the legal ideas of sovereignty, rights, authority systems, and juristic persons. Elster uses his work on the limitations of a strict rationality model to analyze questions about constitutionalism and institutional design (1988), seeing constitutional drafting processes as a "gigantic natural experiment" for analysis of "bargaining, threats and warnings" (1991:447). Buchanan & Tullock (1962) applied public choice theory to the law. These approaches have a strong affinity with law and rationality studies, which divide into several schools.

The Chicago School

When Coase first published *The Problem of Social Cost* (1960), the field of law and economics was barely a blip on the intellectual map. Coase argued that in a world with no transaction costs, the initial assignment of property rights was irrelevant to the final distribution of property. And despite the fact that this looks like an argument that law makes no difference, the article is widely credited with launching the field, particularly the version associated with the University of Chicago and the *Journal of Legal Studies*.

The Chicago school of law and economics evaluates legal rules on the basis of their abilities to promote the efficient use of scarce resources and, in some versions, to produce the greatest amount of wealth in the society as a whole (Posner 1992). Legal rules should, and common law rules largely do, mirror what would happen if an error-free market could determine the outcomes, according to Chicago school theorists. Their approach is relentlessly individualistic, using Gary Becker's particular version of microeconomics for most of the theoretical framework (Becker 1976). It is also very court-centered, focusing on legal doctrine as it has been elaborated by judges as the main object of study. Most of the time, the concrete results of the Chicago school writers are consistent with a libertarian conservativism and, not surprisingly, the approach has generated a large critical literature (Leff 1974, Scheppele 1988), attacking it for being insufficiently sensitive to the variety of values in the law.

The Yale School

Guido Calabresi's book *The Cost of Accidents* (1970) launched the Yale school much the same way that Coase launched the Chicago school. Generally, a group of writers clustered around the Yale Law School and around the *Journal of Law, Economics and Organization* has been concerned with questions of institutional design (Williamson 1975), choices of legal rules (Calabresi & Melamed 1972), and ethical issues in institutional arrangements (Coleman 1988), rather than with working out ideal results from free-market assumptions. The approach tends to be quite institutional and realistic, focusing in particular on the relationship between the administrative state and economic formations. In contrast with the Chicago School, which views government largely as a pathology interfering with well-functioning markets, the Yale School sees public institutions as one organizational form among many which might handle a particular social problem. Rose-Ackerman, for example, argues for a reformist theory of the administrative state that starts from welfare economics rather than from microeconomics (1988). Such an approach generates a concern for social effects as well as individual effects.

The Legal Incentives School

Economists in this group focus on the effects of legal rules on the incentives of individuals who are engaging in rational action. As evidenced in the work of Shavell on tort law (1987), Mnookin & Kornhauser (1979) on bargaining in divorce cases, and in the Polinsky (1989) and Cooter & Ulen (1987) textbooks, scholars in this group use rational choice models to derive the expected effects of alternative legal rules, and then use welfare economics to assess which of competing legal rules produces the most desirable results. Applying the methods of public policy analysis to the study of legal rules, economists of this sort take law to be one of many sources of incentives, constraints, and opportunities.

The Public Choice School

Starting with Buchanan & Tullock (1962), public choice theory examines the collective consequences of individual choice. In legal circles, this traditionally meant thinking about the ways in which individual rationality produced collectively irrational results. But public choice has entered the theoretical fray in law schools most recently with the increasing concern about the rationality of the legislative process and its impact on statutory drafting and interpretation (Farber & Frickey 1991), the rationality of administrative agency decisions

(Eskridge & Ferejohn 1992), and the rationality of judicial review (Ferejohn & Weingast 1992). Critics have complained that these theories fail to take into account important differences across institutions (Rubin 1991), but the ability to use a theory that applies to all institutions regardless of difference is one of the main strengths, proponents claim.

Law and rationality studies have had an enormous impact on law. Many practitioners of this line of scholarship are now federal judges, applying their theories in the course of their judicial decisions. Virtually every major law school has an economist on the faculty to teach economics to law students. And law and rationality studies have had an important influence in rational choice theories in sociology, where law is now more prominently featured as an institutional constraint. In this area, at least, law and sociology are on quite good terms with each other.

CRITICAL JURISPRUDENCE

Politically and methodologically the opposite of law and rationality studies, critical jurisprudence is also flourishing in law schools. Critical jurisprudence comes from the academic left, parallelling the growth of cultural studies (Grossberg et al 1992) and producing an enormous range of writings on law and oppression and on ways of making legal institutions more democratically responsive. Critical jurisprudence embraces a far-flung and large range of scholars who identify themselves as being engaged in critical legal studies, feminist theory, and/or critical race theory. Many critical theorists identify with more than one of these labels, and much exciting intellectual activity these days is happening at the boundaries (Menkel-Meadow 1988, Harris 1990, Rhode 1990, Crenshaw 1989, Torres 1988, Trubek 1984, Johnson 1991).

Critical Legal Studies (CLS)

Starting as a social movement within American law schools in the late 1970s, the group called "The Conference on Critical Legal Studies" created an intellectual home for radical law teachers and by one count in 1989 claimed over 700 articles (Hutchinson 1989). Critical legal studies (CLS) is "influenced by a variety of currents in contemporary radical social theory, but [CLS] does not reflect any agreed upon set of political tenets or methodological approaches" (Kennedy & Klare 1984: 461). Nonetheless, certain critical themes emerge that capture the spirit of much CLS writing.

ATTACK ON LIBERAL LEGALISM   Many CLS writers believe that liberal legal theory, with its conceptions of rights, neutrality, and procedural justice, is an ideological cover for decisions governed by power and the maintenance of inequality (Unger 1986). By speaking in abstract terms, liberal legalism disguises its own fictions: that rules can decide concrete cases, that legal subjects are autonomous individuals, that intentions are sufficient to explain social action (Kelman 1987). Liberal legalism is exposed in CLS writings as a justification machine that serves primarily to reproduce social inequality. (But at least one critic complains that the liberalism CLS attacks is not a version most liberals are defending—Herzog 1987).

THE INDETERMINACY THESIS When judges decide cases, they claim that their results are compelled by the law. But actually, CLS writers argue, law consists of a whole variety of contradictions and inconsistencies, allowing decisions to go either way. Law is logically indeterminate and fails to compel a particular result (Singer 1986). Therefore, judicial decisions cannot be the self-contained models of reasoning that they pretend to be. Instead, they must rest on grounds outside of formal legal doctrine, grounds which are inevitably political (Kennedy 1979, Dalton 1985, Tushnet 1983, Klare 1978).

THE RELATIVE AUTONOMY OF LAW Having unmasked (or "trashed") liberal legal theory and shown that cases cannot be compelled by doctrine, CLS writers argue that law is inevitably tied to politics. Borrowing heavily from both Marx and Weber, critical legal scholars have elaborated a view that law is "relatively autonomous," meaning that although law uses a special form of argumentation that makes it distinct from ordinary politics, it always serves political interests and purposes (Kairys 1990, Gordon 1984). The framework of relative autonomy helps to explain why law may appear to be a self-contained logical system—it does develop according to its own internal rules of operation—but also why law must always be tied to the political.

LEGAL CONSCIOUSNESS Law operates by producing in those subject to it or trained in its use a specific legal consciousness. CLS writers have analyzed both the way in which law sets the terms within which the world is seen and the efforts of those dominated by such visions to escape from these ideologies (Kennedy 1980, Klare 1978).

These themes combine to form a basis for a critical legal practice, devoted to assisting the oppressed and to challenging power, particularly when it masquerades as inevitability. CLS scholars unmask the apparent neutrality of legal premises and show precisely how legal ideas and ideals are constantly being reconstructed to hide their own agendas. And CLS scholars often show the subaltern, subordinated discourses present alongside the authorized ones.

Feminist Jurisprudence

Feminist jurisprudence is centrally concerned with the influence of gender and gendered conceptions of the world on law and vice versa. Since law is a crucial site in which the fight for women's equality has been carried out, feminist jurisprudence has been important in the development of general feminist theory outside of law. Recent collections reveal the impressive vibrancy of feminist jurisprudence (Bartlett & Kennedy 1991, Weisberg 1993, Frug 1992a, Goldstein, 1992).

Most feminists share the view that society is patriarchal, organized and dominated by men, and therefore not necessarily hospitable to women. This dominance can be seen in the way in which gender (the social meaning given to biological sex differences) is employed to mark hierarchy. The role of gender is particularly crucial in law since law regulates all other institutions in a society. Starting from important analyses of areas of the law that were most obviously about women—abortion (Ginsburg 1985, Law 1984, Siegel 1992), rape (Estrich 1987, Olsen 1984), domestic violence (Mahoney 1991), pregnancy (Williams 1984–5), sexual harassment (MacKinnon 1979), employment discrimination (Schultz 1990), work and family issues (Olsen 1983), divorce (Fineman 1991), sexual orientation (Robson 1992), child custody (Fineman 1988), and pornography (Dworkin 1981)—feminist legal theory is now seeing the ways in which law is gendered all the way down, from topics not traditionally thought of as presenting feminist issues, like contracts and torts (Dalton 1985, Bender 1993), to legal education (Menkel-Meadow 1988), to legal methodology (Bartlett 1990), to legal practice (L White 1990, Davis 1991, Scheppele 1992). Feminist legal theory is not only about women; feminist legal theory is now a general theoretical approach to law.

So what does this approach include? Feminists disagree too much to have a common set of answers; what they share is a common framework within which feminist debates occur, emphasizing equality and difference, relations of power, complexities of social position, and subjectivity. They also share a concern with the common question: How can women's situation best be bettered?

EQUALITY VS DIFFERENCE On this question, feminists divide between those who favor treating women equally (in other words, just like men) (Ginsburg 1985) and those who favor treating women differently from men, in order to ensure equality in results (Littleton 1987, Minow 1990). Breaking new ground, "equality feminists" first achieved a series of legal victories in the areas of employment discrimination. This ultimately proved unsatisfying, however, when other barriers, like women's unique reproductive capacities, could not be handled within a strict equality framework. If women had to be treated just like men, then how could they be given maternity leave or pregnancy benefits? "Difference feminists" then argued that formal similarity of treatment would never be enough, because women and men are relevantly different. Such differences needed to be taken into account in fixing legal rules, "difference feminists" argued, or these rules would simply reproduce inequality. Equality could be achieved through differential treatment.

DOMINATION AND SUBORDINATION   Into this debate over equality and difference came another argument: perhaps what mattered was not the formal relation of comparison between men and women, but rather their power relative to each other. Men dominated; women were subordinated. From this, argued Catherine MacKinnon, one could attack the means through which men's domination is achieved: control over sex (MacKinnon 1989). In domination theory, the task of feminism is to end the subordination of women, not simply to make men and women "equal" in some abstract sense (Scales 1986, Colker 1986). Everyone could be equal and oppressed; the task of dominance feminism was to end the oppression.

ESSENTIALISM VS ANTIESSENTIALISM   But while difference and domination were becoming the central analytical tools of contemporary legal feminism, other differences and relations of domination among women themselves began to become apparent. Both dominance and difference theorists were often accused of being essentialist—that is, of defending an idea of woman's "essence" that was the same for all women. Though few feminists overtly defend essentialism, something like essentialism was presumed in early feminist theory as a way of sharpening the primary contrast between men and women. Antiessentialist theory celebrates difference among women and refuses to see "woman" as a unitary social category. This has clearly become the more dominant view in recent years within feminist legal theory, as feminists have examined questions of race, ethnicity, and sexual orientation (Harris 1990, Robson 1992, Matsuda 1989a, Crenshaw 1989, Spellman 1988).

SUBJECTIVITY AND RELATIONALITY   Feminist legal theorists are also now exploring different models of thinking about legal subjects (i) as requiring connections with others rather than seeking separation through claims of autonomy (West 1988, Minow 1990, Nedelsky 1989), (ii) as defined by their subjectivity rather than by objectivist conceptions (Matuda 1989b, Williams 1991), and (iii) as finding that the experience of subordination (Menkel-Meadow 1988) or the sense of an embodied self (West 1988) leads to special insight. These feminists are turning what were once thought to be liabilities of women into sources of strength and illumination, and in so doing, they are reconfiguring the subject of law.

Critical Race Theory

Like feminist legal theory and often closely aligned with it, critical race theory is centrally concerned with questions of oppression, difference, and equality.

Critical race theory had its official beginning in 1989 when a group of scholars of color held a conference in Madison, Wisconsin. Many of these scholars had been previously involved with critical legal studies or with feminist jurisprudence, and the 1989 conference ratified what had already been the case for some time: Critical race theory was a major presence in American legal theory.

Critical race theorists are a diverse group, speaking about many different areas of law in many different voices. Some central themes can be found, however, themes highlighted below in the words of critical race theorists.

"LOOKING TO THE BOTTOM" (Matsuda 1989a): Critical race theorists generally start from the observation that to be a person of color in America is to be oppressed, to have one's subjectivity colonized by others who either silence the opposition of persons of color or speak in their name. Being oppressed creates fundamental disadvantages for those who are so treated. Critical race theory must start from the bottom, by focusing on the experiences and situations of oppressed people of color, giving voice to the concrete experiences of subalterns (Matsuda 1989a, Peller 1990, Johnson 1991).

"WE SEE A DIFFERENT WORLD..." (Lawrence 1990): Because they share experiences of oppression, people of color see the world differently from those who have not had such experiences. With different vision and different voice, scholars of color can bring to legal analysis perspectives that were previously excluded (Lopez 1987, Bell 1987, 1992, Williams 1991).

"A PLEA FOR NARRATIVE" (Delgado 1989) To bring these excluded perspectives to the law, some critical race scholars tell stories about their experiences or the experiences of other people of color to make their presence real in legal scholarship (Bell 1987, 1992, Williams 1991, Scales-Trent 1990, Matsuda 1989b). Overcoming the abstraction of conventional legal analysis and the sanitized versions of facts presented in court decisions, the highly personal stories in these articles break through alleged neutralities.

"EXPLAIN THE SOURCE AND STRENGTH OF MINORITY CONVICTIONS THAT COURTS ... ARE CAPABLE OF BIAS" (Davis 1989: 1559): Some critical race theorists trace the ways in which law undermines people of color, despite official rhetoric to the contrary. Lawrence explains the extraordinary pervasiveness of unconcious racism and shows how it is ignored by courts (1987). Austin traces the material conditions of young women of color and shows how courts fail to recognize them (1989). Davis shows how African Americans interpret legal decisions as "microaggressions" whose cumulative effect is large (1989). Harris analyzes the way that whiteness has been treated as a property right, excluding people of color from making privileged claims (1993). Matsuda has identified "accent discrimination" by showing how the comprehensibility of an accent depends on the hearer as much as the speaker, but courts have not heard this yet (1991).

"MULTIPLE CONSCIOUSNESS AS A JURISPRUDENTIAL METHOD" (Matsuda 1989a) People of color have an ambivalent relationship to law. Sometimes the law helps overcome discrimination, as when Williams reports that having a formal contract can limit the arbitrariness to which people of color are exposed (Williams 1991). But other times the law fails miserably. Matsuda counsels multiple consciousness, being able to think both inside and outside the law. Crenshaw also proposes a multiplicity of identifications in dealing with the combined effects of gender and race (1989). Such accumulated scholarship shows the profound and indelible mark of race in the law.

Critical race theory has come in for criticism (Kennedy 1989), but as a recent bibliography demonstrates, it is more than alive and well (Delgado & Stefancic 1993).

THE LITERARY TURN

Like many disciplines in the 1980s, law reeled from the invasion of literary theory. The new literary theory hit law hard because it challenged fundamental assumptions about the stability of legal doctrine. In the standard view, law was supposed to govern by constraining the future with words written in the past. But the new literary theory showed that all texts, including legal ones, were unstable in their meanings, either because writing always represses what it cannot control (Derrida 1976) or because meaning varies with the relevant "community of interpretation" (Fish 1980). Of course, these observations were broadly consistent with what critical legal studies, feminist, and critical race scholars were also writing about: that claims to objectivity and stability of the law were built on the power of law to suppress alternative viewpoints. The theoretical destabilization of texts and the debates that resulted can be discussed in the general categories of legal interpretation, postmodernism, and narrative jurisprudence.

Legal Interpretation

If, as literary theory demonstrated, texts were unstable, then how could they be shored up again to provide authoritative interpretations? Of course, critical legal scholars were saying that such a thing could not be done at all (Tushnet 1983, Levinson 1982). But other legal theorists tried to come up with ingenious ways to stabilize one of the embarrassing multiplicity of apparently "correct" interpretations any legal text could produce. Each of these efforts resulted in bringing in something from outside the text to accomplish this purpose, and this is where law must be seen as caught in a larger web of cultural processes. Law could no longer be officially portrayed as a closed system of logic immune from social influences.

Much of the fight occurred over interpretation of American law's master text: the US Constitution. Reagan's Attorney General Edwin Meese argued that the only responsible way for a court to interpret the Constitution was by reference to the intentions of the framers (Meese 1988, but see Brest 1980). Supreme Court Justice William Brennan argued that a court must inevitably engage contemporary concerns: "We current justices read the Constitution in the only way that we can: as twentieth-century Americans" (Brennan 1988: 17). Into this debate plunged some substantial fraction of all jurisprudential writing published in the 1980s.

What resulted was a vast catalogue of different strategies of reading and understanding texts. In the 1950s, Wechsler had argued that courts should decide constitutional questions by reference to neutral principles that could be defended regardless of the particular dispute at hand (1959). And Black and Ely tried to argue that one need not look outside the text at all. Staking out "structuralist" positions (albeit different ones), they argued that the meaning of individual clauses in the Constitution could and should be derived either from the internal structure of the overall document or the sense that could be made of the vision of government and society that such a text contained (Black 1969, Ely 1980). Also trying to stay close to the text, Schauer noted that the plain language of constitutional provisions could convey meaning unproblematically to ordinary readers most of the time (1985).

But an assault on these strategies of reading was mounted by a set of authors who were concerned with specifying the social context under which language could be read like that. Fish argued that the idea of a single literal language and a recourse to the text alone only fools the interpreter, since the meaning of words is always supplied by context. While in some circumstances the context may be taken for granted enough to be unproblematic, it is always socially situated in a particular "community of interpretation" that ultimately judges the "reading" to be reasonable or not (1980). Fiss also located grounded readings in the larger community, in the invocation by a judge of public values (1982). Dworkin argued that the relevant context could be constructed by a judge who first developed a justifiable political theory and then read a legal text in light of that theory (1986). And Sunstein argued that one needs to situate texts in the context of the political process that gave rise to them to understand how they might be read (1990). Levinson provides a useful and humorous summary of this literature in his analysis of the "adultery clause of the Ten Commandments" (1985).

In the meantime, other theorists were taking a more cultural view of the interpretation issue. Rather than trying to justify particular answers to particular legal questions, interpretive theorists developed accounts of interpretive practice as an ongoing activity of legal and other social institutions. Starting from the stark proposition, "We inhabit a nomos—a normative world," Robert Cover examined the way in which any community contains within it multiple communities of normative meaning. Legal interpretation links general nomos with particular narrative, but in so doing judges flatten the normative diversity of the social world through exclusion of alternative perspectives (1983). Later, Cover showed how the interpretive acts of judges could be seen as acts of violence since they produced punishment, disruption, and violence in the world (Cover 1986, Sarat & Kearns 1991, 1992).

Other cultural theorists examined how legal representation and broader cultural images both constitute and resist each other. Geertz showed the interpretive fluidity around central legal conceptions in different cultures (1983). JB White explored the disjunctures that result when one system of thinking is translated into another (1990). Scheppele showed how the construction of facts is always an interpretive enterprise (1990). Humphreys shows how much of law could be seen as discourse (1986). The interpretive revolution ran all the way through legal scholarship.

Postmodern Legal Theory

Postmodernism can be described as a theoretical stance that attacks modernism. As an intellectual project, modernism creates order, systems, structures and plans through conceptual neatness and appeals to shared values. Postmodernism is, by modernist standards, messy. It separates images from the objects that such images claim to represent and in so doing denies the possibility of finding truth; it combines cultural shards, textual pieces, imaginaries. Postmodernism defies logic. It, perhaps fittingly, also defies common definition by those who claim to practice it (Schanck 1992).

In some legal postmodernist writing, modernism is equated with "the Enlightenment project" of liberalism, and so postmodernism becomes a critique of liberalism (Schlag 1990). Some postmodernist legal theorists emphasize the social transformation that has broken apart modernist orderings, creating a postmodern condition to which legal interpretation must respond (Balkin 1992). Others emphasize the impossibility of creating legitimate legal interpretations in the face of the now-demonstrated instability of texts (Hunt 1990). As it is used in legal theory these days, postmodernism tends to be a critical discourse. As a result, postmodern scholarship is allied with some aspects of critical legal studies (Peller 1985), feminism (Cornell 1991, Patterson 1992, Frug 1992b), and critical race theory (Thomas 1992), in addition to bringing in strong strands of sociological constructivism (Santos 1987, Eisenstein 1988). Even Derrida himself has turned his attention to the deconstruction of law (Derrida 1992).

Narrative Jurisprudence

Narrative jurisprudence understands legal discourse and the discourse of legal subjects as stories (Scheppele 1989). Recent social theory indicates that people interpret what happens to them narratively by fitting them into story structures (Bruner 1991, Carr 1990). Courts, too, makes sense of things as stories, since they hear cases as elaborations of particular events through story forms (Hastie & Pennington 1991).

Narrative jurisprudence has two distinct strands. In one, linked to some versions of feminism and critical race theory, narrative is the method through which oppressed groups and individuals make their experiences visible in law. "Outsider jurisprudence" (Matsuda 1989b) involves women and people of color telling stories of oppression, sometimes as parables (Bell 1992), sometimes as personal revelations (Williams 1991, Ashe 1989, Scales-Trent 1990), sometimes as a strategy of empowerment (Delgado 1989, Mahoney 1991), sometimes as guide to legal practice (L White 1990), sometimes to reform the law (Matsuda 1989b). These stories are consciousness-raising in the legal literature, making experiences visible that might otherwise not be known to a community that is predominantly white and male (Abrams 1991).

The other strand of narrative jurisprudence analyzes stories that have appeared in legal settings, sometimes to work out what makes some stories more believable than others (Bennett & Feldman 1981, Conley & O'Barr 1990, Scheppele 1992), sometimes to use them as a way of exploring the social context that makes these narratives compelling (Foucault 1975, Ginzburg 1983, Guha 1987, Davis 1987), sometimes to identify their standard forms (Sherwin 1988, Lopez 1984). Bringing methods from the humanities into the analysis of legal stories, narrative theorists try to move away from abstraction to the concrete experiences of particular individuals (Elkins 1985, West 1985).

Stories add in the vividness of detail and context what they may lose in representativeness. Some writers find this disturbing, claiming that the focus on the potentially idiosyncratic individual case obscures larger social patterns (Farber & Sherry 1993, Tushnet 1992).

DISCURSIVE STRUCTURALISMS

Social theorists have been making structuralisms more open to discursive influence through a new emphasis on the social construction of meaning. Where old structuralisms envisioned society as a set of rigid structures off which people bounced like tennis balls, the new discursive structuralisms see society as a dynamic interplay between meaningful action and more enduring social formations. Bourdieu, Giddens, Foucault, and (in one reading, at least) Luhmann have been influential in legal theory by providing a way to think about connections between legal knowledge and social structure.

Practice Theory

Developed through the works of Bourdieu and Giddens, practice theory involves tracing the connections between the daily practice of social agents and the larger structures that those practices constitute, resist, and change. Bourdieu is centrally concerned with the reproduction of social structures through the meaningful activity of agents. From the standpoint of agents, social structures appear as a set of inevitabilities, the naturalized patterns of thinking and doing that constitute a "habitus." But agents create these structures over time by reproducing meaning with the imprint of power (Bourdieu 1977, Bourdieu & Wacquant 1992). In his analysis of the "juridical field," Bourdieu shows how legal concepts and categories form a habitus within which legal practitioners engage the social world and within which struggles over meaning and power are contained (Bourdieu 1987).

Giddens elaborates a view of the "duality of structure," envisioning social structures as both the precondition and result of social practices. Constraining and enabling human agency, social structures comprise generative rules and relationships that social actors use strategically to make their way in the world (Giddens 1979).

Practice theory is starting to catch on among legal theorists, sometimes within a critical legal studies framework and sometimes outside. Coombe (1989), Peller (1985), Boyle (1985), and Francis (1986) are working out applications of practice theory in areas as diverse as sexual violence and debt collection.

Genealogical Inquiries

According to Foucault, genealogies are "histories of the present" that reconstruct the past, showing how knowledge of the "real" and the "inevitable" changes over time. For Foucault, power is inextricably intertwined with knowledge, so that "discourses" (relatively autonomous fields of representation and belief) both shape struggles for power and compete among themselves for dominance in the social world. Law, for Foucault, is a historically situated set of discourses that produce conforming subjects (Foucault 1977, 1978, Hunt 1992).

Foucault's work has produced a growing literature in sociolegal studies that is simultaneously sympathetic and critical. Simon's work on the uses of parole (1993), Constable's book on the genealogy of the mixed jury (1994), and Garland's book on theories of punishment (1990) are particularly creative genealogies of legal practices.

The Amherst School

The Amherst Seminar on Legal Ideology and Legal Process has combined elements of practice theory with Foucauldian insights about the discursive construction of legal consciousness (Silbey 1985, Bumiller 1988, Ewick & Silbey 1992). Members of this interdisciplinary seminar have concentrated on the way in which legal ideologies, the concepts and categories of legal thought, are often negotiated in the process of application (Mather & Yngvesson 1980–1981, Sarat & Felstiner 1986, Harrington 1985). They recognize that legal ideology is found not just in official legal settings like courtrooms, but it is also mobilized and constituted in nonlegal settings as well (Merry 1990, Yngvesson 1989, Brigham 1987). And they explore these processes doing ethnographies, collecting stories, and following the traces of legal discourse in everyday life as well as traces of everyday life in legal discourse.

Autopoesis

Niklas Luhmann at first glance looks like a structural functionalist with his emphasis on systems theory, but on closer reading some of the same discursive structuralist tendencies are apparent. In *A Sociological Theory of Law*, Luhmann describes law as the institution in society that deals with disappointed expectations, both normative and descriptive (Luhmann 1985). When violations occur in what one expects would be done or in what one believes should be done, law is the institution that remedies disappointed expectations by rewriting the world. Most of those who have been influenced by Luhmann focus on the way in which law is constituted as a relatively autonomous system in a differentiated society, emphasizing systemic aspects of law (Teubner 1988). But Luhmann may also be read to say that law is an institution that mediates between expectations and potential future states, between cultural formations and material circumstances.

LEGAL PRAGMATISM

Perhaps exhausted by all of this theorizing, legal scholarship has turned to pragmatism (Brint & Weaver 1991). Pragmatism eschews large conceptual schemes in favor of contextualized knowledge. It starts from the present "here and now," rather than from imagined neutral places and times. It goes somewhere that will make a difference, doing only what is necessary to solve practical problems at hand. It is antifoundationalist, believing that knowledge has only the organization we bring to it and that the search for first principles inevitably turns up nothing very useful. To the pragmatist, truth comprises those things we know that hang together with everything else we believe to be the case. Theory is not what is done on special occasions; theory is what each of us does all the time to make sense of things.

Law, to the pragmatist, is not a pure logical system, but a set of practices: situated, instrumental, sensitive to time and place (Grey 1989, Minow & Spellman 1989). Judges should decide cases without grand schemes, but with sensitivity to the local context of each case (Farber 1988). Legal theorists should stop straining at abstractions and should examine history and culture to understand how law works. And many legal theorists have joined the pragmatist cause, creating alliances between pragmatism and feminism (Radin 1989), the left generally (Baker 1992), and most schools of legal thought. In fact, one commentator noted, "it seems only a slight exaggeration to suggest that a movement which five years ago included almost no one today appears to embrace virtually everyone" (Smith 1990: 409).

AND SOCIOLOGY?

This necessarily brief survey of a wide range of legal theorizing should convince sociologists that many of the same intellectual currents that preoccupy sociologists are also central to jurisprudence. But it should also say more. Social theory has its roots in legal theory, and the agendas of classical social theorists are tied up with jurisprudence. Contemporary social theory is struggling with many of the same issues as contemporary legal theory is, but now, with the differentiation of disciplines, each field is more likely to go it alone. If legal theorists and social theorists followed the developments in each other's disciplines more closely, we each might avoid some blind alleys that the other discipline has already discovered, and we might learn something in the juxtapositions that would otherwise go unnoticed.

ACKNOWLEDGMENTS

Susan Silbey and Leslie Goldstein supplied wonderful advice and detailed comments that only people who also live in this neck of the interdisciplinary woods would be able to provide. I would also like to thank Paul Courant, Avery Katz, Richard Lempert (and his sociology of law graduate seminar), Sanford Levinson, Gianfranco Poggi, and Rachel Rosenfeld for constructive criticism, gentle guidance, and reference wrangling.

Literature Cited

Abrams K. 1991. Hearing the call of stories. *Calif. Law Rev.* 79:971

Ansaldi M. 1992. The German Llewellyn. *Brook. Law Rev.* 58:702

Ashe M. 1989. Zig-Zag stitching and the seamless web: Thoughts on 'reproduction' and the law. *Nova Law Rev.* 13:355

Aubert W. 1969. Introduction. In *The Sociology of Law,* ed. W. Aubert. London: Penguin

Austin R. 1989. Sapphire bound! *Wisc. Law Rev.* 1989:539–78

Balbus ID. 1977. Commodity form and legal form. *Law & Soc. Rev.* 11:571–88

Balkin JM. 1992. What is a postmodern constitutionalism? *Mich. Law Rev.* 90:1966

Baker LA. 1992. 'Just do it': Pragmatism and progressive social change. *Va. Law Rev.* 78:697-

Bartlett K. 1990. Feminist legal methods. *Harvard Law Rev.* 103:829

Bartlett K, Kennedy R, eds. 1991. *Feminist Legal Theory: Readings in Law and Gender.* Boulder: Westview. 446 pp.

Becker G. 1976. *The Economic Approach to Human Behavior.* Chicago: Univ. Chicago Press

Bell D. 1987. *And We Are Not Saved.* New York: Basic Books. 288 pp.

Bell D. 1992. *Faces at the Bottom of the Well.* New York: Basic Books. 222 pp.

Bender L. 1993. An overview of feminist torts scholarship. *Cornell Law Rev.* 78:575

Bennett LW, Feldman M. 1981. *Reconstructing Reality in the Courtroom.* New Brunswisk: Rutgers Univ. Press. 203 pp.

Black C. 1969. *Structure and Relationship in Constitutional Law.* Woodbridge, Conn: Ox Bow Press. 98 pp.

Black D. 1989. *Sociological Justice.* New York: Oxford Univ. Press. 179 pp.

Bourdieu P. 1977. *Outline of a Theory of Practice.* Cambridge: Cambridge Univ. Press. 248 pp.

Bourdieu P. 1987. The force of law: Toward a sociology of the juridical field. *Hastings J. Law* 38:209–48

Bourdieu P, Wacquant L. 1992. *An Invitation to Reflexive Sociology.* Chicago: Univ. Chicago Press. 322 pp.

Boyle J. 1985. The politics of reason: Critical legal studies theory and local social thought. *Univ. Penn. Law Rev.* 685

Brennan W. 1988. The Constitution of the United States: Contemporary ratification. In *Interpreting Law and Literature*, ed. S Levinson, S Mailloux, pp. 13–24. Evanston: Northwestern Univ. Press

Brest P. 1980. The misconceived quest for original understanding. *Boston Univ. Law Rev.* 60:204

Brigham J. 1987. Rights, rage and remedy: Forms of law in political discourse. *Stud. Am. Polit. Dev.* 2:303–40

Brint M, Weaver W, eds. 1991. *Pragmatism in Law and Society.* Boulder: Westview. 400 pp.

Bruner J. 1991. The narrative construction of reality. *Crit. Inq.* 18:1–21

Buchanan J, Tullock G. 1962. *The Calculus of Consent.* Ann Arbor: Univ. Mich. Press

Bumiller K. 1988. *The Civil Rights Society.* Johns Hopkins Univ. Press. 161 pp.

Cain M, Hunt A, eds. 1978. *Marx and Engels on Law.* New York: Academic. 281 pp.

Calabresi G. 1970. *The Cost of Accidents.* New Haven: Yale Univ. Press. 340 pp.

Calabresi G, Melamed AD. 1972. Property rules, liability rules and inalienability: One view of the cathedral. *Harvard Law Rev.* 85:1089

Calhoun C. 1988–89. Social theory and the law: Systems theory, normative justification and postmodernism. *Northwest. Univ. Law Rev.* 83:398–460

Carr D. 1990. *Time, Narrative and History.* Bloomington: Indiana Univ. Press. 189 pp.

Chambliss W, Seidman R. 1982. *Law, Order and Power.* Reading, Mass: Addison-Wesley. 331 pp. 2nd ed.

Coase R. 1960. The problem of social cost. *J. Law & Econ.* 3:1–32

Cohen F. 1935. Transcendental nonsense and the functionalist approach. *Colo. Law Rev.* 35:609–41

Coleman J. 1988. *Markets, Morals and the Law.* Cambridge: Cambridge Univ. Press. 393 pp.

Coleman JS. 1990. *Foundations of Social Theory.* Cambridge: Harvard Univ. Press. 993 pp.

Colker R. 1986. Anti-subordination above all: Sex, race and equal protection. *NY Univ. Law Rev.* 61:1003

Collins H. 1984. *Marxism and Law.* New York: Oxford Univ. Press. 159 pp.

Conley JM, O'Barr WM. 1990. *Rules v. Relationships: The Ethnography of Legal Discourse.* Chicago: Chicago Univ. Press. 222 pp.

Constable M. 1994. *The Law of the Other: The Mixed Jury, Changing Conceptions of Citizenship, Law and Knowledge.* Chicago: Chicago Univ. Press. 184 pp.

Coombe R. 1989. Room for manoever: Toward a theory of practice in critical legal studies. *Law & Soc. Inq.* 14:69–121

Cooter R, Ulen T. 1987. *Law and Economics.* Glenview, Ill: Scott, Foresman. 644 pp.

Cornell D. 1991. *Beyond Accommodation: Ethical Feminism, Deconstruction and the Law.* New York: Routledge. 239 pp.

Cover R. 1983. Nomos and narrative. *Harvard Law Rev.* 97:4

Cover R. 1986. Violence and the word. *Yale Law J.* 95: 1601

Crenshaw K. 1989. Demarginalizing the intersection of race and sex: A black feminist critique of antidiscrimination doctrine, feminist theory and antiracist politics. *Univ. Chicago Legal Forum* 1989:139–42

Dalton C. 1985. An essay in the deconstruction of contract doctrine. *Yale Law J.* 94:977

Davis NZ. 1987. *Fiction in the Archives: Pardon Tales and Their Tellers in Sixteenth Century France.* Stanford: Stanford Univ. Press. 217 pp.

Davis P. 1989. Law as microaggression. *Yale Law J.* 98:1559–77

Davis P. 1991. Contextual legal criticism: A demonstration exploring hierarchy and 'feminine' style. *NY Univ. Law Rev.* 66:1635

Delgado R. 1989. Storytelling for oppositionists and others: A plea for narrative. *Mich. Law Rev.* 87:2411–41

Delgado R, Stefancic J. 1993. Critical race theory: An annotated bibliography. *Virginia Law Rev.* 79:461

Derrida J. 1992. Force of law: The 'mythical foundation of authority.' In *Deconstruction and the Possibility of Justice,* ed. D Cornell,

M Rosenfeld, DG Carlson, pp. 3-67. New York: Routledge
Derrida J. 1976. *Of Grammatology*. Transl. G Spivak. Baltimore: Johns Hopkins Univ. Press
Durkheim E. 1964 (1893). *The Division of Labor in Society*. Glencoe, Ill: Free Press
Dworkin A. 1981. *Pornography: Men Possessing Women*. New York: Perigee Books. 300 pp.
Dworkin RM. 1986. *Law's Empire*. Cambridge: Harvard Univ. Press. 470 pp.
Ehrlich E. 1913. *Fundamental Principles of the Sociology of Law*. New York: Russell & Russell
Eisenstein Z. 1988. *The Female Body and the Law*. Berkeley: Univ. Calif. Press. 235 pp.
Elkins J. 1985. On the emergence of narrative jurisprudence: The humanitistic perspective finds a new path. *Legal Stud. Forum* 9:123
Elster J. 1988. Arguments for constitutional choice: Reflections on the transition to socialism. In *Constitutionalism and Democracy*, ed. J Elster, R Slagstad, pp. 303-23. Cambridge: Cambridge Univ. Press
Elster J. 1991. Constitutionalism in Eastern Europe: An introduction. *Univ. Chicago Law Rev.* 58:447
Ely JH. 1980. *Democracy and Distrust*. Cambridge: Harvard Univ. Press. 269 pp.
Eskridge WN, Ferejohn J. 1992. The Article I, Section 7 Game. *Georgetown Law J.* 80:523-64
Estrich S. 1987. *Real Rape*. Cambridge: Harvard Univ. Press. 160 pp.
Evan W. 1990. *Social Structure and Law: Theoretical and Empirical Perspectives*. New York: Sage
Ewick P, Silbey S. 1992. Conformity, contestation and resistance: An account of legal consciousness. *New Engl. Law Rev.* 26:731
Farber DA. 1988. Legal pragmatism and the constitution. *Minn. Law Rev.* 72:1331-44
Farber DA, Frickey PP. 1991. *Law and Public Choice: A Critical Introduction*. Chicago: Chicago Univ. Press. 159 pp.
Farber DA, Sherry S. 1993. Telling stories out of school: An essay on legal narrative. *Stanford Law Rev.* 45:807
Ferejohn J, Weingast B. 1992. Limitations of statutes: Strategic statutory interpretation. *Georgetown Law J.* 80:565
Fineman MA. 1988. Dominant discourse, professional language and legal change in child custody decisionmaking. *Harvard Law Rev.* 101:727
Fineman MA. 1991. *The Illusion of Equality: The Rhetoric and Reality of Divorce Law Reform*. Chicago: Univ. Chicago Press. 252 pp.
Fish S. 1980. *Is There a Text In This Class?* Cambridge: Harvard Univ. Press

Fiss O. 1982. Objectivity and interpretation. *Stanford Law Rev.* 34:739
Foucault M. 1975. *I, Pierre Riviere, Having Slaughtered My Mother, My Sister and My Brother ... A Case of Parricide in the 19th Century*. Lincoln: Nebraska Univ. Press
Foucault M. 1977. *Discipline and Punish: The Birth of the Prison*. Transl. A Sheridan. New York: Vintage. 333 pp.
Foucault M. 1978. *The History of Sexuality*, Vol. I. New York: Pantheon
Francis C. 1986. Practice, strategy and institution: Debt collection in the English common-law courts 1740-1840. *Northwest. Law Rev.* 80:807-45
Frank J. 1930. *Law and the Modern Mind*. New York: Howard-McCann. 368 pp.
Frank J. 1949. *Courts on Trial*. New York: Atheneum
Friedman L. 1986. The Law and Society Movement. *Stanford Law Rev.* 38:763
Frug MJ. 1992a. *Women and the Law*. Westbury, NY: Foundation Press. 864 pp.
Frug MJ. 1992b. *Postmodern Legal Feminism*. New York: Routledge. 214 pp.
Garland D. 1990. *Punishment in Modern Society: A Study in Social Theory*. Chicago: Chicago Univ. Press. 312 pp.
Geertz C. 1983. Local knowledge: Fact and law in comparative perspective. In *Local Knowledge*, pp. 164-236. New York: Basic Books. 244 pp.
Giddens A. 1979. *Central Problems in Social Theory: Action, Structure and Contradiction in Social Analysis*. Berkeley: Calif. Univ. Press. 294 pp.
Gierke OF. 1934 (1913). *Natural Law and the Theory of Society, 1500-1800*. Cambridge: Cambridge Univ. Press
Ginsburg RB. 1985. Some thoughts on autonomy and equality in relation to Roe v. Wade. *N. Carolina Law Rev.* 63:375
Ginzburg C. 1983. *Night Battles: Witchcraft and Agrarian Culture in the Sixteenth and Seventeenth Centuries*. Transl. J & A Tedeschi. New York: Penguin. 209 pp.
Goldstein L, ed. 1992. *Feminist Jurisprudence: The Difference Debate*. Lanham, MD: Rowman & Littlefield. 286 pp.
Gordon R. 1984. Critical legal histories. *Stanford Law Rev.* 36:57
Grace C, Wilkinson P. 1978. *Sociological Inquiry and Legal Phenomena*. New York: St. Martin's. 307 pp.
Grey TC. 1989. Holmes and legal pragmatism. *Stanford Law Rev.* 41:787
Grossberg L, Nelson C, Treichler P, eds. 1992. *Cultural Studies*. Champaign: Ill. Univ. Press. 788 pp.
Guha R. 1987. Chandra's death. *Subaltern Stud.* 5:135-65
Gurvitch G. 1973. *Sociology of Law*. London: Routledge & Kegan Paul

Hall J. 1963. *Comparative Law and Social Theory*. Baton Rouge: Louisiana State Univ. Press. 167 pp.

Harrington C. 1985. *Shadow Justice*. Westport, Conn: Greenwood. 216 pp.

Harris AP. 1990. Race and essentialism in feminist legal theory. *Stanford Law Rev.* 42:581

Harris C. 1993. Whiteness as property. *Harvard Law Rev.* 106:1707–91

Harris JW. 1980. *Legal Philosophies*. London: Butterworths. 282 pp.

Hastie R, Pennington N. 1991. A cognitive theory of juror decision-making: The story model. *Cardozo Law Rev.* 13:519

Herzog D. 1987. As many as six impossible things before breakfast. *Calif. Law Rev.* 75:607

Holmes OW. 1920. *Collected Papers*. New York: Harcourt Brace & Co.

Humphreys SC. 1986. Law as discourse. *Hist. Anthropol.* 1:

Hunt A. 1978. *The Sociological Movement in Law*. London: Macmillan. 183 pp.

Hunt A. 1990. The big fear: Law confronts postmodernism. *McGill Law J.* 35:507–40

Hunt A. 1992. Foucault's expulsion of law: Toward a retrieval. *Law & Soc. Inq.* 17:1–38

Hutchinson A, ed. 1989. *Critical Legal Studies*. Totowan, NJ: Rowman & Littlefield. 348 pp.

Johnson AM. 1991. The new voice of color. *Yale Law J.* 100:2007–63

Journal of Legal Education. 1988. *Special Issue on Women in Legal Education — Pedagogy, Law, Theory and Practice*

Kairys D, ed. 1990. *The Politics of Law.*. New York: Pantheon. 481 pp. 2nd ed.

Kelley DR. 1990. *The Human Measure: Social Thought in the Western Legal Tradition*. Cambridge: Harvard Univ. Press. 358 pp.

Kelman M. 1987. *A Guide to Critical Legal Studies*. Cambridge: Harvard Univ. Press. 360 pp.

Kennedy D. 1979. The structure of Blackstone's Commentaries. *Buffalo Law Rev.* 28:205

Kennedy D. 1980. Toward an historical understanding of legal consciousness. *Res. Law & Soc.* 3:3

Kennedy D, Klare K. 1984. A bibliography of critical legal studies. *Yale Law J.* 94:461–90

Kennedy R. 1989. Racial critiques of legal academia. *Harvard Law Rev.* 102:1745–819

Klare K. 1978. Judicial deradicalization of the Wagner Act and the origins of modern legal consciousness 1937–1941. *Minn. Law Rev.* 62:265

Kronman AT. 1983. *Max Weber*. Stanford: Stanford Univ. Press. 214 pp.

Law S. 1984. Rethinking sex and the Constitution. *Univ. Penn. Law Rev.* 132:955

Lawrence C III. 1987. The id, the ego and equal protection: Reckoning with unconscious racism. *Stanford Law Rev.* 39:317–88

Lawrence C III. 1990. If he hollers, let him go: Regulating racist speech on campus. *Duke Law J.* 431–83

Leff AA. 1974. Economic analysis of law: Some realism about nominalism. *Virginia. Law Rev.* 61:451–82

Lempert RO, Sanders J. 1986. *An Invitation to Law and Social Science*. New York: Longman. 528 pp.

Levinson S. 1982. Law as literature. *Texas Law Rev.* 60:373

Levinson S. 1985. On interpretation: The adultery clause of the Ten Commandments. *South. Calif. Law Rev.* 58:719

Littleton C. 1987. Reconstructing sexual equality. *Calif. Law Rev.* 75:1279

Llewellyn K. 1930. *The Bramble Bush: On Our Law and Its Study*. New York: Oceana. 192 pp.

Llewellyn K. 1962. *Jurisprudence: Realism in Theory and Practice*. Chicago: Univ. Chicago Press

Lopez G. 1984. Lay lawyering. *UCLA Law Rev.* 32:1

Lopez G. 1987. The idea of a constitution in the Chicano tradition. *J. Legal Ed.* 37:162–69

Luhmann N. 1985. *A Sociological Theory of Law*. Transl. E King, M Albrow. Boston: Routledge. 421 pp.

Luhmann N. 1988–89. Law as a social system. *Northwest. Univ. Law Rev.* 83:136–50

Lukes S, Scull A, eds. 1983. *Durkheim and the Law*. Oxford: Martin Robertson. 241 pp.

MacKinnon CA. 1979. *The Sexual Harassment of Working Women*. New Haven: Yale Univ. Press. 312 pp.

MacKinnon CA. 1989. *Toward a Feminist Theory of the State*. Cambridge: Harvard Univ. Press. 330 pp.

Mahoney M. 1991. Legal images of battered women: Redefining the issue of separation. *Mich. Law Rev.* 90:1–94

Maine HS. 1986 (1864). *Ancient Law*. Tucson: Arizona Univ. Press. 400 pp.

Mather L, Yngvesson B. 1980–81. Language, audience and the transformation of disputes. *Law & Soc. Rev.* 15:775

Matsuda M. 1989a. When the first quail calls: Multiple consciousness as jurisprudential method. *Women's Rights Law Rep.* 11:7–11

Matsuda M. 1989b. Public response to racist speech: Considering the victim's story. *Mich. Law Rev.* 87:2320–81

Matsuda M. 1991. Voices of America: Accent, antidiscrimination law and a jurisprudence for the last reconstruction. *Yale Law J.* 100:1329–407

Meese E. 1988. Address before the D.C. chapter of the Federalist Society Lawyer's Division. In *Interpreting Law and Literature,* ed. S. Levinson, S Mailloux, pp. 25–33. Evanston: Northwestern Univ. Press

Menkel-Meadow C. 1988. Feminist legal the-

ory, critical legal studies and legal education, or 'The Fem-Crits go to law school.' *J. Legal Ed.* 39:61–86
Merry SE. 1990. *Getting Power and Getting Even*. Chicago: Chicago Univ. Press. 227 pp.
Mertz E. 1988–89. Alternative paradigms for legal theory. *Northwest. Univ. Law Rev.* 83:1–9
Minow M. 1990. *Making All the Difference: Inclusion, Exclusion and American Law*. Ithaca: Cornell Univ. Press. 403 pp.
Minow M, Spellman E. 1989. In context. *South. Calif. Law Rev.* 63:1597–51
Mnookin R, Kornhauser L. 1979. Bargaining in the shadow of the law: The case of divorce. *Yale Law J.* 88:950–97
Montesquieu C. 1977 (1748). *The Spirit of the Laws*. Berkeley: Univ. Calif. Press
Nedelsky J. 1989. Reconceptualizing autonomy: Sources, thoughts and possibilities. *Yale J. Law & Feminism* 1:7
Northwestern Law Review. 1988–1989. *Symposium on Law and Social Theory*, pp. 1–472
Olsen F. 1983. The family and the market: A study of ideology and legal reform. *Harvard Law Rev.* 96:1497
Olsen F. 1984. Statutory rape: A feminist critique of rights analysis in feminist legal theory. *Texas Law Rev.* 63:387–432
Pashukanis E. 1978 [1929]. *Law and Marxism: A General Theory*. Transl. B Einhorn. New York: Pluto
Patterson D. 1992. Postmodernism/Feminism/ Law. *Cornell Law Rev.* 77:254
Peller G. 1985. The metaphysics of American law. *Calif. Law Rev.* 73:1151
Peller G. 1990. Race consciousness. *Duke Law J.* 1990:758–847
Polinsky AM. 1989. *An Introduction to Law and Economics*. Boston: Little, Brown. 153 pp. 2nd ed.
Posner RA. 1992. *The Economic Analysis of Law*. Boston: Little, Brown. 772 pp. 4th ed.
Post RC. 1988. Cultural heterogeneity and the law: Pornography, blasphemy and the first amendment. *Calif. Law Rev.* 76:297
Post RC. 1989. The social foundations of privacy: Community and self in the common law tort. *Calif. Law Rev.* 77:957
Pound R. 1911–12. The scope and purpose of sociological jurisprudence. *Harvard Law Rev.* 24:591–619; 25:140–68, 409–516
Radin MJ. 1989. The pragmatist and the feminist. *South. Calif. Law Rev.* 63:1699
Rhode D. 1990. Feminist critical theories. *Stanford Law Rev.* 42:617
Robson R. 1992. *Lesbian (Out)Law: Survival Under the Rule of Law*. Ithaca, NY: Firebrand Books. 185 pp.
Rose-Ackerman S. 1988. Progressive law and economics—and the new administrative law. *Yale Law J.* 98:341
Rubin E. 1991. Beyond public choice: Comprehensive rationality in the writing and reading of statutes. *NY Univ. Law Rev.* 66:1
Rumble WE. 1968. *American Legal Realism*. Ithaca: Cornell Univ. Press
Santos BdS. 1987. Law: A map of misreading. Toward a postmodern conception of law. *Law & Soc. Rev.* 14:279
Sarat A, Felstiner W. 1986. Law and strategy in the divorce lawyer's office. *Law & Soc. Rev.* 20:93
Sarat A, Kearns TR, eds. 1991. *The Fate of Law*. Ann Arbor: Univ. Mich. Press. 290 pp.
Sarat A, Kearns TR, eds. 1992. *Law's Violence*. Ann Arbor: Univ. Mich. Press. 261 pp.
Savigny FK. 1829. *The History of Roman Law During the Middle Ages*. Transl. E Cathcart. Edinburgh: A. Black
Scales AC. 1986. The emergence of feminist jurisprudence: An essay. *Yale Law J.* 95:1373–1403
Scales-Trent J. 1990. Commonalities: On being black and white, different and the same. *Yale J. Law & Feminism* 2:305–27
Schanck PC. 1992. Understanding postmodern thought and its implications for statutory interpretation. *South. Calif. Law Rev.* 65:2505
Schauer F. 1985. Easy cases. *South. Calif. Law Rev.* 58:399
Scheppele KL. 1988. *Legal Secrets: Equality and Efficiency in the Common Law*. Chicago: Univ. Chicago Press. 363 pp.
Scheppele KL. 1989. Telling stories. *Mich. Law Rev.* 87:2073–98
Scheppele KL. 1990. Facing facts in legal interpretation. *Representations* 30:42–77
Scheppele KL. 1992. Just the facts, ma'am: Sexualized violence, evidentiary habits and the revision of truth. *NY Law School Law Rev.* 37:123–72
Schlag P. 1990. Normative and nowhere to go. *Stanford Law Rev.* 43:167
Schultz V. 1990. Telling stories about women and work: Judicial interpretations of sex segregation in the workplace in Title VII cases raising the lack of interest argument. *Harvard Law Rev.* 103:1749
Schwartz RD, Miller JC. 1964. Legal evolution and societal complexity. *Am. J. Sociol.* 74:159
Selznick P. 1968. *Law, Society and Industrial Justice*. New York: Sage
Shavell S. 1987. *Economic Analysis of Accident Law*. Cambridge: Harvard Univ. Press. 31 pp.
Sherwin R. 1988. A matter of voice and plot: Belief and suspicion in legal storytelling. *Mich. Law Rev.* 87:543
Siegel R. 1992. Reasoning from the body: An historical perspective on abortion regulation and questions of equal protection. *Stanford Law Rev.* 44:737
Silbey S. 1985. Ideals and practices in the study of law. *Legal Stud. Forum* 9:7

Simon J. 1993. *Poor Discipline: Parole and the Social Control of the Underclass 1890–1990.* Chicago: Univ. Chicago Press. 284 pp.

Singer J. 1986. The player and the cards: Nihilism and legal theory. *Yale Law J.* 94:10

Smith SD. 1990. The pursuit of pragmatism. *Yale Law J.* 100:409

Spellman EV. 1988. *Inessential Woman: The Problems of Exclusion in Feminist Thought.* Boston: Beacon. 22 pp.

Sunstein CR. 1990. *After the Rights Revolution.* Cambridge: Harvard Univ. Press. 28 pp.

Teubner G, ed. 1988. *Autopoietic Law: A New Approach to Law and Society.* New York: Walter de Gruyter. 38 pp.

Thomas K. 1992. Beyond the privacy principle. *Colo. Law Rev.* 92:1431

Thompson EP. 1975. *Whigs and Hunters.* New York: Pantheon. 312 pp.

Timasheff NS. 1939. *An Introduction to the Sociology of Law.* Cambridge: Harvard Univ. Press

Torres G. 1988. Local knowledge, local color: Critical legal studies and the law of race relations. *San Diego Law Rev.* 25:1043

Tronto J. 1984. Law and modernity: The significance of Max Weber's Sociology of Law. *Texas Law Rev.* 70:109

Trubek D. 1984. Where the action is: Critical legal studies and empiricism. *Stanford Law Rev.* 36:575

Tushnet M. 1983. Following the rules laid down: A critique of interpretivism and neutral principles. *Harvard Law Rev.* 96:781

Tushnet M. 1992. The degradation of constitutional discourse. *Georgetown Law Rev.* 81:251

Unger RM. 1986. *The Critical Legal Studies Movement.* Cambridge: Harvard Univ. Press. 128 pp.

van Zandt D. 1988–89. The relevance of social theory to legal theory. *Northwest. Law Rev.* 83:10–37

Weber M. 1978. *Economy and Society.* Berkeley: Univ. Calif. Press. 1469 pp.

Wechsler H. 1959. Toward neutral principles of constitutional law. *Harvard Law Rev.* 73:1

Weisberg DK, ed. 1993. *Feminist Legal Theory: Foundations.* Philadelphia: Temple Univ. Press. 620 pp.

West R. 1985. Jurisprudence as narrative: An aesthetic analysis of modern legal theory. *NY Univ. Law Rev.* 60:145

West R. 1988. Jurisprudence and gender. *Univ. Chicago Law Rev.* 55:1

White JB. 1990. *Justice as Translation.* Chicago: Univ. Chicago Press. 313 pp.

White L. 1990. Subordination, rhetorical survival skills and Sunday shoes: Notes on the hearing of Mrs. G. *Buffalo Law Rev.* 38:1

Whitman JQ. 1991. Law and the pre-modern mind. *Stanford Law Rev.* 44:205

Williams PJ. 1991. *The Alchemy of Race and Rights: Diary of a Law Professor.* Cambridge: Harvard Univ. Press. 263 pp.

Williams W. 1984–85. Equality's riddle: Pregnancy and the equal treatment/special treatment debate. *NY Univ. Rev. Law & Soc. Change* 13:325

Williamson O. 1975. *Markets and Hierarchies.* New York: Free Press

Yngvesson B. 1989. Inventing law in local settings: Rethinking legal culture. *Yale Law J.* 98:1689

[3]
An Analytical Map of Social Scientific Approaches to the Concept of Law

BRIAN Z. TAMANAHA*

1 *Introduction*

An intractable puzzle brought almost to a standstill the development of theory in the social scientific study of law from the 1950s through the 1970s. The debate over a social scientific concept of law was the central focus of theoretical discussion during this period. The puzzle lies in the fact that the debate seemed incapable of resolution. There appeared to be almost as many concepts of law as there were theorists, with no apparent means to determine which concept, if any, was the correct one.

Legal philosophers have also long been exercised by the question of what law is, as H. L. A. Hart noted on the very first page of *The Concept of Law*.[1] But a lack of agreement has not been as debilitating. Legal philosophers, especially those in the positivist tradition, have the luxury of focusing on state law. Many social scientists, in contrast, consider state law to be an unacceptable starting point because it does not comprise a scientific category, and more so because application of the state law model would result in the conclusion that many societies (historically speaking) did not have law. Especially for legal anthropologists, this smacked of Western ethnocentrism.

This mix of scientism and concern about ethnocentrism resulted in analytical gridlock. Scientists who declared—at the outset of the enquiry—that 'No society is without law',[2] were inevitably led to identify a different concept of law from those scientists who believed that whether or not particular societies have law should be an empirical question, one that can be answered in the negative.

After decades of heated exchanges, with no apparent progress, scholars in the field became frustrated with the issue. The debate over *what is law?* was characterized as 'endless wrangling' which operated 'to the hindrance of more

---

* St John's University School of Law, Jamaica, New York 11439. I would like to thank Donald Black, John Eekelaar, Lawrence Friedman, Marc Galanter, Andre Hoekema, Sally Engle Merry, Gordon Woodman, Jan Wijbe Oosterkamp, Marieke Oderkerk, and Elizabeth van Schilfgaarde for their critical comments on earlier drafts of this work.

[1] H. L. A. Hart, *The Concept of Law* (1961).
[2] S. F. Moore, *Law as Process* (1978) at 215.

fruitful endeavors';[3] as 'arid and unproductive';[4] as a 'sterile' or 'barren topic';[5] as a waste of 'floods of ink';[6] as an exercise which has 'not borne much fruit';[7] and 'like the quest for the Holy Grail'.[8] By the mid-1970s, the general consensus was that 'for the time being, at least, it seems clear that we must displace law from the center of our conceptual focus as we attempt to build social theory'.[9]

Giving up on the issue, however, was costly. It has often been observed that socio-legal studies suffer from underdeveloped theory.[10] Without agreement on the threshold question *what is law?*, the precise object or field to be studied by 'legal' anthropology and 'legal' sociology could not easily be identified,[11] and no foundation existed upon which to construct theory. Although there has been a revival of theory in the field in the past ten years—owing mostly to the application of new social theories like interpretivism and autopoiesis to the study of law—the underlying problems with the conceptualization of law remained, concealed beneath the surface yet exerting an influence.

A second consequence was that the lack of resolution created a state of licence, permitting all sorts of claims to be made in the name of a scientific concept of law. Legal pluralists, for example, have recently made assertions to the effect that they alone hold to an objective, scientific concept of law, that social life is filled with a complex of competing legal orders, and that those who believe that 'law' is linked to the state are suffering from ideological delusion.[12] Another example, from an entirely different perspective, can be found in the growing chorus of claims by social theorists that law is increasingly penetrating all aspects of life, that the life world is becoming juridified or colonized by the law. Without first knowing what law is, however, it is not easy to make sense of, or respond to, these kinds of claims.

Finally, and most important, when the participants involved quit the debate without having come to an understanding of what led to the impasse to begin with, they failed to uncover the lessons hidden within the impasse itself. There were important reasons why the debate could not be resolved, reasons which tell a great deal.

This article will revisit the debate, not as an end in itself, but as a means to get beyond it in a more satisfactory way, and to uncover what remained concealed.

---

[3] Ibid at 224.
[4] J. Comaroff and S. Roberts, *Rules and Processes* (1981) at 4.
[5] I. Hamnett, *Social Anthropology and Law* (1977) at 4.
[6] L. Mair, *Primitive Government* (1962) at 19.
[7] L. Nader, 'The Anthropological Study of Law', 67 *American Anthropologist* 3 at 5 (1965).
[8] A. Hoebel, *The Law of Primitive Man* (1954) at 18.
[9] R. Abel, 'A Comparative Theory of Dispute Institutions in Society', 7 *Law & Society Rev* 217 at 224 (1974).
[10] See, eg, K. Ziegert, 'The Sociology Behind Eugen Ehrlich's Sociology of Law', 7 *International J Sociology of Law* 225 at 235 (1979); R. Simon and J. Lynch, 'The Sociology of Law: Where We Have Been and Where We Might be Going', 23 *Law & Society Rev* 825 at 849 (1989); F. Snyder, 'Anthropology, Dispute Processes and Law: A Critical Introduction', 8 *JL & Society* 141 at 163 (1981); L. Friedman, 'The Law and Society Movement', 38 *Stanford LR* 773 (1986).
[11] A number of other social science disciplines study law, including economic analysis, history, political science and psychology. However, only legal anthropology and legal sociology have specifically grappled with the question of a concept of law, and the discussion herein will therefore be limited to these two fields.
[12] See B. Tamanaha, 'The Folly of the "Social Scientific" Concept of Legal Pluralism', 20 *JL & Society* 192 at 194-9 (1993).

I will survey the dominant social scientific concepts of law, categorize them, and map the relations between these categories. In the course of drawing this map the logic underlying the impasse will be made evident, though I will not stop there. My overarching objective will be to draw out the many implications of the map, which range from insights about the concept of law, to the practice of science, to the sources of social order.

Maps are valuable because they simplify. A map true to every detail would be identical with the terrain covered, and hence superfluous. A distorted or overly simplified map, however, is either misleading or provides no guidance at all. This map will straddle the line between too much and too little by highlighting the important features, then filling in the local detail as they relate to these features. The end product of this mapping exercise will be the outlines of a theoretical foundation for the social scientific study of law.

2 Two Fundamental Categories of the Concept of Law

Although many different concepts of law have been proffered in the social sciences, there is general agreement on the basic alternatives. Usually these are viewed as discrete, self-standing options. Instead, I will show that at the highest level of inclusiveness these concepts can be placed into one of two fundamental categories. The first category sees law in terms of actual patterns of behaviour; the second category sees law in terms of the state law model.

A *First Category: Law Abstracted from Patterns of Behaviour*

Eugen Ehrlich and Bronislaw Malinowski are giants in the field of social scientific approaches to law. Ehrlich has been called the 'inventor' of sociology of law as well as the 'founder' of sociological jurisprudence.[13] And Malinowski's *Crime and Custom in Savage Society* is the single most influential text in the anthropology of law, as well as one of the most widely read texts in anthropology generally.[14] Despite the fact that they worked under markedly different circumstances— Ehrlich as a law professor in a relatively poor, distant part of what was then Austria, Malinowski as a pioneering field researcher among the Trobriand of Melanesia—their concepts of law substantially overlap. The central insight of both analysts was that law consists of and can be found in the regularized conduct or actual patterns of behaviour in a community, association, or society.[15]

This view of law led them to reject the notion that law is connected to the state. Ehrlich asserted:

> It is not an essential element of the concept of law that it be created by the State, nor that it constitute the basis for the decisions of the courts or other tribunals, nor that

---

[13] K. Ziegert, 'A Sociologist's View' in E. Kamenka and A. Erh-Soon Tay (eds), *Law and Social Control* (1980) at 76. E. Schur, *Law and Society: A Sociological View* (1968) at 37.
[14] See I. Hamnett, above n 5 at 6.
[15] See generally L. Pospisil, *Anthropology of Law: A Comparative Theory* (1971) at 28–31.

it be the basis of a legal compulsion consequent upon such a decision. A fourth element remains, and that will have to be the point of departure, i.e. the law is an ordering.[16]

Malinowski made the same point when he contested the belief that law consists of 'central authority, codes, courts, and constables',[17] and insisted that law does 'not consist in any independent institutions';[18] rather law represents 'an aspect of their tribal life'.[19]

Ehrlich believed that society largely consists of social associations at various levels—the family, corporations, business associations or communities, professions, clubs, a school or factory, a farm, the state, and so forth. 'A social association is a plurality of human beings who, in their relations with one another, recognize certain rules of conduct as binding, and, generally at least, actually regulate their conduct according to them'.[20] The 'living law', as Ehrlich famously labelled it, consists of the spontaneously generated inner ordering of these associations. The legal rules of this inner ordering consist of 'rules of conduct'—customary practices which govern the behaviour of persons in the association. Ehrlich emphasized time and again that the investigator finds the law through direct observation of 'concrete usages'.[21] 'The living law is the law which dominates life itself even though it has not been posited in legal propositions... [It] is not the part of the content of the document that the courts recognize as binding when they decide a legal controversy, but only that part which the parties actually observe in life'.[22]

Because Malinowski studied a relatively homogeneous and undifferentiated tribal society, he did not focus directly on associations as such. Nonetheless, he saw law in much the same way. For Malinowski, legal rules consist of 'a class of binding rules which control most aspects of tribal life, which regulate personal relations between kinsmen, clansmen and tribesmen, settle economic relations, the exercise of power and of magic, the status of husband and wife and of their respective families'.[23] Like Ehrlich, Malinowski emphasized that law can be found in actual usages; and his methodological prescription for the scientific investigator of law was remarkably similar to Ehrlich's: 'we are demanding a new line of anthropological field-work: the study by direct observation of the rules of custom as they function in actual life'.[24]

Thus Ehrlich and Malinowski viewed law in essentially the same manner—as the actually followed body of rules which govern the behaviour of members of a social group. They also identified the same basic 'binding mechanism' supporting the law. Both acknowledged the significance of sanction, but denied

[16] E. Ehrlich, *The Fundamental Principles of the Sociology of Law* (1975) at 24.
[17] B. Malinowski, *Crime and Custom in Savage Society* (1926) at 14.
[18] Ibid at 59.
[19] Ibid.
[20] Ehrlich, above n 16 at 39.
[21] Ibid at 85, 501.
[22] Ibid at 497.
[23] Malinowski, above n 17 at 66.
[24] Ibid at 125.

sanction the place of primary importance. As Malinowski put it, 'The binding forces of Melanesian civil law are to be found in the concatenation of the obligations, in the fact that they are arranged into chains of mutual services, a give and take extending over long periods of time and covering wide aspects of interest and activity'.[25] Or as Ehrlich summarized, 'A man therefore conducts himself according to law, chiefly because this is made imperative by his social relations'.[26] Ehrlich and Malinowski both believed that (in addition to simple habit)[27] people followed the law largely due to positive inducement—it was in their interest to do so—rather than from fear of sanction. And in another convergence, both specifically emphasized the role of reciprocity as a major aspect of this positive inducement.[28]

In view of the substantial overlap in approach, it is inevitable that their concepts of law would have shared flaws, and would be subject to the same criticisms. In particular, Ehrlich and Malinowski were confronted with a devilishly difficult problem: how to distinguish specifically legal norms from the many other kinds of norms operative in social life. Legal Realist Felix Cohen observed that 'under Ehrlich's terminology, law itself merges with religion, ethical custom, morality, decorum, tact, fashion, and etiquette'.[29] Both Ehrlich and Malinowski asserted that it was important to make the distinction.[30] Malinowski, however, offered no specific criteria, and it appears that he ultimately abandoned the attempt.[31] Ehrlich suggested that the characteristic feature of the legal norm is *opinio necessitatis*,[32] that is, within the group the legal norm is felt to be 'of great importance, of basic significance'.[33] Obviously this criterion is difficult to apply and is incapable of providing a reliable distinction between legal and non-legal norms.

This has proven to be a dauntingly serious defect, one that prompted most socio-legal scholars to look elsewhere for a concept of law. One commentator even suggested that Ehrlich's notion of the inner ordering of associations 'was quite similar to what anthropologists now mean by "culture pattern"'.[34] Similarly, legal anthropologist Sally Falk Moore concluded that 'the conception of law that Malinowski propounded was so broad that it was virtually indistinguishable from the study of the obligatory aspect of all social relationships'.[35] Despite this flaw, the concept of law articulated by Ehrlich and Malinowski has proven surprisingly

---

[25] Ibid at 67.
[26] Ehrlich, above n 16 at 64.
[27] Ibid at 78; Malinowski, above n 17 at 52.
[28] Ehrlich, above n 16 at 63; Malinowski, above n 17 at 58, 68.
[29] F. Cohen, *The Legal Conscience* (1960) at 187.
[30] Malinowski, above n 17 at 50, 54; Ehrlich, above n 16 at 164–70.
[31] I. Schapera, 'Malinowski's Theories of Law' in R. Firth (ed), *Man and Culture: An Evaluation of the Work of Malinowski*. Edited by R. Firth (1957) 139 at 153.
[32] Ehrlich, above n 16 at 165.
[33] Ibid at 167–8.
[34] Schur, above n 13 at 37.
[35] Moore, above n 2 at 220.

resilient,[36] and has been resurrected in a number of different forms, which I will mention briefly.

The notion of customary law, which Ehrlich drew heavily from when devising his concept of living law, shares the same basic elements and the same problem. There are many different formulations of customary law. Ian Hamnett's definition is representative of the version I am referring to: 'Customary law can be regarded as a set of norms which the actors in a social situation abstract from practice and which they invest with binding authority'.[37] Identical to Ehrlich's and Malinowski's concept, this version of customary law is based upon an abstraction from the actual practices of a group. Analysts of customary law who adopt this version face the perennial problem of trying to distinguish those customs which are 'legal' from those which are not.

Other prominent examples are Marc Galanter's concept of 'indigenous law', which he defines in terms of 'concrete patterns of social ordering';[38] Moore's concept of the spontaneous rule bound order of the 'semi-autonomous social field';[39] and the dominant notion of law postulated within the legal pluralism paradigm.[40] Each of these concepts, in one form or another, focuses on the actual regularized behaviour within groups, and all of them are plagued by an inability to identify the distinctively legal.[41] Sally Engle Merry's objection to the concept of legal pluralism bears this out: 'calling all forms of ordering that are not state law by the name law confounds the analysis'.[42]

The struggle to identify the distinctively legal gave rise to many of the concepts of law in the next category.

B *Second Category: State Law Model of Rules and Institutions*

One of the most influential concepts of law applied in the social sciences is the view that law consists of institutionalized norm enforcement.[43] Max Weber and Adamson Hoebel have produced the most often cited versions of this concept, set out respectively below:

> The term 'guaranteed law' shall be understood to mean that there exists a 'coercive

---

[36] I have limited the discussion to social scientists of this century, mostly because they are the most influential, but also because social scientific approaches to law 'officially' originated at the beginning of this century. R. Pound, *Jurisprudence* (Vol II 1959) at 186–7. However, the view of law herein attributed to Malinowski and Ehrlich has antecedents, especially in the historical school of Savigny (who Ehrlich acknowledges) and the 'social-psychological' school of Gierke and Jellinek. See R. Pound, *Jurisprudence* (Vol I 1959) at 312–20.

[37] I. Hamnett, *Chieftanship and Legitimacy* (1975) at 14.

[38] M. Galanter, 'Justice in Many Rooms: Courts, Private Ordering, and Indigenous Law', 19 *J of Legal Pluralism* 1 at 17–18 (1981).

[39] Moore, above n 2 at 54–81. Moore does not herself apply the term 'law' to the rules she identifies, but others, especially legal pluralists, have interpreted her to this effect. See J. Griffiths, 'What is Legal Pluralism?' 24 *J of Legal Pluralism* 1 at 38 (1986).

[40] Legal pluralists are a diverse group with internal disagreement, and many have not identified the concept of law they adhere to. This assertion is based upon the concept of law set out in an influential and widely cited article about legal pluralism by John Griffiths. Ibid.

[41] Tamanaha, above n 12 at 205–7.

[42] S. E. Merry, 'Legal Pluralism', 22 *Law & Society Rev* 869 at 870 (1988).

[43] See M. Feeley, 'The Concept of Laws in Social Science: A Critique and Expanded View', 10 *Law & Society Rev* 497 at 498 (1976).

apparatus,' i.e., that there are one or more persons whose special task is to hold themselves ready to apply specially provided means of coercion (legal coercion) for the purpose of norm enforcement.[44]

> A social norm is legal if its neglect or infraction is regularly met, in threat or in fact, by the application of physical force by an individual or group possessing the socially recognized privilege of so acting.[45]

These definitions immediately solved the problem faced by Ehrlich and Malinowski. The test for law is based upon the severity (coercion/force) and nature (publically approved and executed) of the sanction imposed upon infraction. Legal norms are only those norms that, when violated, are enforced by publically administered sanctions. All other norms are moral or political or custom or manners or whatever, but not law.

Although the State is not mentioned in either definition, there is a close link between this concept of law and the state law model. The element of socially privileged staff or coercive apparatus is a reference to state bureaucratic legal institutions, stripped of their connection to the State.[46] Norm enforcement is the presumed function of state legal institutions: what courts and police do is visit a sanction, on behalf of the public, upon the violations of norms. This implicit though direct link to the state law model should not be surprising. Weber was trained as a lawyer,[47] and Hoebel credited his concept of law to 'contemporary jurisprudence',[48] citing Hohfeld, Llewellyn, Cardozo and Holmes.

A related version of this concept of law, also popular among socio-legal scholars, was that put forth by Paul Bohannan. The test Bohannan used to distinguish legal from non-legal norms was simply affirmative recognition by the legal institution:

> Customs are norms or rules (more or less strict, and with greater or less support of moral, ethical, or even physical coercion) about the ways in which people must behave if social institutions are to perform their tasks and society is to endure ... Some customs, in some societies, are reinstitutionalized at another level: they are restated for the more precise purposes of legal institutions. When this happens, therefore, law may be regarded as a custom that has been restated in order to make it amenable to the activities of the legal institutions.[49]

Legal institutions are those institutions which settle disputes or counteract violations of rules. In essence this concept of law borrowed from H. L. A. Hart's positivist legal philosophy built around state law. Bohannan's notion of the

---

[44] M. Rheinstein, *Max Weber on Law in Economy and Society* (1954) at 13.
[45] Hoebel, above n 8 at 28.
[46] See Schur, above n 13 at 75. Schur recognized that 'Weber's approach is clearly quite positivistic (his definition is not unlike that of Austin) [except that] he simply refers to a specialized staff, rather than to "the state" or "the sovereign"'.
[47] A. Kronman, *Max Weber* (1983) at 189-93.
[48] Hoebel, above n 8 at 22.
[49] P. Bohannan, 'The Differing Realms of the Law' in P. Bohannan (ed), *Law and Warfare* (1967) 43 at 47.

reinstitutionalization of norms was related to Hart's idea of secondary rules of recognition.[50]

Despite the fact that these concepts appeared to capture general intuitions about the nature of law (at least for those who accepted that law need not be linked to the state), and they avoided the dilemma that led to the rejection of Malinowski's and Ehrlich's concepts, they were not acceptable to the group of social scientists who held to the belief that law is a fundamental social process that exists in all societies. Pre-state societies that lacked an overarching political organization often did not use institutions to enforce norms. Under the criteria suggested above, these societies would not have law.

Dissatisfaction with the implications of these sorts of 'pedigree' tests for law resulted in a slight shift in focus. Since all societies had disputes, and these disputes had to be resolved in some manner, dispute processing became the subject.[51] However, an insistent old problem again arose: how to distinguish legal from political or other forms of dispute processing. Initially, attempts were made to base the distinction on the structure of the institution and on the role played by norms—legal dispute processing institutions involved an authoritative third-party decision-maker and decisions were based upon the application of norms, whereas political dispute processing institutions did not involve a third party and the outcome was determined by power. But these distinctions were later softened or abandoned as untenable.[52] From our post-formalist vantage point, it seems that the line between legal and political is a slippery one.

The focus on dispute processing institutions, as with all concepts of law in this category, was also a product of the state law model. A widely held assumption is that the primary function of courts is to resolve disputes;[53] and a functional description of how state courts are typically constituted and operate results in the institutionalized, third-party, rule-oriented adjudicator model.

Again, as with the preceding concepts, a focus on dispute institutions was unsatisfactory for those whose starting presupposition was that all societies have law. It appears that a number of small-scale, pre-state societies did not use institutions to respond to disputes, and those that did treated rules in a variety of ways. In certain societies a compromise was arranged without the presence of a third party, or rules did not seem to play a primary role, or contests, self-help, or retribution were the responses to disputes.

A clear pattern can thus be found in the above concepts of law, and in their reception or rejection. All of these concepts got away from equating law with state law by identifying a function that state law plays and by providing a functional description of how state legal institutions are constituted and operate.

---

[50] Hart, above n 1 at 89–96.
[51] See R. Abel, above n 9.
[52] See P. H. Gulliver, 'Negotiations as a Mode of Dispute Settlement: Towards a General Model', 7 *Law & Society Rev* 683 (1973).
[53] See J. Gibbs, 'Law as a Means of Social Control' in J. Gibbs (ed), *Social Control: Views from the Social Sciences* (1982) 83 at 95.

No matter how we try to define law, it seems we are continually forced back to the state law model of institutions and norms.

Scholars who are committed to the proposition that all societies have law must reject any notion of law based upon the state law model, in whatever form, because state law was a contingent development that could not be found everywhere, even when described in functional terms. It has proven impossible, however, to come up with an acceptable notion of law that is not ultimately derived from the state law model. State law is the currently dominant paradigm for law. This shared cultural paradigm informs social scientists' intuitions about the nature of law, and it is the underlying source from which these scientists abstract when they strive to produce a scientific concept of law, even when they explicitly set out to escape the state law model.[54]

There is no way out from this conceptual box except to stop talking about law—and that's exactly what many socio-legal scholars, legal anthropologists in particular, did. Various aspects of 'order' and 'dispute' became the objects of study, and 'the word "law" is rarely used in many of these works'.[55] A striking example of the resultant anomalies can be found in Simon Roberts's text *Order and Dispute: An Introduction to Legal Anthropology*, which states in the Preface that 'Despite the sub-title, it must be said that this is not a book about law',[56] and dedicates an entire chapter to explaining 'Why Not Law'. These scholars were mistaken, however, to the extent that they believed that the shift to order and dispute involved a complete 'rejection of a legal mould'.[57] After all, they continued to work in the self-described field of 'legal' anthropology, and they selected 'order' and 'dispute' due to the pervasive belief that what law does is maintain order and respond to disputes.[58] For the purposes of this essay, the main point is they proferred no new concepts of law.

The preceding discussion applies more so to legal anthropologists than legal sociologists. Anti-ethnocentrism and the study of non-state societies, which decisively shaped the anthropological debate, have not been primary concerns of legal sociologists. Closely linked in origin to sociological jurisprudence, legal sociology developed along a path which mostly entailed the application of sociological techniques to the study of different aspects of state law and its relation to society. Thus, the issue *what is law?* was not of especially burning moment. Nonetheless, legal sociologists were influenced by scientism, and this led to the formulation of a concept of law in scientific terms apart from the State.

---

[54] Tamanaha, above n 12 at 201.
[55] S. Roberts, *Order and Dispute: An Introduction to Legal Anthropology* (1979) at 198.
[56] Ibid at 9.
[57] Ibid at 198.
[58] In an important respect a number of legal anthropologists did significantly depart from the state law model. Influenced by interactional social theory, (certain) adherents of what is called the process approach changed their focus from dispute processing institutions (from how society responds to disputes), to look at the process of disputing itself, at the disputants and their constraints and motivations, and at why disputes erupt. See M. Krygier, 'Anthropological Approaches' in Kamenka and Soon-Tay, above n 13 27 at 46-7.

Roscoe Pound's concept of law as social control through the application of force by a politically organized society—also an influential view among earlier legal anthropologists—was and remains (with certain variations) the dominant concept of law in legal sociology. Pound saw a close, almost inseverable connection between state law and social control:

> Today social control is primarily the function of the state and is exercised through law. Its ultimate effectiveness depends upon the application of force exercised by bodies and agencies and officials set up or chosen for that purpose. It operates chiefly through law, that is, through the systematic and orderly application of force by the appointed agents.[59]

Pound's view of law is represented today in the work of Donald Black, who sets his analysis in a more sophisticated scientific framework. Black believes that 'science can know only phenomena and never essences';[60] he concluded that 'the quest for the one correct concept of law or for anything else "distinctively legal" is therefore inherently unscientific'.[61] From this standpoint the question *what is law?* was not an analytical one; rather, it was just a matter of designating the phenomenon to be studied by legal sociologists. Thus Black simply stipulated that 'law is governmental social control',[62] thereby sidestepping the entire debate.

This position nicely immunized Black from conceptual criticism (though not from objections about application or use value), but it is not entirely ingenuous. Black readily crosses over to apply his definition to other contexts, for example, to declare that legal anthropologists studied stateless societies 'where law, by definition, cannot exist'.[63] His instrumentally justified definition, however, requires that he not extend beyond the bounds of his own brand of legal sociology, at least not without first justifying the superiority of his definition relative to these other fields also.

A related sociological concept of law started with institutionalized social control, but placed special emphasis on the presence of formalized rules or doctrines. As Philip Selznick put it, 'We should see law as endemic in all institutions that rely for social control on formal authority and rule-making'.[64] According to this view, the characteristic which distinguishes law is 'legality', a particular orientation pursuant to which rules form restraints or limitations on decisions or actions.[65] This concept of law—which was derived from the 'rule of law' ideology that has shaped the Western legal tradition—was applicable beyond the state to many private institutions, yet was still able to distinguish those that are rule-bound (and hence legal) from those that are not.

---

[59] R. Pound, *Social Control Through Law* (1942) at 25.
[60] D. Black, 'The Boundaries of Legal Sociology', 81 *Yale LJ* 1086 at 1092 (1972).
[61] Ibid.
[62] D. Black, *The Behavior of Law* (1976) at 2.
[63] D. Black, 'Social Control as a Dependent Variable' in D. Black (ed), *Toward a General Theory of Social Control* (Vol 1, 1984) 1 at 2.
[64] P. Selznick, *Law, Society and Industrial Justice* (New York 1969) at 7. P. Selznick, 'The Sociology of Law', 9 *International Encyclopedia of the Social Sciences* 51 (1968).
[65] See R. Cotterrell, *The Sociology of Law* (1984) at 45–6.

A final concept of law in the social sciences, adhered to mainly by Marxists but also taken for granted by many sociological researchers in the trenches, was the view that law must be seen in terms of state power.[66] According to this perspective—as the mass of lawyers, legislators and judges would attest to without hesitation—law is state law.

3 Positivism and Behaviourism, the Gap Problem and New Approaches

To begin the task of mapping the relations between the above two categories, it is important to note what they had in common, and how they differ from more recent approaches to the concept of law. Almost all of the scientists who preferred the above concepts of law adhered to the core tenets of scientific positivism, and many adopted one or another version of behaviourism.

Scientific positivists believe that social phenomena can and should be studied through application of the objectivistic methodology of the natural sciences, with its emphasis on observation, measurement, data gathering and quantification. Pursuant to positivism, the goals of scientific enquiry are to produce explanations based upon the formulation of causal laws. Until the relatively recent rise of interpretivism[67]—which argues that the natural science model is inappropriate for the study of social phenomena, that instead of trying to formulate explanations based upon causal laws we must strive to understand the social action or event at issue by paying attention to the meaning for the social actors involved—positivism represented the almost universal view of what it meant to be doing science, including among the social scientists who studied law.

Behaviourism exists in its own right as one branch of scientific positivism, but it also serves as a methodological orientation applied by other versions of positivism. Social behaviourism (behaviourism in its own right) insists that it is inherently unscientific to try to guess what is going on in the minds of social actors, and that such psychic feats are anyway unnecessary—social phenomena can be understood and explained simply by constructing laws based upon the relations between observed patterns of behaviour. Donald Black is virtually alone among socio-legal scholars in adhering to this extreme version. Other versions of positivism, like structuralism or functionalism, focus on behaviour as a means to identify the structures in society or to determine how the functions of subsystems are satisfied. Like social behaviourism, this more limited form of behaviourism insists that social scientists must focus on what people do—on how people actually behave rather than on what they say. Many proponents in both categories of the concept of law adhered to this view. As I emphasized,

---

[66] Ibid at 41.

[67] The basic tenets of interpretivism are that social reality is largely constructed upon our ideas and beliefs, and that these ideas and beliefs are socially generated and shared through our participation within and socialization by groups or interpretive communities. See D. Hiley, J. Bohman, and R. Shusterman (eds), *The Interpretive Turn: Philosophy, Science, Culture* (1991). For an example of interpretivism applied to the study of law, see B. Tamanaha, *Understanding Law in Micronesia: An Interpretive Approach to Transplanted Law* (1993).

both Ehrlich and Malinowski focused on patterns of actual behaviour. Hoebel called his own method 'legal behaviourism',[68] and declared that the 'anthropological approach to law is flatly behaviouristic'.[69]

Their shared orientation to the observation of actual behaviour must not obscure a crucial difference between the two categories of the concept of law: they identified and settled upon different realms of behaviour as their object of focus when locating 'law'. For the first category, the relevant behaviour was that of people within the community or social group; whereas for the second category the relevant behaviour was that of the legal actors or the legal institutions themselves.

Despite this difference, proponents in both categories shared the same basic objective in their focus on actual behaviour: to distinguish the *real* law from that which merely was claimed to be law. Ehrlich saw patterns of social behaviour as the real law of the community, not the unknown or ignored legal norms set forth in the civil code; Malinowski was concerned to separate the real law from the often unreliable statements of rules made by informants, and believed 'the only way to discover the discrepancy between the ideal of law and its realization, between the orthodox version and the practice of actual life, is to play close and extended attention to the latter'.[70] With a similar purpose, Hoebel included the element of 'regularity' of enforcement (which was derived from Holmes' prediction theory of law) in his concept of law to identify and separate the real law from among the many norms espoused but not acted upon by legal institutions.[71] Pound, and more generally the Legal Realists, urged the very same focus on the actual behaviour of legal institutions for the same reason.

These observations point to another notable similarity between the two categories of the concept of law, though again with a significant difference. Both categories relate to what is known as the 'gap problem'. For a time the gap problem was 'the central issue for studies about law'.[72] Curiously, it is seldom recognized that there are two distinct versions of the gap problem. One version is the gap between state legal rules (or the rules cited as binding by non-state 'legal' institutions) and *what people in the community actually do*, the rules they actually follow in the course of social life. Many of the concepts of law in the first category highlighted this first gap. A second version is the gap between state legal rules (or the rules cited as binding by non-state 'legal' institutions) and *what the legal institutions actually do*, which norms they in fact enforce and how they do so, regardless of what they claim. Many of the concepts of law in the second category highlighted this second gap.

Their role in relation to the gap problem reveals the special power of behaviour-oriented approaches to law, regardless of which category they fall into—they have an inherently critical edge. They serve as checks or reminders that the rules

---

[68] Hoebel, above n 8 at 23.
[69] Ibid at 5.
[70] Krygier, above n 58 at 40.
[71] Hoebel, above n 8 at 22-3.
[72] R. Abel, 'Law Books and Books About Law', 26 *Stanford LR* 175 at 189 (1976).

we espouse are one matter, but how people in a group actually behave, or what legal actors actually do, are an entirely different matter. Although behaviourism has lapsed into disfavour with the modern turn to interpretation, this valuable quality must not be forgotten.

The distinguishing characteristic of the handful of novel social scientific concept of law that have been elaborated in recent years is precisely their departure from the earlier focus on behaviour, towards a greater emphasis on meaning or on the symbolic realm. Niklas Luhmann's autopoiesis, for example, views law as 'a system of meaning',[73] not as a set of institutions. Law is present whenever someone communicates, or even thinks, in legal terms. This approach to the concept of law opens up entirely new realms of enquiry. Its radically different look, however, should not create the impression that two categories of the concept of law I have identified have been surpassed or overcome. To identify law as a system of meaning still requires that we be able to distinguish this system from, say, the economic system or the political system, which requires that we identify criteria for what law is.

Luhmann's concept of law is openly parasitic upon the state law model, because autopoiesis defines law in terms of 'the law's unique *binary code of lawful/ unlawful, legal/illegal*'.[74] 'Any act or utterance that codes social acts according to this binary code of lawful/unlawful may be regarded as part of the legal system, no matter where it was made and no matter who made it.'[75] But the very ability to say (or think) that something involves 'lawful/unlawful' or 'legal/illegal' presupposes the existence of law—presupposes that there is an existing source which generates this binary code such that it can be invoked (acted, uttered or thought). For Luhmann, as I will demonstrate in a later Part, that source is what either state law or non-state 'law' (defined as institutional norm enforcement) dictates about lawfulness and legality.

What this new concept of law—and others like it—does is alter the dimension referred to in the second category, away from the former flat orientation to just behaviour, in the direction of the more complex dimensions of meaning and communication. But it is still firmly anchored in the second category. Indeed, for the present, at least until the meaning of law dramatically changes, anyone who wishes to formulate a social scientific concept of law will necessarily produce some variation of one or both of the two categories of the concept of law, because these categories take up the two sides of the same fundamental belief about law.

4 *Born of the Same Fundamental Belief*

Both categories were born out of the single article of faith that has dominated our understanding of law at least since Hobbes threatened that life without law would be 'solitary, poor, nasty, brutish and short'. That is: *law maintains social*

---
[73] M. King, 'The Truth About Autopoiesis', 20 *JL & Society* 218 at 226 (1993).
[74] Ibid at 223 (emphasis in original).
[75] Ibid.

order. Regardless of the many sharp disagreements which divided the scholars in the debate over the concept of law, there was universal agreement on the point that law is the primary mechanism of social control which preserves the normative order of society.[76] Sharing this baseline, the two categories of the concept of law identified opposite starting points.

Ehrlich and Malinowski were explicit about their belief that what law did—the function of law—was maintain social order.[77] And in an often quoted phrase, Malinowski observed that law should be defined 'by function and not by form'.[78] Malinowski studied a society that had no state law; Ehrlich was struck by the irrelevant and often alien rules contained in the Austrian Civil Code. Life in the societies they studied was nonetheless quite orderly, and it appeared that people engaged in their affairs with hardly a thought about institutionally enforced sanctions. Thus they examined social life, identified what they found to be the source of order, and appended to that source the label 'law'. The syllogistic-like chain of reasoning involved operates like this: the function of law is to maintain social order; social order can be found in regularized patterns of actual behaviour; the binding mechanism maintaining these patterns of behaviour is the complex of social obligations (ie reciprocity); *ipso facto*, legal norms are the norms abstracted from actual patterns of behaviour and the mechanism of law resides in the social relations themselves. The defining characteristic of the concepts in the first category was they took seriously law's *claims* to be or represent or embody the normative order of society.

In contrast, all of the concepts of law in the second category were derived from the state law model alone, applying functional analysis at different levels to eliminate the trappings of the State. Institutionalized norm enforcement was a functional description of what the state legal apparatus (legislature, courts and police) presumably does; institutionalized dispute-processing was a functional description that isolated upon just the court (which is the primary organ of law in the Anglo-American legal tradition). Taken one step further—to render explicit the implicit reasoning involved—the presumed function of enforcing norms is to maintain the normative cohesion of society; the presumed function of resolving disputes is to restore peace in society, thereby maintaining order. The defining characteristic of the concepts in the second category was that they took for granted that the state law model was the epitome of law, and they assumed (without checking) that institutional norm enforcement or dispute processing played the dominant role in maintaining order in society.

That is the explanation for how these competing categories of the concept of law came about. The key aspect to the concepts in the first category was that their proponents worked their way up from the context of achieved social order.

---

[76] See Pospisil, above n 15 at 24.
[77] See B. Malinowski, 'A New Instrument for the Interpretation of Law—Especially Primitive', 51 *Yale LJ* 1237 (1942) ('The sociologist and the ethnographer on the other hand must primarily be interested in the working of social control, that is, in the maintenance of order.'); E. Ehrlich, 'The Sociology of Law', 36 *Harvard LR* 130 (1922).
[78] B. Malinowski, 'Introduction', in Hogbin, *Law and Order in Polynesia* (1934) at lxiii.

The key aspect to the concepts in the second category was that the scholars involved started and stayed with the state law model, redescribed in functional terms.

In effect, each category staked out a position directly critical of the other: the first category said to the second, 'you are wrong if you believe the source of normative order in society is to be found in the activities of coercive institutions'; the second said to the first, 'what you are talking about is not what we mean by law because it brings in all of social life, not matching our intuitions about what law is, and rendering it impossible to identify the distinctively legal'.

Each side was essentially correct in their critique of the other. The problem lay not in what they were saying, but in the belief they shared. They can be reconciled only by giving up this belief. If 'law' means the publicly approved, institutional enforcement of norms (which is the scientific abstraction of the common meaning of law today), then 'law' (meant as such) is not the only or even the primary generative mechanism of normative order in society.

5 *Functional Analysis Cannot Answer* What is Law?

As the above description indicates, proponents of both categories of the concept of law applied functional analysis. A great deal of confusion exists, however, because the label functionalism encompasses several different kinds of analysis. I will distinguish two basic versions of functionalism.

The first kind, briefly alluded to earlier, is Functionalism (with a capital F) from the field of sociology. Durkheim is the acknowledged progenitor of this version. Its basic postulate is that society should be viewed as an organism with interdependent parts. Each part satisfies an essential function that contributes to the survival of the whole. Malinowski was one of the pioneers and most extreme theorists of Functional analysis,[79] though Functionalism is not limited to the first category of the concept of law. Talcott Parsons and Niklas Luhmann, whose views of law fit the second category, have been important Functionalist theorists.[80]

For our purposes the relevant aspect of Functionalism is the fact that the role and nature of law are determined *a priori*, by virtue of the function it is deemed to serve in the context of the overall social system. Under Functionalism, the characteristics of law are not specific to any actual legal system; rather, they are analytically specified according to a given theorist's abstract construction of the elements of a social system (as such) and its functional needs. Almost invariably, Functionalism holds that the function of law is to maintain order in society.[81]

---

[79] See B. Malinowski, *A Scientific Theory of Culture* (1944). For a critique of Malinowski's version of functionalism see R. K. Merton, *Social Theory and Social Structure* (1968) at 84–6. An influential critique of functionalism generally and Malinowski in particular can be found in C. Hempel, 'The Logic of Functional Analysis' in C. Hempel, *Aspects of Scientific Explanation* (1965) 297.

[80] See T. Parsons, 'The Law and Social Control' in W. Evan (ed) *The Sociology of Law* (1980) 60. N. Luhmann, *A Sociological Theory of Law* (1985).

[81] See P. Wilkinson, 'The Potential of Functionalism for the Sociological Analysis of Law' in A. Podgorecki and C. Whelan, *Sociological Approaches to Law* (1981) 67.

Functionalism has thus built into its systems analysis the problematic shared belief about law I identified in the preceding Part.

The second kind I will label Functional Realism,[82] to recognize the lead role Pound and the Legal Realists played in formulating it. As Felix Cohen described it, Functional Realism was a product of different influences in philosophy and the sciences, including logical positivism and pragmatism. It amounts to a general eschewing of meaningless concepts and questions and metaphysical entities ('transcendental nonsense').[83] According to Functional Realism, the significance of all things are determined by their actual consequences. Pound described it as 'asking not merely what law is and how it has come to be but what (in all its senses) it does, how it does it, and how it may be made to do it better'.[84] This consequentialist approach led many Functional Realists to adopt Holmes' definition of law: 'The prophesies of what the courts will do in fact, and nothing more pretentious, are what I mean by law'.[85] Functional Realism is best understood not as a coherent theory, but as a reaction to obscurantist conceptualizing, combined with a faith in scientific observation. The basic point is an admonition to pay close attention to reality, which led to the earlier described emphasis on the observation of actual behaviour.

Contrary to the belief of its adherents, Functional Realism, and indeed all forms of functional analysis, are incapable of answering the question *What is Law?*. The answer must always be given or assumed. Observe Holmes' definition of law as what a *court* does; to start with a court is to presuppose that a court is the locus of law. In essence, Functional Realism says: *law is what law does*.[86] But to find out what law does (its function), we must first posit that which is doing (the object whose function we are examining)—we must presuppose what law is.

We could instead start by positing the function (maintain social order) and work backwards to locate the object (law), just as Ehrlich and Malinowski did. This reverse analysis would work, however, only if a single object alone served the posited function. Otherwise we would be left with a choice among several objects with no function-based criteria by which to identify *the* object at issue, precisely the problem Malinowski and Ehrlich could not surmount. Any attempt to locate criteria for law—for the distinctively 'legal'—necessarily presupposes what law is, for only by already knowing what law is can we identify its distinctive characteristics. Hence the inevitable resort to the state law model, which provides our current paradigm for 'law'.

In response to sharp criticism (of Malinowski in particular) about the logic of functional analysis applied to social systems, later Functionalist theory disavowed

---

[82] Hoebel used this label to describe his own work, above n 8 at 5.
[83] See F. Cohen, 'Transcendental Nonsense and the Functional Method' and 'The Problems of a Functional Jurisprudence' in F. Cohen, above n 29 at 33–76, 77–94.
[84] Pound, above n 36, vol 1 at 349.
[85] Holmes, 'Path of the Law', 10 *Harvard LR* 457 at 461 (1897). Cohen, above n 29 at 61–5.
[86] Llewellyn put it thus: 'What these officials [judges, sheriffs, jailers, lawyers] do about disputes is, to my mind, the law itself'. K. Llewellyn, *The Bramble Bush* (1930).

the notion that a single object alone serves a given function, and acknowledged the existence of functional equivalents or alternatives.[87] Thus the problem I have identified is endemic to functionalist thought.

The point bears repeating: functional analysis of whatever variety is incapable of providing an answer to the question *What is Law?*. 'Law' must be posited *before* functional analysis can be engaged to enquire what it does, how it does it, and what its consequences are; we can instead posit the function (maintain social order), but then we must still come up with criteria to distinguish the distinctively 'legal' phenomena from among the other kinds of phenomena (including culture, reciprocity and language) which serve this function; which means, again, we must already know what law is. Whichever way we begin, we either end up with the state law model (which leads to the conclusion that certain societies did not have law) or we stop talking about 'law'. And therein lies the logic that led to the impasse in the debate over the concept of law.

6 *Existing in Tension*

Although the two categories of the concept of law are in agreement on several core aspects—a belief about the nature of law, resort to functional analysis, an orientation to the scientific observation of actual behaviour—they exist in tension with one another. The first sign of this tension is that each category stakes out a position directly critical of the other, as described earlier. There are three further signs.

For one, these categories are *competitors*. Many of the concepts of law in the second category were reactions to the inability of Malinowski and Ehrlich to isolate satisfactorily the distinctively legal. The two categories cannot easily be combined, because application of the criteria used in the second category would eliminate much of what Ehrlich and Malinowski (especially) would want to call law.

Another sign of this tension is evident in the *polemical thrust* directed by the first category against the second. I have already mentioned Ehrlich's attack on codification. Customary law has always existed in tension with state law, especially with its connotations of pre-existing state law and being closer to the people. Galanter offered indigenous law by way of contrast to state law. And legal pluralists are among the most vociferous critics of the perceived hegemonic impulses of state law. Although these polemics were mostly directed at state law, Malinowski's insistence on the irrelevance of institutions extends the polemical opposition of the first category to the second category as a whole.

A third sign of tension consists in the *contrasting objects* they centred upon. The first category was oriented towards the behaviour of people in social groups or society, the second category towards the behaviour of legal actors within legal institutions. The first category focused on regular or routine behaviour, the

---

[87] Merton, above n 79 at 86–91.

second category on institutionalized reactions to disruptions of this routine. The first category saw the binding mechanism of law in the complex of social relations, the second category in the institutionalized imposition of sanctions.

These signs of tension indicate that the relationship between the two categories of the concept of law is an uneasy one. Yet they are mixed together all the time. Look at the very first entry for 'law' in Webster's Dictionary:

> i(a) a binding custom or practice of a community: a rule or mode of conduct or action that is prescribed or formally recognized as binding by a supreme controlling authority or is made obligatory by a sanction (as an edict, decree, rescript, order, ordinance, statute, resolution, rule, judicial decision, or usage) made, recognized, or enforced by the controlling authority.[88]

The part before the colon refers to the first category, for custom and practice always involves what people actually do; the part after the colon refers to the second category, the state law model of law. But we now know there is no automatic correspondence between the two, and if anything the relationship is often one of antagonism.

Although the dictionary can be excused for a lack of subtlety, even sophisticated legal theorists have used concepts of law from both categories at the same time, not recognizing their incongruity, as I will show in the upcoming discussion of Luhmann's concept of law. The belief that these two categories are internally connected or otherwise strongly correlated runs deep—it is a product of the ideology that law represents the consensual normative order of society.

7 *A Brief Excursus on the Concept of Social Control*

A prominent feature of the discussion thus far is the persistence with which the terms social order and social control keep popping up. Law is thoroughly understood in terms of these notions. Thus a brief excursion into the sociological literature on social control—the modern scientific terminology we apply to the old problem of social order[89]—will help identify the boundaries of the map.

Much of the background discussion can be avoided at the outset by observing that, despite the close association between ideas about law and about social control, there is general consensus on the point that law is distinct from social control—the relationship between the two is not one of identity or equivalence. Law (at least state law) performs many functions besides social control, including, *inter alia*, enabling or facilitative, performative, status conferring, defining, legitimative, integrative, distributive, power conferring, and symbolic;[90] and there are many forms of social control besides law. For various reasons we have often lost sight of both halves of this non-identity. A functional definition of law as

---

[88] *Webster's Third New International Dictionary of the English Language Unabridged* (1981).
[89] M. Janowitz, 'The Intellectual History of "Social Control"' in J. S. Rouek (ed) *Social Control for the 1980's* (1978) 20 at 30.
[90] See L. Nader and B. Yngvesson, 'On Studying the Ethnography of Law and its Consequences' in J. Honingmann (ed) *Handbook on Social and Cultural Anthropology* (1973) 883 at 908–9; Feeley, above n 43 at 503–8.

social control tends to obscure any other functions law may perform,[91] and the continuing influence of Hobbes' dicta, combined with a law-centred perspective, misled many to believe that law was 'the only important mechanism' of social control.[92] Sociological studies have helped loosen the grip of this view, though a strong residual belief in it remains.

'The study of social control has traditionally been a central aspect of the sociological enterprise.'[93] As is standard fare in the social sciences, a number of different meanings have been attached to the term, and it has gone through various phases of development. Fortunately, just two basic senses of the term have been dominant throughout.

According to Morris Janowitz, in an influential formulation, the 'classical' sense of social control referred to the 'capacity of a society to regulate itself'.[94] Janowitz claimed that this meaning dominated from the inception of the sociological discussion of the concept, at the early part of this century, until it was replaced in the 1930s by a narrower meaning of social control as 'the processes of developing conformity'.[95] Janowitz argued that the classical sense retained its vitality during this period, and has recently begun to re-emerge, sometimes under the rubric of 'social regulation'. Donald Black offered a slightly different chronology, but used the same two basic meanings. For Black the early meaning of social control referred 'broadly to virtually all of the human practices and arrangements that contribute to social order and, in particular, that influence people to conform';[96] whereas the more recent meaning 'refers more narrowly to how people define and respond to deviant behaviour'.[97]

These two senses of social control resulted in alternative emphases. Those (mostly social psychologists) who saw social control as the process of developing conformity to social practices identified socialization as the primary mechanism of social control.[98] Education, in particular, but also the family, television, advertising, and so forth, are the means by which attitudes and values are inculated in members of a community or society. Internalization by individuals of shared cultural orientations determines many of the customary patterns of behaviour that prevail within a group.[99] This form of social control has been characterized as internal control: whereby 'the individual himself is motivated to conform in his behaviour (conscience, conditioning processes, attitudes, indoctrination, socialization)'.[100]

---

[91] See Krygier, above n 58 at 38–9.
[92] L. Coser, 'The Notion of Control in Sociological Theory', in Gibbs (ed), above n 53 13 at 14. Coser added that early sociological investigators have taught us that among the various mechanisms of social control, law 'is one of many, and possibly not even the most important one'. Ibid.
[93] A. Horwitz, *The Logic of Social Control* (1990) 1.
[94] Janowitz, above n 89 at 20.
[95] Ibid.
[96] Black, above n 63 at 4.
[97] Ibid at 5.
[98] See Coser, above n 92 at 14–19.
[99] J. Roucek, 'The Concept of Social Control in American Sociology', in Roucek (ed), above n 89 3 at 4–5.
[100] Ibid at 12.

Those who instead saw social control as societal responses to deviance tended to emphasize the role of rules and institutions, and the presence of compulsion as a means to insure conformity.[101] Many studies were conducted on state institutions, such as the police, juvenile courts, mental hospitals, and reformatories. The degree of coercion or repression involved was often a central focus for these works.[102] This form of social control has been characterized as external control: controls 'imposed from without'.[103]

The parallels between these two versions of the concept of social control and the two categories of the concept of law I set out earlier are plainly evident. Internal control matches up with the first category (regularized patterns of behaviour), and external control with the second category (institutionalized norm enforcement or dispute processing). The basic difference is that in both instances the sociological approach to social control casts a broader net.

Ehrlich and Malinowski were well aware of the overarching influence of socialization. They both recognized the significance of education in generating conformity,[104] and Malinowski even discussed 'cultural determinism'.[105] Trying to get at 'law', Ehrlich and Malinowski narrowed their focus to the considerable space for alternative courses of action left open by socialization. Likewise, although the response to deviance branch of social control overwhelmingly focused on state institutions, sociological studies have also been done on informal forms of coercive social control. These differences aside, the parallel remains a strong one.

The two categories I have identified appear to reflect a basic (albeit not always recognized) divide that runs through the legal as well as sociological literature: the consensus/coercion dichotomy.[106] Recent efforts to break down this dichotomy, especially those which highlight the phenomenon of coercively generated consensus, alter the dichotomy from a sharp one to a matter of degree, but do not entirely eliminate it.

8 Luhmann's Attempt to Overcome the Divide

An examination of Niklas Luhmann's sophisticated concept of law, which appears to fall into both categories at once, will help test whether the divide is as sturdy as it seems. Luhmann articulated his concept of law in his earlier work, but carried over the basic elements of this concept when he shifted to autopoietic analysis.

---

[101] Ibid at 12–13.
[102] See Horwitz, above n 93 at 4–5.
[103] Roucek, above n 99 at 12.
[104] See Ehrlich, above n 16 at 78 ('The social norms give shape and form to the individuality of man.'); Schapera, above n 31 at 142–3.
[105] Ibid at 143.
[106] A. Hunt, 'Dichotomy and Contradiction in the Sociology of Law' in A. Hunt, *Explorations in Law and Society* (1993) at 58–89. Hunt argued that this dichotomy exists *within* each theorist's concept of law. I have shown that it also exists at the most general level across concepts of law as well.

Luhmann defined law as the '*structure of a social system which depends upon the congruent generalisation of normative behavioural expectations*'.[107] He asserted that the function of law is to limit or resolve incongruencies of expectation which arise in every society in the course of interaction between people. 'Law is in no way primarily a coercive order, but rather a facilitation of expectation.'[108] These expectations are based upon generalized norms, and incongruencies arise when the generalizations break down or when people act against the generalized norm. Luhmann stated:

> We are not returning to the popular thesis that there have been societies without law either in the history of mankind or even in crosscultural comparisons of the present (namely, those which do not have a coercive state apparatus). Rather, our functional concept of law makes it clear that law fulfils a necessary function in every meaningfully constituted society and must therefore always exist. The development of law is not to be understood as the step from the pre-legal to legal forms of societies, but as a gradual differentiation and functional independence of law.[109]

Thus, according to Luhmann, law is not primarily coercive and exists in all societies (thereby falling into the first category), and law evolves as society does to become institutionalized (thereby falling into the second category).

Luhmann recognized the problems with his concept of law. He asserted that the 'areas of custom and law are by no means equivalent, although the precise delimitation can only be made at a concrete and empirical level'.[110] However, he offered no criteria upon which to make the delimitation. He went on to admit: 'It is more difficult to establish a clear delineation between law, language and its accessories (eg rules of spelling). Although it may be intuitively clear that law is not identical with language, it takes some reflection to find the crucial point of difference.'[111]

Needless to say, this is the Malinowski/Ehrlich problem with a vengeance. Like Malinowski and Ehrlich, he was unable to distinguish law from custom; and just as their concepts appeared to encompass even 'culture patterns' or 'the obligatory aspects of all social relationships', Luhmann's concept cannot clearly be distinguished from language! The inability of functional analysis to make such distinctions, as I established earlier, is inevitable whenever functional alternatives are present, and results in a totalizing impulse (swallowing up all of the other functional alternatives) that cannot be contained.

Although Luhmann suggested a few ways to distinguish law from language, in the end he pointed to the development of legal institutions as an 'important step ... which permits a clearer separation between law and language, truth, art and rational practice'.[112] Luhmann thus shifted to the second category of the

---

[107] Luhmann, above n 80 at 82 (emphasis in original).
[108] Ibid at 78.
[109] Ibid at 83.
[110] Ibid at 81.
[111] Ibid.
[112] Ibid at 83.

concept of law to solve his problems with locating the distinctively legal. Thereafter, Luhmann's discussion is almost entirely related to law in its differentiated form.

As the flow of his argument reveals, when struggling through the problem in the course of a few pages of analysis, Luhmann actually replicated the debate over the concept of law. The answer to whether he successfully straddled the two categories of the concept of law rests upon how we interpret his evolutionary sequence. According to Luhmann's description, prior to the differentiation of society and the emergence of a differentiated law, there was a kind of primordial soup in which law, custom, and language (among others) all served the function of stabilizing behavioural expectations, and could not be sharply distinguished from one another.

An alternative interpretation is this: if they all served the same function, and if there were no clearly identifiable criteria by which to distinguish among them, then there was no distinction to be made in the primordial period. There was no-thing 'law' which underwent a continuous evolutionary development from the very beginning of the existence of social groups. There was primordial soup before differentiation, and something else after. With the differentiation of society, the emergence of institutions, and the separation of public and private realms, entirely new social phenomena arose.

The only apparent reason for Luhmann to insist that law exists even when it has no separate identity was to preserve the coherence of his *a priori* constructed Functionalist paradigm, which built law in as an inherent part of a social system. Social analysts can legitimately maintain that all societies (including undifferentiated ones) require mechanisms to co-ordinate normative expectations. The dubious move is the separate assertion that what fills this function is, by definition, 'law'. Without this additional assertion, however, Luhmann cannot claim that all societies or social systems have 'law'.

Luhmann straddled the divide in the only way possible, by altering midstream what he meant by 'law', applying the first category meaning to societies lacking in differentiation and the second category to those with differentiation. However, this shift in meaning is not a satisfactory solution to his problem because even after the emergence of 'legal' institutions, language and custom (as well as other factors) still substantially contributed to maintaining 'the congruent generalization of normative behavioural expectations', and therefore must still be considered 'law' consistent with Luhmann's explicit, non-coercion based definition of law, which he did not give up when shifting to the focus on institutions. Under Luhmann's analysis, after differentiation, society contains two fundamentally distinct phenomena going by the label 'law', one non-coercive and the other coercive. Besides creating an ambiguity at the core of his theory, this simultaneous usage is affirmatively and perhaps dangerously misleading insofar as it analytically clothes a coercive phenomenon within a non-coercive one. Any successful attempt to overcome the two categories must be consistent in the meaning it applies to the term 'law'.

The divide is a resilient one. Indeed, the forms of 'law' identified by these categories regularly coexist in the social arena, both temporally and spatially, with different scopes of application, belying any suggestion that they are related to one another through evolutionary descent.

9 Outline of the Map, Legal Versus Social Scientific Perspectives

A preliminary outline of the map can now be provided. Although I began the map focused on social scientific concepts of law, it turns out that the territory covered by the map is actually that of social order. The two categories of the concept of law stand as prominent features set at opposing corners of this shared terrain.

The first category is located squarely upon regularized conduct, what people actually do, the patterns of behaviour they engage in on a routine basis; it sits on a base which at its broadest includes socialization. The second category is centred upon publicly organized institutional reactions to disruptions of regularized conduct; it sits on a base that broadly includes non-institutional (ie shaming, ostracism) reactions as well. The line where these two respective bases meet is a fuzzy one, drawn where positive inducement and negative sanction tend to support and feed into one another, where external and internal control intermingle, where coercion has a role in generating consensus.

A general action sequence is involved, which can be divided into three phases—routine conduct, disruption, and social reaction to disruption—with the first category of the concept of law applicable to the first phase and the second category to the third phase.[113] The following table should help clarify matters:

Concept of Law	Phase	'Legal' Mechanism	Sociological Studies	Sociological Mechanism	Effective Moment
First category—lived norms	Patterned or regular conduct	Complex of social obligations	Internal control—conformity	Socialization	Proactive (shaping conduct)
Second category—enforced norms	Social reaction to disruption of regular conduct	Institutionally imposed sanction	External control—response to deviance	Coercive application of power	Reactive (following disruptive conduct)

The table makes abundantly clear that the two categories are thoroughly distinct in nature. What shapes routine conduct is an entirely different matter

---

[113] This three part action sequence is similar to that observed by the Process school, as set out in Victor Turner's four stages of a social drama. V. Turner, *Dramas, Fields, and Metaphors: Symbolic Action in Human Society* (1974) at 37–41.

from what happens when society responds to the disruption of routine conduct.

Neither state law nor institutionalized norm enforcement or dispute processing (the second category) *of themselves* directly result in or generate regularized patterns of behaviour (the first category).[114] The former is not the underlying operative mechanism of the latter. Institutionalized norm enforcement can give rise to regularized behaviour only if it is incorporated into the socialization process or if it becomes a part of the complex of social obligations leading to the behaviour. There must be an intimate internal link between the two categories if what comes after (institutionalized response to breach) is to have a role in shaping what came before (routine conduct).

This link will be elaborated upon in a moment. First I should note the very different look the above table presents from the lawyer's typical view of law. According to the widely held legal positivist view of law, as articulated most ably by H. L. A. Hart, legal norms are all those norms legitimately recognized as such by legal actors, including code provisions promulgated in advance of enforcement activities. Thus many a lawyer reader will deny that state law has only a reactive presence.

The response to this objection is that the lawyer reader is correct within the self-understanding of law as articulated by legal positivism, an understanding which is essential to those who are functionaries within a given legal system. However, as I emphasized in the discussion of behaviourism, many of the social scientific concepts were set up in opposition to legal positivism, with the express purpose of identifying and separating out those legal norms actually lived by members of the community, or actually enforced or applied by legal institutions, from among those 'paper only' legal norms merely declared as such but not reflected in social behaviour or regularly enforced by legal institutions. These approaches deny the label 'law' to unobserved or unenforced norms because they have no role in the maintenance of social order. According to legal positivism, however, as long as the rule of recognition is satisfied, even paper only norms are entirely valid legal norms.

Social scientific concepts of law carve up the world of norms quite differently from legal positivism, to the extent that state law norms have no special status when viewed from the scientific perspective. Those norms actually lived by members of the community (regardless of whether they are codified in state law) fall into the first category, and are effective pro-actively since they lead to behaviour; those norms regularly enforced by legal institutions fall into the second category, and are reactive since enforcement actions are seldom undertaken prior to a breach.

The contrast between the legal positivist and the social scientific point of view is critically important. They operate in different realms of activity—legal practice versus social scientific practice. Both views are entirely legitimate when kept

---

[114] An institution itself consists of the patterned behaviour of those whose complex of actions make up the institution. What is meant here, however, is the influence of institutional enforcement in generating compliant behaviour in society at large.

within the boundaries of their respective practices, and neither view has authority over the other. Untold confusion has resulted in socio-legal studies from the failure to recognize the practice-based and practice-bound validity of both views, the most recent manifestation of which are assertions by legal pluralists that the lawyer's view of law is the product of ideological delusion, and inferior to the scientific view of law.

10 Two Theses about the Link between the Two Categories

Building upon norms, two separate theses provide the link between the two categories: a thesis about the source of legal norms, and a thesis about social engineering through law.

The first thesis about the connection between the two categories of the concept of law holds that institutionally enforced norms (the second category) are derived from actually lived norms (the first category), that lived social rules are the source of enforced legal rules.[115] This view of the source of legal norms can be traced at least as far back as Savigny's argument that legal rules reflect the legal consciousness of the people, and it is consistent with the self-understanding of the Anglo-American common law tradition that common law rules gradually developed out of existing social practices that were recognized by courts.

Ehrlich, who extensively cited Savigny, and promoted the common-law system as the ideal one, exemplified this thesis in his assertion that rules for decision (rules applied by courts) often are—and should be—derived from rules of conduct (actually lived rules).[116] Indeed, his major criticism of codification was that the act of codification, combined with the tendency towards abstraction exhibited by codifiers, freezes rules for decision while rules for conduct continue to develop, thus resulting over time in a growing gap between the living law and state law.

An even more direct claim that legal rules are derived from social rules can be found in Hoebel's and Bohannan's concepts of law. Hoebel began by asserting 'A social rule is legal if . . .', and Bohannan asserted that 'law may be regarded as a custom that has been restated' for the purposes of the legal institution. Thus the thesis of the social origin of enforced legal norms applies equally to state law as well as to non-state institutions of norm enforcement or dispute processing.

A critical link between the two categories is provided by this thesis. If the norms applied by state law or by institutionalized norm enforcement are derived from actually lived norms, then the rules applied at the reactive stage of institutional enforcement will directly correspond to the rules which shape behaviour at the pro-active stage. Strictly speaking, however, it is not the actual

---

[115] Lived social rules are also 'law', according to the first category. To avoid confusion, however, since both categories claim the label 'law', I will now refer to first category rules as social rules and second category rules as legal rules. This terminology has been adopted because it more closely matches the understanding of readers, not because I intend to deny the claim of the first category to the label 'law', although it does reveal that confusion easily arises in relation to the first category's application of the term law.
[116] Ehrlich, above n 16 at 121–36.

influence of the legal rules but the fact of correspondence to lived social rules which matters. Enforcement of the legal rules does not itself generate the behaviour,[117] though legal endorsement of the social rules may be a reinforcing factor in their continued socialization.

This initially plausible thesis is weakened—at least with regard to state law—when we recognize that the history of legal development around the world substantially consists of the transplantation of norms and institutions from one society to another, either through natural diffusion, colonial imposition or voluntary borrowing.[118] Furthermore, legal institutions often formulate or mould norms to fit the internal demands of legal discourse, sometimes rendering them unrecognizable in relation to lived social norms. Neither the alien origin of norms nor their legalistic phrasing, however, are the final determinative factors, since the key for the second category is how they are actually enforced. Judges applying the mix of available rules often come up with an outcome that matches prevailing social norms regardless of what the legal norms actually say. But this does not solve the further problem that many societies or groups consist of different subcommunities each with their own bodies of sometimes competing norms. Therefore, even assuming that judges' decisions match lived social rules, the outcomes may still conflict with other (competing) bodies of lived social rules.

Finally, many actually enforced legal rules—like the annual reporting requirements imposed upon corporations, or jurisdictional requirements for courts—have nothing to do with actually lived social norms, but rather exist for a multitude of other social purposes, or are generated by the needs of legal discourse itself. Many enforced legal rules relate to and are solely the product of other legal rules, and have no connection in origin or application to social behaviour.

Thus the first thesis is contingent upon several factors, each of which is fraught with difficulties, as is reflected by the pervasive presence of the gap problem. Commercial transactions are the one area where there often is a match between lived social norms (actually followed business practices) and the norms enforced by legal institutions, in Ehrlich's time as well as our own. This is in part because legal actors have more often paid attention to prevailing business practices (as with the Uniform Commercial Code), and in part because the particular content of the rules governing transactions is often less important than the fact that everyone follows the same format. Thus business practices are more easily modified to meet changes in the law. Gaps exist even here, however, as Stuart Macaulay showed in his study of the non-contractual relations in business.[119]

The second thesis about the connection between these two categories is the

---

[117] See K. Llewellyn, *Jurisprudence* (1962) at 401–2. ('law observance, so called, to be generally effective requires that folkways in conformity with the purposes of the law concerned shall have been first developed. It is the folkways, not the law, which are known; it is the folkways, not the law, which our present scheme of things offers some guaranty of people learning and following'.)

[118] See A. Watson, *Legal Transplants: An Approach to Comparative Law* (1974).

[119] S. Macauley, 'Non-Contractual Relations in Business: A Preliminary Study' 28 *Am Sociological Rev* 55 (1963).

reverse of the first thesis. This thesis holds that law instrumentally shapes routine behaviour in virtue of its authority as law, or due to the fear of sanction that supports the law—legal rules thereby create new lived social rules.

When social engineering through law is successful, two different mechanisms are involved. In the short term it operates by altering the complex of social obligations (usually by changing the perceived costs or benefits attached to existing courses of action); in the long term, once the new pattern of behaviour is established, it operates through continued socialization of the new pattern of behaviour reflected in (now) lived social rules.

The problem with this thesis is that attempts at social engineering through law have a notable failure rate.[120] A threshold barrier is communication of the legal rules. In a truism that is repeated as often as it is forgotten: 'most of us are vastly ignorant of the law, and are continually violating or disregarding the law'.[121] Lest you forget: 'we do not know what the law is',[122] at least not much beyond the bare minimum that we should pay our taxes, and shouldn't steal from or physically harm others. Even the fact that a given set of legal rules are enforced does not of itself assure that they are widely known. 'It is certain that law does not secure obedience except in so far as it is known.'[123] Ironically, outside of legal professionals, the persons most knowledgeable about legal rules and procedures (within a narrow band) are those least likely to abide by them: recidivists.

Another problem is that prevailing social rules resist the new behaviour required by the law, as Sally Falk Moore demonstrated in her notion of the semi-autonomous social field. In these situations the enforced legal rules must compete with existing social rules which have the marked advantage of being the rules already actually followed. Aside from the symbolic authority which attaches to law, and in the absence of positive inducements, law has only the threat of sanction to secure compliance. But as Ehrlich observed, in most everyday behaviour 'the thought of compulsion by the courts does not even enter the minds of men'.[124]

A third problem is that, with regard to both state law and non-state institutions, legal rules are often articulated only after the fact, in the course of the institutional response to the dispute. 'It is on such occasions [after break down] that existing values and norms are likely to be articulated and, in the course of debate,

---

[120] The most dramatic example of this failure can be found in the law and development movement, which urged law as a means to alter social relations and lead the way to development in developing countries. See D. Trubek and M. Galanter, 'Scholars in Self-Estrangement: Some Reflections on the Crisis in Law and Development Studies in the United States', 1974 *Wisconsin LR* 1062 (1974).
[121] Cohen, above n 29 at 87.
[122] Llewellyn, above n 117 at 401.
[123] Cohen, above n 29 at 87. For an elaboration of this obvious point, see R. Seidman, 'The Communication of Law and the Process of Development', 1972 *Wisconsin LR* 686 (1972). It must be emphasized that this ignorance is not limited to lay people. As a former public defender, and then state attorney general, I seldom knew in advance what the law was in any given case. At most I had general ideas about the possibly applicable rules, and I knew where to look to find the law.
[124] Ehrlich, above n 16 at 21. K. Llewellyn, above n 117 at 401 ('Rarely, very rarely, we check conduct, or embark on conduct, or modify conduct, with a conscious eye to the law'.).

consciously or unconsciously reformulated to accommodate the situation which has arisen'.[125] Rules articulated (or reformulated) later cannot govern behaviour which comes before, as losing parties to a dispute have sometimes loudly complained. Although the newly articulated rules can influence later behaviour, the populace will have good reason to be suspicious of reliance upon the such rules.

Yet another problem with this second thesis comes from the typical form of legal norms. At least with regard to state law, a large proportion of enforced legal norms do not prescribe an affirmative course of routine conduct, and many of those that do have a facilitative or enabling function rather than a social control function. For example, a statute that punishes murder does not give rise to any routine patterns of conduct. A nimble retort might be that not killing is itself a pattern of behaviour. But the point remains that—except in a nightmarish (and short-lived) community where people are socialized to routinely kill—the negative statute did not give rise to this non-behaviour; rather, it never occurs to most people to kill to begin with, and thus the statute itself is irrelevant.

A final problem with this thesis is that it assumes a commitment as well as capacity on the part of the law announcer, the law enforcer, and the law applier (roles that can be distributed or held by one person or group) to effectuate the content of the rules. Many legal rules are proclaimed for mostly symbolic purposes, with no intention on the part of legal actors to enforce the paraded norms. And on many occasions, even when the commitment exists, legal institutions simply lack the power to enforce the rules. Because they are not actually enforced, these norms would not qualify under the second category of the concept of law anyway, but it is important to be reminded of these reasons when addressing the failure of law to give rise to lived social norms.

These objections should not be interpreted to indicate that legal rules do not influence behaviour. They most assuredly do in a myriad of ways, often unanticipated by the promulgators of the rules. Frustratingly for the law issuers, newly enforced legal rules often give rise to actual patterns of behaviour which are designed by the participants to get around the legal rules so that pre-existing patterns of behaviour can continue in substance or effect. These objections more narrowly suggest that, for a variety of reasons, it is quite a formidable task for enforced legal norms (the second category) directly and intentionally to result in corresponding lived social norms (the first category).

Many of the above points can be expeditiously illustrated by the recent US Supreme Court case *Bowers v Hardwick*.[126] A Georgia statute prohibited sodomy, defined as 'any sexual act involving the sex organs of one person and the mouth or anus of another'. Obviously this prohibition, which reflected the moral views of a part of the community, was not consistent with the sexual behaviour of many Georgians, especially but not limited to homosexuals. Prior to the publicity engendered by the case, probably few people were aware of the existence of the

---

[125] Roberts, above n 55 at 43.
[126] 478 US 186 (1986).

prohibition, which Georgia officials did not actively enforce. The decision enforcing the legal rule undoubtedly had little if any effect on reducing the incidence of sodomy, though perhaps more people thereafter closed their curtains.

The conclusion from an examination of these two theses is that the link between the two categories of the concept of law is a complex and often tenuous one. No doubt, with regard to specific systems or contexts, many points of correspondence can be found. The objective of the foregoing analysis was not to deny that the link exists, but to suggest that the link is much more problematic than is usually assumed. The common belief that law represents the consensual normative order of society seduces us into taking for granted that there is a link between lived social norms and the norms enforced by legal institutions. Often that is not the case.

This conclusion exposes a flaw in the concepts of law formulated by Hoebel and Bohannan, and others who defined law as social norms enforced by legal institutions or as reinstitutionalized custom—in effect they analytically merged lived social norms and enforced legal norms,[127] thereby removing from scrutiny the uncertain relationship between the two.

11 A Concept of Law Based upon the Union of Both Categories

The final step in drawing the map is to consider the implications of formulating a single concept of law out of the union of both categories of the concept of law. The preceding Part focused on the *empirical* links between the two categories. Here I will explore what results when they are joined on a *conceptual* level, by formulating a concept of law which includes only those norms that are actually enforced by publicly approved coercive institutions, *and* only when the norms so enforced are also reflected in the actual social behaviour of the group.[128]

This joinder is quite instructive. Because the scopes of application of the two categories are not coextensive, joining them sharply narrows the band of what qualifies for the label 'law'. This narrowing comes on top of the fact that each category, in its own way, already restricts the use of the label law on behavioural grounds, banning non-lived or non-enforced rules from being considered 'law'. One consequence of this scientific approach was to remove ideals from the domain of law—as reflected in the Realists' controversial stance that they must set aside the *ought*, at least temporarily, while scientifically investigating what *is*.

The immediately beneficial effect of joining the two categories is it dramatically

---

[127] In their defence it might be said that they were defining non-state 'law' and legal institutions, and in such instances there is an internal connection between social norms and legal norms, at least more so than with regard to state law. The problem with this response is, first, if indeed differences exist they must be established through investigation; and second, they cannot be investigated unless the two are kept analytically separate to begin with.

[128] Responding to an earlier draft of this article, Gordon Woodman suggested this union as a suitable scientific definition for law. Letter of 19 August 1994. A similar kind of joinder has occasionally been proposed by legal theorists. Joseph Raz argued that Hans Kelsen required a degree of efficacy (that is, behaviour had to actually conform to it) for a state legal norm to be valid. J. Raz, *The Authority of Law* (1979) 85–90.

restricts the scope of the first category of the concept of law, eliminating most of the many lived social norms it encompasses which we do not normally think of as 'legal'. But there is a price to pay: the claim that all societies have law must be given up, for the same old reason that some societies did not use publicly approved institutions to enforce norms. This explains why the coherence of Luhmann's concept of law, which referred to both categories, could not be saved by being interpreted as a union of the two categories rather than as an unacknowledged shift in meaning from the first category to the second—his Functionalist framework prohibited him from granting the possibility that certain societies lacked law.

The joinder drastically cuts back on the second category of the concept of law in an even more revealing way. Earlier I asserted that many enforced legal norms have no relation to actually lived social norms. The examples are legion. Consider standard tax codes filled with a complex body of rules. Some of these rules are designed to shape routine behaviour, like the hefty tax imposed on cigarettes to reduce smoking or the tax on gas to inhibit driving. But many other tax rules have the purpose of raising revenue or redistributing income. These latter rules cannot be considered to give rise to any lived social rules, except in the limited sense (involving only a handful of the total body of tax rules) that people file their tax returns and pay the amount due by the legally designated day. Another example involves laws governing marriage. Many of these legal rules also do not give rise to lived social rules; rather their primary effect is to create a new status recognized in law, to which a variety of consequences are attached. The same can be said of the massive volume of legal rules that apply to corporations, many of which do not even refer to social behaviour. Their most dramatic effect is to grant life (or at least existence) to entirely new entities.

These kinds of phenomena and the rules which produce them form a substantial bulk of what law—state law, and often non-state 'legal' institutions and rules as well—actually does. However, they would all be excluded if a scientific concept of law were based upon the union of the two categories of the concept of law, because they have nothing to do with lived social rules and would thus fail to satisfy the requirements of the first category.

This implication of the union is particularly revealing insofar as it again raises a crucial limitation of the scientific concepts of law in both categories. They were constructed around the notion of social order. This orientation resulted in an emphasis on various aspects of the control of social behaviour. When the focus was on simple societies perhaps this emphasis was appropriate. But only a part of the activities of state legal institutions—largely the part dealing with criminal law—fall within this limited focus, and the same could be said of many non-state institutions of norm enforcement.

The social order lens thus artificially constricted the scope of scientific enquiry into law and legal phenomena. Law today does much more than social control. With the increasing differentiation of society and the internal development of state law, social control-based concepts of law lacked the analytical capacity to keep up with the change. This is not to say that it was wrong to focus on social control. As this map reveals, many essential insights were produced by the two categories of the concept of law.

12 Reading the Map and the 'Centrality of Law' Thesis

Assuming social order is largely comprised of regularized patterns of behaviour, the foregoing analysis suggests that in general all forms of institutionalized norm enforcement or dispute processing (including state law) play a relatively small role in generating social order, at least in comparison to the influence of socialization, habit, and the complex of social obligations. This disproportion is simply a reflection of the greater degree to which internal control influences most behaviour relative to external control—the greater degree to which we do things because we want to, not because we are forced to by sanction or fear of sanction.

It would appear that the map is not divided into territories of equal size. The base upon which the first category of the concept of law sits extends to three corners of the map, with the base of the second category left to occupy the last remaining corner. A map of this sort can be drawn for entire societies or for communities or groups, whenever institutionalized norm enforcement is present. Different societies or communities, and the same society under different circumstances, differ with regard to the relative proportion of these bases. But most long-term, stable communities should have a greater proportion of the first category to the second.[129] Perhaps only totalitarian societies would have this proportion reversed.

If correct, this conclusion sits in apparent conflict with an influential thesis about the modern condition currently sweeping through the community of socio-legal scholars. Alan Hunt summarized this thesis:

> In a variety of different expressions contemporary social theory points to the thesis that the law continues to occupy an increasingly central and organizing place, whether for good or ill, in advanced capitalist democracies.... For such diverse figures as Weber, Poulantzas, Habermas, and Luhmann are to be found distinct, but related, versions of a thesis that state law has been an increasingly central feature of modernity. Whether expressed as the advance of legal rationality, the centrality of the 'juridico-political instance', the process of 'juridification', or as the 'positivization' of a self-referential legal system, these are all variants of what I call the centrality of law thesis. Another very popular version of this general thesis is that of 'legalization' that makes the general point that legal regulation penetrates more pervasively into social life.[130]

---

[129] These observations should not be mistaken for Donald Black's thesis that law is inversely related to other means of social control. Black, above n 62. My observations about the relative proportions between the first and second categories need not remain in inverse relation. For example, it is easily conceivable that a society with a high degree of other social control might also have an ambitious, strong arm leader who expands the power and activity of legal institutions to achieve his own pursuit of power in the name of society. In this situation there would be a high degree of the first category, without any compensating reduction in the second. There is no cap on the total quantum of coercive and non-coercive forms of social control operative in a given society.

[130] Hunt, above n 106 at 12–13 (citations omitted).

The 'centrality of law' thesis described by Hunt applies to the second category of the concept of law, specifically to state law.

Hunt's description combines several different theses under one name. If the thesis is that state bureaucratic legal institutions are increasing in size and specialization, along with the number of legal professionals and the volume of law books, and that law has increasingly become rationalized as Weber described, and positivized and autonomous (at least relatively) as Luhmann describes, there is much evidence to support it. Note, however, that these observations relate primarily to changes in state law itself. The material growth of law and its continued internal development, which accompanies the growth and differentiation of society, says nothing about a relative increase in the actual reach of law.

If the thesis is that the coercive activities of state legal institutions (second category of the concept of law) have taken over from and increased in proportion relative to non-coercive sources of social behaviour (first category of the concept of law)—that the iron grip of law is closing ever in upon us—as Habermas' notion of juridification and Hunt's final sentence appear to indicate, it is highly questionable. People still generally do not know what the law is, and still give no thought to it when engaging in routine behaviour. And application of the coercive power of the state legal apparatus remains a marginal phenomenon relative to the mass of social interaction. As Hunt cautioned, 'It remains important, because of the inflated self-aggrandisement of legal discourses, to chip away at the myth of legalism and not to assume that law makes much difference to lived relations'.[131]

The latter version of the centrality of law thesis is especially dubious when one considers a phenomenon that has emerged in cities around the world, from Washington DC to Paris: the almost total impotence of the state legal apparatus within certain urban pockets surrendered to the control of gangs or local warlords, or simply left to a state of anarchy. The beleaguered residents of these abandoned regions would not easily be persuaded that their social life was being colonized by state law.

The mistake lies in taking the undeniable explosion of legal forms, and the increasing adoption by private institutions of legal procedures like due process requirements, for an intensification of law's interference in our everyday lives. These changes are part and parcel of the rationalization of society along the trajectory identified by Weber. The increase in legal forms is a reflection of the modern penchant for the typification of transactions and for intercourse in writing. To be sure, this penchant is substantially driven by the fact that law prefers and imposes typification (especially for substantial or commercial transactions), and recognizes and often requires the written form. However, the essential resulting change is that we increasingly conduct and embody our transactions in a regularized format. This standardization of transactions is

[131] Ibid at 327.

more a process of rationalization (in terms of efficiency and uniformity) than legalization. And the legalization it entails is largely facilitative in nature rather than oppressive.[132] Besides, for the most part legal institutions and legal rules are passive, lying in wait until sought out and invoked by users, which can hardly be characterized as an intrusion or penetration by law itself.

A positivist view of law leads us to see these changes as involving an expansion of law. From within the legal positivist perspective this is correct, and would be irrefutably confirmed by a glance at shelves overflowing with codes and legal regulations. But a social scientific view of law, with its focus on observation of the behaviour of legal institutions, suggests that a real tightening of the iron grip of law would involve an actual increase in the application of the power of the state legal apparatus into the everyday lives of citizens, as has occurred and continues to occur in totalitarian societies.

Those who fear that law is increasingly penetrating the life world are perhaps also swayed by the astonishing expansion of law in the cultural arena, from daily news coverage of sensational or important cases, to popular television programmes like 'L.A. Law', to the O. J. Simpson trial—broadcast live and watched by millions. This is the age of the symbolic ascendance of law. Ordinary social discourse, which used to take place in various traditional or moral terms, is increasingly couched in legal terms. But law as a cultural symbol and mode of cultural discourse has a life of its own quite apart from (though interacting with) what the state legal apparatus actually does.

The advantage of interpretive oriented approaches to law is their capacity to account for this meaning based dimension; that does not, however, imply discarding the behaviour oriented approaches, which insist that we must keep an eye on the material effects of law. Because Luhmann's autopoiesis sees law in terms of communication, it suffers from precisely this limitation: conflating discourse about law with law itself, it loses direct touch with the realm of institutionalized coercion. What needs to be investigated is the complex mix of interrelations among the expansion of law as a mode of cultural discourse, the increasing rationalization of transactions through legal means, and the scope and nature of the coercive activities of legal institutions, and this will require contributions from both interpretivist and behaviourist social science.

Whether the centrality of law thesis is correct is an empirical question that cannot be determined by the analytical map alone. The map only suggests that we have compelling reasons to be sceptical of the most sweeping version of the thesis, and it reveals that the notion of the legalization of society encompasses several qualitatively distinct processes, which can be benign, beneficial, or threatening depending upon their nature and how they operate.

---

[132] Oliver Wendell Holmes made a complementary point when he observed that Austin's 'command' theory is inadequate because it fails to recognize that private law rules 'create options' rather than lay down commands. See T. Grey, 'Holmes and Legal Pragmatism' 41 *Stanford LR* 787, 831 (1989).

13 Final Observations

Donald Black was correct when he concluded that science can know only phenomena not essences. Yet he went on to make an essentialist claim about law when he declared that 'law *is* governmental social control'. His concept was artificially constricting in two directions: it removed from the field of enquiry all those other functions law provides, and it conceptually eliminated the possibility that the Government has other mechanisms of social control besides law. Black should have just said 'governmental social control' is an important phenomenon which must be studied.

The same is true of 'institutionalized norm enforcement', 'institutionalized social control', 'institutionalized dispute processing', 'living law', 'concrete patterns of social ordering', and all of the other many variations of scientific concepts of law. Each such concept created a legitimate and useful framework—an analytical tool—that allowed scientists to compare and study various phenomena in relation to the functions or criteria identified.

The error in each case was to take the additional step and assert that a given concept *is* law. This move limited our ability to observe and analyse law to the parameters proscribed by the social scientific framework. When, for example, law is defined as the institutional enforcement of social norms, the question 'Do legal institutions in fact enforce social norms?' is analytically precluded, for an affirmative answer to this question is a presupposition of what it means to be a legal institution. Likewise, from their respective functionalist perspectives, the following questions are incoherent: 'Do legal institutions resolve disputes?' 'Does law effect social control?' These are not just academic questions.[133] Analysts have observed that the presence of law sometimes *produces* disputes.[134] The analytical map and sociological studies suggest that law is not the most important mechanism of social control, and that social control may not be the most important function law fulfills. Yet the belief that law fundamentally involves social control persists in the scientific as well as legal literature, sturdily resisting all evidence to the contrary. By their nature, all functionalist concepts inhibit an enquiry into whether law fulfills the stated function, for law has been defined in terms of that function.

What law is and what law does cannot be captured in any single scientific concept. The project to devise a scientific concept of law was based upon the misguided belief that law comprises a fundamental category. To the contrary,

---

[133] In his recent book Richard Posner raised a related set of questions:
'I am not sure law has an expressive function—that is, a function of creating or reinforcing a set of social norms or an ideology. That law affects behaviour not only directly, by altering attitudes and through them behaviour is an article of faith for most legal professionals, especially judges and professors. But consistent with the lack of scientific curiosity that is so marked a characteristic of legal thought, the legal profession has for the most part neither participated in conducting nor even paid any attention to (even to the extent of criticizing) studies designed to confirm or refute the existence of such consequences. The lack of evidence that these consequences exists—even the evidence that they do not exist—has failed to shake the profession's faith.'
Posner, *The Problems of Jurisprudence* (1990) at 213–14.
[134] Schur, above n 13 at 84.

law is thoroughly a cultural construct, lacking any universal essential nature.[135] Law *is* whatever we attach the label *law* to. It is a term conventionally applied to a variety of multifaceted, multifunctional phenomena: natural law, international law, primitive law, religious law, customary law, state law, folk law, people's law, and indigenous law on the general level, and an almost infinite variety on the specific level, from the state law of Massachusetts to the law of the Barotse, from the law of Nazi Germany to the Nuremberg trials. If there is a shared trait to the various phenomena which carry the tag 'law', it's that they all lay claim to legitimate authority, to rightful power. This quality more than anything else is what makes law—in all of its many incarnations—so potentially dangerous.

Scientists should study these phenomena to discover what they do, or what we do with them, and to learn why the label 'law' is attached to them (what is—politically, rhetorically, symbolically—gained thereby), rather than attempt to squeeze them into narrow conceptual categories. This study will certainly be facilitated by the construction of comparative frameworks like 'institutionalized norm enforcement', as long as these frameworks are not then taken to *be* law. Unfortunately, the increasingly popular concept of legal pluralism is grounded upon precisely this error, and revives all of the old problems surrounding the social scientific concept of law.

There is an obvious irony in ending up at essentially the same place socio-legal scholars stood a generation ago when they collectively gave up attempts to define law. The difference is they walked away in frustration, leaving matters in a state of confusion and licence rather than resolution. Now we know what went wrong and why. And splaying open the innards of the puzzle that led to the impasse in the debate over the concept of law has helped lay a framework for future theoretical work in the field.

---

[135] This claim does not deny that the ideal of law in a given community may indeed have an essential nature that can be analytically identified. Lon Fuller's *The Morality of Law* (1964) is an attempt at specifying the essential elements of law. However, this is the nature of the ideal of law as it exists within the Western liberal rule of law tradition. If in the distant future this tradition prevails around the world, then there will be one (world) cultural version of law, and its essential nature will be much as Fuller describes.

[4]

Why Must Legal Ideas Be Interpreted Sociologically?

ROGER COTTERRELL*

Sociology of law and socio-legal studies are sometimes declared unable to give insight into the nature of legal ideas or to clarify questions about legal doctrine. The idea that law has its own 'truth' – its own way of seeing the world – has been used to deny that sociological perspectives have any special claim to provide understanding of law as doctrine. This paper tries to specify what sociological understanding of legal ideas entails. It argues that such an understanding is not merely useful but necessary for legal studies. Legal scholarship entails sociological understanding of law. The two are inseparable.

I. SOCIOLOGY OF LAW AND LEGAL IDEAS

A modern myth about sociological study of law survived until quite recently, encouraged from within legal philosophy and by some legal sociologists themselves. According to this myth an inevitable division of labour governed legal inquiry. While lawyers and jurists analysed law as doctrine – norms, rules, principles, concepts and the modes of their interpretation and validation, sociologists were concerned with a fundamentally different study: that of behaviour, its causes and consequences. Hence, the legal sociologist's task was solely to examine behaviour in legal contexts.[1] Sociology could contribute

---

1 See, for example, D. Black, *The Behavior of Law* (1976), treating legal sociology as the study of governmental social control. Correspondingly, Hans Kelsen wrote of sociology's role as that of inquiring 'into the causes and effects of those natural events that . . . are represented as legal acts.' See H. Kelsen, *Introduction to the Problems of Legal Theory* (1992) 13. In his final work, he asserted that such a legal sociology 'does not describe the law, but rather law-creating behaviour and law-observing or law-violating behaviour. See H. Kelsen, *General Theory of Norms* (1991) 301.

* *Professor of Legal Theory, Queen Mary and Westfield College, University of London, Mile End Road, London E1 4NS, England*

Earlier versions of this paper were presented at the Socio-Legal Studies Association Conference, University of Wales, Cardiff in April 1997 and at the Nordic Forum for the Sociology of Law, Landskrona, Sweden in June 1997. I am grateful to David Nelken for much valuable discussion and incisive criticism. Also to Per Stjernquist, Alan Norrie, Peter Fitzpatrick, Hanna Petersen, Vincenzo Ferrari, Grazyna Skapska, and Jørgen Dalberg-Larsen for particular comments.

little to the understanding of legal ideas, abstracted from their effects on specific actions. In this sense sociology of law conducted inquiries peripheral or even *external* to law as lawyers understood it. Legal sociologists often avoided lawyers' disputes or theories about the nature of doctrine as such.[2] They studied primarily practices of dispute processing, administrative activity or law enforcement, or social forces operating on legislation, especially as a result of the actions of particular law-making or policy-advocating groups.

That this division of labour was in no way inevitable is clear from the briefest glance at the work of the classic founders of sociology of law. While Max Weber saw sociology's object as the study of social action, he treated the nature of legal ideas and the variety of types of legal reasoning as central to his sociological concern with law.[3] Émile Durkheim intended that the enterprise of understanding law as doctrine should itself become a field of sociology, so that lawyers' questions would eventually be reformulated through sociological insight.[4] For Eugen Ehrlich, the lawyer's understanding of law would be simultaneously subverted and set on surer foundations by means of sociological inquiry into popular understandings of legal ideas.[5] Leon Petrazycki considered that law should be studied as a variety of forms of consciousness and understanding.[6] Equally, numerous contributions to legal philosophy, including modern realist jurisprudence in Scandinavia, the United States of America, and elsewhere, showed that jurists had serious concerns with behaviour in legal contexts in their efforts to grasp the nature of legal ideas.

To remove a focus on legal doctrine from sociological inquiry would prevent legal sociology from integrating, rather than merely juxtaposing, its studies with other kinds of legal analysis. Without this focus, sociological observation of behaviour might influence policy expressed in legal doctrine; but this would amount not to a sociology of law but to a diversity of sociological information presented to legal policy-makers.[7] The old claim that social science should be 'on tap rather than on top' in legal inquiries reflected the idea that sociology and other social sciences were debarred

---

2 Vilhelm Aubert's work provides a significant exception. See, for example, V. Aubert, 'The Structure of Legal Thinking' in *Legal Essays: A Tribute to Frede Castberg*, eds. J. Andenaes et al. (1963) 41–63; and C. M. Campbell, 'Legal Thought and Juristic Values' (1974) 1 *Brit. J. of Law and Society* 13–30.
3 M. Weber, *Economy and Society* (1968) part 2, ch. 8.
4 É. Durkheim, Letter to the Director of the *Revue néo-scholastique*, in É. Durkheim, *The Rules of Sociological Method and Selected Essays on Sociology and its Method* (1982) 260; É. Durkheim, *Textes 1: Élements d'une théorie sociale* (1975) 244.
5 E. Ehrlich, *Fundamental Principles of the Sociology of Law* (1936).
6 L. Petrazycki, *Law and Morality* (1955).
7 Nothing in this paper should be taken as denying the worth of sociological studies of behaviour in legal contexts. In my view, these kinds of studies have produced insights of the greatest significance and should continue to occupy a central place in social inquiries about law. My argument here is, however, that the sociological interpretation of legal ideas should have a central place within legal studies generally, and that it is important for socio-legal scholarship and for legal scholarship in general that this place should be claimed.

from offering insight into the *meaning* of law (as doctrine, interpretation, reasoning, and argument). Hence, in so far as proponents of legal sociology accepted the myth of an inevitable division of labour, they were tempted to argue defensively that lawyers' debates on doctrine were trivial or mystificatory, and that real knowledge about law as a social phenomenon was gained only by observing patterns of judicial, administrative or policing activity, lawyers' work and organization, or citizens' disputing behaviour. Correspondingly, opponents of legal sociology hastened to dismiss it as unable to speak about *law* at all; fated to remain for ever 'external' and thus irrelevant to legal understanding.

The assumption that there could be no serious rapprochement between legal and sociological views of law often depended on each side in the dispute characterizing the other in excessively positivistic terms.[8] Thus, jurists often ignored scholarship expressing well established sociological positions: for example, that action is to be understood in terms of its subjective meaning to those engaged in it; that social life is structured by symbols, or constituted as forms of collective understanding; that social order is explicable in terms of social rules continuously created and recreated in human interaction; or that society may be understood as a system of communication.[9] Similarly, social science sometimes treated lawyers' legal understanding as entirely positivistic. Law for the lawyer was often seen by sociologists as a kind of datum (rules or regulations). Social processes central to lawyers' experience – interpretation, argument, negotiation, presentation, influence, decision-making and rule-formulating – were often underemphasized in characterizing the lawyer's outlook on the nature of law as doctrine.

II. IS SOCIOLOGY'S 'TRUTH' POWERLESS?

Criticisms of legal sociology's capacity to understand legal ideas have become more sophisticated, though they have not changed their fundamental character. It is now widely accepted that sociological inquiry is valuable and necessary in illuminating the social or historical processes that shape legal doctrine. Hans Kelsen, for example, moved from a position largely dismissive of sociology's relevance in the study of legal ideas[10] to recognize an important role for legal sociology in explaining the causes and consequences of ideological phenomena reflected in law, and especially the idea of justice.[11] It is now evident that legal ideas can be understood as the outcome of

8 D. Nelken, 'The Truth About Law's Truth' in *European Yearbook in the Sociology of Law 1993*, eds. A. Febbrajo and D. Nelken (1994) 87–160, at 107.
9 N. Luhmann, 'Communication as a Social System', in N. Luhmann, *Ecological Communication* (1989) 28–31.
10 Kelsen, op. cit. (1992), n. 1 (originally published 1934) 13–14.
11 H. Kelsen, 'The Pure Theory of Law and Analytical Jurisprudence' in H. Kelsen, *What is Justice? Justice, Law and Politics in the Mirror of Science* (1957) 266–87, at 270; H. Kelsen, *General Theory of Law and State* (1945) 174.

historical, cultural, political or professional conditions which sociological studies are able to describe and explain.

The most powerful current critique of legal sociology – the one which this paper seeks to examine and respond to – does not deny that sociological inquiry can, in its own ways, explain aspects of legal doctrine. It argues rather that sociology has *no privileged way of approaching legal ideas* – no specially powerful insight which can prevail over others. Because of this, it has no way of plausibly claiming that its interpretations are better than those which lawyers themselves can give. It therefore becomes an open question why a sociological view should be adopted in preference to any other. In other words, the claim is no longer that law cannot be understood in sociological terms. It is: why should we want to do so? What is to be gained by doing so, especially for lawyers, or other participants (for example, litigants or just lay citizens) in legal processes?

These questions are sharpened with additional claims. It is sometimes suggested that sociology is an exceptionally weak and inadequate explanatory discourse. For example, it is claimed to have 'an intriguing inability to constitute its field of study.'[12] The concept of 'the social' thus remains 'remarkably unexamined' in socio-legal studies and, it is said, no longer provides a focus for them.[13] On the other hand, law is now seen by those sceptical of sociology's interpretive capacities as having an intellectual power and resilience which protects it from social science's earlier 'imperial confidence' that it could know law better than law knew itself.[14]

In a rich discussion of relationships between law and scientific (including social science) disciplines, David Nelken describes the efforts of these disciplines to tell 'the truth about law' as being confronted now with law's own 'truth'.[15] What he means is that law has its own ways of interpreting the world. Law as a discourse determines, within the terms of that discourse, what is to count as 'truth' – that is, correct understanding or appropriate and reliable knowledge – for specifically legal purposes. It resists scientific efforts to interpret it away (for example, in economic cost-benefit terms, psychological terms of causes and consequences of mental states, or sociological terms of conditioning social forces). None of these interpretations, it is claimed, grasps law's own criteria of significance.

When law borrows from scientific disciplines or practices it appears to do so as it sees fit, taking what it deems useful, on its own conditions, for its own purposes.[16] Concepts borrowed are often transformed, turned into

---

12 P. Fitzpatrick, 'Being Social in Socio-Legal Studies' (1995) 22 *J. of Law and Society* 105–12, at 107.
13 id., p. 106.
14 D. Nelken, 'Can There Be a Sociology of Legal Meaning?' in *Law as Communication*, ed. D. Nelken (1996) 107–28, at 108–9.
15 Nelken, op. cit., n. 8, p. 107.
16 id., pp. 101–2.

'hybrid artifacts', tailored to legal use.[17] And law goes on the offensive. It provides its own explanations of the social world. It interprets social life in its own terms.[18] Law is said to provide truth for itself, for its purposes, which cannot be swept away by sociology, but with which sociology's interpretations are fated merely to co-exist. Because of this, sociology cannot reshape legal understanding; it provides at best a resource of ideas from which law may borrow if it finds reasons to do so. In a different sense from before, social science is again 'on tap, but not on top'.

From the standpoint of sociology the problem is not merely that its insights can be made to seem irrelevant to legal understanding. It is not just the unpleasantness of rejection that dominates this scenario, but also the frustration of attempting the impossible. The argument goes as follows. As sociology tries to understand law, law disappears, like a mirage, the closer the approach to it. This is because as sociology interprets law, law is *reduced to sociological terms*. It becomes something different from what it (legally) is; or rather, from what, in legal thought, law sees itself as being. How can legal ideas be understood sociologically without, in the process, being turned into sociological ideas?[19] The 'legal point of view', as Robert Samek called it in a neglected discussion of related themes,[20] disappears; subsumed into a sociological viewpoint and lost. It cannot be grasped sociologically because it is *not* sociological. It is a specifically *legal* point of view.

Legal sociology's potential is also challenged from another standpoint. For more than a decade, concern among progressive legal scholars has been less and less with how law is produced by society (the traditional outlook of legal sociology) and increasingly with the way 'society' is produced by law.[21] Not only can law stand alone from sociology with its own basis of understanding, taking or leaving social scientific insights as it sees fit, but it is said to be able also to create the central objects of inquiry – the very ontological basis – of sociology itself. According to some influential scholars,

---

17 G. Teubner, 'How the Law Thinks: Toward a Constructivist Epistemology of Law' (1989) 22 *Law and Society Rev.* 727-57, at 747.
18 Jan Broekman makes the claim forcefully:
   ... those elements of social reality that are under the grip of legal thinking are *structurally altered*. Transformations have occurred. This simply means that the one reality is not the other. Legal provisions form a unique whole of its own kind which is a special category of human experience. One cannot understand a contract or a delict unless one recognizes one's being as *de iure*.
   See J. Broekman, 'Revolution and Commitment to a Legal System' in *Enlightenment, Rights and Revolution: Essays in Legal and Social Philosophy*, ed. N. MacCormick and Z. Bankowski (1989) at 323.
19 Nelken, op. cit., n. 14, p. 112. For example, legal explanations of criminal conduct are in terms of responsibility. When the matter is considered sociologically in terms of causation of patterns of criminal activity through social or economic conditions, legal questions of responsibility may sometimes be partly or even wholly displaced.
20 R. Samek, *The Legal Point of View* (1974).
21 D. Nelken, 'Beyond the Study of "Law and Society"? Henry's *Private Justice* and O'Hagan's *The End of Law*' [1986] *Am. Bar Foundation Research J.* 323-38, at 325.

law has no need, and no possibility, of doing more than creating its own normative understanding of its social environment.[22] But, in a more radical view, law is also seen as responsible, partly at least, for *creating the social categories which sociology itself must work with*.

For example, the problematic idea of 'society' is said to be actually established by law's methods of determining social inclusion and exclusion. Peter Fitzpatrick argues that law renders society possible, 'thus reversing the foundational claims of the sociology of law'.[23] His assertion refers mainly to law's role in marking an identity for and boundaries of the entity thought of as political society. But, more generally, law can be considered to express or structure the experiences that make up the essential texture of social life. Far from law being coloured by the social context that sociology brought into legal study, context is 'assumed and reproduced in law as a bearer of traditions, or of ideological constructions, or forms of discourse.'[24] Thus, law, to a significant extent, actually constitutes social reality.

For these reasons a sharp line between the legal and the social can no longer be drawn; a 'more holistic understanding' is required.[25] Legal ideas constitute a form of social knowledge in themselves. The often neglected point that legal speculations once provided prototypes for early forms of social theory[26] acquires a new significance.

Certainly, some scholars in sociology of law continue to ask for evidence of law's ideological effects and to nurse doubts about law's capacity to influence social consciousness.[27] The demands and doubts are unsurprising given that the postulated direction of influence *from* legal ideas as shaping forces in social life fits uneasily with legal sociology's traditional assumption that society shapes law, and that effects of law on society are always specific matters for empirical study. But newer approaches to the relationship between the 'legal' and the 'social' refuse to see law and society as somehow

22 N. Luhmann, 'Closure and Openness: On Reality in the World of Law' in *Autopoietic Law: A New Approach to Law and Society*, ed. G. Teubner (1988) 335–48.
23 Fitzpatrick, op. cit., n. 12, p. 106.
24 Nelken, op. cit., n. 21, p. 325.
25 id., pp. 325, 338.
26 See D. R. Kelley, *The Human Measure: Social Thought in the Western Legal Tradition* (1990); W. T. Murphy, 'The Oldest Social Science? The Epistemic Properties of the Common Law Tradition' (1991) 54 *Modern Law Rev.* 182–215; S. P. Turner and R. A. Factor, *Max Weber: The Lawyer as Social Thinker* (1994).
27 L. M. Friedman, 'The Concept of Legal Culture: A Reply', in *Comparing Legal Cultures*, ed. D. Nelken (1997) pp. 33–9, at 37–9. In his paper, Friedman criticizes me for specifying the content of 'legal ideology in general' (p. 37), in other words, for appearing to essentialize legal ideology as something with a determinate, constant character in all times and places. But I offer no such specification and try to indicate only some particular ideological elements in contemporary Western law. There is surely no constant content of 'legal ideology in general'. The content of legal ideology may vary greatly from one legal environment to another. Neither does legal ideology necessarily form any kind of unity in relation to a particular legal system or society. See, generally, R. Cotterrell, *Law's Community: Legal Theory in Sociological Perspective* (1995).

separate or even competing spheres of influence. They more often treat as self-evident that law constitutes social life to a significant degree by influencing the meanings of basic categories (such as property, ownership, contract, trust, responsibility, guilt, and personality) that colour or define social relations. Hence, when the nature of socio-legal studies is considered, it is said to be no longer clear (and perhaps never was) whether the enterprise is legal, social or a mixture of the two.[28] The field remains undefined; conceptual clarity seems sacrificed to a need to avoid deep controversies about the foundations of social scientific inquiries about law.[29]

What then should be made of the effort to understand legal ideas (elements of legal doctrine and the reasoning and forms of interpretation that surround them) sociologically? This paper argues that the main problems, set out above, that are said to undermine this effort are in fact, despite their apparent seriousness, solvable or ultimately false. They do not stand in its way. But they do very properly demand that the nature, aims, and methods of sociological inquiry be clarified. Nevertheless, the claim to be made here is not merely that the effort to understand legal ideas sociologically is appropriate. My claim is that the *only* way to grasp these ideas imaginatively as ideas about the organization of the social world is through some form of sociological interpretation.

In the remainder of this paper an attempt is made to address the issues raised above for sociological understanding of legal ideas by analysing the two main apparent sources of difficulty to which these issues relate. The first of these is the nature of law's own 'truth' – its capacity to interpret the world in its own way. What is this 'truth' which, it is suggested, law produces or inhabits? What is to be made of the claim that law knows itself better than sociology can know it? Can we, indeed, speak of law 'knowing' or 'thinking' anything?[30] The second source of difficulty is the need to clarify what is meant by the effort to gain 'sociological understanding'. What kind of understanding is envisaged here? What is sociology's 'truth', or in Nelken's phrase, what kind of 'truth about law' can sociology offer? Does this, for example, imply a need to subsume law as a discipline under the hegemony of another academic discipline, such as sociology?

I argue that no such implication is required. Indeed, it would entirely miss the point. Disciplinary boundaries should be viewed pragmatically; indeed, with healthy suspicion. They should not be prisons of understanding. The term 'sociological' is necessary to keep firmly in mind certain definite foci in interpreting law, but these foci and their authoritative definition are not the property of any particular academic discipline. Participants in law – not just lawyers but all those who seek to use legal ideas for their own purposes, to promote or control the interests of others, or more generally for public

28 Fitzpatrick, op. cit., n. 12, p. 105.
29 Compare Nelken, op. cit., n. 14, p. 108.
30 Compare Teubner, op. cit., n. 17.

purposes of direction or control – understand legal ideas in practical terms. The aim in what follows is to show that the most practical view of legal ideas is one informed by sociological insight. Legal ideas are properly understood sociologically.

III. DOES LAW HAVE ITS OWN WAY OF SEEING THE WORLD?

In a recent paper, Jack Balkin offers an explanation of law's resilence when faced with the interpretive claims of other disciplines.[31] He argues, echoing earlier writers,[32] that law[33] is inherently weak as an academic field. It is highly susceptible to invasion by other disciplines. Although sociology is one such invader, the disciplines that, in the United States of America, have recently been most successful in invading law have been economics, history, philosophy, political theory, and literary theory.[34] Balkin's explanation of why law is so easily invaded is that it 'is less an academic discipline than a professional discipline. It is a skills-oriented profession, and legal education is a form of professional education.'[35] Law does not have a 'methodology of its own'[36] and borrows methodologies from any discipline that can supply them. On the other hand, because law is researched and taught in settings that are never far from the professional demands of legal practice, it cannot be entirely absorbed by any other discipline. Its professional focus compensates for the lack of a purely intellectual one.

Thus, even economic analysis of law, by far the most successful recent intellectual invader of the American law school, cannot completely colonize law because its disciplinary direction ultimately diverges from law's professional orientation. There simply is no place in the vocationally organized environment of academic law for the reproduction of the sophisticated research skills and statistical methods that the research culture of advanced economics requires. The law school thus takes what it needs from economics, or any other discipline, simplifying and packaging the insights or methods on offer and presenting them for law's own purposes. Law is continuously invaded but, Balkin asserts, cannot be conquered.

This is an essentially sociological account of law's disciplinary resilience, in terms of the organization of legal education, professional training, and the recruitment and socialization of law professors. Consequently, the

---

31 J. M. Balkin, 'Interdisciplinarity as Colonization' (1996) 53 *Washington and Lee Law Rev.* 949–70.
32 See, for example, R.A. Posner, 'The Decline of Law as an Autonomous Discipline 1962–1987' (1987) 100 *Harvard Law Rev.* 761–80.
33 Balkin's discussion is limited to the United States context, but the analysis seems more generally applicable.
34 Balkin, op. cit., n. 31, p. 965.
35 id., p. 964.
36 id., p. 966.

178

account is susceptible to sociological rebuttal. Balkin does not explain any reasons inherent in the nature of legal ideas or understanding as to why law cannot be conquered by social science. The factors are merely organizational. The law school environment and the legal profession provide this resistance. He offers no argument as to why these organizational factors must continue to operate. Indeed, law is portrayed as so weak as a discourse that it invites continuous change in the way it is taught, learned, and understood. Balkin gives no reason why American law schools should not ultimately turn into graduate schools in applied economics (and it can be recalled that Harold Lasswell and Myres McDougal once seriously advocated[37] turning them into advanced schools of policy science). If law has no special characteristics as a discourse, method or body of knowledge, it is unclear why law schools must continue to take their current form. Balkin's argument does not explain law's resilience.

In making the claim that law is 'not, strictly speaking, an academic subject',[38] Balkin means that it lacks a methodology of its own. But, in fact, law in contemporary Western societies does embody quite specific methods of intellectual practice: for example, methods of presenting a case in court, of drafting a brief, of marshalling evidence, of citing and reasoning with precedents. A stronger claim for law's weakness would be that it lacks any of the usual intellectual marks of disciplinarity: controlling master theories, distinctive methods of intellectual debate, established paradigms of research practice, familiar epistemological and ontological positions or controversies.[39] But it might be said that law has *some* important indicators of its own intellectual outlook or orientation. For its purposes they count as providing coherence for its practices. These indicators give it a way of interpreting the world; at least the world as it exists in relation to law's purposes.

The strongest current arguments for law's capacity to declare sociological understanding of legal ideas irrelevant are arguments emphasizing these kinds of indicators. In one way or another, these indicators make possible what Nelken terms 'law's truth'. When attempts are made to specify the indicators, however, they seem remarkably limited. They may amount to no more than a consistent focus in any context on marking a distinction between the 'legal' and the 'illegal'; right and wrong in terms of specifically legal definitions.[40] Otherwise, law might be said to be distinctively concerned with institutional rather than brute facts, and with considerations of authority, integrity, fairness, justice, acceptability, and practicability. It has to use 'arbitrary cut-off points' in argument, and often chooses not to look behind its presumptions. It seeks to provide certainty and to relate to common sense.

---

37 H.D. Lasswell and M.S. McDougal, 'Legal Education and Public Policy: Professional Training in the Public Interest' (1943) 52 *Yale Law J.* 203–95.
38 Balkin, op. cit., n. 31, p. 966.
39 Compare Cotterrell, op. cit., n. 27, ch. 3.
40 N. Luhmann, 'The Coding of the Legal System' in *State, Law and Economy as Autopoietic Systems*, ed. G. Teubner and A. Febbrajo (1992) 145–85.

It may adopt or reject scientific (including social scientific) knowledge or reasoning in order to pursue these objectives. It gathers and presents facts in ways tailored to adjudicative needs.[41] It operates by means of practical reasoning and argumentation that may be more or less specific to its governmental, dispute processing or social control tasks. But any enumeration of characteristics of law's truth will miss the point for 'what truth means for law is the result of its own processes.'[42] 'Ultimately,' as Arthur Leff puts it, 'law is not something we know but something that we do.'[43] It is not grasped by description from 'outside' but by working and thinking within it.

But does this argument really go much further than Balkin's more directly stated point that law's social conditions of practice determine the forms of knowledge appropriate to it? The difference seems to be that it is not just the law school, the profession, and constraints on the professoriat that are said to reproduce law's ways of interpreting the world. It is apparently law in a more abstract sense that does this. Changing any of the specific social settings of law that Balkin emphasizes would not alter the fact that the legal point of view is distinctive.

Thus law tends to become, in arguments about 'law's truth', an abstract site of understanding removed from particular kinds of social locations. For some writers, such as Niklas Luhmann, law's truth is that of a communication system not tied to any specific empirical settings. These scholars treat law as a discourse but typically do not stress the potential diversity of legal discourses of particular lawyers in particular courts, particular claimants or defendants in relation to specific claims, or particular political actors pursuing their special interests or projects or promoting their particular values. Law in some abstract sense is presented as having a unified, cohesive mode of understanding, a distinctive viewpoint, or a specific style of interpretation or reasoning.

From a sociological standpoint, however, it is an empirical question how far and in what forms this cohesion, distinctiveness or specificity may exist. Lawyers operating between different legal systems can experience different 'truths' of law, and sometimes have difficulty in establishing a shared discourse. Even within the same system, outlooks on almost all matters legal may sometimes differ radically as between different participants in legal processes. As Balkin suggests, there may be much disagreement on matters of method no less than on the interpretation of particular matters of doctrine. And it contributes little to envisage all these actual or potential disagreements as part of an ongoing conversation on the justice or integrity of law. Such a conversation may exist only because the structure of political power forces those who wish to have access to or protection from that power to adjust their claims and arguments. It may force them to press these claims

---

41 See, generally, Nelken, op. cit., n. 8, pp. 99–100.
42 id., p. 103.
43 Quoted id., p. 99.

and arguments in ways that distort the particular legal 'truth' which they would otherwise wish to express.

Law's basic 'truth' may be merely the *provisional, pragmatic consensus* of those legal actors who are perceived at any given time to be supported by the highest forms of authority within the legal system of the state. Another way of putting the matter would be that there is no 'law's truth', no single legal point of view, but only the different – sometimes allied, sometimes conflicting – viewpoints expressing the experience, knowledge, and practices of different legal actors and participants. What links all of these as 'legal' in some official sense is their varied relationships with matters of government and social control and with institutionalized doctrine bearing on these matters.

Undoubtedly law is presented professionally as a more or less unified, specialized discourse. But, as Balkin notes, it is an intellectually vulnerable, open discourse, liable to invasion by many kinds of ideas, including sociological ones. Ultimately, it is given discursive coherence and unity only because its intellectual insecurity, its permanent cognitive openness, is stabilized by *political fiat*.[44] The political power of the state which guarantees the decisions of certain official legal interpreters, puts an end to argument, determines which interpretive concepts prevail, asserts favoured normative judgments as superior to all competing ones, and guarantees normative closure by the threat of official coercion.[45] The *voluntas*, or coercive authority, of law, centralized by political structures and organized through legal hierarchies, stabilizes and controls potentially unlimited, often competing and conflicting, elaborations of *ratio* – reason and doctrinal principle – in a host of diverse sites and settings of legal argument and interpretation.

Seen in sociological perspective, this is the nature of law's truth as a unified, distinctive discourse; a contingent feature of particular social environments. Sociological interpretation both reveals law's character and is, like many other forms of knowledge, available to enrich law's debates, colour its interpretations, and strengthen or subvert the strategies of control to which legal discourse is directed. Sociological insight is simultaneously inside and outside legal ideas, constituting them and interpreting them; sometimes speaking through them and sometimes speaking about them; sometimes aiding, sometimes undermining them. Thus a sociological understanding of legal ideas does not reduce them to something other than law. It expresses their social meaning *as law* in its rich complexity.

At the same time, as noted earlier, law defines social relations and influ-

---

44 Compare Hobbes's formulation: 'It is not wisdom, but authority that makes a law.' See T. Hobbes, *A Dialogue Between a Philosopher and a Student of the Common Law*, ed. J. Cropsey (1971) 55.
45 Thus, as Robert Cover puts it, the problem that requires a court to make an authoritative legal ruling is not that the law is unclear but that there is *too much law*. Courts (and especially the ultimate courts of appeal in a legal system) exist 'to suppress law, to choose between two or more laws, to impose upon law a hierarchy.' See R. Cover, 'The Supreme Court 1982, Foreword: *Nomos* and Narrative' (1983–4) 97 *Harvard Law Rev.* 4–68, at 40.

ences the shape of the very phenomena that sociology studies. Thus legal and other social ideas interpenetrate each other. A line between law and society is, as has been seen, no longer capable of being sharply drawn. Law constitutes important aspects of social life by shaping or reinforcing modes of understanding of social reality. It would be remarkable if the power of law as officially guaranteed ideas and practices could have no such effects. One might indeed wonder what law as an expression of power is for, if not for this. But a sociological perspective makes it possible to *observe and understand* this effect of legal discourses and situate it in relation to the social effects of other kinds of ideas and practices. Law constitutes society in so far as it is, itself, an aspect of society, a framework and an expression of understandings that enable society to exist. A sociological perspective on legal ideas is necessary to recognize and analyse the intellectual and moral power of law in this respect. To interpret legal ideas without recognizing, through sociological insight, this dimension of them would be to understand them inadequately. It would be to treat them as less significant and less complex than they are made to appear in a broader sociological perspective.

IV. WHAT IS A SOCIOLOGICAL PERSPECTIVE?

Is it, however, really necessary to invoke the word 'sociological' here? Why privilege sociology? Nelken[46] argues that sociology is sometimes presented as supreme only by downgrading law's disciplinary status. He doubts that sociology can ultimately transcend its own methods of argument and style. The legal sociologist may stand too close to sociology to understand law. And, in any case, why should a sociological, rather than, for example, an economic or psychological viewpoint be favoured?[47] Why should sociology impose *its* understandings? On the other hand, if it does not do so, its analyses of law can be criticized as being parasitic on law's own definitions of 'the legal'.[48]

But most of these problems surely disappear once it is recognized that use of the word 'sociological' does not imply adherence to the distinct methods, theories or outlook of the academic discipline called sociology. It is appropriate to claim that a sociological perspective is indispensible in orienting oneself, whether for practical (participatory) or theoretical purposes, to contemporary law as a social phenomenon. But the term 'sociological' must be taken in a methodologically broad and, at the same time, theoretically limited sense. This rejects any implication of attachment to a specific social scientific or other discipline. Sociological understanding of legal ideas is

---

46 Nelken, op. cit., n. 8, p. 125; Nelken, op. cit., n. 14, p. 115.
47 id. (1994), p. 125.
48 C. Pennisi, 'Sociological Uses of the Concept of Legal Culture' in *Comparing Legal Cultures*, ed. D. Nelken (1997) 105–18, at 107.

transdisciplinary understanding.[49] But it is properly termed sociological because it consistently and permanently addresses the need to reinterpret law *systematically and empirically* as a *social* phenomenon. This terminology also suggests, however, that a legal outlook can itself be sociological, involving a systematic, empirical view of the social world, though it need not be so. As noted earlier, sociological understanding is simultaneously inside and outside legal ideas.

The essence of a sociological interpretation of legal ideas lies in three postulates. First, law is to be seen as an entirely *social* phenomenon; law as a field of experience is to be understood as an aspect of social relationships in general, as wholly concerned with the co-existence of individuals in social groups. Secondly, the social phenomena of law must be understood *empirically* (through detailed examination of variation and continuity in actual historical patterns of social co-existence, rather than in relation to idealized or abstractly imagined social conditions). And thirdly, they must be understood *systematically*, rather than anecdotally or impressionistically; the aim is to broaden understanding from the specific to the general. It is to be able to assess the significance of particularities in a wider perspective; to situate the richness of the unique in a broader theoretical context and so provide orientation for its interpretation.

A sociological perspective could be defined and clarified in relation to other perspectives that are relevant to law. Literary fiction, for example, undoubtedly provides much insight into social relations in novels or short stories. But it does not usually claim to offer systematic interpretation of social phenomena. Its great power is in the rich presentation of particularity in a way that evokes general interest. The telling of stories, the evocation of mood, character and circumstances can present human individuality as simultaneously a matter of unique and universal experiences.[50] Fiction can offer to the reader a means of reflecting on the nature of the social world. It does this when it inspires the conviction that its ideas extend social experience – the experience or observation of the reader, either direct or vicarious.

Fiction contributes to sociological ideas when it creates in the reader the sense that its stories, characterizations, and evocations, or certain elements in them, can be used to interpret or inform aspects of social experience. The reader may empathize with characters or imagine situations as if they were presented as factual reports of experience. Empathy and imagination supply empirical reference for fiction, and give it its power to supply insight into 'the human condition' in some sense. Thus fiction presupposes for its success some plausible reportage of human experience. Hence the line between fiction and non-fiction is itself problematic. But a story or a characterization – whether fictional or non-fictional – does not, in itself, provide the means

---

49 Cotterrell, op. cit., n. 27, ch. 3.
50 Compare É. Durkheim, *Textes 2: Religion, morale, anomie* (1975) 323–4.

for generalizing from the particular; hence it typically remains an unsystematic, untheorized account of individual or social circumstances. It offers, at its best, a richly detailed presentation of particularities of human experience, made profound by its capacity to attract empathy and engagement.

One might characterize typical orientations of many intellectual disciplines specifically in relation to the systematic, empirical and social aims and orientation of sociological inquiry. By contrast with the latter, theology's dominant concerns, for example, are not entirely social. A focus on relationships between human beings may be derived from a primary focus of the relation of humans to spiritual things – 'the central mystery of faith and unbelief'.[51] The approach is only partly empirical, in the senses referred to earlier; but usually generalized and often systematic and theoretically oriented.[52] Much the same contrast with sociological inquiry might be sketched in very broad terms as regards philosophy as a discipline. Perhaps the most basic focus here is on self-knowledge,[53] systematic reflection on general human experience in all its forms, not all of this experience necessarily being encompassed in social relations and not all being capable of illumination through empirical study.

Art's aesthetic creations do not offer systematic insight into the nature of the social world. 'For the artist, there are no laws of nature or history that must always be respected',[54] but the insights inspired may nevertheless be powerful when the observer of art or the participant in artistic experience finds points of real or imagined empirical reference on which the power of artistic creativity is sensed as focusing. Again, history is usually determinedly empirical and richly related to the understanding of social life, but may limit its effort to be explicitly systematic or generalized in its portrayal of 'the social', in order to achieve a multifaceted insight into particular people, actions, developments or events similar to that offered by the rich evocations and descriptions of great fiction.

As a final example, economics combines a concern with the empirical and a determinedly systematic and theoretical outlook with its own distinctive focus on the social. But, for all the contemporary claims of some economists to be able to analyse every aspect of social life in rational choice terms, economic analysis concerns itself with only certain aspects of social relations, or tends to reduce their complexity to a single model or strictly limited range of models.[55] From many legal participant perspectives, and certainly from sociological perspectives, these models appear inadequate to encompass the *entirety* of legal aspects of social life.

Approaches to legal inquiry that are set up as in some way *opposed* to sociological perspectives are, *to the extent that they are presented in this*

---

51 S. Neill, *The Interpretation of the New Testament 1861–1961* (1966) 347.
52 See, for example, id., pp. 336–48.
53 E. Cassirer, *An Essay on Man* (1944) 1.
54 É. Durkheim, *Moral Education* (1961) 270.
55 Compare A. Rosenberg, 'Can Economic Theory Explain Everything?' (1979) 9 *Philosophy of the Social Sciences* 509–29.

competitive way, often ultimately more restricted forms of understanding of law as a social phenomenon to the extent that they actually exclude sociological insight in certain ways. Otherwise, most productively, these other approaches are best seen as allied with and (in so far as they seek to offer social insight) even appropriately organized by means of a (perhaps implicit) sociological perspective. They should be treated as specialized co-workers with sociological inquiry.

Equally, sociological inquiry needs to be open and receptive to a variety of forms of legal inquiry that are not generally thought of as sociological. It must recognize their special power and merit and draw from and interact with them. Sometimes, indeed often, these forms of inquiry produce sociological insights while declaring justifiably that their ideas and approaches are directed to quite different purposes, and founded on quite different bases, from those that they associate with sociological studies.

A sociological perspective is thus not exclusive of or separate from the perspectives offered by the various disciplines mentioned above. Indeed, it may be contributed to by all of them, and by others. And it does not need to derive or seek its justification from the traditions of academic sociology, which nevertheless provide much important material to inform it. It is justified by the fact that for practical purposes law is appropriately understood as a social phenomenon, a phenomenon of *collective human life*: an expression and regulation of communal relationships; a means of codifying, being systematically aware of, working out, planning, and co-ordinating the relationships of individuals who co-exist in social groups. One important aspect of this is that, in some respects (but not all), law is thought of – and experienced – as an external, constraining force on the individual: a social fact, in Durkheim's sense.[56] Something set apart from individual life, and acting on it as a social force.

Again, for practical purposes of thinking and working with law, understanding it as an aspect of society and using that understanding to control conditions of social life as best they may be controlled, it is essential that understanding of law should be *systematic and general*, theorized and organized. At the very least, this is necessary to manage both legal doctrinal and social complexity. Theorizing legal ideas is not a separate enterprise from theorizing the nature of social life. It is an aspect of a single but unending endeavour. Because systematic understanding of law is necessary, systematic understanding of social phenomena generally is required. A sociological perspective must, by its nature, seek an integrated, continually broadening view of what it studies.

Finally, such a perspective needs to be *empirically grounded* – based on observation of the diversity and detail of historical experience. Speculation about the nature of or the meaning of legal ideas which does not relate its inquiries to historical experience in this way is impractical and may lack

---

56 Durkheim, op. cit. (1982), n. 4.

point since it ignores the specificity of the contexts in which the meanings of legal doctrine are shaped. Thus, while the demand for systematic understanding exerts pressure towards generalization and the broadening of perspectives, the requirement for empirical foundations of understanding exerts pressure to reject broad speculation which ignores or generalizes beyond what the detail of particular experience and observation can support as plausible.

Is the claim that law should, as a practical matter, be understood in a perspective that emphasizes the social, the systematic, and the empirical a philosophical or an empirical claim? Ultimately it is a claim that thinking about law in this way offers the most general possibilities for encompassing the widest range of participant perspectives on law. Thus, it is an empirical claim since it makes assertions about the nature of legal experience. At the same time it can be considered a philosophical claim because it asserts that legal experience is usefully interpreted in a certain light; in relation to certain constant concerns, elaborated in many different ways in different times and places. For example, it is possible to think of law in an asocial manner, as a kind of pure calculus unrelated to any idea of social relations. But it is hard to do so and for most legal participants – that is, people who have experience of law or involvement with it in some way – it may be difficult to see great value in doing so.

Again, it is possible to renounce any connection between law and a wish to make knowledge systematic. Weber wrote of 'kadi justice' as a form of legal interpretation or decision-making that rejects any aspiration to subsume particular instances within general categories.[57] Yet most legal experience of which we have historical and contemporary knowledge seems to value the aspiration towards system in law – whether as rational codification, wise consistency in the administering of justice, the citizen's or subject's ability to predict legal outcomes, aspirations towards simplicity or clarity in legal doctrine, an effort towards standardization or unification of law, or the control of arbitrariness. The aspiration has not always been for rational systematization, and rationality takes different forms. Sometimes the aspiration goes no further than a demand for some stability or certainty of outcome; or some possibility of generalization. But in most legal experience, this aspiration towards system is present in some form and is recognized in the development of law and its practice.

So too with a concern for the empirical. Like the concerns with the social and the systematic, this can be considered a fundamental component of most legal experience in all times and places for which knowledge is available. Law is often created in substantial ignorance of the empirical conditions of its application. It might be supposed that this has been a problem for all legal systems and societies beyond a certain size and level of social complexity. Yet most legal experience recognizes or is connected with circumstances

---

57 Weber, op. cit., n. 3. pp. 976–8.

of interpretation and application of legal ideas to specific instances. Law is generally understood as significant in experience only if applied and related to specific contexts. In some sense this is the other side of law as system: law as the 'wilderness of single instances'. It can be claimed that the effort to draw legal ideas from practices of resolving problems in particular empirical settings or to adapt and refine these ideas in application to such problems has been at the heart of most participant experience of law. It is possible to think of law in isolation from specific empirical references and the effort at systematization continually pulls law away from the particularities of context. But most legal experience does not avoid some concern for the empirical as a central aspect of law.

The task of interpretation in law, which might also be thought of as a fundamental aspect of legal experience, can be seen in this light as part of the never-ending activity of balancing the empirical and systematic, and doing so by drawing on continually changing conceptions of law's nature as a social phenomenon; its nature as an aspect of social life, to be related to other aspects. Legal interpretation in this sense is the aspect of legal participation that is concerned with reconciling or balancing concerns with the social, the systematic and the empirical in law.

V. HOW SHOULD LEGAL IDEAS BE INTERPRETED?

The term 'sociology of law' remains useful as a label for identifying a vitally important body of research on legal processes and as an important focus of self-identification for scholars committed to extending this research. But it is a somewhat unsatisfactory and misleading term when it is used to refer to the sociological study of legal ideas. It often suggests a sub-discipline or a specialism, a branch of sociology or a distinct compartment of legal studies. In considering the interpretation of legal ideas it would be better to speak of sociological perspectives or insights, or sociological understanding or interpretation.

Sociological interpretation of legal ideas is not a particular, specialized way of approaching law, merely co-existing with other kinds of understanding. Sociology of law in this particular context is a transdisciplinary enterprise and aspiration to broaden understanding of law as a social phenomenon. It certainly insists on its criteria of the social, the systematic, and the empirical, reflecting – as will be further illustrated subsequently – the conviction that these criteria are inscribed in some sense and in some degree in participant understandings of the nature of law itself as a social phenomenon. It seeks to go beyond many such understandings. But sociology of law is otherwise *inclusive* rather than exclusive. Sociological insight is found in many disciplinary fields of knowledge and practice.

If sociological inquiries about law have an intellectual or moral allegiance, then this is to law itself – that is, to its enrichment through a radical broadening of the perspectives of the varied participants in legal processes, practices, and forms of knowledge.[58] Sociological inquiry is critical because it insists that the legal perspectives of many of these participants (whether lawyers or non-lawyers) are *insufficiently* systematic and theoretically informed or sensitive to empirical variation, and have *too narrow* an awareness of law's social character. But it is also constructive because it cannot merely condemn existing legal ideas without also asking at all times how law might be *reinterpreted* and so re-imagined and reshaped consistently with its social character, when understood better in a broader sociological perspective.

It should be clear that the discussion above of sociological understanding of legal ideas takes for granted the need to reject the familiar dichotomy between internal and external views of law, or between insider and outsider perspectives. This dichotomy is familiar within legal philosophy. Its assertion is a device that accompanies the false assertion of the uniqueness of 'law's truth'. As Nelken properly points out,[59] the internal-external distinction is, for the most part, merely a feature *internal* to lawyers' thinking. It reflects especially a professional self-image in terms of a special kind of reasoning and understanding.[60] When legal thinking is understood sociologically, the distinction disappears between internal (legal participant) views of law and external (for example, social scientific observers') views. It is replaced by a conception of partial, relatively narrow or specialized participant perspectives on (and in) law, confronting and being confronted by, penetrating, illuminating, and being penetrated and illuminated by, broader, more inclusive perspectives on (and in) law as a social phenomenon.[61]

It might be asked what happens to justice and legal values in sociological

---

58 Compare Hubert Rottleuthner's assertion, in an address to lawyers, that:
> sociological research can . . . help us to look beyond our daily routines . . . As sociologists of law we go beyond the individual field of experience . . . we transcend the individual perspective . . . we establish correlations systematically instead of relying on unproved everyday theories. And by using a different frame of reference we point out new aspects to which inadequate attention has been given in your legal practice . . . we offer a cognitive background for your daily work.

See H. Rottleuthner, 'Sociology of Law and Legal Practice' in *Legal Culture and Everyday Life*, ed. A-J. Arnaud (1989) 77–84 at 79, 82. These claims seem justified apart from the suggestion that sociological knowledge contrasts with *unproven* theories. I prefer to say that it cannot provide 'proof' but rather potential enlightenment – a deeper understanding – by reinterpreting everyday understandings in a broader, more systematic, more consciously empirical perspective. And, of course, it offers this not just for lawyers but for legal participants generally.

59 Nelken, op. cit., n. 8, pp. 111–2.
60 Cotterrell, op. cit., n. 27, ch. 5.
61 In this context Philip Lewis's concept of 'representations' – forms of understanding ('description and accounts') present in legal thinking with regard to social institutions, practices and relations – seems useful. It highlights types of social knowledge that become a part of legal thought, so that, to this extent, legal and social understanding blend into each other as inseparable. See P. Lewis, 'Notes for a Socio-Legal Jurisprudence', in *European Yearbook in the Sociology of Law 1988*, ed. A. Febbrajo et al. (1988) 209–26.

understanding. Can a sociological understanding of legal ideas address questions of justice? The answer is, clearly, yes. It was noted earlier that sociological insight should both inform and interpret legal ideas. The question of whether sociology is 'inside' or 'outside' law becomes redundant. It is both inside and outside; and so the inside-outside demarcation is meaningless in this context.[62] The line between law and society, and thus between legal and sociological interpretation becomes indistinct. Law constitutes society in certain respects; social understanding informs law in certain ways. But in so far as sociological interpretation of legal ideas relates them to the entire context of social relationships in general it focuses attention on the patterning of those relationships, which is the specific concern of justice.

Justice is a perception of social relations in balance. It is one aspect of a sense of social cohesion or integration.[63] The radical broadening of perspective which sociological interpretation seeks makes it possible to enrich understandings of the social conditions of justice. The consistent focus of sociological inquiry on the social, the systematic, and the empirical provides the essential dimensions of this enriched understanding. Sociological inquiry cannot abolish disagreement as to what justice demands in any particular situation. But it can reveal the meaning of justice claims in a broader perspective by systematically analysing the empirical conditions that provide postulates underlying these claims.

If sociological interpretation of legal ideas is to be characterized in these ways, can we say anything concrete and specific about its *methods*? As noted earlier, settled methodology is the unifying feature which, according to Jack Balkin, law so crucially lacks. Can such a settled methodology be attributed to sociological inquiry?

The answer must recognize a crucial claim made earlier. This is that, if sociological inquiry about legal ideas is to be treated as having any specific intellectual allegiance, it is to law as a social phenomenon, not to an academic discipline of sociology or to any other social science discipline. Hence the sociological understanding of legal ideas reflects methodologically law's own fragmentary and varied methodological characteristics as understood by those who participate in or are affected by legal practices. This is inevitable because of the interdependence of legal and sociological understanding referred to earlier. Sociological interpretation extends legal analysis; it broadens the perspectives of legal participants.

It does not necessarily *replace* those perspectives or *contradict* them by the use of a specific methodology foreign to the diverse methods already used by legal participants. If it did so *generally* this would be to replace law with sociology; to fall into the trap which, as noted earlier, has been said by some commentators to ensnare all sociological attempts to grasp law's

---

62 See R. Cotterrell, 'Law and Community: A New Relationship?' (1998) *Current Legal Problems*, forthcoming.
63 Compare É. Durkheim, *The Division of Labour in Society* (1984) 77.

truth. Thus, the methodology of sociological understanding of legal ideas is the deliberate *extension* in carefully specified directions of the diverse ways in which legal participants themselves think about the social world in legal terms. It seeks radically to extend the already partially systematic and empirical characteristics of this legal thinking, and thereby sets out to transform legal ideas by reinterpreting them.

An illustration may help to clarify this argument. The English law of trusts has developed a strange impasse in one narrow and somewhat arcane area of legal doctrine. While property can be held on trust by trustees to benefit individuals or groups of individuals in a wide variety of ways, English law, unlike some other common law jurisdictions, has declared that property may not be held on trust for abstract non-charitable purposes – for example, to promote press freedom, or sport outside an educational context.

When it is asked why English law takes this particular stance on private purpose trusts and how the law in this area should be developed in the light of the precedents, answers are not particularly straightforward. The cases refer to particular private purpose trusts as illustrations, and offer various reasons for a tradition of judicial hostility to them. The matter is dealt with by the courts partly by looking at what has been decided in the past, partly by detailing technical problems that would be faced by law if private purpose trusts were to be declared generally valid (for example, problems of enforcement), and partly by offering policy arguments about the social or economic rights and wrongs of allowing particular kinds of trusts to be set up.

Legal thinking in this area is empirical up to a point, looking at what has been decided and the specific judicially stated circumstances in which particular decisions were taken. It considers how law in this area has been and can be enforced. It tries also to be systematic, seeking general principles which can unite the judicial approaches taken (but it ultimately admits failure, declaring that cases in which some private purpose trusts have been upheld are anomalous). It is also aware of the nature of the law in this field as an expression of social relations. Thus, it considers policy; for example, the social and economic pros and cons of restrictions on alienation of property and of particular kinds of testamentary freedom. But legal analyses do not seem to remove the deep-rooted controversies surrounding the law in this area. Commentators take a variety of positions on the issues, some supporting the general legal hostility to private purpose trusts, others declaring it unjustified. And the controversy has continued for decades. In other jurisdictions matters have been dealt with by legislative reform.

A sociological approach to doctrine in this area attempts to extend established methods of legal thought in new, relatively unfamiliar ways.[64] First, it puts the development of doctrine into a far wider historical context,

---

64 R. Cotterrell, 'Some Sociological Aspects of the Controversy Around the Legal Validity of Private Purpose Trusts' in *Equity and Contemporary Legal Developments*, ed. S. Goldstein (1992) 302–34; R. Cotterrell, 'Trusting in Law: Legal and Moral Concepts of Trust' (1993) 46 *Current Legal Problems* 75–95.

noting the changing social and economic contexts in which trust law as a whole has developed. By this means it suggests that the institution of the trust has been thought of in ways that have changed radically over time. This change becomes recognizable when attention shifts from the development of a particular line of precedents, as in orthodox legal analysis, to changing patterns of legal ideas about the nature of trusting relationships seen as interrelated with broader social, economic, and moral ideas. Thus, the inquiry broadens the idea of law as a social phenomenon by treating legal ideas as an aspect of social ideas in development. This is not to reduce the former to the latter, but to see each as inseparable from the other.

Similarly, empirical inquiry is broadened beyond the observation of previous decisions to include much wider observation of the particular social contexts and implications of these decisions. It considers their relation with other legal developments in areas that may be legally distinct from but socially interconnected with the area of private purpose trusts, viewed as an area of legally structured social relationships. Thus, sociological inquiry seeks a broader, systematic view of the law by reinterpreting the relationships of ideas which the lawyer identifies. It puts them into an intellectual context that allows the identification of other relationships and other connections. And these in turn help to explain the law as it stands and point to ways of rethinking and developing it.

When sociological inquiry is used in the ways outlined above it ceases to appear as the pursuit of a methodology alien to law, or the invocation of a competing academic discipline with the aim of colonizing law. It is seen as the radical extension and reflexivity of legal participants' understanding of law. Viewed in this way, it appears as a necessary means of broadening legal understanding – the systematic and empirical understanding of a certain aspect of social life which is recognized as 'legal'.

It procedes from participant understandings, but because it seeks to *systematize* legal understanding beyond the needs of particular participants, it goes beyond their perspectives. For example, it certainly does not reject – but does not treat (for its purposes) as adequate – personal or anecdotal accounts of legal experience, particular narratives which cannot be generalized. Because it treats very seriously the requirement that systematizations of legal or social knowledge must be grounded in *empirical* observation, it resists speculations that it considers as taking inadequate account of empirical variation. And because it emphasizes law's character as a *social* phenomenon, it examines law's social character far more extensively and broadly than most participants need to do. Hence, for example, it is led to extend its conception of the legal as a social phenomenon beyond the forms of law familiar to lawyers or some other categories of legal participants.[65]

---

65 Some sociological theories of legal pluralism offer the clearest examples here. They often suggest a vast *diversity* of legal knowledge, consciousness, authority, and experience which tends to be obscured by the orthodox typical focus of lawyers' practice and legal education on uniform law applied by official national and state courts. See Cotterrell, op. cit., n. 62.

Viewed in this way the enterprise of sociological interpretation of legal ideas is not a desirable supplement but an essential means of legal understanding. Legal ideas are a means of structuring the social world. To appreciate them in this sense and to recognize their power and their limits, is to understand them sociologically.

[5]

Analytical Jurisprudence Versus Descriptive Sociology Revisited

Nicola Lacey*

"Notwithstanding its concern with analysis the book may also be regarded as an essay in descriptive sociology; for the suggestion that inquiries into the meanings of words merely throw light on words is false. Many important distinctions... between types of social situations or relationships may best be brought to light by an examination of the standard uses of the relevant expressions and of the way in which these depend on a social context, itself often left unstated."[1]

"Decade after decade, Positivists and Natural Lawyers face one another in the final of the World Cup (the Sociologists have never learned the rules)."[2]

"It was Oliver Wendell Holmes who argued most influentially, I think, for... 'external' legal theory: the depressing history of social-theoretic jurisprudence in our century warns us how wrong he was."[3]

"No one in the current debate [over the concept of law] advocates a social-scientific concept of law that best promotes our systematic understanding of the emergence and maintenance of social structures[4] *.... Specifically, the concept of law that concerns the philosophers of law emphasizes the legal order, the set of prohibitions, requirements, and permissions that prevail in a society rather than the institutions of the legal regime that promulgate, enforce, and maintain the legal order. Phrased differently, the philosophical debate over the concept*

---

* Professor of Criminal Law and Legal Theory, London School of Economics; Adjunct Professor of Social and Political Theory, Research School of Social Sciences, Australian National University. I am grateful to Lizzie Barmes, Hugh Collins, Roger Cotterrell, Ronald Dworkin, Moira Gatens, Leslie Green, Stephen Guest, Lewis Kornhauser, George Letsas, Brian Leiter, Liam Murphy, James Penner, Philip Pettit, Simon Roberts, Brian Tamanaha, and William Twining for comments on and discussion of this paper. An earlier draft was delivered as the Leon Green Lecture at the University of Texas Law School in March 2005. The paper was also discussed at the Colloquium on Legal, Political, and Social Philosophy at University College, London; the Center for Law and Public Affairs at Princeton University; and the 2005 W.G. Hart Workshop at the Institute of Advanced Legal Studies, University of London. I am grateful to the audiences on each of these occasions for their constructive feedback.

1. H.L.A. HART, THE CONCEPT OF LAW, at v (1961).
2. Tony Honoré, *Groups, Laws and Obedience, in* OXFORD ESSAYS IN JURISPRUDENCE 1 (A.W.B. Simpson ed., 1973).
3. RONALD DWORKIN, LAW'S EMPIRE 75 (1986).
4. Lewis A. Kornhauser, *Governance Structures, Legal Systems, and the Concept of Law,* 79 CHI.-KENT L. REV. 355, 355 (2004).

of law treats the legal order as a largely autonomous set of norms rather than as an artifact of functioning institutions of the governance structure."[5]

In this Essay, I revisit the protracted, inconclusive and sometimes unedifying debate prompted by H.L.A. Hart's famous claim in the Preface to *The Concept of Law* that the book might be regarded as a contribution not only to analytical jurisprudence but also to descriptive sociology. Drawing on my work as Hart's biographer,[6] I shall review his own reflections on the claim, the arguments of legal theory to which his claim gave rise, and the reasons for thinking that the structure of his own theory prevented him from following through on the insights from which his claim proceeded. My motivation, however, is not primarily that of the biographer or the intellectual historian. Rather, this general interpretive question about Hart's work connects with some long-standing interests that have informed my own work in jurisprudence and criminal law theory. While bearing in mind Freud's view of the biographer's relationship with his or her subject as "a heady brew of Oedipal triumph and sibling rivalry,"[7] I shall use my engagement with Hart's biography and intellectual legacy as the jumping-off point for a further examination of the relationship between the analytic and sociological approaches to legal theory, and of the relative contributions of philosophy, history, and the social sciences to our systematic understanding of the nature of law. Are legal philosophers like Dworkin justified in dismissing the achievements of sociotheoretic jurisprudence as "depressing," or in regarding sociological legal theorists, as Honoré suggests, as playing an entirely different game? Or, to put the question in Kornhauser's terms, does it make sense to seek a theory of the "legal order"—that is, prevailing legal norms—independent of a theory of the "legal regime," i.e., the institutions that generate and enforce those norms?

My argument will proceed in three stages. First, I shall examine Hart's original claim, interpreting it in light of the archival materials—particularly Hart's working notebooks—which were available to me as his biographer. I shall then consider the role of this dual ambition in Hart's later development of his own theory of law. In this stage I shall argue that the structural features of Hart's theory, as well as his insistence on the primacy, or even on the exclusive relevance, of analytic philosophical method to jurisprudence, prevented him from building upon his original insight that a theory of law might be taken as a genuine contribution to sociology. Ironically, Hart's emphatic recapitulation of the essentially descriptive nature of his legal theory in the posthumously published Postscript[8] took him, if anything,

---

5. *Id.* at 375.
6. NICOLA LACEY, A LIFE OF H.L.A. HART: THE NIGHTMARE AND THE NOBLE DREAM (2004). For reviews that take up the themes discussed in this Essay, see Keith Culver, *H.L.A. Hart: A Life in the Perspective of Law and Philosophy*, 44 OSGOODE HALL L.J. (forthcoming 2006), and Frederick Schauer, *(Re)Taking Hart*, 119 HARV. L. REV. 852 (2006).
7. ADAM PHILLIPS, DARWIN'S WORMS 90 (1999).
8. H.L.A. HART, THE CONCEPT OF LAW 238–76 (2d. ed. 1994) (1961).

further from his original insight, and it underlines the rather limited extent to which his theory built up its promise of a social or institutional theory capable of illuminating the ways in which the conception of law reflected in usage "depend[s] on a social context."[9] Yet, after decades of a mutual lack of interest (tinged on both sides with a shade of contempt), the productive dialogue between philosophical and socio-legal theory glimpsed in the Preface has, I shall argue, now begun to flourish. Today, Hart's original insight is more widely appreciated, perhaps as a result of the increasingly stark contrast between his accessible style of legal philosophy and the more abstract and technical style of some of his positivist successors.

In the second stage of the paper, I shall consider the relationship between Hart's idea that legal theory had to do with both analytical jurisprudence and descriptive sociology, and what might be called the project of special as opposed to general jurisprudence. The revival of a philosophically sophisticated special jurisprudence—a mode of conceptual analysis very different from the arid jurisprudential pondering on concepts such as ownership and possession that he skillfully lampooned in "Definition and Theory in Jurisprudence"[10]—is generally considered to be one of Hart's most important long-term contributions to legal theory. And while it is most often associated with his normative work—notably *Punishment and Responsibility*[11]—the vast monument of *Causation in the Law*,[12] as well as the interplay of the normative and the analytic in this aspect of Hart's work, testify to the relevance of this special jurisprudence to his analytical project. In suggesting that here, too, there was an implicit (and incompletely realized) social dimension to Hart's work, I am moving beyond any claim of his own. But I argue that the claim in the Preface is of great relevance to his analysis of legal concepts such as causation, intention, or negligence, and of higher level concepts such as responsibility that, he argued, underpin these legal concepts. Indeed, I contend that it may be easier to get a clear view of the mutual dependence of analytic–conceptual and social–institutional aspects of legal theory through a discussion of "micro" rather than "macro" legal theory.

In the final stage of the paper, I develop the argument of the second stage through three case studies within special jurisprudence, each of them the subject of Hart's work. First, I shall consider the idea of causation in legal discourse; second, the idea of responsibility in criminal law; and finally, the idea of corporate personality and responsibility. Through these case studies, I shall argue that a full understanding of legal concepts (and, by extension, legal rules, principles, and doctrines) can only be attained by

---

9. *Id.* at v.
10. H.L.A. Hart, *Definition and Theory in Jurisprudence*, 70 LAW Q. REV. 37 (1954).
11. H.L.A. HART, PUNISHMENT AND RESPONSIBILITY: ESSAYS IN THE PHILOSOPHY OF LAW (1968).
12. H.L.A. HART & A.M. HONORÉ, CAUSATION IN THE LAW (1959).

supplementing philosophical analysis with a study of the social institutions and contexts in which those concepts, rules, and arrangements are embedded. Accordingly, my argument is that if legal theorists want to escape the sort of isolation or irrelevance risked by a view of jurisprudence as autonomous, they should abandon Hart's insistence that analytic philosophy[13] is its exclusive disciplinary resource. I conclude that a view of analytic and sociological jurisprudence as mutually dependent would be more intellectually satisfactory than the philosophical imperialism that currently characterizes the field.

I. Hart's Claim and Its Limits

A. Interpreting Hart's Claim

On its face, Hart's prefatory claim to be contributing to descriptive sociology as well as analytical jurisprudence is surprising. A philosopher by training as well as by deepest disposition, Hart also worked in an environment in which the status of the social sciences in general, and of sociology in particular, was relatively low. The diaries that he kept during his year at Harvard in 1956–1957 provide an amusing testament to the low esteem in which he held both sociology and sociological jurisprudence,[14] though the proof that this year afforded him of their currency in the top U.S. law schools, as well as his desire to escape his reputation for "formalism," may help to explain the gesture to sociology four years later.[15]

Herbert Hart was never a man to use words lightly; his ideas were, after all, molded at the feet of H.W.B. Joseph[16] and then fired in the kiln of Austinian linguistic philosophy.[17] We must therefore assume that the Preface's claim was a considered one. Hence it is highly significant.

---

13. Clearly, not all philosophical methods would invite the criticism that I voice in this paper. For example, Brian Leiter has argued that post-Quinean naturalism sees philosophy as sitting in tandem with the natural and social sciences, and hence as centrally concerned with constructing just the sort of dialogue for which I argue in this paper. Brian Leiter, *Beyond the Hart–Dworkin Debate: The Methodology Problem in Jurisprudence*, 48 AM. J. JURIS. 17 (2003). Much contemporary jurisprudence, however, continues to be informed by an analytic philosophy committed to its own autonomy, and it is therefore vulnerable to the critique developed in this paper.

14. In the autumn of 1956, he wrote to his wife, Jenifer: "How [my Harvard law students] *love* everything beginning with the syllable 'soc-'!', but 'After the initial shock of my accent and my refusal to do sociology, and natural law, they seem to enjoy linguistics and comparisons of law with the rules of Baseball: They'll be raging positivists before we're 'thru' and then there'll be a row. But the atmosphere is very stimulating: every point of view is advanced and they adore debate." LACEY, *supra* note 6, at 185.

15. *See* H.L.A. Hart, *Philosophy of Law and Jurisprudence: Britain (1945–52)*, 2 AM. J. COMP. L. 355 (1953). With a largely American audience in mind, Hart mounted a spirited defense of the distinctive importance of analytical jurisprudence as compared with the Realist, sociologically oriented legal theory current in the United States at that time.

16. *See* LACEY, *supra* note 6, at 22–39.

17. *Id.* at 112–51.

Certainly, Hart's reference to "descriptive sociology" was a gesture to the Austinian precept that an understanding of linguistic usage illuminates the world. But my own view is that it was more than this, and stood for his determination to move beyond the conceptually rigid positivisms of Austin and Kelsen, with their peremptory bundling of inconveniently shaped legal phenomena into the conceptual straitjacket of their theories, and, failing that, their banishing of such phenomena to other disciplines. It represented his commitment, in other words, to producing a commonsensical, "social fact" theory of law: a theory of law that would speak to the existence of varied social phenomena, accommodate social realities, and "fit the facts."[18] But Hart's own final statement of his position goes further yet. In one of his notebooks of the late 1980s, while accepting that he had been mistaken in making such a broad claim, he argued that a better formulation would have been that the book provided the "normative concepts required for a descriptive sociology."[19] This suggests a wider ambition to facilitate a degree of complementarity between jurisprudence and the social sciences, and an aspiration that jurisprudence be of use to social scientists and socio-legal scholars.

As the take-up of Hart's theory in works of legal anthropology attests,[20] social science research can usefully deploy, and indeed needs, conceptual accounts of the phenomena being studied. But, as is equally reflected by the social sciences' lively criticism of *The Concept of Law*, Hart's contribution had limits.[21] Although the techniques of analytic philosophy may establish that law is simply one form of social rule, the further question of just what is distinctive about legal as opposed to other social rules can only be understood in terms of historical and social facts about the particular features of legal modes and institutions of governance in which *The Concept of Law* shows relatively little interest. As Brian Tamanaha has said,[22] Hart's theory is torn between a thoroughgoing conventionalism that attempts to theorize

---

18. HART, *supra* note 6, at 80. For a different interpretation of the claim and its implications for Hart's theory, see Veronica Rodriguez-Blanco, *A Defence of Hart's Semantics and Nonambitious Conceptual Analysis*, 9 LEGAL THEORY 99–124 (2003).

19. Hart's late notebooks are not systematically dated, so it is impossible to put a precise date on this formulation. It accords, however, with the broad position outlined in his interview with David Sugarman in 1988 (an interview in which he also confessed to having suffered the "Oxford disease" of "an excessive distrust" of sociology!). David Sugarman, *Hart Interviewed: H.L.A. Hart in Conversation with David Sugarman*, 32 J. L. & SOC'Y 289, 289–93 (2005).

20. *See, e.g.*, Paul Bohannan, *The Differing Realms of the Law*, AM. ANTHROPOLOGIST, Dec. 1965, at 33.

21. The book's claim to contribute to descriptive sociology was immediately questioned, with one early reviewer, B.E. King, arguing that "Professor Hart's great talents for linguistic analysis may . . . have a conservative effect on legal theory" and that "[t]he point at issue is really one as to the scope of jurisprudence: whether as a social science it is to be brought under the theoretical umbrella of sociology—or whether, as mainly a study of judicial technique, it is to remain under the shadow of logic and linguistics." B.E. King, *The Basic Concept of Professor Hart's Jurisprudence: The Norm out of the Bottle*, 1963 CAMBRIDGE L.J. 270, 277, 300.

22. BRIAN TAMANAHA, A GENERAL JURISPRUDENCE OF LAW AND SOCIETY 135 (2001).

any phenomenon treated as law within a social group, and a more essentialist position that assumes that law has some core and invariant structural features. This is a tension that is also reflected in *Causation in the Law*, where Hart moves between the project of analyzing legal usage, on the assumption that the context in which causal concepts are used dictates the meaning of causal terms, and the idea that there is an essential core to causation.[23]

Hart's legal theory has also been argued to display a functionalism that invites confusion between analytic and historical claims. The distinction between primary and secondary rules, for example, can be taken as either a conceptual or a functional distinction. In a conceptual sense, it is a distinction between structurally different forms of rule. In a functional sense, it is a distinction between rules with different social purposes. And the account of the emergence of secondary rules as "curing the defects" of a system of primary rules, if taken as a historical claim, is both inaccurate and implicitly serves to represent, as the acme of "civilization," the contours of a modern western legal order. According to the more radical of these critiques,[24] the status of *The Concept of Law* as a work of description is questionable, and the very project of seeking to answer, in a general and universally applicable way, the question "what is law?" is fundamentally misconceived.

Hart's defense against these objections was clear, if unlikely to satisfy his critics. It was simply that these sociological and historical questions were not the ones that he set out to answer. Rather, his was essentially a philosophical project, and its allusion to "descriptive sociology" was an unfortunately misleading attempt to signal his move away from the more rigidly conceptual theories of John Austin and Hans Kelsen in favor of an approach that helps us to look at the complex social phenomenon of law. Similarly, in his response to Bodenheimer's critique in the *Pennsylvania Law Review* that Hart's positivism neglected the importance of disciplines other than philosophy, Hart emphasized the distinction between theories of law and the law itself. While legal practice could undoubtedly be improved by a systematic appreciation of the insights of other disciplines, legal theory, Hart insisted, was an autonomous intellectual approach in which philosophy was the appropriate disciplinary resource.[25]

---

23. This perhaps reflected Herbert Hart's and Tony Honoré's different approaches. *See infra* note 91.

24. *See, e.g.*, PETER FITZPATRICK, THE MYTHOLOGY OF MODERN LAW (1992).

25. Edgar Bodenheimer, *Modern Analytical Jurisprudence and the Limits of Its Usefulness*, 104 U. PA. L. REV. 1080, 1086 (1956); H.L.A. Hart, *Analytic Jurisprudence in Mid-twentieth Century: A Reply to Professor Bodenheimer*, 105 U. PA. L. REV. 953, 974 (1957). Yet, in defending himself against Bodenheimer's charge that his position ultimately undermined jurisprudence by redefining jurisprudential questions as ones about the usage of terms in particular legal contexts—a charge that is structurally similar to the "paradox of analysis" critique often mounted against Austinian linguistic philosophy—Hart sounded less than fully convinced by his own position. His argument

Yet there is an interesting question about the influence of a certain genre of sociological theory on Hart's work. As I discovered during the course of my work on his biography, Hart was almost certainly influenced by his reading of Max Weber. In Hart's copy of *On Law in Economy and Society*,[26] Weber's comments that "[c]onduct ... can be oriented on the part of actors toward their *idea* of the existence of a *legitimate order*" and that "only then will an order be called 'valid' if the orientation toward [its] maxims occurs, among other reasons, also because it is ... regarded by the actor as in some way *obligatory* or *exemplary* for him" are annotated with several comments and underlinings—Hart's usual method of indicating a close reading and passages to which he intended to return. And Weber's discussion of the variety of ways in which conduct may be orientated towards certain maxims within an order is marked "Good, like it, likely to be useful." Other margin notes imply that Hart's reading of Weber fed into his formulation of the internal aspect of rules: the notes include "reasons for accepting/reasons for obeying ... *external*/personal," and Weber's claim that "an 'externally' *guaranteed order* may also be guaranteed 'internally'" is heavily marked.[27]

This strand of social theory in Hart's work is not unique. His friend Jean Floud pressed him on why he had not taken more seriously the great early sociologists Max Weber and Emile Durkheim, and it was under Floud's influence that he read Durkheim and began to think about the implications of his thought for criminal law.[28] But despite the insight Hart gained from Weber and his decision to commission a book entitled *Law in Society* for the Clarendon Law Series, Hart's reaction to these sorts of ideas was never particularly positive. This is illustrated by his essay "Social Solidarity,"

---

was that students of substantive law can learn to use terms of legal art and to predict their effects without understanding their conceptual structure or normative function. But this sounded dangerously like an unstable theoretical division of labor that would carve up the teaching of law and jurisprudence between, respectively, the Realists and the philosophers. From his own point of view, this was surely to concede too much.

26. MAX WEBER, ON LAW IN ECONOMY AND SOCIETY 3 (Max Rheinstein ed., Edward Shils trans., Harvard University Press 1954) (1925). I am grateful to John Finnis for alerting me to these annotations. *See* LACEY, *supra* note 6, at 230–31. I am also grateful to Frances Olsen for tracing the relevant volume in the library of the Hebrew University, Jerusalem, to which Hart bequeathed his books.

27. *See* BRIAN Z. TAMANAHA, REALISTIC SOCIO-LEGAL THEORY 157 (1997) (discussing Weber's grasp of the importance to social science of understanding the ideas and beliefs of social actors); *see also* ANTHONY T. KRONMAN, MAX WEBER (1983). When asked by John Finnis about the influence of Weber on his account of the internal aspect of rules, Hart claimed rather that it was Peter Winch's *The Idea of a Social Science and Its Relation to Philosophy* that had shaped his ideas. PETER WINCH, THE IDEA OF A SOCIAL SCIENCE AND ITS RELATION TO PHILOSOPHY (1958). As Garry Runciman has pointed out to me (in private correspondence), Hart's actual references to Winch are to his discussions of Mill, Oakeshott, and Wittgenstein, and not to his discussion of Weber. It is perhaps a sign of how weak a hold even Winch's philosophical engagement with the social sciences had on Hart's intellectual imagination that when interviewed by David Sugarman late in life he could not remember having read Winch's book. Sugarman, *supra* note 19.

28. *See* LACEY, *supra* note 6, at 260.

published in 1967.[29] In this paper, Hart returned to Devlin's argument that without legal enforcement of the common morality, a society risks disintegration.[30] In *Immorality and Treason*[31] and *Law, Liberty and Morality*,[32] Hart had launched a devastating philosophical onslaught on Devlin's position. This time, he considered the argument from a sociological point of view, drawing an analogy between Devlin's thesis and Talcott Parsons' and Durkheim's accounts of social systems' maintenance of shared values.[33] He set out Durkheim's distinction between "mechanical solidarity"—the underpinning of social stability by means of substantially shared values, often reflected in criminal law—and "organic solidarity"—the underpinning of social stability by means of a complementarity of functions, often reflected in a preference for civil law regulation.[34] While criticizing Durkheim's suggestion that a predominance of organic solidarity is a mark of civilization, he noted a strong analogy between Devlin's thesis and Durkheim's account of criminal punishment as the symbolic expression (and repression) of what is most deeply disapproved—in Durkheim's term, the *conscience collective* of a social order.[35]

But what kind of evidence, Hart asked, could support such a thesis? On the one hand, there would be comparative historical data about the decline of societies that failed to use such penal mechanisms—primitive agrarian societies, perhaps. But here the problems of systematic comparison, he suggested, are overwhelming. For example, can we assume that the conditions of stability for industrial societies are comparable with those of premodern social orders? On the other hand, we might look to psychological data showing that a failure to enforce core morality leads to either (1) permissiveness, which in turn leads to a general loss of individual self-control and hence indirectly to social disorder, or (2) moral pluralism of such a radical kind as to lead to a general weakening of the necessary minimum content of morality. Hart argued that neither kind of evidence in fact exists. Read sociologically, therefore, Devlin's argument cannot be sustained. This essay is of particular interest in that it demonstrates a rather thin reading of the relevant social theory. For example, Hart all but ignores Durkheim's argument about the functional affinity between certain values and the requirements of organic solidarity and social differentiation in complex modern societies, thus facilitating the superficial analogy with Devlin.[36] Moreover, Hart's argument represents an attack not merely on Devlin's

---

29. H.L.A. Hart, *Social Solidarity and the Enforcement of Morality*, 35 U. CHI. L. REV. 1 (1967).
30. *Id.* at 2.
31. H.L.A. Hart, *Immorality and Treason*, LISTENER, July 30, 1959, at 162.
32. H.L.A. HART, LAW, LIBERTY AND MORALITY 18–19 (1963).
33. Hart, *supra* note 29, at 4–5.
34. *Id.* at 5.
35. *Id.* at 6–7.
36. *See* ROGER COTTERRELL, ÉMILE DURKHEIM: LAW IN A MORAL DOMAIN (1999).

thesis but on sociological method in general. Hart suggested that sociology can never match the test of empirical rigor it sets for itself. His view boils down to the idea that because the social sciences can never produce evidence as compelling as the evidence produced by the natural sciences, the social sciences are not worth pursuing. This is a convenient rationalization for staying firmly within an analytic philosophical method, and for distancing the complex question of how our theories relate to the social phenomena that they conceptualize. But Hart was, after all, a philosopher, and he worked within a philosophical community—notably the Oxford group of "linguistic philosophers"—that conceived its own boundaries narrowly.

B. *The Impact of the Incompletely Realized "Social Fact" Dimension of Hart's Theory on the Later Development of His Ideas*

Interesting questions can be raised, however, about the impact of the incomplete nature of Hart's espousal of a social science dimension to jurisprudence on the development of his own theory. Inevitably, *The Concept of Law* was subject to a barrage of criticism from a number of different directions. As we have seen, Hart was relatively impervious to historical and sociological criticism, precisely because he saw his project as philosophical and therefore immune to the charge of having ignored issues that seem central to historians and social scientists. As far as he was concerned, any concession to these critics would have been an abandonment of the central idea of his book and a move towards something akin to Legal Realism.[37] The empirical assumptions underlying his theory—that law facilitates survival and that a legal system's existence depends on a baseline of effectiveness—along with the "social context" on which he claimed that linguistic usage depended, remained at the most abstract level. But Hart was significantly more troubled by criticism from the opposite direction, notably from natural lawyers who saw his restricted notion of the acceptance needed to underpin the existence of a legal system and with it of legal obligations as drawing a line that could not be held. The notes that were insufficiently complete to be included in the published version of the Postscript to *The Concept of Law*, for example, were concerned with what we might call the moral critique of positivism, notably in the guise of John Finnis's argument about the inevitability of evaluation in the selection implicit in descriptive theory.[38] Another concern was Finnis's argument—a natural lawyer ironically hoisting Hart on his own sociological petard—that an acceptance of the idea that law is geared to human coexistence should dictate that those with a morally based internal attitude be accorded theoretical priority as a

---

37. It is arguable that Hart's concern to distinguish his position from that of Legal Realism derived from a misconstruction of Realism as a theory of law as opposed to specifically a theory of judicial behavior. *See* Brian Leiter, *Legal Realism and Legal Positivism Reconsidered*, 111 ETHICS 278 (2001).

38. JOHN FINNIS, NATURAL LAW AND NATURAL RIGHTS 11–18 (1980).

central case, because only with a core of such people can a system gain the sort of stability necessary to that basic function.[39]

Hart's working notebooks reveal the intensely sad struggle of the last decade of his life to resolve the problem of legal obligation and explicate a positivist conception of law's normativity that would satisfy critics like Ronald Dworkin and John Finnis. They also reveal that this struggle found its roots in a sense of intellectual dissatisfaction with his own account that stretched back to his work in *The Concept of Law*. From his very earliest notes, Hart anticipated that the idea of obligation, generated by the key internal/external distinction, would be central to and distinctive of his theory:

> Obligation as the differential of modern nature of law but caricatured by command. This is likely to become central idée maitresse of the book. What principles are may become clear in course of reading Warrender... [I]n this can I draw my distinction between the command habit caricature and the far more central notion of rule-like acceptance.[40]

Identifying the issue was not, however, the same as solving it:

> There is something odd, possibly something mistaken in position which I have taken v. 2 that the essence/structure of a legal system rests on acceptance of central/certain authority as binding..... Perhaps all I need to convey is that the obligation is strictly *obligation*... i.e.: narrower than belief in moral goodness. But? there is a muddle (in me) I suspect here.[41]

As John Finnis put it in an interview, Hart felt that there was "dark or dangerous territory" whichever way he looked out from the precarious middle position that he had carved out in *The Concept of Law*.[42] He felt the space for normativity that he had delineated was perilously close to a concession that legal obligation was a species of moral obligation.[43] This explains why he felt so vulnerable to Dworkin's critique, especially as it developed so as to give increasing importance to the moral as opposed to institutional dimension of legal reasoning.[44] As the Postscript shows, Hart's

---

39. *Id.*; *see* LACEY, *supra* note 6, at 231, 335–37, 347–52 (citing and discussing Hart's late notebooks).

40. LACEY, *supra* note 6, at 228 (citing Hart's personal notebooks).

41. *Id.*

42. *Id.* at 336.

43. *Id.* On the tensions in Hart's method in relation to law's normativity, see Stephen R. Perry, *Hart's Methodological Positivism*, *in* HART'S POSTSCRIPT: ESSAYS ON THE POSTSCRIPT TO THE CONCEPT OF LAW 311–54 (Jules Coleman ed. 2001). Hart's struggles over the concept of legal obligation give further evidence of his faith in the capacity of philosophical analysis to produce definitive resolutions. Yet, as Liam Murphy argued persuasively in his remarks at the New York launch of my biography of Hart (draft comments on file with the author), it might be argued that certain concepts—legal obligation among them—are inherently equivocal and not susceptible of being captured in a single, coherent conceptual analysis.

44. This development is discernible in Dworkin's work. *See* RONALD DWORKIN, TAKING RIGHTS SERIOUSLY (1977); *see also* DWORKIN, *supra* note 3.

response was to insist with ever greater vehemence on the essentially descriptive nature of his project. But with this insistence came an increasingly radical split between the descriptive-analytical jurisprudence that he saw himself as providing (in this part of his work) and both evaluative—natural law theory, Dworkin—or positive—sociological, historical, economic, political—forms of jurisprudence that draw part of their data or inspiration from beyond law as defined in positivist terms. And his new position, I suggest, made the inchoate nature of the "social" aspect of his original theory still more vivid.

In his struggle to come to terms with Dworkin's new account of his own position in *Law's Empire*, Hart focused his attention on an argument that is superficially attractive but ultimately not entirely satisfactory. This was the argument that Dworkin's projects and his own were fundamentally different and might even be understood as complementary to one another. "New approach," he wrote in a notebook in late 1985: "reply to Dworkin by making case for a *general descriptive JP*."[45] *The Concept of Law*, he repeatedly asserted, is "*NOT* a branch of justificatory moral or political theory."[46] While *Law's Empire* advances an ideal vision and a legitimating argument for a certain conception of law, it neither engages in, nor undermines the validity of, the project of producing a general, universally applicable and fundamentally descriptive theory of law such as Hart himself sought to provide. He thought that this descriptive project could survive what he now recognized to be a further complication: that the

> description ... will involve *selection* of some elements for a cluster and the selection will be *evaluative* (not morally) in sense of answerable to some criteria of *importance* (Raz [though in fact this point is made more forcefully by Finnis]) and among these will be "relevance to moral judgment". So though description and evaluation are different they are in such ways connected.... This is parallel though different from Aristotle's real definition and "real essence" where the elements in the definition are seen as *necessarily combined*....[47]

Since disputes about what elements could satisfy the implicit criterion used to select the "central case" would inevitably make such descriptive analysis controversial, these controversies, he recognized, would have to be accommodated as "pivotal rather than borderline" cases.[48]

With the move towards a division of labor between his and Dworkin's theory—the one descriptive and the other justificatory—Hart escaped one element of his dilemma: he avoided the need to synthesize and comment on every aspect of Dworkin's theory, and was able instead to organize his

---

45. LACEY, *supra* note 6, at 351 (citing and discussing Hart's personal notebooks).
46. *Id.*
47. *Id.*
48. *Id.*

thoughts more firmly around a defense and elaboration of his own views. But in doing so, he faced the difficulty that Dworkin himself roundly denied the possibility of compatibility,[49] and continued to insist that his theory contradicted some central tenets of *The Concept of Law*. Hart risked, therefore, giving the impression that he was simply failing to respond to Dworkin's challenge. More importantly, in focusing his argument on the representation of his own theory as entirely descriptive, he was turning his back on an insight that he had powerfully defended in his early work but dropped out of his later writings. This was the insight, that Hart put with particular force in the Holmes lecture,[50] that there was a strong *moral* case for espousing the inclusive, positivist concept of law according to which even morally unappealing standards may count as fully valid legal rules.[51] In 1957, his argument had been that the clarity gained by a differentiation of legal and moral standards had both intrinsic moral and intellectual merit and political advantages. It was honest to be clear-sighted about the different considerations at play for citizens confronted with evil laws: first, are they legally valid; second, should they be obeyed? And this clear-sightedness would be more likely to foster the reflective approach to obedience to the state's legal orders that properly underlies liberal citizenship and a robust attitude toward tyranny. Why had these persuasive arguments disappeared from later statements of his position? One can only speculate, but it seems likely that he recognized that they were claims the ultimate proof of which depended on further moral argument or empirical data. And in constructing his legal philosophy Hart was, as all the evidence shows, reluctant to involve himself in the investigation of such wide-ranging questions.[52]

In moving more firmly in a descriptive direction, Hart had also—ironically—moved further from the insights that informed the genuinely institutional or social fact aspect of *The Concept of Law*. For example, in

---

49. As is evident, for example, from the early chapters of *Law's Empire*. DWORKIN, *supra* note 3.

50. H.L.A. Hart, *Positivism and the Separation of Law and Morals*, 71 HARV. L. REV. 593, 593–629 (1958).

51. For different developments of this approach, see TOM CAMPBELL, THE LEGAL THEORY OF ETHICAL POSITIVISM (1996); Liam Murphy, *The Political Question of the Concept of Law*, in HART'S POSTSCRIPT, *supra* note 43, at 371; and—in explicit terms of the political case for positivism as discouraging quietism in relation to state power—Liam Murphy, *Concepts of Law*, 30 AUSTRALIAN J. LEGAL PHIL. 1, 9–19 (2005), observing that "the best place to locate the boundary of law is where it will have the best effect on our self-understanding as a society, on our political culture." *See also* Frederick Schauer, *Positivism as Pariah*, in THE AUTONOMY OF LAW 31 (Robert P. George ed., 1996); Jeremy Waldron, *Normative (or Ethical) Positivism*, in HART'S POSTSCRIPT, *supra* note 43, at 410.

52. As Ronald Dworkin would later put it in one of his many assaults on positivism's limited scope, "[P]ositivists are drawn to their conception of law not for its inherent appeal, but because it allows them to treat legal philosophy as an autonomous, analytic, and self-contained discipline." Ronald Dworkin, Book Review, *Thirty Years On*, 115 HARV. L. REV. 1655, 1656 (2002) (reviewing JULES COLEMAN, THE PRACTICE OF PRINCIPLE: IN DEFENSE OF A PRAGMATIST APPROACH TO LEGAL THEORY (2001)). My question is whether any legal theory that regards its disciplinary resources as exclusively based in analytic philosophy can escape some version of this dilemma.

struggling to respond to the issue about the inevitability of selection in theory construction in the passage quoted above, Hart reaches for the Aristotelian notion of essence rather than a Weberian notion of paradigms or ideal types. The genius of *The Concept of Law* was its success in drawing together insights from such intensely different traditions as these. But as soon as Hart tried to develop the theory in a more elaborate way, the tensions began to show. Hart's priority was philosophical success and not usefulness to the social sciences. Yet the exit that he glimpses in that passage—the rationalization of selection criteria in terms of the notion of importance, which must be kept separate from a morally evaluative selection criterion—reaches back to the baseline sociological and functional assumption of *The Concept of Law* that law's social role is to facilitate human survival through peaceful coexistence.[53] But the way forward is blocked, because any elaboration of such a criterion would depend on a far richer conception of the social functions of law and of its institutional base than that which Hart provided or was interested in providing. The puzzle here is not so much that Hart was relatively uninterested in detailed facts, but that he was uninterested in the typologies characteristic of the more theoretical paradigms in the social sciences, (which were later put to good jurisprudential purpose in, for example, Roberto Unger's early work).[54]

Certainly, positivist theorists—notably Joseph Raz[55]—have occasionally ventured into the terrain of postulating the varied social functions of law and, to some extent, the institutional structures needed to realize them. But the terrain is more usually occupied by sociological jurists and anthropologists of law, and perhaps for good reason. For the richer the characterization of law's social basis—its institutional forms, its various types of rules, its role, and its functions—the less plausible is any theoretical claim to universality.[56] Hart wanted to maintain the claim to universality as well as descriptiveness. In doing so, he ended up with the worst of both worlds. On the one hand, he produced a theory whose commitment to a social fact dimension meant that it did indeed reflect certain specific features of institutionalization—a fact that already compromised its universality. His

---

53. Selection, in other words, need not be evaluative in a strong or moral sense, but may rather regard itself as answerable to social-scientific data. William Twining has argued: "There is no good reason why a legal positivist should not interpret social practices and institutions in terms of their point. 'Point' in this context is about motive, purpose, or expectation rather than actual consequences. On this interpretation, a thin functionalist . . . is not committed to any of the fallacies about law that gave Functionalism a bad name . . . ." William Twining, *A Post-Westphalian Conception of Law*, 37 LAW & SOC'Y REV. 199, 240 (2003); *see also* Leiter, *supra* note 13, at 49–51 (discussing the Naturalist Method and its application to Hart's methods).
54. ROBERTO MANGABEIRA UNGER, LAW IN MODERN SOCIETY (1976).
55. JOSEPH RAZ, *The Functions of Law*, *in* THE AUTHORITY OF LAW 163 (1979).
56. This is, of course a general methodological issue for all social sciences, as the history of anthropology shows with particular force.

theory, after all, fits most comfortably with a centralized state legal order.[57] On the other hand, in the grip of the ambition for universality, he failed to deliver any rich paradigm of law's institutional form. This difficulty perhaps also explains why, despite the fact that the working notebook for *The Concept of Law* anticipates that the book would consider the varieties of laws,[58] no such consideration found its way into the book itself, with the distinction between power-conferring and duty-imposing rules standing in for the entire panoply of both normative and functional varieties among legal standards.[59] The capacity of a fuller articulation of the institutional dimensions of law to compromise universality perhaps also explains Hart's notoriously under-developed account of adjudication: an under-development which allowed Dworkin, unencumbered by this particular methodological postulate,[60] to provide a more textured account to which Hart had difficulty in responding. But it is hard not to feel that a more ambitious and Weberian deployment of the central case technique might have allowed Hart to make at least some further progress in squaring this particular theoretical circle.

In the decades that followed the publication of *The Concept of Law*, an unfortunate and intellectually obstructive hostility grew up between many legal theorists of an analytic or philosophical temper and those committed to socially grounded versions of legal theory. Among many proponents of "critical legal studies" and feminist legal theory,[61] as well as some socio-legal or "law and society" scholars, Hart came to symbolize the intellectual narrowness and arrogance of philosophical jurisprudence. His claim to have produced "an essay in descriptive sociology" fanned, ironically, the flames of hostility.[62] Positivism was linked strongly with formalism, and the general

---

57. *See infra* text accompanying note 67 (arguing that particular conceptions of law must have empirical support).

58. *See* LACEY, *supra* note 6, at 223 ("This would . . . bring out the *multiplicity* of kinds of law: *Substantive*; Crime and Private; *Jurisdiction*; *Procedure*; *Evidence*; Constitutional (Grundnorm) and drive away the obsession with Command . . . .").

59. While the working notebook anticipated, for example, an elaboration of the distinction between substantive and procedural rules, no such argument is to be found in *The Concept of Law*. The distinction between power-conferring and duty-imposing rules stands in for a much wider variety of functional distinctions (facility-creating, dispute-resolving, symbolic enunciation of standards, authority-conferring and so on), while also marking the very different, conceptual distinction between rules in which an enacted standard of behaviour can be distinguished from a sanction (criminal law for example) and rules in which no such conceptual distinction can be drawn (the law of contract: as Hart himself noted in his criticism of Kelsen, the concept of validity is intrinsic to that of contract and cannot be equated to that of sanction for noncompliance without conceptual as much as functional distortion).

60. Or, at least, by the particular version of universality claimed by Hart.

61. For a discussion, see NICOLA LACEY, UNSPEAKABLE SUBJECTS 4–11 (1998). The feminist hostility to positivism was misdirected in so far as the constructivist temper of legal positivism sits comfortably with both feminist commitment to social constructionism and the deployment of law for projects of feminist reform.

62. *See* FITZPATRICK, *supra* note 24, at 208 (finding that "Hart's attempt to preserve law from an involving use and context fails, except as myth"); THE JURISPRUDENCE OF ORTHODOXY (Philip Leith & Peter Ingram eds., 1988).

assumption was that socio-legal and critical legal studies scholars had no need of jurisprudence in the analytic tradition. But, intellectually, these are spurious battle lines, and over the last decade, happily, they have begun to disintegrate. Several influential scholars are reopening the effort to find a common cause across the philosophy/social science divide, motivated by the thought that there is a genuine complementarity and scope for productive debate claim—the very thought that prompted Hart's claim. While Brian Tamanaha[63] has sought to push Hart's approach further in the direction of its constructionist or conventionalist aspects and away from its functionalism and essentialism, providing a broader "socio-legal positivist" conception of law that purports to fulfill many of the aims that Hart saw as central to his own jurisprudence, sociological jurists such as Niklas Luhmann and Gunther Teubner have developed sociologies of law[64] that have a strong philosophical component (indeed that, in Luhmann's case, sometimes seem indistinguishable from the most thoroughly philosophical account!). William Twining's recent work on legal theory[65] shows a similarly eclectic embrace of different methods and disciplinary resources, while Hamish Ross has traced the echoes of classical social theory in the work of legal philosophers including Kelsen and Hart.[66] In a recent paper, Simon Roberts has even gone so far as to question the broadening out of conceptions of law beyond the state in the work of scholars like Tamanaha and Twining in response to the long-running debate about legal pluralism, arguing on empirical grounds in favor of giving just the kind of priority or distinctiveness to state law for which legal pluralists have so long criticized Hart.[67] And most consistently

---

63. BRIAN TAMANAHA, A GENERAL JURISPRUDENCE OF LAW AND SOCIETY (2001). In relation to the themes of this paper, see Twining, *supra* note 53. *See also* Kenneth Einar Himma, *Do Philosophy and Sociology Mix? A Non-essentialist Socio-legal Positivist Analysis of the Concept of Law*, 24 O.J.L.S. 717 (2004) (comparing Tamanaha's socio-legal positivist theories to Hartian positivism).

64. NIKLAS LUHMANN, A SOCIOLOGICAL THEORY OF LAW 9–22 (Martin Albrow ed., Elizabeth King & Martin Albrow trans., Routledge & Kegan Paul 1985) (1972); GUNTHER TEUBNER, LAW AS AN AUTOPOIETIC SYSTEM (Zenon Bankowski ed., Anne Bankowska & Ruth Adler trans., 1993).

65. WILLIAM TWINING, GLOBALISATION AND LEGAL THEORY (2000); *see also* William Twining, *General Jurisprudence*, *in* LAW AND JUSTICE IN GLOBAL SOCIETY 563–608 (M. Escamilla & M. Saavedra eds., 2005); Twining, *supra* note 53.

66. HAMISH ROSS, LAW AS A SOCIAL INSTITUTION (2001); Hamish Ross, *The* Pure Theory of Law *and Interpretive Sociology* or *A Basis for Interdisciplinarity*, *in* LAW AND SOCIOLOGY: (CURRENT LEGAL ISSUES VOL. 8) (forthcoming May 2006). See also, for a philosophical approach defending the relevance of empirical knowledge to Hart's conceptual project, Veronica Rodriguez-Blanco, *A Defence of Hart's Semantics As Nonambitious Conceptual Analysis*, 9 LEGAL THEORY 99 (2003).

67. Simon Roberts, *After Government? On Representing Law Without the State*, 68 MOD. L. REV. 1, 20–23 (2005). Roberts argues that pluralist conceptions of law beyond the state risk diluting the analytic purchase of the concept of law, depriving comparative social science of tools to make important distinctions between centralized, hierarchical, and governing-oriented normative systems, and genuinely negotiated normative orders. *Id.* at 20–24. Hence, in his view Hart's concept of law indeed has an empirical and ethnographic basis, albeit one that Hart himself failed to elaborate. While questions may be raised about the sharpness of the distinction drawn by Roberts— in particular in relation to negotiated aspects of state legal orders—his argument that particular

of all, Roger Cotterrell has argued for a mutually respectful and informed division of labor between sociological jurisprudence and analytic jurisprudence.[68] At the level of general jurisprudence, then, it seems that the promise of a productive dialogue glimpsed in the Preface to *The Concept of Law* is finally being realized. But can the debate about the relationship between philosophy and the social sciences in our understanding of law be so easily laid to rest?[69] In the following section, I turn from general to special jurisprudence and suggest that the idea of a straightforward division of labor may oversimplify the relevant issues.

II. Philosophy and the Social Sciences in Hart's Special Jurisprudence

"If it is to be effective as a guide to criticism and reconstruction, a normative model must build on . . . experience."[70]

Judged in terms of book sales and scholarly citations, *The Concept of Law* is Hart's most important work. In terms of influence on legal scholarship, his contributions to particular jurisprudence must be regarded as of virtually equal significance. From the insights in his inaugural lecture about the need to escape an arid definitional approach in favor of a view of legal entities as created by rules; through the linguistic philosophy-inspired early analysis of responsibility, rights, and, with Tony Honoré, causation; to the analysis of concepts such as intention and negligence, contributing to a normative theory of criminal justice in *Punishment and Responsibility,* Hart's work transformed the jurisprudential analysis of the building blocks of legal doctrine as surely as it revived general analytical jurisprudence. This work paved the way for a revived interest in the "philosophical foundations of the Common Law," and remains at the core of the now burgeoning fields of criminal law, contract, and tort theory in Britain, North America, Australia, and New Zealand.[71]

On the face of it, Hart's contributions to the analysis of the philosophical foundations of legal doctrines might be associated with a gradual move towards a greater concentration on normative issues in the latter part of his academic career: from *Definition and Theory*[72] and

---

conceptions of law can and must claim empirical support is persuasive and consistent with my argument in this paper.

68. *See* ROGER COTTERRELL, LAW'S COMMUNITY (1995). Cotterrell has also identified a "sociological drift" in Hart's legal theory. *See* ROGER COTTERRELL, THE POLITICS OF JURISPRUDENCE 94–96 (1989).

69. As doubted, for example, by Lewis Kornhauser. *See* Kornhauser, *supra* note 4.

70. PHILIP SELZNICK, THE MORAL COMMONWEALTH 360 (1992).

71. *See, e.g.,* JULES COLEMAN, RISKS AND WRONGS (1992); Alan Norrie, *'Simulacra of Morality'? Beyond the Ideal/Actual Antinomies of Criminal Justice, in* PHILOSOPHY AND THE CRIMINAL LAW 101, 125–26 (Antony Duff ed., 1998).

72. Hart, *supra* note 10.

Causation[73] to *Law, Liberty and Morality*,[74] *Punishment and Responsibility*[75] and the fine political philosophy essays of the *Essays in Jurisprudence and Philosophy*.[76] Of course, this is an over-simplification: Hart's early fascination with Plato and work on essays such as *The Ascription of Responsibility and Rights*[77] and *Are There any Natural Rights?*[78] demonstrate not only a close concern with normative issues but also the intimate relationship between the analytic and the normative in this aspect of his work, in which conceptual clarification and ground-clearing are motivated by moral concerns. Moreover, some of the most important essays in *Punishment and Responsibility*[79] were written relatively early in his career.[80]

These examples suggest that Hart always saw his normative and analytic work as feeding into each other: the analytic ground-clearing and clarity of the latter laying foundations for the former, but the former, perhaps, providing the motivation for the enterprise in the first place. There is a connection here with his early insistence in the Holmes lecture on the status of positivism as a moral project: being clear about important distinctions — the distinction for example between what the law requires us to do and what morality requires us to do—was itself of moral value to Herbert Hart. Reading his diaries, one has the sense that to him clarity was an almost overweening virtue, something that held the power of both an aesthetic and an ethic, and this is certainly one of the threads that bound his fascinating relationship with J.L. Austin.[81] Conversely, he continued to work on classic issues of analytical jurisprudence throughout his life, as is shown not only by several of the *Essays on Bentham*[82] and the posthumously published Postscript, but also by the evidence from his notebooks and the Oxford University lecture lists that he was writing and lecturing on both Kelsen and Hohfeld (work of which no trace has survived).[83]

Nonetheless, there is some truth in the superficial observation that Hart's work turned more to the normative in later years. Certainly, this had to do in part with psychological factors and moral dispositions, notably his

---

73. H.L.A. HART & A.M. HONORÉ, CAUSATION IN THE LAW (1959).

74. HART, *supra* note 32.

75. HART, *supra* note 11.

76. H.L.A. HART, ESSAYS IN JURISPRUDENCE AND PHILOSPHY (1983).

77. H.L.A. Hart, *The Ascription of Responsibilities and Rights*, 49 PROC. ARISTOTELIAN SOC'Y 171 (1949).

78. H.L.A. Hart, *Are There Any Natural Rights?*, 64 PHIL. REV. 175 (1955).

79. HART, *supra* note 11.

80. The essays were originally published between 1958 and 1967, but Hart was working on drafts and delivering lectures that were early versions during his year at Harvard in 1956–57. LACEY, *supra* note 6, at 190–91.

81. *See* LACEY, *supra* note 6, at 132–48.

82. H.L.A. HART, ESSAYS ON BENTHAM: STUDIES IN JURISPRUDENCE AND POLITICAL THEORY (1982).

83. *See* LACEY, *supra* note 6, at 260.

strong sense of duty to engage in worthwhile work. Using his philosophical talents to make a case for the liberal values and principles in which he so strongly believed helped to provide what he saw as a necessary justification for an academic's abstraction from political life. But it had also to do with his increasing perplexity about how to respond to critics of his account of law's normativity in *The Concept of Law*, which favored a turn to a genre of work in which the normative and the analytic sit in more comfortable relation than they do in Hart's general jurisprudence. Even in *Causation*—the work of Hart's most touched by Austinian linguistic philosophy and steadfastly analytic in ambition—we see in Hart's emphasis on the centrality of voluntary human conduct to the legal attributions of causation the seeds of the liberal theory of agency and responsibility that dominates his normative criminal law theory. We also see the method, yet clearer in *Punishment and Responsibility*, of moving back and forth between linguistic usage and conceptual clarification. In the criminal law essays, the ambition to produce the most satisfactory possible account of the values immanent within the relevant social practices puts this aspect of Hart's work—as was reflected in Dworkin's review of *Punishment and Responsibility*[84]—much closer to the latter's approach to jurisprudence.

The turn to particular jurisprudence, with its increasing emphasis on moral issues, may therefore have offered Hart some respite from his perplexities about the concept of legal obligation and from what in his gloomier moments he feared might be the impasse in his general jurisprudence. But what of the other aspect of his dilemma: the relationship between the aspiration to theorize law as genuinely normative and the commitment to producing a "social fact" account? This dilemma, I want to suggest, is yet more acute in the context of particular than of general jurisprudence. For the tension between the "conventionalist" and the "essentialist" aspects of Hart's analysis is thrown into sharp relief by the method of moving back and forth between actual usage and philosophical refinement adopted in *Causation* and, to a somewhat lesser degree, in his criminal law theory essays. The whole burden of Hart's work here is premised on the idea that what is at issue is the analysis of concepts that are "live" in the sense that they form a part of existing, "realized" and "functioning," social (legal) institutions and practices. Yet, as in his general jurisprudence, the shape, texture, and history of those institutions are all but ignored. In Hart's general jurisprudence, the content of the "momentary legal system" of legal positivism—that is, all the rules of a system valid at any moment of time—can, other than in exceptional cases such as revolutionary situations, be identified independently of any reference to the "non-momentary legal system"—an entity subsisting over time and identified in terms of a complex and shifting combination of values and institutional

---

84. Ronald Dworkin, *Morality and the Law*, N.Y. REV. OF BOOKS, May 22, 1969, at 29.

arrangements.[85] Similarly, in his special jurisprudence, Hart assumes that the concepts of causation, responsibility, intention, or negligence can be analyzed independently of any consideration of their development within particular systems over time or their functions in relation to particular systems. In the next section, my goal is to question this assumption. I shall also suggest that an analysis of issues within Hart's special jurisprudence can give us a better sense of the relationship between jurisprudence and the social sciences than can a critique of the general theory of law in relation to which Hart himself floated the idea. This is because it can focus our attention on the criteria of answerability implied by the claim to produce a theory *of* legal concepts such as causation and responsibility.

III. Case Studies in Special Jurisprudence: Causation and Responsibility in Context

A. Causation[86]

Hart and Honoré's *Causation in the Law* is a monumental analysis of the idea of causation in criminal law, the law of torts, and the law of contract. Following Hart's exchanges with Herbert Wechsler at Harvard in 1956 and 1957, the book's argument was reconstructed in opposition to the influential school of thought that Wechsler represented and that Hart and Honoré call "causal minimalism."[87] Causal minimalism claims that there is no *sui generis* concept of causation deployed in law beyond the "factual" idea of causation as a *sine qua non*—as all the conditions but for which an event would not have happened or a consequence would not have occurred. Beyond this "but for" sense of causation, the minimalist claims, decisions about how to attribute causal liability are based on policy considerations such as efficiency or moral considerations such as fault.

As against this, Hart and Honoré insist that law operates with a distinctive notion of causation richer than that of "but for" causation. They argue, however, that most philosophical analyses of causation are inapposite to explain the legal uses of the term, because they focus on causation in the context of science, and hence seek to identify general laws of causation. This is a mistake, because no such invariant, general laws can govern the identification of causes in the essentially particularistic legal context. In law, causation is a many-faceted notion: it has to be traced not to one overarching principle but to many principles and subprinciples clustering around the

---

85. *See* JOSEPH RAZ, THE CONCEPT OF A LEGAL SYSTEM 34, 187 (2d ed. 1980) (1970) (defining "momentary legal systems" and distinguishing them from "(non-momentary) legal systems"); *see also* John Finnis, *Revolutions and the Continuity of Law*, *in* OXFORD ESSAYS IN JURISPRUDENCE (A.W.B. Simpson ed., 1973).

86. Much of the argument section is a revised and expanded version of the account sketched in my biography of Hart. LACEY, *supra* note 6, at 211.

87. *Id.* at 212; *see also id.* at 187–88.

centrally recognized bases for attributing causal responsibility. These central cases themselves connect with widespread, common sense understandings of causation reflected in linguistic usage. According to Hart and Honoré, voluntary human action is the centrally significant variable in the attribution of legal causal responsibility. The central case is that of action intentionally aimed towards a particular end that it produces, or done with foresight that that end will occur. Secondary but important cases are those in which a person provides an opportunity for a result to be created (for example, leaving a house unlocked with the result that a burglary occurs) and in which a person incites or assists another person to produce a certain effect (for example, persuading or helping another person to kill a third person). Where, however, another voluntary human act intervenes between one human action and a consequence—particularly if that second act is "abnormal" or unexpected or where another abnormal event such as an "act of god" like a storm or earthquake intervenes—the law will generally regard the causal chain as being "broken."

At the level of method, *Causation in the Law* represents a thoroughgoing application of the linguistic philosophical analysis to law. For Hart and Honoré's approach is to seek to unearth the principles underlying judges' use of causal language—itself often metaphorical, as in the familiar idea of a "chain of causation" being "broken"—and to explore the relationship between this judicial usage and more general, common sense understandings of causation embedded in linguistic usage in particular contexts. Hence they analyze hundreds of cases, drawing out common approaches to elicit general principles, and identifying a core meaning of causation that reaches across different contexts. *Causation in the Law* presents a spirited defense of the idea that causation in law is indeed a distinctive ground for the attribution of liability, and a persuasive critique of the causal minimalist position as collapsing questions of the ground of liability (causation) into questions about its scope or extent (policy factors affecting the extent of damages or the scope of the rule), and, in doing so, as blurring what they argue to be the proper division of labor between judge and jury, between law and fact.[88] This is, of course, itself a law-specific, institutional claim.

---

88. Morton White, persuaded by Herbert Wechsler to review the book for the influential Columbia Law Review, wrote to Hart in September 1960:

> This is just a fan note to express my great admiration for Causation in the Law. It is a splendid piece of work which I find myself in agreement with whenever my ignorance of the law does not prevent me from following the argument.... I hope you will not be too disappointed by your failure to get a review from a lawyer in so important a legal journal, but there may be some compensation in the fact that your philosophical views may receive more accurate exposition than a judge or a law professor might be likely to give them.

LACEY, *supra* note 6, at 213–14. Hart's reply reveals the extent to which he still regarded himself as a philosopher and the judgment of his philosophical peers as the true measure of his achievements:

Yet, *Causation* marks the limits as well as the strengths of the Austinian version of linguistic philosophy, and presents a significant example of the differences between the Oxford school and the genre of linguistic philosophy being developed in Cambridge by Ludwig Wittgenstein. The two shared a distrust of metaphysics and were agreed on the Wittgensteinian precept, "don't look for the meaning, look to the use." But their interpretation of this injunction differed markedly. The difference was not merely the Oxford School's stylistic preference for precision and simplicity, though this certainly contrasted sharply with Wittgenstein's elliptical, oblique approach in the *Philosophical Investigations*.[89] It was also a substantive difference of understanding about how use and meaning are connected, and about the ways we can use, in Austin's words, "a sharpened awareness of words to sharpen our perception of, though not as the final arbiter of, the phenomena."[90] Although this formulation was qualified—language is "not the final arbiter"—the Oxford School's assumptions about the power of an analysis of language to contribute to our understanding of the world was significantly less cautious than the approach prevailing at Cambridge.

The relationship between language and meaning was, for neither School, a matter of metaphysics; nor did either School adhere to the view that words in some sense reflect fixed conceptual truths. Rather, the fluidities of usage were taken to mark important practical distinctions, and the claim was that in clarifying these, we come to a better understanding of phenomena. But Wittgenstein and the Oxford philosophers differed in their response to what is known as the "paradox of analysis": the fact that if language speaks for itself, it is not clear that philosophical analysis is either necessary or capable of being applied to linguistic usage without doing violence to its meaning. For philosophical analysis is itself a distinctive form of usage. How, then, can linguistic usage criticize the incoherence of the linguistic practice that it takes as its material? Here we confront an issue at the core of "philosophical foundations" scholarship: when we claim that our account is an account *of* a concept or phenomenon that has a "real" social existence, what, precisely, are the criteria of accountability involved? How many aspects of the phenomenon—appeals to "causation" in legal contexts

---

I was delighted to get your letter and very happy that you like our book. It is wonderfully good of you to spend your time and energies reviewing it. You are of course right: the lawyers won't understand the analytical part until they are shown by someone who does. There have been 2 or 3 quite appreciative reviews here but only one by a lawyer. (It seems to sell quite well in spite of its price and length). Really I can't say how pleased we are that *you are to review it and I much prefer* it to a legal review.

Id.

89. LUDWIG WITTGENSTEIN, PHILOSOPHICAL INVESTIGATIONS (1953). First published in English in a translation by Elizabeth Anscombe in 1953, *Philosophical Investigations* had certainly come to Hart's attention by the time he was working on *Causation*. LACEY, *supra* note 6, at 215.

90. HART, *supra* note 1, at v (paraphrasing J.L. AUSTIN, PHILOSOPHICAL PAPERS 130 (J.O. Urmson & G.J. Warnock eds., 3rd ed. 1979)).

in this instance—are we allowed to jettison as mistaken or confused? How, in other words, do we square the normative/conceptual clarification aspect of the philosophical enterprise with its positive aspect? Hart and Honoré grappled with this problem at several points in *Causation*. One spectacular example is their departure from the general tenet of looking to usage to discern significance in their scorching critique of lawyers' appeal to the concept of "active force," which they castigated as "obfuscating" rather than as a helpful way of distinguishing among "but for" causes.[91]

More generally, there are discernable differences between the Wittgensteinian and the Austinian approaches in Hart and Honoré's attitude toward the legal "contexts," without appreciation of which, they argue, it is impossible to grasp the distinctive shape of the concept of causation in law. *Causation* is about "causation talk" in particular contexts rather than "causation," understood as a metaphysical concept. Its method, then, assumes the answerability of philosophical analysis to institutional context.[92] The book's central argument is that a focus on judicial language can elucidate discrete principles of causation that are conceptually distinct from the broader patterns of attribution. Causation, it is argued, is an autonomous condition of attribution, not to be collapsed with policy factors like economic impact, distribution of loss, and implications for the parties' incentives, which often restrict the ambit of attributions of responsibility. Three important sub-claims include: (1) legal usage of causal terms is multiple, generating a "family" of interrelated causal concepts, rather than a single principle; (2) this variety of legal notions of cause is in turn related to features of the legal context, particularly to the need to provide causal accounts of particular events (i.e., cases); and (3) for this reason, scientific concepts of cause, which focus on generalizations, are of no use to lawyers. Hart and Honoré argue that moral and historical notions of cause are more like legal notions than scientific notions. Because philosophers have focused

---

91. It seems likely that there was some difference between the two authors in relation to this tension between their assumption that there is a "core notion of causation" and their idea that the context in which causal concepts are used makes all the difference to the meaning of causal terms. Honoré's approach appears to have been less wholehearted in its espousal of linguistic philosophy and more Kantian: a view that would have inclined him to the idea of a contextually invariant core to causation. During one discussion between the two, Hart described Honoré's view as *naturrechtlich*, i.e., inspired by a natural law approach. LACEY, *supra* note 6, at 210. (Honoré resisted the suggestion.) Another key difference would have been Honoré's argument for "outcome responsibility"—the idea that we are truly responsible for the outcomes of our actions even when they are "accidental" in the sense that we could not have done otherwise than we did. Honoré's argument is that the results of our actions become a part of our sense of identity. Tony Honoré, *Responsibility and Luck: The Moral Basis of Strict Liability*, in RESPONSIBILITY AND FAULT 14 (1988). This would have been anathema to Hart, who defended the view that we are responsible only for the things that we choose to do, in the sense that we had a fair opportunity to do otherwise. Despite its obvious relevance to legal causation, it is therefore not surprising that the idea of outcome responsibility does not appear in *Causation*.

92. *Cf.* Nancy Cartwright, *From Causation to Explanation and Back*, in THE FUTURE FOR PHILOSOPHY 230 (Brian Leiter ed., 2004).

on scientific theories, they have not contributed substantially to moral, historical, or legal understandings of causation.

These sub-claims help illuminate the issues that the "descriptive sociology/analytical jurisprudence" axis raises for particular jurisprudence. Hart's and Honoré's claim that the specific context in which causal statements are made is relevant to their meaning or force makes this clear. And this claim takes a variety of forms. First, causal explanation is not the same as causal attribution. The explanatory statement that a fire came about through the combination of naked flame, combustible material, and oxygen in the air employs a notion of cause different from the attributive statement that the person holding the match caused the fire. Secondly, the point of view from which a statement is made will affect the causal account given. For example, a political activist might attribute a drought to a governmental failure to address environmental concerns, while a meteorologist might attribute it to weather. Thirdly, the detailed factual context will affect the causal account given. While we normally would not cite the presence of oxygen in the air as a causal factor in a fire, we would do so if the fire occurred in a factory where the productive process was such that oxygen had to be specifically excluded. Finally, the disciplinary context in which a causal statement is made will affect its meaning. Causation in law is not the same as causation in morals, and it is very different from causation in science. In each of these examples, the claim that context makes a difference invokes a different sense of the word "context": first, as conceptual context; second, as the interest or point of view of speaker; third, as the discipline within which causal statement is made; and fourth, as the factual context within which causal statement is made. And, as Hart and Honoré sometimes note, these four different contextual factors will often interact. For example, in the disciplinary context of medicine, it will make a difference whether a doctor is making a diagnosis or prescribing a course of treatment.

But, having identified these various nuances within the central argument that context makes all the difference to the way in which causal language is used and causal concepts developed, how, and how far, do Hart and Honoré push this claim? The main description that they offer of what is distinctive about the legal context is that it is concerned—unlike science—with particulars. This is hardly a rich characterization because, for one thing, it does not serve to distinguish law from morality. Beyond this, Hart and Honoré simply inundate us with a huge amount of actual linguistic data. This data is almost exclusively drawn from appellate case law. The reader is not given a systematic analysis of the institutional, practical, professional, or social context in which that legal language was used. In Wittgenstein's terms, there is no exploration of the social practices or forms of life within which the causal language game is embedded. Hart and Honoré do not, for example, explore the nature of the judicial role. And despite the inclusion of data from the United Kingdom, the United States, and Germany, there is little discussion of how differing judicial roles or procedural systems in those countries might affect the development of legal concepts.[93] There is therefore no sense in which the book could claim to give a comparative analysis. Nor does *Causation* build up any systematic picture of the significance to be accorded to which of the areas of the common law causation talk is embedded in: the very different social roles of contract, crime, and torts are relatively faintly sketched, and no developed typology is attempted. Although Hart is often thought of as having had an institutional or social theory of law, *Causation*'s exploration of that institutional framework is relatively thin. Law is analyzed as a body of doctrine rather than as a social practice, and "usage" is understood as the language that makes up the doctrines.

Hart's and Honoré's Austinian approach contrasts significantly with the approach that might be drawn from Wittgenstein's *Philosophical Investigations*.[94] Wittgenstein circled—in an elliptical style that alienated many analytical philosophers—around a problem that Hart himself never quite confronted. The problem was the precise nature of the relationship not just between language and behavior, but more specifically between linguistic usage and its context. In contrast with Hart and Honoré's limited conception of context, Wittgenstein understood context to include a whole range of variables from the individual mind through to social institutions and practices—teaching, game-playing, customs, experience. This comparison between Wittgensteinian and Austinian approaches to linguistic philosophy does not mean that Wittgenstein himself was any more attentive to social context than Austin, or Hart and Honoré. Despite his injunctions about the limits of philosophy, Wittgenstein was, after all, a philosopher, and his method was analytic rather than empirical. His own reaction to these insights was to adopt a famously defeatist view of the power of philosophy, rather than to launch a case for the social sciences. The point is that a more socially contextualized approach is implied by, and could be constructed through, a supplementation of Wittgenstein's work, as could a more equal and intimate relationship between philosophy and other disciplines.

It is therefore legitimate to ask what kind of a book *Causation* would have been had it been written by a linguistic philosopher inspired more by Wittgenstein than by Austin. I would argue that we could expect it to have explored questions such as (1) the institutional factors that restrict the extent to which judges will appeal to pragmatic or policy arguments, (2) their sensitivity to the need to legitimate their decisions, and (3) their system-specific understanding of their constitutional role. As an empirical matter,

---

93. This seems especially relevant to any analysis of the prominence of "causal minimalism" in American scholarship and judicial practice as compared, for example, to its appeal in Germany or France.

94. In making this point, I do not mean to imply that Wittgenstein's ideas had no impact on the argument of *Causation*. For example, as Tony Honoré has suggested to me in correspondence, the book's approach is significantly more systematic than that which Austin himself might have been expected to take.

these institutional factors not only shape the appeal to policy in causation cases but also the development of causal concepts.

The appeal to language does indeed, as Hart and Honoré saw, bring contextual factors into play. But it is far from clear that they were justified in confining their attention to language in the sense of the meaning to be elicited from usage, analyzed from the page, rather than moving on to think about the way in which the contexts of usage—normative, institutional, political, and so on—shape the development of the meaning as well as the force of statements. Hart and Honoré reduced linguistic usage to a body of doctrine rather than seeing it as a social practice that takes place within a context, the specific nature of which requires investigation because it inflects the relevant concepts. It is interesting to speculate on what difference it would have made to Hart's further work, and to *The Concept of Law* in particular, had he taken a broader, Wittgensteinian approach. Given Wittgenstein's emphasis on the embeddedness of language games within social practices and forms of life, it is likely that there would have been positive effects on the development of a genuinely social or institutional understanding of law. It is also equally interesting to consider the reasons that prevented Hart from pursuing this line. Certainly, an impatience with what he saw as Wittgenstein's scandalously obscure style of writing would have been one factor. A loyalty to Austin—and perhaps even a desire to please him—was probably another. But still another reason is more substantial: if fully pursued, the Wittgensteinian message—as Wittgenstein himself recognized—undermines the pretensions of philosophy as the "master-discipline" that illuminates our access to knowledge about the world. For once the notion of "context" is made broader, the inexorable conclusion is that illumination of legal practices lies not merely within an analysis of doctrinal language; it lies equally within an attempt to locate the analysis within some general account of the history and social role of the institutions and the power relations within which that usage takes place. In other words, a full acceptance of the implications of Wittgenstein's thought would have threatened Hart's idea of the philosophical boundaries of jurisprudence.

B. *Responsibility*

It is hardly an exaggeration to say that Hart's theory of responsibility,[95] as grounded in a set of cognitive and volitional capacities, along with its associated theory of the mens rea principle in criminal law,[96] forms the starting point for virtually all subsequent work in the field. Responsibility, in Hart's sense, guarantees the justice of criminal punishment by restricting punishment to those who had a fair opportunity to conform their behavior to

---

95. *See* H.L.A. HART, *supra* note 11.

96. Mens rea is "the state of mind that the prosecution, to secure a conviction, must prove that the defendant had when committing a crime." BRYAN A. GARNER, A DICTIONARY OF MODERN LEGAL USAGE 556 (2d ed. 1995).

the precepts of criminal law. Granted, his theory of punishment, with its theoretically disaggregated general justifying aim and principles of distribution, cannot provide any effective normative guidance on when, if ever (as Hart contemplated), the "compromise" of prima facie unjust "strict" liability would be justified by compensating utilitarian aims.[97] But within the confines of the presumption of a requirement of mens rea, his account of responsibility provides both a remarkably accurate fit with late Twentieth Century Anglo-American criminal law, and a persuasive rationalization for the contribution of proof of responsibility to the legitimacy of the criminal sanction.

Yet in relation to his theory of criminal responsibility, as much as in relation to his and Honoré's work on causation, the project encounters some methodological complications that stem once again from Hart's ambivalence about the extent to which his account should be grounded in an understanding of the wider practice within which appeals to responsibility are embedded. Unlike *Causation, Punishment and Responsibility* draws only sparingly on actual legal materials. But the message is clearly that the account of capacity-based responsibility is the best account of responsibility to be drawn from criminal law. Yet Hart is not much interested in the institutional features of criminal law that underpin the emergence of this notion of responsibility: once elicited, "responsibility" is implicitly invested with an objective or even metaphysical status that is at odds with his professedly linguistic and socially grounded method.

To see the intimate links between the development of legal concepts and their institutional basis, however, we have only to engage in some fairly basic historical or comparative research. To take a historical example, the modern, agency-based notion of capacity–responsibility which Hart articulates finds strong voice in various forms within Enlightenment political and moral philosophy from the late seventeenth century onwards. Yet it finds almost no expression in even the most systematic accounts of the common law until much later.[98] In Blackstone's *Commentaries*, for example, there is virtually no "general part" of the criminal law elaborating principles of responsibility. Yet more significantly, even in J.F. Stephen's late nineteenth-century draft code,[99] the articulation of general conditions of liability, including principles of responsibility and "excusing conditions," is vestigial. Yet only seventy years later, Glanville Williams produced a treatise of several hundred pages on "the general part" of criminal law,[100]

---

97. For further discussion, see NICOLA LACEY, STATE PUNISHMENT 46–56 (1988).

98. For a more detailed discussion, see Nicola Lacey, *In Search of the Responsible Subject of Criminal Law*, 64 MOD. L. REV. 350–71 (2001), and Nicola Lacey, *Responsibility and Modernity in Criminal Law*, 9 J. POL. PHIL. 249 (2001).

99. J.F. STEPHEN, A DIGEST OF THE CRIMINAL LAW (1883).

100. GLANVILLE WILLIAMS, THE GENERAL PART OF CRIMINAL LAW (2d ed. 1981). I am grateful to Tony Smith for alerting me to the fact that Williams originally planned a four-volume

which had assumed such centrality that he never bothered to write the planned sequel on criminal law's "special part"—i.e., its offenses. The principle of responsibility as Hart understood it, that might have been thought to be central to criminal law doctrine at least since the Enlightenment, and that did form a key part of the modern codes of the continent of Europe from the late eighteenth century on, found its way into English criminal law doctrine only a hundred years later.

The explanation, as I have argued in detail elsewhere, has two dimensions. The argument proceeds from the hypothesis that the principle of responsibility plays two key roles in the current system of criminal law. First, it legitimates the state's imposition of criminalizing power, in the context of liberal expectations about individual freedom and the proper limits of state power. Second, once the precise conditions of responsibility are delineated in legal doctrines, it serves as a coordinating device, specifying the forms of knowledge or evidence that may be produced in the courtroom. This helps to explain the late emergence of doctrines of capacity responsibility in English criminal law. Looking first at the legitimating role of criminal responsibility, the argument is that the liberal, democratic, and humanist sentiments that necessitate an appeal to individual responsibility to legitimize criminal law were relatively weak in Britain at the end of the eighteenth century, except in relation to the most serious of crimes such as murder. In this context, as the legal historian John Langbein has argued, the criminal justice system operated with something closer to a presumption of guilt than a presumption of innocence.[101] To put it differently, the functional notion of responsibility in criminal law practice was closer to a notion of responsibility for character—those with bad reputations were much more likely to be prosecuted and almost certain to be convicted—than to a notion of responsibility as founded in an investigation of capacity in the sense of fair opportunity to conform to the law on this occasion. The law reform debates that produced the various Criminal Law Commissioners' Reports during the first part of the nineteenth century strongly reflect the legitimating appeal of modern ideas of capacity–responsibility among the elite,[102] but the remarkable fact is that criminal law itself managed perfectly well without articulating it. This is not, of course, to say that the notion of capacity responsibility was historically irrelevant to the practice of criminal law. For example, though there was no legal definition of insanity until the middle of the nineteenth century, juries were clearly acquitting or, from 1800 onward, awarding special verdicts to defendants who presented as insane, no doubt on

---

work, with additional volumes on offenses against property, persons, and the state. The success of the one volume as a self-standing work is, however, highly significant.

101. John H. Langbein, *Shaping the Eighteenth Century Criminal Trial: A View from the Ryder Sources*, 50 U. CHI. L. REV. 1 (1987); *see also* JOHN H. LANGBEIN, THE ORIGINS OF ADVERSARY CRIMINAL TRIAL (2003).

102. *See* K.J.M. SMITH, LAWYERS, LEGISLATORS AND THEORISTS: DEVELOPMENTS IN ENGLISH CRIMINAL JURISPRUDENCE 1800–1957 (1998).

the basis of their incapacity. But—and here is the problem for Hart's method—it cannot thereby be claimed that there is a fully formed concept of responsibility at work in criminal *law* understood in strictly positivist terms. A legal doctrine of responsibility developed only gradually, spurred on by a perceived legitimation deficit that became increasingly acute as, among other things, democratic sentiments and practices spread.

Of equal relevance to the sociotheoretic dimension of special jurisprudence is the coordination aspect of the principle of responsibility in criminal law. Just as the early nineteenth century English common law had no pressing legitimation need for an across-the-board requirement of proof of mens rea, neither did it have an institutional structure that could have managed such proof. The idea of human capacity as the proper and feasible object of proof in a courtroom, though it came more quickly in civil than in criminal law, depended on a complex infrastructure that was still in its infancy. At a minimum, this included (1) a systematic law of evidence; (2) regular representation by lawyers capable of presenting and developing doctrinal arguments; (3) law reporting that allowed emerging doctrines to be communicated across courts; and (4) a system of appeals allowing the interpretation of emerging doctrines to be challenged, tested, and clarified. Of these minimum institutional conditions, only the second was in place by 1850.[103] Law reporting developed interstitially, the law of criminal evidence was not put on a statutory footing until 1898, and a system of criminal appeals was not in place until 1907.[104] Furthermore, these developments in legal institutions were themselves embedded in, and premised on, a cluster of broader social, economic, and political developments. Principal among these developments were industrialization and urbanization, which prompted both a decline in the reliability of local and informal structures of control and information-gathering and gave a new impetus to the state's interest in crime control; changes in political and cultural sentiments which underpinned increasing revulsion against the arbitrary and bloody features of the "ancien regime" in criminal justice; the increasing centralization and administrative competence and ambition of the state.

These factors, and many others, fundamentally changed the nature of criminal law, at once underlining the need for a clearly articulated notion of individual responsibility and pushing the borders of criminal liability to encompass new areas in which the costs of proof of responsibility were seen as disproportionate to the regulatory functions that criminal law was being asked to perform. From the mid-nineteenth century on, English criminal law, unlike the criminal law of many of its European neighbors, had two very different features that were often in tension with one another. First, it

---

103. A general right to legal representation was introduced in 1836.

104. For a detailed discussion see Lacey, *Responsibility and Modernity in Criminal Law*, *supra* note 98, and LANGBEIN, *supra* note 101..

continued to be regarded as a quasi-moral system, embodying widely shared social norms thought to be of key importance. Second, it came to be used by government, and to some extent regarded by citizens, as a relatively neutral, instrumental tool of social regulation.[105] The shifting balance between these two features of criminal law must be central to any interpretation of doctrines of criminal responsibility.

Someone anxious to defend Hart's approach to theorizing criminal responsibility will retort that none of this in any way threatens either the normative credentials of his account or its applicability to late twentieth century English criminal law. The first point may be conceded, though it seems obvious that the normative recommendations of particular principles such as responsibility are to some degree founded in social facts—facts not only about human beings but also about the shape of the social world—and vary in their relative strength along with those founding conditions. But even a full concession does not rescue Hart's account from the need to attend to the broader social and institutional context that shapes the significance of doctrines of responsibility in criminal law. His account purports to be not merely normative, but also to have explanatory power. Historical, comparative, or socio-legal understandings of the role of responsibility in criminal law that affect our interpretation of its shape and relative importance in criminal law are therefore factors that his account cannot ignore.[106] For they help us to understand, explain, and even predict the ways in which judges and legal decision-makers interpret and apply the concept. As Hart's enterprise in special jurisprudence implicitly concedes, one does not have to be a Legal Realist or deny the distinctively normative, or action-guiding quality of law to take the view that legal theory has this sort of explanatory aspect.

The argument for a more socially grounded jurisprudential analysis of responsibility can be related back to Hart's general jurisprudence, particularly to his relatively parsimonious conception of law as a system of more or less formally articulated rules. As Dworkin famously discussed in relation to Hart's theory of adjudication, Hart showed little interest in the operation of the discretion that he saw as characterizing "hard cases."[107] *A fortiori*, the operation of the range of discretionary powers that shape factors such as which cases come to court and how they are prosecuted stood well

---

105. Think, for example, of the role of criminal law in regulating public health or safety both directly and indirectly by acting as a backup to licensing provisions. On the origins of the summary jurisdiction and strict liability, see LINDSAY FARMER, CRIMINAL LAW, TRADITION AND LEGAL ORDER 74–82 (1997).

106. The same, of course, is true of other concepts such as punishment. For an account that weaves historical and philosophical analysis together, see John Gardner, *Crime in Proportion and in Perspective*, in FUNDAMENTALS OF SENTENCING THEORY 31–52 (Andrew Ashworth & Martin Wasik eds., 1998).

107. Ronald Dworkin, *Hard Cases*, 88 HARV. L. REV. 1057 (1975). *See generally* DWORKIN, *supra* note 44.

beyond his delineated terrain. Yet there are powerful reasons for thinking that the full significance of legal concepts such as responsibility can only be understood in light of precisely these surrounding forms of power and decision-making, that contribute significantly to the balance criminal law strikes at any particular time between its competing quasi-moral and regulatory aspects. This point may be illustrated by two examples.

First, even within the terrain of criminal law in which a relatively robust responsibility or *mens rea* requirement exists—such as the law of murder or theft—other features of legal doctrine (notably the scope of defenses), as well as the typically rather limited time frame in which an offense is situated and the constraints rules of evidence place on the kinds of information that may be presented to the court—may compromise the investigation of individual responsibility in a full sense.[108] To take a recent and controversial example, the tendency to frame domestic violence prosecutions in relation to single incidents marginalizes the relevance of the experience of background factors such as long-term domestic abuse to the volitional dimension of responsibility, resulting in a finding that victims of such abuse are fully responsible for an ultimate attack on their abuser.[109] In several jurisdictions, this situation has recently been reversed.[110] Putting aside the merits of this change in the law of provocation and self-defense, and the very limited extent to which criminal defenses incorporate factors in a defendant's background that might be thought to compromise their cognitive or volitional capacities, the legal realization of responsibility depends not merely on the articulation of a liability rule but on a cluster of other assumptions and discretionary powers that must be understood if the meaning and significance of responsibility in criminal law is to be appreciated.

The second, converse example has to do with strict liability offenses. These, of course, are the most controversial features of criminal law from the point of view of a normative theory of responsibility. Yet, intriguingly, a welter of empirical evidence suggests that the actual prosecution of these offenses is overwhelmingly focused on people or organizations whom the prosecuting authority views as responsible in something like the capacity sense.[111] Although this does not necessarily weaken the case for a

---

108. On the relevance of time frames for interpreting criminal law, see Mark Kelman, *Interpretive Construction in the Substantive Criminal Law*, 33 STAN. L. REV. 591 (1981).
109. *See* John Gardner & Timothy Macklem, *Compassion Without Respect? Nine Fallacies in* R v Smith, 2001 CRIM. L. REV. 623; Donald Nicolson & Rohit Sanghvi, *Battered Women and Provocation: The Implications of* R. v Ahluwalia, 1993 CRIM. L. REV. 728.
110. See, for example, in relation to England and Wales, R v. Smith, (2000) 4 All E.R. 289 (H.L.). For further discussion, see NICOLA LACEY, CELIA WELLS & OLIVER QUICK, RECONSTRUCTING CRIMINAL LAW 768–801 (3d ed. 2003).
111. KEITH HAWKINS, ENVIRONMENT AND ENFORCEMENT: REGULATION AND THE SOCIAL DEFINITION OF POLLUTION (1984); LACEY ET AL., *supra* note 110, at 637–58; W.G. Carson, *White-Collar Crime and the Enforcement of Factory Legislation*, 10 BRIT. J. CRIMINOLOGY 383 (1970).

responsibility requirement in the law itself,[112] legal theorists should be interested in the ways in which broad social attitudes and power relations conduce to or against the realization of ideas and ideals of responsibility in the enforcement as much as in the letter of criminal law. This militates in favor of a broader view of law than that adopted in Hart's descriptive jurisprudence.

These arguments about the relevance of the social bases for legal ideas such as responsibility to jurisprudence have decisive implications for the normative aspect of special jurisprudence. For if conceptual ideas have institutional and other conditions of existence—if, for example, a notion of capacity responsibility can only be realized in criminal law on the basis of certain institutional developments and in the context of a cluster of social and cultural conditions—this has clear implications for the pursuit of our normative project. To the extent that the ambition of special jurisprudence is to affirm, and not merely to delineate, certain key legal concepts, we must surely be interested in the conditions that facilitate—or hamper—their institutional realization. Yet Hart's version of special jurisprudence rests at the abstract level of institutional structures and pays little attention to what Lewis Kornhauser has called "realized institutions" inhabited by particular individuals, and none whatsoever to "functioning institutions" situated and operating in a specified social and physical environment.[113] To the extent that such "functioning institutions" are a necessary condition for the realization of our concepts, this is a deficit in Hart's theory. This point is further illustrated by the third case study of corporate criminal responsibility.

C. Corporate Criminal Responsibility: The Social and Institutional Basis[114]

In both jurisprudential scholarship and legal doctrine, a human individual is generally assumed to be the subject of modern systems of criminal law in and beyond the common law world. The elaborated notions of conduct and responsibility, as suggested by the Latin tags *actus reus* and *mens rea*, have been worked out in relation to assumptions about individual human beings, their agency and responsibility, the scope and limits of their capacities for voluntary conduct, and in relation to a moral theory that follows from these basic assumptions about human beings. Much the same is true of the subject of criminology. Though criminologists have, since the publication of Sutherland's pioneering work,[115] typically taken a greater interest in corporate crime than have academic criminal lawyers, the

---

112. The prosecutorial discretion that strict liability offenses expand may be subject to various forms of abuse.

113. KORNHAUSER, *supra* note 4, at 362–64.

114. For a more detailed discussion of the issues discussed in this section, see Nicola Lacey, PHILOSOPHICAL FOUNDATIONS OF THE COMMON LAW: *Social Not Metaphysical, in* OXFORD ESSAYS IN JURISPRUDENCE 17 (Jeremy Horder ed., 2000).

115. EDWIN H. SUTHERLAND, WHITE COLLAR CRIME (1949).

framework within which they have done so—that of "white collar crime"—implicitly sets up the individual offender as the primary focus of the analysis. Criminology moves between what might be called organizational and occupational conceptions of corporate crime, and, in both Sutherland's work and subsequent research, it is the occupational conception that has dominated.[116] This occupational focus is usually on managers, and it is reflected in, for example, the nature of the public debate on the notorious cases of corporate financial wrongdoing in the United States and Britain in recent years. However, this implicit methodological individualism seems to have been gradually displaced in relation to fatal disasters such as the sinking of the Herald of Free Enterprise and a number of rail crashes, in which a discourse more closely focused on the corporation as a collectivite entity with its own legal and moral identity, appears to be emerging.[117]

However, the paradigmatic subject of criminal law remains the individual human being. This means that in both doctrinal scholarship and legal theory, the debate about the liability of corporations is marked by a sustained use of metaphors, contrasts, and images that depend upon the analogies and disanalogies between corporate and human persons. In the criminal law sphere, sometimes the analogies of action, conduct, agency, and effects in the world are emphasized so as to argue in favor of liability.[118] At other times, the disanalogies of lack of soul, mind, intentions, moral capacity, and physical body are emphasized so as to argue against liability, or in favor of a distinct regulatory scheme.[119]

My focus here is an assumption underlying both the analogies and disanalogies, and bearing on the nature of our normative and analytic projects within special jurisprudence. This is the idea that the legal personality of individual human persons is real, or, rather, not fictitious in a sense that corporate personality is. Does this assume that at least some legal concepts reflect invariable logical or moral truths about the world? This view is one of the main targets of Hart's constructionist argument about legal concepts in his "Definition and Theory."[120] Though Hart's argument makes it clear that even if some legal concepts apparently have more straightforward "counterparts in the world of fact" than others, this is of, at most, indirect relevance to their constitution as legal persons. Legal

---

116. *See* JOHN HAGAN, CRIME AND DISREPUTE (1994).

117. *See* CELIA WELLS, CORPORATIONS AND CRIMINAL RESPONSIBILITY (2d ed. 2001).

118. *See, e.g.*, Pamela H. Bucy, *Corporate Ethos: A Standard for Imposing Corporate Criminal Liability*, 75 MINN. L. REV. 1095 (1991); C.V. Clarkson, *Kicking Corporate Bodies and Damning Their Souls*, 59 MOD. L. REV. 557 (1996).

119. *See, e.g.*, Peter Arenella, *Convicting the Morally Blameless: Reassessing the Relationship Between Legal and Moral Responsibility*, 39 UCLA L. REV. 1511 (1992); G.R. Sullivan, *The Attribution of Culpability to Limited Companies*, 55 CAMBRIDGE L. J. 515 (1996).

120. This is an argument that is, significantly, almost exactly reproduced in Lord Hoffmann's conception of the company as "rules," and of rules as the distinctively legal mode of existence, in the *Meridian Global Funds* case. Meridian Global Funds Management Asia Ltd. v. Securities Comm'n, (1995) All E.R. 918 (P.C.).

personality is not descriptive in a simple sense; it makes reference to the conditions under which it is true to say that some social phenomenon—human, corporate, or other—may be held liable in law.[121] Few legal theorists today would admit to holding the position taken by Michael Moore, who asserts that legal concepts are built of a bedrock of natural kinds that, for the purposes of criminal responsibility, include human beings and exclude corporations.[122]

In analyzing the philosophical foundations of corporate legal personality, Hart therefore stepped neatly around *metaphysical* questions about the reality of corporate entities. But can such an analysis avoid addressing *social* questions about the operation of, and attitudes towards, corporate bodies? In emphasizing the construction of corporate legal personality by analogy with individual human personality, Hart sometimes appears to have assumed that the project of seeking a "counterpart in the world of fact" is *more* misconceived for corporations than for humans as subjects of criminal law. And there is an important sense in which this is true. But it is true for historical, and therefore contingent, reasons: it is a persuasive *interpretation of modern criminal law* because English criminal law categories have been historically constructed primarily with human beings and with moral ideas about human responsibility in mind. The "general principles of criminal law" respond to a particular legitimacy problem in liberal polities: the justification of state punishment of individuals. Yet, as we saw in relation to his general analysis of responsibility, Hart shows little interest in the relationship between those legal conceptions and the social, moral, or economic environment in which they have developed. Hence the implication often appears analytic rather than interpretive. This part of "Definition and Theory" therefore provides a good illustration of his inclination towards the analytical jurisprudence as opposed to descriptively sociological pole of his dual method. Hart's focus is law's normative conception of the person rather than the social developments that provide the environment (and often impetus) for that legal conception, and he assumes that the two are quite separate. Indeed, there are moments when Hart comes close to the logical or metaphysical view about corporations that it is his purpose to reject. Probably the most vivid example

---

121. Hart, *supra* note 10 at 23. See also Dworkin's robustly antimetaphysical approach to group personification in LAW'S EMPIRE. DWORKIN, *supra* note 3, at 168–75 (recognizing the corporation as having a form of moral agency while asserting that it is a creature of the practices of thought and language in which it figures rather than having any independent metaphysical existence).

122. MICHAEL S. MOORE, PLACING BLAME 18–23, 623 (1997); *see also* JOHN FINNIS, *The Priority of Persons*, *in* OXFORD ESSAYS IN JURISPRUDENCE 1 (Jeremy Horder ed., 2000).

is his reference to "corporate spirit" as a "secret of success and not a criterion of identity."[123]

The assumption that individual human beings are the obvious or typical subjects of criminal law must be understood, then, as historically specific and as grounded in particular social practices. Moreoever, it must be so understood if it is to be consistent with Hart's approach towards corporate responsibility. It is tied up with an interpretation of criminal law as a social practice geared to making judgments about blame, responsibility, and wrongdoing—judgments that are closely articulated with the humanist discourse of moral agency. Within this vision of criminal law, the imposition of corporate liability involves a form of anthropomorphism. But, from a social science point of view, this is only one aspect of the Nineteenth and Twentieth Century criminal law. The criminal law's meaning as a system of quasi-moral judgments exists alongside its status as a regulatory or even administrative system, and the relationship between these two aspects of criminal law is arguably one of the most important keys to understanding its operation and development.[124] In today's world, a criminal law that lacks a conception of corporate responsibility has gradually become unacceptable, and the longstanding recognition of corporate liability for regulatory crimes of strict liability is being overtaken by a stronger conception of corporations' quasi-moral responsibility for "real crime." Though the corporation is a legal creation, it has a social being, and it is no surprise that the genesis of the corporation as a significant social actor is gradually producing a legal framework adequate to explicating the role of corporations in the fields in which they are influential. These fields include various forms of economic production; contracting; harmful practices; and, perhaps, wrongdoing.

If we are interested in the philosophical foundations of law and of other social institutions, we must be concerned with the structure and dynamics of how these social institutions operate and hence (potentially) with literature in political science, sociology, and economics, as well as with the more obviously relevant interdisciplinary literature on corporate governance. And if we agree with Hart that attributions of criminal liability are a legal or political matter and not a matter of logic, we should not follow him in holding that practices or conceptions of attribution can be analyzed without adverting either to the circumstances in which questions about holding collectivities socially responsible are raised or to details about the actual workings of the relevant collectivities. This is because it is a mistake to think that law can afford to ignore insights into the operation of the institutions

---

123. HART, *supra* note 10, at 46. In fact, law reform proposals in several jurisdictions have since adopted something close to corporate spirit as a central element in the construction of corporate criminal liability.

124. LACEY, WELLS & QUICK, *supra* note 110; Nicola Lacey, *Contingency, Coherence and Conceptualism*, in PHILOSOPHY AND THE CRIMINAL LAW: PRINCIPLE AND CRITIQUE (R.A. Duff ed., 1998); *see also* LINDSAY FARMER, CRIMINAL LAW, TRADITION AND LEGAL ORDER (1997) (tracing the development of regulatory criminal laws in the nineteenth century).

whose practices it seeks to shape, or that the structure of those practices places no constraints on the development of adequate legal policy. Both policy and theory are, in short, answerable to context. A radical separation between the analytic and the contextual will, therefore, occlude our understanding of law. If this is persuasive, a further set of questions moves on to the agenda of criminal law theory: questions about how criminal law should respond to the fact that corporations are organized in different ways and operate in very different social, institutional, and economic contexts.[125]

Finally, although a proper consideration is beyond the scope of this paper, I want to raise a further theoretical issue regarding corporate criminal responsibility and bearing on the necessity of grounding our understanding of legal concepts in the institutional context and social practices in which they are embedded. This is what might be called a comparative question, in both a cultural and a historical sense. In thinking about the available regulatory possibilities and the appropriateness of attributing criminal responsibility, we are constrained, just as we are in relation to criminal responsibility, by the differing institutional structure of corporations and by the differing socio-economic and political environments in which corporations operate. For example, basic questions such as the employment tenure of corporate managers, the incentives structuring corporate careers, the accountability structure within the corporation, and the attitude toward profits and financing will all affect regulatory possibilities.[126] This sort of comparative analysis is often ignored in criminal law theory. In the United Kingdom there has been a baffling reluctance to investigate the relevance of an intriguing literature in corporate governance about the impact of changes in corporate structures for

---

125. For example, is the variation in corporate structure and agency significantly greater than that of human agency, and, if so, what does this imply for criminal law's aspiration to embody general and universally applicable standards and methods of attribution? For an illuminating discussion of the possibility of tailoring criminal justice to corporate structure and compliance record, see John Braithwaite & Brent Fisse, *Varieties of Responsibility and Organizational Crime*, 7 LAW & POL'Y 315 (1985). *See also* BRENT FISSE & JOHN BRAITHWAITE, CORPORATIONS, CRIME AND ACCOUNTABILITY (1993).

126. *See, e.g.*, John Kay & Aubrey Silberston, *Corporate Governance*, NAT. INST. ECON. REV. 84 (1995); Paul Windolf & Jürgen Beyer, *Co-operative Capitalism: Corporate Networks in Germany and Britain*, 47 BRIT. J. SOC. 205 (1996). For a useful general assessment of the relevance of theoretical models in the social sciences for socio-legal studies, see Julia Black, *New Institutionalism and Naturalism in Socio-legal Analysis: Institutionalist Approaches to Regulatory Decision Making*, 19 LAW & POL'Y 51 (1997). The interaction between possibilities for criminal liability and corporate structure has been most effectively addressed in the work of John Braithwaite and Brent Fisse. *See* FISSE & BRAITHWAITE, *supra* note 125; Brent Fisse & John Braithwaite, *The Allocation of Responsibility for Corporate Crime: Individualism, Collectivism and Accountability*, 11 SYDNEY L. REV. 468 (1988); *see also* MARK BOVENS, THE QUEST FOR RESPONSIBILITY: ACCOUNTABILITY AND CITIZENSHIP IN COMPLEX ORGANISATIONS (1998); JAMES S. COLEMAN, POWER AND THE STRUCTURE OF SOCIETY (1974); JOSEPH MCCAHERY, CORPORATE CONTROL AND ACCOUNTABILITY: CHANGING STRUCTURES AND THE DYNAMICS OF REGULATION (Sol Picciotto & Colin D. Scott eds., 1993). On one specific regulatory difficulty flowing from the development of complex corporate networks made up of legally separate collectivities, see Hugh Collins, *The Ascription of Legal Responsibility to Groups in Complex Patterns of Economic Integration*, 53 MOD. L. REV. 731 (1990).

practices of legal attribution. This is perhaps because it is assumed that the attribution of criminal responsibility is, at its core, a non-consequentialist normative question, independent of the contingencies of particular corporate arrangements.[127] Yet the social facts about corporate structure are important to the moral, as much as the practical, appropriateness of imposing criminal liability for reasons that are analogous to the relevance of empirical understandings about human agency and psychology to individual criminal responsibility. Whatever the dimensions of our moral aspirations, we must believe that it is consistent with a plausible interpretation of the world. Hence there are strong reasons to think that legal theorists' debates about the future of corporate criminal responsibility should be informed not only by normative political and moral theory but also by both theoretical and empirical work in the social sciences.[128]

D. The Institutional Deficit in the Analysis of Law's Philosophical Foundations: Descriptive Sociology Versus Analytical Jurisprudence Revisited

In this paper, I have argued not for a sociological methodology in jurisprudence, but rather for a general commitment to theorizing law as a *social* phenomenon.[129] This commitment brings with it a focus upon the historical development of legal orders and their interaction with social, cultural, political, and economic context. Neither analytical nor normative jurisprudence can afford to dispense with these insights. It makes no sense, to put it in Kelsen's terms, to try to "discover the specific principles of a sphere of meaning"[130] independently of the socio-historical context in which that sphere exists. Therefore, "the enterprise of sociological interpretation of legal ideas is not a desirable supplement but an essential means of legal understanding."[131]

The project of analyzing philosophical foundations of legal doctrines and arrangements is rooted firmly in the tradition of analytical jurisprudence revived by Herbert Hart.[132] Yet the commitment to analyzing "the common

---

127. This point is central to the argument of G.R. Sullivan, *The Attribution of Culpability to Limited Companies*, 55 CAMBRIDGE L.J. 515 (1996).

128. This is, of course, a different argument from my broader contention about the need to theorize law sociologically.

129. *See* Roger Cotterrell, *Why Must Legal Ideas Be Interpreted Sociologically?*, 25 J. LAW & SOC'Y 171, 183 (1998).

130. *See* HANS KELSEN, AN INTRODUCTION TO THE PROBLEMS OF LEGAL THEORY 481 (Bonnie Litschewski Paulson & Stanley L. Paulson trans., Clarendon Press 1992) (1934). For further discussion of the relationship between normative and sociological jurisprudence, see Hans Kelsen, *The Pure Theory of Law: Its Methods and Fundamental Concepts*, 50 L.Q. REV. 474, 480–81 (1934).

131. *See* Cotterrell, *supra* note 129, at 188, 192.

132. In associating "philosophical foundations" with a focus on analytical rather than sociological jurisprudence, I am concerned in the first instance with descriptive or interpretive aspects of the project. The persuasiveness of straightforwardly prescriptive claims will generally

law"—indeed, in many of its manifestations, to analyzing specific aspects of the common law—implies a vision of law as the sort of spatially and historically specific phenomenon that is susceptible of social-scientific inquiry. The values and ideals of a political society change over time. Conceptions of conduct, agency, and responsibility shift. Geo-political and economic circumstances change. The implications of these and many other factors for not only the substance but also the conceptual framework and even the idea of law, are an important object of research.

This idea of legal systems as developing over time and within complex social, economic, cultural, and political environments is captured well by Joseph Raz's idea of the "non-momentary legal system."[133] Raz's argument is that the identity of the nonmomentary system is determined primarily by its content rather than by its criteria for the identification of valid legal standards. It is the latter—the normative conditions under which a momentary legal system exists—that is the proper object of analytical jurisprudence. This object, so the argument goes, can be theorized independently of any consideration of the nonmomentary system to which it belongs. Raz may be taken to imply that the social-theoretic analysis of law can be neatly bracketed off from the analytic, and that in tracing the philosophical foundations of, for example, English criminal law, we have no need for any broad understanding of the social functions or meaning of criminalization as a connected sequence for practices, for the historical development of the values informing those practices, or for the conceptual frameworks in terms of which they have been carried forward. This resolute distancing of social and historical context is reproduced in analyses of philosophical foundations that are concerned with the moral coherence of particular common law doctrines. The result is that law is implicitly misrepresented as founded, actually or ideally, on a metaphysics—that is, on a moral or conceptual structure whose validity transcends space and time.

Aspects of Hart's theory opened up a set of possibilities for a more socially grounded theory of law, or for a jurisprudence founded in the social

---

also depend upon social factors, but the relationship in which I am primarily interested is the one implied by the ways in which theories present themselves as characterizations of the legal world as it is or proceed on the basis of assumptions about that world. The nature of the relationship between "descriptive," "interpretive," and "prescriptive" aspects remains, of course, one of the central issues of legal theory, not least because—as many "descriptive" theorists acknowledge, and as discussed in the first section of this paper—the criteria for selection among legal phenomena to be theorized are inevitably shaped by the theorist's values or point of view. *See* COLEMAN, *supra* note 71; FINNIS, *supra* note 38; MOORE, *supra* note 122; Joseph Raz, *Two Views of the Nature of the Theory of Law: A Partial Comparison*, 4 LEGAL THEORY 249 (1998); *see also* Peter Cane, *Markets and Morals in Contract and Tort*, 13 LEGAL STUD. 396 (1993) (reviewing JULES COLEMAN, RISKS AND WRONGS (1992)); George Fletcher, *Corrective Justice for Moderns*, 106 HARV. L. REV. 1658 (1993) (same).

133. RAZ, *supra* note 85.

sciences, and of use to them.[134] For a variety of reasons, only some of which I have been able to review in this paper, he was unable or unwilling to fully pursue these possibilities. But the emergence in contemporary legal theory of genres of work in both general and special jurisprudence that seek to blend the insights of philosophical and sociological approaches to both explanatory and normative ends may truly claim to be part of Herbert Hart's intellectual legacy. Indeed, they may be argued to resonate more strongly with his broad and enlightened vision of the role of the legal theorist than do some of the more strictly philosophical contributions that predominate in the field of analytical jurisprudence today.

---

134. *See* Martin Krygier, *The Concept of Law and Social Theory*, 2 OXFORD J. LEGAL STUD. 155 (1982).

[6]

LEGAL RESEARCH AND THE SOCIAL SCIENCES

Christopher McCrudden

FOUR overlapping research agendas form the bulk of current academic legal scholarship in Britain. First, *the understanding and internal coherence of legal concepts and legal reasoning*: how legal concepts fit together, the consistency of the use of concepts in different areas of law, the extent to which general principles can be extracted from legal reasoning that can be used to predict or guide future legal decision-making. Secondly, *the meaning and validity of law*: the examination of what makes law different from, or similar to, other normative systems. Typically, this has involved questions such as:

— "What is law?"
— "How far are issues of ethics or morality part of legal reasoning?"
— "How does a set of normative principles come to be thought of as 'legal'?"
— "How does law differ from other social institutions and practices?"

Thirdly, *the ethical and political acceptability of public policy delivered though legal instruments*: the consideration of issues such as whether specific legal interventions are acceptable when assessed against external moral, ethical or political principles, or what should be the appropriate legal response where none exists at the moment. Policy prescription is thus often encountered in legal scholarship, sometimes addressed to the courts, sometimes to policy makers in government. Fourthly, *the effect of law*. What effect, if any, does law have on human behaviour, attitudes, and actions? How does it have these effects? Are some institutional mechanisms for delivering legal outcomes more appropriate or effective than others? Each of these four sets of issues can be studied in a purely domestic legal context, such as England and Wales, or at the European level, internationally or comparatively, as a contemporary issue, or historically.

Which, if any, of these questions engage a legal academic in "social scientific" research?

LEGAL RESEARCH AND THE "SCIENTIFIC METHOD"

We can distinguish two broadly contrasting approaches to science that are frequently on display in discussions of social science methodology.[1] The

---
[1] See further H.J. Berman, "The Origins of Western Legal Science" (1977) 90 Harvard L.R. 894 at 931.

first, older, model of science, perhaps best exemplified in some areas of mathematics, acquires knowledge on the basis of constructing logically coherent conclusions from elementary principles. The techniques used are argument, conceptual clarification, logic, and discussion. The second uses the term "science" to mean the generation of knowledge by *empirical investigation* of natural phenomena, often using laboratory investigation. The distinction, then, between the older and newer forms of scientific enquiry is that the former is based largely on logical argumentation, the latter on empirical examination of the phenomenon, and the testing of theoretical hypotheses.

Doctrinal Analysis

Over the past few centuries, Western legal academics often thought they were being scientific in the first sense.[2] They considered, in other words, that they were studying law using reason, logic and argument. They adopted methods that date back at least to the scholastic philosophers. The methodology adopted is one that concentrates on the primacy of critical reasoning based around authoritative texts. But this is not simply textual analysis, at least in common law systems, for the idea of law as a *practice* is deeply embedded. The core of this type of legal research concentrates on issues of legal coherence, what is sometimes called "black letter law", or "doctrinal legal analysis", adopting an *internal* viewpoint, the meaning of which will be considered subsequently.

Although sometimes much disparaged by non-lawyers (and by some legal academics) as narrow, the ability to engage in this type of research is what most often marks out what are perceived by one's legal colleagues as "good lawyers" from "bad lawyers".[3] This type of work concentrates substantially on the first set of research questions that I mentioned above. Crucially, traditional legal analysis adopts an "internal" approach. The internal approach is the analysis of legal rules and principles taking the perspective of an insider in the system. As David Ibbetson has written:

> "Its sources are predominantly those that are thrown up by the legal process: principally statutes and decided cases, supplemented where possible with lawyers' literature expounding the rules and occasionally reflecting on them."[4]

An external approach, in contrast, is the study

---

[2] For a discussion in the United States' context, see H. Schweber, "The 'Science' of Legal Science: the Model of the Natural Sciences in Nineteenth Century American Legal Education" (1999) 17 Law and Hist. R. 421.

[3] For a robust defence of such work, see A. Burrows, *Understanding of the Law of Obligations: Essays on Contract, Tort and Restitution* (1998), pp.112–114.

[4] D. Ibbetson, "Historical Research in Law", in P. Cane and M. Tushnet (eds), *Oxford Handbook of Legal Studies* (2003) 863 at p.864.

"of the law in practice, of legal institutions at work in society rather than legal rules existing in a social, economic, and political vacuum."[5]

I want to use this distinction to draw out different strands of legal scholarship, although, ultimately, I shall argue that the distinction is useful mainly for heuristic purposes, and that much recent legal scholarship adopts both approaches.

An internal approach, then, dominates traditional doctrinal scholarship. It often involves the close analysis of decisions by the higher judiciary, often at the appellate level, and legislation of various kinds. The task for doctrinal analysis is often to attempt to understand how these various elements fit together, to attempt to draw out the patterns of normative understanding that enable us to see the wood and the trees together as constituting a working whole.[6] Frequently, however, doctrinal analysis often takes another form, in which the writer attempts to argue that this or that is the "best" solution to a particular problem, "best" meaning having the best fit with what already exists. Often, the analysis concentrates on questions of law in "hard cases," and how in practice these should be addressed. In this hermeneutic approach, the language used by legal academics is heavily dominated by terms such as coherence, fit and analogy.

What marks out this type of analysis is the attempt to render the law intelligible, but sometimes also to show the multiple possible readings and contradictions of existing "law". The combination of norms, concepts and institutions, and their interplay, is mother's milk to academic lawyers.[7] Looked at from the social science perspective, and using social science terminology, legal academics are constantly constructing explanatory "models" from the legal material at their disposal, models that they then test against that legal material. There are more or less agreed criteria of what are reasonable or unreasonable readings, although it is sometimes difficult to articulate these with any precision and they are subject to change.

I do not want to mislead, however. It is clear that though there are similarities with model building in the social sciences, there are also considerable differences: doctrinal legal models are causal models, and they are empirically tested, but in only a very limited sense; in addition, legal model-building takes place within a normative context, and is likely to include normative elements.

---

[5] *ibid.*
[6] A.W.B. Simpson, "The Rise and Fall of the Legal Treatise: Legal Principles and the Forms of Legal Literature" (1981) 48 U.Chi.L.R. 632.
[7] J. Bell, book review, (2004) 53 I.C.L.Q. 1049.

Another crucial point is that the approach to legal research that I have identified frequently proceeds from a view of the legal system as either completely autonomous or, more usually, *relatively* autonomous. This means that behind such analysis, as Ibbetson says,

> "lurks the assumption that law constitutes a sufficiently autonomous field of experience or discourse that it can legitimately be described by reference to its own sources."[8]

But, the question of what constitutes the appropriate sources of legal analysis is often profoundly contested. So too is the issue of their relative weight or cogency.[9] In particular, the extent to which its sources include materials other than cases and statutes varies over time, and between countries. To what extent can accepted sources include considerations of justice, morality or utility? Or policy analysis? Or social science evidence on the effects of regulations? When they do, then the "internal" approach to legal analysis will, perforce, include these considerations within their domain. The notion of internal legal analysis is therefore potentially highly flexible. How far any jurisdiction considers particular sources as relevant is one that is likely to be substantially determined by the (changing) consensus of academic and practising lawyers and judges.[10]

Doctrinal work of this sort is not necessarily antagonistic to engagement with other disciplines. Indeed, several law faculties in the United Kingdom have long had relationships with the other disciplines that we would now consider at the core of the *humanities*, such as classics, history, philosophy, and political theory. These disciplines are being seen as contributing to the scientific study of law in the first sense, in contributing to the endeavour of applying logic, reason and argument to a body of material considered legal. Much of this involvement with other disciplines is perceived as useful because it contributes to better "internal" legal analysis.

LAW AND PHILOSOPHY

Undoubtedly, however, the flowering of the most recent phase of close working relationship between law and the humanities in Britain began in Oxford after the Second World War. By the 1950s, Oxford law was significantly influenced by developments in philosophy, and has remained so since then. The work of H.L.A. Hart revolutionised the study of the philosophy of law. This was true in at least two respects. First, it introduced a degree of philosophical sophistication, hitherto unknown

---

[8] Ibbetson, cited above fn.4, at p.863.
[9] W.L. Twining, "Legal Reasoning and Argumentation" *Inter. Encyl Soc. Behav. Sci.* (2004) 8670 at p.8671.
[10] S. Sedley, book review, [1999] C.L.J 627 at 628.

in England, into consideration of doctrinal legal analysis, such as the work of Hart and Honoré on causation.[11] Secondly, it revolutionised consideration of the second set of research issues: the question of what the relationship is between the normative system that is law and other normative systems, such as morality. Hart adopted the view that there is no necessary connection between law and morality, and that law consists of a series of rules that are regarded as law by virtue only of being recognised as such by social and political elites, what he called "officials of the system".[12] For Hart, the range of legal materials available to judges meant that legal rules sometimes ran out. When they did run out, judges then resorted to other arguments in order to decide cases, including policy arguments.

A third major strand in Hart's work, and those of his successors, is the critique of what we might call legal policy from a philosophical perspective, and using philosophical tools, the third set of research questions. So, for example, Hart's work on the acceptable reach of the criminal law in areas such as abortion, and homosexuality, and in the proper purposes and scope of punishment, left an indelible mark on the legal research agenda in the United Kingdom,[13] where lawyers and philosophers have worked happily together on a wide range of legally-informed philosophical critiques of legal concepts and policy, ranging from minority rights, to euthanasia. Debates over these issues continue to flourish, providing an area of primary research as well as influencing more indirectly the approach to doctrinal legal analysis.

SOCIAL SCIENCES AND LEGAL RESEARCH

But what is the role of the *social* sciences (excluding philosophy) in legal research? What, first, do we mean by the social sciences? At one level, the answer is clear. We mean to include, at least, the disciplines of sociology, political science (including normative political theory), economics, anthropology, statistics and psychology. For the purposes of this paper, however, it may be more useful to distinguish, following Murphy,[14] between, first, the more empirical branches of each of these disciplines; secondly, the more interpretative and phenomenological branches of the social sciences; and thirdly, more social theory-based approaches. Each of these three developments within the social sciences has impacted on legal research. Each is sceptical that either an analytical

---

[11] H.L.A. Hart and A.M. Honoré, *Causation in the Law* (1959).
[12] H.L.A. Hart, *The Concept of Law* (1961).
[13] H.L.A. Hart, *Law, Liberty and Morality* (1963); H.L.A. Hart, *Punishment and Responsibility: Essays in the Philosophy of Law* (1968).
[14] W.T. Murphy, "Law: History of its Relation to the Social Sciences" *Inter. Encycl Soc. Behav.* (2004), 8521 at p.8522.

philosophical approach of the type pioneered by Hart, or doctrinal legal analysis, are up to the task of explaining law in all its richness, and thus each has contributed to a set of critiques of law. Importantly, social scientific approaches to legal research are often dominated by an "*external*" approach.

This "external" turn led to the growth of three approaches to legal scholarship, widely seen as antagonistic to each other. The first is generally termed socio-legal studies (within which, for these purposes, I include criminology). In the British context socio-legal work and criminology has frequently drawn on the more empirical side of sociology and psychology, although some of its work has been influenced by phenomenology and hermeneutics. The second was the development of Critical Legal Studies, drawing on social theory and particularly influenced by the Frankfurt School. The third, and more recent, development is the law-and-economics movement, which draws more substantially on microeconomics, particularly rational choice. Each of these has affected the methodology of some current legal research.

Socio-legal Research

Those who developed *socio-legal* research usually argued that a more rounded picture will be gained only if we seek to adopt a more scientific understanding of law, using the term science in the second sense to mean the generation of knowledge by *empirical investigation*. This approach often emphasised the disparity between "law in the books" and "law in action", to use the phrase first coined by Roscoe Pound in 1910.[15] It examines the role of law, attempting to discover whether patterns can be identified after collecting and organising facts based on observation. Socio-legal studies focuses on the question, as Eekelaar and Maclean have put it,

> "of relating how the form and content of the law (as may be found in statements of law in legal textbooks), which are matters for intellectual comprehension and interpretation, move beyond such *intellectual* existence into social reality."[16]

Legal rules are not self-enforcing, in other words; they must be mobilised. What socio-legal studies is, exactly, is heavily contested but at its core, I understand it meant originally the use of empirical social science disciplines such as sociology, anthropology, social psychology and political science to investigate and understand legal phenomena and the role of law in society, on the basis of both multi-disciplinary and

---

[15] R. Pound, "Law in Books and Law in Action" (1910) 44 Am.L.Rev. 12.
[16] J. Eekelaar and M. Maclean, *A Reader in Family Law* (1994), at p.2.

inter-disciplinary work. In contrast to the doctrinal scholarship and current analytical legal philosophy, this socio-legal work often concentrates on the routine in the legal process, rather than the hard case, and the operation of law by actors at the lowest levels of the legal hierarchy, rather than at the appellate level, attempting to come up with "general predictions about when law affects society, in what ways and under what conditions."[17]

CRITICAL LEGAL STUDIES

The second major external approach in legal scholarship has sometimes been termed "post empiricist scholarship",[18] one example of which is Critical Legal Studies ("CLS"). This was a loose collection of American legal scholars, originally influenced by the wilder aspects of American Legal Realism, 1960s Marxism, and the growth in social and literary theory of what can broadly be called post-modernism. This heady brew, which spread to Britain in the 1980s, led to scepticism about the role of internally based legal reason. It emphasised the importance of understanding the constructed nature of what we think of as objectivity. It was, essentially, sceptical that the older understanding of science, namely the role of reason, has any real claim to validity or truth in legal studies. Such critics argued that traditional legal philosophy conceals "the fundamental indeterminacy of legal decision-making"[19] and legal doctrine masks the law's hegemonic function, ensuring the dominance of social and economic elites. It was equally critical of empirical socio-legal research. Whilst great fun for the participants, CLS's critique of ideology blazed during the 1980s, but has now generally faded, apart from some few bastions in the United States. At its best, it brought to light the role of power relations in the generation of knowledge and, perhaps, in particular, the importance of understanding the role of gender and race in that process. It left in its wake the importance of identity issues in legal studies, heavily influenced by feminist legal scholarship, critical race theory, and a scepticism about rights-talk. *Methodologically*, although not politically, CLS tended to be relatively conservative, usually resorting to doctrinal analysis in practice, though one leavened with social theory, an external perspective, and a radical political agenda. Only in the (sometimes rather irritating) use of personal narrative as a way of "situating" the author can they be said to have contributed anything methodologically novel to legal scholarship.[20]

---

[17] Centre for Socio-Legal Studies, "Theory and Method in Socio-Legal Research" (2004), available at: *www.csls.ox.ac.uk*.

[18] A. Sarat, "Off to Meet the Wizard: Beyond Validity and Reliability in the Search for a Post-Empiricist Sociology of Law" (1990) 15 Law Soc. Inq. 155.

[19] Twining, cited above fn.9, at p.8672.

[20] See E. Rubin, "Legal Scholarship" (2004) *Int. Encycl Soc. Behav. Sci.* 8677 at pp.8679–8681.

LAW AND ECONOMICS

The third major external approach in legal scholarship has been *law and economics*. It is probably the single most important methodology in American legal scholarship, other than traditional doctrinal scholarship, and is applied to all areas of legal concern. In Britain, however, neo-classical economics is almost entirely absent from academic legal study, except in such sub-disciplines as competition law, and to a lesser extent labour law, company law and regulation. What, then, is it about microeconomics and rational choice models that appear at once so powerful, and yet so alien to British legal scholarship? Our starting point must be rational choice theory. At its core, I understand rational choice to posit the relatively simple idea that, in general, individual human beings know what is best for them, in the sense that they are rational utility maximisers. They "have goals and make choices intended to achieve their goals."[21] Human beings calculate the costs and benefits of their actions. They choose those actions that they expect will best serve their goals, given the available evidence. The power of the theory is its apparent universality, its testability and its importance in a wide range of social situations, if it is correct. When combined with the application of rigorous mathematical modelling, and the application of computer-assisted analysis of large quantities of data, the more it looks as if the social sciences can come closer to the second conception of science. The theories that are developed are universal theories, not bounded in time or relevant only to one jurisdiction, as much of legal research is. The emphasis on goals and choices

> "contrasts with sociological and psychological [and therefore socio-legal] approaches that treat behaviour as a response to organisational norms, social pressures, or inner drives."[22]

Perhaps the most famous article of the genre, certainly among the most cited articles in American law journals, and in many ways the start of the modern law and economics movement, provides a useful illustration of the method. Ronald Coase's article, "The Problem of Social Cost", was published in 1960 and is among the most important theoretical statements in law and economics.[23] This is what lawyers would probably say it meant: Coase's theorem holds that when transaction costs are zero or very low, bargaining will lead to the efficient use of resources, regardless of the law. Certain insights flow from this. First, if the desired legal outcome is efficiency, there may be circumstances in which that goal will be achieved without any need for law. Secondly, in certain circumstances, the law may

---

[21] M.P. Fiorina, "Rational Choice in Politics" (2004) *Int. Encycl Soc. Behav. Sci.* at p.12760.
[22] *ibid.*
[23] R. Coase, "The Problem of Social Cost" (1960) 3 J. Law Econ. 1.

actually impede or make more costly an efficient outcome. Thirdly, where transaction costs are high, achieving an efficient outcome may depend on law. Economists would probably describe the theorem somewhat differently, substituting the idea of "property rights" for "law" in the description I have given. Indeed, it is noticeable that in academic writing on the institutional turn in economics that "property rights institutions" seem frequently to be used as a substitute for "legal institutions". My own view is that a richer idea of the institutional complexities at work would be captured by more explicit reference to legal institutions, a point I shall return to subsequently. The Coase theorem has generated a huge literature and could be the basis for a profitable paper by itself, which I shall not attempt here.

Instead, I shall concentrate on two common criticisms, from socio-legal scholars in particular, about rational choice models as applied to legal phenomena. The first is that such an approach, based on methodological individualism, is incompatible with research that concentrates more on systems and institutions. The second common criticism is that law and economics often seems to have a political agenda that is politically neo-liberal. Neither of these criticisms is convincing, in my view. The unease about law and economics lies elsewhere than in methodological concerns or perceived political bias. My sense is that this unease, apart from simple ignorance of economics, often arises from its important role in generating what Duxbury has called "the counter-intuitive impulse".[24] By this he means that law and economics is often most powerful when it challenges legal and political orthodoxy. "Over and again, lawyer-economists", he says, "want to warn us that things are not as they might at first appear."[25] Indeed, sometimes they turn out to be the opposite of what orthodox thinking supposes. This can often challenge deeply held views. In short, law and economics is reviled for much the same reason that law and economics scholars often revel in their reputation: they rather like being the *enfants terribles* of the legal academy. And to the extent that the function of scholarship is to afflict the intellectually comfortable, it seems to me that they can play an exceptionally important role.

CHARACTERISTICS OF "EXTERNAL" LEGAL RESEARCH

These three "external" approaches—socio-legal studies, critical legal studies and law and economics—despite their many differences, have several characteristics in common. The first involves a broadening of the disciplinary background of the research community involved.

---

[24] N. Duxbury, "A Century of Legal Studies", in P. Cane and M. Tushnet (eds) *Oxford Handbook of Legal Studies* (2003), 950 at p.961.
[25] *ibid.*, at p.961.

In considering the research carried out using the older methods of legal research, it is clear that most of the researchers are lawyers.[26] Research in law, however, is not now any longer the "preserve of the academic lawyer alone, but has attracted scholars from across the social sciences, especially sociologists, economists, and psychologists."[27] Secondly, these approaches tend to regard the appropriate research agenda as encompassing all four of the issues mentioned earlier, thus occupying some of the territory originally thought to be the preserve of doctrinal lawyers.

Most importantly for our purposes is their third common characteristic: the adoption of a much more explicitly "external" perspective when viewing the operation of legal phenomena. In this sense, they often proceed from a view of the legal system as either entirely or (more usually) partly determined by the same type of forces that affects other non-legal social phenomena. Law, therefore, can and should be examined using the same tools and methodologies as are used to study any other political, social or economic practice. They reject the assumption that law is autonomous, or largely so. At the more extreme edges of each of these approaches, law is viewed as *simply* politics, or as *simply* economics, or as *simply* sociology. What we see, in other words, is the growth of an approach to law that may challenge the idea of legal scholarship as a separate craft. They tend to set up an apparently irreconcilable tension with important aspects of traditional legal scholarship, in particular doctrinal legal analysis.

END OF "INTERNAL" LEGAL RESEARCH?

Are we seeing, then, the end of a specifically legal sphere, where legal research "steadily succumbs to the influence of the social and behavioural sciences"?[28] Some, like Richard Posner have encouraged such a development.[29] Others have decried it; in 1990, Ruth Deech objected to the apparent regard that law reformers were paying to social science. The influence of social scientists had led, she asserted, to an apparent reduction in the "intellectual challenge and content of the law."[30] But I do not believe that this is occurring. Rather, I agree with Rubin, who argues that these apparently irreconcilable approaches in legal research are now "being significantly eroded" by developments in each.[31]

---

[26] J. Baldwin and G. Davis, "Empirical Research in Law", in P. Cane and M. Tushnet (eds), *Oxford Handbook of Legal Studies* (2003), 880 at p.881.
[27] *ibid.*
[28] Murphy, cited above fn.14, at p.8525.
[29] R.A. Posner, "The Decline of Law as an Autonomous Discipline 1962–1987" (1987) 100 Harvard L.R. 761.
[30] R. Deech, "Divorce Law and Empirical Studies" (1990) 106 L.Q.R. 229.
[31] Rubin, cited above fn.20, at p.8677.

There are several significant developments that contribute to my sense that legal research now embraces a pluralism of methodological approaches. These developments have had the effect of moderating important elements of legal research dominated by both "internal approaches" and "external approaches", creating opportunities for closer working across these boundaries, and between law and the social sciences. What is emerging are approaches that combine both the internal and the external approaches that I have distinguished up to this point, pinpointing what is distinctive about law as a social construction, *as well as* examining its inter-relationship with other social phenomena.

CURRENT LEGAL SCHOLARSHIP AND THE ACCEPTANCE OF METHODOLOGICAL PLURALISM

Without attempting to be comprehensive, we can mention some developments as particularly important, beginning with the social science side. There have, first, been important evolutions in economics and political science that render it more sympathetic both to traditional legal scholarship, and legal philosophy. Rational choice theory is now more open to the role that institutions and organisations play in individual decision-making. Studies in institutional economics of the type carried out by Douglass North[32] and Oliver Williamson[33] seem close to the organisational and institutional approach that dominates research on legal phenomena.

A second development has been the incorporation of some findings of recent behavioural economics into legal research.[34] This has been important both in challenging the approach to rationality inherent in previous law and economics, and in leading to attempts to set up experimental testing. If people are irrationally attracted to current endowments, or irrationally influenced by the way choices are presented, then this has important implications for legal decision-making. There is now also considerably greater recognition that cognitive science may require deep revisions to economic models of the human decision-maker. The periodic recurrence among economists of replacing the more radical assumptions of economic man with models of bounded rationality and bounded selfishness, and the recognition of the importance of institutional and organisational context to decision-making, make joint working considerably more likely.

A major development within law and economics scholarship has reflected this, namely the study of whether internalised norms "exercise powerful effects that conflict with the self-interest, or at least the

---

[32] D. North, *Institutions, Institutional Change and Economic Performance* (1990).
[33] O.E. Williamson, *The Mechanisms of Governance* (1996).
[34] C. Jolls, C. Sunstein and R. Thaler, "A Behavioral Approach to Law and Economics" (1998) 50 Stanford L.R. 1471.

immediate self-interest, of the author."[35] In a famous book testing the Coase theorem, Robert Ellickson studied the way in which cattle ranchers and farmers in Shasta County in California, handled disputes about the harms caused by cattle trespassing on farmland.[36] In general, he found the Coase theorem to be limited in its ability to predict how disputes would be handled in practice. The study discovered that the Coase theorem over-emphasised the importance of law in certain circumstances. Although they knew there was law that could have governed their relationship, few of the farmers or the cattle ranchers actually knew what the law was, or had regard to it in practice. Rather, they ordered their relationships on the basis of *social* norms, rather than law. There was bargaining but, contrary to expectations perhaps, it was not bargaining in the shadow of the law, but without law. It also demonstrated that the social norms of Shasta County overcame the immediate self-interest of the farmers and ranchers.

Within socio-legal studies, the turn to supplementing empirical work with more theoretical approaches, has also meant that socio-legal scholars have increasingly engaged with other approaches. Themes drawn from Critical Legal Studies have influenced several British socio-legal scholars. But Critical Legal Studies has also become more sophisticated. Some Critical Legal scholars, such as Robert Gordon,[37] are much more likely to accept claims to law's partial autonomy, accepting the existence of some degree at least of insulation in the activities of lawyers and judges. A separate development within socio-legal studies, drawing on systems theories, has also resulted in considerable attention being paid to what might be distinctive about the legal system. First developed by Luhmann,[38] and refined by Teubner,[39] this approach views law as a more or less closed normative system in which norms are generated and sustained within the system itself, thus emphasising the autonomous aspects of legal thought in a way that previously would have seemed unlikely from a sociological perspective. Ironically, this brings socio-legal scholarship closer to doctrinal legal scholarship than in the past.

So too, within those approaches to legal scholarship that previously adopted more of an internal perspective, several developments have occurred that have opened up the possibility of greater rapprochement with external approaches. First, legal philosophy has increasingly focussed on the political theory aspects of the third research issue mentioned above, increasing the opportunity for external perspectives to be engaged with that are neither legal nor philosophical. Particularly in the critique

---

[35] Rubin cited above fn.20.
[36] R. Ellickson, *Order Without Law: How Neighbors Settle Disputes* (1991).
[37] R. Gordon, "The Independence of Lawyers" (1988) 68 Boston U.L.R. 1; R. Gordon, "Critical Legal Histories" (1984) 36 Stanford L.R. 57.
[38] N. Luhman, *Law as a Social System* (2004).
[39] G. Teubner (ed.), *Autopoietic Law: a New Approach to Law and Society* (1988).

of legal policy, Hart and his successors have appeared somewhat more comfortable in using social science literature derived from economics or sociology. Hart himself, for example, worked with David Soskice, the economist, on abortion.[40] Sociology and economic approaches are now increasingly influencing legal philosophy.[41] The approach to law in doctrinal legal scholarship is also changing in ways that allow for increased multi-disciplinary work. In the past, doctrinal legal analysis has concentrated on "state-centred" law, meaning the law that derives from, and is accepted by, the institutions of the nation state. Traditional doctrinal analysis, whether in a particular state's legal system, or in comparative law, often emphasised the extent to which law was the result of a country's unique history or culture. Even traditional ideas of international law were essentially state-centred, seeing international law as developing mostly either from state practice, or from the acceptance of treaties by states. This was seen as at odds with the desire of increasingly dominant social science approaches that stress the need for generalisation. Economists, after all, do not see the utility of economics as limited to the country in which a theory was developed.[42] Intriguingly, however, legal academics are increasingly questioning this state-centredness, and "there are indications . . . that this theoretical preoccupation with state structures, state institutions, and state laws may now be in decline." [43] The importance of European legal scholarship, of human rights law, of the use of such concepts as "soft law", of the growing conversation between judges in different jurisdictions, of globalisation, all point to developments that weaken the state-centred-ness of traditional legal categories. As Bell writes, "The conventional hierarchies of norms is being challenged by ideas of 'networks' of normative orders."[44] This development links with traditional socio-legal work on legal pluralism, which argues that the state does not have a monopoly on what we mean by law, to create synergies between internal and external perspectives on law in fields as diverse as comparative law and criminal law.[45]

Thirdly, much traditional doctrinal legal analysis now relaxes its view of the autonomy of law, drawing on economic and socio-legal insights increasingly easily. Now, the seamless integration of insights from other

---

[40] D. Soskice and H.L.A. Hart, "After the Act": *The Guardian*, May 3, 1972. See also D. Soskice with T.J. Trussell, *Effects of the Abortion Act*, British Journal of Hospital Medicine (1973).

[41] For example the extensive presence of M. Weber in J. Finnis, *Natural Law and Natural Rights* (1980).

[42] T.S. Ulen, "A Nobel Prize in Legal Science: Theory, Empirical Work, and the Scientific Method in the Study of Law" [2002] U.Ill.L.R. 875 at 895.

[43] H.P. Glenn, "A Transnational Concept of Law", in P. Cane and M. Tushnet (eds), *Oxford Handbook of Legal Studies* (2003), at p.839.

[44] Bell, cited above fn.7, at p.1049.

[45] See, *e.g.* N. Lacey and L. Zedner, "Discourses of Community in Criminal Justice" (1995) 22 J.Law Soc. 93.

disciplines into legal scholarship is sufficiently common for it to be unremarkable, although it is still more common in some areas than others. As Collier has recently argued:

> ". . . there now exists a commonly held view within legal studies that the majority, if not all, university law schools can usefully be characterised as embracing a broadly 'liberal', pluralistic approach to legal education and scholarship."[46]

Cownie observes, drawing on her research, "We're all socio-legal now."[47]

Seen from this perspective, then, the broad insights of the external approaches are increasingly being incorporated into traditional British legal scholarship. This is not to say that all legal academics are adopting an external perspective. Some areas of law, such as public law, family law and labour law seem more likely to engage with these perspectives than other areas. Nor am I arguing that all are engaging in empirical work themselves. Rather, my argument is that those engaging in doctrinal legal analysis much more frequently than before are ready to support, and sometimes to test their doctrinal or theoretical models by drawing on social science influenced information. Should this methodological pluralism be regarded as a strength or a weakness in current legal scholarship? Does it show an immature desire to derive comfort by leavening legal research with undigested parts of other more prestigious disciplines? My own view is contrary to the thrust of such questions. In my view it demonstrates, instead, a mature openness to other disciplines that demonstrates a welcome self-confidence.

But we should not be blind to outside criticism. Our assessment of our research should not be limited to the views of other lawyers. In particular, it should include the assessments of other social scientists working on related topics. If they are not persuaded of the utility of what we are doing, perhaps particularly of our methodologies, we need at least to know why. But that assumes that other social scientists actually know of the work we produce, and have assessed it, and frequently this is not the case. We need to develop strategies that bring our work much more frequently to the attention of those in cognate areas, not least in order to ensure that the approaches we take, and the results we achieve, make sense.

ONE-WAY TRAFFIC?

Thus far, I have concentrated on what the social sciences can do for law. What about the flip side of the coin? What can legal research do

---

[46] R. Collier, "Research Capacity, Critical Social Science and the Paradox of Socio-Legal Studies", 43 *Socio-Legal Newsletter* (Summer 2004), at p.3.

[47] F. Cownie, *Legal Academics: Culture and Identities* (2004).

for the social sciences? We know that, in the past, legal studies have made an important contribution to the development of other social science disciplines. Now, however, if one views the relationship between law and other disciplines as akin to that between neighbours, then the relationship seems one-sided. Law increasingly uses insights from the other social sciences but, with some limited exceptions, mainstream social scientists neither perceive themselves as studying legal phenomena nor (apparently) do they see themselves as able to gain any significant insight from legal scholarship.

There are several problems with convincing social scientists that legal research has anything to contribute to the social sciences. Institutionally, academic law sits uncomfortably somewhere between humanities and the social sciences in universities, although particular legal academics are more likely to see themselves as closer to one rather than the other.[48] Legal academics, in my experience at least, seldom appear to talk about methodology in the context of their research, whereas other social scientists often place particular importance on methodological issues. There is another problematic element: the apparently almost complete blindness to the potential relevance of legal issues in much social science research. The absence of explicit consideration given to law and legal institutions in much mainstream social sciences research is puzzling. The role of one of the primary methods of organising social life seems to be left outside consideration. Why is that the case? Several explanations are possible. The first explanation may lie simply in the apparent aridity of legal research, its apparent absence of interest in theory, and its apparent closeness to legal practice (all *false* assumptions as I hope I have shown). Academic law may seem too intimidating and technical, too specific, too detailed and too parochial to have much to offer to approaches that are attempting to bring clarity, simplicity, elegance, and generalisation. And yet, the other social sciences are equally complex. In much social science research, there appears to be fairly regular reference to the other social (and often natural) sciences without embarrassment, demonstrating the extent to which where there is a will, there is a way.

An explanation for law's virtual exclusion from the modelling of the other social sciences may be sought at a deeper level. Is it to be found in the assumption that law is, ultimately, unimportant? Is law simply "superstructural", as Marxist historical materialism used to assert, only the outward manifestation of much deeper social and behavioural processes that should attract social science research instead? In this perspective, law becomes the symptom not the cause. Legal research is impliedly missing the point, reifying the legal at the expense of the real determinants of the

---

[48] W.L. Twining *et al.*, "The Role of Academics in the Legal System", in P. Cane and M. Tushnet (eds), *Oxford Handbook of Legal Studies* (2003), p.920.

social. However, in 1997, Professor Goodhart, a professional economist, argued that although the scale of law on the economy was pervasive, law was "rarely examined in any depth by economists". He illustrated his argument with an analysis of how often there was discussion of the legal system in mainstream textbooks on economics. In the classic textbook Samuelson's *Economics* (currently 800 pages), one-quarter of one page addressed the legal framework of the economic system and three-quarters of a page considered the influence of economics on law.[49]

Treating law as epiphenomenal may not be the only problem. Investigating the legal dimensions of an issue in social science research may be seen as requiring a close working relationship with legal academics. Is this a price too high to pay, perhaps? Fiona Cownie has described how the "predominant notion of academic lawyers [by those from other disciplines] is that they are not really academic."[50] Drawing on interviews with other British academics by Becher some time ago, she describes how one interviewee summed up the attitude to legal academics. They are seen as "arcane, distant and alien—an appendage to the university world."[51] Their personal qualities are described by other academics as "dubious": "they are variously represented as vociferous, untrustworthy, immoral, narrow, arrogant and conservative."[52] Their scholarly attitudes are described as "unexciting and uncreative, comprising a series of intellectual puzzles scattered among 'large areas of description'."[53] The work Cownie quotes is a little dated, so one might hope that these views represent past attitudes, but this cannot be guaranteed.

There is no point in complaining if legal scholarship really has nothing to contribute to mainstream social scientific work. I will argue, however, that law has indeed something to offer and that the failure to engage with legal scholarship leads to a more intellectually impoverished social science than need be the case. This is not an argument for legal imperialism. Nor is it my aim to produce some artificial synthesis of the various disciplinary approaches. Rather, it is to argue that engagement with the diversity of different social sciences approaches, including law, produces a stronger social science. What, then, can legal scholars bring to the table of social science research?

I suggest, tentatively, that in at least four respects legal research may be able to contribute to social science research. First, doctrinal and philosophical consideration of law can help provide conceptual clarity

---

[49] C.A.E. Goodhart, "Economics and the Law: Too Much One-Way Traffic?" (1967) 60 M.L.R. 1 at 4, 7.

[50] F. Cownie, "Researching (Socio) Legal Academics", (2004) 42 Socio-Legal Newsletter 1.

[51] *ibid.*

[52] *ibid.*

[53] *ibid.*, quoting T. Becher, *Academic Tribes and Territories: Intellectual Enquiry and the Culture of Disciplines* (1989), p.30.

and specificity about particular sets of social norms and social concepts that occur in both the legal and social contexts.[54] Many examples spring to mind: the concept of "obligation", the idea of a "promise", different forms that "rules" take and how they differ from other cognate concepts, the concept of a "right", and the idea of "discrimination". Legal scholars, in ways that are of general relevance, have extensively considered all these. Those whose empirical work is built upon hypotheses that involve such concepts but do not incorporate legal insights do so at their peril. Legal work provides a treasure trove of conceptual resources. Without reference to legal philosophical clarity, hypotheses are likely to be much less clear, and therefore much less testable in certain areas. Now, sometimes, the response to this argument is that social science research needs simple concepts, because otherwise the methodological tools available cannot cope. If that is a valid point, then the lack of sophistication of the available methodological tools needs to be addressed, if they cannot cope with the complexity of real life.

Secondly, and less obviously, where law or legal concepts or legal institutions *are* recognised by the social scientist to play a role in the theory that is being developed for testing, the tendency within both economics and sociology is to view law too often as a datum, as fact, unproblematic, and one-dimensional. Where lawyers are involved in an empirical project, the tendency, in my experience, is to ask lawyers to identify "the law," stripped of complexity, and preferably in the form of a rule or obligation that is specific to a limited social setting.[55] If legal academic work shows anything, it shows that an applicable legal norm on anything but the most banal question is likely to be complex, nuanced and contested. Law is more often in the process of becoming, than settled. Law is not a datum; it is in constant evolution, developing in ways that are sometimes startling and endlessly inventive, as Doreen McBarnet has demonstrated in her work on "creative compliance".[56] That is its fascination. Anyone engaged in research that involves the formulation or testing of propositions incorporating legal issues who does not understand this will produce results, however satisfying otherwise, that are fundamentally flawed.

Thirdly, and less obvious, social scientists who are not lawyers are perhaps less likely to recognise when law is playing an important role in the social and economic phenomena they are attempting to analyse.

---

[54] W.L. Twining, "Have Concepts, Will Travel: Analytical Jurisprudence in a Global Perspective" (2005) 1 Inter. J. Law in Cont. 5.

[55] Edelman and Suchman discuss this in their work on the relationship between "law and society" and organisational studies: L.B. Edelman and M.C. Suchman, "The Legal Environments of Organizations" (1997) 23 Ann.R.Soc. 479; L.B. Edelman and M.C. Suchman, "When the Haves Hold Court: Speculations on the Organizational Internalization of Law" (1999) 33 Law Soc.R. 941. I am grateful to Philip Lewis for drawing my attention to this.

[56] D. McBarnet, *Crime, Compliance and Control* (2004).

The best example is probably to be found in the context of theories of regulatory behaviour, where there is an extensive legal literature demonstrating the inadequacies of public choice theories as explanations for how regulatory decisions are made. In the main, this literature argues that the organisational context is usually too often ignored or underplayed in public choice theories, and of course the organisational context is a specifically legal one. It is hard to appreciate the organisational constraints without understanding the extent to which the legal limits within which organisations operate affect their behaviour. In short, as Mary Dudziak has argued, law does not simply reflect social context, but also shapes it. Writing of the litigation against school segregation in the United States, she observes that "the 'social context' to which law . . . was responsive turns out to be constructed, in part, by the law . . . itself. . ."[57] So many of the ideas and categories through which we understand the world are in part legally determined: marriage, war, crime, to take but three examples. There is a sort of paradox here: law is the product of its social context, yet the social context is itself in part a product of law.[58]

Fourthly, and perhaps most controversial, legal researchers often pride themselves on being able to see the need for a normative dimension in inter-disciplinary research. Particularly where such research leads to policy proposals, legal academics view their training in navigating practical decision-making, normative principles, and institutional considerations as equipping them to play an important complementary role to other social science disciplines, perhaps particularly those with a more descriptive, empirical bent.

CONCLUSION

I have argued, then, that developments within legal scholarship and developments within the other social sciences mean that the time has probably never been better for inter-disciplinary research, and increased cross-fertilisation. Indeed, at a time when the social sciences appear to be fracturing, separating from each other into smaller and smaller sub-disciplines, and when increasing calls are heard for greater communication between the social sciences leading to more interdisciplinary and multi-disciplinary work, developments within the legal academy are of broader relevance. Legal research and legal scholarship now provides an interesting model of how interdisciplinary and multidisciplinary work in the social sciences and the humanities can be done. The attempt to reconcile and join up the different social sciences and the humanities is not just

---

[57] M.L. Dudziak, "The Court and Social Context in Civil Rights History, Review Essay: From Jim Crow to Civil Rights: The Supreme Court and the Struggle for Racial Equality, Michael J. Klarman" (2005) 72 U.Chi.L.R. 429 at p.444.
[58] A.W.B. Simpson, "Analysis of Legal Concepts" (1964) 80 L.Q.R. 535.

an aspiration in legal scholarship, it is currently taking place; slowly and painstakingly, of course, but it is happening. The opportunity is there for us to make it work better.

Legal research has engaged with the more recent social sciences in ways that would have seemed unlikely even 50 years ago. Socio-legal studies, sociology of law, law and economics must now be seen as integral to legal research. The social sciences can (and do already), therefore, contribute significantly to legal research. But, more controversially, legal research should contribute significantly to the social sciences. The most productive relationship between law and the social sciences, therefore, is one in which each contributes to the other, with two-way, rather than one-way, traffic.

CHRISTOPHER MCCRUDDEN.[*]

---

[*] Professor of Human Rights Law, University of Oxford; Fellow of Lincoln College, Oxford. I am most grateful to the many colleagues with whom I have discussed the topic and who read previous drafts. This paper was first given as part of a series of public lectures to celebrate the opening of the Oxford Social Sciences Centre.

LT Legal methodology; Legal research; Socio legal studies

[7]

IS LAW REALLY A SOCIAL SCIENCE? A VIEW FROM COMPARATIVE LAW

GEOFFREY SAMUEL*

THE question to be pursued in this article has the merit of simplicity even if the response to it proves somewhat complex. The question is this: is law truly a social science? This may seem an odd question to many in the common law world since it is not uncommon, at least in England, for law schools to find themselves located in faculties of social science. Moreover there are a number of individuals, perhaps a considerable number in common law departments and faculties throughout the world, whose research and scholarship undoubtedly qualifies as social science research. So, before one can even begin to reflect upon the question to be pursued in this paper, a preliminary question must first be asked. Why should one wish even to pose the question?

This question will be considered by way of introduction and it will be followed by a section setting out the arguments as to why law might be regarded as not being a social science. Counter arguments will be discussed in further sections, but one particular difficulty will then be highlighted. Law, like traditionalist theology, is a discipline that is governed by the authority paradigm and it is this paradigm that restricts it in its capacity to make an epistemological contribution to social science thinking. However not all jurists are, or at least ought to be, trapped within this paradigm. Comparative legal studies, for example, have to be interdisciplinary and have to operate outside of the authority paradigm if they are to be taken seriously. Moreover such studies can generate, so it will be argued in this article, new ideas with regard to methodology and epistemology. So, by way of conclusion, it will be suggested that the answer to the question of whether law is a social science is an ambiguous one.

---

* Professor of Law, Kent Law School, University of Kent, UK. This article is partly based on the Beatty Annual Lecture in Jurisprudence and Public Policy delivered to the McGill University Faculty of Law on 26 October 2005 and on papers delivered at the London School of Economics, Edinburgh University and Fribourg University. The author would like to thank all of those who have commented either on the papers or on earlier drafts of this article.

I. INTRODUCTION: WHY THE QUESTION?

The primary reason why the question has been posed is to be found in a relatively recent book published in France under the editorship of Jean-Michel Berthelot and entitled *Épistémologie des sciences sociales*.[1] Now it is clear that what constitutes a social science in France is somewhat different from the position in the United Kingdom, for the English do not tend to treat disciplines such as history and philosophy as social science subjects; they are usually regarded as falling within the humanities. This distinction is of course of great importance and raises of itself fundamental discipline issues.[2] Nevertheless the point to be stressed for the purposes of this present article is that it is still striking that Berthelot has no chapter on law.[3] This exclusion is due neither to oversight nor to the lack of anyone in France capable of writing a sophisticated entry on legal epistemology, for there is a short work by a French law professor that, adapted, might have made an excellent contribution to the Berthelot book.[4] The exclusion results from a deliberate decision taken by Professor Berthelot not to include law.

To do justice to Berthelot, he did not, it seems, arrive at his decision without considerable reflection nor in fact does he actually state that law is not a social science.[5] Indeed he indicates that had more space been available he might well have invited a contribution on law.[6] What he does do, however, is to advance a theoretical argument in which he asserts that law (together with political science) is different from the other social sciences in that "the legal and political sciences are made up in the main of normative judgments and their foundations". This, he says, makes them different in terms of their perspective. The disciplines that Berthelot includes in his book are all "drawn towards problematising the forms of interaction between

---

[1] Presses Universitaires de France, 2001 (hereinafter cited as *Épistémologie*). A review of this book by Wanda Capeller, who also gives consideration to the question of whether or not law is a social science, can be found in [2003] *Droit et Société* 215. This review is followed by a short response from Jean-Michel Berthelot at 227. The death of Professor Berthelot was reported in *Le Monde* 14 February 2006. Reference should also be made to W.T. Murphy, *The Oldest Social Science? Configurations of Law and Modernity* (Oxford 1997). Professor Murphy is equally sceptical about the claim that law is a social science.

[2] It has to be pointed out of course that what constitutes a social science is of itself a highly difficult and debated issue, as is the question of the distinction between the social sciences and human sciences (humanities). Indeed, there is the whole issue of whether or not "social science" (and equally "human science") constitutes a discipline in itself or is simply an amalgam of individual disciplines: see *e.g.* A Renaut, "Humanisme et Sciences Humaines", in S Mesure and P Savidan (eds.), *Le Dictionnaire des Sciences Humaines* (Paris 2006), 584. Although this present article will not investigate directly these issues and debates (if only because of space constraint), it is nowhere being suggested that these questions and debates are irrelevant to the issues that are discussed.

[3] See Capeller, above note 1, p.224ff.

[4] See *e.g.* C. Atias, *Épistémologie du Droit* (Paris 1994).

[5] See also Berthelot [2003] *Droit et Société*, pp.227–228.

[6] Berthelot, *Épistémologie*, pp.11–12.

'*actants*', whatever name one gives them (agents, actors, speakers, social forces, or indeed institutions)". Law and politics, in contrast, "seek to explain the factors which determine a normative universe and to understand the reasons which the actors have to adhere to it." These 'textual sciences', as he calls them, no doubt make many references to the social sciences in general, but, he asserts, either "they define themselves through a specific object, approached in an interdisciplinary fashion or they make use of a hermeneutical and textual programme which is not their own."[7] The focal point for the social sciences that are included in his collection is, in brief, *interaction*[8] and it is this notion of interaction that permits one to construct a conceptual apparatus that, says Berthelot, will lead to a schematisation capable of transcending, at least to some extent, the individual social sciences in order to act as a basis for a more general epistemological discussion.[9] In other words Berthelot is excluding law on epistemological grounds.[10]

Is he right to do this? This of course is just another way of asking, at the epistemological level, whether or not law is a social science. Yet it might be worth reflecting at the outset not just upon Berthelot's reasoning but also upon law as a discipline. If one looks at textbooks on, say, sociology one is struck by the fact that much of what counts as knowledge is, to a greater or lesser extent, about methodology.[11] In saying this, one is not in any way implying anything pejorative about this (or any other) social science. Indeed, it is one of the objectives of the present article to establish method as a serious and central part of knowledge.[12] What one is saying is that the different schools of

---

[7] *Ibid.*, p.12.
[8] *Ibid.*
[9] *Ibid.*, p.13.
[10] Professor Murphy makes a similar point. He says that "to claim that law is a social science is to conflate distinctive epistemic styles, and to overlook the crucial difference which "positivity" makes to the character of the knowledge of society.... Between these two modes or epistemic styles, the gulf is immense...": Murphy, above note 1, at p.152. However Murphy is taking a rather different approach to the problem than Berthelot. He focuses on the relationship between the common law tradition and the modern social sciences and as a result sees the epistemic problem as "the Congruences [*sic*], Harmonies, and Concordances of the common law tradition" in contrast to "the production of performance indicators and the diagnosis of social problems" (p 152). This is an interesting and perhaps important point, but it may be that in terms of methodology the gulf between the two "epistemic styles" is not as great as Murphy claims. Central to Murphy's thesis is his assertion that "it is the enterprise of statistics, rather than economic theory, which has changed the world to which those involved in public affairs are orientated" (p 153). To premise the distinction between law and social science just on this statistics point is, as the totality of Berthelot's work surely indicates, too restrictive; moreover it is, perhaps, taking a too restrictive view of social science knowledge. As one French commentator puts it, as indispensable as statistics may be to the sociologist, they "cannot however be a substitute for sociological reasoning: mathematics do not have explanatory or comprehension power": O. Martin, "Mathématiques, Méthodes Quantitatives et Sciences Humaines", in Mesure and Savidan (eds.), *Le Dictionnaire des Sciences Humaines*, 750, 751. With respect, Professor Murphy's epistemological thesis is possibly too naive.
[11] See *e.g.* J.-P. Delas and B. Milly, *Histoire des pensées sociologiques* (2nd ed., Paris 2005).
[12] See also G. Samuel, "Taking Method Seriously" (2007) 2 Journal of Comparative Law 94 and 210.

sociology, knowledge of which is a central part of the discipline, are characterised by differences of what might be called method. However "method" here means more than just forms of reasoning such as induction and deduction or analogy and types of argumentation. It is, also, more than statistical method.[13] The term is employed to embrace what Berthelot calls schemes of intelligibility and what Thomas Kuhn called paradigms.[14] In other words, method merges with epistemology, this latter "discipline" itself raising a variety of questions about differing approaches.[15]

There is another reason for posing the question about whether or not law is a social science. In an essay devoted to the American jurist and comparative lawyer John Henry Wigmore, Annelise Riles makes the point that this jurist "made his scholarly name as an expert in the field of evidence, and his serious and still-popular treatise is a standard performance in that formalist genre".[16] Yet, she says, when it came to comparative law his work was seen as displaying a "dogged amateurism".[17] Now Riles uses this essay to make the point that amateurism is in fact a "defining methodological trait" not just of Wigmore's work, but of twentieth century comparative law in general.[18] "A consideration of Wigmore's life and scholarship", she concludes, "suggests that if amateurism is defined as a failure to analyse, then comparative law is inherently amateuristic." And, she adds, it "cannot be otherwise as long as our discipline remains comparative *law* that is, a discipline grounded in the culture of legal formalism, rather than comparative politics, literature, aesthetics or anthropology."[19] The second reason why the question of whether or not law is a social science thus becomes important in as much as it impacts directly on comparative law. If the comparatist cannot claim to be a social scientist it would seem that he or she would be ill-equipped to handle those disciplines other than formal law listed by Riles.

Pierre Legrand, equally, has asserted that the essence of comparative legal studies is its interdisciplinarity,[20] but his analysis

---

[13] *Cf.* Murphy, above note 1, p.155.
[14] T. Kuhn, *The Structure of Scientific Revolutions* (2nd ed., Chicago 1970). It is not being suggested here that schemes of intelligibility and paradigms are different ways of describing the same phenomenon or methods. As this article will hopefully indicate, schemes and paradigms are not to be confused one with the other.
[15] This merging of method and epistemology is evident in a work devoted to the method of undertaking a literature review: see C. Hart, *Doing a Literature Review* (London 1998).
[16] A. Riles, "Encountering Amateurism: John Henry Wigmore and the Uses of American Formalism", in A. Riles (ed.), *Rethinking the Masters of Comparative Law* (Oxford 2001), 94 at p.97.
[17] *Ibid.*, p.98.
[18] *Ibid.*, p.94.
[19] *Ibid.*, p.125.
[20] P. Legrand, *Le Droit Comparé* (Paris 1999), pp.27–32.

develops this point in a particularly pertinent way. Legrand argues that interdisciplinarity is vital because the comparison of formal legal rules is a meaningless exercise; what matters are the cognitive structures – the legal mentality – that lie beneath this surface.[21] And in order to discover these structures, or legal mentality, the comparatist must adopt a hermeneutical method instead of relying either on a causal analysis or on functionalism.[22] This methodological point should not pass unnoticed because it offers a direct link with the work of Jean-Michel Berthelot. One of Berthelot's major contributions to social science epistemology is his enumeration of six schemes of intelligibility which, according to the philosopher of science Gilles-Gaston Granger, offers real epistemological insights into all the human sciences.[23] What Pierre Legrand is indicating is that the comparatist must be *au fait* with social science epistemology, with works like *Épistémologie des sciences sociales*. Now this is not to imply that merely being familiar with social science methodology and epistemology is enough to turn comparative law into a social science. Yet if the comparatist is able to make an independent contribution to this methodology and epistemology it at least would offer a platform from which the jurist could begin to take issue with Berthelot's exclusion of law from the epistemological investigation. Can such an independent contribution be made? One possibility is to argue that many of the methods now employed by social scientists were formulated by jurists. This is an argument that will be pursued in the present article (an argument that will involve a defence of Donald Kelley's thesis). A second possibility is to move from the diachronic to the synchronic and argue that legal thought is still capable of making an independent contribution. This is an argument that (for reasons of space) will be pursued in a future paper.

II. Arguments against Law as a Social Science

Berthelot's central reason for excluding law from his social science epistemological investigation is that it is a discipline that is preoccupied with normative judgments and not with human interaction and behaviour as such. The object is a body of norms and not humans as an interacting social reality.[24] If one looks at the make up of most law programmes in Europe it would seem that Berthelot has a point. Law degrees in both civilian and common law faculties consist largely of learning what the law is; the emphasis is on learning rules

---
[21] *Ibid.*, p.28.
[22] *Ibid.*, p.31.
[23] G.-G. Granger, *La Science et les Sciences* (2nd ed., Paris 1995), pp.90–92.
[24] Berthelot. *Épistémologie*, p.12.

and these rules in turn have been described as the ontological and epistemological basis of legal knowledge.[25] As for the law professors themselves, their role, at least traditionally, has been to produce textbooks. These of course are guides to what the law is, but in addition they are supposed to be more than mere guides, "for they seek not only to arrange the cases systematically but to extract from them the general principles of the law and to show how those principles may be developed."[26] When taken together with law articles this *doctrine* plays a fundamental role in the formation of a legal system.[27] Perhaps the Research Assessment Exercise has, in the United Kingdom at least, changed expectations to some extent,[28] but it is still difficult to imagine that this organising role of the legal academic has fundamentally changed. Thus the United Kingdom judges certainly see the academic endeavour as being the search for principle[29] and in France "doctrine has as its mission to comment on positive law: therefore it comprehends only the professionals of law and only to the extent where they undertake this task of commentary".[30]

The writing of textbooks is, accordingly, regarded as being scientific since the academic is engaged in an exercise of reductionism.[31] This latter term has been described by one French philosopher specialising in theories of knowledge as "the epistemological strategy consisting of putting into action the concepts and methods destined to unify an area of knowledge which has had to fragment and diversify in order to understand its objects".[32] Common lawyers may not go as far as civilians in the quest for symmetry, structure and rationality in the organisation of legal knowledge,[33] but a considerable proportion of the academic literature in the common law world displays these tendencies.[34] Indeed, it has been argued that one reason why codification of English law never happened was because of the rise of the law faculties in England and Wales which resulted in an

---

[25] See *e.g.* P. Orianne, *Apprendre le Droit* (Brussels 1990), pp.153–155; F. Cownie, *Legal Academics: Cutlure and Identities* (Oxford 2004), p.35. The position is now more complicated in the common law world as two French jurists note: P. Jestaz and C. Jamin, *La Doctrine* (Paris 2004), pp.265–269. Professor Cownie's book provides a good up-to-date overview of legal education in the UK. As for the epistemological assumption that legal knowledge consists of rules and (or) norms: see *e.g.* J.-L. Bergel, *Méthodologie Juridique* (Paris 2001), p.30.
[26] H.F. Jolowicz, *Lectures on Jurisprudence* (London 1963), p.314.
[27] *Ibid.*, p.315.
[28] Cownie, above note 25, pp.135–141, 200.
[29] Robert Goff, *The Search for Principle*, reprinted in W. Swadling and G. Jones (eds.), *The Search for Principle: Essays in Honour of Lord Goff of Chieveley* (Oxford 1999), 313.
[30] Jestaz and Jamin, above note 25, p.171.
[31] *Ibid.*, pp.228–232.
[32] J.-M. Besnier, *Les Théories de la Connaissance* (Paris 1996), p.102.
[33] P Legrand, "Are Civilians Educable?" (1998) 18 Legal Studies 216.
[34] For a useful insight into the nineteenth century foundations of this rationalisation of English law, see N. Duxbury, *Frederick Pollock and the English Juristic Tradition* (Oxford 2004).

epistemological reorientation towards the rule model of law.[35] As far as the civil law is concerned, then, one of the arguments against law being regarded as a social science might be said to be grounded in its quest for natural science status.[36]

Now the problem facing law in the quest for this status is that the theories produced by academic lawyers cannot be falsified, this falsification method being one of the key tests, according to Karl Popper, for qualifying a theory as scientific.[37] The only alternative epistemological test is to associate law with the non-empirical science of mathematics where the test is one of coherence rather than correspondence.[38] The search for coherence in law has of course been such a dominant part of continental legal doctrine – it was one of the major preoccupations of legal scholars from the Humanists to the Pandectists[39] – that it might be the theme that sums up the whole of civilian legal history. Civilian legal thought has been the movement from an *ars judicandi* to a *mos geometricus*; that is to say a movement from judging to inference, the latter requiring, if the syllogism is to be viable, an ever more perfected rational organisation of law.[40] And even if civilian doctrine has moved on from this logical formalism – which it undoubtedly has – one legacy of this continental legal history is the association of law with scientific rationality. Whereas the Glossators and the Post-Glossators considered that the authority of law was to be found in the existence of the Roman texts themselves, which in turn were ultimately linked to the authority of God, the effect of the humanist revolution was to create an epistemological shift. The authority of law gradually became embedded in its scientific rationality with the result that one form of authority became replaced by another.[41] As far as the medieval jurists were concerned the texts themselves were authoritative just like the Bible or the *Qur'an* and the validity of the knowledge contained in these texts arises from their consensual acceptance as being the Word of God.[42] But for the jurists

---

[35] S. Hedley, "How has the Common Law Survived the Twentieth Century?" (1999) 50 Northern Ireland Legal Quarterly 283.
[36] Jestaz and Jamin, above note 25, pp.141–146. One should note that Murphy's book (above note 1) is concerned almost exclusively with the common law and does not really embrace the history of civilian legal thought.
[37] See generally K. Popper, *The Logic of Scientific Discovery* (London 1959; reprinted 2002).
[38] L. Soler, *Introduction à l'Épistémologie* (Paris 2000), pp.43–45.
[39] See P. Dubouchet, *Sémiotique Juridique: Introduction à une Science du Droit* (Paris 1990); F Wieacker, *A History of Private Law in Europe* (trans. T Weir, Oxford 1995); O. Jouanjan, *Une Histoire de la Pensée Juridique en Allemagne* (Paris 2005).
[40] Jouanjan, *Pensée Juridique en Allemagne*.
[41] P. Stein, *Roman Law in European History* (Cambridge 1999), pp.79–82.
[42] W. Ullmann, *The Growth of Papal Government in the Middle Ages* (2nd ed., London 1962), pp.359–366. "Not the least significant feature of the medieval period", writes Ullmann, "is the great reliance placed upon authority: authority – *auctoritas* – either in the shape of custom or tradition, or preferably in that of documentary evidence. The value of an *auctoritas* increased proportionately with its age: the older the *auctoritas* the more weight and greater standing it had" (pp.359–360).

who succeeded the medieval doctors one part of the authority was to be found in the "scientific" or systematic coherence of law because this rationality provided not just the deductively valid solutions but, in doing this and thus freeing judging from subjective bias, the very authority that gave law its validity.[43] Another dimension of law's authority was of course provided by the political (constitutional) validity of the source of the texts considered legal.[44]

In seeking therefore the status of a science law might be said to have become so preoccupied with its own internal organisation that, as a knowledge discipline, it has completely isolated itself from social reality.[45] By this is meant not that law fails to take account of social fact; it certainly does take account of fact and how it does this is an aspect that needs particular attention.[46] What is meant is that law as a body of knowledge has nothing to contribute, epistemologically speaking, to our knowledge of the world as an empirical phenomenon. Law does not, in other words, take as its object social reality – or at least an aspect of social reality – so as to produce a model that increases our knowledge of this reality. Law has as its object only itself.[47] It is in this sense a narcissistic science that is of little interest intellectually speaking to those outside of the discipline, save perhaps to those social scientists interested in studying the corps of lawyers as a social phenomenon itself.[48]

One might object to this assertion in saying that law does in fact have as its object an important social phenomenon, namely justice or, failing that, norms as a social "fact". Legal rules, concepts and institutions exist, it might be argued, to give expression to justice. However one difficulty here is that if justice is itself to be defined by law, then one is back to the problem of law as its own object. Alternatively if justice is a phenomenon that exists independently of law one will need to turn to other social science disciplines – for example to economics, moral philosophy, political theory or whatever – in order to give substance and definition to the phenomenon.[49] And in doing this one comes up against Berthelot's observation that law either defines itself "through a specific object, approached in an

---

[43] Wieacker, above note 39, pp.199–204, 213–215; Jestaz and Jamin, above note 25, pp.141–157. Murphy claims that with regard to the common law it is the medieval *auctoritas* that is still the guiding paradigm: Murphy, above note 1, pp.93–101.
[44] In the Roman sources what pleased the ruler (emperor, prince or king) had force of law: D.1.4.1.pr. However this text famously goes on to locate the ultimate source of sovereign power in the *populus* who had transferred this authority to the emperor via the *Lex regia*.
[45] Indeed the epistemological "purification" of law was one of the objectives of a section of the German Historical School: see generally Jouanjan, above note 39.
[46] C. Atias, *Épistémologie Juridique* (Paris 1985), pp.129–132.
[47] *Ibid.*, pp.31–36.
[48] For another view of the irrelevance of law see Murphy, above note 1, p.175.
[49] The definition of justice provided by the Roman texts, namely *suum cuique tribuendi* (Ulpian D.1.1.10.pr), begs more questions than it answers.

interdisciplinary fashion" or it makes "use of a hermeneutical and textual programme which is not [its] own."[50] Norms as a social phenomenon acting as the object of a "legal science" is equally problematic in that what constitutes the ultimate source of such norms is a concept that is either metaphysical[51] – for example Kelsen's *Grundnorm*[52] – or seemingly empirical, for example Hart's rule of recognition[53] or some other social source.[54] In other words, law is either creating its own epistemological validity or is relying upon a sociological phenomenon that cannot itself be explained by legal knowledge. Accordingly Berthelot's rejection of law as a social science capable of contributing to an epistemology of social sciences does seem, at first sight, difficult to refute.

III. METHODOLOGICAL POSSIBILITIES

If law itself, that is to say law as a system of propositions, seems unpromising as the basis for candidature to the category of social science, could the methods associated with the discipline prove of greater interest? Here the history of legal thought is more ambiguous since it could well be said that the methods used by the generations of jurists from Roman to modern times have of themselves had an important impact on social science thinking.[55] No doubt it could be argued that these methods have in truth been fashioned outside the discipline of law and thus, following Berthelot, they are simply further evidence of lawyers approaching their own texts through recourse to other disciplines. Yet if one looks at the history of the civil law as a history of changing methods it is possible to discern a number of factors that ought to be of interest to social science epistemology.

---

[50] Berthelot, *Épistémologie*, p.12.
[51] Atias, *Épistémologie Juridique*, above note 46, p.33.
[52] On which see M. Troper, *La Philosophie du droit* (Paris 2003), pp.47–50. Troper describes the *Grundnorm* as "une décision épistémologique" (p 49).
[53] H.L.A. Hart, *The Concept of Law* (2nd ed., Oxford 1994), pp.94–95, 100–110.
[54] On this point see J.W. Jones, *Historical Introduction to the Theory of Law* (Oxford 1940), pp.222–223. Interestingly Jones says here that the "science of law may be a social science – it may even be, in the words of Saleilles, the social science *par excellence* – but it is not the whole of sociology" (p 222). On the *Grundnorm* see Jones, pp.226–227; and on the metaphysical aspects of Kelsen's pure theory see pp.211–212, 232–233.
[55] This was no doubt true of Roman law: see J. Ellul, *Histoire des Institutions: 3 - Le Moyen Age* (9th ed., Paris 1982), pp.26–28. Note in particular Ellul's comment: "Le droit devient une sorte de réalité imposée au donné social, le mettant en forme, et finissant en somme par devenir plus « vrai » que les faits" (p 27). It was certainly true of medieval jurisprudence: see generally W. Ullmann, *Law and Politics in the Middle Ages* (London 1975). And it is true of the humanists as well: see *e.g.* D.R. Kelley, *The Beginning of Ideology: Consciousness and Society in the French Reformation* (Cambridge 1981). Murphy, however, is sceptical since he sees an epistemological break between legal thought and modern social science thinking, the latter being based on statistical thinking. See Murphy, above note 1. However Murphy is focusing on the common law rather than the civil law and possibly puts far too much emphasis on the epistemological importance of statistics. They are by no means irrelevant to epistemology in the social sciences (and he thus makes a good point), but they are not definitive of contemporary methodology if Berthelot and others are to be believed.

Indeed one might start with Berthelot's collection itself. Despite the absence of a chapter devoted to law, one might note that in the contribution from an historian there is right at the start a reference to Donald Kelley.[56] There is no doubt about Kelley's credentials as an historian, but he is equally a jurist best known for his work on the French humanists. In particular he has argued that these sixteenth-century academics were not just jurists; they were the founders of modern historical research methods and thus hold an important position in the epistemology of history.[57]

Indeed Kelley, as jurist, is important for his view that law is not just a social science but one that is central to social thought in general. "If the book of nature is 'written in the language of mathematics' (as Galileo thought)", he writes, "the book of human nature in its social forms has been written, in the most practical contexts, in the language of the law."[58] Whether Berthelot was aware that Kelley seems to be advancing a thesis about the place of law in social science epistemology somewhat at odds with his own argument is an interesting question. Had Kelley been invited to contribute a chapter to *Épistémologie des sciences sociales* the American academic would no doubt have re-quoted Walter Ullmann's remark that "medieval jurisprudence was forced to elucidate some basic principles about society, and was thus led to consider topics which, under modern conditions, would be dealt with, not by lawyers, but by the sociologist."[59] Jurists, it would seem, once did the work of sociologists; not only did they fashion the modern research methods but they equally provided a *grille de lecture* for understanding early modern European society.[60]

It might at this point be useful to turn to Berthelot's own major contribution to social science methodology and epistemology. For it is this social theorist who has to date provided one of the most coherent accounts of the methodological schemes of intelligibility through which social scientists analyse the object of their investigations, namely society and social fact. According to Berthelot the question to ask is this: "what are the ontological and epistemological principles presupposed by the various existing research programmes?"[61] His response to this question is to assert that if one studies the main

---

[56] J. Revel, "Les Sciences Historiques.", in Berthelot, *Épistémologie*, 21 at p.25.
[57] D. Kelley, *Foundations of Modern Historical Scholarship* (New York 1970).
[58] D. Kelley, *The Human Measure: Social Thought in the Western Legal Tradition* (Cambridge, Mass. 1990), p.12. However note Murphy's specific dissent from this comment by Kelley: Murphy, above note 1, pp.3–4.
[59] W. Ullmann, *The Medieval Idea of Law as Represented by Lucas de Penna* (London 1946), p.163; quoted in Kelley, *The Human Measure*, at p.12.
[60] See *e.g.* Ellul, above note 55.
[61] Berthelot, *Épistémologie*, pp.483–484.

sociological schools six different *principes* – or, as another sociologist puts it, *grilles de lecture*[62] – can be *dégagés*. They are:

the *causal* scheme (if x, then y or $y = f(x)$); the *functional* scheme (S→X→S, where one phenomenon X is analysed from the position of its function – X→S – in a given system); the *structural* scheme (where X results from a system founded, like language, on disjunctive rules, A or not A); the *hermeneutical* scheme (where X is the symptom, the expression of an underlying signification to be discovered through interpretation); the *actional* scheme (where X is the outcome, within a given space, of intentional actions); finally, the *dialectical* scheme (where X is the necessary outcome of the development of internal contradictions within a system).[63]

These schemes are, of course, in need of much elaboration and explanation if their epistemological and methodological importance is to be fully appreciated.[64] But for present purposes it will hopefully suffice if they are developed only in a limited way in relation to law. The point here is not so much to examine the schemes themselves, as important as they are;[65] what needs to be stressed is the relationship between these methodological and epistemological *grilles de lecture* and the claim that law is (or is not) a social science.

It should be immediately evident that these schemes of intelligibility have a direct relevance for law in that they encapsulate all the various methods used in legal reasoning and analysis. Tort lawyers spend much time applying causal and *actanciel* methods in the analysis of case law problems – the classic "actional" approach being an analysis utilising the "reasonable man" or "le bon père de famille" – just as those writing judgments may make use of functional methods (for example policy reasoning or the application of the mischief rule in statutory interpretation) in place of a hermeneutical analysis (what did the legislator mean or what was the will of the legislator or testator?).[66] The dialectical scheme finds expression not just in the legal maxim *audi alteram partem* but equally in a whole range of conceptual and category dichotomies such as the distinctions between public and private law, real and personal rights, corporeal and incorporeal property and so on.[67] At the level of legal theory structuralism,

---

[62] C. Giraud, *Histoire de la Sociologie* (2nd ed., Paris 2000), pp.86–123.
[63] Berthelot, *Épistémologie*, p.484.
[64] For a more developed treatment see G. Samuel, *Epistemology and Method in Law* (Aldershot 2003), pp.295–334.
[65] G Samuel, Taking Method Seriously, above note 12.
[66] For an "actional" approach to remoteness of damage see *Overseas Tankship (UK) Ltd* v. *Morts Dock* and *Engineering Co Ltd (The Wagon Mound (No 1))* [1961] A.C. 388 where the Privy Council adopted the test of foreseeability of the reasonable man in place of an objective causal analysis (directness test). As for statutory interpretation and methodology, one might profitably look at *Birmingham CC* v. *Oakley* [2001] 1 A.C. 617, where different schemes of intelligibility seem very much in evidence.
[67] J.-L. Bergel, *Théorie Générale du Droit* (4th ed., Paris 2003), n° 253.

intermixed with hermeneutics, finds one of its most perfect developments in nineteenth-century German legal thinking, as a new work by a French jurist so clearly reminds us.[68] But this "transcendental nonsense" was to be displaced in American legal theory by an appeal to "the functional approach".[69] In the civil law world, however, a structural analysis remains (in some quarters at least) very much in vogue.[70] The history of theory and method in law could, in other words, be explained by reference to Berthelot's schemes.

This would not have surprised Berthelot of course, for, as we have seen, he asserted that lawyers make use of social science methods. Yet what might be more of a surprise is the argument that, diachronically speaking, it is not always a question of lawyers adopting and adapting schemes from disciplines outside law. It is a question, as Kelley asserts, of the history of methods and the history of law often marching very much hand-in-hand. Where but in the *Digest* does one find a rich source of "social science" methodology from the ancient world? Admittedly with respect to the natural sciences the position is more complex in that it is in Greek philosophy and mathematics – in particular in the writings of Aristotle – that one looks for the foundations of the scientific mind.[71] But what is of fundamental importance with respect to the social sciences are the institutional concepts to be found in the work of the Roman jurists. Notions such as *obligatio* and *dominium* were not just important ideas in themselves; when combined with the institutions of *persona*, *res* and *actiones* they created a structural system in which individual owners and contractors were integrated into a social whole itself given expression by concepts such as the *respublica*, *fiscus* and *ius publicum*. This whole was genuinely a system in that it was capable, as has been illustrated elsewhere,[72] of creating its own elements which then became integrated into the social system as realities. Thus the moment a *universitas* became capable of bringing an *actio* in its own name, it effectively became a *persona*; equally as soon as an *actio in rem* was available in respect of a *ius* this latter became a form of intangible property (*res incorporalis*).[73] One is not talking here merely of relatively passive systems capable of creating other conceptual elements such as intellectual property and corporate legal persons. Such structural thinking was integrated into legal reasoning itself.

---

[68] Jouanjan, above note 39.
[69] F. Cohen, "Transcendental Nonsense and the Functional Approach" (1935) 35 Columbia Law Review 809.
[70] Orianne, above note 25, pp.271–286.
[71] Granger, above note 23, pp.21–22.
[72] See Samuel, *Epistemology and Method in Law*, above note 64.
[73] G Samuel, *The Foundations of Legal Reasoning* (Antwerp 1994), pp.171–190.

This structural thinking manifests itself in legal reasoning in a number of ways. First it is to be found in the way the reasoning of the Roman jurists is often centred on the question of whether or not an *actio* is available and against whom; this institution, in other words, regularly acts as a vehicle for discussing more substantive issues such as blame, cause and (or) risk.[74] Secondly, although the jurists seem often to be discussing problems at the level of fact, these facts are usually organised in terms of concepts that might appear descriptive but are actually more schematic in their structure. For example, the jurist Paul tells us that it is not just the owner of stolen property who has the *actio furti* but anyone who has an "interest" in the thing, such as a hirer.[75] What is being constructed here is a model based upon the institutions of *persona* and *res* in which the person who is entitled to the action is delineated either by the legal (institutional) relationship of ownership (*dominium*) or by the existence of an *interest*.[76] This notion of an interest is of course one that was much later to become a key concept in economic theory,[77] but the idea that the social science model of "individuals" endowed with an economic "interests" is a creation of the discipline of economics is, historically speaking, not true. Economists may talk of how the notion of an interest allows one to evaluate society and its individuals in terms of economic relations and function,[78] yet it is not the lawyers who have appropriated the term from economists. Rather it is economists making use of a model of social reality fashioned by Roman jurists.

A third way in which structural thinking manifests itself in Roman legal reasoning is through categories. These categories were partly rooted in what the Romans perceived as social reality, but, and this is the point to be stressed, only partly. As Ulpian says of the law of contracts, *natura enim rerum conditum, ut plura sint negotia quam vocabula*.[79] That there are more transactions in the real world than are capable of being represented in the established categories of contracts, suggests clearly that one is dealing with a rationalised model rather than working directly on the facts. Indeed, as another jurist points out, facts, unlike the laws, are not something capable of being grasped by the mind, for law is definite while facts are not.[80] Accordingly the reasoning of the Roman lawyers is one of negotiating an adequate correspondence between a reasoning model – consisting of institu-

---

[74] One famous example is D.9.2.52.2.
[75] D.47.2.86.
[76] A variation on the interrelation of legal institutions and relations is to be found in D.47.2.60: here the *actio furti* interrelates with interest and contract.
[77] A. Leroux and A. Marciano, *La Philosophie Économique* (Paris 1998), pp.15–18.
[78] *Ibid.*, pp.17–18.
[79] D.19.5.4.
[80] D.22.6.2.

tions (*personae*, *res* and *actiones*), institutional relations (*obligationes*, *dominium*, *possessio* and so on) and empirical concepts (interests, damage, fault, fraud and the like) – that insinuates itself within the facts and the actual facts themselves. Are these texts to be found in the *Digest* really just about normative judgments? Surely they are as much about "human interaction and behaviour" as any other social science? At all events these texts certainly invite one to reflect upon a fundamental epistemological challenge that is to be found in all of the social sciences. What is the relationship between the knowing *intellectus* and the *res* that forms the object of knowledge?

As for the schemes of intelligibility themselves, they equally are to be found in the reasoning of the Roman jurists. A causal analysis of facts operates both as a constituent of liability in cases of, in particular, wrongful damage[81] and, in combination with a hermeneutical approach, as a means of interpreting legal texts. An example of this latter kind of reasoning is evident in the discussion concerning the interpretation of the aedilicean edict imposing a duty upon sellers of slaves to disclose any disease or other defect. What becomes clear in the discussion of particular cases is that the jurists distinguish between symptoms and disease; and thus in answer to the question whether a bed-wetting slave is diseased the jurist replies that it depends. If the problem arose because, say, the slave was drunk or too lazy to get up that is not a disease; if the defect was caused by a problem with the bladder then this would amount to a disease and the buyer would be entitled to rescind the sale.[82] A similar causal analysis is applied to other symptom problems.[83] A functional dimension can also provide a logical premise in that if every defect is considered a disease – for example missing teeth – it would give rise to a situation where whole classes of people, for instance the elderly, would have to be considered diseased.[84] Structuralism is particularly evident in the Institutes: Gaius constructs his work with constant reference to genus and species[85] and points out the error of confusing the two levels.[86] Hermeneutics even attracts its own chapter in the *Digest*: what do words *signify*?[87] A dialectical analysis may also be adopted in respect of factual situations to aid, for example, the interpretation of a word. Thus in an attempt to define accurately a "fugitive" one Roman jurist asserts that a distinction must be made between a "fugitive" and a "wanderer",

---

[81] See *e.g.* D.9.2.11.pr.
[82] D.21.1.14.4.
[83] See *e.g.* D.21.1.13.4.
[84] D.21.1.11.
[85] See *e.g* G.3.89.
[86] See *e.g.* G.4.1.
[87] D.50.16.

the latter indulging merely in aimless roaming about and time-wasting.[88] A statement (*dictum*) must equally be distinguished from a *promissio*,[89] just as a specific assertion must be differentiated from failing to speak.[90] Making sense of both *les mots et les choses* is often aided, in other words, by simple oppositions.

The identification of these schemes in the Roman texts may seem, today, obvious if not trite; but the point to be made here is that the Roman jurists were just as involved in *un engagement ontologique* as any modern social scientist, and long before theorists used such terms to describe the epistemological complexities of contemporary social science.[91] But the jurists did more than just engage with the facts of society. As Kelley observes, the "distinctive language of sociology was created through a sort of distillation from social and legal conventions at hand – beginning with the obvious designations of personality, property, action, inheritance, custom, contract, domination, sacred and civil law, public and private law, law-making and law-finding, codification and administration, and other commonplaces of the old Gaian system."[92] Kelley might well have added that the distinctive methodology of the social sciences (that is schemes of intelligibility) is equally just as much a distillation from the legal methods that were at hand in the *Digest* and the *Institutes*. Of course modern French and German legal theory, with its emphasis on texts, norms and on axiomatic structures, might seem kilometres from *un engagement ontologique*, which of course it is. Yet had Berthelot looked beyond modern legal theory – had he appreciated that "sociology was ... the ghost of jurisprudence past"[93] – he might have realised that the real methodological and epistemological challenge for jurists is in the diversity of legal activity[94] and in the very place where social fact and legal knowledge meet, namely in the deciding of cases.[95]

IV. Paradigms

However, the challenge of social science epistemology does not begin and end with schemes of intelligibility, as Berthelot's own rich writing makes clear.[96] The schemes usually combine so as to give expression to a governing paradigm, the term itself being used by Berthelot –

---

[88] D.21.1.17.14.
[89] D.21.1.19.2.
[90] D.21.1.52.
[91] *Cf.* Berthelot, *Épistémologie*, p.517.
[92] Kelley, *The Human Measure*, above note 58, p.275.
[93] *Ibid.*
[94] A point emphasised by Atias, above note 4, pp.23–28. This little book would have made an excellent chapter in Berthelot's *Épistémologie*.
[95] Atias, above note 4, at p.119.
[96] See in particular one of his own chapters in Berthelot, *Épistémologie*, pp.457–519: "Programmes, Paradigmes, Disciplines: Pluralité et Unité des Sciences Sociales".

although he actually abandons the expression[97] – to mean "an ill designated class weakly formulated but nevertheless powerfully significant in its attitudes and behaviours".[98] In fact the term, usually attributed to Thomas Kuhn,[99] is notoriously difficult to define and is often summed up as a "vision of the world", a "way of seeing"[100] or a "*cadre de pensée*".[101]

In the social sciences one possible use of the term "paradigm" is to give expression to a number of fundamental epistemological dichotomies such as the ones between holism and individualism, order and chaos and nature and culture. Take first of all the opposition between a whole and its parts whose paradigmatic and epistemological status is often traced back to the nominalist revolution associated (possibly incorrectly) with William of Ockham.[102] Does society exist as an ontological reality – as a "thing" – or are there only individuals? The question is fundamental both in the natural and social sciences because the difference of levels reveals differences of information. For example statistical modelling might well reveal that there is a greater preponderance of disease x in communities situated near factories y. This is clearly valuable information, but operating at this holistic level there is a great danger that one might conclude that y is the cause of x, a dangerous assumption. An analogous problem arises in the social sciences: statistics may well reveal that it is the children of middle class families who dominate the higher education institutions but such a correlation does not explain the causes of this phenomenon. In order to search out such an explanation it is necessary to adopt a different methodological paradigm; the social scientist must think in terms of the individual and examine the causes in relation to individuals within families.[103] One has to move, in other words, from structural models (statistics) to causal and actional schemes. The dichotomy has political implications as well since social theorists such as Marx – who saw society in terms of class – are likely to generate a different kind of political hypothesis than theorists such as Weber who saw society in terms of individuals.[104] In short, so important is this paradigm dichotomy between holism and individualism that it has attracted a chapter to itself in Berthelot's *Épistémology des sciences sociales*.[105]

---

[97] Berthelot, *Épistémologie*, p.468.
[98] *Ibid.*, p.457. But *cf.* p.469.
[99] T. Kuhn, *The Structure of Scientific Revolutions* (2nd ed., Chicago 1970).
[100] J. Pheby, *Methodology and Economics: A Critical Introduction* (London 1988), p.37.
[101] Berthelot, *Épistémologie*, p.468.
[102] See now B. Tierney, *The Idea of Natural Rights* (Atlanta 1997).
[103] See generally R. Boudon and R. Fillieule, *Les Méthodes en Sociologie* (12th ed., Paris 2002), pp.41–90.
[104] S. Gordon, *The History and Philosophy of Social Science* (London 1991), pp.479–480.
[105] B. Valade, "De l'Explication dans les Sciences Sociales: Holisme et Individualisme", in Berthelot, *Épistémologie*, at p.357ff.

Yet as Yan Thomas reminds us, the debate has its roots in Roman law.[106] In a text that must have fascinated the medieval doctors a Roman jurist describes a case that was put to him concerning the appointment of judges for a hearing. As some judges had been excused and others appointed in their place the question arose as to whether this replacement process meant that a different court had been constituted.[107] The jurist responds that even if all of the judges had been replaced it would still be the same court and he justifies this by reference to other examples where a thing remains the same although the parts change. An army legion and a community are always the same despite the turnover of personnel. However the most striking example is that of the boat whose every plank is gradually replaced over the years; the boat, says the jurist, is the same boat even if every single plank has been replaced.[108] Now at the level of legal reasoning this dichotomy between a whole and its parts is of fundamental importance because the institutional system, based upon relations between persons (*personae*) and things (*res*), continually has to move from the group to the individual.

For example the institutional system envisages a society in which individual persons own individual things. But what amounts to an individual "thing"? The response of a Roman jurist to this question is that there are three kinds (*genera*) of things: there are things that have a single spirit such as a stone, slave or beam of wood; there are things that are made up (*quod ex contingentibus*) of other "cohering" (*inter se cohaerentibus constat*) things, such as a ship or a house; and there are things made up of individual entities (*quod ex distantibus constat*) like a people (*populus*), legion or flock.[109] All this is set out by the jurist because it has real practical consequences given the existence of property concepts in the institutional system. With respect to usucapion – the acquiring of ownership of a thing through long possession in good faith – the first kind of thing presents no problem, but, of course, the other two do. What if one possesses tiles or bricks that later become incorporated in someone else's building?[110] What if one possesses a plot of land on which there is a lost gold ring: does one also possess the ring?[111] Then there is the problem of the flock. According to one jurist although a flock does exist in nature (*natura*) as a thing[112] one cannot obtain ownership of it through usucapion in

---

[106] Y. Thomas, "L'Extrême et l'Ordinaire: Remarques sur le Cas Médiéval de la Communauté Disparue", in J.-C. Passeron and J. Revel (eds.), *Penser par Cas* (Paris 2005), 45 at p.55.
[107] D.5.1.76.
[108] See also D.46.3.98.8; D.44.2.7.pr.
[109] D.41.3.30pr.
[110] D.41.3.30.1.
[111] *Ibid.*
[112] And see D.30.1.22.

the same way as with individual things; it is the individual animals that are possessed and not the flock.[113] Analogous problems arise with respect to *res judicata*. If one has unsuccessfully claimed for a ship can one subsequently claim for all its planks?[114] Or if one has claimed for a flock and failed can one then claim for several individual head of cattle?[115]

It is not of course being asserted here that the Romans were indulging in some kind of social science epistemological reflection. What they were doing, however, was to engage with social fact and it is in the context of this very engagement that the elements that make up epistemological debate start to reveal themselves. This is true with respect to the other paradigm dichotomies as well. We have already seen that the Romans began to be aware of a difference between order and chaos with respect to the distinction between mistakes of fact and mistakes of law; the law can and should be definite while fact can baffle the wisest of people.[116] It is not unreasonable, then, to assume that the Roman notion of *ratio iuris* – the term is to be found in the *Digest*[117] – amounted to a rationalised social order even if certainty was to be preferred on occasions over this rationality.[118] What is not rational ought not to be extended by analogy.[119] Moreover the force of law, be it in respect of custom or statute, is justified by reference to a kind of social contract acceptance within the *populus*. *Nam quid interest suffragio populus voluntatem suam declaret an rebus ipsis et factis?*[120] The will of the people declares itself not just through voting but equally by their actions.

This kind of reflection provokes the next paradigm question, if only because it is of course debatable whether these ideas about the *populus* have any basis in social reality. What Berthelot calls *le pôle naturaliste* is "that which considers that social phenomena are an extension of natural phenomena and not requiring specific explanation". It is, as he says, sufficient "for analysis to determine the mechanisms on which they depend".[121] Is law the product of nature or culture? One can thus oppose to this naturalist paradigm that of culture. As for this latter paradigm, "they are the cultural norms and values of the group or of the society which, through the mediation of socialisation, enculturation or inculcation, define the sense of behaviour or, according to certain definitions, practices".[122] Are ideas

---

[113] D.41.3.30.2.
[114] D.44.2.7pr.
[115] D.44.2.21.1.
[116] D.22.6.2.
[117] See *e.g.* D.1.3.14.
[118] See *e.g.* D.1.3.20.
[119] D.1.3.39.
[120] D.1.3.32.1.
[121] Berthelot, *Épistémologie*, at p.498.
[122] *Ibid.*, at p.247.

of social contract, legal rationality (*ratio iuris*), legal knowledge (*scientia iuris*)[123] and the transfer of sovereignty (*Lex regia*) cultural or natural phenomena? It might be tempting to say that this paradigm debate takes one beyond the Roman texts themselves in that any opposition between Roman society as culture and Roman law as *naturalis ratio* is not obviously to be found in the texts. Yet in developing an institutional 'system' around *persona*, *res* and *actio* the question arises as to whether this system has transcended Roman law. Is it not a system capable of applying to any body of rules irrespective of time and culture? Indeed is it not the system upon which the whole of the modern civilian private law tradition is based?

While not denying the importance of the link between culture and law, Alan Watson makes the point that Justinian's *Institutes* – which reproduces the Gaian plan[124] – "was the basic text for beginning law students throughout Europe for hundreds of years, and gave them their concepts and structures."[125] And without this introductory book – this "nutshell" as he calls it – the subsequent reception of Roman law into modern Europe would have been "a great deal more difficult and would have been very different".[126] Watson subsequently concludes by expressing a certain scepticism with respect to the link between law and culture. In what sense, he asks does Gaius' *Institutes*, reflect Roman pagan, and (via Justinian) later Christian, society? Indeed he goes on to issue a challenge. Can anyone produce "one scrap of evidence that the *Institutes* is in any way indicative of the specific religious, political, economic or social conditions of early Byzantium"?[127] And he concludes that had the *Institutes* reflected Byzantine society, "it would have been influential in the west only with difficulty."[128] The implication here is that in order to understand legal concepts and law's systemic rationality one does not need to study legal culture as such; one needs to study the Gaian system and its elements in a synchronic fashion in order to understand its scientific or natural *essence*, as indeed the German jurists were to do with an extraordinary vigour.[129]

This view has not gone unchallenged. Arguing from the position of the cultural paradigm, Pierre Legrand is scathing in his criticism of the idea that law can be transplanted from one culture to another or can be studied in terms of similarity between rules from different

---

[123] D.1.2.2.35.
[124] J.1.2.12.
[125] A Watson, "The Importance of 'Nutshells'" (1994) 42 American Journal of Comparative Law 1, 10.
[126] *Ibid.*, p.18.
[127] *Ibid.*, p.21.
[128] *Ibid.*
[129] On which see Jouanjan, above note 39.

cultures.[130] Such thinking is "the result of a particularly crude apprehension of what law is and of what a rule is".[131] As far as this comparatist is concerned rules are the product of a particular culture and as a result cannot be studied simply in terms of a bare propositional statement. "There is", he says, "more to ruleness than a series of inscribed words which is to say that a rule is not identical to the inscribed words".[132] Rules as words are simply the "surface" of the law and as such one needs to adopt a deep hermeneutical approach in order to get below this surface – this layer of words as signifiers – to discover the *mentalité* in which positive law is anchored.[133] Legrand defines this mentality as the cognitive structures that underpin the rules and the job of the comparatist is to reveal them "*à travers une «comparaison à étages»*."[134] One can switch the point of view in saying that any "manifestation of posited law thus exists as the unknowing articulator or vector of a cultural sensibility which, while it is actually inscribed in the textual fragments themselves, requires the comparatist's ampliative acts of interpretation to come to light."[135] The job of the comparatist is, then, not one of disembodying aspects of law from its cultural embeddedness – it is not a matter of detaching from say the *Institutes* a system-as-entity – because "the specificity of legal discourse lies precisely in its *embeddedness*".[136] This "venture into cultural hermeneutics"[137] represents a shift not just at the level of schemes of intelligibility – away from structuralism and from causality as logical necessity – but equally at the level of the paradigm because transmissions between cultures do not take place via "some transcendent, supra-individual entity".[138] It is not a question of *essence* existing as some kind of detached *res*.

Now it has to be stressed at once that the point of raising this paradigm debate is not to enter into the debate itself. The point is to show how the paradigm debate itself is the result of nothing less than an engagement with the facts of social reality. Whether one agrees with Watson or not – or equally whether one agrees with Legrand or not – is hardly the matter in issue here. What matters is that both jurists are engaged in an exercise that has as its object not just texts but the "*interactions entre actants*".[139] This is particularly evident in the work

---

[130] See *e.g.* P. Legrand, "The Impossibility of 'Legal Transplants'" (1997) 4 Maastricht Journal of European and Comparative Law 111.
[131] *Ibid.*, at p.113.
[132] *Ibid.*, at p.115.
[133] Legrand, *Le Droit Comparé*, above note 20, p.28.
[134] *Ibid.*
[135] P Legrand, Comparative Legal Studies and the Matter of Authenticity (2006) 1 Journal of Comparative Law 365, 371.
[136] *Ibid.*, p.372 emphasis in the original.
[137] *Ibid.*, p.378.
[138] *Ibid.*, p.386.
[139] Cf Berthelot, *Épistémologie*, at p.12.

of Professor Legrand whose reflections on comparative legal studies are specifically aimed at providing a deep hermeneutical alternative to a comparative law "which [just] engages in the juxtaposition of substantive and adjectival posited law".[140] Yet even Professor Watson's thesis is capable of being envisaged as much more than *une science du texte* exercise trapped within *un univers normatif*.[141] As Kelley points out, the Gaian system "entailed not only moral priorities and a means of ordering reality but also a characteristic mode of perceiving, of construing, and potentially of controlling the social field."[142] It is a system that can be seen at one and the same time as an entity that is trans-cultural (for those who subscribe to the nature paradigm) and as an epistemological structure that integrates itself within the facts of social reality.[143] This integration becomes in itself an epistemological framework for understanding *les interactions entre actants* – and indeed for understanding the relations between *actants* and things. The "categories of person-thing-action constitute, first implicitly and later explicitly, what might be regarded as the metaphysical (or metanomical) foundations of Roman social thought" and, given the later developments, "they may also be regarded as a system rivalling the naturalistic construction of Aristotelianism, as another version of the many-faceted contrast between Physis and Nomos – of primary and secondary nature."[144] In short the epistemological implications of the Gaian system for the social sciences cannot be underestimated.

V. THE AUTHORITY PARADIGM

It might at this stage be tempting, then, to conclude that Professor Berthelot made an error of judgment in excluding law from his epistemological investigation of the social sciences. When approached diachronically the discipline of law has its own distinct contribution to make to social science epistemology. However this diachronic dimension is not a paradigm or orientation[145] that represents the approach of most lawyers, even with respect to those working in law faculties. Most jurists – in Europe as a whole at least – adopt a synchronic approach to their discipline and such an approach is

---

[140] Legrand, above note 135, p.393.
[141] Cf Berthelot, *Épistémologie*, at p.12.
[142] Kelley, *The Human Measure*, above note 58, p.49.
[143] See further Samuel, *Epistemology and Method in Law*, above note 64.
[144] Kelley, *The Human Measure*, above note 58, p.49.
[145] The dichotomy between a diachronic and synchronic approach can be regarded as a paradigm question given the relative imprecision of the term "paradigm". It is certainly an "epistemological approach": see R. Blanché, *L'Épistémologie* (3rd ed., Paris 1983), pp.33–39. But it might be better to regard it as operating at a level even higher than a paradigm in that it is less a way of seeing the world and more an approach to knowledge itself.

supported by the weight of legal theory.[146] Historical jurisprudence, in the common law world, enjoys little emphasis in today's jurisprudence textbooks[147] and few graduates will leave their law faculties with a knowledge of the contributions made to their discipline by for example Gaius, Ulpian, Bartolus, Cujas, Domat, Pothier and (or) Savigny.[148] Students tend to learn what the law is rather than how law has been constructed as a discipline. In many ways one should not be surprised by this. As has been mentioned earlier, law's quest for scientific status has resulted in the emphasis being put on coherence and this has encouraged what Robert Blanché terms (for the natural sciences) *une analyse directe*, that is to say a static or synchronic view of a science's contemporary structure.[149]

In the common law world it is probably true to say that this emphasis on law as science is treated with much scepticism and the great majority of jurists working in Anglo-American law faculties would no doubt prefer to see their discipline associated with the social sciences.[150] Nevertheless the influence of civilian thinking on legal theory ought not to be underestimated[151] and with the growth of law as an academic subject in England and Wales from the end of the nineteenth century the law-as-rules model increasingly has come to dominate common law thinking.[152] Indeed, for Richard Susskind, "one fundamental assumption… should be articulated: that *rules* do and should play a central role in legal science, legal knowledge representation, and in legal reasoning." For "[o]verwhelming authority for this proposition can be found in legal theory, and even a philosopher such as Dworkin, who has questioned the sufficiency of rules for legal decision-making, does nevertheless himself seem to presuppose a predominant place for them, as MacCormick has shown."[153] The result of this theorising is that students spend much of their time examining legal texts and trying to make sense of them using what might be termed shallow hermeneutical[154] and (or) structural

---

[146] See in particular Ronald Dworkin's comment about the irrelevance of history to legal theory: R. Dworkin, *Law's Empire* (London 1986), p.14.
[147] P. Stein, "The Tasks of Historical Jurisprudence", in N. MacCormick and P. Birks (eds.), *The Legal Mind: Essays for Tony Honoré* (Oxford 1986), 293.
[148] Knowledge of these jurists will no doubt vary from system to system and so it would be misleading to say that every law graduate will be ignorant of the civil law's rich historical tradition. However, this said, because the law degree plays an essential role in the qualification of practitioners in the civilian tradition this inevitably means that the law curriculum is dominated by what might be called the foundational doctrinal subjects.
[149] Blanché, above note 145, p.34.
[150] See generally Cownie, above note 25. See also K. Gray and S. Gray, "The Rhetoric of Reality", in J. Getzler (ed.), *Rationalizing Property, Equity and Trusts* (London 2003), 204.
[151] See generally P. Stein, *Legal Evolution: The Story of an Idea* (Cambridge 1980).
[152] See Hedley, above note 35. And see also Gray and Gray, above note 150.
[153] R. Susskind, *Expert Systems in Law* (Oxford 1987), pp.78–79.
[154] The term "shallow" is used here to differentiate this kind of interpretative approach from the one advocated by Professor Legrand in respect of comparative legal studies: see Legrand, above note 135. See also Murphy, above note 1, p.94.

methods.[155] One is not inviting the contemporary law student to examine a statute or a judgment as a signifier for a deep cultural mentality; what the student is invited primarily to do is to read a legal text in such a way that she will know what the law "is" and be able to apply it to relevant factual situations. Of course this "is" aspect, and the methodology that now accompanies it, is no doubt more critical in its orientation in the common law faculties than in the High Court.[156] As Christopher McCrudden has recently observed, referring to Fiona Cownie's work, "We're all socio-legal now",[157] an expression that recalls William Twining's comment that "we are all Realists now".[158] What these expressions indicate is that rules and concepts – the law – is now studied, in many common law jurisdictions, in their (its) social, political and (or) economic context and even the foundational subjects may well be approached, if not from a "law and..." perspective, then at least in a context that emphasises law's functional role.[159] The emphasis in the common law faculties is now more on functionalism than conceptualism (structuralism), although, as we shall see, the late Professor Birks attempted to reverse this trend.[160]

Yet it has to be asked to what extent this social functionalist emphasis has effected a shift of paradigm. Certainly it has encouraged a more social science orientated enquiring approach towards legal rules and concepts and this shift away from formalism has impacted upon the judiciary as well.[161] Indeed some English judges are even prepared to pay lip service to, for example, the law and economics school.[162] But what it has not done is to encourage a more sophisticated attitude towards methodology and epistemology.

Imagine three students from the same town and acquainted with each other leave for university, one to study sociology, one to study cinema and the third to read law. Towards the end of their courses, which they have pursued very diligently, they meet to discuss the

---

[155] Orianne, above note 25, pp.271–286.
[156] *Cf.* Vinelott J in *Derby* and *Co v Weldon (No.5)* [1989] 1 W.L.R. 1244, 1250.
[157] C. McCrudden, "Legal Research and the Social Sciences" (2006) 122 L.Q.R. 632, 645 referring to Cownie, above note 25. Professor Cownie's rich and interesting work on academic lawyers can certainly be described as social science research, and important social science work; but she would probably be the first to say that her book is not about to be adopted as a standard text in any of the foundational subjects required by the professions.
[158] W. Twining, *Karl Llewellyn and the Realist Movement* (London 1973), p.382. The actual quote is: "Realism is dead; we are all realists now".
[159] Cownie, above note 25, pp.197–199.
[160] Peter Birks' work is discussed critically by the present author in "Can Gaius Really be Compared to Darwin?" (2000) 49 I.C.L.Q. 297 and in "English Private Law: Old and New Thinking in the Taxonomy Debate" (2004) 24 O.J.L.S. 335.
[161] In *Watts v. Aldington* (1993) Steyn L.J. said, "In a less formalistic age it is now clear that the question... is a policy issue" in that more than one "solution is logically defensible" and "good sense, fairness and respect for the reasonable expectations of contracting parties suggests that the best solution" is one which "at least has the merit of promoting more sensible results than any other solution" (quoted in *Jameson* v. *CEGB* [1997] 3 W.L.R. 151, 161).
[162] See G. Samuel, *Cases and Materials on Torts* (Exeter 2006), pp.57–59.

content of what they have studied. The sociology student will certainly be able to distinguish functionalism from structuralism, holism from methodological individualism and, probably, a causal approach from a hermeneutical one. These methods are associated with the very construction of the subject.[163] The film studies student might be a little less aware of all these different schemes of intelligibility and paradigms as they relate to social fact, but will be very knowledgeable about the various methods and techniques individual film-makers have contributed to cinema since its inception. She will be able to discuss the individual methodological techniques and styles made by, say, John Ford, Alfred Hitchcock, Douglas Sirk and Alain Resnais. Moreover the film studies student will be well-trained in critical theory and will almost certainly be able to distinguish a structuralist analysis from a hermeneutical one[164] and may well be aware of the importance of dialectics in cinema.[165] What will the law student know of the methodology of her discipline? She will, perhaps, be able to distinguish between deduction and induction and may well be able to discuss the various approaches towards statutory interpretation. If she has studied legal theory she will also be aware of the important contribution made by a number of the more recent jurists about the formal sources of legal rules. Indeed, she may well be aware of Dworkin's chain novel analogy with respect to legal reasoning.[166] But the chances are she will know almost nothing about methodology outside of the authority paradigm and little about schemes of intelligibility despite their relevance to law.[167]

In terms of a governing paradigm, the law graduate, in short, will be analogous to some narrowly educated theology graduate.[168] Indeed the kind of methodological movements to be found in the history of the civil law can mirror to some extent those found in religious disputes. Take for example the idea of "fundamentalism". According to Karen Armstrong, the American Protestant "fundamentalists wanted to go back to basics and reemphasize the 'fundamentals' of the Christian tradition, which they identified with a literal interpretation of Scripture and the acceptance of certain core doctrines."[169] One cause of this back-to-basic movement had been the various attempts in nineteenth-century America to marry theology with science. However, as Armstrong notes, once "theology tried to turn itself into science, it

---

[163] See J.–M. Berthelot, *La Construction de la Sociologie* (6th ed, Paris 2005).
[164] See *e.g.* M. Wallington, "Pasolini: Structuralism and Semiology", 1969(3) Cinema 5; W. Wright, *Sixguns and Society: A Structural Study of the Western* (Berkeley 1975).
[165] J. Kitses, *Horizons West* (London 1969), p.11.
[166] Dworkin, *Law's Empire*, above note 146, pp.228–232.
[167] On this last point see Samuel, *Epistemology and Method in Law*, above note 64, pp.295–334.
[168] Jestaz and Jamin, above note 25, p.167.
[169] K. Armstrong, *The Battle for God: Fundamentalism in Judaism, Christianity and Islam* (London 2004), p.x.

could only produce a caricature of rational discourse, because these truths are not amenable to scientific demonstration."[170] Thus "systematic theology" did not look for meaning beyond the words of the Bible; instead it attempted to produce a closed and coherent system from which all Biblical truths could be inferred by the use of reason brought to bear on words that had an absolute authority.[171] Indeed earlier in the century one theologian had used these scientific methods – particularly mathematics – to "prove" that the Second Coming of Christ would occur in 1843.[172] The attempt to marry law and science, particularly in nineteenth-century Germany, in many ways echoes this religious methodology. Some German Roman lawyers brought the same scientific method to bear on the Roman law texts and induced out of them that the legal system is conceptually perfect, without any gaps whatsoever, just "like the order of nature".[173] Law was a system, analogous to mathematics, consisting of axioms from which all other norms, together with the solutions to case law problems, could be logically deduced. Hermeneutics had given way to conceptual causality.[174]

Admittedly it was not some sort of legal "fundamentalism" as such that was to provoke the reaction to this *Begriffsjurisprudenz*. It was, in the common law world at any rate, a shift to functionalism preached by the American Realists.[175] However Realism has provoked, in its turn, something of a return-to-science movement, at least by the late Peter Birks and his followers. This movement is one where the importance of "scientific" legal classification is being reemphasised accompanied by a reassertion of deductive methodology.[176] And even outside this movement, a shallow hermeneutical (and structural) approach – dominated, as McCrudden says, by "terms such as coherence, fit and analogy"[177] – remains the traditional methodological technique in doctrinal legal scholarship,[178] especially in the civil law world.[179]

The paradigm that dominates this methodology is perhaps revealed once again by the epistemological orientation of theology. "Human

---

[170] *Ibid.*, p.141.
[171] *Ibid.*, pp.141–142.
[172] *Ibid.*, pp.90–91.
[173] Jouanjan, *Une histoire de la pensée juridique en Allemagne*, above note 39, pp.224–225.
[174] *Ibid.*, p.229.
[175] Cohen, Transcendental Nonsense, above note 69.
[176] See e.g. P Birks, "Equity in the Modern Law: An Exercise in Taxonomy" (1996) 26 University of Western Australia Law Review 1, at pp.4–6.
[177] McCrudden, above note 157, p.634.
[178] *Ibid.*
[179] Professors Jestaz and Jamin note that in France one of the characteristics of legal doctrine is its divorce from the human sciences; it is a question of *la dogmatique*: Jestaz and Jamin, above note 25, pp.172–174.

beings, in nearly all cultures," says Karen Armstrong, "have long engaged in a rather strange activity." And she continues:

> They have taken a literary text, given it special status and attempted to live according to its precepts. These texts are usually of considerable antiquity yet they are expected to throw light on situations that their authors could not have imagined. In times of crisis, people turn to their scriptures with renewed zest and, with much creative ingenuity, compel them to speak to their current predicament.[180]

Scriptural texts, in other words, become the unique and sole source of, if not all knowledge, then a considerable part of it. From the historical perspective, this observation by Armstrong certainly seems of some relevance with respect to the foundations of the Western legal tradition. The medieval Roman lawyers, as we have seen, regarded their texts in the same way as theologians regarded theirs.[181] Of course, today, lawyers are just as likely to abandon their texts (especially those protecting individual rights) in times of crisis and most do not regard such legal writing as the source of anything more than legal knowledge (that is to say they do not regard the texts as having anything more than a positivistic authority).[182] Nevertheless, within this narrow disciplinary limit, the legal text is given special status and it is these texts that are the primary source of all knowledge. In addition their authority – if not their styles, quality and function – is not open to question. And even legal philosophy has largely devoted itself to identifying, and thus implicitly supporting the authority of, the "valid" source of the normative propositions expressed in these documents.[183] In short what theology can contribute to legal epistemology is to help emphasise, by way of analogy, the extent to which law as a discipline is trapped within an authority paradigm, in turn seemingly making it an intellectually unattractive candidate when it comes to any serious investigation into social science epistemology.

VI. Escaping the Authority Paradigm

Professor McCrudden – drawing inspiration no doubt from Professor Cownie's book[184] – is of the view that this "internal" approach (as he and others term it) is breaking down to some extent and is merging

---

[180] K. Armstrong, Unholy strictures, *The Guardian*, August 11, 2005.
[181] Note also the actual importance of theological sources to the Western legal tradition: H. Berman, *Law and Revolution: The Formation of the Western Legal Tradition* (Cambridge, Mass. 1983), pp.165–198.
[182] Atias makes this point more elegantly: see *Épistémologie Juridique*, above note 46, pp.35–36.
[183] For an overview see Jestaz and Jamin, above note 25. See also S. Toddington, "The Emperor's New Skills: The Academy, The Profession and the Idea of Legal Education", in P Birks (ed.), *Pressing Problems in the Law: Volume 2: What Are Law Schools For?* (Oxford 1996), 69.
[184] Cownie, above note 25.

with an "external" approach, in particular socio-legal studies, critical legal studies and law and economics.[185] This may be true, but one wonders to what extent these external references are likely to provoke a significant epistemological shift within the discipline of law.[186] Berthelot, it may be recalled, at no point denies the importance of social sciences to law. "Sciences of the text have to make numerous references to the social sciences", as he says, "but either they define themselves in relation to a specific object, approached in a multi-disciplinary fashion, or they lay claim to a hermeneutic and textual programme which is not their own".[187] In short one might be expanding the authority paradigm but not escaping from it.

Can, how might, and should this escape happen? By these questions one is asking how lawyers might take their methodology (and thus epistemology) beyond the limits imposed by the authority paradigm, always assuming that going beyond these limits is desirable.[188] Now, as far as the practitioner is concerned, the necessity for such an escape is by no means evident. However for academic lawyers the position is different in that a number of them do, presumably, want to be taken seriously by their colleagues in other disciplines.[189] And, if this is the case, jurists will need to take method more seriously.[190] Yet even if a majority of academic lawyers are content to remain within the authority paradigm – to be traditionalist "theologians" rather than social scientists – there is one group that cannot. Comparative lawyers, if they are to say anything meaningful, must work within a spirit of enquiry rather than authority, for the exercise of comparison – if it is to do anything other than merely *dégage* some trans-national "science" (an exercise that often results in legal imperialism) – cannot be conducted in terms of authority.[191] Comparative legal studies is obliged, in other words, to be interdisciplinary[192] and this implies that comparatists must be social scientists and not "theologians".[193]

---

[185] McCrudden, above note 157, p.640.
[186] Note J.W. Jones' comment (writing in 1940) with respect to the law and economics school: "It is enough to say that, however far back we trace economic relations, we never get completely away from some compulsive system of rules which is difficult to describe otherwise than as law": *Historical Introduction to the Theory of Law*, above note 54, p.264.
[187] Berthelot, *Épistémologie*, at p.12.
[188] *Cf.* Birks, above note 176.
[189] McCrudden, above note 157, p.646.
[190] *Ibid.*
[191] P Legrand, How to Compare Now (1996) 16 Legal Studies 232; P Legrand, Comparer [1996-2] Revue Internationale de Droit Comparé 279.
[192] Legrand, *Le droit comparé*, above note 20, pp.27–32.
[193] Although in fairness to modern theological thinking a comparative approach is now seen as essential: see *e.g.* M. Burger and C. Calame (eds.), *Comparer les Comparatismes: Perspectives sur l'Histoire et les Sciences des Religions* (Lausanne 2006). By "theologian" in the context of this present article is meant one who never questions the authority of a holy text.

If, then, escape is on the agenda, perhaps law schools should start by looking in much more diachronic depth at the construction of their discipline. The history of the civil law, as we have already mentioned, is largely a history of changing methods and a better appreciation of these methods and the changes that have occurred with respect to them would endow law students with a perspective that might allow them at one and the same time to appreciate the relationship between law as knowledge and as methodology and how changes in method can effect changes of substance.[194] As Robert Blanché has asserted with regard to the natural sciences, history "offers a good means of analysis in separating, by the date and by the circumstances of their appearance, the various elements which have contributed to form little by little the notions and principles of... science".[195] One is not talking here, as he goes on to say, of a history of events but the history of ideas which cannot be written in the same style, "for the links are not of the same nature in the two cases".[196] The ideas have to be "grasped, so to speak, from the inside" in a manner that is philosophic rather than descriptive.[197]

For example, the force of authority paradigm itself has not always been of the same epistemological nature. As far as the Glossators and Post-Glossators were concerned, the authority was primarily textual – although authority came to attach also to the celebrated jurists (or at least to their writings) – and thus their methods were orientated towards explaining the content of the texts, cross-referencing and ironing out the contradictions. Hermeneutics and dialectics were the two primary methods applied to this written source material.[198] The French humanists of the sixteenth century effected a complete revolution in that they brought quite different methods to bear on the Roman material; they developed what today we would regard as the modern historical methods.[199] They no longer saw the Justinianic compilation as a timeless authority but as a historical document whose contents had been fashioned at different time periods. In fact so different were some of their methods that several humanist jurists were dismissed as being philologists and grammarians rather than lawyers.[200] Yet this historical scholarship was equally to generate a

---

[194] A good overview of these changing methods from the 11th to the 20th centuries can be found in Jones, above note 54.
[195] Blanché, *Épistémologie* above note 145, p.36.
[196] *Ibid.*, p.38.
[197] *Ibid.*
[198] See on this methodology: W. Ullmann, *Law and Politics in the Middle Ages*, above note 55, p.87 and W Ullmann, *The Medieval Idea of Law as Represented by Lucas de Penna*, (above note 59), pp.112–113. See also M. Bellomo, *The Common Legal Past of Europe 1000–1800* (trans. LG Cochrane, Washington 1995), p.181.
[199] See generally Kelley, *Foundations of Modern Historical Scholarship*, above note 57.
[200] Jones, above note 54, pp.42–43.

new kind of authority, that of the *essence* – that is to say the internal coherence – of law. As far as some of the humanists were concerned, the Roman materials had been corrupted by the intellectual vulgarity of the compilers, and subsequently by the medieval Roman lawyers, and what was needed was a method that would expose the systematic nature of law as understood (so the humanists believed) by the great classical Roman jurists.[201] Having been "exposed" – in effect constructed by the humanist jurists on the basis of the Gaian institutional plan[202] – this coherent model became, by the force of its rationality, a new authority.[203]

The methodological effect, in other words, was dramatic. The authority paradigm was no longer just a matter of textual authority; it was equally a scientific authority whose epistemological basis, borrowed from mathematics, was internal coherence.[204] Legal academics had been endowed with a new role and one that would prove infinite given the inherent ambiguity of language. Their job was to fashion an ever more coherent and closed structure of legal axioms so as to create a logic model from which solutions could be deduced with confidence and whose authority would be guaranteed by the authority of the syllogism.[205] Causality (*ratio iuris*) became the scheme of intelligibility that would endow hermeneutics (*interpretatio iuris*) with its "scientific" respectability.[206]

The authority of scientific rationality found, seemingly, its most perfect expression in codification.[207] Yet the moment a code came into force there was something of a shift back within the authority paradigm from rationality to textual authority. As Donald Kelley has observed with respect to the *Code civil*:

> [T]he imperial will would emanate mathematically, concentrically, and inexorably from its legislative source and reflect back on its national foundation. Few questioned the principle of *la volonté générale*. The main question was: How was this force to be expressed, explained, and applied? The crux of the matter was the age-old legal problem of 'interpretation,'… Corresponding to the thirteenth-century glossators was the so-called exegetic school (*école de l'exégèse*), which also took a narrow-minded construction of the text and tended to make a fetish of the 'intention' of

---

[201] J.-L. Thireau, *Introduction Historique au Droit* (Paris 2001), pp.223–226, 232–238.
[202] Kelley, *The Human Measure*, above note 58, p.196.
[203] H.F. Jolowicz, *Roman Foundations of Modern Law* (Oxford 1957), pp.61–81. Peter Birks, in more recent times, tried to import such an "authoritative" structure into the common law: see *e.g.* P. Birks, "Definition and Division: A Meditation on *Institutes* 3.13", in P. Birks (ed.), *The Classification of Obligations* (Oxford 1997), 1.
[204] Dubouchet, *Sémiotique juridique*, above note 39, pp.37–70.
[205] Jouanjan, above note 39, pp.222–230.
[206] Kelley, *The Human Measure*, above note 58, p.198.
[207] See eg D. Bureau, "Codification", in D. Alland and S. Rials (eds.), *Dictionnaire de la Culture Juridique*, Paris 2003, 225, 227.

the imperial redactors. The *exégètes* more or less avoided recourse to history but had an advantage over the medieval glossators: they had access to a record of the debates of the original editors [of the *Code civil*], assembled authoritatively in the analysis published by Jacques Maleville in 1805.[208]

Modern jurists continue therefore to be trapped within a paradigm whose foundational basis is two-fold. There is the authority of the text itself, an authority continually buttressed by appeals to democracy, certainty and (or) the "rule of law".[209] And there is the authority of coherence; law is a rational science in that it provides a model which is capable both of explaining law as an epistemological phenomenon and of predicting solutions to each and every legal problem.[210]

Certainly it would be completely misleading to claim that contemporary civil lawyers still equate law and legal method with mathematics. As Professor Bergel asserts, the reduction of law to a set of equations is a delusion. "It comes up against insurmountable method difficulties" and, he continues, "would anyway be contrary to the essential purpose of any legal system".[211] But what this two-fold authority paradigm does foster – and this indicates the great intellectual power of a paradigm – is an extraordinary restraining power at the level of schemes of intelligibility. Causal, functional, structural, hermeneutical, actional and dialectical approaches are indeed all employed by lawyers and jurists alike. Yet instead of providing a diversity of *grilles de lecture* through which *difference* can be explained with respect to legal texts, facts and theories regarding the legal system itself they are used, instead, as a means of subverting difference.[212] The authority paradigm combines logic, function, interpretation, individualism, system and dichotomy in such a way as to construct a methodological and epistemological model of law in which society – that is the society created by the Gaian model – is seemingly as predictable as the behaviour of comets or the planets.[213] And such a model has the great advantage that it is not open to testability. Its disadvantage is that it creates a closed model of

---

[208] D.R. Kelley, *Historians and the Law in Postrevolutionary France* (Princeton 1984), pp.43, 47.
[209] See eg Y. Gaudemet, "Légalité", in Alland and Rials (eds), *Dictionnaire de la Culture Juridique*, above note 207, 917.
[210] Common lawyers might not subscribe to the idea of law as a deductive model, but, as McCrudden observes, they still reason on the basis of reason and logic: McCrudden, above note 157, p.633.
[211] J.-L. Bergel, *Méthodologie Juridique* (Paris 2001), p.145.
[212] Professor Murphy makes the point that the common law is governed by what might be called the "medieval authority paradigm"; the "literature it [the common law] resembles, in other words, is medieval literature, not modern novels, chain or otherwise": Murphy, above note 1, p.95.
[213] Thus differences of reasoning between judges often results from differences in schemes of intelligibility or even paradigms: see on this point G. Samuel, *Foundations of Legal Reasoning* (Antwerp 1994) and *Epistemology and Method in Law*, above note 64. However these differences are masked by the structure and authority of the reported judgments.

knowledge that isolates it from the other social sciences. This kind of law is, arguable, not social science.[214]

CONCLUSION: IS LAW A SOCIAL SCIENCE?

Can one conclude, accordingly, that law is not a social science? Before responding directly to this question the point must be made, once again, that the question is aimed at the discipline of law and not at individuals working within the discipline. There is no suggestion whatsoever that law faculties lack genuine social scientists producing research that is unquestionably social science research.[215] Indeed there is much good research of this nature emerging from law schools, just as good social science research from outside law is having an impact within the discipline. In this sense, then, law faculties are making an important contribution to social science knowledge. The question is aimed at law as a discipline, that is to say law as it is perceived by those outside the subject, such as the late Professor Berthelot, and by those internal to law who talk in terms of a traditional "internal" approach to the subject.

To take a recent example, one might consider the vast scholarly effort in the United Kingdom devoted to restitution law since this effort has generated debates about classification and taxonomy in law in turn raising questions that can be regarded as epistemological.[216] This writing might well be of value to students and practitioners of law, and the point of referring to it here is not imply that it is valueless. But if this work were to be considered from Professor Berthelot's perspective two questions arise. What real social relevance does any of this scholarship actually have to an understanding of social knowledge? And what major contribution have the papers concerning legal coherence and taxonomy made to epistemology? It is arguable that had this restitution and taxonomy scholarship been brought to the attention of Professor Berthelot he would have been convinced of the correctness of his decision to exclude law from his project for the reasons he sets out in *Épistémologie des sciences sociales*. Even from the perspective of comparative law – an important perspective since the idea of a separate category of restitution within the law of obligations based on the principle of unjust enrichment is a civilian import[217] – the restitution scholarship, or some of it, can be regarded as amateurish. Can Gaius really be compared with Darwin as one

---

[214] See also (and generally) Murphy, above note 1.
[215] See *e.g.* Cownie, above note 25.
[216] For an overview see P. Birks, *Unjust Enrichment* (Oxford 2003).
[217] See generally J. Beatson and E. Schrage, *Cases, Materials and Texts on Unjustified Enrichment* (Oxford 2003).

leading restitution lawyer was constantly suggesting?[218] In short, this type of scholarly pursuit, as valuable as it might be, is not *social science* scholarship and if, in turn, this restitution scholarship is to be regarded as typical high quality law research – the "paradigm" legal research – then it is difficult to escape from the conclusion that this type of law is not a social science. The research tells us nothing about society itself and is concerned only with the logical and hermeneutical implications of the unjust enrichment principle being regarded as an axiom whose authority cannot be questioned.

However the debate does not end here because there is one area seemingly "internal" to law as a discipline that cannot, if it is to have any credibility, be governed by the authority paradigm. The area in question is comparative law. This field of law studies cannot be governed by the authority paradigm because "comparative law", as the words themselves suggest, are governed by two questions. What is "comparison" and what is "law"? Neither of these questions can be adequately investigated or employed within the limits of the authority paradigm.

The comparison question requires the jurist first to consider the role of comparison as an epistemological tool in itself – an exercise that simply cannot be conducted within the framework of the traditional "internal" doctrinal methodology[219] – and secondly to reflect upon the objects of comparison. Again this second aspect of comparison cannot be tackled using only the reasoning tools of induction, deduction, analogy and coherence. What is required is an investigation of the ontological and (or) epistemological focal points of legal knowledge. Should one, for example, be comparing rules, norms, factual situations, values, institutions, categories, concepts, reasoning methods, systems structures, words, *les unités épistémologiques*[220] or what? And what are the paradigms within which these focal points are to be approached: is it a matter, say, of nature or culture or order of chaos? In addition there are other serious methodological issues that attach to the exercise of comparison. Should one presume similarity or difference? Should one take an insider or an outsider approach? Is the functional approach the primary method to be adopted or are there alternatives? And, indeed, what are these alternatives? These are extremely complex and controversial questions that are beginning to generate a sophisticated literature in comparative legal studies.[221] And whatever one thinks of

---

[218] On which see further G. Samuel, above note 160.
[219] See generally C. Vigour, *La Comparaison dans les Sciences Sociales : Pratiques et Méthodes* (Paris 2005).
[220] On which see Atias, *Épistémologie du droit*, above note 4, at pp.77–85.
[221] See *e.g.* the Legrand references cited above; and see generally P. Legrand and R. Munday (eds.), *Comparative Legal Studies: Traditions and Transitions* (Cambridge 2003); Riles (ed.), *Rethinking the Masters of Comparative Law*, above note 16.

this literature, there is no doubting its independence from the authority paradigm.

Exactly the same can be said about the "law" aspect of comparative law. It might be tempting to think that comparatists will be confined to the parameters set by legal theorists, parameters often functioning within the authority paradigm.[222] But comparative lawyers are not preoccupied with fashioning a unified theory of law. Quite the opposite in fact, for they require "theories" of "laws" rather than a theory of law since the imposition of a unified theory normally amounts to legal imperialism.[223] The comparative lawyer who approaches the common law – or the legal systems of Africa or China – as a set of Kelsenian norms is likely to produce work not just of limited value to comparative legal studies but of a type that might actively mislead jurists.[224] No doubt some may think that these assertions are open to challenge, yet they are not raised here to provoke or to be defended (here) as such. They are raised simply to make the point that comparative law, when reflecting upon the nature of law, cannot do this from within the traditional authority paradigm.

Comparative legal studies, if it is to make a serious contribution to knowledge in general, must employ comparison as an epistemological tool and this epistemological dimension carries over, of course, into the "law" question as well. Comparative lawyers are thus engaged in a continual exercise that can be classed as epistemological and this is an exercise that cannot be categorised within dichotomies such as that between knowledge that is "internal" and "external" to law. Professor Berthelot's schemes of intelligibility are, for example, neither purely "external" to law (since judges and legal theorist employ different schemes) nor purely "internal". The comparative lawyer as epistemologist is viewing dichotomies such as the internal-external one from a different level than those operating as traditional doctrinal jurists or as social science scholars working within law faculties. In addition the comparative lawyer operates, or should operate, from the perspective of an enquiry paradigm. She is engaging with persons and things (and often actions) at one and the same time as legal constructs and as economic, political, social (including cultural) and psychological

---

[222] Much legal theory is concerned with the valid sources of legal rules and the isolation of the legal from the non legal. This is very much an exercise conducted within the authority paradigm, although of course certain jurisprudential orientations such as the Critical Legal Studies movement can legitimately claim to be working within an enquiry paradigm. Note the interesting observations with respect to the clash of these two paradigm approaches in Cownie, above note 25, pp.42–47.
[223] This point is developed in G. Samuel, "Droit Comparé et Théorie du Droit" [2006.57] Revue Interdisciplinaire d'Études Juridiques 1.
[224] P Legrand, "The Same and the Different", in Legrand and Munday (eds.), above note 221, 240 at p.304.

constructs.[225] This is why the comparative legal studies deserves to qualify as a social science and this is why it is to be regretted that there is no contribution from a comparative lawyer in *Épistémologie des sciences sociales*.

In short, whether or not law is to be regarded as a social science is a paradigm question. Legal literature of the type that can be classed as having been produced from within the authority paradigm is not social science literature since it is not motivated by a spirit of enquiry into the nature of the social. Legal literature from outside the paradigm is more ambiguous, some, if not all, qualifying as social science scholarship.

---

[225] In what ways might the comparative lawyer make a contribution to social science epistemology? Limits on space dictate that this question cannot be pursued in the present article; it will be the subject of a future paper. However suffice it to say here that one way in which law as a discipline might contribute to social science epistemology is with regard to the schemes of intelligibility identified by Professor Berthelot. He identifies six such schemes, but it is arguable that this list is longer and that a seventh scheme based on "objects" or "commodification" is a possible *grille de lecture* of social fact (for example intellectual property and the notion that a person can "own" her ideas). If this is correct, it would be an example of how lawyers, working outside of the authority paradigm, could contribute to social science epistemology. As mentioned, this point will be developed in a future article.

Part II
Common Problems: Modes of Explanation of Behaviour

[8]
HOW THE LAW THINKS: TOWARD A CONSTRUCTIVIST EPISTEMOLOGY OF LAW

GUNTHER TEUBNER

I. JABBERWOCKY

Twas bryllig, and the slythy toves did gyre and gymble in the wabe: all mimsy were the borogoves; and the mome raths outgrabe.
American law professor commenting on Niklas Luhmann, "The Unity of the Legal System"

European and American scholars of law and society apparently have problems in communicating with each other. To invoke Lewis Carroll's authority on a piece of legal theory indicates how serious the problems are. After all, traced to its true origins, "Jabberwocky," the famous "Stanza of Anglo-Saxon Poetry" (Carroll, 1855; 1871: 191), means "weeks of woe" in its original German version (Scott alias Chatterton, 1872). And inextricably involved in the interpretation of the poetry is a certain Hermann von Schwindel . . .

This lack of mutual understanding is only a recent phenomenon. Communication was still easy when Merton's regime of middle-range theories was governing law and society. There was a consensus that from the patient observation of the real law in the real world, a body of nonspeculative, nonmetaphysical theories would evolve. And this consensus was reflected in a common, sober, professional, comprehensible language. However, with the "Return of Grand Theory," (Skinner, 1985), with the invasion of poststructuralism, critical theory, discourse theory, and autopoiesis in the sociolegal world, the unified discourse of law and society is falling apart again into different cultural provinces. The deplorable result is a fragmentation of theory languages, the "Jabberwocky" of sociolegal theory.

Obscurity of language, then, is the most common critical comment on those recent European theory fashions, be they of Parisian, Frankfurtian, or Bielefeldian origin. The language is said to be overly complex, often incomprehensible, and to conceal usually

---

For helpful criticism I would like to thank Zenon Bankowski, Klaus Eder, Michael Donnelly, Reiner Grundmann, Christian Joerges, Wolfgang Krohn, Giandomenico Majone, Neil MacCormick, David Nelken, Helga Nowotny, Alessandro Pizzorno, Joyce Reese, Gerhard Roth, Philip Selznick, Sean Smith.

trivialities behind a smoke screen of trendy words like legal discourse, communicative rationality, and legal autopoiesis.

Of course, bad translations play an unfortunate role in this exchange of ideas. And national cultural contexts are still so diverse today that the transplantation of a theory from one context to the other leads to a degree of incomprehensibility that can only be gradually reduced by careful explanation. And one should also concede that sometimes personal idiosyncracies of theorists render their texts needlessly difficult to understand. However, the core of the problem lies elsewhere. It is a question of whether the language is complex enough to match the complexity of the subject matter. The new theories on law claim to construct sociolegal realities that cannot be adequately expressed by ordinary language. For them, to give in to the demands of easy comprehensibility would be to compromise on the content of their message.

Let us take a concrete example. In the context of legal autopoiesis, several authors are working on a new theory of the legal person (collective actor, corporate personality; cf. Luhmann, 1984: 270ff.; Teubner, 1988a: 130ff.; Knyphausen, 1988: 120ff.; Hutter, 1989: Ch. 4; Ladeur, 1989b; Vardaro, 1990). In their language, "the social reality of a legal person is to be found in the collectivity: the socially binding self-description of an organized action system as a cyclical linkage of identity and action." What? More Jabberwocky? Do organizations think? How can they have the capacity to describe themselves? Linkage of identity and action? All this sounds like those infamous mystifications of collectivities. Obviously, collectivities do not act, but only individuals, and it is nothing but individual actions that are aggregated into collective action. So why not go back to Max Weber's more sober and comprehensible formulation of the same subject matter?

> These concepts of collective entities . . . have a meaning in the minds of individual persons, partly as of something actually existing, partly as something with normative authority. This is true not only of judges and officials, but of ordinary private people as well. Actors thus in part orient their action to them, and in this role such ideas have a powerful, often a decisive, causal influence on the course of action of real individuals. (Weber 1978: 14).

But is it still the same? Certainly, one can now easily understand the words. The message, however, is lost. The novelty of the construction lies in the following issues that depart point by point from the world views invoked by ordinary language:

1. Organizations do not consist of human individuals as members, but of communications, more precisely of decisions as their self-constituted elements.
2. Organizations do "think." It is through internal communication that they construct social realities of their own, quite apart from the reality constructions of their individ-

ual members. In short, organizations are epistemic subjects.
3. Organizations are not *per se* capable of collective action. They transform themselves into collective actors by communicatively constituting their identity.
4. The capacity for collective action emerges when organizations in their collective identity produce actions and, vice versa, organizational action produces their collective identity.

Obviously, these four issues suggest a social reality of the legal person that lies far beyond the well-known territories of fiction, group or entity theories of corporate personality (for the ongoing discussion in terms of those classical theories, cf. Horwitz, 1985; Dan-Cohen, 1986; Schane, 1987; Roos, 1988).

This example should have made clear that the above-mentioned communication problem is not due to obscurity in language but to the limited capacity of our language to express the construction of newly perceived social realities. This, at least, is what the following new theories on law—post-structuralism, critical theory, and autopoiesis—have in common. It is true that Michel Foucault, Jürgen Habermas, and Niklas Luhmann "gyre and gymble in the wabe," but they do so because they imagine social realities whose reconstruction clearly goes beyond the limits of ordinary language. What makes them seemingly incomprehensible is their radical departure from epistemological premises that are deeply embedded in contemporary thinking on law and society, particularly, from what Pizzorno (1989) polemically calls the reification of a "metafisica quotidiana"—epistemological realism and methodological individualism. Although poststructuralism, critical theory, and the theory of autopoiesis develop quite different visions of modern law, they converge in their antirealism and their anti-individualism.[1]

One should hasten to add that antirealism does not mean epistemological idealism, and anti-individualism does not mean methodological holism/collectivism. We are not confronted with a revival of the old dichotomies realism/idealism and individualism/collectivism that dominated the legal theory debates in the first half of the twentieth century. It is neither Kelsen nor Duguit who

---

[1] Given the humanistic orientation of critical theory, it might sound strange to characterize this theory as anti-individualistic. However, we are not talking about moral-political options, but theory constructions. In a threefold sense, this theory is anti-individualistic: (1) in its critique of methodological individualism in economic and rational actor theories, (2) in its replacement of monological theories of norm formation by dialogical ones, (3) in locating the discourse in the center of cognition, and not the classical epistemological subject (cf. "communicative versus subject-centered reason" in Habermas, 1987a: Ch. 11; and Habermas, 1984: Ch. 3 in general).

730   HOW THE LAW THINKS

is on the agenda of legal theory today. Rather, in the return of Grand Theory, epistemological realism is transformed into a new epistemological constructivism, and the agents of methodological individualism are replaced by constructs such as discourse, social self-reflection, and self-organization. What does this radical reorientation of social theory mean for law?

For law, the crucial point is the combination of both the change in epistemology and the new perception of individuality: constructivism rules out the naive reality assumption that human actors through their intentional actions make up the basic elements of society. From this combination follow the main theses of this article:

1. Under a constructivist social epistemology, the reality perceptions of law cannot be matched to a somehow corresponding social reality "out there." Rather, it is law as an autonomous epistemic subject that constructs a social reality of its own.
2. It is not human individuals by their intentional actions that produce law as a cultural artifact. On the contrary, it is law as a communicative process that by its legal operations produces human actors as semantic artifacts.
3. Since modern society is characterized on the one side by a fragmentation into different *epistèmes*, on the other side by their mutual interference, legal discourse is caught in an "epistemic trap." The simultaneous dependence on and independence from other social discourses is the reason why modern law is permanently oscillating between positions of cognitive autonomy and heteronomy.

"Social construction of reality" apparently has become, after Berger and Luckmann (1966), received wisdom in sociology (see, e.g., Bloor, 1976; Latour & Woolgar, 1979; Knorr-Cetina, 1984; Gilbert & Mulkay, 1984; Collins, 1985; Fuller, 1988). However, our three theses show that there is a more profound version of social epistemology than the usual understanding of how social institutions, scientific communities, and laboratory cultures influence individual perception. There is more to social epistemology than the "interests" of social agents that are responsible for the manipulation of knowledge (Barnes, 1974). The three new theories under consideration here—poststructuralism, critical theory, and theory of autopoiesis—have radicalized the notion of the "social" in social cognition which is worthwhile being examined in our context of legal cognition. What is the precise meaning of the somewhat ambiguous statement that law constitutes an autonomous reality? Similarly, what is meant by saying that the individual is a mere construct of society and law? And, above all, how does the law "think"?

II. DISCOURSE AND AUTOPOIESIS

It is comforting, however, and a source of profound relief to think that man is only a recent invention, a figure not yet two centuries old, a new wrinkle in our knowledge, and that he will disappear again as soon as that knowledge has discovered a new form (Foucault, 1974: xxiii).

Not only are law and economics irritated by Michel Foucault's antirealist and anti-individualist provocation, but most strands of social theory that are influencing modern legal thought feel uncomfortable with poststructuralism's decentering of the subject. Under the enormous influence of the "founding fathers" of methodological individualism, Hayek (1948, 1973) and Popper (1953), the quasi-natural reality of individual human actors is assumed by contemporary economic and social theories, such as theories of microfoundations (Weintraub, 1979; Nelson, 1984) and rational actor theories (Elster, 1983, 1985), which demand that any collective phenomenon be reduced to intentional actions of human individuals. In an analogous fashion, the reduction of social macrophenomena to characteristics of individuals is quasi-axiomatic for sociological behaviorism (Homans, 1961). But also for sociological theories on law in the tradition of Max Weber's interpretive sociology, the reality of the acting individual is a fundamental assumption. "After all, the actions of individuals form society" (Aubert, 1980: 119). And even social theorists pursuing structuralist and systemic approaches feel compelled to correct them with an infusion of individualism (e.g., Crozier and Friedberg, 1977; Giddens, 1987: 98ff.; for the legal system, Febbrajo, 1985: 136; Kerchove and Ost, 1988: 157ff.; Ost, 1988: 87).

And it is indicative of the epidemic character of the individual-as-reality-syndrome that even critical legal authors who are deeply influenced by Foucault's ideas and enthusiastically take over his political messages plainly refuse to draw the epistemological consequences. Duncan Kennedy, in his recent analysis of legal indeterminacy (1986: 518) reveals a highly individualist bias for the reflective legal subject and law's communicative aspects. Thus, concentrating on the individual judge's reflections and strategic considerations, he is as far away from a discourse analysis as are his "liberal" adversaries. And Robert Gordon (1984: 117ff.) explicitly rejects the anti-individualist tendencies in structuralism and poststructuralism as undermining the humanistic intentions of critical legal thought.[2]

What makes this combination of realism and individualism in contemporary legal thought so viable is not so much its inherent

---

[2] There are important exceptions among the critical scholars who develop serious alternatives to the prevailing individualism, above all Thomas Heller (1984, 1988) and David Kennedy (1985). But these exceptions confirm our rule: it is their language, even in their own intellectual circles, that has to struggle with the Jabberwocky syndrome.

virtues but the lack of credible alternatives. The traditional alternatives, epistemological idealism and methodological collectivism, are seen as unattractive—and rightly so. But is it true that the only available alternatives are those that read "as if these impersonal structures had a life of their own and human beings were enslaved to the needs of that life-cycle, building or demolishing as the World-Spirit might dictate" (Gordon, 1984: 117)?

As I will discuss in the following pages, there are alternatives to the prevailing realist and individualist modes of thinking. From the diffuse contemporary movement toward "social construction of reality" and "decentering of the subject," I would like to single out three theorists who have contributed to a more profound understanding of sociolegal cognition and who represent at the same time the most important intellectual strands in Western Europe: Michel Foucault (poststructuralism), Jürgen Habermas (critical theory), and Niklas Luhmann (theory of autopoiesis). What they have in common is to replace the autonomous individual, not with supra-individual entities, but with communicative processes. They differ, however, in their identification of the new cognizing unit. In Habermas's version of critical theory correspondence theories of truth are overturned by consensus theories and "intersubjectivity" takes the place of the epistemic subject. Foucault and Luhmann are even more radical in their disenchantment of the human individual. For Foucault, the human individual is nothing but an ephemeral construction of an historically contingent power/discourse constellation, which dictates the *epistème* of a historical epoch. Luhmann completely separates psychic processes from social ones and perceives the human individual in society as a communicative artifact, as a product of self-observation of social autopoiesis. The new epistemic subjects are autopoietic social systems.

III. JÜRGEN HABERMAS: INTERSUBJECTIVITY AND CONSENSUS

To arrive at a legal epistemology that really deserves its name, three important changes in our perception of law and society have to be made: first, from realism to constructivism; second, from individual to social construction of reality; and third, from law as a rule system to law as an epistemic subject. While the first one leads to a certain modification of Kantian positions, the other two changes break new ground in social and legal theory. The second change reveals the social foundations of cognition in a more radical way than traditional sociology of knowledge ever has done, and the third one attributes to the discursive practices of law the production of an autonomous social reality.

In this reorientation of social and legal cognition Habermas's theory of communicative rationality (Habermas, 1971a, 1971b, 1974, 1975, 1984, 1987a, 1987b, 1988) plays a prominent role. Habermas's key concept of "rational discourse" highlights the crucial role of procedure in empirical and normative cognition and at the same time his "universal pragmatics" takes account of the social dimension in moral and legal cognition, as against a predominantly individualist epistemology.

Habermas rejects traditional correspondence theories of truth (from Aristotle to Tarski) according to which statements are true if they correspond to an external reality. Instead, he follows a consensus theory of truth, which declares as the criterion of truth the "potential" consensus of all discourse participants (Habermas, 1971b: 123, 1973: 211). This move, of course, creates the need to identify an independent criterion in order to distinguish true from false consensus. Going through a sequence of different criteria, Habermas finally finds it in the presupposition of an "ideal speech situation" which in itself is defined by certain formal and procedural characteristics (Habermas, 1984: Ch. 3).

It is this proceduralization of the truth criterion which has rendered Habermas's discourse theory so important for law (see for example, Alexy, 1978: 219ff.; Günther, 1988). It makes the theoretical-empirical discourse of the sciences directly comparable to the practical-normative discourse in politics, morals, and law: their validity claims depend on the correctness of procedure (Habermas, 1984: Ch. 3). And it opens the way to a rethinking of the modernity of law in which Max Weber's thesis of the materialization of formal law is replaced by concepts of proceduralization of law (Habermas, 1985: 215ff., 1987c: 1; Wiethölter, 1985, 1986; Günther, 1988; Frey, 1989: 55ff.; Joerges, 1989; Ladeur, 1989a; Preuss, 1989).

Habermas's other main contribution to an epistemology of law is to take account of the social element in empirical and normative cognition. His philosophy attributes "epistemic authority" no longer to the autonomous subject, but to the communicative community (Habermas, 1983: 26; 1988: 63ff., 80). While traditional epistemology situates cognition exclusively in the consciousness of the (empirical or transcendental) subject, Habermas recognizes that cognition is basically a communicative process. "Intersubjectivity" takes the place of the Kantian epistemic subject. It is the authentic consensus of the communicative community and not the consciousness of the autonomous individual that determines truth in cognitive and normative issues. Thus Kant's famous question: "What are the conditions for the possibility of cognition?" is redirected from the conditions of consciousness to those of communication. And even transcendentalism becomes socialized: the new *a priori* is represented by the "ideal speech situation," the presupposition of which is a condition of the possibility of communication (Habermas, 1971b: 136; 1983: 53; 1984: Ch. 3).

However, the "*a priori* of the communicative community" (Apel, 1973, 1988; Böhler, 1985) is at the same time one of the great problems of this theory. With the apriorization of certain features of communication, Habermas attempts to escape from the "paradoxes of self-reference" (Wormell, 1958; Quine, 1976; Krippendorff, 1984; Barwise and Etchemendy, 1987) that necessarily emerge from his hierarchy of discursive justification. The core of Habermas's theory is in the self-application of discursive practices: the procedures of discourse can be justified only by discourse whose procedures in turn have to be justified by discourse.[3] And in order to avoid infinite regression or circularity, Habermas resorts to communicative transcendentalism.

Closely related to the transcendentalist foundation of rational discourse are the ambiguities of "intersubjectivity" that represent the other principal unresolved problem in Habermas's account of social cognition. What is meant: elements or relation? Consciousness or communication? Psychic or social processes? Habermas's epistemic subject oscillates between these two positions without ever finding its identity in either world (for the controversy on intersubjectivity versus communication, see Habermas, 1987a: Ch. 12, 1988: 95ff.; Luhmann, 1986c: 41ff.). It seems as if Habermas again attempts to avoid the paradoxes of self-reference in discourse, this time by changing the system reference. If discourse can be founded on discourse only recursively, need it not then be founded on human consciousness?

IV. MICHEL FOUCAULT: DISCOURSE AND *EPISTÈME*

Foucault's ideas on discourse and power can be read as a radicalization of Habermas's epistemological position. Indeed, Foucault directly attacks what we have just described as the main unresolved problems in Habermas's account: the foundation of discourse in a communicative *a priori*, and the ambiguous role of individual consciousness in intersubjectivity. Foucault's main contribution to a social epistemology is to liberate the core concept of "discourse" from any transcendental or psychic foundation. Of course, this does not save him from the traps of self-referentiality. Foucault's escape is at the same time the most famous and the weakest point of his theory—the ubiquity of power.

Foucault's starting point is constructivist: reality is not something external to cognition, but is constituted, "constructed" by cognition itself. However, in sharp contrast to the classical tradition, it is not the individual consciousness of the subject that constitutes reality. Nor is it intersubjectivity, as in Habermas's theory, the communicative result of interaction between human actors.

---

[3] The problem of infinite regression/circularity in Habermas's theory of discursive justification is perhaps most clearly expressed in Habermas, 1971b: 123 ff., and 1973, 255 ff.

Rather it is "discourse"—an anonymous, impersonal, intention-free chain of linguistic events (Foucault, 1972: Ch. 2). One should hasten to add that this is not a structuralist position (see Dreyfus and Rabinow, 1982: 44ff.). Discourse in Foucault's account is much richer than the abstract orders of signs in structuralism. It is social practice, not social structure; it is *parole*, not *langue*. The basic elements of the discourse are not signs, but *énoncés*, that is, social usage of language that constructs reality. The task of discourse analysis does not consist, in Foucault's words, of "treating discourses as groups of signs (signifying elements referring to contents or representations) but as practices that systematically form the object of which they speak" (Foucault, 1972: 49). Discourse is both event and structure, "a stream of linguistic events in space and time as well as a highly selective organization of linguistic events" (Honneth, 1985: 164). And it is this historically contingent social practice of discourse that dictates the *épistémè* of a certain historical epoch, that defines the conditions for the possibility of cognition, not in an atemporal universal manner, but temporally, concretely, locally (Foucault, 1974: Ch. 2, 3, 7, for the sciences, 1979, for law).

Such a radical social epistemology has no place for individual consciousness and the intentional actions of human subjects and no need for an *a priori* foundation. The human subject is no longer the author of the discourse. Just the opposite: the discourse produces the human subject as a semantic artifact (Foucault, 1974: Ch. 9). At the same time, discourse formations are historically contingent, lacking any *a priori* foundation. Every society has its own order of truth, its own politics of truth.

Now, it would be a consequence of this way of thinking that discourse formations, those highly autonomous social practices, would themselves produce the criteria for their own transformation. Dreyfus and Rabinow, for example, clearly see this necessary self-referentiality as a condition for structural change of discourses: Since "he is committed to the view that discursive practices are autonomous and determine their own context . . . he must locate the productive power revealed by discursive practices in the regularities of these same practices. The result is the strange notion of regularities which regulate themselves" (1982: 84). Foucault, however, stops short of those paradoxes of self-reference. He withdraws from the necessary consequences of his own construct and introduces the concept of power in order to externalize self-referential relationships. In his later thinking, he gives up the idea of the autonomous discourse as the new epistemic subject and resorts to the ubiquity of power as a quasi-transcendental foundation of discursive practices (for a critique, see Honneth, 1985: 168ff.; Habermas, 1987a: Ch. 10).

V. NIKLAS LUHMANN: CONSTRUCTIVISM AND AUTOPOIESIS

The paradoxes of self-reference seem to be the principal obstacle to the development of an authentically social epistemology. Habermas and Foucault have made important contributions, but the radical consequences of their ideas seem to be blocked by self-referential structures (circularity, tautology, infinite regression, paradox) in their specific versions of discourse theory. How can rational discourse be justified, if not by rational discourse itself (Habermas)? How can those discourse formations that govern the *épistème* of a whole historical epoch be transformed if not by those discourse formations themselves (Foucault)? Both authors are well aware that these questions necessarily lead to paradox, but their solution is to avoid the paradox at any cost. Of course, in the end, the paradoxes of self-reference cannot be avoided; they simply reappear at the termination of their escape route. When Habermas finds the transcendental foundation of communication in the distinction between the ideal speech situation and real speech situations, is this distinction, then, in itself empirical or is it transcendental? Alternatively, when he reintroduces the subject to the discourse, the classical paradoxes of the self-reflecting subject are obviously bound to reappear. When Foucault identifies the foundations of discourse in ubiquitous power-constellations he does so at the price of the self-referential paradoxes of power.

The theory of autopoiesis (Maturana and Varela, 1980; von Förster, 1981; Luhmann, 1984) deals with these paradoxes of self-reference in a different way: Do not avoid paradoxes, but make productive use of them! If social discourses are autopoietic systems, that is, systems that recursively produce their own elements from the network of their elements, then they are founded on that very self-referentiality that Habermas and Foucault are desperately trying to avoid (Luhmann, 1986a: 172; 1986d: 129; 1988b: 153). As autopoietic systems, discourses cannot but find justification in their own circularity and cannot but produce regularities that regulate themselves and that govern the transformation of their own regularities. The paradox of self-reference then, is not a flaw in our intellectual reconstruction of discourse that we have to avoid at all costs, but is its very reality that we cannot avoid at all. And the recursive application of operations to the results of these very operations does not necessarily lead to paradoxical blockage paradox or to sheer arbitrariness, but, under certain conditions, to the emergence of "eigenvalues" (Förster, 1981: 274; 1985: 36). From continual recursive "computation of computation," social discourses "blindly" learn those modes of operation that are valid in coping with their environment to which they have no direct access (for an elaboration of these somewhat jabberwocky remarks, see Teubner, 1989).

The epistemological consequence is a radical constructivism (Piaget, 1971; Glasersfeld, 1975, 1981, 1985; Maturana & Varela, 1980; Förster, 1981; Luhmann, 1984: 647ff.; Roth, 1984, 1987; Arbib & Hesse, 1986; Schmidt, 1987). Any cognition—be it psychic or social, be it scientific, political, moral, or legal cognition—is a purely internal construction of the outside world; cognition has no access whatsoever to reality "out there." Any cognitive activity—be it theory or empirical research—is nothing but an internal construction by the cognizing unit; and every testing procedure that pretends to examine the validity of internal constructions against outside reality is only an internal comparison of different world constructions.

In this radicalized version of the "social construction of reality," there is no place for individual action and thought (for the relation of individual and social observation, cf. Luhmann, 1983: 1; 1985: 402; 1986b: 313). Social autopoiesis is exclusively based on communication—defined as the synthesis of utterance, information, and understanding—that recursively reproduces communication (Luhmann, 1984: 193ff., 1986b: 172 ff.). Social construction of reality is sharply separated from psychic construction of reality. Here lies the important difference from Habermas, who in the ambiguous concept of intersubjectivity blends communication and consciousness, and also from Foucault, for whom the subject is nothing but a historically contingent construct of shifting discourse/power constellations. For the theory of autopoiesis, psychic processes form a closed reproductive network of their own—psychic autopoiesis—accessible only to themselves and inaccessible to any communication. Communication in turn forms a closed autoreproductive network of its own—social autopoiesis—accessible only to communication and inaccessible to any psychic processes. Certainly, human individuals reappear in this world of communication, but only as communicative constructions, as semantic artifacts, that have no correspondence to consciousness, to the autopoietic processes in the psychic world (Luhmann, 1984: 158ff., 1986b: 313ff.). Psychic and social processes do coexist; they are "coupled" by synchronization and coevolution, but there is no overlap in their operations. There is nothing but a symmetry of reality constructions: psychic processes produce mental constructs of society, and social processes produce communicative constructs of the psyche.

In these two aspects—radicalization of constructivism and deindividualization of discourse—Luhmann is expanding on what Habermas and Foucault have developed in their versions of social epistemology. However, there is a third aspect in Luhmann's theory of autopoiesis that clearly goes beyond discourse analysis in its Parisian or Frankfurtian version—this is the view of modernity as an irreconcilable conflict of different *epistèmes* (Luhmann, 1988a: 335ff.). While Foucault sees in history the ruptures of discourse formations that dictate one paradigmatic society-wide *episteme* for a certain historical epoch, and interprets the modern epoch as the governance of one pervasive "subjectivist" *episteme* following the Kantian revolution (Foucault, 1974: Ch. 9f.; 1979: Ch. 4), Luhmann views modernity as the fragmentation of society into a plurality of autonomous discourses, as the multiplication of *epistemes* in society. The crucial feature of modern society is the loss of a unifying mode of cognition. Society is seen as fragmented into a multiplicity of closed communicative networks. Each communicative network constructs a reality of its own that is, in principle, incompatible with the reality constructions of other networks. At the same time, there is a multiplication and fragmentation of individualities that corresponds to the multiplication and fragmentation of social discourses. On the basis of its specific code and programs, each specialized communicative network produces "persons"—semantic artifacts of individual actors—to which actions are attributed (Luhmann, 1984: 155ff.). The "Multiple Self" (Elster, 1986; Etzioni, 1988) is the product of the fragmentation of social discourses in modernity.

This fragmentation of society into different *epistemes* is one of the strongest points in Luhmann's theory—and at the same time its "blind spot." The emphasis on fragmentation, differentiation, separation, closure, and self-reference of social *epistemes* creates problems, to say the least, as to how their interconnection, interference, openness, and hetero-reference can be theoretically reconstructed (for a more detailed critique, see Teubner, 1990). Unlike Habermas and Foucault who, at any cost, try to avoid the traps of self-reference, Luhmann courageously faces self-referential realities in law and society. He even declares law to be founded on the paradoxes of self-reference (Luhmann, 1988b). But a theory that deals extensively with self-reference, may ultimately be caught in the self-created closure of self-referential constructions. And the obvious problem that autopoiesis theory has to face is how to deal with the interrelations of different autonomous *epistemes*, their conflicts, their incompatibilities, their interferences (for first steps in this direction, see Luhmann, 1988a, 1990). The open questions for a theory of fragmented *epistemes* are: Is there something like an epistemic minimum in modern society that serves as a common base for the autonomization of social discourses? Does one find covariation or even co-evolutionary trends among autonomous social *epistemes*? Or is the only way to connect them through the reconstruction of an *episteme within the framework of another episteme*? These questions will reappear when we examine in detail, on the basis of the foregoing discussion, how a constructivist epistemology of the law reconstructs legal cognition in its conflict with other modes of cognition in society (see below VII and VIII).

VI. LAW—AN EPISTEMIC SUBJECT?

How does the law think? Mary Douglas, in a recent book, has again raised the old question: *How Institutions Think* (1986). After an exciting flirtation with Emile Durkheim's "collective consciousness" and Ludwig Fleck's "Denkkollektiv," she finally finds her way back to good old individualism: Of course, it is the individual member of the institution that thinks. However, his/her thinking is influenced by institutional context. In this version of social epistemology, the social element is represented by socialization of the individual mind. That's it. Collectivism is banned and individualism happily survives after a healthy dose of socialization.

From our selective reconstruction of Habermas, Foucault, and Luhmann on social epistemology, the picture changes dramatically. It is true that individual cognition is shaped by social institutions such as law, through socialization (and here constructivism would add that since there is no access from communication to consciousness, socialization can only be self-socialization). But this is only half the story. The other half is that institutions such as law do "think" independently from their members' minds. The law autonomously processes information, creates worlds of meaning, sets goals and purposes, produces reality constructions, and defines normative expectations—and all this quite apart from the world constructions in lawyers' minds. Such a constructivist legal epistemology is at the same time nonindividualist and noncollectivist. It needs no recourse to individual actors and intentions; at the same time, it does not presuppose the existence of a supra-individual collective entity, "Denkkollektiv," "conscience collective," World III, legal consciousness, *Weltgeist* . . .

Law is communication and nothing but communication. By this very conceptualization it is possible to avoid the traps of methodological individualism that would define law as a set of rules constraining individual action and that, apart from the catchall phrase of unintended consequences, has no tool with which to analyze of the autonomy of the social, not to speak of the "legal proprium" (Selznick, 1968). At the same time it avoids the traps of collectivism that views law as a supra-individual subject and that cannot explain who is, in fact, acting in the name of the *Weltgeist*.

The precise construction is as follows (for an elaborate discussion of the characteristics of autopoietic law, see Teubner, 1988b, 1988c, 1990). Law is defined as an autopoietic social system, that is, a network of elementary operations that recursively reproduces elementary operations. The basic elements of this system are communications, not rules; law is not, as analytical-normativist legal theories have it, a system of rules. On the other hand, the sociological-realist definitions of law as a system of legal professionals and organizations are problematic as well, because they see human actors as the basic elements of law and other social institutions.

740 HOW THE LAW THINKS

The self-reproductive character of law as a social process becomes intelligible only if one chooses communications as the law's basic elements. Law as an autopoietic social system is made up neither of rules nor of legal decisionmakers, but of legal communications, defined as the synthesis of three meaning selections: utterance, information, and understanding. These communications are interrelated to each other in a network of communications that produces nothing but communications. This is what is basically meant by autopoiesis: the self-reproduction of a network of communicative operations by the recursive application of communications to the results of former communications. Law as a communicative network produces legal communications.

Legal communications are the cognitive instruments by which the law as social discourse is able to "see" the world. Legal communications cannot reach out into the real outside world, neither into nature nor into society. They can only communicate about nature and society. Any metaphor about their access to the real world is misplaced. They do not receive information from the outside world which they would filter and convert according to the needs of the legal process. There is no instruction of the law by the outside world; there is only construction of the outside world by the law. This is not to say that the law arbitrarily "invents" social reality. A constructivist perspective should not be confused with "methodological solipsism" (Fodor, 1980); it rather looks for a "middle path" between representationalism and solipsism (Varela, 1984: 217). Legal constructivism, then, presupposes the "existence" of an environment for the law. The point is not a monadological isolation of the law, but the autonomous construction of legal models of reality under the impression of environmental perturbations. Legal order from social noise!

What about the world perceptions of lawyers and lay people? Is it not their aggregation that forms the collective world view of the law (cf. the actor-based objections against an autopoietic law by Febbrajo, 1985: 134ff.; Kerchove and Ost, 1988: 157ff.; and Ost, 1988: 87ff.)? Of course, the communicative process of law needs lawyers and lay people; it would not work without their intentions, strategies, and actions. But their ("subjective," internal, psychic) intentions never enter the ("objective," external, social) communication of law. They only make up part of the psychic processes, accompanying the social process of law and co-evolving with it. Law as a communicative process is not accessible to any of those accompanying psychic processes of lawyers and lay people, and, vice versa, it has no access to them. They work only as "perturbations," as "chocs exogènes" (Kerchove and Ost, 1988: 159) under the pressure of which the communicative process of law builds up its own autonomous order and creates the world of legal meaning (cf. Förster, 1981; Teubner, 1990).

But does the law as a social process not constantly deal with real people? Is the law not driven by actual motives, strategies, actions of clients, professionals, judges, and legislators? Does the law not constantly refer to mental states of real people, to their intentions, goals, consent, dissent, errors, negligence, *mens rea*? Obviously the law does so. But the "persons" the law as a social process deals with are not real flesh-and-blood people, are not human beings with brains and minds, are not the above mentioned autopoietic psychic systems. They are mere constructs, semantic artifacts produced by the legal discourse itself. Mental states are "in reality [sic!] constructs of practical discourses, necessary for the formation of communicative circles, of discursive communities" (Pizzorno, 1989: 9).

As social constructs, they are indispensable to legal communication, because law as a social process needs to attribute communication to actors (individual or collective ones) in order to continue its self-reproduction. But these "actors" are only role-bundles, character-masks, internal products of legal communication (for an elaboration on collective actors, see Teubner, 1988a: 133ff.; 1988c: 66ff.). The densely populated world of legal persons, the plaintiffs and defendants, the judges and legislators, the parties to a contract, the corporations and the state, is an internal invention of the legal process. Not only the corporation, but any legal person—be it collective or individual—is nothing but that famous "artificial being, invisible, intangible, existing only in contemplation of law," discovered by Chief Justice Marshall in the celebrated case of *Dartmouth College* v. *Woodward*, 4 Wheaton 518, 627 (1819).

So human actors have a "double identity" in the world of autopoiesis. While in their social existence, they are pale constructs of autopoietic social systems, among them the law; in their psychic existence, they are themselves vibrant autopoietic systems. It is plainly wrong to argue, as some critics do, that autopoiesis dehumanizes society (Grünberger, 1987), has no place for actors and intentions (Schimank, 1985: 421; Mayntz, 1986; Ost, 1988: 87ff.; Rottleuthner, 1988: 122), does not account for the individual as epistemic subject (Podak, 1984: 734; Frankenberg, 1987: 296), and represents a "dehumanisation totale du droit" (Grzegorczyk, 1989: 12). The point is not the individual subject withering away, but the multiplication of centers of cognition. Social discourses are the new epistemic subjects that compete with the consciousness of the individual. Insofar as autopoiesis insists on the epistemic autonomy of a multiplicity of social discourses, it takes part in "decentering the subject," that is, moving the subject away from its privileged position as the sole and ultimate center of cognition. To repeat, if we talk about human actors in the law we have to distinguish carefully between the autopoietic reproduction of human consciousness, that is, the operative reality of psychic processes, and the autopoietic reproduction of the social life of law in which human actors are not elements but constructed social realities.

VII. THE EPISTEMIC TRAP

While discourse analysis in the tradition of Foucault sees the modern epoch in the grip of one pervasive *episteme* (Foucault, 1972: Ch. 2; 1974: Ch. 9) and views law like other disciplines only as a particular expression of the power/knowledge complex (Foucault, 1979: Ch. 4), autopoiesis theory characterizes modern society as fragmented into multiple autonomous *epistemes* (Luhmann, 1988a: 335ff.; 1990). Autopoiesis thus throws modern legal discourse into an irreconcilable conflict between epistemic autonomy and heteronomy (for two types of cognitive conflict between social systems, see Teubner, 1989, 1990). The dynamics of social differentiation force legal discourse to produce reality constructions of its own, but the very same dynamics make law dependent upon a multiplicity of competing autonomous *epistemes*.

The epistemic autonomy of law results from the fragmentation of modern society that drives the law into second order autopoiesis (for elaboration, see Deggau, 1988: 128; Heller, 1988: 283; Ladeur, 1988: 242; Teubner, 1988b: 217; 1988c: 60). In the dynamics of social evolution, self-referential relations are multiplying within the legal process, culminating in a hypercyclical linkage of the law's components. The law becomes autonomous from general social communication. It develops into a closed communicative network that produces not only legal acts as its elements and legal rules as its structures, but legal constructions of reality as well. The autonomy of modern law refers primarily to its normative operations that become independent from moral and political normativity (cf. Mengoni, 1988: 15); and secondarily, autonomy refers to the law's cognitive operations that—under the pressure of normative operations—construct idiosyncratic images of reality and move them away from the world constructions of everyday life and from those of scientific discourse (for an elaboration on the "facts of law," see Nerhot, 1988).

In this context, Baudrillard (1976: Ch. II) speaks of "hyperreality" as a movement from reality-dependent theory to theory-dependent reality. In an autopoietic reformulation, one would describe this process as an autonomization of specialized social discourses in which reality constructions of general social communication are increasingly replaced by reality constructions of the specialized discourses. The legal discourse invents and deals with a juridical "hyperreality" that has lost contact with the realities of everyday life and at the same time superimposes new realities to everyday life. It is an "efficacité quasi magique," as Bourdieu calls it, which law possesses in its practices of "world making" (Bourdieu, 1986: 13). Grzegorczyk (1989: 21) speaks of the law as a "hermeneutique officielle du monde" that organizes the social world. "Institutional facts" such as corporate personality, contract, and the will, are only the tip of an iceberg of legal reality constructs drifting in an ocean of "brute facts" of diffuse social communication. Legal discourse increasingly modifies the meaning of everyday world constructions and in case of conflict replaces them by legal constructs.

From a constructivist perspective, there is no way to challenge the epistemic authority of law, neither by social realities themselves, nor by common sense, nor by scientifically controlled observation. A social epistemology on a constructivist basis can explain why law appears to be an "essentially self-validating discourse" which one should expect to be "largely impervious to serious challenge from other knowledge fields" (Cotterrell, 1986: 15). It is simply naive to invoke social "reality" itself against legal conceptualism, against the "heaven of legal concepts" (Jhering, 1884: 245) or against the law's "transcendental nonsense" (Cohen, 1935: 809). There is no direct cognitive access to reality. There are only competing discourses with different constructions of reality. And all that Jhering and Cohen have to offer is their own transcendental nonsense in a different heaven of legal concepts. Is there any reason to believe that *Freirecht*, sociological jurisprudence, or legal realism have made the legal discourse more realistic? Not at all. They have not moved legal concepts closer to social reality "out there." They have just replaced one conceptual jurisprudence with another conceptual jurisprudence. "Social interests," the atoms of realistic jurisprudence, are unreal fictions, artificial semantic products, just as much as the "legal subjects," the atoms of classical jurisprudence.

"Law and society" and "law and economics" are not doing any better if they pretend to invoke the authority of controlled scientific observation against the lawyers' "mystifications" of the social world (see for example, Aubert, 1980: 117ff.; 1983: 98ff.; Rottleuthner, 1980: 137ff., for sociology; Adams, 1985, for economics). If epistemological constructivism does anything it is to deconstruct the claims of modern science to having privileged access to reality (Bloor, 1976; Barnes, 1974). Science does not discover any outside facts; it produces facts. "Science is in a literal sense constructive of new facts" (Arbib & Hesse, 1986: 10). Radical constructivism maintains that "science produces a construction of the world which is validated by its distinctions and not by the world as such. Thus, science cannot claim the authority to discover the only and the correct access to the real world and to communicate this to others" (Luhman, 1988c: 2, 9). If we can believe constructivist reconstructions of the scientific process, then the celebrated controlled experiment is not what it pretends to be, a test of an internal theory against external reality, but is a mere internal coherence test comparing two constructs that are produced according to different procedural requirements: the logic of theoretical reasoning and the logic of the laboratory.

Let us take an example. Social science theory on the relation between organization and collective action is not in any way superior to legal doctrine on the relation between the corporation and legal personality; both are discursive artifacts whose construction is not arbitrary, but rationally guided by specific codes and programs. Similarly, empirical facts about dysfunctions in organizational life, hard facts that result from scientifically controlled inquiry, are in no sense more "true" than legal facts about the violation of corporate duties that are produced under the firm guidance of the rules of law of evidence. In both cases, rational procedures and conventions of factual inquiry lead to empirical statements about reality. They serve as "hard" evidence confirming or refuting "soft" claims based on theoretical speculations or on legal reasoning. And if these empirical facts conflict with each other—which is not so rare—then there is no superiority of scientific constructs over legal constructs, as some sociologists would like to have it (Opp, 1973). Epistemic authority is claimed by both scientific discourse and legal discourse—and rightly so. What a naive realism would call the observation of "facts" is in both cases the production of artifacts whose truth is guaranteed by formalized procedures of factual inquiry, procedures that differ considerably in law and science. These procedures in turn are conventions, not arbitrary ones but structural selections which reflect choices made in the history of scientific and legal discourse.[4]

The epistemic authority of legal discourse is an undeniable fact of modernity, and we have found ways and means to cope with the fact of multiple truths—scientific truth, legal truth, political truth. *Res judicata* is the classical example of an institutionalized conflict between legal facts and scientific facts. Even if it can be proven with scientific evidence that a factual statement in a legal procedure is blatantly wrong, that factual statement of the court—and even worse, its legal, economic, and social consequences—will not be reversed (apart from very few, narrowly defined exceptions) unless the procedural requirements are fulfilled and the appeal procedures exhausted. Obviously, scientific facts collide with legal facts, but we are used to living with this collision, rationalizing it by invoking higher values, like legal certainty, or appealing to the relativism of our cultural provinces.

However, things are not quite so easy. Windscheid's notorious "lawyer as such," who is entitled by the law of social differentiation not to be "concerned with ethical, political, or economic considerations" (1904: 101), is forced by the same law to give up the entitlement and to incorporate those nonlegal considerations into

---

[4] Thus, the resulting relativism of different social discourses is not "anything goes" relativism. It is a relativism that invites to "raise the status of the other 'mythologies' by a more careful investigation of their methodological and cognitive credentials" and to examine "the various kinds of criteria of acceptability that apply to different kinds of constructed models and myths" (Arbib and Hesse, 1986: 10).

his/her autonomous reasoning. This is what I would call the "epistemic trap" of modern law. Law is forced to produce an autonomous legal reality and cannot at the same time immunize itself against conflicting realities produced by other discourses in society.

The underlying reason for this confusion is "interference," that is, the mutual diffusion of law and other social discourses (cf. Mengoni, 1988: 23). This is one of the most challenging problems for autopoietics if this theory intends to avoid the fallacies of solipsism and monadism (see above V). Although the legal discourse is closed in its self-reproduction and produces its own constructions of reality, it remains always social communication and uses the general social constructions of reality and influences general social communication by its specific world constructions. Any legal act is at the same time—*uno actu*—an event of general social communication. One and the same communicative event, then, is linked with two social discourses, the specialized institutionalized discourse of law and the diffuse and general social communication. Interference of law and other social discourses does not mean that they merge into a multidimensional super-discourse, nor does it imply that information is "exchanged" among them. Rather, information is constituted anew in each discourse and interference adds nothing but the simultaneity of two communicative events (for details, see Teubner, 1989, 1990). Thus juridical constructs are exposed to the constructs of other discourses in society, particularly to the constructs of science. They are exposed to a test of "social coherence" that replaces the old fiction of a test of correspondence with outside reality.

In the world of nonlegal communication, legal constructs inevitably lose in this epistemic competition. Here, science has the advantage of having specialized in procedures for purely cognitive operations, while law uses cognitive operations only secondarily and has, thus, shaped the procedures of cognition in a different institutional context. But what about the world of legal communication in courtrooms, law offices, and legislative chambers? Here, the legal discourse claims to be entitled to "enslave" cognitive operations according to normative context and institutional purpose. The "empirical" models of legal communication are in the firm grip of "strategic" and "operative" models (for an elaboration of the mutual constraints exerted among different internal models of the outside world, see Teubner, 1982: 96 ff.). However, it is the institutional context of the legal process itself that produces an internal contradiction. While it requires idiosyncratic reality constructions through legal communication, it forces legal communication to reconstruct the scientific constructs of reality and to expose—even within the law's empire—juridical constructs to the "higher" authority of science in cognitive questions. The conflictual character of legal procedures—litigation as well as legislation and scholarly disputes—forces legal discourse to examine any piece of new knowledge produced outside the legal world only if it is "relevant" to the law. Any practicing lawyer who did not challenge legal evidence in the light of a new scientific research method would act against his/her interests and violate his/her professional duties. In the legislative process, political opponents on, say, health legislation will challenge legal measures once there is credible scientific evidence that the presupposed nexus between a disease and certain causal factors does not exist. And scholars in law and economics reap their highest reputational profits when they inform courts about their naive prescientific models of human behavior and propose scientifically proven alternatives.

The epistemic trap of modern law, therefore, produces a challenge of the first order to legal doctrine, legal theory, and legal sociology. Relentlessly, legal doctrine—through the mouths of judges and law professors—comes up with positive proposals on how to escape from the trap. Reflexively, legal theory helps to broaden the escape routes, generalizing particular solutions and importing supportive knowledge from other disciplines. And positive legal sociology zealously studies the correlations between those legal semantics and the broader sociocultural context, while it remains the privilege of critical sociolegal studies to "trash" those attempts, to demonstrate to lawyers in a merciless deconstructive analysis that they are still in the old trap.

VIII. ESCAPE ROUTES

To renounce epistemic authority, at least partially, would be the easiest way for legal discourse to escape from these troubles. Indeed, Luhmann who probably underestimates the possibility of conflict in authority among social *epistèmes*, seems to favor this escape route when he discharges the law from reexamining everyday interpretations and scientific constructs, like "woman," "cylinder capacity," "inhabitant," "thallium." "Should questions such as whether women, etc., really exist arise, they can be turned aside or referred to philosophy" (Luhmann, 1988a: 340). Unfortunately, such a clean separation of social spaces does not exist. Moreover, with such a division of labor among social discourses one would not exploit the richness of the autopoiesis concept, and would have to face empirical counter-evidence. In the day-to-day practice of legal decisionmaking, law is constantly forced to decide autonomously on cognitive questions that are supposedly within the competence of scientific inquiry or of common sense. If the normative context of law requires cognitive statements on specific matters, then it is true that the law may start its operations with common sense understanding and with reference to science. But whenever in the legal process these cognitive statements become controversial—and this is usually the case for the politically and legally "hot" issues—then law can no longer turn them aside or refer them to philosophy. Then, *hic et nunc*, the legal process must provide for procedures to settle these divergences, and must make a decision that is based on a legal determination of those questions, even if they are controversial or actually non-determinable in the sciences. More particularly, political and juridical conflicts in the environmental law area requiring much extralegal scientific and technical expertise show the great degree to which legal decisions have to be based on a specifically juridical assessment of scientific controversies or have to be made without any guidance from scientific results (cf. for the German situation, Kitschelt, 1984; Wolf, 1986; Winter, 1987).

The other main escape route from the law's epistemic trap is the integration of law and social sciences. Instead of clearly separating the realms of juridical cognition from those of scientific cognition, the legal discourse is supposed to incorporate social knowledge into its world constructions and permanently revise legal models of social reality according to the accumulation of knowledge in the social sciences. From the times of Jhering, Geny, and Pound to the most recent variations of the "law and . . ." movements, this has been the most challenging intellectual adventure of modern legal thought.

What can legal epistemology learn from almost a hundred years of experimentation with "law and social sciences"? Although social science thinking has been remarkably successful in influencing legal practice (see for example, Cotterrell, 1984: 253 ff.), the great expectations of legal enlightenment raised in academia have been dashed in the courtrooms. Psychiatry, sociology, policy analysis, and economic analysis have successfully entered the legal sphere, but the result is not a greater degree of isomorphy of law and social reality that would result in more rational legal policies. Rather, the social science enlightenment of law has resulted in unanticipated consequences—the production of hybrid artifacts with ambiguous epistemic status and unknown social consequences.

"Interest analysis," for example, is a surprising success of the efforts of "sociological jurisprudence" to replace formalist, conceptually derivative legal reasoning (for a recent analysis of the German and French practice in administrative law and its sophisticated interpretation, see Ladeur, 1984: 11ff., 57ff.). Today, interest analysis practically dominates legal decisionmaking in the courts: the courts analyze legal conflicts in terms of underlying conflicting social interests and "balance" them against each other according to standards that they infer from legislative goals expressed in a comparable context. But what is sociological about this type of sociological jurisprudence? No sociologist whatsoever would dare to follow lawyers in their attempts to conceptualize, operationalize, and empirically identify those phenomena called "social interests" that figure prominently in legal decisions (e.g., the legal concerns of creditors, debtors, neighbors, corporations, regions, states), not to speak of the juridical methods of "balancing" them. There are just too many explicit and implicit normative assumptions based on a complex network of legal-doctrinal considerations that enter into legal interest analysis. Simply put, juridical interest analysis cannot be legitimated from the standpoint of sociological theories or methods. In practice, interest analysis is a new conceptual jurisprudence that originally was subsidized by social science constructs but has been gaining its autonomy for a long time. It may very well be that "interest analysis" contains elements of a new legal rationality (in terms of flexibility, openness, and learning capacity, see Ladeur, 1984: 216ff.), but they are surely different from the original goals of sociological jurisprudence, and they evolve by institutional experimentation, not by the incorporation of sociological knowledge.

"Policy analysis" tells a similar story. Basically, it is a method of decisionmaking inspired by the instrumental use of social science knowledge (for a recent statement, see Albert, 1986: 34ff.). Define the goals consented upon in the political process, determine the factual conditions of the regulatory situation, choose among the regulatory instruments according to nomological knowledge about means-ends relations, take into account side effects, and, if you can, learn from practice about unanticipated consequences and perverse effects! But what has legal practice made of this "rational jurisprudence"? The lawyers have simply shifted their scholastic methods of doctrinal reasoning from the level of rules to the level of "policies," purposes, goals, and principles supplanting social science analysis by the obscure hermeneutics of "teleological" interpretation. Legal consequentialism has in practice become a caricature of a scientifically controlled, causal analysis supported by empirical evidence (in Germany cf. the lively debate on *Folgenkontrolle*, Luhmann, 1974; Lübbe-Wolff, 1981). What counts as a relevant consequence of a legal rule or decision derived from legal doctrine, is in a circular fashion defined by legal doctrine itself. Thus doctrine that originally was supposed to be controlled by its social consequences, now controls its social consequences. Moreover, the rational calculation of probable consequences of decisionmaking in practice turns out to be nothing but the commonsense projection of judges. And consequentialism is taken seriously only on the level of rules and not on the level of individual decisions that are in practice never reversed if the calculation of consequences turns out to be wrong. Again, we are faced not with social science in law but with a new type of legal doctrine dealing with "policies" as the new legal artifacts that replace old-fashioned rights and duties.

One could continue with the "poverty of psychiatry." Is it conceivable, from the point of view of a positivist science, that a psychiatric expert give an opinion of how to distinguish, abstractly and/or concretely, between guilt and causality (see for example, Prins, 1980: Ch. 2)? Although from a scientific standpoint any notion of individual guilt is nothing but a "trans-scientific issue"—questions that are unanswerable by science (see Weinberg, 1972; Majone, 1979, 1989: 3ff.)—forensic psychiatrists routinely give such opinions because they allow the law to "enslave" the basic concepts of their discipline.

"Economic analysis of law" is a more recent battlefield for epistemic competition. It has yet to be seen whether economic imperialism will prevail or, vice versa, whether juridical dogma will colonize economic thought. Especially in the hands of economizing lawyers, analytical concepts of economics undergo a subtle (and often not so subtle) change into normative constructs that serve as cornerstones for legal-doctrinal edifices. If, for example, one examines the new legal economics literature on the firm as a nexus of contracts (e.g., Alchian & Demsetz, 1972; Fama & Jensen, 1983; Clark, 1985; Schanze, 1986, 1987; Roos, 1988), what is left from the methodological principles of economics, formulated by Williamson (1987): theoretical openness, readiness to learn from other fields of experience, refutability of implications and exposure to empirical falsification? Judge Easterbrook's piece "Corporations as Contracts" (1988) in any case is a prototype of ideological orthodoxy, doctrinal rigidity, and conceptual immunization against contradicting experience.

These polemical remarks should not be misunderstood. They are not meant to defend the purity of scholarly conceptualization against strategic misuse by lawyers with ulterior motives. On the contrary, they are meant to demonstrate that social science constructs are not only transformed or distorted, but constituted anew, if they are incorporated into legal discourse.[5] They are not imported into the law bearing the label "made in science," but are reconstructed within the closed operational network of legal communications that gives them a meaning quite different from that of the social sciences. It is not a question of the same thing being looked at from different angles, appropriately to different disciplinary interests, methods, etc. (Aubert, 1980: 117ff., 1983: 98ff.; Rottleuthner, 1980: 137ff.). This would be to presuppose an underlying reality that is capable of unifying the diverse aspects stressed in different disciplines and of deciding between conflicting descriptions. Rather, the differences are to be found in the realities themselves that are produced by different discourses and that can be neither unified nor reconciled.

Thus the incorporation of social science knowledge is not really an escape from what we called the epistemic trap of modern

---

[5] "Much depends on noticing that law's autonomy lies not in its freedom from being influenced by external causes and influences but in the way in which it incorporates and responds to them" (Nelken, 1987).

law. It does not solve the conflict between juridical and scientific realities, but adds a new reality that is neither a purely juridical construction nor a purely scientific construction. The constructs of sociological jurisprudence, legal economics, "legal politology," and the like, are hybrid creatures, produced in the legal process with borrowed authority from the social sciences. However, epistemic authority and responsibility are no longer with the social sciences but with the law. And their "truth," their social adequacy, their viability will be decided no longer in the process of scientific inquiry but in the process of legal communication. For instance, certain psychoanalytic constructs, as well as fully deterministic models in psychology, will never be viable constructs in a juridical world that is based upon assumptions of individual guilt and responsibility. Or to take another field, the relative success of legal economics compared to sociological jurisprudence has probably nothing to do with the intrinsic "scientific" values of the models involved, but with their structural affinity to traditional legal doctrine. If courts considering questions of, say, negligence, public policy, fairness, or properties of the "reasonable man" resort to "social norms," a sociological conceptualization would require time, energy, and money for extended empirical research, while an economic conceptualization in terms of transaction costs requires an armchair.

It would be wrong, however, to view the incorporation of social knowledge as "irrational." Given the inherent tension between scientific and juridical realities and the authority of modern sciences, it seems quite rational for the law to attempt to make the legal reality constructs at least compatible with recent developments in the sciences. In this respect, law resembles religion (for a constructivist account of the conflict between science and religion, see Arbib & Hesse, 1986: 16ff., 197ff.). For legal dogma and theological dogma alike, it is advisable to keep the world of faith compatible with the world of scientific truth. However, there is more to the integration of law and social sciences than merely making contradictory world constructions compatible. The "law and . . ." movement, it should be admitted, has benign effects for the decisionmaking quality of modern law in terms of justice and utility. The most recent results of the social sciences and the permanent challenge which they represent can serve as a "variety pool" for legal innovation. It is a tremendously rich source for an ongoing reconstruction of the legal world, comparable only to the richness in what people find litigable and which creates legal conflicts. However, what happens to those constructs once they enter the legal scene is no longer in the hands of the social sciences. Selection and retention of these variations is the job of legal evolution.

There are indications today that this legal reconstruction of scientific knowledge, if carried too far, becomes risky in itself. In the environmental law area, for example, Gerd Winter (1987) felt a growth in the "judges' anxiety" about technical risk assessment and other legal incorporation of scientific findings together with a tendency to reduce the scope of legally relevant issues. This looks like a return to the first mentioned escape route in the permanent oscillation between epistemic autonomy and heteronomy. However, there are other attempts to cope with this situation, experimentation with a third solution, a kind of middle path between the two main escape routes. These more promising attempts can be summarized in the following formula. Law cannot take over full epistemic authority and responsibility for the reality constructions involved, but at the same time it does not totally delegate epistemic authority to other social discourses. Rather, as a precondition for the incorporation of social knowledge, the legal system defines certain fundamental requirements relating to procedure and methods of cognition.

A case in point is the decision of the German Supreme Court on codetermination in economic organizations (*Bundesverfassungsgericht, BVerfGE* 50, 290). For years, constitutional lawyers had judged the constitutionality of labor participation on the basis of its economic effects—in terms of efficiency of the firm, performance of the West German economy, and its position in international competition. In this way, the collective actors involved, that is, firms, employer associations, labor unions, government, and parliament, had prepared short legal reality constructions in their briefs with detailed scenarios about the socioeconomic consequences of codetermination, either with catastrophic or beneficial consequences, whichever was appropriate to their position (see Badura *et al.*, 1977: 137ff., 246ff.; Kübler *et al.*, 1978: 35ff., 99ff., 145ff., 197ff.). In addition, economic and sociological experts had been mobilized on both sides. The court refused to take a substantive position on these scenarios about possible consequences and resorted to a "procedural" solution. Instead of confirming or rejecting reality constructions, the court allocated risks of information and risks of prediction among the collective actors involved, including the court itself, and created a new legal duty for the legislature: to reverse its decisions if the predictions on which they were based should turn out to be wrong (for an in-depth analysis of such a "proceduralization" of institutional cognition, see Wiethölter, 1985, 1986, 1989; Frey, 1989: 103ff.; cf. also Majone, 1979, 1989). In several more recent decisions this tendency has been strengthened: to abstain from a material constructions of reality and to proceduralize the legal solution; to delegate epistemic authority to different collective actors, that is, regulatory agencies, private firms, labor unions, research institutions, interest associations, governmental organizations, parliament, courts; to allocate risks of information and prediction; to define procedures and methods; to decide which collective actor must bear the "burden of proof" for reality constructions; and to define responsibilities for failures in information and prediction (see for environmental law, *BVerfGE* 49, 89; for corporation law, *BVerfGE* 72, 155; for the law of property, *BVerfGE* 74, 264).

To a certain degree, a constructivist perspective would favor such attempts to "proceduralize" the conflict between epistemic autonomy and heteronomy in modern law. Indeed, when correspondence theories of truth have to be replaced by consensus theories and coherence theories, when the authority of science is based only on its internal procedures of validation, when institutional contexts like the law are condemned to epistemic autonomy and cannot resort to external authorities, then practical and theoretical attention must focus on the procedures that dictate the premises, content, and consequences of institutional constructions of social reality.

GUNTHER CURT MAX TEUBNER is Professor of Law in the University of Bremen and the European University Institute Firenze. He is the author of numerous works in law and society, including *Dilemmas of Law in the Welfare State* (1985), *Juridification of Social Spheres* (1987), *Autopoietic Law* (1988), *State, Law, Economy as Autopoietic Systems* (1990).

REFERENCES

ADAMS, Michael (1985) *Ökonomische Analyse der Gefährdungs- und Verschuldenshaftung*. Heidelberg: Decker and Schenck.
ALBERT, Hans (1986) "Law as an Instrument of Rational Practice," in T.C. Daintith and G. Teubner (eds.), *Contract and Organisation: Legal Analysis in the Light of Economic and Social Theory*. Berlin: de Gruyter.
ALCHIAN, Armen A., and H. DEMSETZ (1972) "Production, Information Costs and Economic Organization," 62 *American Economic Review* 777.
ALEXY, Robert (1978) *Theorie der juristischen Argumentation: Die Theorie des rationalen Diskurses als Theorie der juristischen Begründung*. Frankfurt: Suhrkamp.
APEL, Karl-Otto (1973) "Das Apriori der Kommunikationsgemeinschaft und die Grundlagen der Ethik," in K. O. Apel, *Transformation der Philosophie*. Frankfurt: Suhrkamp.
——— (1988) *Diskurs und Verantwortung: Das Problem des Übergangs zur postkonventionellen Moral*. Frankfurt: Suhrkamp.
ARBIB, Michael A., and Mary B. HESSE (1986) *The Construction of Reality*. Cambridge: Cambridge University Press.
AUBERT, Vilhelm (1980) "On the Relationship between Legal and Sociological Concepts," in E. Blankenburg, E. Klausa and H. Rottleuthner (eds.), *Alternative Rechtsformen und Alternativen zum Recht*. Opladen: Westdeutscher Verlag.
——— (1983) *In Search of Law: Sociological Approaches to Law*. Oxford: Robertson.
BADURA, Peter, Fritz RITTNER, and Bernd RÜTHERS (1977) *Mitbestimmungsgesetz 1976 und Grundgesetz: Gemeinschaftsgutachten*. München: Beck.
BARNES, Barry (1974) *Scientific Knowledge and Sociological Theory*. London: Routledge and Kegan.
BARWISE, Jon, and John ETCHEMENDY (1987) *The Liar: An Essay in Truth and Circularity*. New York: Oxford University Press.

BAUDRILLARD, Jean (1976) *L'échange symbolique et la mort.* Paris: Gallimard.
BERGER, Peter L., and Thomas LUCKMANN (1966) *The Social Construction of Reality: A Treatise in the Sociology of Knowledge.* New York: Doubleday.
BLOOR, David (1976) *Knowledge and Social Imagery.* London: Routledge and Kegan.
BÖHLER, Dietrich (1985) *Rekonstruktive Pragmatik: Von der Bewußtsein philosophie zur Kommunikationsreflexion: Neubegründung der praktischen Wissenschaften und Philosophie.* Frankfurt: Suhrkamp.
BOURDIEU, Pierre (1986) "La force du droit: Elements pour une sociologie du champ juridique," *Actes de la recherche en sciences sociales* 3.
CARROLL, Lewis (1871) *Through the Looking Glass and What Alice Found There* (cited after the edition of 1960, Bramhall House, New York) London: Macmillan.
—— (1855) "Stanza of Anglo-Saxon Poetry," *Misch-Masch.*
CLARK, Robert C. (1985) "Agency Costs Versus Fiduciary Duties," in J. W. Pratt, and R. J. Zeckhauser (eds.), *Principals and Agents: The Structure of Business.* Boston: Harvard Business School Press.
COHEN, Felix S. (1935) "Transcendental Nonsense and the Functional Approach," 35 *Columbia Law Review* 809.
COLLINS, Harry (1985) *Changing Order: Replication and Induction in Scientific Practice.* Beverly Hills: Sage.
COTTERRELL, Roger (1984) *The Sociology of Law: An Introduction.* London: Butterworths.
—— (1986) "Law and Sociology: Notes on the Constitution and Confrontation of Disciplines," 13 *Journal of Law and Society* 9.
CROZIER, Michel, and Erhard FRIEDBERG (1977) *L'acteur et le systeme: Les contraintes de l'action collective.* Paris: Seuil.
DAN-COHEN, Meir (1986) *Rights, Persons, and Organizations: A Legal Theory for Bureaucratic Society.* Berkeley: University of California Press.
DEGGAU, Hans-Georg (1988) "The Communicative Autonomy of the Legal System," in G. Teubner (ed.), *Autopoietic Law: A New Approach to Law and Society.* Berlin: de Gruyter.
DOUGLAS, Mary (1986) *How Institutions Think.* Syracuse, NY: Syracuse University Press.
DREYFUS, Hubert L., and Paul RABINOW (1982) *Michel Foucault: Beyond Structuralism and Hermeneutics.* Chicago: University of Chicago Press.
EASTERBROOK, Frank (1988) "Corporations as Contracts." Conference paper, presented at Stanford Law School, 1988.
ELSTER, Jon (ed.) (1986) The Multiple Self. Cambridge: Cambridge University Press.
—— (1985) *Making Sense of Marx.* Cambridge: Cambridge University Press.
—— (1983) *Explaining Technical Change.* Cambridge: Cambridge University Press.
ETZIONI, Amitai (1988) *The Moral Dimension: Toward a New Economics.* New York: Free Press.
FAMA, Eugen F., and JENSEN, Michael (1983) "Agency, Problems and Residual Claims," 26 *Journal of Law and Economics* 327.
FEBBRAJO, Alberto (1985) "The Rules of the Game in the Welfare State," in G. Teubner (ed.), *Dilemmas of Law in the Welfare State.* Berlin: de Gruyter.
FODOR, J. A. (1980) "Methodological Solipsism Considered as a Research Strategy in Cognitive Psychology," 3 *Behavioral Brain Science* 63.
FÖRSTER, Heinz von (1985) "Entdecken oder Erfinden? Wie Läßt sich Verstehen Verstehen?" in A. Mohlar (ed.) *Einführung in den Konstruktivismus.* München: Oldenbourg.
—— (1981) *Observing Systems.* Seaside, CA: Intersystems Publications.
FOUCAULT, Michel (1979) *Discipline and Punish.* New York: Vintage/Random House.
—— (1974) *The Order of Things: An Archaeology of the Human Sciences.* London: Tavistock.
—— (1972) *The Archaeology of Knowledge.* New York: Harper Colophon.

754 HOW THE LAW THINKS

FRANKENBERG, Günter (1987) "Der Ernst im Recht," 20 *Kritische Justiz* 281-307.
FREY, Reiner (1989) *Vom Subjekt zur Selbstreferenz: Rechtstheoretische Überlegungen zur Rekonstruktion der Rechtskategorie*. Berlin: Duncker and Humblot.
FULLER, Steve (1988) *Social Epistemology*. Bloomington: Indiana University Press.
GIDDENS, Anthony (1987) *Social Theory and Modern Sociology*. Stanford: Stanford University Press.
GILBERT, Nigel, and Michael MULKAY (1984) *Opening Pandora's Box*. Cambridge: Cambridge University Press.
GLASERSFELD, Ernst von (1985) "Konstruktion der Wirklichkeit und des Begriffs der Objektivität," in H. Gumin and A. Mohlar (eds.), *Einführung in den Konstruktivismus*. München: Oldenbourg.
—— (1981) "An Epistemology for Cognitive Systems," in G. Roth and H. Schwegler (eds.), *Self-Organizing Systems: An Interdisciplinary Approach*. Frankfurt: Campus.
—— (1975) "Radical Constructivism and Piaget's Concept of Knowledge," in F. B. Murray (ed.), *Input of Piagetian Theory*. Baltimore: University Park Press.
GORDON, Robert W. (1984) "Critical Legal Histories," 36 *Stanford Law Review* 57.
GRÜNBERGER, Hans (1987) "Dehumanisierung der Gesellschaft und Verabschiedung staatlicher Souveränität: Das Politische System in der Gesellschaftstheorie Niklas Luhmanns" in I. Fetscher and H. Münkler (eds.) *Pipers Handbuch der politischen Ideen*. München: Piper.
GRZEGORCZYK, Christophe (1989) "Système juridique et réalité: Discussion de la théorie autopoiétique du droit," 33 *Archives de philosophie du droit*.
GÜNTHER, Klaus (1988) *Der Sinn für Angemessenheit: Anwendungsdiskurse in Moral und Recht*. Frankfurt: Suhrkamp.
HABERMAS, Jürgen (1988) *Nachmetaphysisches Denken: Philosophische Aufsätze*. Frankfurt: Suhrkamp.
—— (1987a) *The Theory of Communicative Action. Lifeworld and System: A Critique of Functionalist Reason*. Vol. 2. Boston: Beacon Press.
—— (1987b) "Wie ist Legitimation durch Legalität möglich?" 20 *Kritische Justiz* 1.
—— (1985) "Law as Medium and Law as Institution," in G. Teubner (ed.), *Dilemmas of Law in the Welfare State*. Berlin: de Gruyter.
—— (1984) *The Theory of Communicative Action*. Vol. 1: *Reason and the Rationalization of Society*. Boston: Beacon Press.
—— (1983) *Moralbewußtsein und kommunikatives Handeln*. Frankfurt: Suhrkamp.
—— (1975) *Legitimation Crisis*. Boston: Beacon Press.
—— (1974) *Communication and the Evolution of Society*. Boston: Beacon Press.
—— (1973) "Wahrheitstheorien," in H. Fahrenbach (ed.), *Wirlichkeit und Reflexion*. Pfullingen: Neske.
—— (1971a) *Knowledge and Human Interest*. Boston: Beacon Press.
—— (1971b) "Vorbereitende Bemerkungen zu einer Theorie der kommunikativen Kompetenz," in J. Habermas and N. Luhmann, *Theorie der Gesellschaft oder Sozialtechnologie—Was leistet die Systemforschung*. Frankfurt: Suhrkamp.
HAYEK, Friedrich A. (1973) *Law, Legislation, and Liberty*, Vol. 1: *Rules and Order*. London: Routledge and Paul.
—— (1948) *Individualism and Economic Order*. London: Routledge.
HELLER, Thomas (1988) "Accounting for Law," in G. Teubner (ed.), *Autopoietic Law: A New Approach to Law and Society*. Berlin: de Gruyter.
—— (1984) "Structuralism and Critique," 36 *Stanford Law Review* 127.
HOMANS, George C. (1961) *Social Behavior: Its Elementary Forms*. London: Routledge and Kegan.
HONNETH, Axel (1985) *Kritik der Macht: Reflexionsstufen einer kritischen Gesellschaftstheorie*. Frankfurt: Suhrkamp.
HORWITZ, Morton (1985) "Santa Clara Revisited," 88 *West Virginia Law Review* 173.

HUTTER, Michael (1989) *Die Produktion von Recht*. Tübingen: Mohr und Siebeck.
JHERING, Rudolf von (1884) *Scherz und Ernst in der Jurisprudenz*. Leipzig: Breitkopf und Haertel.
JOERGES, Christian (1989) "Politische Rechtstheorie and Critical Legal Studies," in C. Joerges and D. Trubek (eds.), *Critical Legal Thought: An American-German Debate*. Baden-Baden: Nomos.
KENNEDY, David (1985) "Critical Theory, Structuralism, and Contemporary Scholarship," 21 *New England Law Review* 209.
KENNEDY, Duncan (1986) "Freedom and Constraint in Adjudication: A Critical Phenomenology," 36 *Journal of Legal Education* 518.
KERCHOVE, Michel van de, and François OST (1988) *Le système juridique entre ordre et desordre*. Paris: Presses Universitaires de France.
KITSCHELT, Herbert (1984) *Der kologische Diskurs: Eine Analyse von Gesellschaftskonzeptionen in der Energiedebatte*. Frankfurt: Campus.
KNORR-CETINA, Karin (1984) *Die Fabrikation von Erkenntnis: Zur Anthropologie der Naturwissenschaft*. Frankfurt: Suhrkamp.
KNYPHAUSEN, Dodo zu (1988) *Unternehmungen als evolutionsfähige Systeme: Überlegungen zu einem evolutionären Konzept für die Organisationstheorie*. Herrsching: Kirsch.
KRIPPENDORFF, Klaus (1984) "Paradox and Information," in B. Dervin and M. Voight (eds.), *Progress in Communication*. Norwood: Ablex.
KÜBLER, Friedrich, Walter SCHMIDT, and Spiros SIMITIS (1978) *Mitbestimmung als gesetzgebungspolitische Aufgabe*. Baden-Baden: Nomos.
LADEUR, Karl-Heinz (1989a) "The Law of Uncertainty," in C. Joerges and D. Trubek (eds.), *Critical Legal Thought: An American-German Debate*. Baden-Baden: Nomos.
――― (1989b) "Zu einer Grundrechtstheorie der Selbstorganisation des Unternehmens," in *Festschrift für Helmut Ridder*. Neuwied: Luchterhand.
――― (1988) "Perspectives on a Post-Modern Theory of Law," in G. Teubner (ed.), *Autopoietic Law: A New Approach to Law and Society*. Berlin: de Gruyter.
――― (1984) *"Abwägung"—Ein neues Paradigma des Verwaltungsrechts: Von der Einheit der Rechtsordnung zum Rechtspluralismus*. Frankfurt: Campus.
LATOUR, Bruno and Steve WOOLGAR (1979) *Laboratory Life: The Construction of Scientific Facts*. Princeton: Princeton University Press.
LÜBBE-WOLFF, Gertrude (1981) *Rechtsfolgen und Realfolgen*. Freiburg: Alber.
LUHMANN, Niklas (1990) "The Coding of the Legal System," in A. Febbrajo and G. Teubner (eds.) *State, Law, Economy as Autopoietic Systems*. Milano: Giuffrè.
――― (1988a) "Closure and Openness: On Reality in the World of law," in G. Teubner (ed.), *Autopoietic Law: A New Approach to Law and Society*. Berlin: de Gruyter.
――― (1988b) "The Third Question: The Creative Use of Paradoxes in Law and Legal History," 15 *Journal of Law and Society* 153.
――― (1988c) *Wissenschaft*. Bielefeld: Typosript.
――― (1986a) "The Autopoiesis of Social Systems," in F. Geyer and J. van der Zouwen (eds.) *Sociocybernetic Paradoxes*. London: Sage.
――― (1986b) "The Individuality of the Individual: Historical Meaning and Contemporary Problems," in T. C. Heller, M. Sosna, and D. E. Wellbery (eds.), *Reconstructing Individualism: Autonomy, Individuality, and the Self in Western Thought*. Stanford, CA: Stanford University Press.
――― (1986c) "Intersubjektivität oder Kommunikation: Unterschiedliche Ausgangspunkte soziologischer Theoriebildung," 54 *Archivio di Filosofia* 41.
――― (1986d) "The Theory of Social Systems and Its Epistemology: Reply to Danilo Zolo's Critical Comments," 16 *Philosophy of the Social Sciences* 129-134.
――― (1985) "Die Autopoiese des Bewußtseins," 36 *Sociale Welt* 402.
――― (1984) *Soziale Systeme: Grundriß einer allgemeinen Theorie*. Frankfurt: Suhrkamp.

——— (1983) "Individuum und Gesellschaft," 39 *Universitas* 1.
——— (1974) *Rechtssystem und Rechtsdogmatik*. Stuttgart: Kohlhammer.
MAJONE, Giandomenico (1989) *Evidence, Argument and Persuasion in the Policy Process*. New Haven: Yale University Press.
——— (1979) "Process and Outcome in Regulatory Decision-Making," in C. H. Weiss and A. Barton (eds.), *Making Bureaucracies Work*. Beverly Hills: Sage.
MATURANA, Huberto R., and Francisco J. VARELA (1980) *Autopoiesis and Cognition*. Boston: Reidel.
MAYNTZ, Renate (1986) "Steuerung, Steuerungsakteure und Steuerungsinstrumente: Zur Präzisierung des Problems," 70 *HiMon-DB*. Siegen: Universität.
MENGONI, Luigi (1988) "La questione del 'diritto giusto' nella societa postliberale," 11 *Fenomenologia e Societa Diritto ed Etica Pubblica* 14.
NELSON, Alan (1984) "Some Issues Surrounding the Reduction of Macroeconomics to Microeconomics," 51 *Philosophy of Science* 573.
NERHOT, Patrick (1988) "The Fact of Law," in G. Teubner (ed.), *Autopoietic Law: A New Approach to Law and Society*. Berlin: de Gruyter.
OPP, Karl-Dieter (1973) *Soziologie im Recht*. Reinbek: Rowohlt.
OST, François (1988) "Between Order and Disorder: The Game of Law," in G. Teubner (ed.), *Autopoietic Law: A New Approach to Law and Society*. Berlin: de Gruyter.
PIAGET, Jean (1971) *The Construction of Reality in the Child*. New York: Ballantine.
PIZZORNO, Alessandro (1989) "Spiegazione come re-identificatione," in L. Sciolla, and L. Ricolfi (eds.), *Il soggetto dell'azione: Paradigmi sociologichi e immagini dell'attore sociale*. Milano: Angeli.
PODAK, Klaus (1984) "Ohne Subjekt, ohne Vernunft: Bei der Lektüre von Niklas Luhmanns Hauptwerk 'Soziale Systeme'," 7 *Merkur* 733.
POPPER Karl (1953) *The Poverty of Historicism*. London: Routledge and Kegan Paul.
PREUSS, Ulrich K. (1989) "Rationality Potentials of Law: Allocative, Distributive and Communicative Rationality," in C. Joerges and D. Trubek (eds.), *Critical Legal Thought: An American-German Debate*. Baden-Baden: Nomos.
PRINS, H. (1980) *Offenders, Deviants or Patients? An Introduction to the Study of Socio-Forensic Problems*. London: Tavistok.
QUINE, Willard V. (1976) *The Ways of Paradox*. Cambridge, MA: Harvard University Press.
ROOS, Carl Martin (1988) "Corporate Personality and Contractual Structure: Legal Aspects on the Firm as a Nexus of Treaties," Uppsala: Manuscript.
ROTH, Gerhard (1987) "Die Entwicklung kognitiver Selbstreferentialität im menschlichen Gehirn," in D. Baecker *et al.* (eds.), *Theorie als Passion*. Frankfurt: Suhrkamp.
——— (1984) "Erkenntnis und Realität: Das Gehirn und seine Wirklichkeit," in G. Pasternack (ed.), *Erklären, Verstehen, Begründen*. Bremen: Universität.
ROTTLEUTHNER, Hubert (1988) "Biological Metaphors in Legal Thought," in G. Teubner (ed.), *Autopoietic Law: A New Approach to Law and Society*. Berlin: de Gruyter.
——— (1980) "Diskussionsvotum zum vorstehenden Beitrag," in E. Blankenburg, E. Klausa, and H. Rottleuthner (eds.), *Alternative Rechtsformen und Alternativen zum Recht*. Opladen: Westdeutscher Verlag.
——— (1979) "Zur Methode einer folgenorientierten Rechtsanwendung," *Archiv für Rechts- und Sozialphilosophie*, Beiheft 13. Wiesbaden: Steiner.
SCHANE, Sanford A. (1987) "The Corporation is a Person: The Language of a Legal Fiction," 61 *Tulane Law Review* 563.
SCHANZE, Erich (1987) "Contract, Agency, and the Delegation of Decision Making," in G. Bamberg and K. Spreman (eds.), *Agency Theory, Information, and Incentives*. Berlin: Springer.
——— (1986) "Potential and Limits of Economic Analysis: The Constitution of the Firm," in T. Daintith and G. Teubner (eds.), *Contract and Organisation: Legal Analysis in the Light of Economic and Social Theory*. Berlin: de Gruyter.

SCHIMANK, Uwe (1985) "Der mangelnde Akteurbezug systemtheoretischer Erklärungen gesellschaftlicher Differenzierung—Ein Diskussionsvorschlag," 14 *Zeitschrift für Soziologie* 421.
SCHMIDT, Siegfried (ed.) (1987) *Der Diskurs des Radikalen Konstruktivismus.* Frankfurt: Suhrkamp.
SCOTT, Robert (1872) "The Jabberwock Traced to Its True Source," *Macmillan's Magazine,* February.
SELZNICK, Philip (1968) "Law: The Sociology of Law," 9 *International Encyclopedia of the Social Sciences* 50.
SKINNER, Quentin (1985) *The Return of Grand Theory in the Human Sciences.* Cambridge, England: Cambridge University Press.
TEUBNER, Gunther (1990) "Social Order from Legislative Noise? Autopoietic Closure as a Problem for Legal Regulation," in G. Teubner and A. Febbrajo (eds.), *State, Law, Economy as Autopoietic Systems.* Milano: Giuffrè.
——— (1989) "And God Laughed . . .: Indeterminacy, Self-Reference, and Paradox in Law," in C. Joerges and D. Trubek (eds.), *Critical Legal Thought: An American-German Debate.* Baden-Baden: Nomos.
——— (1988a) "Enterprise Corporatism: New Industrial Policy and the 'Essence' of the Legal Person," 36 *American Journal of Comparative Law* 130.
——— (1988b) "Evolution of Autopoietic Law," in G. Teubner (ed.), *Autopoietic Law: A New Approach to Law and Society.* Berlin: de Gruyter.
——— (1988c) "Hypercycle in Law and Organization: The Relationship between Self-Observation, Self-Constitution and Autopoiesis," *European Yearbook in the Sociology of Law* 43.
——— (1982) "Generalklauseln als sozio-normative Modelle," in H. Stachowiak (ed.), *Bedürfnisse, Werte und Normen im Wandel.* Bd. 1. München: Fink and Schöningh.
VARDARO, Gaetano (1990) "Before and Beyond the Legal Personality: Group Enterprises and Industrial Relations," in D. Sugarman and G. Teubner (eds.), *Regulating Corporate Groups in Europe.* Baden-Baden: Nomos.
VARELA, Francisco J. (1984) "Living Ways of Sense-Making: A Middle Path for Neuro-Science," in P. Livingstone (ed.), *Disorder and Order: Proceedings of the Stanford International Symposium.* Saratoga, CA: Anma Libri.
WEBER, Max (1978) *Economy and Society.* Berkeley: University of California Press.
WEINBERG, Alvin M. (1972) "Science and Trans-science," 10 *Minerva* 209.
WEINTRAUB, E. Roy (1979) *Microfoundations: The Compatibility of Microeconomics and Macroeconomics.* Cambridge: Cambridge University Press.
WIETHÖLTER, Rudolf (1989) "Proceduralization of the Category of Law" in C. Joerges and D. Trubek (eds.), *Critical Legal Thought: An American-German Debate.* Baden-Baden: Nomos.
——— (1986) "Social Science Models in Economic Law," in T. Daintith and G. Teubner (eds.), *Contract and Organisation: Legal Analysis in the Light of Economic and Social Theory.* Berlin: de Gruyter.
——— (1985) "Materialization and Proceduralization in Modern Law," in G. Teubner (ed.) *Dilemmas of Law in the Welfare State.* Berlin: de Gruyter.
WILLIAMSON, Oliver E. (1987) "The Contractual Logic of Internal Organization." Firenze: EUI Conference paper.
WINDSCHEID, Bernhard (1904) "Die Aufgaben der Rechtswissenschaft," in B. Windscheid, *Gesammelte Reden und Abhandlungen.* Leipzig: Duncker.
WINTER, Gert (1987) "Die Angst des Richters bei der Technikbewertung," 20 *Zeitschrift für Rechtspolitik* 425.
WOLF, Rainer (1986) *Der Stand der Technik.* Opladen: Westdeutscher Verlag.
WORMELL, C. P. (1958) "On the Paradoxes of Self-Reference," 67 *Mind* 267.

[9]

Law And Spontaneous Order: Hayek's Contribution to Legal Theory

A. I. OGUS*

Ten years ago, I observed that the work of Friedrich von Hayek had been unjustifiably neglected by legal writers in this country.[1] Notwithstanding the impact and influence of New Right theorists in the period since then,[2] the situation has not altered significantly.[3] This is all the more surprising because, particularly in his later works, Hayek addresses issues central to legal theory: the nature of law and the state, justice, constitutional structures, and the rival merits of common law and legislation.

Of course, Hayek's exploration of law has been, in no sense, a separate enterprise; rather, it is but one part of an overarching unified restatement of liberalism, having at its base a theory of knowledge and scientific inquiry, which is developed systematically first in relation to economic decision making and systems and then to the political order as a whole. In this paper I shall focus on Hayek's contribution to legal theory as expounded principally in his last major work *Law, Legislation and Liberty*[4] but will attempt to place that in the context of his general theory of society, as it was developed throughout his intellectual career. After a short account of Hayek's approach to social science methodology, I show how he uses an epistemological theory to develop two models of social organization: spontaneous order, which he identifies with the market and with common law, and rational constructivism, which is associated with a planned economy and regulatory law. Hayek's main thesis is that it is only the first of these which, by preserving liberty subject only to universal rules of just conduct, can guarantee the progress of human civilization. I argue that the normative dimension of this assertion is fundamentally flawed but that, as an explanatory model of the development of law, Hayek's theory merits serious attention.

---

* *Professor of Law, The University, Manchester M13 9PL, England.*

This paper is the second in a series dealing with the work of theorists who have substantially influenced contemporary understanding of law and society. (See previously H. Collins, 'Roberto Unger and the Critical Legal Studies Movement' (1987) 13 *J. of Law and Society* 387.)

I. THE METHODS OF SOCIAL SCIENCE

Hayek's method of analysing society has its origin in the Kantian conception that individuals cannot observe phenomena 'externally'; the human mind is as much a part of the natural and social environment as that which is being studied.[5] Social reality, then, cannot be 'explained' by an objective, intellectual process. The subjectivist theory was central to the Austrian school of economics, in which Hayek was trained and from which he derived much of his early inspiration.[6] In contrast to the classical economists, the Austrians concluded that resources had no objective 'value', determinable by reference to, for example, labour and capital input. 'Value' was, instead, a matter of individual subjective preferences and choice. Hayek developed the notion in his own economic work[7] but, more significantly, applied it to the whole of social sciences.[8] Since the subject-matter of the latter was composed entirely of human action and interaction which was, in turn, the result of attitudes, beliefs, and motives, objective analysis was impossible and therefore 'scientistic':

> Not only man's [sic] action towards external objects but also all the relations between men and all social institutions can be understood only in terms of what men think about them. Society as we know it is, as it were, built up from the concepts and ideas held by the people; and social phenomena can be recognized by us and have meaning to us only as they are reflected in the minds of men.[9]

How, then, is the social scientist to derive an understanding of society and social institutions? Hayek's answer is by means of a 'compositive' method: groups of structurally connected elements can be selected out of the totality of observed phenomena, revealing the regularities, pattern, or general order of human behaviour.[10] A strict Austrian would argue that the complexity of variables inherent in human behaviour and motivation precludes the possibility. No doubt aware of the risk of undermining the importance of his own essay in prophesy (in the highly influential *Road to Freedom* he had spelt out what he saw as the implications for the future of current trends in political institutions),[11] Hayek in his later writing reached a different, and perhaps not entirely satisfactory, conclusion. While specific predictions about complex phenomena (such as the price of a particular product at a particular time) cannot be made, nevertheless a theory derived from observing broad patterns of behaviour under certain conditions may enable us to expect those patterns to recur if the conditions prevail – and in principle the hypothesis is testable, or at least falsifiable in the Popperian sense.[12] Hayek's sweeping generalizations about the human condition stand or fall with this methodological assumption; some would argue that its inherent vagueness makes it difficult to distinguish between scientific prediction and pure speculation.[13]

II. TWO MODELS OF SOCIAL ORGANIZATION

The anti-rationalist thrust of Hayek's approach to social science methodology applies to action as well as thought and is at the heart of his social theory.

Knowledge of the innumerable facts which make up the human condition is necessarily widely dispersed and fragmentary. Individuals making decisions about courses of action can at best rely on limited information normally pertaining to localized environments. Interaction and co-operation with others are, of course, essential, but this does not imply a planned or directive form of social organization. The *spontaneous order* which emerges is self-generating or endogenous:[14] it is not deliberately brought about and has no explicit purpose; rather it results from the instinctive adoption of certain (often unformulated) rules. This idea of unplanned order is exemplified by the development of human language but also by animal life, for example in the insect societies of bees, ants, and termites.[15]

For society to exist, the rules must be habitually obeyed, but to overcome the Hobbesian dilemma which arises when self-interest conflicts with the common goal compulsion may be necessary:

> Some such rules all individuals of a society will obey because of the similar manner in which their environment represents itself to their minds. Others they will follow spontaneously because they will be part of their common cultural tradition. But there will be still others which they must have to be made to obey, since, although it would be in the interests of each to disregard them, the overall order on which the success of their actions depends will arise only if these rules are generally followed.[16]

Although, therefore, representatives of the community might have to enforce the rules, under a spontaneous order their specific content is not to be designed. Because the relationship between individual rules and the overall order is so complex, no individual is able to predict what will or will not succeed. Rules are best left, by a process of evolutionary selection, to adapt to changes in the environment.

The spontaneous order model of social organization is to be contrasted with *rational constructivism* which assumes that human institutions are capable of serving human purposes, and in the past have successfully done so, only if they are deliberately designed.[17] For Hayek, this view, which has infused social and political thought since Descartes, is deeply fallacious: it fails to recognize that the human mind is a part of, and therefore cannot transcend, spontaneous order; and it results from the synoptic delusion: 'the fiction that all the relevant facts are known to some one mind, and that it is possible to construct from this knowledge of the particulars a desirable social order'.[18]

1. *The Market as Spontaneous Order*

The earlier part of Hayek's career was devoted to pure economic theory[19] – he held the Tooke Chair in Economic Science at London University from 1931 to 1950 – and his notion of spontaneous order was developed first in relation to the market.[20] The latter is an unplanned process whereby individuals make use of decentralized and fragmented knowledge, limited normally to localized information about prices and costs, to advance their own interests in competition with others. The basis of the competitive market order is, then, a system for communicating information: individuals respond to signals, the prices which reflect peoples' needs for products (demand), with profits rewarding those whose skill, or perhaps luck, enables them to adapt best to those signals. They need know nothing of why demand changes, still less of the economy as a whole. The 'marvel' of prices is: 'how little the individual participants need to know in order to be able to take the right action. In abbreviated form, by a kind of symbol, only the most essential information is passed on and passed on only to those concerned.'[21]

Planned economic systems fail simply because no individual, or set of individuals, can have the knowledge required to co-ordinate the activities of producers and consumers; and, in any event, economic progress is dependent on individuals being rewarded for successful experimentation with what is wholly or partially unknown.[22]

While these ideas may be largely shared by neo-classical economists, Hayek diverges from their traditional theory by not relying on assumptions either of the perfect knowledge of economic actors, or of perfect competition. The phenomena of the market process are always in a state of flux. An individual entrepreneur may, for example, offer a new product, guessing from information about other products that there will be sufficient demand for it; if her or his guesswork is good, she or he will enjoy an initial monopoly power but, unless there are barriers to entry, that will not last. This view of the market as a dynamic process led Hayek to be highly critical of the neo-classical obsession with supply and demand equilibrium and allocative efficiency:[23] a model in which, responding to stable preferences, resources are assumed to gravitate towards such an equilibrium distorts the reality of economic behaviour, because there is an inherent tendency for agents, in the light of newly-acquired knowledge, to move away from this state. Since Hayek's approach does not lend itself to econometric modelling of the kind which now dominates the economics discipline, it is perhaps not surprising that his work is neglected by contemporary economists.[24]

2. *Common Law as Spontaneous Order*

The germs of Hayek's identification of the common law with spontaneous order may be found in *The Road to Serfdom*[25] and *The Constitution of Liberty*[26] where he views 'genuine' law as possessing a generality and thus abstracted from particular circumstances of time and place. Further, and in sharp opposition to Austinian jurisprudence, 'law' is distinguished from 'command' in that it does not presuppose a sovereign who issues it; as such, it is a part of the unplanned order.

The subject is explored in considerable depth in *Law, Legislation and Liberty*, the larger part of the first volume being devoted to it.[27] Law-making is here portrayed as a continuous, adaptative process dealing with unforeseen consequences:

> The parts of a legal system are not so much adjusted to each other according to a comprehensive overall view, as gradually adapted to each other by the successive application of general principles to particular problems – principles, that is, which are often not even explicitly known but merely implicit in the particular measures which are taken.[28]

The individual judge functioning within this process is more an 'unwitting tool ... than a conscious initiator'. The judge's task is to apply the general principles of law, not to question them. Stability ensues because, in applying the general to the particular, the judge will interpret it in such a way as to render it consistent with other general principles and thus generate coherence.[29]

The principles themselves are 'universal rules of just conduct'.[30] This means, in the first place, that there is an equality before the law, in that particular groups within society are not the subject of specific prescription or specific dispensation. Secondly, the principles do not purport to provide a concrete solution to all the many (and unknowable) contingencies which may arise. Thirdly, they are purpose-independent; their application in particular instances is not designed to achieve particular social or economic ends. Rather, they reflect the practices which have evolved in the spontaneous order and, as such, should, in general, conform to the expectations which the parties would have 'reasonably formed because they corresponded to the practices on which the everyday conduct of the members of the group was based'.[31] Granted, however, the fact that in an ever-changing environment some individuals will be exploiting new knowledge, it will be impossible (and inappropriate) to protect all expectations. The aim, then, is to *maximize* the possibility of expectations in general being fulfilled and, as we shall see, for Hayek this implies laying down for each individual a range of permitted actions (liberty) by designating ranges of objects over which the individual has control and rights of disposal (property).[32]

Legislation is frequently, though not always, used as an instrument of rational constructivism. It performs this function when it lays down rules designed to achieve particular ends or supplements positive orders that something should be done, or creates, or confers powers on, an agency for this purpose.[33] Hayek is here referring to what we would call regulatory law,[34] though confusingly he uses the term 'public law', thereby failing to appreciate that part of public law, for example that governing judicial review of administrative action, contains 'universal rules of just conduct'. In contrast to the rules evolving under spontaneous order, regulatory measures are purpose-specific, often by means of targeting rules (or exemptions from rules) on specific groups, thus infringing equality before the law, and typically attempting to lay down a comprehensive set of solutions for all foreseeable contingencies, impliedly assuming omniscience in the sovereign ruler.

Hayek's concern to identify law under the spontaneous order with the common law does not, however, lead him to the position that legislation should be dispensed with altogether.[35] Of course, statute law may, in part, be a codification of the principles of private law which have evolved through judicial decisions.[36] More than this, Hayek recognizes that legislation may be necessary to correct judge-made law where the latter is too slow to adapt to wholly new circumstances; this can occur because developments cannot be reversed if judges are not to disappoint reasonable expectations created by earlier decisions. Most significantly of all, in a passage which is frequently overlooked, he concedes that judicial error, and therefore the need for legislation, may result from the fact that 'the development of the law has lain in the hands of members of a particular class whose traditional views made them regard as just what could not meet the more general requirement of justice'; and he instances labour law, landlord and tenant law, and creditor/debtor law as fields where judges were drawn almost exclusively from the class of one of the interested groups.[37]

III. BLUEPRINT FOR THE 'GREAT SOCIETY'

As we have seen, Hayek's approach to social science, while preventing him from formulating specific predictions about human behaviour by inductive or deductive means, nevertheless enables him to make broad generalizations, derived from observations of 'patterns' of events. The main thesis of *Law, Legislation and Liberty* involves such a generalization:

> ... that a condition of liberty in which all are allowed to use their knowledge for their purposes, restrained only by rules of just conduct of universal application, is likely to produce for them the best conditions for achieving their aims; and that such a system is likely to be achieved and maintained only if all authority, including that of the majority of the people, is limited in the exercise of coercive power by general principles to which the community has committed itself.[38]

Hayek's blueprint for the Great Society[39] is drawn, of course, from the spontaneous order model. Its constituent parts now call for examination.

1. *Liberty*

Liberty is not viewed by Hayek as an end in itself, but as the means to an end – human progress.[40] Whether or not civilization is 'better' as a result of increased wealth, there is an overwhelming demand for material progress of this kind and it cannot be achieved without liberty. For social progress, each individual should be able to act on her or his own particular knowledge for her or his own particular purpose. Since there is inevitable ignorance as to many of the factors on which the pursuit of individual purposes rests, 'liberty is essential in order to leave room for the unforeseeable and unpredictable'.[41] The goal should be the maximization of opportunities for individuals to learn of facts hitherto unknown, even though, of course, this involves the risk of failure as well as of success.

The concept of liberty employed here is, it should be noted, a restricted one.[42] It means freedom from coercion by others but does not extend to freedom in the political sense of people participating in the choice of government. It insists that individuals have some private sphere protected against interference by others, but this does not imply that society is to guarantee that each individual has access to a minimum amount of resources. In this respect Hayek differs from those libertarians who argue that some material support for disadvantaged persons may be necessary if they are to exercise political rights.[43] It is true that he accepts as inevitable government action to deal with extremes of poverty but the justification is not 'liberty', still less 'citizenship'; rather it is in the interests of those 'who require protection against acts of desperation on the part of the needy'[44] – an explanation which is more fully explored in Marxist analsysis.[45] The essence of the 'private sphere', therefore, is not the possession of property ('freedom may be enjoyed by a person with practically no property of his own'[46]) but the right to use assets which are possessed, for which purpose freedom and enforceability of contracts are vital. Assets are acquired as rewards for merit, as determined by the market. Inheritance is defended simply because it arises from the natural instincts of parents and if it is prevented those instincts will manifest themselves in less attractive ways, for example nepotism and corruption.[47] It follows that Hayek accepts historical patterns of entitlements as a given and makes no attempt, in the manner of Nozick,[48] to justify them.

Clearly there must be some exceptions to freedom from coercion. We have already seen that compulsion to obey the rules of the spontaneous order, the common law, is necessary. Defence of a society against external enemies is another uncontroversial justification for governmental control. But it may come as a surprise to Hayek's critics to learn that he is, by no means, an advocate of the 'minimal state' and that there is a wide range of regulatory measures that he is prepared to tolerate.[49] Most cases arise as a result of market failure, notably externalities, that is, where some of the adverse or beneficial consequences of an activity are not reflected in the prices which agents charge, thus leading to an overproduction, or underproduction, of the activity in question.[50] It is on this ground that he rationalizes, for example, centralized provision of roads[51] and the public financing of education. More generally, since information is a commodity not easily supplied by the market but facilitates the working of that process, he recognizes the appropriateness of building regulations, pure food law, the certification of certain professions, and some safety and health regulations – intervention of this kind 'certainly assists intelligent choice and sometimes may be indispensable for it'.[52]

Nevertheless, he is quick to point out important limitations. First, while regulatory legislation inevitably involves some departure from the ideal of universal rules of conduct, to mitigate the evil certain general requirements of justice, such as the avoidance of arbitrary discrimination, ought to be observed. Secondly, though the public financing of some services may be justified, it does not follow that government should necessarily itself provide them – hence the argument for publicly funded education vouchers valid for private institutions. In short, it should be recognized that the adoption of collective measures involves resorting to an inferior method of provision and the spontaneous mechanism of the market should be relied on as much as possible.[53]

2. *The Rule of Law*

A continual theme in Hayek's work from *Road to Serfdom* through to *Law, Legislation and Liberty* has been that liberty is not a natural state but is rather created and preserved by the 'rule of law'. The latter mirrors closely the concept familiar from Dicey's work[54] and asserts as meta-legal requirements that laws should be universal, known and certain, and should apply equally to all.[55] Viewed as such, the rule of law has suffered a marked decline in the twentieth century. The original concept of *Rechtsstaat*, a product of the liberal movement, which demanded subservience of the state to the meta-legal principles of the rule of law was displaced by a purely formal interpretation which required only that all state action be authorized by the legislature. Hayek is ruthless in his criticism of developments in legal thought which he considers contributed to this decline: the overwhelming success of legal positivism – 'the "pure theory of law" . . . expounded by Professor H. Kelsen signalled the definite eclipse of all traditions of limited goverment';[56] the violent attacks on the certainty of law by Jerome Frank – 'it was the young men brought up on such ideas who because the ready instruments of the paternalist policies of the New Deal';[57] and the literature outlining an antirule-of-law doctrine promulgated by a group of 'socialist lawyers and political scientists' including Ivor Jennings and W. A. Robson.[58]

For Hayek, the institutions and practices of the administrative/welfare state infringe the meta-legal principles in several important respects. Collectivist economic measures cannot be accommodated to general principles which prevent arbitrariness:

> The planning authority . . . must provide for the actual needs of people as they arise and then choose deliberately between them. It must constantly decide questions which cannot be answered by formal principles only, and in making these decisions it must set up distinctions of merit between the needs of different people.[59]

In making these decisions, the authority and its subordinate agents must inevitably possess and exercise considerable discretionary powers. The rule of law would insist that such discretion be constrained by a system of administrative law which enables the judiciary to review the substance of the action by reference to general principles; but the courts' concern is, in general, limited to the question whether the particular action was formally authorized by legislation.[60]

These arguments familiar to, and much debated by, administrative lawyers do not call for detailed consideration here; suffice it to observe that Hayek would probably find unpersuasive the view that the principles of judicial review developed in our legal system – particularly the '*Wednesbury*'[61] principle of reasonableness – fit his model,[62] and would be even more hostile to the opinion which casts doubt on the alleged superior wisdom of the ordinary courts and, therefore, on extensive judicial activism.[63]

3. Constitutional Constraints

The need to impose constraints on government action arises nor merely because such action inevitably infringes the meta-legal principles of the rule of law. As Hayek has argued in his later work, it is a consequence also of the weaknesses of traditional democratic structures. If, as we have seen,[64] power must be conferred on representatives of the community in order to avoid the Hobbesian dilemma created by conflicts of self-interest, it does not follow that the existence of democratic institutions representing majority opinion is able to solve that dilemma. Given the unlimited power of legislative bodies to enact regulatory measures conferring benefits on particular groups, a government commanding the majority of votes in those bodies will need to offer such measures to those on whose support it relies. Groups with common interests will, then, co-ordinate and organize themselves to demand benefits. Thus:

> ... in the course of this century an enormous and exceedingly wasteful apparatus of para-government has grown up, consisting of trade associations, trades unions and professional organizations, designed primarily to divert as much as possible of the stream of governmental favour to their members.[65]

The concept of parliamentary sovereignty, particularly the Westminister model, is the root cause of the problem. The classical theory of representative government took the wrong direction: the equal claims of democratic government and democratic legislation led to a situation in which the powers of the two branches were effectively combined and to a revival of the 'monstrous' establishment of an absolute power not restricted by any rules.[66] Democracy in this form is a sham; it is 'increasingly becoming the name for the very process of vote-buying, for placating and remunerating those special interests which in more naive times were described as the "sinister interests" '.[67]

At the same time as Hayek was formulating these ideas, a highly sophisticated and influential version of them was being developed by the public choice school of economics.[68] Because most of this analysis is predictive – what consequences flow from different institutional arrangements – the economists involved have tended to fight shy of adumbrating reform proposals. Hayek is not so cautious. In the third volume of *Law, Legislation and Liberty* he outlines an ideal constitution which, in his view, would solve the problems.[69] The key to his model is the establishment of two representative bodies with different functions. The Legislative Assembly would be charged with maintaining and developing 'proper' law which, throughout this work, Hayek identifies with spontaneous order, that is the universal rules of just conduct. As such, its role would be sharply contrasted with that of the Government Assembly which would be concerned with organizing the apparatus of government and making decisions about the use of resources entrusted to the government. Crucially, the second body would be bound by the rules of just conduct laid down by the first, so that it could not issue any orders to private citizens which did not follow 'directly and necessarily' from the rules emanating from the latter.[70] Consistently with the theory of spontaneous order that the rules of just conduct should be purpose-independent, they should be determined by opinion (what is right or wrong) and not by interests. To achieve this, it is obviously desirable that the members of the Legislative Assembly should be insulated from the demands of pressure groups. Hayek therefore suggests that they should be elected for long periods, for example fifteen years. After this period, they would not be eligible for re-election, nor indeed forced to earn a living in the market; rather, they would be assured of continuous public employment as lay judges. To reflect contemporary standards of right and wrong, the members would be elected by all persons in the community of the same age, say forty-five years old. Finally, a constitutional court would be entrusted with the task of resolving disputes about the proper competence of each of the two assemblies and, to preserve independence from government, its judges would be elected by a committee of former members of the Legislative Assembly.

4. *Justice*

If, for Hayek, law properly so called comprises 'universal rules of just conduct', such as evolve through common law decisions or, in his ideal constitution, by the Legislative Assembly, what is their content? What makes them 'right' or 'wrong'? What is 'justice'? Since justice is a part of the constantly evolving spontaneous order, we cannot expect, and certainly do not receive, concretized answers to these questions; to provide such would smack of rational constructivism. In the second volume of *Law, Legislation and Liberty*, appropriately titled *The Mirage of Social Justice*, Hayek therefore concentrates on how just rules should be 'discovered' and what is *not* 'justice'.

The rules of just conduct are abstract guides to behaviour in a world in which most of the particulars are unknown.[71] They command general assent since they correspond to general usage. Internal consistency and application over a reasonably long period are important qualities, because they become the basis of planning by individuals. The function of the rules is to protect ascertainable domains within which the individual is free to act, rather than to determine particular courses of action; consequently, they are typically negative in character.[72] Likewise, since knowledge of the importance of particular ends for particular individuals is lacking, the test of justice is also negative:

> ... justice is ... emphatically not a balancing of particular interests at stake in a concrete case, or even of the interests of determinable classes of persons, nor does it aim at bringing about a particular state of affairs which is regarded as just.[73]

Utilitarian evaluations are therefore dismissed as being constructivist fallacies.[74]

Hayek would prefer his concept of justice not to be identified with 'natural law', which as typically used denotes some deontological theory.[75] Nevertheless, the manner in which the rules, and notions of justice, develop is the result of a 'natural' process, in the anti-positivist sense of that being independent of deliberate choice by sovereign wills: it is 'natural selection' through evolution which determines the success and the justice of the rules. (I shall return to this crucial proposition in the next section of the paper.)

Only human conduct, and that which affects others, can be considered just or unjust. The action of governments and other organizations can be so qualified but not the order (or situation) of society as a whole since, in terms of Hayek's theory, a state of affairs, the particulars of a spontaneous order, cannot be the intended aim of individual actions.[76] This leads to the enormously important, and also highly controversial, rejection of concepts of social, or distributive, justice:

> '[S]ocial justice' will ultimately be recognized as a will-o'-the wisp which has lured men to abandon many of the values which in the past have inspired the development of civilization.[77]

For Hayek, the term has no meaning except under systems where rulers arrogate to themselves power to determine the impossible – what is good – and in which individuals are ordered what to do. In a social order under which people are free to experiment by extending knowledge and thereby enabling improvements to be made to the general wealth of all, the inevitable price is that individuals and groups risk unmerited failure. To replace a system of rewards determined by the market would halt progress. Further, 'rational constructivist' attempts to distribute resources on the basis of 'justice' are doomed to failure because we lack objective criteria for determining and comparing 'merit' or 'need'. As the failure of medieval systems to locate just prices and just wages reveals, 'value to society' is immeasurable except by market methods; nor can the need of one individual, for example, to decent housing, be compared with that of another, for example, to relief from pain. Decisions on such matters inevitably lead to arbitrariness. They also result in infringement of the universal rules of just conduct since people would be treated differently according to their apparent material situation:

> The distributive justice at which socialism aims is thus irreconcilable with the rule of law, and with that freedom under the law which the rule of law is intended to secure.[78]

IV. CRITIQUE: THE NORMATIVE DIMENSION

1. *The Problem of Values and Evolution*

In my account of Hayek's work I have attempted to show how he develops his evaluative framework for social institutions, and hence also his highly critical judgements of some forms of social and political arrangements, from an epistemological base. What is good for mankind cannot be known and rational plans for the future cannot be made; institutions should therefore be appraised in terms of their capacity to foster explorations into the unknown and to disseminate the findings. But a crucial question is raised as to the normative content of this theory. It is through addressing this question that we can locate what I believe to be the fundamental weaknesses in Hayek's work.

Hayek argues that the spontaneous order is value-neutral. Values are a product of, and may be altered by, evolutionary processes:

> It is not only in his knowledge, but also in his aims and values that man is the creature of civilization; in the last resort, it is the relevance of these individual wishes to the perpetuation of the group or the species that will determine whether they will persist or change.[79]

What is 'good' or 'bad' is thus a question of what proves to be effective in terms of survival. Within any given society there will be competition between different groups and individuals with different sets of aims and values:

> Whether a group will prosper or be extinguished depends as much on the ethical code it obeys, or the ideals of beauty or well-being that guide it, as on the degree to which it has learned to satisfy its material needs.[80]

Cultural development is thus seen as involving conflicts of norms, with natural selection operating to resolve the conflicts.

This Darwinian approach is paralleled by the current fashion to apply socio-biological models of evolution to legal and economic institutions[81] and by the well-known thesis of Priest,[82] among others, that the litigation process generates a natural tendency for common law rules to evolve towards efficiency, as those disadvantaged by inefficient rules will have the incentive to challenge then until they are overturned.[83] These other exponents of evolutionary models typically use them as explanatory or descriptive devices. In contrast, Hayek's central purpose is to argue that the liberty inherent in spontaneous order *should* be preserved by the universal rules of just conduct which constitute the rule of law. Clearly this proposition has a normative character and thus must be posited on some moral value, presumably that of liberty. But this opens the door to a number of powerful objections, which may be considered in increasing order of importance.

First, it has been argued that the rule of law, even under Hayek's own definition, 'universal rules of just conduct', is compatible with a system that does not uphold liberty but rather permits highly oppressive policies.[84] This objection may perhaps be overridden if, as has been suggested, the test of 'universalizability' implies not merely a consistency of treatment between similar cases but also that the rules should be impartial as to the interests and preferences of all concerned.[85] Secondly, liberty cannot stand by itself as the sole moral value being invoked. Hayek, it will be recalled, regards liberty as essential for the progress of civilization. Inevitably, he postulates as a goal the maximizing of the welfare of mankind as a whole,[86] thus rendering himself vulnerable to the many well-known criticisms of utilitarianism.[87] Thirdly, the implicit notion that rules are morally appropriate simply because they are the result of undesigned evolutionary processes is, to say the least, extremely dubious.[88] Survival is no test of moral worth and the theory can be used to justify any set of rules which develop over time. In so far as the evolutionary-utilitarian criterion is identified with the capacity to sustain the maximum human population, it leads to the absurd proposition that the system which can support the largest population is also the best.[89] The outcome of competition between groups with different sets of aims and interests may be determined by accident, local factors, and also less morally-neutral conditions, such as the exploitation of power or use of force;[90] and, were it otherwise, how can the considerable differences between the rules operating in differing societies be explained? Given these difficulties, it would seem that

Hayek, if he wishes to adhere to his 'Blueprint for the Great Society', is forced to argue for the 'rational' adoption of his ideal order, a course of action which he would, of course, wholeheartedly have to condemn as being itself 'rational constructivism'.[91]

2. *Social Justice and Universal Rules of Just Conduct*

Many – I count myself among them – must find morally offensive Hayek's rejection of any notion of social, or distributional, justice[92] and the arguments he marshals in support of the thesis are not his strongest. The proposition that 'justice' can apply only to human conduct (and not states of affairs) would seem to be a semantic one, because it rests on his own definition of justice which does not accord with common usage.[93] The fact that it may not be possible objectively to determine need otherwise than according to the market criterion of ability to pay should not lead to the conclusion that that method of allocation is necessarily more just. The prices that individuals are willing to pay are as much a reflection of their wealth position as of the intensity of their desire for the goods in question and, as such, constitute an imperfect measure of social welfare. As Calabresi and Bobbitt have so eloquently demonstrated, allocation purely by reference to the market method may be acceptable for washing powders but is intolerable for the 'tragic choices' forced on society by the scarcity of some resources, for example kidney machines;[94] and perhaps the argument holds for many choices which are less than tragic. In a moral, if not a formal, sense market-based decisions on such resources are as arbitrary as those grounded in other criteria.

Even if we were to accede to Hayek's meta-legal requirement that legislation should accord with the 'universal rules of just conduct', it is far from clear why redistributive measures should be regarded as necessarily infringing those rules.[95] To prescribe that all citizens must be guaranteed access to a minimum amount of resources, sufficient to enable them to participate actively in the community or that all those with income above a certain threshold should pay taxes would seem to be no less 'universal' than to insist that all occupiers of premises owe a common duty to lawful visitors to see that they are reasonably safe in using the premises.[96] There is an evident difficulty in reaching firm conclusions on this matter simply because Hayek is vague on the degree of generality required for his universal rules and, indeed, is loth even to offer examples.[97] But, from an historical perspective, one may legitimately inquire how the principles of common law could properly satisfy the test of 'equality' when in practice they were formulated in relation only to the claims of individuals who had the means and willingness to take legal proceedings in the higher courts. Conversely, as in more recent times access to those courts has been facilitated by legal aid and other developments, judges have clearly allowed distributional goals to influence the formulation of general principles, for example, the broadening of tort liability to accord with loss-distributing techniques such as insurance[98] and the attempts to modify contract obligations in the light of fairness considerations.[99]

Hayek's unqualified preference for general judicial principles provokes more criticism. These principles are, of course, intended to foster economic growth by meeting the parties' reasonable expectations but the very unpredictability of the application of a general principle to specific facts will often hinder planning which is so essential for that growth. It has been demonstrated that the economically optimal precision of rules typically requires a much greater degree of specificity than Hayek's model would allow.[100] More seriously, perhaps, in an age when fast-expanding technology poses immense threats to the environment and human welfare, universal rules of just conduct can hardly provide the protection which members of society will demand against uncontrolled experimentation.

V. CONCLUSION

For the reasons outlined in the last section, my conclusion is that the normative dimension of Hayek's work is untenable. As an explanatory model of the development of political and legal institutions, his epistemologically-based theory of spontaneous order, while weakened by a tendency to push arguments too far, represents an important contribution to our understanding of law and certainly does not deserve its neglect by legal theorists. The insistence on the limits to human knowledge and hence on the constrained ability 'rationally' to control behaviour, particularly by regulatory measures, provides a powerful antidote to the more optimistic views expressed by Weberians and others. We might not agree with the specific characteristics which Hayek attributes to the common law in his 'universal rules of just conduct', notably the undue focus on a restrictive notion of liberty, but these very assertions force us to reflect on, and explore further, the sets of values which give integrity to that law. Indeed, once liberated from the stranglehold resulting from that insistence on liberty, those retaining faith in regulatory systems of law should accept the challenge and attempt to articulate the principles and values around which such systems might plausibly cohere.

NOTES AND REFERENCES

1 A. I. Ogus, 'Economics, Liberty and the Common Law' (1980) 15 *J. Society of Public Teachers of Law* 55.
2 N. P. Barry, *The New Right* (1987).
3 The only leading legal theorist who appears to have grappled seriously with Hayek's writings is Professor Neil MacCormick. See, particularly, *Legal Right and Social Democracy* (1982), ch.1 and 'Spontaneous Order and Rule of Law: Some Problems' (1986) 35 *Jahrbuch des Öffentlichen Rechts der Gegenwart* 1. The literature on Hayek of other disciples is, in contrast, voluminous: a useful bibliography is to be found in J. Gray, *Hayek on Liberty* (2nd ed. 1986) 210–49.
4 F. A. Hayek, three volumes: *Rules and Order* (1973); *The Mirage of Social Justice* (1976); and *The Political Order of a Free People* (1979).
5 Hayek, op. cit., n. 4 (1973), p. 17.

6   T. C. Taylor, *The Fundamentals of Austrian Economics* (2nd ed. 1980).
7   For example, 'Economics and Knowledge' (1937) 4 *Economica* 33, reprinted in F. A. Hayek, *Individualism and Economic Order* (1949) ch. 2.
8   F. A. Hayek, *The Counter-Revolution of Science* (1952).
9   id., pp. 34-5.
10 id., p. 39.
11 'Although history never quite repeats itself, . . . we can in a measure learn from the past to avoid a repetition of the same process': F. A. Hayek, *The Road to Serfdom* (1944) 1.
12 F. A. Hayek, *Studies in Philosophy, Politics and Economics* (1967) 17, 28.
13 cf. E. Butler, *Hayek* (1983) 147.
14 Hayek, op. cit., n. 4 (1973), ch. 2.
15 Hayek, op. cit., n. 12, p. 69.
16 Hayek, op. cit., n. 4 (1973), p. 45.
17 Hayek, op. cit., n. 12, ch. 5; op. cit., n. 4 (1973) ch. 1.
18 Hayek, op. cit., n. 4 (1973), p. 14.
19 His major pre-war publications were: *Prices and Production* (1931); *Monetary Theory and the Trade Cycle* (1933); *Profits, Interest and Investment* (1939). I am not concerned in this paper with Hayek's anti-Keynesian work on money, credit, and trade cycles; on this, see F. Machlup, 'Hayek's Contribution to Economics' in *Essays on Hayek*, ed. F. Machlup (1977) 19-33.
20 Hayek, op. cit., n. 7, chs. 2, 4; see also op. cit., n. 4 (1976), ch. 10.
21 Hayek, op. cit., n. 7, p. 86.
22 id. chs. 7-9; Hayek, op. cit., n. 4 (1976), pp. 1-5.
23 Hayek, op. cit., n. 7, ch. 5.
24 J. Gray, 'Hayek, the Scottish School and Contemporary Economics' in *The Boundaries of Economics*, eds. G. C. Winston and R. F. Teichgraeber (1988) 66-8.
25 Hayek, op. cit., n. 11, p. 57.
26 F. A. Hayek, *The Constitution of Liberty* (1960) ch. 10.
27 Hayek, op. cit., n. 4 (1973), chs. 3-6.
28 id., p. 65.
29 There is an obvious parallel here with Dworkin's 'law as integrity' (R. M. Dworkin, *Law's Empire* (1986)), though under the latter, the Herculean judge is expected to interpret the general principles in the light of his perceptions of changing views of justice.
30 Hayek, op. cit., n. 4 (1973), p. 131.
31 id., pp. 96-7.
32 id., p. 107.
33 id., p. 125.
34 cf. Ogus, op. cit., n. 1, p. 56.
35 Using Hayekian arguments, this extreme position is taken in B. Leoni, *Freedom and the Law* (1961).
36 Hayek admits that legislation can increase the certainty of the law but 'this advantage is more than offset if its recognition leads to the requirement that *only* what has thus been expressed in statutes should have the force of law' [his italics]: op. cit., n. 4 (1973), p. 116.
37 id., p. 89.
38 id., p. 55.
39 Deliberately adopting this term, as used by Adam Smith, among others: cf. op. cit., n. 4 (1973), p. 138, n. 11.
40 Hayek, op. cit., n. 26, chs. 2-3.
41 id., p. 29.
42 id., pp. 11-13.
43 A. E. Buchanan, *Deriving Welfare Rights from Libertarian Rights* (1979). See also C. Bay, 'Hayek's Liberalism: The Constitution of Perpetual Privilege' (1971) 1 *Political Science Rev.* 110-23.
44 Hayek, op. cit., n. 26, p. 285: hence the case for compulsory social insurance.
45 V. George and P. Wilding, *Ideology and Social Welfare* (1976) ch. 5.

46 Hayek, op. cit., n. 26, p. 141.
47 id., p. 91.
48 R. Nozick, *Anarchy, State and Utopia* (1974).
49 Hayek, op. cit., n. 4 (1979), ch. 14.
50 cf. A. I. Ogus and C. Veljanovski, *Readings in the Economics of Law and Regulation* (1984) 64–5.
51 Except where, as in long-distance highways, tolls are practicable: Hayek, op. cit., n. 4 (1979), p. 44.
52 id., p. 62.
53 id., p. 46.
54 A. V. Dicey, *Law of the Constitution* (10th ed. 1961).
55 Hayek, op. cit., n. 11, ch. 6; Hayek, op. cit., n. 26, ch. 14.
56 Hayek, op. cit., n. 26, p. 238. For an extended criticism of Kelsen and legal positivism, see op. cit., n. 4 (1976), pp. 44–56.
57 Hayek, op. cit., n. 26, p. 247.
58 id., p. 241, referring, in particular to the former's *The Law and the Constitution* (1933) and the latter's *Justice and Administrative Law* (3rd ed. 1951).
59 Hayek, op. cit., n. 11, p. 55. See also op. cit., n. 26, pp. 227–8.
60 id., pp. 213–4.
61 *Associated Provincial Picture Houses Ltd.* v *Wednesbury Corp.* [1948] 1 K. B. 223.
62 H. W. R. Wade, *Administrative Law* (6th ed. 1988) 33–4 and ch. 12.
63 P. Craig, *Administrative Law* (1983) 30–1.
64 *Supra.*
65 Hayek, op. cit., n. 4 (1979), p. 13.
66 id., pp. 36–7.
67 id., p. 32.
68 Notably, J. M. Buchanan and G. Tullock, *The Calculus of Consent: Logical Foundations of a Constitutional Democracy* (1962) and J. M. Buchanan, *The Limits of Liberty: Between Anarchy and Leviathan* (1975). For a review of the literature, see D. C. Mueller, *Public Choice* (1979), and for its application to British institutions see R. C. O. Matthews (ed.), *Economy and Democracy* (1985).
69 Hayek, op. cit., n. 4 (1979), ch. 17. He is, however, reluctant to propose that a country with a 'firmly established constitutional tradition' should adopt his model: p. 107.
70 id., p. 119.
71 Hayek, op. cit., n. 4 (1976), p. 1.
72 Exceptionally, where individuals are placed in close community with others, positive duties may arise, the most prominent example being family law: op. cit., n. 4 (1976), p. 36.
73 id., p. 39.
74 id., pp. 17–23.
75 cf. J. M. Finnis, *Natural Law and Natural Rights* (1980).
76 Hayek, op. cit., n. 4 (1976), p. 33.
77 id., p. 67.
78 id., p. 86.
79 Hayek, op. cit., n. 26, p. 36.
80 id., p. 36.
81 See, generally, R. O. Zerbe (ed.), *Evolutionary Models in Economics and Law*; (1982) 4 *Research in Law and Economics.*
82 G. L. Priest, 'The Common Law Process and the Selection of Efficient Rules' (1977) 6 *J. Legal Studies* 65.
83 In an interesting extension to this theory, P. H. Rubin has argued that statute law will have a similar property, since under certain conditions those disadvantaged by inefficient rules may find it cheaper to lobby the legislature than to litigate: 'Common Law and Statute Law' (1982) 11 *L. Legal Studies* 205.
84 J. Raz, 'The Rule of Law and Its Virtues' (1977) 93 *Law Quarterly Rev.* 185.
85 Gray, op. cit., n. 3, pp. 61–8.

86 More specifically maximizing the chances of members of society to achieve unknown purposes: Hayek, op. cit., n. 12, pp. 173–5. It should be noted that though Hayek describes utilitarianism as a 'constructivist fallacy' (op. cit., n. 4 (1976), pp. 17–23), he is there referring to the use of hedonistic calculus to evaluate *particular* rules, rather than systems as a whole.
87 Usefully summarized in J. L. Coleman, *Markets, Morals and the Law* (1988) ch. 4.
88 cf. S. Gordon, 'The Political Economy of F. A. Hayek' (1981) 14 *Canadian J. Economics* 470.
89 Gray, op. cit., n. 3, p. 141.
90 Bay, op. cit., n. 43.
91 cf. MacCormick, op. cit., n. 3 (1986).
92 A reaction which he anticipated: op. cit., n. 26, p. 306.
93 D. Miller, *Social Justice* (1976) 17–20.
94 G. Calabresi and P. Bobbitt, *Tragic Choices* (1978).
95 D. Miller, 'Review of *Law, Legislation and Liberty, vol. II: The Mirage of Social Justice*' (1977) 4 *Br. J. Law and Society* 142; MacCormick, op. cit., n. 3 (1986) p. 13.
96 Occupiers' Liability Act 1957 s. 2.
97 Though at one point he notes that freedom of contract, inviolability of property, and the duty to compensate another for damage caused by fault invariably feature in contemporary systems of private law: op. cit., n. 4 (1976), p. 40.
98 P. Cane, *Atiyah's Accident Compensation and the Law* (4th ed. 1987) p. 234. For a striking example of distributional influences on negligence claims, see the recent House of Lords decision *Smith* v *Eric Bush* [1989] 2 All E.R. 514, where in formulating the duty owed by surveyors to house purchasers the judges draw a clear distinction between inexpensive houses and other property.
99 H. Collins, *The Law of Contract* (1986) ch. 9.
100 I. Ehrlich and R. Posner, 'An Economic Analysis of Legal Rulemaking' (1974) 3 *J. Legal Studies*; A. I. Ogus, 'Quantitative Rules and Judicial Decision Making' in *The Economic Approach to Law*, eds. P. Burrows and C. Veljanovski (1981) ch. 9.

[10]

The Normativity of Law

Lewis A. Kornhauser, *New York University School of Law*

1. Introduction

Over the past 40 years, economic analysis of law has transformed both the practice and understanding of law. Economic analysts have examined and illuminated virtually every substantive and procedural area of law and, in doing so, have clarified not only the positive analysis of legal rules and institutions but also the normative structure of legal doctrines and legal institutions. Recently, a spate of empirical and experimental work has greatly increased knowledge of how legal institutions actually function and of the effects of legal rules on behavior.

Economic analysis of law initially met great hostility within the legal academy and the legal profession. The extraordinary success of its research program has quieted that hostility, though one may observe occasional outbursts in the legal literature.[1] Nevertheless, a deep chasm exists between the economic approach to legal rules and institutions and the

---

This is the presidential address presented at the American Law and Economics Association meeting in New Haven on May 7, 1999. The financial assistance of the Filomen d'Agostino and Max E. Greenberg Research Fund of the New York University School of Law is gratefully acknowledged. Richad Craswell, John Donohue, John Ferejohn, Mark Geistfeld, Liam Murphy, Mitch Polinsky, Ricky Revesz, and Larry Sager commented on an earlier draft. I also benefited from conversations with Jean-Pierre Benoit and comments by participants at the Stanford Law and Economics Program Free Lunch seminar.

Send correspondence to: Lewis A. Kornhauser, New York University School of Law, 40 Washington Square South, New York, NY 10012. Fax: (212) 995-4341; E-mail: lewis.kornhauser@nyu.edu.

1. For an example, see Judge Edwards's (1998) attack on Richard Revesz's study of ideological voting on the D.C. Circuit (1997) and Revesz's reply (1999).

more traditional approach. Many distinguished academic lawyers and legal philosophers view law very differently than economic analysts do.

In this article, I address a central element of the traditional approach to law that, I believe, explains a significant portion of the gap between the two approaches to law. I consider one of several questions that are, in the legal-philosophical literature, encompassed in the problem of the normativity of law: What role should legal rules play in an agent's practical deliberations?[2]

Legal philosophers generally treat this question as a normative one. The answer they provide, however, implicitly serves as a descriptive model of how law influences behavior. This legal model of how law influences behavior differs greatly, at least on its surface, from the economic model of how law influences behavior. Illuminating the differences between the economic and jurisprudential models of how law influences behavior, then, identifies an important source of the tension between the two approaches.

My aim, however, is not primarily to explain the origins of the intellectual tension. Rather, I investigate the jurisprudential model because I hope it may help explain the behavior of public officials (and other agents who act within institutional roles). Economic models of public officials, particularly of federal judges, have often foundered when the analyst must specify the preferences that the official seeks to maximize.[3] Judges and civil servants moreover face few clear incentives but they do, from a legal point of view, act under complex, if ill-specified, legal obligations. Understanding the jurisprudential theory of how obligation should influence the agent's deliberations may indicate how to model that behavior.

I proceed as follows. First, I sketch the jurisprudential theory. Second, I contrast it with current, standard economic model. Next, I offer some more general remarks about modeling obligation.

---

2. The rubric "the normativity of law" includes several other inquiries. In addition to the question considered here, it encompasses questions such as "What reason does an agent have to obey the law?" and "When is an agent justified in obeying the law?" Economic analysis of law illuminates these questions as well and I hope to treat them elsewhere. Traditional discussions of these issues appear in, for example, Raz (1994), Schauer (1991) and Soper (1996, 1998).

3. For a discussion of the objectives of judges see Cooter (1983) and Posner (1993).

2. The Jurisprudential Account of Obligation

In this section I discuss the jurisprudential accounts of the role that obligation plays in the practical deliberations of an agent. The first subsection provides some background. The second subsection sketches Joseph Raz's (1975) account of the role an authoritative rule should play in practical deliberation. Though Raz's account is offered normatively, I then suggest that it captures certain intuitions concerning how individuals actually respond to legal rules. In the final subsection, I consider some of the strengths and weaknesses of this account understood as a theory of behavior.

2.1. Background

When an agent has an obligation, she faces a "requirement" to perform or refrain from performing an action. At issue here is the nature of this requirement and how it influences behavior. Various terms refer to requirements of this nature. "Obligation" is synonymous with "duty." The term "norm" or "mandatory norm" is often used synonymously as well. I shall also use these terms interchangeably.

Obligations have a variety of sources. Some are legal; some are moral; some are social. I am under both a legal and moral obligation not to steal, but the legal obligation as embedded in the law of contract to perform my promises is not coextensive with my moral obligation to keep my promises. I may have a social obligation to give up my seat on a bus to an elderly person but I probably do not have a legal obligation to do so and I may not have a moral one either.

It is not obvious that obligations from different sources should influence behavior in the same way or conform to the same logic of practical deliberation (Hart, 1982). My discussion assumes that differences among types of obligation are relatively unimportant; thus, though the discussion is directed primarily at legal obligation, much of the argument applies to obligations of any type. Moreover, Raz's account of the role of obligation in practical deliberation, does not distinguish between legal and moral obligation.

The discussion here thus has some overlap with the growing literature on informal social norms (e.g., Bernstein, 1992, 1993, 1996; Cooter, 1997; McAdams, 1996, 1997; E. Posner, 1996a, 1996b, 1997, 1998.) That literature, however, addresses a number of questions not considered here; for example, the authors seek to explain the origins of social norms. Moreover, this literature largely assumes that social norms influence behavior in the way that standard economic models assume that law influences behavior.

Most Anglo-American legal philosophy prior to 1960 offered a sanction theory of obligation. A sanction theory of obligation offers a prudential account of how legal rules influence an agent's behavior. This account contends that individual obeys the law in order to avoid a sanction; obedience is in her self-interest.[4] This account is obviously congenial to an economist who also grounds motivation in self-interest. The reason to obey the law was thus prudential rather than moral and specific to (the sanction of) a particular rule.

H. L. A. Hart (1961), however, offered several important objections to this account. For example, Hart noted that some, often important, legal rules carried no sanction. In private law, he pointed to enabling regimes such as contract, corporations, and the law of estates and trusts that permitted individuals to create obligations for others. Failure to comply with the law, in these contexts, often resulted in the *invalidity* of the agent's action rather than a sanction. More importantly, in public law, rules constituting the structure of government such as those governing an electoral system, did not carry sanctions with them. They nonetheless imposed obligations on public officials. The probability, or even existence of a sanction, Hart therefore argued, was not necessary for the existence of a legal rule. Further, the existence of a sanction is not sufficient to create a duty in general. A tax on gasoline, for example, imposes additional costs on drivers, but it does not create a duty not to drive.

Hart's own account of obligation and the normativity of law focuses on the attitudes and behavior of public officials rather than all individuals. He acknowledges that many, if not most, private citizens will regard law as Holmes's bad man does—as a set of orders backed by threats or, to phrase Holmes's position in a more economic fashion, as a set of incentives. Explanations of how law influences the behavior of private individuals

---

4. Hacker (1973) identifies three varieties of sanction theories of duty: (1) the probabilistic one emphasized in the text; (2) an imperatival one in which the sanction is commanded in the event that conduct does not conform to the norm; and (3) a justificatory one in which noncompliance justifies the imposition of a sanction.

may rely more heavily on a sanction theory of duty while the theory to be outlined below plays a lesser role. For public officials, the sanction theory does not seem either to explain the behavior of public officials or to justify it.

Hart's critique of the Austinian account of the grounds of the normativity of law is more successful than his own substantive answer to the question. The analysis in Hart (1961) emphasized the "internal aspect of rules," which Hart elaborated as a particular attitude of acceptance of or commitment to the rule. His discussion, however, did not clearly articulate the nature or content of the reason that an individual would have for obeying a particular legal rule. Subsequent commentary has sought to resolve these ambiguities.

2.2. Raz's Account

Economic accounts of practical reason assume that the agent has a well-defined preference relation over the set of actions available to her that permit a representation of these preferences as a preference over outcomes and a set of beliefs that conform to the axioms of probability theory. The agent then chooses the action that maximizes her expected utility.[5] Obligation must then influence behavior in one of the four ways: by altering payoffs, beliefs, preferences, or the choice set.

Noneconomic accounts of practical reason proceed differently. They elaborate the set of reasons that an individual should consider and the way in which these reasons should be weighed in order to reach an all-things-considered judgment concerning what action to undertake. Phrased in this fashion, the economic and non-economic accounts of practical reasons might be complementary. This complementarity would be particularly evident if one identified the individual's reasons for action simply as the different sets of concerns and interests that she had. One identifies the agent's reasons for action, that is, with the desires, concerns, and interests that motivate her rather than with some "objectively" given desires, concerns or interests that might or might not actually motivate her. The noneconomic account of practical reason would then provide a

---

5. The axiomatic underpinnings of subjective expected utility require that the agent's underlying preference satisfy six axioms that include completeness, transitivity, and independence. See, for example, Savage (1954).

construction of the individual's preference relation from the individual's underlying concerns.[6]

Raz's (1975) account of the role of norms in practical deliberation begins with an account of reasons for action but it diverges from the account of all-things-considered judgments mentioned above. First, while the above account assumes that all reasons have the same logical status, Raz distinguishes between first-order and second-order reasons. A first-order reason for action is simply a consideration that weighs for or against the undertaking of a particular action. A second-order reason for action, by contrast, concerns the manner in which first-order reasons for action should be combined. A second-order reason for action, for example, might specify the weight that should be accorded some consideration. Raz's account of the role of norms focuses on *exclusionary* reasons which are second-order reasons for action that direct the decision maker to exclude—or to put a weight of zero on—some class of first-order reasons for action.

Second, Raz argues that a norm serves as both a first-order reason to undertake (or not to undertake) a particular action and a second-order reason to exclude certain other first-order reasons for action. An example may help to clarify ideas. Suppose that Liza must decide how to spend her Saturday afternoon. She may either visit her aged aunt or help Freddy organize an academic conference. She considers the first-order reasons for each option: Her aunt is alone and, unless she visits, will have no company for the week; she likes Freddy and the conference will promote her career. All things considered, she thinks it best to help Freddy. Suppose, however, that, earlier in the week, prior to Freddy's suggestion that she help him, Liza had promised her aunt to visit. The promise acts as an exclusionary reason that directs Liza to ignore "ordinary" first-order reasons for action. Now the balance of reasons dictates that she visit her aunt because the reasons that weigh in favor of visiting Freddy are excluded from consideration.

Raz argues that legal rules, if accepted by the agent as authoritative, play a similar role in practical deliberation as promise did in the example: they exclude "normal" first-order reasons from the agent's deliberation.

---

6. Such a construction might not be possible unless the underlying concerns satisfy certain conditions. Alternatively, one might want to impose conditions on the construction. For a brief discussion, see Kornhauser (1998).

Notice that, on this understanding of its role in practical deliberation, legal rules would play a dramatically different role in influencing the behavior of individuals than they do under the incentive view generally adopted by economic theory. The view of legal rules as incentives treats the (expected) sanction for noncompliance as one reason on a par with other costs and benefits that will flow from her action.

2.3. Strengths and Weakness of the Account

Raz offered his accounted of exclusionary reasons as part of a normative theory of practical deliberation, or rationality, rather than as a descriptive account of how individuals actually reason practically. A normative account of practical rationality, however, must satisfy the requirement that "ought implies can;" it must be *possible* for an individual to treat rules as exclusionary reasons and for her actions to be governed by the offered account of practical reason. This requirement then suggests that one interpret the exclusionary reasons theory of how rules enter practical deliberation as a descriptive, rather than a normative one.

Moreover, one of the strengths of Raz's account derives from its success in capturing certain intuitions about behavior in general and legal behavior in particular. Intuition suggests that some people, in some circumstances, *actually* treat rules as exclusionary reasons. It is this actuality that poses a challenge to economic theory to capture within its preference theory this effect of rules on action.

To motivate the claim that *some* people actually treat legal rules as exclusionary reasons, I offer a simple example that, I believe, many noneconomists find suggestive. Consider the effects of a legal rule barring the emission of sulfur dioxide above some threshold level. An economic analysis suggests that an individual will treat the legal rule as simply presenting a first-order reason for action. Specifically, when the individual compares a noncompliant level of emissions to a compliant one, she will now include the expected costs of noncompliance in her assessment of the choice of noncompliance. If the expected costs outweigh the expected benefits, she will comply; otherwise she will not comply.

An agent who reasons as the exclusionary reason account of practical deliberation dictates will proceed very differently. She will consider the rule as a first-order reason not to emit above the threshold. She will also see the rule as excluding normal profit calculations from her decision procedure.[7] Thus, the fact that the (economic) benefits of emissions above the threshold exceed the expected costs of noncompliance would not constitute a reason for the agent not to comply. Consequently, if individuals accept law as authoritative and deliberate (and act on the basis of their deliberations) as the exclusionary reason account dictates, the distribution of emission levels regulated by a tax should differ from the distribution of emission levels regulated by a civil or criminal fine. Specifically, the fine should induce more compliance than the tax because, while the agent may treat the tax as a first-order reason to weigh against her other revenues and costs, the fine-imposing rule excludes this comparison.[8]

This analysis captures the common intuition that an emission tax differs from a rule that imposes an equivalent civil or criminal penalty for noncompliance. Some critics of environmental taxes, for example, object to a tax because it *permits* emissions above the threshold, whereas a fine *prohibits* emissions above a threshold. Conceivably, their concern is driven only by the symbolism of a permission; more plausibly the critic believes that agents will act differently when subject to a permission than when subject to a prohibition.

Similar intuitions underlie the difference in response that individuals have to violations of obligations as opposed to exercises of permissions. Suppose that a jurisdiction wishes to restrict access to a beach. It may do so in two distinct ways. It may designate a parking area and charge a high fee for parking there. Alternatively, it may prohibit cars at the beach and enforce this with a fine equal to the parking fee under the other regime. When parking is permitted, individuals are authorized to weigh the parking fee against other first-order reasons for actions. When cars are banned at the beach, by contrast, these other first-order reasons are excluded from consideration.

---

7. The rule presumably does not exclude all reasons for emissions above the threshold. In an emergency, for example, failure to emit above the threshold might threaten the health or safety of a larger number of employees while emission would have only a small effect on a larger number of people. The threat to the employees would not be excluded by the legal rule.

8. An economist might, of course, explain any difference in behavior under the two rules in terms of an additional psychic or other non-pecuniary cost that agent suffers when a fine is imposed. I consider this strategy in more detail below. I note here only that the strategy has an ad hoc air in the absence of an account of the size and source of this nonpecuniary cost that is independent of the induced behavior. The text addresses this approach below in its discussion of the "additional cost" model of obligation.

These examples suggest that the exclusionary reason account does have some descriptive as well as normative appeal as a theory of how law influences behavior. Raz's account of obligation, however, is radically incomplete both normatively and descriptively and dramatically inaccurate descriptively.

The theory, as thus far elaborated, for example does not explain how conflicts among obligations are to be resolved. When the law's command disagrees with an agent's conscience, for example, what behavior does the Razian theory predict, or even recommend? Similarly, when the content of the obligation is ambiguous or unclear, the theory provides little guidance concerning the agent's response to such ambiguity.

More seriously, as formulated, the theory, though it permits an obligation to be overridden and hence not determinative of action, always predicts compliance with one's obligations (or at least the obligations that agent accepts or to which she is committed). Obviously, individuals sometimes do not meet their obligations.

3. Assessing the Jurisprudential Account of Obligation against the Economic Account

3.1. An Economic Account of Obligation

Most economic analysts of law implicitly adopt the sanction theory of obligation that Hart criticized. The sanction theory might take many forms within an economic model. One might, for instance, model obligation as an incentive in which non-compliance imposes an external cost. I shall consider here an early model of that type in which Cooter (1984) attempted to incorporate the insights of Hart into economic analysis of law. Equally, however, one might model obligation as a constraint—a tactic that is equivalent to modeling it as an incentive where the penalty for non-compliance is infinite. Finally, one might model obligation as preference; in the next section I shall consider attempts to capture obligation with the idea that non-compliance imposes an internal "utility" cost on the agent.

At this point, however, it may be useful to compare briefly Cooter's account to Raz's account of the role of obligation. In Cooter's (1984) analysis, the distinction between obligation and incentive lies not in the distinction between first-order and second-order reasons but in the size of the (official) penalty for noncompliance. Specifically, Cooter argues that small changes in the price—the "penalty" associated with "noncompliance" with an incentive—may induce significant changes in behavior while small changes in the sanction, the "penalty" associated with non-compliance with an obligation, induce little or no changes in behavior. Sanctions, Cooter says, are discontinuous but prices are not. So, from Cooter's perspective, a strict liability regime in tort creates an incentive while a negligence regime imposes an obligation.

One might object to Cooter's characterization of the difference between obligation and incentive on several grounds. First, most lawyers I think regard the rules of strict product liability as imposing obligations on manufacturers to produce safe products rather than creating an incentive for safety. Indeed, the imposition of large punitive damages on Ford Motor Company for its use of cost-benefit analysis in its decision not to move the gas tank of the Pinto might be regarded as punishing Ford for treating the obligation imposed by the law as a first-order reason for action rather than as a second-order reason for action that excludes the usual cost-benefit calculation.

Second, Cooter's distinction rests on a particular interpretation of the damage rule under negligence. At least in some cases, and arguably in all, a negligent defendant is responsible for the damage *caused by* her negligence (see Kahan [1989] for discussion). On this interpretation, negligence rules also create incentives because the damage rule, though nondifferentiable at the standard of care, is continuous.

Here, however, I am largely interested in the structural differences between Cooter's and Raz's account of obligation. Raz's distinction between obligation and incentive ignores the consequence of non-compliance. Instead, Raz points to the roles that obligation and incentive play in the individual's practical deliberation. Raz agrees with Cooter about the role of incentives in deliberation: An incentive is simply a first-order reason for action like all other first-order reasons. Unlike Cooter, who treats obligation simply as a *stronger* first-order reason for action, Raz argues that obligation excludes at least some reasons from consideration. I next consider whether this difference in formulation has predictive consequences.

3.2. Variant Predictions

From a positive point of view, the exclusionary reasons account of how law influences behavior has greater interest the more divergent its predictions are from those of the economic theory of behavior under law. In this subsection, I suggest several different predictions of the two theories; I argue that the variant predictions cannot be captured in a simple economic model of the sanction theory of obligation.

The prior discussion already identified one predictive difference between the Razian and economic theories of how law influences behavior: compare two regimes that differ only in the form that imposes a sanction. So, if one holds the penalty for noncompliance as well as the likelihood of detection and conviction constant, one should observe more compliance under a liability rule (or a criminal fine) than under a tax.

An economic model that assumed that the agent incurred a cost additional to the official sanction when she failed to comply with an obligation would account for this discrepancy.[9] Call such a model an "additional cost" model. Such a model might also account for a second predictive difference. Suppose the size of the penalty varies. Then, the predicted change in compliance levels of a population will, under the legal-rules-as-incentive theory, be greater than the predicted change in compliance levels under the legal-rules-as-exclusionary reasons theory. Indeed, a literal reading of the exclusionary reason account would predict that compliance remains unchanged as the penalty levels vary from zero to infinity because the exclusionary reason account ignores the penalty levels entirely.

An additional cost model (as well as Cooter's theory) predicts, however, that changes in the probability of detection of a wrong, holding the penalty constant, will have the same effect as changes in the penalty level, holding the probability of detection constant. That is, under the legal-rules-as-incentive theory, a reduction in the probability of detection is equivalent to a proportionate reduction in the size of the penalty for noncompliance. Consequently, less enforcement implies less compliance. Under the legal-rules-as-exclusionary-reason account, detection, like the size

---

9. The suggested model modifies Cooter's account which distinguishes obligations from (costly) permissions in terms of the official sanction. The suggested model assumes that noncompliance with an obligation imposes an additional cost, either in the form of external stigma, or in the form of internal "guilt". For a model of this type, see for example Rasmusen (1996).

of the penalty, plays no role in the agent's deliberations. Consequently, the level of compliance should be largely independent of the enforcement level.

The different consequences of changes in the enforcement level of the two theories suggests that an additional cost model of norm violation requires that the agent suffer the additional cost of noncompliance "internally" or "psychically" rather than through external agencies. Further elaboration of the exclusionary reasons account, however, suggests that even this economic characterization of obligation may not succeed in capturing the exclusionary reasons account.

Suppose for example that the content of the rule is uncertain—that is, some action is not clearly proscribed or permitted by the rule. In the emission example, one might imagine that the prohibited emissions are not clearly defined and the permissibility of emitting some specific chemical is unclear. In this circumstance, the legal-rules-incentives theory predicts that the agent will choose on the basis of the expected penalty for emission with the probability weights given by her beliefs concerning the judgment on the permissibility of emissions by the relevant enforcement authority. The legal-rules-as-exclusionary-reasons theory, by contrast, would presumably direct the agent to consider the reasons underlying the rule in order to determine *her* (rather than the *enforcement authority's*) belief about the permissibility of emission. She should then act on her judgment of the content of the norm.[10]

These differences in prediction suggest that one cannot capture the behavioral consequences of the exclusionary reasons model of the influence of law on behavior with a simple model that treats noncompliance with the norm as the imposition of an additional cost on the agent.

---

10. This difference parallels a difference noted by Rabin (1995) between treating obligation as a preference and treating it as a constraint. He argues that, if obligation is modeled as a preference, the agent has an incentive not to gather information that might lead to the discovery of an obligation that would restrict her ability to fulfil her other preferences. If one models obligation as a constraint, then, Rabin argues, the agent should acquire information as long as the marginal benefit of information acquisition exceeds the cost of information acquisition.

3.3. Differences in the Normative Implications of the Two Accounts

The economic and the jurisprudential also differ in their implications for evaluation of conduct and states of affairs. I consider briefly two such differences here.

Recall the two examples that distinguish a permission and an obligation. In one, a tax on emissions permitted pollution while the fine proscribed it. Similarly, a parking fee permitted parking at the beach, but a fine banned it. When the law permits an action, it accepts that wealthy individuals may differentially exercise the permission—pay the parking fee or the tax. When the law proscribes an action with a fine, wealth still makes non-compliance more economically feasible than compliance. The wealthy can better afford to pay the fine just as the tax or fee impose less onerous burdens. Social evaluation of differential levels of compliance across wealth classes, however, are very different. They are no longer acceptable.

Economists generally, and economic analysts of law in particular, usually adopt a *welfarist* approach to evaluation. Welfarist evaluation assesses states of affairs solely with respect to the well-being of individuals within those states of affairs. Economists make two further evaluative assumptions. First, they assume that well-being is defined in terms of an agent's preference relation. Second, they assume that the preference relation that determines the agent's motivation—that is his *motivational* preferences— is the relevant preference relation for evaluation of the agent's well-being.

When one models obligation as preference, one undermines either the first or second assumption concerning the relation of preference and well-being. Compliance with an obligation does not improve the agent's well-being. An opposite conclusion would suggest that the agent could increase her well-being by multiplying the obligations with which she must comply. Even when it is the case that the agent is better off when individuals generally comply with a particular obligation than when they do not, the agent is usually better off still when others comply but she does not.

3.4. A Further Difficulty with Sanction Models of Obligation

The prior subsections indicate that the exclusionary rule model of how law influences behavior differs from economic models of how law influences behavior. The two classes of model yield different predictions. A deeper problem with modeling law's normativity as a sanction, however, exists. In models of the response of private individuals to legal rules, a sanction theory may be perfectly reasonable. Many private agents such as corporations are clearly best modeled as profit maximizers and most private individuals are likely to have a purely instrumental view toward the law. Moreover, in these contexts, it is often reasonable to consider the content of the legal rule as given exogenously. At least two difficulties arise when the model is extended to public officials, particularly those officials whose actions determine in part the content of the legal rule.

First, with respect to most of their duties, public officials face few explicit, formal sanctions but a large number of duties. Various forms of bribery and corruption are banned; in addition, the officials are subject to supervision within a hierarchy. On the other hand, most public officials are protected from dismissal by civil service regulations. Similarly, legislators face few sanctions for non-compliance with the myriad rules that govern legislative behavior that play such a large role in models of positive political theory.[11]

Federal judges present a particular striking example of the phenomenon. They have life tenure during which their salaries cannot decrease. They face little bureaucratic supervision, and the prospects of promotion are slim.[12] How do they decide cases? Many scholars (McNollGast, 1995; Revesz, 1998) argue that they seek to promote their own policy views; philosophers of law, and some legal scholars (Kornhauser, 1992a, 1992b, 1995), elaborate the logic of judicial reasoning which judges are obligated to follow. The political science account relies on a preference theory, but the legal account implicitly relies on some unspecified theory under which the content of the obligation rather than its sanction influences action. The political science account would therefore expect federal judges appointed for life to behave differently than those state judges elected for a term while the legal account generally regards the two sets of judges as reasoning within a set of identical obligations.

---

11. In positive political theory models the sequence of actions is particularly important. This sequence embodies the analyst's understanding of the rules followed in the enactment of legislation.

12. There is some weak evidence, however, that federal judges in fact respond to promotion incentives. See, for example, Higgins and Rubin (1980) and Cohen (1991, 1992).

At least one of these rules, *stare decisis*, has been modeled along standard economic lines in at least two different ways; but neither relies on sanctions. Rasmusen (1994) shows, in a restrictive model, that, in a sequential game in which each judge in a sequence of judges wish to have her views prevail in the future, an equilibrium of the game is one in which the judges "honor" *stare decisis* in the sense that each gives effect to the prior decisions of her predecessors. On this account, the legal norm is not modeled as a sanction but is understood as an equilibrium of the game. I discuss this approach below.

Heiner (1986) has modeled *stare decisis* as an optimal decision rule for imperfect decision makers under uncertainty. Again, the idea of a sanction plays no role. Rather the judge, given her preferences, adheres to the rule because, under it, she does best. Heiner's explanation for *stare decisis* then lies in his assumption concerning judicial preferences; on his view, the judges apparently have an unexplained obligation to (or preference for) minimize errors.

The second difficulty with sanction models is more general. It questions the feasibility of reducing the influence of law on the behavior of all public officials (and private individuals) to incentives. The argument, articulated in Basu (1998), is straightforward. Compare two "global" games that social agents might play; where a global game is a "general equilibrium" model of the society in which no (social) rules are exogenous. One of these games—call it "the law game"—has law and legal institutions, while the other—call it "the anarchic game"—does not. These two games cannot differ in terms of the available strategy sets or payoffs to the agents because any action (or strategy) available to an agent who, in the law game acts as a "public official," is available to the same agent in the anarchic game. Conversely, the actions available to a player in the anarchic game are available to the corresponding player in the law game. Moreover, the payoffs associated with any vector of strategies adopted by all players will be identical. Phrased differently, it appears that the law game and the nonlaw game are identical; the set of players is identical, the strategy set of each player is identical in the two games; the game tree of the two games is identical; and the players receive identical payoffs when the vector of adopted strategies is identical.

It is therefore not the games that differ because legal rules, from this perspective, are not texts but behavior. Moreover, the behavior is endogenous to the model rather than constitutive of it. The games cannot differ, but the relevant game might have multiple equilibria that differ in some systematic way from each other. On this account we would identify one equilibrium as a "law equilibrium" and another equilibrium as an "anarchic" (or "nonlaw") equilibrium. On the other hand, we might identify law in one game with some extra-game theoretical aspect of the situation that has some effect on the choice of equilibrium.

4. Modeling Obligation

The previous section suggested that attempts to model obligation as an incentive, as a constraint, or in an additional cost model will not be wholly successful. In this section, I consider two other tactics. The first, suggested by the prior discussion of endogenous legal rules, considers how one might regard law as equilibrium. The second considers a more extensive reformulation of the agent's preference relation to capture the idea of obligation.

I should reemphasize at this point, however, the complexity of normative phenomena. This complexity undoubtedly will require a variety of different models. Some of these, at least in circumstances in which the normative rules are taken as exogenous, may be adequately captured in models that treat legal rules (or other norms) as incentives or as constraints.

The idea of obligation raises several questions for economists. One might for example seek to explain the content of obligations: which norms will emerge under what circumstances? A similar question arises when one observes that, in most social circumstances, a large number of obligations from a variety of sources, are urged on individuals. One might seek to explain why an agent acknowledges some obligations but not others. This problem, for example, was latent in the discussion of Raz's exclusionary reason account of obligation and in the analysis of the distinction between a tax and a fine. The state imposes fines on many actions; New Yorkers, for example, obviously do not treat the prohibitions on double parking or jaywalking as exclusionary reasons. If they pay any attention to them at all, they weigh the expected fine against the other first-order reasons for action.

Further, it is not clear that all obligations influence behavior in the same way. Obligation might encompass a number of different behavioral phenomena, each of which should be modeled differently. For instance, obligations that serve to coordinate behavior might require a different explanation than ones that have redistributive consequences.

4.1. Law and Equilibrium Analysis

The discussion of sanction theories of obligation identified two other, related, accounts of law. Both treat law as an equilibrium phenomena. One account, however, merely identifies law with one feature of an equilibrium, while the other considers law as an extra–game theoretical element that determines which equilibrium in the game will be played.

4.1.1. Law As Equilibrium. Some models of law economic analysis of law seem to regard the legal rule not as a factor that explains an agent's behavior or a social phenomenon but as an aspect of equilibrium behavior itself. So for example, Bicchieria (1994, p. 232) defines a norm as "a behavioral regularity R that satisfies two conditions (1) "Almost every member of P [the population] prefers to conform to R on the condition (and only on the condition) that almost everyone else conforms too. (2) Almost every member of P believes that almost every other member of P conforms to R."[13]

This view of norms generally and law in particular is inadequate for several reasons. First, it is overinclusive. It characterizes some behavior that results from complex structure of incentives that one may not see as normative. Consider, for example, Akerlof's (1976) model of caste. In his model, failure to conform to the caste rules leads to ostracism. As a consequence, condition 1 is satisfied for each individual. Similarly, in equilibrium, condition 2 is satisfied. Or, consider Green and Porter's model of collusion under uncertainty (1984). In their model, firms collude tacitly in an environment in which deviations from the agreed on price might arise from violations of the agreement or from chance. In equilibrium firms adopt a complex behavior of compliance and punishment.

Second, this conception of law does not tie the behavior to the text that announces the law in any way. Consider, for example, the jaywalk-

---

13. She acknowledges that her definition does not capture the idea of norms that are meant to serve as standards of behavior.

ing laws in New York City. These laws are duly enacted and, on occasion, enforced. Yet, these laws do not qualify as norms under Bicchieria's definition. An individual's motivation to conform may be detached from the motivation that derives from the conformity of others.[14] Nor, given the rate of noncompliance, most do not believe that almost everyone in the population complies with the laws.[15]

The definition of law thus seems underinclusive because many of the behaviors induced by legal rules violates either condition (1) or condition (2). Rates of noncompliance for many laws are high and known to be high by the population subject to them. Yet, in some instances at least, the fact that the law exists still motivates some individuals to comply with it. Similarly, for some rules, the fact that most others comply provides an incentive for the individual not to comply. Consider, in this regard, public health laws that require universal vaccination. If most people comply and are vaccinated, the risk of infection to a nonvaccinated individual falls. When it gets sufficiently low, the risk of contracting the disease through infection will be less than the risk of adverse side-effects from the vaccination. The individual would prefer not to comply with the norm. One might make a similar argument with respect to other rule such as those banning fraud. When the incidence of fraud is low, precaution against fraud is low. Consequently, frauds may be easier to perpetrate. Moreover, one might argue that, whatever the incidence of fraud, the individual's motivation to comply with law depends not on her beliefs about the rate of compliance but on her beliefs about the likelihood of detection, prosecution and conviction.

Finally, and most important, this conception of law leaves legal rules without explanatory power. On this account, legal norms are simply features of an equilibrium; they do not explain why that equilibrium exists or how it came to be selected from among all potential equilibria. Yet,

---

14. At least, the interrelation of individual motivations to conform is complex. In California, compliance with the jaywalking laws is much greater. This may result from stricter enforcement, or it may result from a different sense of what is expected.

15. There is some ambiguity concerning the phrase "almost everyone conforms to the rule." New York City records a large number of burglaries each year. As a consequence individuals invest money in locks and other security devices. Is there an expectation of general conformity to the prohibition on burglary? In one sense, yes, because most people do not commit burglaries; moreover even those that do commit burglaries do not do so at every opportunity.

in general, we think that law matters. When Congress enacts stricter regulations concerning auto emissions, we expect changes in a wide range of behaviors ranging from the research and development activities of auto manufacturers and oil refineries to the purchasing and driving patterns of individuals. On this account law is not a *feature* of an equilibrium but a partial explanation as to why that equilibrium was reached.

4.1.2. Law as Equilibrium Selection. The alternative equilibrium account of law does attribute some explanatory role to law: The legal structure identifies which of many equilibria the players will in fact adopt. The enactment of a law results in the institution of a new equilibrium. The mechanism through which this shift among equilibria is accomplished is not articulated. One can say only that legal rules affect beliefs so that individuals can determine which of the available equilibria will be played.

In some instances, legal rules do indeed seem to influence directly individual beliefs about which equilibrium will be played. Consider the New York City "pooper scooper law" enacted in 1978. This law required dog owners to clean up after their dogs. Though the City did not devote many resources to the enforcement of the rule, enactment dramatically affected the cleanliness of New York streets.

The explanatory power of other rules, however, seems at first glance to depend on more than the effect of the enactment of the law on individual beliefs. It might be that dog owners changed their behavior only because of the incentive provided by the expected sanction for non-compliance with the law. This expected sanction, however, arises from the change in beliefs of public officials occasioned by enactment of the new ordinance. Enactment of the ordinance, on this account, changes the beliefs of various officials who now coordinate their actions to enforce the law. It thus does not capture the way in which an exclusionary reason works.

4.2. Modeling Obligation as Preference

A model of choice starts with a set of objects or options and a preference relation on that set. The first question that confronts the analyst, then, concerns the specification of the set of options that the agent faces. In most economic problems, the analyst assumes that the agent differentiates among actions or states of the world on only a limited set of context-independent features, usually the "economic" or pecuniary costs and benefits of a particular action or state of the world. So, for example, economists regard a tax and fine as equivalent because they usually assume that only the (expected) cost of non-compliance is relevant to the decision maker.

To model obligation, then, one might simply broaden the domain of preference and assume, as the additional cost model essentially does in a naive way, that the agent has a preference to comply with the obligation. To succeed, however, this approach must overcome two complications. First, in order to define the domain of preference appropriately, one requires a complete specification of the obligation to identify the features of a situation that the agent finds relevant to her deliberation. As many legal obligations—e.g., judicial obligations—are controversial, such specification will be difficult, if not impossible. Second, one must understand how the agent "trades off" her interest in compliance with her other interests. Actual trade-offs, as manifested for example in judicial decision, exhibit a complex pattern of adherence and non-adherence to obligation. This pattern is difficult to specify ex ante while ex post specification appears ad hoc.

The earlier example that distinguished between a tax and a fine or a user fee and a fine suggested several features of the domain of preference and some consistency conditions that a preference to comply must satisfy. The domain of preference must include the legal form of the regulation. Moreover, the argument suggested that, for some range of sanctions, the agent should conform to the norm largely without regard to the size of the sanction. This condition restricts the set of possible preferences.

Ideally, the domain of preference should satisfy several conditions. It should be simple, as in the usual context-independent specification of preferences over net wealth because the context of individual action is often incompletely specified. (For a discussion see Baigent, 1995.) In addition, the analyst should have reasons to specify the decision relevant criteria that comprise the domain of preference that are independent of the phenomena under investigation. The specification of the domain of preference in the additional cost model fails this latter condition; it seems to be an ad hoc specification of concern. It is not clear, however, that one can expand the domain of preference in a principled way when norms and obligations are endogenous.

5. Concluding Remarks

Economic analysis of law has greatly increased our understanding of legal rules and institutions through its focus, both theoretical and empirical, on how law influences behavior. Continued progress will depend on our ability to refine and extend the theory of how law influences behavior.

In this article, I have identified two related challenges to the economic theory of how law influences behavior. The primary challenge arises from the extension of economic analysis of the behavior of private individuals to the behavior of public officials and lawmakers. Public officials act under legal obligations that may impose few sanctions for non-compliance. Moreover, public officials create and enforce legal rules so that simple sanction models of legal behavior that assume exogenously given legal rules prove inadequate.

Second, I have compared a "legal" model of how law influences behavior to the economic model. This model generates different predictions and has different normative implications. To the extent that it actually describes the behavior of public officials and private individuals, it presents a challenge to economists to capture this phenomenon in our theoretical net.

References

Akerlof, George. 1976. "The Economics of Caste and of the Rat Race and Other Woeful Tales," 90 *Quarterly Journal of Economics* 599–617.

Baigent, Nicholas. 1995. "Behind the Veil of Preference," 46 *Japanese Economic Review* 88–101.

Basu, Kaushik. 1998. "The Role of Norms and Law in Economics: An Essay on Political Economy," Cornell Working Paper 461.

Bernstein, Lisa. 1992. "Opting Out of the Legal System: Extralegal Contractual Relations in the Diamond Industry," 21 *Journal of Legal Studies* 115–57.

———. 1993. "Social Norms and Default Rules Analysis," 3 *Southern California Interdisciplinary Law Journal* 59–90.

———. 1996. "Merchant Law in a Merchant Court: Rethinking the Code's Search for Immanent Business Norms Merchant Law in a Merchant Court: Rethinking the Code's Search for Immanent Business Norms" 144 *University of Pennsylvania Law Review* 1765–1821.

Bicchieria, Cristina. 1994. *Rationality and Coordination.* Cambridge: Cambridge University Press.

Cohen, Mark A. 1991. "Explaining Judicial Behavior or What's 'Unconstitutional' about the Sentencing Commission?" 7 *Journal of Law, Economics, & Organization* 183–99.

———. 1992. "The Motives of Judges: Empirical Evidence from Antitrust Sentencing," 12 *International Review of Law and Economics* 13–30.

Cooter, Robert D. 1983. "The Objectives of Private and Public Judges," 41 *Public Choice* 107–32.

———. 1984. "Prices and Sanctions," 84 *Columbia Law Review* 1523–59.

———. 1997. "Normative Failure Theory of Law," 82 *Cornell Law Review* 947–79.

Edwards, Harry T. 1998. "Collegiality and Decision Making on the D.C. Circuit," 84 *Virginia Law Review* 1335–70.

Green, Edward J., and Robert H. Porter. 1984. "Non-Cooperative Collusion under Imperfect Price Information," 52 *Econometrica* 87–100.

Hacker, P. M. S. 1973. "Sanction Theories of Duty," in A. W. B. Simpson, ed. *Oxford Essays on Jurisprudence.* Oxford: Oxford University Press.

Hart, H. L. A. 1961. *The Concept of Law.* Oxford: Oxford University Press.

———. 1982. "Legal Duty and Obligation," in *Essays on Bentham.* Oxford: Oxford University Press.

Heiner, Ronald. 1986. "Imperfect Decisions and the Law," 15 *Journal of Legal Studies* 227–61.

Higgins, Richard A., and Paul H. Rubin. 1980. "Judicial Discretion," 9 *Journal of Legal Studies* 129–38.

Kahan, Marcel. 1989. "Causation and Incentives to Take Care under the Negligence Rule," 18 *Journal of Legal Studies* 427–47.

Kornhauser, Lewis A. 1992a. "Modeling Collegial Courts. I: Path Dependence," 12 *International Review of Law and Economics* 169–85.

———. 1992b. "Modeling Collegial Courts II: Legal Doctrine," 8 *Journal of Law, Economics and Organization* 441–70.

———. 1995. "Adjudication by a Resource-Constrained Team: Hierarchy and Precedent in a Judicial System," 68 *Southern California Law Review* 1605–29.

———. 1998. "No Best Answer?" 146 *University of Pennsylvania Law Review* 1599–1637.

McAdams, Richard H. 1996. "Group Norms, Gossip, and Blackmail," 144 *University of Pennsylvania Law Review* 2237–92.

———. 1997. "The Origin, Development, and Regulation of Norms," 96 *Michigan Law Review* 338–433.

McNollGast. 1995. Politics and the Courts: A Positive Theory of Judicial Doctrine and the Rule of Law," 68 *Southern California Law Review* 1631–83.

Posner, Eric A. 1996a. "Law, Economics, and Inefficient Norms," 144 *University of Pennsylvania Law Review* 1697–1744.

———. 1996b. "The Regulation of Groups: The Influence of Legal and Nonlegal Sanctions on Collective Action," 63 *University of Chicago Law Review* 133–97.

———. 1998. "The Strategic Basis of Principled Behavior: A Critique of the Incommensurability Thesis," 146 *University of Pennsylvania Law Review* 1185–1214.

Posner, Richard A. 1993. "What Do Judges and Justices Maximize? (The Same Thing Everybody Else Does)," 3 *Supreme Court Economic Review* 1–41.

Rabin, Matthew. 1995. "Moral Preferences, Moral Constraints, and Self-Serving Biases," Berkeley Department of Economics Working Paper No. 95–241.

Rasmusen, Eric. 1994. "Judicial Legitimacy: An Interpretation as a Repeated Game," 10 *Journal of Law, Economics, and Organization* 63–83.

———. 1996. "Stigma and Self-fulfilling Expectations of Criminality," 39 *Journal of Law and Economics* 519.

Raz, Joseph. 1975. *Practical Reason and Norms*. London: Hutchinson & Co.

———. 1994. "Authority, Law, and Morality," in *Ethics in the Public Domain*. New York: Oxford University Press.

Revesz, Richard L. 1997. "Environmental Regulation, Ideology, and the D.C. Circuit," 83 *Virginia Law Review* 1717–71.

———. 1999. "Ideology, Collegiality, and the D.C. Circuit: A Reply to Chief Judge Harry P. Edwards," 85 *Virginia Law Review* 805–52.

Savage, Leonard J. 1954. *Foundations of Statistics*. New York: Doyer.

Schauer, Frederick. 1991. *Playing by the Rules*. Cambridge, MA: Harvard University Press.

Soper, Philip. 1996. "Law's Normative Claims," in Robert P. George, ed. *The Autonomy of Law*. Oxford: Oxford University Press.

———. 1998. "Two Puzzles from the Postscript," 4 *Legal Theory* 359–80.

[11]

USING THE CONCEPT OF LEGAL CULTURE

David Nelken[*]

1. The Meaning of Legal Culture

Legal culture, in its most general sense, is one way of describing relatively stable patterns of legally oriented social behaviour and attitudes. The identifying elements of legal culture range from facts about institutions such as the number and role of lawyers or the ways judges are appointed and controlled, to various forms of behaviour such as litigation or prison rates, and, at the other extreme, more nebulous aspects of ideas, values, aspirations and mentalities. Like culture itself, legal culture is about who we are not just what we do.

Enquiries into legal culture try to understand puzzling features of the role and the rule of law within given societies. Why do the UK and Denmark complain most about the imposition of EU law but then turn out to be the countries which have the best records of obedience? Conversely, why does Italy, whose public opinion is most in favour of Europe, have such a high rate of non compliance? Why does Holland, otherwise so similar, have such a low litigation rate compared to neighbouring Germany? Why in the United States and the UK does it often takes a sex scandal to create official interest in doing something about corruption, whereas in Latin countries it takes a major corruption scandal to excite interest in marital unfaithfulness!? Such contrasts can lead us to reconsider broader theoretical issues in the study of law and society. How does the importance of 'enforcement' as an aspect of law vary in different societies? What can be learned, and what is likely to be obscured, by defining 'law' in terms of litigation rates? How do shame and guilt cultures condition the boundaries of law and in what ways does law help shape those self-same boundaries?

These few examples are enough to suggest that findings about legal culture can have both theoretical and policy implications. But there may even be more straightforwardly practical advantages.

---

[*] Distinguished Professor of Legal Institutions and Social Change, University of Macerata, Italy; Distinguished Research Professor of Law, Unversity of Wales Cardiff; and Visiting Professor of Law, LSE. This is a revised version of a paper that was presented as a keynote address to the Australian Association of Legal and Social Philosophy conference (July 18-20 2003). I should like to thank Professor Peter Crane and Professor Tom Campbell for their kind invitation, Professor Dimity Kingsford-Smith for graciously suggesting the idea, and Professor Jeremy Webber for his 'reply' to the paper.

Knowing more about differences in legal culture can actually save your life! One well-travelled colleague who teaches legal theory likes to tells a story of the way crossing the road when abroad requires good knowledge of the local customs. In England, he claims, you are relatively safe on pedestrian crossings, but rather less secure if you try to cross elsewhere. In Italy, he argues, you need to show about the same caution in both places; but at least motorists will do their best to avoid actually hitting you. In Germany, on the other hand, or so he alleges, you are totally safe on the zebra crossing. You don't even need to look out for traffic. But, if you dare to cross elsewhere, you risk simply not being 'seen'...

The sort of investigations in which the idea of legal culture finds its place are those which set out to explore empirical variation in the way law is conceived and lived rather than to establish universal truths about the nature of law, to map the existence of different *concepts* of law rather than establish *the* concept of law. [1] In employing the idea of legal culture in comparative exercises geared to exploring the similarities and differences amongst legal practices and legal worlds the aim is to go beyond the tired categories so often relied on in comparative law such as 'families of law' and incorporate that attention to the 'law in action' and 'living law' which is usually missing from comparative lawyers' classifications and descriptions. [2]

But the concept of legal culture is certainly not a simple one. Not only is it used in a variety of ways, some authors have even suggested that it is so misleading that it should be abandoned. In this paper I shall first address two of the key issues surrounding the use of this term. Firstly, what should we consider to be the unit of legal culture? In a period of increasing globalisation is it still appropriate that it be the nation state? Secondly, how should the term legal culture figure in our explanations? Is it a separable variable to be set against other causal factors, or is it a rather an invitation to interpret what is distinctive about the way law works and is experienced in different places? After summarising some of the general literature on these issues I shall then re-examine them with reference to empirical research I am engaged on which concerns court delays[3] in Italy. Italian drivers may indeed be relatively quick witted in avoiding accidents, but if we should ever be so unfortunate

---

[1] See Brian Tamanaha, *A General Jurisprudence of Law and Society* (2001).
[2] See eg David Nelken, 'Understanding/ Invoking Legal Culture' David Nelken (ed), special issue on *Legal Culture, Diversity and Globalization* (1995) 4 *Social and Legal Studies* 435-452; David Nelken (ed) *Comparing Legal Cultures* (1997) 58-88; and David Nelken, 'Comparative sociology of law' in Reza Benakar and Max Travers (eds), *Introduction to Law and Social Theory*, (2002) 329-344.
[3] I shall have to leave to another occasion the problems in using the term delay as if it were a self-evident fact, rather than a contested and contestable label implying that someone finds a length of waiting time unacceptable. Likewise, I shall not discuss here the harm caused -*even in Italy*- by legal procedures that are over *too* quickly.

as to be caught up in one it is important to know that we may have to wait as much as 14 years for a verdict. In many other European countries waiting time tends to be measured in months rather than years; yet despite this apparently creaking court system Italy is a leading economic power. How far can using the concept of legal culture explain or make sense of such differences in the heart of Europe? I shall conclude by saying something about what legal delay can tell us about the relationship between legal culture and general culture in Italy. Any study of this sort can at best provide only part of the picture. But hopefully even this will be sufficient to remind us of the ethnocentricity of many of our ideas regarding the role and the rule of law.

a) The Unit of Legal Culture

Articles,[4] and books[5], very interesting ones, continue to identify legal culture with the nation state, and collections of studies of legal culture likewise use this as their organising theme[6]. But rather than limit ourselves to the state level, patterns of legal culture can and must also be sought both at a more micro as well as at a more macro level. At the sub-national level the appropriate unit of legal culture may be the local court, the prosecutor's office, or the lawyer's consulting room. Differences between places in the same society may often be considerable. Legal culture is not necessarily uniform (organisationally and meaningfully) across different branches of law.[7] Lawyers specialising in some subjects may have less in common with other lawyers outside their field than they have with those abroad. At the macro level, historical membership of the continental or common law world transcends the frontiers of the nation state. And, increasingly, the implications of these memberships are being challenged and reworked by globalising networks of trading and other interchanges. We also need to explore what have been described as the 'third cultures' of international trade, communication networks and other trans-national processes.[8]

---

[4] Eric Feldman, 'Patients' Rights, Citizen Movements and Japanese Legal Culture' in David Nelken (ed) (1997) note 2, 215-236, and Eric Feldman, 'Blood Justice, Courts, Conflict and Compensation in Japan, France and the United States', in (2001) 34 *Law and Society Review* 651-702.

[5] See eg John Bell, *French Legal Culture* (2002); Ehrhard Blankenburg and Freek Bruinsma, *Dutch Legal Culture* (2nd. edition) (1994); David Johnson, *The Japanese way of Justice* (2002).

[6] See Volkmar Gessner, Armin Hoeland, and Casba Varga (eds), *European Legal Cultures* (1996).

[7] John Bell, note 5

[8] See eg Francis Snyder, 'Governing Economic Globalisation: Global Legal Pluralism and European Law' (1999) 5 *European Law Journal* 334-374; Guenther Teubner, 'Global Bukowina: Legal Pluralism in the World Society', in Guenther Teubner ed. *Global Law without a State*, (1997) 3-38; Guenther Teubner, 'Legal Irritants: Good Faith in British Law or How Unifying Law Ends up in

Given the extent of past and present transfer of legal institutions and ideas, it is often misleading to try and relate legal culture only to its current national context. [9] For example, some American authors have mistakenly tried to explain, as examples of 'Japanese' legal culture, standard features of Continental European systems which date back in Japan there only to their borrowing of these legal institutions in the last century. Many aspects of law are the result of colonialism, immigration and conquest. Non- European countries frequently have mixed or pluralistic legal systems which testify to waves of colonial invasions or imitations of other systems.[10] Deliberate attempts at the socio- legal engineering of so called 'Legal transplants' can range from single laws and legal institutions to entire codes or borrowed systems of law [11]. Law may be remade by wider national culture; but it can also itself help mould that culture. Many current legal transfers can be seen as attempts to bring about imagined and different *futures*, rather than to conserve the present (as the transplant metaphor might suggest). Hence ex- communist countries try to become more like selected examples of the more successful market societies, or South Africa models its new constitution on the best that Western regimes have to offer rather than on constitutional arrangements found in its nearer neighbours in Africa. The hope is that law may be a means of resolving current problems by transforming their society into one more like the source of such borrowed law; legal transfer becomes part of the effort to become more democratic, more economically successful, more secular - or more religious. In what is almost a species of sympathetic magic borrowed law is deemed capable of bringing about the same conditions of a flourishing economy or a healthy civil society that are found in the social context from which the borrowed law has been taken.

The adoption of dissimilar legal models is perhaps most likely where the legal transfer is imposed by third parties as part of a colonial project and/or insisted on as a condition of trade, aid, alliance or diplomatic recognition. But it has also often been sought by elites concerned to 'modernise' their society or otherwise bring it into the wider family of 'civilised' nations. Japan and Turkey are the most obvious examples.[12] Even in Europe some of the laws and legal institutions that people think of as

---

New Divergences', (1998) 61 *Modern Law Review* 11-32; Yves Dezalay and Bryan Garth, *Dealing in Virtue* (1996).

[9] David Nelken, ' Comparativists and Transferability', in Pierre Legrand and Roderick Munday (eds), *Comparative Legal Studies: Traditions and Transition* (2003)

[10] Andrew Harding, 'Comparative Law and Legal Transplantation in South East Asia', in David Nelken and Johannes Feest (eds), *Adapting Legal Cultures* (2001), 199-222.

[11] David Nelken, Towards a Sociology of Legal Adaptation,' in David Nelken and Johannes Feest (eds), note 10, 4 -55.

[12] See the contributions to Andrew Harding and Elsin Orucu (eds), *Comparative law for the 21st century* (2002) and Michael B. Likosky, (ed), *Transnational Legal Processes* (2002).

most typically their own are the result of imitation, imposition or borrowing.[13] Much domestic law in the 19th Century, such as the law of copyright, was mainly invented as a response to its existence elsewhere. There are Dutch disputing mechanisms which are in fact a result of German imposition during the occupation, and which have been abandoned in Germany itself.[14] Hence, in advance of empirical investigation it would be wrong to assume any particular 'fit' between law and its environing national society or culture. In addition, the nation state has now to come to terms with the impact of globalisation.[15] For some writers, we inhabit a 'deterritorialised world'; we can participate via the media in other communities of others with whom we have no geographical proximity or common history [16]Hence, 'all totalising accounts of society, tradition and culture are exclusionary and enact a social violence by suppressing contingent and continually emergent differences'. Instead we must face the 'challenges of transnationalism and the politics of global capitalism or multiple overlapping and conflicting juridiscapes.[17]

Claims about the decline of the nation state can no doubt be taken too far. Given the boundaries of jurisdiction, politics, and language, the nation state does make a convenient starting point for comparing legal culture. It is an empirical question how far legal culture at the national level is modified by what happens at other levels. Common influences, cultural interchange and increasing economic interdependence (or in many cases just dependence) can all produce similarities. But, simultaneously, 'increasing homogenisation of social and cultural forms seems to be accompanied by a proliferation of claims to specific authenticities and identities'[18] We also need to take care that our comparisons do not fall into the vices of Occidentalism or Orientalism, of making other cultures seem either necessarily similar or intrinsically 'other'.[19] Given that culture is, to a large extent, a matter of struggle and disagreement, the purported uniformity, coherence or stability of given national cultures will often be no more than a rhetorical claim projected by outside observers or manipulated by elements within the culture concerned. Much that goes under the name of culture is no more - but

---

[13] See Brad Sherman, 'Remembering and Forgetting: The Birth of Modern Copyright Law', in David Nelken (ed.), 1997 note 2, 237-266.

[14] Alex Jettinghoff, 'State Formation and Legal Change: On the Impact of International Politics', in David Nelken and Johannes Feest, (eds), note 10, 99-116

[15] Antoine Garapon, 'French Legal Culture and the Shock of 'Globalization', in David Nelken (ed), 1995, note 2, 493-506

[16] Rosemary J Coombe, 'Contingent Articulations: a Critical Studies of Law', in Austin Sarat and Thomas Kearns (eds), *Law in the Domains of Culture* (2000).

[17] ibid.

[18] Marian Strathern, *Shifting Contexts: Transformations in Anthropological Knowledge* (1995) 3.

[19] Maureen Cain, 'Orientalism, Occidentalism and the Sociology of Crime' (2000) 40 *British Journal of Criminology* 239-260.

also no less- than 'imagined communities' or 'invented traditions', though these may of course be real in their effects). There is therefore some danger of reifying national stereotypes, (as in the earlier examples of driving practices in different societies?), as there is of failing to recognise that legal culture, like all culture, is a product of the contingencies of history and is always undergoing change.[20] It is enough to think of the transformations in attitudes towards 'law and order' from Weimar to Hitlerian Germany. In terms of the case study that follows it is worth remembering that Italian judges in the 1920's and 30's had virtually no backlog of cases.

One of the most pressing tasks of the comparative sociologist of law is to try and capture how far in actual practice what is described as globalisation in fact represents the attempted imposition of a one *particular* legal culture on other societies. Some leading authors argue that we are now seeing convergence towards a modern type of legal culture,[21] and is particular the recent growth of prestige of the Anglo American model which is spread by trade and the media. The Anglo- American model is seen to be characterised by its emphasis on the care taken to link law and economics (rather than law and the State), procedures which rely on orality, party initiative, negotiation inside law, as well as more broad cultural features such as individualism and the search for security through legal remedies. [22] Others insist that nation states remain recognisably distinctive, with the extreme of 'adversarial legalism' located only in the USA. [23] It has been observed that much of the 'ideal' model does not accurately describe how the law operates at home, for example the American legal and regulatory system in practice often relies on inquisitorial methods. National versions of the Continental legal system embodied in ready packaged Codes are also being exported, especially to the ex-communist world. In addition, the ideals represented by the 'rule of law' itself, as a way of providing certainty and keeping the state within bounds, seem increasingly outdated for the regulation of

---

[20] see David Nelken (1995) 2.

[21] Lawrence Friedman, 'Is there a Modern Legal Culture?' (1994) *Ratio Juris,* 117. See also David Garland, *The Culture of Control* (2000), who, in the admittedly restricted area of criminal justice, argues that American legal responses epitomise those required by 'late modern society ', and are bound to arrive to other advanced democracies if they have not already done so.

[22] See Wolf Heyderbrand, 'Globalization and the Rule of Law at the end of the 20th Century', in Alberto Febbrajo, David Nelken, Vittorio Olgiati (eds), (2001) *Social Processes and Patterns of Legal Control: European Yearbook of Sociology of Law, 2000* 25-127.

[23] Robert Kagan, *Adversarial Legalism: The American Way of Law* (2001); David Nelken, ' Beyond Compare? Criticising the American Way of Law' (2003) 28. *Law and Social Inquiry* 181-213.

international commercial exchange by computer between multinationals which are more powerful than many of the governments of the countries in which they trade.[24]

What does seem undeniable is the extent to which legal culture is becoming ever more what we could call 'relational'. With increasing contact between societies there are ever more opportunities to define one's own legal culture in terms of relationships of attraction to or repulsion from what goes on in other societies. For example, when comparative European prison rates first began to be published in the 1980's, Finland, which came high in the list, decided to cut back on prison building, whereas Holland felt entitled to build more. What mattered was to stay within the norm. Likewise, for many European countries the continued use of the death penalty in the USA serves as a significant marker of the superiority of their own legal culture.

b. What is the Concept of Legal Culture good for?

Let us assume that we can identify which unit -or, better, units- of legal culture we want to study. Our second set of questions concern how we should employ the concept in the context of our investigations. What is the point in calling a particular pattern of behaviour or ideas legal culture, and what follows from this? We could use this term, like others such as 'legal system' or ' legal process', as no more than scholarly shorthand for pointing to a set of activities or problems. But if we want to utilise legal culture in explanatory enquiries we shall have to go further than this. The question is how much further? . Culture is one of those words which it is particularly difficult to define and easy to abuse.[25] Within anthropology the process of producing accounts of other cultures is increasingly contested.[26] How can we avoid the ever-present danger of circular argument ? (They do it that way because that is how they do it in Japan, in Holland or wherever). Is it best to use the term legal culture only as a residual explanation when other explanations run out?[27]

Roger Cotterrell has argued that the term legal culture is too vague and impressionistic a concept to be useful in constructing explanations.[28] Lawrence Friedman, the acknowledged father of the term,

---

[24] See William E Scheuerman, 'Globalization and the Fate of Law ', in David Dyzenhaus (ed), *Recrafting the Rule of Law: The Limits of Legal Order* (1999), 243-266
[25] Adam Kuper, *Culture: The Anthropologists Account* (1999).
[26] James Clifford and George Marcus, *Writing Culture: The Poetics and Politics of Ethnography* (1986).
[27] Tony Prosser 'The State, Constitutions and Implementing Economic Policy: Privatisation and Regulation in the UK, France and the USA', in David Nelken (ed) (1995) note 2, 507-516.
[28] Roger Cotterrell, in David Nelken (ed) (1997) note 2, 13-32.

replies that it is no worse than other overarching social science concepts. Even if the concept as such is not measurable it covers a wide range of phenomena that can be measured.[29] In its role in explanations, legal culture can serve to capture an essential intervening variable in influencing the type of legal changes which follow on large social transformations such as those following technological breakthroughs.'[30] More generally, 'legal culture determines when, why and where people turn for help to law, or to other institutions, or just decide to 'lump it".[31] It would be a finding about legal culture, he says, if French but not Italian women were reluctant to call the police to complain about sexual harassment. The issue of legal delay, as we shall see also lends itself to analysis for this purpose.

Friedman is also the author of the classic distinction between 'internal' and 'external' legal culture. On the one hand, 'internal legal culture' refers to the ideas and practices of legal professionals; 'external legal culture,' on the other hand, is the name given to the opinions, interests, and pressures brought to bear on law by wider social groups. Friedman has increasingly argued that the importance of 'internal legal culture' as a factor in explaining socio- legal change tends to be exaggerated, usually by legal scholars who have an investment in doing so. He has preferred to concentrate on the importance of external legal culture and has given especial attention to the increasing public demand for legal remedies - what he calls the drive to 'Total Justice'[32] - produces legal and social change. Some of the most stimulating if controversial work in this field, however, has been designed to show, *pace* Friedman, that patterns of legally related behaviour are less the result of the way 'folk culture' shapes the demand for legal relief and more the consequence of the institutional possibilities provided. There has been considerable debate for example about how far the comparatively low use of courts in Japan should be explained in terms of a specifically widely felt Japanese (and, more generally Asian) religious based, cultural reluctance to going to law, or whether it is more a result of a deliberate set of government created disincentives to litigation[33] An important study of litigation rates in Europe seeks to explain why the Netherlands has one of the lowest, and Germany one of the highest, litigation rates, despite being so similar culturally and even interdependent economically.[34] The

---

[29] Lawrence Friedman, 'The Concept of Legal Culture: A Reply', in David Nelken (ed) (1997) note 2, 33-40.
[30] Friedman ibid.
[31] Friedman, ibid.
[32] Lawrence Friedman, *Total Justice* (1985), and see also Lawrence Friedman *The Republic of Choice: Law, Society and Culture* (1990).
[33] See eg Valerie Hamilton and Joe Sanders *Everyday Justice: Responsibility and the Individual in Japan and the United States* (1992).
[34] Ehrhard Blankenburg, 'Civil Litigation Rates as Indicators for Legal Culture', in David Nelken (ed) (1997) note 2, 41-68.

answer given is that these rates depend less on what people want from law than on the availability of other institutional possibilities for dealing with their disputes and claims. The Netherlands, it is argued, as compared to Germany, possesses a much wider range of 'infrastructural' avenues for disposing of cases in ways that do not require court litigation.[35]

The mainstream social science explanatory approach to legal culture typically seeks to assign causal priority between competing hypothetical variables. The interpretative approach, on the other hand, is more concerned to understand how aspects of legal culture resonate and fit together. It sees its task as faithfully translating another system's ideas of fairness and justice and making proper sense of its web of meanings. In the search for holistic meaning the insistence on distinguishing internal from external legal culture, or the 'demand' for law from the 'supply' of law, is likely to obscure more than it reveals.[36] Whereas the first approach uses various aspects of legal culture to explain variation in levels and types of legally related behaviour such as litigation or crime control, the second approach seeks to use evidence of legally relevant behaviour and attitudes as an 'index' of legal culture. It aims at providing 'thick descriptions'[37] of law as 'local knowledge'[38]. In testing its hypotheses the mainstream approach seeks a sort of socio-legal Esperanto which abstracts from the language used by members of different cultures, preferring for example to talk of 'decision-making' rather than 'discretion'. The rival strategy, concerned precisely with grasping linguistic nuance and cultural packaging, would ask whether and when the term discretion is used and what different nuances it carries. [39]

Scholars who adopt the interpretative approach contrast the different meanings of the 'Rule of law', the 'Rechtstaat', or the 'Stato di diritto', the Italian term 'garantismo' versus 'due process', or 'law and order' as compared to the German 'innere sicherheit'; they unpack the meaning of 'lokale justiz' as

---

[35] As an illustration of the lack of conceptual clarification in this field we may note that the infrastructural alternatives that Blankenburg (1997) note 34, calls legal culture' others would describe as 'structural factors', precisely in contrast to cultural ones.

[36] David Nelken 'Puzzling out Legal Culture: A Comment on Blankenburg,' in D. Nelken ed. (1997) note 2, 58-88.

[37] Clifford Geertz, 'Thick Description: Towards an Interpretive Theory of Culture,' in Clifford Geertz *The Interpretation of Culture,* (1973).

[38] Clifford Geertz., *Local Knowledge: Further Essays in Interpretive Anthropology* (1983)

[39] 'Legal culture' is not itself an indigenous term. But in Italy it is very common (especially when referring to the South) to speak of the 'culture of legality', by which is meant the project of extending 'jurisdiction' and the difficulty of gaining social acceptance of the need to live life within the constraints of legal rules.

compared to 'community crime control' [40]They try to grasp the secrets of culture by focusing on key local terms, which are almost, but not quite, untranslatable. Blankenburg himself explores the meaning of the term 'beleid' in Holland that refers to the more or less explicit policy guidelines followed by trusted government, criminal justice personnel and public organisations in general.[41] They examine the idea of the State in common law and Continental countries so as to understand, for example, why litigation is seen as essentially democratic in the USA and as anti- democratic in France. For this approach, concepts both reflect and constitute culture; as in the changes undergone by the meaning of 'contract' in a society where the individual is seen as necessarily embodied in wider relationships [42], or the way that the Japanese ideogram for the new concept of 'rights' came to settle on a sign associated with 'self interest' rather than morality.[43]

An interpretative stance is more ready than the mainstream explanatory approach to treat culture as part of a flow of meaning, 'the enormous interplay of interpretations in and about a culture' [44] to which the scholar herself also contributes. It is also less interested in drawing a definitional line between legal culture and the rest of social life because it sees this less as a problem for the observer to solve than an aspect of the way legal culture actually works as it reflexively constructs the boundaries of law- in - society. Common law systems, for example, tend to look focus more on the link between law, economics and society, Civil law systems principally on that between law, politics and society. [45] In some civil law legal regimes, as compared to the Anglo American pragmatic - instrumental view of law, law may be deliberately treated as more of an ideal aspiration than as a blueprint for guiding behaviour, either because of deference to the State project of representing the collective will, or under the influence of religious traditions and philosophical idealism. This may partly explain the successful spread of Anglo - American lawyering.[46]

---

[40] Lucia Zedner 'In Pursuit of the Vernacular: Comparing Law and Order Discourse in Britain and Germany', in David Nelken (ed) 1995 note 2, 517-534.
[41] See Blankenburg and Bruinsma, note 5.
[42] Jane K Winn, 'Relational Practices and the Marginalization of Law: Informal Practices of Small Businesses in Taiwan ' (1994) 28 *Law and Society Review*, 193- 232.
[43] Eric Feldman (1997), Note 4.
[44] Jonathan Friedman *Cultural Identity and Global Process* (1994)
[45] This is one reason why it is difficult to accept the Luhmann- Teubner systems theory of law which tries to posit a constant relationship between the legal and other social sub-systems in all modern societies, see David Nelken, 'Beyond the Metaphor of Legal Transplants? Consequences of Autopoietic Theory for the study of Cross-Cultural Legal Adaptation' , in Jiri Priban and David Nelken (eds) *Law's New Boundaries: The Consequences of Legal Autopoiesis,* (2001), 265- 302.

[46] See Maria- Rosaria Ferrarese *Le Istituzioni della Globalizzazione* (2000).

2. Legal Delay in Italy: A Case Study

Civil cases in 1999 took *on average* 5 years to go through the first trial stage, and over 9 years for both the first and appeal stage (which is essentially a retrial of the facts).[47] There is also a further and regularly used final appeal stage on legal points that can be taken to the numerous sections of the Supreme Court. Penal cases can take only a little less time. At the start of 2000 as many as 3,500,000 civil cases and 5,400,000 penal cases were awaiting trial. Can the idea of legal culture help us make sense of all this? What can this case study show us about the value of the concept? As promised, I shall be concentrating in particular on the intersections amongst different units- or levels- of legal culture, as well as on the role of the concept as an explanatory tool and an invitation to explore meaning. I shall take these two issues in turn.

a) The need for a multi- level analysis

---

[47] It is difficult to find an Archimedean lever for studying legal culture. Explanations of legal culture cannot just be based on explaining 'rates' of legal activity since knowledge of how culture works is required to make sense of these 'rates' and decide their signifiucance for comparative purposes. See David Nelken, note 36, and David Nelken 'Comparing Criminal Justice' in Mike Maguire et al, *The Oxford Handbook of Criminology* (3rd edition), 175-202. These official figures therefore obviously need considerable interpretation. For some purposes they overestimate the time required, whereas for others they may even underestimate it! The figures report the *average* time taken by all cases in each tribunal and include those that finish by agreement between the parties or for other reasons before a sentence is delivered. Yet further time is required for 'depositing' the sentence of the judge, and even more for actually carrying out the court's judgment and getting your money and property back. For a series of reasons, that have to do with the lack of court bailiff resources and the competition from private and even illegal actors, the actual 'recovery' of the debt is the most problematic stage of the legal process. After the 1995 civil justice reform designed to shorten waiting time hundreds of thousands of cases, some of which are quite legally complex ones, awaiting trial at the time of the reform, were assigned to a sort of legal bureaucratic limbo (the so called 'sezione stralcio') where they are still slowly being disposed of by poorly paid lawyers deputising as honourary judges.

The problem of legal delay in Italy is largely perceived and presented as a national problem. But there is certainly also considerable variation at the local court level around the country. The time courts took to dispose of civil cases from their case loads ranged from around six to eleven years, and the courts in the South were almost always consistently longer. For example, according to the Ministry of Justice statistics for the Civil courts in 1999, the shortest period was found in the small town of Bolzano in the (Austrian influenced) far North of the country, where first stage trials took on average around four and half years and the process of appeal court hearing took around a further year and half (making a total 6.20 years). The court with the record for the longest trials was Caltanisetta, a small town in Sicily where, on average, cases took seven and half years for the first trial stage, and a further five and a half for the appeal stage (total time 13.15 years). In some, mainly southern, courts bankruptcy or inheritance disputes can still involve more than one generation of lawyers. In others, legal culture may be 'behind' the level of efficiency reached in those parts of the country. The small University town where I work is situated in wealthy and peaceful part of Central Italy. But the head of the local lawyers association was reported in June 2003 as protesting about the fact that after initial hearings the following hearing date for civil trials can only be fixed for dates between 2007 and 2011 (!) (And in most normal cases six hearings are required.)

Nonetheless, these national differences do not negate the existence of a relatively high level of court delay in Italy, as compared to other European countries. And, if anything, there is *more* in common in legal culture across the country than in many other aspects of national culture. As a relatively young State there are significant differences in many other aspects of national culture between the North, the Centre and the South. The similarities in legal culture, on the other hand, derive from the sharing of common rules, procedures and nationally appointed judges as well as aspects of institutional practice and law in action, such as the way lawyers are paid. Indeed, law is often deliberately used as a nationalising and centralising force to correct for the 'backwardness' of outlying areas.

On the other hand, it is impossible to understand the factors that shape court delays in Italy without looking beyond national boundaries. The current working of Italian criminal justice is moulded by doctrinal scholarship which reflects, on the one hand, the long standing hegemony of German penal law, which is still unchallenged amongst the law professors of substantive criminal law, and, on the other hand, the more recent influence of Anglo-American ideas which have come in as a result of the introduction of a large number of accusatorial elements in the penal process. This certainly complicates any effort to characterise Italian criminal justice merely in terms of other aspects of the same culture. Proposed remedies for court delays are more likely to come from abroad than from within Italy. This is true, for example, the introduction of so called 'Justices of the Peace' as a more rapid jurisdiction for first level civil cases, which again drew on the Anglo-American tradition.

Sometimes such 'borrowing' may even exacerbate delay For example, this was true of the effects of the 1989 new code of criminal procedure on delays on the penal side. This famous reform was the first to introduce a fully- fledged accusatorial system into a Continental legal system. But it came up against the reluctance of the judges and prosecutors working in the system to lose control of the trial. It was modified early on by a restrictive decision handed down by the constitutional court, which feared that organised crime would otherwise be able to exploit the considerable new procedural advantages it gave to the accused.[48] Part of the justification for the reform was the stimulus it would give to speeding up trials by allowing a variety of quicker alternatives including plea bargaining. But alternatives to full trial are adopted in less than a third of cases. The main problem is that the new protections for the accused that characterise the adversarial system were simply added to the previous ones characteristic of the older inquisitorial type of system. The system now seeks to incorporate protections designed to foreground the forensic heat of the adversarial trial *together* with reliance on double checking by different judges in the three stages of trial that include the right to a full rehearing of the facts on appeal. Even relatively trivial criminal cases can need to be viewed by as many thirty people with legal training. Bureaucratic procedural requirements include complex notification rules for all parties to the trial that can be easily manipulated if the accused changes his address or lawyer regularly. What this means is that there is little incentive for lawyers to use any of the alternatives to trial. By holding out and exploiting all procedural rights there is a good chance that the case will be time- blocked before it runs its full course of all three trial stages.

At the macro level, however, it is the role played by the super- national Strasbourg court of Human Rights that is of particular interest for our purposes. The right to a trial within a reasonable period is one of the fundamental rights of the Convention of Human Rights (Article 6) that this Court seeks to protect. In 1999, when there were over forty signatories to this convention, there were no less than 6885 appeals from Italy awaiting decision, almost all of which concerned legal delay. This represented over 20% of the total from all countries for breaches of all the various provisions of the Convention. Italian representation at later stages was even higher. 36% of all sentences handed down were findings of guilt against Italy for cases involving unreasonable delay in its trial processes. The Italian state was condemned to pay so called moral damages to almost all the successful applicants. The Strasbourg Court itself got into difficulty in handling all these appeals within a reasonable period and set up Committees to overhaul its machinery in an attempt to catch up with its backlog!

---

[48] Grande, Elizabetta, 'Italian criminal justice: borrowing and resistance', (2000) vol xlvlll *Amer. J. of Comparative law*, 227-260.

The cases that reach Strasbourg are not necessarily representative of Italian court cases in general, but it is by no means only the extreme cases that arrive there. To provide some empirical evidence on these matters I carried out an analysis of a sample of 50 court sentences cases handed down by the court in the late 1990's. This revealed that delays ranged from four to eighteen years. Most cases were on the civil side. Penal cases tend to end by the case becoming time bound ('prescription') and the accused person often tends to leave it there. But interestingly, no more than a seventh of the sample involved anything like commercial disputes. Most cases involved individuals in dispute with large organisations. The Italian state usually tried to defend the cases at Strasbourg on the grounds of court overload, but this defence was always rejected. At a conservative estimate as many as a fifth of court cases in Italy take longer than the time Strasbourg considers reasonable. Absent particular reasons of legal complexity a good part of the Italian system could in theory automatically just be transferred to Strasbourg after a certain period of normal waiting time! The Court has responded to the annual assault of cases by treating the Italian state as a 'persistent offender', placing it under surveillance and threatening to exclude it from the Council of Europe. The only other signatory treated in this way is Turkey, for its continuing maltreatment of the Kurds. Justice delayed is often justice denied, but it is questionable whether excessive court delay is the same sort of breach as human rights as torture.

The role of the Strasbourg court well illustrates the complexities of charting the relationship between the local and the global in studying legal culture. Because 'law' is at the same time both agent and object of globalisation it becomes difficult even for participants in legal systems to know where the boundaries of the jurisdiction stop. On the one hand the Strasbourg court is an institution whose jurisdiction allows it override local legal regimes. In the Italian case the court even seems be engaged in something like an attempt to standardise modern court systems and 'normalise' Italy's deviant approach to legal procedure and court practice. On the other hand, because Italy was a willing signatory to the convention we could consider the European Court as no more than a higher level court of appeal of the *same* legal culture. Importantly, even if not as such an element of the *legal system,* this idea of resorting to law as the antidote to abuse of power is also a central part of the belief system of many judges, lawyers and jurists within the Italian legal culture itself. But Strasbourg is still a rather special court. According to one Italian 'human rights' lawyer who specialises in taking cases to Strasbourg who was interviewed in 2000 "... the European Court, the Court is almost a 'Court of Miracles' because it seems to be an organisation which is outside time and space. You can go there to punish the powerful. Because that is what it is all about we could say that what it offers is revolutionary, even anarchic justice " The lawyer went on to add that the actual damages that the Strasbourg court awards to someone "crushed by the national legal system" were far too low to compensate for what can have been lost.

It would be premature to conclude that European harmonisation of court delay is round the corner or that Italy is about to get its house in order.[49] Some home- grown remedies have been introduced. There have been significant 'managerial' type reforms aimed at combining different levels of criminal court and reducing the number of hearings in civil cases. Gains in speed in new civil cases did result from the re-routing of pre 1995 cases to be dealt with by honorary judges. Judges who are found responsible for breaching bureaucratic time limits in writing their judgments now risk having to pay damages and not, as previously, only criticism, as a result of internal disciplinary hearings by the Supreme Judicial Council. But the basic weaknesses of the system have not been touched. In addition, however, Italy has also taken more questionable measures to stave off criticism from Strasbourg. In 1999 the so- called Pinto Law (Legge Pinto) was passed. As a result cases of alleged delay now have first to be submitted to the court of appeal of the nearest district, where decisions are then supposed to be provided within four months. This holds back recourse to Strasbourg and aims to prevent parties from seeking remedies that place Italy in a bad light internationally and cost the government money in moral damages. But this new trial stage of course itself adds to delay, and there are additional limits to the remedies provided. At a conference on legal delay in the criminal courts held at Padua that I attended recently, the way the courts are applying the legge Pinto was described as ' diabolical'.[50] For example, unlike in actions before the Strasbourg court it is necessary within Italy to prove that delay has led to material damage and the expenses of bringing the action are not reimbursed. So cases are still going to go to Strasbourg.

More recently, a new constitutional right to reasonable length trials was included in the framework of the so- called ' just trials ' revision of the constitution. Significantly, however, this does not give rise to private actions against the state as with the Strasbourg court[51]. No thought was given to how to make this right effective, nor how to ensure its priority in relation to the other rights and procedural protections being introduced simultaneously whose tendency was actually to lengthen court processes. Judges have told me that they have begun to use this new principle as a means of 'closing' stale cases where, from a strictly formally point of view this would have been problematic. Lawyers defending politicians and organised criminals also try to invoke this as a right when their clients have been waiting a long time (often because of their own delaying tactics) for their trials to end. But any real commitment to the aim of 'speedy trials' must be suspect in the light of the

---

[49] Other case studies, for example of the implementation of IMF standards or international conventions etc., would likely turn up similar dialectics of change and resistance.
[50] The Padua Conference on Reasonableness in the length of trials 30-31 May 2003.
[51] Italian legal (and political) culture is one where rights are often not related to effective resources. For example female judges (an ever increasing proportion of the magistracy) are guaranteed excellent paid maternity leave but no substitute is supplied for them at this time and the cases they are responsible for are usually just put on hold.

continuing and even increasing emphasis on multiplying points and methods of procedural rights and controls. For most of the trial lawyers I have been interviewing in the course of my research on this topic the average time taken for court cases in Italy is something they have adapted to and take for granted. The exceptional cases for them are the ones that overrun the Italian norm, because of more than normal problems in the availability of judges, administrative errors by the cancelleria, the number of parties involved, the need for complicated expert evidence, difficulties in obtaining the collaboration of parties or witnesses, unfair tactics used by the other side, legal complexities and so on. .

b) Explaining and interpreting legal delay in Italy

What happens in Italy is not merely a result of Italian culture and legal culture. But it is certainly also very much connected to other aspects of the Italian context. What (other) aspects of culture and society explain court delay in Italy? What can an interpretative approach tell us about the attitudes and behaviour which help produce such delays? As we shall see, one strategy of explanation concentrates on identifying the possible causes of delay and give each the weight it deserves. The second seeks more to understand different ways of thinking about law.

To a degree the length of legal processes is the result of purely legal factors. The requirement of three court stages (two of these on 'the facts'), the number of supreme courts (which often in practice re-try cases), the length of judge's verdicts ('motivations' as they are called on the continent), and the prestige of jurists' commentary as a potential source of law, all encourage legal uncertainty. The judge's role in civil trials is central, as it is in France, but in Italy they are expected to write much longer 'motivations' of their decisions. Judges explain that they can only get round to thinking about the case and writing their sentences once all the facts have come in. Lawyers who used to write brief requests now use their computers to state their claims at great length. Moreover, once it has accumulated, delay itself produces more delay and uncertainty.

Media discussions attribute the 'blame' to way people abuse the sytem. Either the problem is the laziness, arrogance or managerial ineptitude of judges, or it is the avidity of lawyers, the litigousness of disputants or the disinterest or self interest of politicians, In academic discussions the most cited cause is undoubtedly the fact that the number of judges has nowhere near kept pace with the increasing rate of litigation in the post war period. In terms of what Friedman calls 'external legal culture', the argument is that the 'supply' of law has simply not kept up with public demand. Since the last world war there has been a seven fold increase in the number of civil cases filed whereas the number of judges has less than doubled.[52] Many more cases arrive at the courts than can possibly be dealt with by the number of judges available, and court hearings are for this reason scheduled well into the future for the earliest court calendar date available. Crucially, then, delay is not a result of the time actually spent on dealing with the cases, but is instead the accumulated product of all the 'dead' periods (calculated in months or even years) that are allowed to pass between the relevant court sessions.

A second important cause of delay is said to be the large increase in the number of lawyers which has grown up to satisfy, but which may also stimulate, this public demand. According to some statistics there are now as many as 150 thousand lawyers though not all of them are in practice. Entrance examinations for becoming lawyers, by contrast to those for judges, are extremely easy. The way that lawyers are paid, on the basis of each legal act they perform, is also said to encourage drawing out cases [53] On the one hand, there is no state financed legal aid, and hence no possibility for limiting cases litigated with public subsidy to those considered meritorious. On the other, the costs for litigation, especially in comparative context, can be considered relatively low and do not serve as much of a deterrent to litigation. Once cases are under way lawyers rarely aim at settlements before the case reaches court, in part because delay comes to represent a goal in itself.· On the civil side, delay for one person is stay of execution for another, and, in both the civil and penal process, postponement of the day of reckoning is exactly what at least one party is seeking to obtain. The relatively low proportion of cases which lawyers settle before trial is also said to be explained by the fact that in Italy there is 'no culture of compromise'. The last chapter of a recent review of alternative dispute arrangements in Italy has the title (in Italian) 'Conciliation as set out by the Code- a ruined past, a bankrupt present and a highly uncertain future'.[54]

Other background institutional factors are also worth noting. In terms of government spending the Italian court system is starved of resources and those that are available are sometimes skewed by political considerations as by the difficulty in rationalising the distribution of tribunals across the country in terms of effective demand. The court administration struggles to cope with its workload often relying on antiquated information technology, and at least some of the generally poorly paid

---

[52] Sabino Cassese, 'L'esplosione del diritto. Il sistema giuridico italiano dal 1975 al 2000', in XXVIII/I (2001) Sociologia Del Diritto, 55-66. Cassese, a leading authority on public law, links this to both to economic change and the 'explosion' of law. An earlier empirical study argued that patterns of economic growth and court overload in Italy were not well correlated and that aspects of internal legal culture seemed to be better predictors, see Stefania Pellegrini, *La Litigiosità in Italia, un Analisi Sociologica-Giuridica* (1997), 24.

[53] Daniele Marchesi, *Avvocati, Magistrati, Litiganti* (2002).

[54] Stefania Pellegrini,. *La Giustizia Civile Dentro e Fuori dal Tribunale* (2000).

employees are affected by the formalistic ethos which characterises much public employment in Italy. The self governing judicial parliament has its work cut out to defend judicial autonomy from political attack and has neither the resources nor the know how to run the courts as a public service. There is little support amongst judges for a managerial approach to running Italian courts. The heads of courts are never chosen for managerial ability and often lack it, and those who are, formally speaking, their subordinates have a high level of constitutionally guaranteed independence. There is no small claims court, though recently Justices of the Peace have been recruited and given a role in dealing with low value cases. But they too are now accumulating a backlog . These weaknesses at the formal level are made up for by the existence of what Blankenburg called 'infrastructural alternatives'. [55] Only the very rich can afford judicial arbitration and there are still only relatively few mediation schemes set up by local chambers of commerce.

In addition, however there are also what could call structural factors. Here the major argument would be that legal delays are in the interest of the powerful. But the evidence for this is equivocal. Take first the politicians. Governments save money by not spending on the courts, and, indirectly, the voters benefit in lower taxes- assuming they pay them. Delay, and its consequence, queuing, is then one way to ration a scarce resource. Some of the cases of worst delay actually involve government trying to avoid cashing pension or other promises. In general, Italian governments tend to govern through leniency rather than efficiency and order[56]. Yet, on the other hand, governments pay a high price in legitimacy for the poor functioning of the courts, especially after the procession of cases going to Strasbourg. And the court system has a high degree of political, though not financial, autonomy from the executive. Even the Ministry for Justice relies on judges seconded to the Ministry for drafting and supervising legal reforms.

Working out the relationship between delay and economic interests is similarly complicated. For Weber (and his modern followers) a predictable and well functioning legal system is an essential part of the infrastructure of capitalism. Yet economic interests in Italy put up with a high level of disorganisation and delay. The largest businesses, it is true, can and do have recourse to arbitration, using judges and / or distinguished jurists, as a way of resolving their disputes. But this is a costly solution as a percentage of the value of the case has to be paid in return for quick justice. The large majority of Italy's economy, however, relies on small business, and they would surely benefit from a more expeditious and responsive court system.. Delay mainly helps those in the wrong who can use court delay as means to postpone payment (or prison), especially, as has happened, when the

---

[55] Ehrhard Blankenburg, note 34
[56] Dario Melossi, 'The 'economy of illegalities: Normal crimes, Elites and Social Control in comparative analysis', in David Nelken (ed) *The Futures of Criminology*, (1994), 202-219.

interest on funds that can be obtained in the market place is higher than the legal interest which has to be paid when the case is eventually settled.

Of course, once this type of system exists, those working within or alongside it, and those caught up as parties, may all sometimes have vested interests in delay. Having found ways to benefit from it they may also willingly perpetuate the current situation. Judges and lawyers, sometimes in implicit collusion, may gain advantages by taking things slowly; the judge can postpone the moment of writing the sentence, the lawyer can keep more cases on the go than could possibly be handled in a system with more stringent temporal requirements. What is more, the consequent unpredictability of legal remedies provides a niche for intermediaries or mediators, such as politicians and professionals, debt collection agencies, accident specialists, in the North, and, in addition, organised criminals the South. These play a vital role in bringing parties together, acting as guarantors,[57] and resolving at least some cases of non compliance for example by taking over or recovering debts. Banks gain from acting as depositors in long drawn out bankruptcy cases. For their part large corporations, get round court inefficiencies by taking independent action to disconnect supply or reclaim debts owed. Those who are 'repeat players'[58] in the legal system can choose when it suits them to engage in litigation and can opt for delaying tactics or early settlement as it suits them. They have the power to make others wait and have time on their side. It is often said, though usually without any direct evidence to back it up, that economic actors also tolerate the current inefficient system because they feel it could be to their advantage if they were ever to find themselves the side with the weaker case. Certainly, there is ample proof that some powerful actors, including leading politicians and businessmen, do fear that they might one day come within the reach of the criminal courts and so have an interest in a trial system which offers room for maneuver and delay. It is hard (if not impossible) to envisage a legal system that on the one hand had long drawn out criminal trials but rapid civil ones. Nonetheless to argue that the present delays are more in the interests of economic actors than otherwise still seems to be going too far. The widely read and authoritative financial daily, *il Sole 24 ore*, which is owned by the *Confindustria* employers' association, certainly treats delay as a serious problem and it regularly denounces the inefficiency of Italy's courts. Indeed this newspaper is the main public source of information about court delay.

In Friedman's terms, the question remains, why does the pressure of 'external legal culture' not produce a more responsive and efficient system? To explain this we must focus more carefully on the 'internal legal culture' of jurists and practitioners and try to make sense of their attitudes and actions.

---

[57] In Continental systems the profession of notaries plays a vital institutionalised role in guaranteeing the validity of documents and transactions such as those involved in the sale or purchase of property and the construction of companies.

[58] Marc Galanter, ' Why the haves come out ahead' 1974 8 Law and Society Review, 95-160

From the President of the Republic down, public discourse is uniformly and repetitively critical of legal delay. At each ceremonial opening of the legal year the head judge of the Legal system and the heads of individual court districts ritually deplore delay. Indeed they use the level of backlog as a measure of the progress they have (or have not) achieved in the running of their courts. Ministers of Justice likewise underline this problem as their priority. But most of the jurists who construct and debate procedural reforms are opposed, as a matter of principle, to treating law as only or mainly a matter of good management. Many such jurists see it as a pre-eminent task for law not to compromise its ideals and procedures. For example, The Padua conference on reasonable trial lengths, was punctuated by unflattering references to Bentham, utilitarianism, managerialism, and pragmatism. And mention of some trials in Denmark taking no more than twenty-three days were greeted with laughter!·

Legal processes are seen to need lawyer's expertise. By comparison with Anglo American legal cultures lay participation in judicial matters is highly restricted and even Justices of the Peace are required to have law degrees. Sometimes delay is admitted to be just an unfortunate side- effect of what fair procedure requires. But, more often, ' Law' and 'administration' are presented as potentially competing discourses, and the transformation of law into administration a danger to be exorcised. A distinction is sometimes made between 'effectiveness' (which is relative to aim), and acceptable, and 'efficiency ' which is assumed to sideline questions of ideal aims into sordid questions of costs and benefits. Because the law must be equal for all, there is resistance to introducing special procedures for different types of cases at either a formal or informal level. Greater effort is dedicated to maintaining the greatest possible right to trial before a professional judge than in any other comparable common law or civil law systems. Interestingly, delay itself may even be seen as valuable. One experienced family lawyer whom I interviewed said it was right for family separation cases to take the time they did because of all the emotions involved. [59] And a speaker at the Padua conference on legal delay offered a variety of reasons why delay could be considered valuable in criminal cases. [60]

Jurists become highly learned in the arts of procedure. Some even snub their colleagues who deal with mere substantive law! When practising in the courts as lawyers they are skilled in using the time

---

[59] By contrast the Strasbourg court of Human Rights sees delay in cases involving personal status as particularly heinous.

[60] He argued that delay could helps the victim get over the effect of the crime; that the trial is (and should be) the punishment for the offender; and that the passage of time allows the judge to see the effects of the crime on the victim and society. In general, delay creates a necessary distance to both the victim and the offender and may make conciliation and mediation possible. Where appropriate it allows the victim and society to see that they were 'co-responsible' for the crime.

factor as one of the key pragmatic and practical considerations which facilitates the exchange and compromise needed to gain advantage in the cases they defend. But they almost never discuss these practicalities when engaged in politico- legal debate. By contrast, on the criminal side especially, at the level of actual practice many judges and prosecutors do try to indicate priorities and introduce 'virtuous' organisational practices so as to prevent what they see as distortions of legal procedure from leading to paralysis of the system. These include the use of 'do it yourself' techniques that hide behind the 'myth of obligatory prosecution' of all reported crimes, in an effort to avoid falling foul of time- limitation rules. [61] Rather than being credited with keeping the system going, however, resort to these practices is seen as bordering on the employment of legally improper and discreditable discretion.

As this suggests, it would be a mistake to draw too sharp a contrast between 'external legal culture' with its demand for accessabile and speedy justice, and a unified 'internal legal culture' with its disdain for other than self regarding legal values. Apart from the interests in greater through put of some of those in the system (especially those in Directive roles), accessible and speedy justice are also legal values in themselves which can and do find some way of being recognised by the system. The question is rather *how* the Italian legal system defines acceptable and unacceptable delay through its rules, jurisprudence and everyday practice. At the level of legal doctrine, for example, there are different time limits for penal and civil cases, special rules for urgent civil cases, and special procedures for certain types of cases. In Italy the legislator has given priority to cases where workers risk losing their jobs. By contrast, in the New York courts, which were the first to be studied socio- legally, priority was given to business cases, and it was this which allegedly led to increasing delay in other kinds of cases.[62] If any remedies for delay are to take effect they will have to engage with the autopoietic definitions of the system, both in doctrine and the 'law in action', for it these that determine how it allocates its scarce resources. [63]

---

[61] David Nelken and Letizia Zanier, 'Tra norme e prassi: durata del processo penale e strategie degli operatori del diritto', forthcoming in <u>Sociologia del diritto</u>.

[62] Harry Kalven and Harry Zeisel, *Delay in the Courts* (1959).

[63] Reducing legal delay requires an understanding of how to co-ordinate the times of all the actors involved, legal and otherwise. The process cannot move faster than that of its slowest component. But there is no reason why the courts have to be the slowest of these. See Thomas Durkin, Robert Dingwall, William LF Felstiner, *Plaited Cunning: Manipulating Time in Asbestos Litigation* (1990).

Equally, the legal procedural values which help produce delay are shared by political elites and many others in the wider society. This is particularly clear on the penal side. In fact, no analysis of legal culture in Italy would do more than scrape the surface if it did not reckon with the historically shaped mutually interlocking distrust of the state found both on the Right and the Left. After the war there was an understandable reaction against the role of State run courts during the excesses of Fascism. In addition it was unclear whether it would be the Communists or the Christian Democrats who would prevail electorally, and hence which of these would be obliged to endure the hegemony of their ideological enemies. The post war constitution granted judges and prosecutors high degree of constitutionally entrenched autonomy and self-government and over the next thirty years an ambitious scheme of self-governing autonomy of the judges was put into place. Increasingly this autonomy from the state came to favour the Communist party that was permanently excluded from the changing government coalitions put together by the Christian Democrats. And eventually it allowed prosecutors and judges to bring down all the parties of government simply by applying established criminal law.[64]

The fear of placing discretion in the hands of political opponents continues to justify the maintenance of unrealistic, redundant and mutually controlling institutions with high procedural safeguards. At the Padua conference a leading law professor sympathetic to the Berlusconi government and active in politics said in his presentation that he would not feel 'protected' if Italy was to remove the appeal stage in criminals cases, even though it is functionally redundant under the newly introduced accusatorial system.' In this culture and at this time', he said, 'we do not benefit from the settled political consensus characteristic of Anglo - Saxon polities'. A law professor on the Left, on the other hand, argued that, in order to avoid the power to prosecute coming under the control of (corrupt) governments it was necessary to maintain the rule of obligatory prosecution, despite the fact that this is either a fig leaf for discretionary decision making or the cause of unmanageable delay. Better that delay serve as the 'functional equivalent' of discretion than allow one's political rivals the choice of who to prosecute, or let off. In this as in so many other ways structure and culture are symbiotic.

---

[64] See for example, 'David Nelken 'A Legal Revolution? The Judges and Tangentopoly,' in Stephen Gundle and Simon Parker (eds) *The New Italian Republic: From the fall of the Berlin wall to Berlusconi* (1995), 191-206; David Nelken 'Judicial Politics and Corruption in Italy' in David Nelken and Mike Levi (eds) *The Corruption of Politics and the Politics of Corruption*: special issue of the *Journal of Law and Society* (1996), 95-113, and David Nelken ' Il significato di Tangentopoli: La risposte giudiziaria alla corruzione e i suoi limiti ' in Luciano Violante (ed) *Storia d'Italia 14: Legge, Diritto e Giustizia*, (1997), 597- 627.

It could be objected that delays in the civil courts have less to do with the degree of autonomy possessed by prosecutors and more to do with the general weaknesses of the public administration. But it is what happens in the criminal courts that sets the agenda for court reform. Moreover, criminal courts handle a far wider range of issues than is true in Anglo - American polities. As just one example, lawyers in tort claims in road accident cases regularly rely almost entirely on the evidence collected by the public prosecutor in connected criminal proceedings. And criminal courts have regularly drained resources from the civil courts as they responded to the emergencies of terrorism, organised crime, and, more recently political corruption.

3. Legal delay, Legal culture and General culture in Italy

What else can legal delay tell us about the connection between legal culture and other aspects of daily life in Italy as compared to elsewhere? Certainly, the rhythms of law and life are in some ways similar. From a comparative perspective, many aspects of social life also move more slowly in Italian culture than in Northern Europe or the USA. Relationships typically depend on family or family -like group allegiances that take a long time to build up. People, are slow to leave home, they like to live near where they grew up and to keep very close contact with their families. Ties that are slow to build are also difficult to end. For the groups that occupy key roles in social, economic and political life, co-option is the norm, seniority is of considerable importance, and merit is gained to a large extent simply by *waiting* ones turn. In matters which involve government or public agencies queuing is inevitable, the case file must be followed through all it stages, and it may sometimes be necessary to intervene, personally or preferably through an important intermediary, to secure a successful outcome. There is much in common between the inefficient and over bureaucratised justice system and the cumbersome and deliberately unresponsive bureaucratic machine that takes refuge in legal formalities and is uninterested in outcomes. Many of the delays attributed to inefficient courts, so called 'malgiustizia', in fact represent efforts by the courts to deal with the results of poor administration or so- called 'maladministrazione'.

On the other hand, we should be wary of treating the slowness of court processes in Italy as just an extension of patterns in the wider culture. In its private sector, Italian firms provide fierce international competition on delivery dates and service; the delay of the courts therefore seems rather to be indicative of the much complained of differences between the 'public' sector and the 'private' sector, another aspect of the poor infrastructure that Italian business has to tolerate. Even more than is the case in many other modern societies everyday social and economic life follows its own patron - client logics behind a veneer of state legal norms. Social actors may resort to law as a weapon so as to challenge or at least delay decisions that would otherwise take place according to these other norms. For the weak -as well as for the powerful -delay may sometimes be a solution and not always a problem.

But those who have only legal remedies to rely on can in some senses be held 'to blame' for not being in sufficiently good standing in wider social hierarchies or groupings as to be able to use more privileged routes or alternatives to vindicate their claims. It is appropriate that those using legal remedies put up with the considerable time these take to bear fruit. An important consequence, even if not necessarily the cause, of court delay is thus the way it reinforces such dependence on social hierarchy[65], and maintains the importance of group allegiances as compared to the individualistic assertion of rights. Whatever other benefits they might bring, more effective court dispute mechanisms might replace or attenuate such bonds.. Delay may also be integrative in other, yet stranger, ways. In the Italian context for example it allows everyone, including politicians and state employees, to blame 'the state' and feel united against it!

Legal delay in Italy should therefore be treated not just as an indicator of waiting times but also as a measure of the distance between legal culture and general culture. This 'gap' is in part deliberate, as in the way the criminal law tries to maintain principles of impersonal equality before the law at all stages of the penal process precisely because elsewhere clientilistic and other particularistic practices are so widespread. But it means more generally that the courts are often quite out of touch with widely accepted practices. Thus in Italy a central issue of late has been the question of where the role of the judges does (and should) stop and that of other authorities begin. This has led to a running battle between the judiciary and the politicians. Every day the newspapers carry stories about allegedly improper inference by one side with the prerogatives of the other. On the one hand the judges see themselves as preventing the powerful escaping the exercise of 'jurisdiction', as they term the boundaries of law's empire; on the other hand, some politicians complain of the exercise of political biased interventions by the judges.[66]

In the end, the lengthy court delays of the Italian legal system may be one price to be paid for what is an extreme form of legal independence from political control. Courts in this type of polity (and the legal culture which goes with it) can, if needs be, take action against the most powerful in the land.

---

[65] Douglas Hay, in *Albion's Fatal Tree* (1976), provides a brilliant interpretation of the reason why the increasing passage of legislation carrying the death penalty in 18th Century England was accompanied by relatively low implementation of this penalty (especially after the possibility of transportation). He explains that, because avoidance of the death penalty required the obtaining of a 'pardon', its 'latent function ' was to reinforce the systems of hierarchical dependence by which those of lower status were reminded that they might one day need to turn for help to their social superiors.
[66] David Nelken, 'Legitimate Suspicion? Berlusconi and the Judges', in Paulo Segatti and J. Blondel (eds) *The Second Berlusconi Government* (2003), 112-128.

But, clearly, this level of activism cannot be sustained on an everyday basis without upsetting those social norms that are geared to the reproduction of social hierarchies. The *Tangentopoli* anti–corruption investigations themselves demonstrate both the exception and the rule as far as the place of legal delay within legal culture is concerned. In the special political circumstances of the early 1990's (in particular the collapse of the Iron curtain), ruling politicians lost legitimacy as soon as the newspapers released the information that they had been sent 'advice' that legal proceedings were being taken against them for corruption. But most of these cases then took a large number of years to actually run their course and virtually no one went to jail. The cycle of corruption scandals has now come to an end. The current Berlusconi government has found that there is much to gain from exploiting and increasing the possibilities of postponing cases where its own legitimacy and interests are at stake. At the same time, however, it regularly accuses the judges of being the major cause of disgraceful delays.[67]

---

[67] Ibid.

[12]

THE LAW AS A SOCIAL PRACTICE:
*Are Shared Activities at the Foundations of Law?**

Matthew Noah Smith
Yale University

A central tenet of positivism is that social practices are at the foundations of law. This has been cashed out in a variety of ways. For example, Austin argues that, among other practices, a habit of obedience to a sovereign is at the foundations of law, and Hart argues that at the foundations of law is the converging attitudes and behaviors of a class of relevant officials. Since Hart, some prominent positivists have employed either David Lewis's analysis of conventions or Michael Bratman's theory of shared cooperative activities to develop new accounts of the social practices that are at the foundations of law, whatever those foundations might be. In this paper, I identify five features characteristic of the Lewisean and Bratmanian models of social facts—models of what I call *hypercommittal* social practices. I then show that models of social facts that have these features ought not to be used to explain the way in which a social practice is at the foundations the law. I conclude that hypercommittal social practices such as Lewisean conventions or Bratmanian shared activities are not at the foundations of law.

I. INTRODUCTION

The legal theorist Scott Shapiro puts it well: "Legal philosophers never tire of saying that the law is a social practice. But what precisely does this dreary bit of jurisprudential boilerplate mean?"[1] One approach among analytic legal philosophers when answering this question has been to employ either David Lewis's analysis of conventions or Michael Bratman's analysis of joint intentional actions and shared cooperative activities to explain how law is social practice.[2]

---

*I thank Jules Coleman, George Bealer, James Woodbridge, and Troy Cross for valuable conversations about these issues. I also thank the participants of the 2006 Analytical Legal Philosophy Conference at UCLA and two anonymous referees for extremely helpful comments on earlier drafts of this paper.

1. Scott Shapiro, Legal Practice and Massively Shared Agency (unpublished manuscript), at 1.

2. For a representative sample of the Lewisean approach, *see* Gerald Postema, *Coordination and Convention at the Foundations of Law*, 11 J. LEGAL STUD. 185 (1982); Jules Coleman, *Negative and Positive Positivism*, 11 J. LEGAL STUD. 139 (1982); Gerald Postema, *Conventions at the Foundations of Law*, in 1 THE NEW PALGRAVE DICTIONARY OF ECONOMICS AND THE LAW 465–472 (P. Newman ed., 1998); Jules Coleman, *Incorporationism, Conventionality and the Practical*

But there is an ambiguity here. For what are legal philosophers talking about when they say that the law is a social practice? Since the publication of H.L.A. Hart's *The Concept of Law*, contemporary positivists are often just talking about the rule of recognition.[3] Hart argues that a rule of recognition is at the foundation of law and that the rule of recognition exists only when it is practiced by the relevant officials. The mystery philosophers of law faced, then, was to explain what it meant for a rule of recognition to be practiced by the relevant officials (a gesture in the direction of the internal point of view is quite clearly insufficient). To resolve this mystery, some philosophers appeal to Lewis's account of conventions or to Bratman's account of shared agency. Often, the choice of framework—Lewisean, Bratmanian, or some other framework—and the tweaks to that framework for analyzing the rule of recognition as a social practice are designed to address one of the battery of arguments that Ronald Dworkin and like-minded philosophers have launched against Hartian positivism.[4]

With one or two exceptions, those who have attempted to develop a theory of how the rule of recognition is a Lewisean convention or a Bratmanian shared activity have abandoned this project.[5] Accordingly, some legal theorists who were once leading proponents of the view that the rule

---

Difference Thesis, in HART'S POSTSCRIPT 99–148 (Jules Coleman ed., 2001); and ANDREI MARMOR, POSITIVE LAW AND OBJECTIVE VALUES (2001), esp. ch. 1. *See also* Eerik Lagerspetz, THE OPPOSITE OF MIRRORS: AN ESSAY ON THE CONVENTIONALIST THEORY OF INSTITUTIONS (1995), ch. 7. Postema, who was the first to use a Lewisean framework to explain how rules of recognition are social rules, presumes that the function of rules of recognition is the resolution of recurrent coordination problems. But one need not adopt this view to be a conventionalist about the law. This is important because Leslie Green has provided a very strong argument against taking fundamental legal rules—rules of recognition—to be Lewisean conventions whose function is to solve a recurrent coordination problem. *See* Leslie Green, *Positivism and Conventionalism*, 12 CAN. J. LAW & JURISPRUDENCE 35 (1999). Marmor, *id.*, argues that one can be a conventionalist without endorsing the view that the aim of the rule of recognition is resolution of recurrent coordination problems. Lewis's account of conventions is found in DAVID LEWIS, CONVENTION: A PHILOSOPHICAL STUDY (1969). For a representative sample of the Bratmanian approach, *see* Christopher Kutz, *The Judicial Community*, 11 PHIL. ISSUES 442 (2001); Scott Shapiro, *Laws, Plans, and Practical Reason*, 8 LEGAL THEORY 387 (2002); and JULES COLEMAN, PRACTICE OF PRINCIPLE (2001). For Bratman's views, *see* MICHAEL BRATMAN, FACES OF INTENTION (1999), chs. 5–8.

3. H.L.A. HART, THE CONCEPT OF LAW (Raz and Bullock, eds., 2d ed., 1994).

4. *See* RONALD DWORKIN, *Model of Rules I*, in TAKING RIGHTS SERIOUSLY 14 (1977); and *Model of Rules II*, in *id.*, 46. *See also* RONALD DWORKIN, LAW'S EMPIRE (1986). Postema and Coleman, in their groundbreaking articles (Postema, *Convention and Coordination at the Foundation of Law*, *supra* note 2; and Coleman, *Negative and Positive Positivism*, *supra* note 2) that established this approach to analyzing the way in which the rule of recognition is a social rule, were responding to some of Dworkin's objections to Hart. There have been too many epicycles of this debate to cite all the relevant literature. I do not mean to suggest that Razian objections to Hart have not played a role in shaping how people have thought about the rule of recognition as a social practice. But by a wide margin, Dworkin's objections and the objections of those who are sympathetic to Dworkin's position—whatever the merit of these objections—have been the primary source of the hurdles philosophers of law have had to clear in their reflections about how to conceive of the social practice of the rule of recognition.

5. The most important exception is MARMOR, *supra*, note 2, who defends a modified Lewisean conventionalist account of the rule of recognition.

of recognition is some kind of conventional social norm have turned their attentions away from working out how rules of recognition in particular are social practices and back toward the old question of working out how the foundations of law are social practices, whatever those foundations might be.[6] In this paper, I argue against continuing to employ certain models of social practices to explain how the foundations of law are social practices.

When exploring this issue, one must be careful to distinguish claims about the social practices at the foundations of law based upon purported conceptual truths about law (e.g., Raz argues that a conceptual truth about the law is that it claims authority and so the social practices at the foundation of law must be ones that somehow allow for such a claim) and claims about social practices at the foundations of law based upon claims about law that are not conceptual truths (e.g., there is often disagreement among legal officials about the criteria of legal validity and so the social practices at the foundation of law must not be fatally disrupted by such disagreement).[7] In this article, I defend a view based upon claims about the law that I do not take to be conceptual truths. In particular, I argue that given some noncontroversial facts about contemporary legal systems, a certain class of models of social facts of which the Bratmanian theory of shared activity and Lewisean model of conventions are members—models of what I call *hypercommittal*[8] social practices—ought not to be used to explain the way in which the law is a social practice.[9] Looking closely at Bratman's view in particular, I identify five features that I take to be characteristic of hypercommittal social practices. I argue that many legal systems fail to have these features. On the basis of this, I conclude that conceptual analyses of social practices as hypercommittal ought not to be employed as frameworks to analyze how the foundations of law are social practices. In short, I aim to show that the foundations of law are not hypercommittal social practices (from here on,

---

6. *See* Shapiro, *Law, Plans, and Practical Reason*, *supra* note 2, in which Shapiro argues for a Bratmanian theory of legal authority; and Shapiro, Legal Practice as Massively Shared Agency, *supra* note 1, in which Shapiro argues for a novel theory of legal institutions as social practices. In COLEMAN, PRACTICE OF PRINCIPLE, *supra* note 2, Coleman's suggestion that we might analyze the rule of recognition as a Bratmanian shared activity turns out to be a suggestion that we analyze legal systems as Bratmanian social practices (I say more about this below). Gerald Postema now focuses his attention on the overall practice of the law and not just the rule of recognition. *See* Gerald Postema, *Law's Melody*, 7 ASSOCIATIONS 227 (2003); and *Melody and Law's Mindfulness of Time*, 17 RATIO JURIS 203 (2004). *See also* Kutz, *supra* note 2.

7. Conversations with Jules Coleman have helped me to see the wide-ranging significance of this point.

8. Shelly Kagan first used this term in a Yale Law School seminar in the Spring 2006 semester when discussing Shapiro, Legal Practice and Massively Shared Agency, *supra* note 1.

9. Two other important members are Margaret Gilbert's and Raimo Tuomela's theories of social practices. Gilbert's main work is MARGARET GILBERT, ON SOCIAL FACTS (1989). She discusses Hart at length in GILBERT, SOCIALITY AND RESPONSIBILITY (2000), ch. 5. A relevant sample of Tuomela's view is Raimo Tuomela & Kaarlo Miller, *We-Intentions*, 53 PHIL. STUD. 367 (1988). Neither Gilbert's nor Tuomela's views have been incorporated into Anglo-American jurisprudence to the degree to which Lewis's and Bratman's have been.

when I use the phrase "the law is a social practice" and phrases like that, I mean something like "the foundations of law are social practices").[10]

My conclusion may be reminiscent of Dworkin's criticisms of Hartian positivism (and his criticisms of positivism in general). In brief, Dworkin argues that there is far too much disagreement in the practice of law for the foundations of law to be conventional social norms. My line of argument, although focused on disagreement, is nonetheless distinct from Dworkin's and therefore does not suffer from some of the well-known problems from which his suffer.[11] Thus although some Dworkinians may find my skeptical conclusions about taking the foundations of law to be a social practice to be old news, I believe I am offering a novel set of arguments.

Before diving into the body of the discussion, I shall introduce an important caveat. Nothing I say in this paper is meant to be an objection to Lewis's theory of conventions or Bratman's theory of shared activities. My only goal is to raise worries about analyzing the social practices at the foundations of law using the Lewisean or Bratmanian frameworks. Neither Lewis nor Bratman ever argue that all social practices should be analyzed according to their respective models. In Lewis's case, he is interested entirely in conventions understood as solutions to iterated coordination problems and he makes clear that he does not take every social practice to be a solution to an iterated coordination problem.[12] Bratman also self-consciously describes his project as modeling shared agency only and not all social practices.[13]

The paper proceeds as follows. In Section II, I give a formal account of what we mean by the claim that the law is a social practice. In Section III, drawing on Joseph Raz's work, I give a very brief and preliminary formal explanation of what people in legal systems do. Sections IV and V are the heart of the paper. In these sections, I give an overview of the Bratmanian theory of shared activity, I give an example of its use as a framework for an analysis of legal institutions, I identify five defining features of the Bratmanian framework, and finally, I explain why the Bratmanian

---

10. To be clear, my argument does not rest on the claim either that the law in some community is identical to a social practice or that the law is identical to some set of legal institutions.
11. Dworkin's misreading of Hart in Dworkin, *Model of Rules II*, supra note 4, is well known. For a recent and relevant criticism of the semantic sting argument, see Kenneth Einar Himma, *Ambiguously Stung: Dworkin's Semantic Sting Reconfigured*, 8 LEGAL THEORY 145 (2002).
12. See LEWIS, *supra* note 2, ch. 1.
13. Although he suggests that his analysis can be extended to cover large-scale social practices when he writes in *Shared Cooperative Activity* in BRATMAN, *supra* note 2, at 94:

> Such shared cooperative activities can involve large numbers of participating agents and can take place within a complex institutional framework—consider the activities of a symphony orchestra following its conductor. But to keep things simple I will focus here on shared cooperative activities that involve only a pair of participating agents and are not the activities of complex institutions with structures of authority.

See also *I Intend that We J* in BRATMAN, *supra* note 2, at 144, in which Bratman asks whether his account of shared agency picks out just one species of shared agency from a broader genus of shared agency. He says nothing of institutions or large-scale social practices.

analysis of shared activities is a poor framework for analyzing modern legal systems.

II. SOCIAL PRACTICES

When we say that the law is a social practice, we are making two claims. First, we are saying that the law is to be understood in terms of something that people do. That is what we mean when we say that the law is a social *practice*. Second, we are saying that the law is to be understood in terms of something that people do together. That is what we mean when we say that the law is a *social* practice. So what we need to explain when we say that the law is a social practice is what it is that people in legal systems do together and how it is that they do it together.

In a trivial way, everyone who is alive, insofar as they are doing something, is doing something together, namely being alive. But that just reflects an ambiguity in the term "together." Sometimes (but not all the time) we say people are doing something together if we use the same term to describe what it is that they are doing and they are doing that thing contemporaneously. So everyone in New York City who is at this moment riding the subway is riding the subway together. This is very loose usage and applies just as well to animals as it does to persons: cows graze in a pasture together, and alligators sun on the riverbank together. The stricter sense in which we use the term "together" to describe people's activity is when there is some kind of *systematic unity* to the activity, for example as when friends share a meal together or musicians play music in a band or orchestra together.[14]

When philosophers try to explain social practices, most of their energy is spent on trying to explain what is going on when we do things together in the stricter sense I describe above—the sense in which there is a systematic unity of the activity. It is fair to say, then, that the philosophy of social practices is primarily an inquiry into the systematic unity of social practices. This is what Bratman seeks to explain when he gives an analysis of joint intentions and shared cooperative activity.[15] This is a worthwhile project because it is mysterious how it is that individuals, who are not separable components of a superagent, manage to do things together in ways that exhibit the systematic unity described above.

On the other hand, what it is that we do together (as opposed to what it is to do something together) when we do things together is not really in its own right a subject of philosophical analysis. For there are innumerably many and heterogeneous things we can do together, from painting a house to

---

14. Some of these examples are from Postema, *Law's Melody, supra* note 6, at 227.
15. For example, Bratman writes in *Shared Intention* in BRATMAN, *supra* note 2, at 110: "Supposing, for example, that you and I have a shared intention to paint the house together, I want to know in what that shared intention consists." Bratman aims to explicate what makes the shared intention *shared*, i.e., what gives the systematic unity characteristic of sharing to a collection of intentions held by individual persons.

participating in a massive legal system. The only philosophically interesting generalizations we can make about the class of things we can do together will be made when working out what it is to do something together. Nonetheless, it is important when talking about a specific institution to spell out what people are doing together in that institution so that we have an idea of where to look for the systematic unity.[16]

So when we say that the foundations of law are social practices, we are saying something like the following: there are foundational components of the law that should be understood as systematically unified activities. Perhaps the rule of recognition is a legal entity that should be understood as a social practice. Certainly, legislatures, courts and administrative agencies such as police departments and prisons are, for the most part, social practices and so are systematically unified activities. We have no single term that comfortably refers to all and only these components of the law that are social practices. Nonetheless, I shall use the term "legal institution" to refer to those features of the law that the positivist takes to be susceptible to analysis as a social practice. This is an imperfect solution, because there are some legal institutions that are not best understood as social practices and there are features of the law that may be analyzable as social practices but that are not best understood as institutions. But it will do for my purposes. An analysis of legal institutions as social practices therefore involves giving an account of both the activities constitutive of the institution and the systematic unity of those constitutive activities.

III. WHAT PEOPLE DO IN LEGAL INSTITUTIONS

Drawing heavily on Joseph Raz's formal discussion of institutionalized systems of norms, I stipulate here a simple, general account of what people do in legal institutions.[17] The point of this account is to pick out some characteristic activities constitutive of legal institutions and not to give a definition or a list of necessary and sufficient conditions for some activity to be an activity in a legal institution.

---

16. For example, suppose we are trying to explain the systematic unity of the institution of baseball teams (as a class of social practice). It is important to specify what the activities of baseball teams are when explaining the systematic unity of baseball teams. For a baseball team may also regularly have an NCAA March Madness basketball pool. But this is not part of the social practice that is part of the social practice constituting baseball teams, because regularly engaging in basketball pools is not a standard thing people do when they are on baseball teams together (even though basketball pools may also be a social practice). Citing participation in the basketball pool as part of a general account of the institution of a baseball team would therefore be an error (even if it might be relevant for a more specific historian's account of the institution that is some particular baseball team).

17. *See, esp.,* Joseph Raz, Practical Reason and Norms (2d ed. 1990), at 123–148. *See also* Raz's criticisms of Kelsen in Raz, The Concept of a Legal System (2d. ed., 1980), at 95–109; and his discussion of the relation of law and state in Raz, The Authority of Law (1979), at 97–102. For the law claiming legitimate authority, *see* Raz, Authority of Law, ch. 1.

The Law as a Social Practice:

Legal institutions are, broadly speaking, relatively stable integrated social practices that make possible the creation and/or application (i.e., the production, interpretation, and/or enforcement) by third-party formal agents of rules governing a bounded domain of agents not entirely coextensive with the domain of third-party formal agents. Thus institutions are stable social practices that (a) have some kind of internal, self-sustaining structure that ensures stability and integration; (b) provide guidance to those governed by the institution by the production, propagation, and/or enforcement of rules; (c) include formal agents whose practices sustain the institution and apply the rules of the institution.[18] Let us call the third-party formal agents *officials of the institution* (or just *officials*).[19] Officials are third-party agents in the sense that they create and apply rules that, for the most part, govern agents other than themselves (although the rules they create and apply might govern other officials). There is one set of rules that establishes the institution and governs the functioning of the institution. And there is one set of rules created and/or applied by the officials of the institution that govern private individuals (and some officials qua officials).[20] Both sets of rules are legal rules, or, as we often call them, *laws* (I do not mean to assume here that all laws are strictly speaking rules and not Dworkinian-style principles). Let us, more or less following Hart, call the second set of rules *primary rules*.[21] And for ease of exposition, let us take it to be the case that primary rules are directed at private individuals (even though they may just as often be directed at officials, corporations, and other institutions). The most distinctive (although neither only nor necessary) job of officials is to settle disputes among private individuals about primary rules, in particular disputes about what the primary rules require of the private individuals.[22] In some cases, this will require officials creating and/or applying laws that are members of the first set of rules, namely, those that structure the institution. In most cases, though, the officials will simply apply existing primary rules.

---

18. This view is designed to rule out as institutions informal conventional norms such as conversational norms and governance by consensus of the sort Quaker communities seek to achieve. On conversational norms, *see* ERVING GOFFMANN, RELATIONS IN PUBLIC (1980).

19. Following Joseph Raz, I leave aside for another day spelling out the identifying characteristics of officials. In particular, the most difficult thing to spell out is what it is for an official to be a formal official as opposed to an informal official. This is a very difficult question to answer and one that I need not settle now, given the purposes of this paper (although I have something to say about this below). *See* Raz, PRACTICAL REASON, *supra* note 17, at 133. I later include as officials of legal institutions practicing private attorneys.

20. Once again, I follow Raz here. *See id.*

21. I take primary rules not only to be simple rules directed at individual agents but also rules that set priorities and targets, allocate resources, and stipulate long-term plans governing those who engage in some practice. Here I am following Edward Rubin in his discussion of administrative agencies. *See, e.g.*, Edward Rubin, *Law and Legislation in the Administrative State* 89 COLUM. L. REV. 369 (1989); and Edward Rubin, *It's Time to Make the Administrative Procedure Act Administrative*, 89 CORNELL L. REV. 96 (2002).

22. RAZ, AUTHORITY OF LAW, *supra* note 17, at 132–137.

I assume that the legal institutions in which contemporary philosophers of law are interested are modern legal institutions. In such institutions, the officials are not only judges and legislators but also are lawyers, police officers, officers of the court, and bureaucrats in administrative agencies that are created by legislation in order to apply policies that have been duly legislated. I also assume that the population of officials is a heterogeneous population composed of people from diverse backgrounds, from different generations, and with different political commitments.

We can summarize, in dirty simplicity, the activity that is characteristic of legal institutions as follows: officials create and apply primary rules. So when a positivist seeks to explain how legal institutions are social practices, he seeks to explain how officials create and apply laws *together*. Or, to put it in more complex terms: the positivist seeks to explain how it is that a collection of very many and very different people can create and apply laws in a manner that displays the systematic unity necessary for those activities of creating and applying laws to constitute the social practice of a legal institution. This is where Bratman's theory of joint intentional and shared cooperative activities comes in.

IV. THE BRATMANIAN FRAMEWORK

There is more than one theory of social practices. But some very important Anglo-American legal philosophers have appealed to either the Lewisean theory of conventions or the Bratmanian theory of shared activity as preferred theories of social practices.[23] Both theories explicate social practices by appeal to explicit beliefs, knowledge, and/or intentions of agents. In this section, I explore this feature of these theories by way of a discussion of the Bratmanian analysis of shared activity. Although I do not discuss Lewis's theory, those familiar with it—or at least with how it has been deployed by analytic legal philosophers—will see that my reflections about Bratman's account apply to Lewis's as well.

A. Overview

Bratman identifies the following two conditions that must be met by agents in order for their activities to have the kind of systematic unity that a shared activity has:

(i) *Mutual responsiveness*: . . . each participating agent attempts to be responsive to the intentions and actions of the other, knowing that the other is attempting to be similarly responsive. Each seeks to guide his behavior with an eye to the behavior of the other, knowing that the other seeks to do likewise.

---

23. *See* references at note 2.

(ii) *Commitment to joint activity*: ... the participants each have an appropriate commitment (though perhaps for different reasons) to the joint activity, and their mutual responsiveness is in the pursuit of this commitment.[24]

If several persons' activity displays these features, then they are engaged in what Bratman calls "joint intentional action."[25]

This is a weak form of shared activity that does not rise to the level of cooperation. To see why, imagine two line cooks working in a professional kitchen. Each wants to see the other fail in front of the chef so that she can get a promotion, but neither can succeed on her own, because cooking dinner in a professional kitchen requires at least two people working together. So each has to play her part as long as the other plays her part (lest the chef sees one failing to play her part and then fires her on the spot), but neither will help the other out if the other fails to do her part. The two competitive line cooks in this example are not being cooperative, because in cooperative activity, which Bratman calls "shared cooperative activity," there is a commitment to mutual support. Bratman defines the condition in this way:

(iii) *Commitment to mutual support*: ... each agent is committed to supporting the efforts of the other to play her role in the joint activity. If I believe that you need my help to find your note [if singing a duet together] (or your paintbrush [if painting a house together]) I am prepared to provide such help; and you are similarly prepared to support me in my role. These commitments to each other put us in a position to perform the joint activity successfully even if we each need help in certain ways.[26]

When the first two—and better yet, all three—of these conditions are met with respect to some action, then the action will have the systematic unity of a social practice.

So how is it that at least two, if not all three, of these conditions can be met with respect to some action, J? Bratman explains how these three conditions can be met by developing a theory of shared intentions. His view is that it is in virtue of agents sharing intentions that an activity in which they are engaged is a shared activity. So Bratman explains the systematic unity of shared activity by appeal to shared intentions. Shared intentions, which are a state of affairs in which individuals' intentional states are interrelated in a certain way, have three roles. First, they coordinate individual intention action so as to achieve the aim of the shared intention. Second, shared intentions regulate our "subplans" so that they do not conflict (or, in Bratman's terms,

---

24. *See* Bratman, *Shared Cooperative Activity, in* BRATMAN, *supra* note 2, at 94–95.
25. Bratman names actions that meet these two conditions *jointly intentional actions* (JIAs) in *id.* at 104. Some of the caveats that apply to SCAs, though, surely apply to JIAs, such as, for example, the caveat that rules out what Bratman calls "pre-packaged cooperation" in *id.* at 106.
26. *Id.*

so that they mesh). Third, shared intentions are the backdrop against which bargaining about how to achieve the shared end proceeds.

What exactly are these shared intentions that make an activity a shared activity? Bratman is very careful to analyze shared intentions to J by way of meshing subplans in what he calls a "cooperatively neutral" manner. The reasons he does this are first, that Bratman rejects the possibility of a superagent intending to J; and second, that Bratman notes that it would be circular to explain shared agency by appeal simply to agents intending to cooperate. Instead, Bratman explains what a shared intention to J is in terms of each agent intending that all relevant agents achieve the same end (J-ing) by way of each acting in accordance with her own subplan that meshes with the subplans of the relevant other agents.[27] Thus Bratman's theory of shared intention, boiled down to a nutshell, is the following: agents have a shared intention to J when each agent has the intention to perform J with the other agents who intend to J, all by way of meshing subplans, which are components of an overall plan whose aim is J-ing.

What makes shared intentions *shared* is that they are *coreferential* and *interreferential*: the intentions reference the same end (and so are coreferential) and the intentions reference each other (and so are interreferential).[28] The interreferentiality of the intentions is due to the fact that Bratmanian mutual responsiveness is not responsiveness primarily to how other parties act but to the other parties' *intentions* to J by way of meshing subplans. In order that I can be responsive to your intentions, I must represent your intentions in my intentions (and so that you can be responsive to my intentions, you must represent my intentions in your intentions).[29] These interlocking intentions constitute the systematic unity within which mutually responsive and supportive actions occur.[30]

Here is Bratman's formalized analysis of the attitudes essential to a shared activity (SCA):

(1)(a)(i) I intend that we J.
(1)(a)(ii) I intend that we J in accordance with and because of meshing subplans of (1)(a)(i) and (1)(b)(i).

---

27. Bratman says a great deal more about this in *Shared Intention* and *I Intend that We J*, in BRATMAN, *supra* note 2. None of this is relevant to the objections I raise, although I will likely remind some readers of the objections Bratman addresses in these two articles.

28. This is what sets Bratman's shared intentions apart from mere we-intentions (as Searle calls them). We-intentions can be a single person's intention that we J without the other people in the extension of the "we" having that intention as well. Bratman's shared intentions are knit together by their co- and interreferentiality. On we-intentions, *see* JOHN SEARLE, *Collective Intentions and Actions, in* INTENTIONS IN COMMUNICATION (Cohen, Morgan, & Pollack eds., 1990), at 401–415.

29. In *Shared Intention*, in BRATMAN, *supra* note 2, at 123, Bratman writes: "[Shared intention] is a state of affairs that consists primarily in attitudes (none of which are themselves the shared intention) of the participants and interrelations between those attitudes."

30. Bratman writes, in *id*. at 112: "Our shared intention, then, performs at least three interrelated jobs: It helps coordinate our intentional actions; it helps coordinate our planning; and it can structure relevant bargaining."

(1)(b)(i) You intend that we J.
(1)(b)(ii) You intend that we J in accordance with and because of meshing subplans of (1)(a)(i) and (1)(b)(i).
(1)(c) The intentions in (1)(a) and in (1)(b) are not coerced by the other participant.
(1)(d) The intentions in (1)(a) and (1)(b) are minimally cooperatively stable.[31]
(2) It is common knowledge between us that (1).[32]

Bratman, acknowledging that the systematicity of the *intentions* is what provides the systematic unity of the shared activity, writes:

> It is the web of intentions cited in (1) that ensures the commitments to the *joint* activity characteristic of SCA.[33]

It is the systematicity—the webbiness—of these intentions as spelled out in (1) that constitutes the shared intention and makes possible the joint activity.[34] It is important that the systematicity is not a product of mere common knowledge. Rather, it is almost entirely product of the interreferentiality of the agents' mental states. The common-knowledge requirement may be an additional necessary condition to complete the theory, but common knowledge is ubiquitous in unshared activity as well and so is not an interesting component of shared activities.[35]

---

31. This is the condition ensuring commitment to mutual support.
32. Bratman, *Shared Cooperative Activity, in* BRATMAN, *supra* note 2, 105.
33. *Id.* at 102 (emphasis added). The point Bratman is making in this brief passage is not what ensures commitment to some action but what ensures commitment to a particular kind of action, namely, a shared activity. What ensures commitment is a matter of the reasons each agent takes herself to have for performing the shared activity, and this is not something with which Bratman is concerned (or could possibly have much to say).
34. To complete the overview of Bratman's position, let me state his definition of shared cooperative activity (in *id.* at 106):

For a cooperatively neutral J, our J-ing is an SCA if:

(A) we J;
(B) we have the attitudes specified in (1) and (2); and
(C) leads us to (A) by way of mutual responsiveness (in the pursuit of our J-ing) of intention and in action.

Conditions (A) and (B) are not relevant for my purposes because (A) adds only a success condition and (B) is already contained in the text accompanying footnote 32. (C) is of some interest because it makes explicit the causal connection between each agent's beliefs and intentions and her J-ing.

35. Consider a variation on Searle's example in which people sitting on the grass in the park suddenly get caught in a downpour and so all jump up and run for shelter. In the variation, each intends to run for shelter, each sees every other person running for shelter, and each correctly believes that every other person has the intention of running for shelter (and that every person believes that every other person has the intention of running for shelter). So the common-knowledge requirement is easily met, but this is quite clearly not a shared activity. *See* Searle, *supra* note 28.

B. Legal Institutions as Bratmanian Shared Activities

I will now explore one concrete example of a Bratmanian analysis of legal institutions in order to illustrate how Bratman's theory is used to analyze the way in which legal institution are social practices. The example is Jules Coleman's account of legal institutions as Bratmanian shared cooperative activities.[36] Although Coleman claims that this account is an account of how the rule of recognition is a shared cooperative activity, he is in fact wrong about his own view. For upon close inspection we can see that what Coleman is proposing is not a view about rules of recognition but of how *legal institutions* are shared cooperative activities.

Here is the most complete statement by Coleman of his view that the rule of recognition is a shared cooperative activity:

> Judges coordinate their behavior with one another through, for example, practices of precedent, which are ways in which they are responsive to the intentions of one another. The intention of an appellate court is that its decisions be binding on lower courts. Lower-court judges typically respond to these intentions by treating higher-court judges' decisions as constraints on their own behavior. The best explanation of judges' responsiveness to one another is their commitment to the goal of making possible the existence of a durable legal practice (though judges may have different reasons for thinking that a durable, sustained legal practice is desirable). Abiding by a practice of precedent is one way in which each judge helps the other do his part in fulfilling the aims of a legal practice.[37]

The parties who are engaged in the shared activity here are judges, so they are the ones who have an intention that they J together. But what is this J that the judges are intending to do together? Here is the rub. What the judges intend to do together is not merely to apply the criteria of legality, which is all that judges would be doing together if they had the shared intention that they follow the rule of recognition together. Rather, on Coleman's view, what the judges intend to do together is the business of "a durable legal practice."[38] The shared activity of the judges is the activity described in Section III above, namely, the application (and sometimes the creation) of primary rules *as well as* the application of secondary rules such as the rule of recognition.

---

36. In COLEMAN, PRACTICE OF PRINCIPLE, *supra* note 2, at 95–102. Coleman has since abandoned this account, but not on the grounds I present here. I am avoiding Shapiro's account of legal authority because it is too involved to spell out and I need only a sketch to serve as an example.

37. *Id.* at 97.

38. Coleman also describes the aim of the officials as the creation and sustenance of law:

> The practice of officials necessary to create and sustain law is a more general form of social coordination [than a Nash equilibrium solution to a game of partial conflict], a form that is otherwise familiar to us. Bratman has a plausible and attractive account of such practices and of their possibility conditions. (*Id.*)

So we have established who is engaged in the shared activity and what the shared activity is. What about the interlocking intentions? Let us begin with the coreferring intentions to J. Coleman carefully follows Bratman here when he points out that judges must explicitly share the intention to J together, which in this case must be an explicit intention to apply primary rules together: "...when [judges] participate jointly in SCA, [they] must share an intention that converges on a common goal—even if [their] reasons or motives for doing so are importantly different."[39] Coleman does not say how it is that judges manage to share this intention, but it seems uncharitable to suppose that there would be a problem explicating how this is achieved. This, then, accounts for the coreferentiality of judges' intentions.

But merely having coreferential intentions to J together is not sufficient; the agents must also have interreferential intentions, in particular, intentions to J together by way of meshing subplans. For example, if you and I intend to wash dishes together, we must have meshing subplans so that we can wash dishes *together* as opposed to the activity of washing dishes merely at the same time and in the same place. For example, suppose I have the subplan of soaping and rinsing and you have the subplan of drying (as opposed to both of us having the subplan of drying the dishes and neither having the subplan of soaping and rinsing the dishes). In order for us to wash dishes together, each of us must know of the other's subplan that is part of our larger shared plan to wash dishes together. That is, each of us must have intentions that successfully refer, somehow, to the other's intentions to wash the dishes. How, then, do the judges successfully form these sorts of intentions? According to Coleman, judges' subplans mesh when their decisions in the cases they hear and the published opinions explaining these decisions mesh in the appropriate manner. Judges' subplans are therefore expressed through the making of decisions and the production and publication of opinions, which in turn become precedent.

But, as noted above, it is not enough for shared activity that subplans mesh but that they mesh because of the general intention to J together (the judges' decisions might end up meshing only accidentally). For example, if we are going to wash dishes together, then it is not enough if it merely luckily turns out to be the case that I soap and rinse the dishes and then you dry them. Rather, I must intend to soap and rinse the dishes in accordance with your intention that we wash the dishes together and in accordance with your subplan to dry the dishes; and you must intend to dry the dishes in accordance with my intention that we wash dishes together and in accordance with my subplan to soap and rinse the dishes. Similarly, the decisions produced by judges must be, in some sense, components of the

---

39. *Id.* I have replaced the first-person plural in the original text with the term "judges" and the third-person plural because I take Coleman to be giving an analysis of how judges engage in shared cooperative activity.

overall plan to apply primary rules together. So each judge issues a decision (i.e., intends to do her part in the shared activity of applying laws) in accordance with all other judges' intentions that all judges apply laws and in accordance with all other judges' decisions. The meshing of judicial decisions with precedent is what it is for the subplans of the agents who are officials in a legal institution to mesh.

Finally, Coleman stresses how the judges' shared intention to apply rules provides a backdrop against which bargaining about how to achieve this shared end proceeds. This is how Coleman proposes to explain how there can be disputes about the content of the rule of recognition without such disputes undermining the shared activity that constitutes the legal institution.[40] In sum, then, Coleman's employment of the Bratmanian framework to analyze legal institutions involves judges sharing an intention to apply primary rules together. This shared intention plays a role in the mental lives of individual judges so that they form intentions (i.e., issue decisions and write opinions) in a way that makes possible the joint application of primary rules. In particular, this shared intention to apply primary rules allows for the formation by individual judges of intentions (i.e., the making of particular decisions and writing of particular opinions) that mesh, like, for example, lower-court judges intending their decisions to be consistent with the opinions of higher-court judges.

Thus Coleman employs the Bratmanian theory of shared activities to explain how legal institutions are social practices. He argues that judges have a certain kind of shared intention that knits together their activities into a shared action. As a result, their activities as judges have a systematic unity, and it is on the basis of this that the legal institution of which the judges are a part is a social practice.

In this section I summarize one way in which the Bratmanian framework has been used to explicate the way in which legal institutions are social practices. In the next section, I identify five core features that I believe this kind of analysis possesses. I then argue in the final section that analyses of social practices that are hypercommittal, such as Bratman's analysis of shared activity, which are used as frameworks for explaining how legal institutions are social practices in the way in which Coleman has done, are inadequate for the task.

C. Analysis

I focus on five features of Bratman's view of shared activities.[41] These five features are characteristic of what I am calling hypercommittal social

---

40. *See id.* at 97–98.
41. I think that Bratman's analysis of shared intention has these five features because his analysis of shared intention is meant to mirror his analysis of an individual's intention. Bratman writes: "Just as an individual's intention helps to 'organize and unify her individual agency over

practices. Because I take these to be central features of Bratman's view, each one of the five features would be a feature of any variation on a Bratmanian explanation of how legal institutions are social practices. Furthermore, at least one of these five features is characteristic of any theory of hyper-committal social practices, including Lewisean conventionalism, Gilbert's theory of cooperative activity, and Tuomela's theory of we-intentions. These features are also related to robust common-knowledge requirements that all these theories have, but I do not think that they are necessitated by that requirement.[42]

Before leaping in, I must note an important distinction between beliefs and intentions. Beliefs and intentions are distinct from one another primarily because they have different directions-of-fit (briefly put, beliefs aim at fitting the world as it is, whereas intentions aim at making the world fit to the content of the intention). If the direction-of-fit of a propositional attitude is a significant factor with regard to the content of the propositional attitude, those who wish to explain systematic unity of social practices in terms of the inter- and coreferentiality of the content of intentions owe us a more robust semantics of intentions and, in particular, a sketch of a theory of how intentions refer in the manner that facilitates co- and interreferentiality.[43] Some of the barriers to co- and interreferentiality I highlight below are therefore general problems that must be addressed in any theory of hypercommittal social practices.

The first characteristic feature of a Bratmanian analysis of social practices is *conceptual agreement* of the participating agents, by which I mean both extensional and intensional agreement of the agents' relevant beliefs and intentions.[44] If two parties are going to engage in a shared activity successfully, then each must have the intention "I intend that we J," which should be understood at least partially in terms of the intention "I intend to J in response to her intention to J." At first blush it seems sufficient for shared activity if the two parties' concepts of *J-ing* are extensionally equivalent.[45] And if this were sufficient, then full conceptual agreement would

---

time,' shared intention helps 'to organize and to unify our intentional agency."' *Shared Intention, in* BRATMAN, *supra* note 2, at 112.

By modeling shared agency on individual agency, then, Bratman presumes a level of semantic and epistemic transparency that one finds in individuals but which may not be the norm in larger groups.

42. Lewis's theory of conventions is the most well known and has among the strongest common-knowledge requirements. *See* LEWIS, *supra* note 2, at 52–68. But for comments on the demands of the common-knowledge requirement, *see* note 35.

43. The semantics of intentions that Bratman offers us is primarily a set of possibility conditions restricting the domain of possible contents of intentions. *See I Intend that We J* in BRATMAN, *supra* note 2, at 142–161. *See also* DONALD DAVIDSON, *Intending, in* ESSAYS ON ACTIONS AND EVENTS (1980), at 83–102.

44. A related issue is discussed in much greater depth in Jules Coleman & Ori Simchen, *"Law,"* 9 LEGAL THEORY 1 (2003).

45. For the J-ing that concerns us happens in the actual world and not in some merely possible world.

not be required because there can easily be cases of extensional equivalence with intensional divergence (e.g., "the current vice president of the United States" and "the man who shot Harry Whittington in February 2006" were in early 2006 extensionally equivalent but not intensionally equivalent). But what makes shared actions *shared* are the interlocking attitudes constitutive of shared intention. In particular, each party's intention must refer to the intention of the other party: "I intend to J in response to her intention to J" must be such that "her intention to J" refers to the other party's intention to J.[46] But in order to refer successfully, the intension of "J" in "her intention to J" has to be the same as the intension of "J" in my intention to J, or else my concept *her intention to J* will not get mapped onto her intention to J. Mere coextensionality will not do.[47] Thus, for parties who are J-ing together in an SCA, their concepts of J-ing have to be intensionally equivalent as well as extensionally equivalent.[48]

For example, suppose you say to me while we are standing on a basketball court and you are holding a basketball, "Let's play some ball." I respond, "Okay, let's play some ball." Now, it turns out that by "play some ball" you mean "practice one-on-one drives to the basket" and I mean "play pickup basketball." So although at first blush our intentions mesh—we both have the intention that we play some ball—upon closer inspection, it looks like you actually have the intention that *we practice one-on-one drives to the basket* and I actually have the intention that *we play pickup basketball.*[49] Our intentions are not intensionally equivalent even if they turn out to be extensionsionally equivalent in this instance (we might say that our intentions have the same "implementation conditions" but are not intentions to do the same thing).[50] In fact, prior to acting on our divergent intentions, we will have no reason to believe that we lack conceptual agreement, and it is even unlikely that once we engage in our activity we will gain new evidence for the belief

---

46. Another way to say this is to say that our intentions are not mediated entirely by the action we intend to perform but are in fact more directly related in virtue of the fact that they refer to each other. This makes sense because it is not entirely clear how our intentions can be connected solely in virtue of their object being an action that has not yet realized. Bratman writes: "In SCA each agent intends that the group perform the joint action in accordance with and because of meshing subplans of each participating agent's intention that the group so act." *Shared Cooperative Activity,* in BRATMAN, *supra* note 2, at 100.

47. So this is just another way to put the old Fregean point that within *de dicto* contexts there cannot be substitution *salva veritate* by merely coreferring terms.

48. Arguably, intensional equivalence is more important, because Bratman puts more weight on responsiveness to the intentions of others than on responsiveness to the actions of others.

49. It is worth noting here that we may never discover that we had different intentions because, as there are only two of us, practicing one-on-one drives and playing pickup basketball end up getting realized in more or less the same way.

50. In fact, they are not even extensionally equivalent. For each of us is playing a different game because the rules governing each of our behaviors are different. You are playing by the rules governing practicing one-on-one drives to the basket, and I am playing by the rules governing pickup basketball. So each of us is doing something different from the other even though it *looks* as though we are playing the same game. This is why I introduce the neologism "implementation conditions" instead of extension equivalence. I thank George Bealer for very illuminating discussions on this point.

that we lack conceptual agreement. So the situation is bleak: we not only lack conceptual agreement, we also lack reasons to believe that we lack conceptual agreement. Given these conditions, our intentions can easily fail to refer to each another and continue to fail to refer to each other even once we begin to engage in our respective actions. Thus, absent clear and public conceptual agreement, the systematic unity of our activities is blocked.[51]

Now this problem of conceptual disagreement can easily be rectified through limited communication. But this just makes clear that full conceptual agreement requires some sort of *commitment to conceptual agreement*. Parties who seek to share agency in the Bratmanian fashion must be committed both to establishing conceptual agreement and then, once it is established, to sustaining that conceptual agreement. Absent such commitment, if the joint activity extends over a long enough period of time, there is a strong possibility that the parties engaged in the shared activity may slowly come to have differing understandings of what they are up to. This, in turn, can lead to a case in which the parties merely appear to share intentions, as in the playing of pickup basketball/practicing one-on-one drives case.

This suggests an additional problem. For the commitment to sustain conceptual agreement looks like another shared activity. This threatens to build into Bratman's account of shared activity an infinite regress. Someone might respond that this agreement need be neither fixed nor maintained through the intentional action of the cooperating agents. This would avoid the regress. This seems perfectly fine—it is more or less what happens in normal language use. One might further argue that the threat of deviation from conceptual agreement once it has been fixed is so limited that *commitment* is hardly necessary. For one might argue that the threat of "semantic drift" is so minimal that parties can lack commitment without conceptual divergence emerging. This seems a reasonable position to adopt, as well.[52] But I shall argue that in the case of analyzing legal institutions as shared activities, we cannot be sanguine about appealing to unintentionally adopted conventions and the lack of pressure on conceptual agreement.

---

51. There is an even deeper problem faced by any account that is based upon the coreferentiality intentions of the agents. Let an intention be a relation, I, between an agent, a, and an action, r: aIr. Because intentions are future-directed, r cannot be a past or existing action. One cannot intend to do what one is already doing or what one has already done (although one can intend to continue doing what one is already doing). This has the following consequence: intentions cannot, strictly speaking, corefer. A solution is to say that r is an *act-type*, and so intentions corefer by referring to the same act-type. This solution, though, drags us into a new nest of problems in philosophy of language and metaphysics because act-types are presumably abstract objects.

52. It is worth noting that the Lewisean analysis of convention as found in LEWIS, *supra* note 2, is not an analysis of the *unintended* adoption of a convention. In fact, he has rather robust common-knowledge requirements, to which many objections have been lodged. *See, esp.*, Tyler Burge, *On Knowledge and Convention*, 84 PHIL. REV. 249 (1975). Some of my objections to a Bratmanian analysis of legal institutions are the distant products of reflections inspired by Burge's objections to the Lewisean common-knowledge requirement.

The third important feature is what I shall call *epistemic agreement*. Bratman writes:

> In SCA I will see each of the cooperators, including me, as participating, intentional agents. If this obliges me to include the efficacy of your intention and subplans in the content of my relevant intention, then it also obliges me to include the efficacy of my own intention and subplans in this content.[53]

In order for me to include the efficacy of your intention and subplans in the content of my relevant intention, then I need to have a reasonably accurate belief about what the contents of your intention and subplans are. Even if you have not yet worked out your subplans and we will need to bargain over them at a later date, at that later date I would *then* need to have reasonably accurate beliefs about the subplans you are considering adopting.[54] The same must be said about your beliefs about my intention and subplans. This becomes quite explicit in Bratman's explication of how it is possible for a person to intend that she and someone else J together (or from the perspective of that agent and her friend, how it is possible that I intend that we J). Bratman writes that when I intend that we, for example, paint:

(1a) I intend that we paint.
(1b) You intend that we paint.
(2) My intention is *known* to you, and yours is *known* to me.
(3a) The persistence of (1a) depends on my continued *knowledge* of (1b): if I did not *know* that (1b) I would not intend that we paint.
(3b) The persistence of (1b) depends on your continued *knowledge* of (1a): If you did not know that (1a) you would not intend that we paint.
(4) We will paint but only if (1a) and (1b).
(5) (1)–(4) are common *knowledge* between us.[55]

So what is required for shared intention and shared action is not only that there is conceptual agreement with respect to concepts deployed with respect to the activity to be shared but that the agents have more or less correct beliefs about each other's subplans and intentions.[56] This is more than mere conceptual agreement, because we can share a concept without

---

53. *Shared Cooperative Activity*, in BRATMAN, *supra* note 2, at 100 (emphasis removed from "including me").
54. *See Shared Intention*, in *id.* at 121ff.
55. *I Intend That We J*, in *id.* at 153 (emphasis added).
56. Bratman notes, in *id.* at n. 14, that he has excluded mention of meshing subplans for ease of exposition. Bratman writes:

> I ignore here the idea that in shared intentions we each intend that the activity proceed by way of meshing subplans of each of our intentions. This idea is central to my overall view, but can be safely put to one side in a discussion of the... objections [being dealt with in this article].

sharing subplans or intentions in which the concept is deployed. For example, we can share the concept *playing ball* but we need also both to believe correctly that the other intends to play ball if we are to get the appropriately systematic web of intentions characteristic of shared intention and shared activity. Bratman seems to think that this is not difficult to achieve and so he writes:

> it seems reasonable to suppose that in shared intention the fact that each has the relevant attitudes is itself out in the open, is public.[57]

But I will argue below that we will have good reason to doubt this supposition in the case of large-scale institutions like legal institutions.

As in the case of conceptual agreement, there also needs to be *commitment to epistemic agreement.* Consider conditions (3a) and (3b) above: the persistence of shared intention depends upon continued true belief by the relevant agents about each other's relevant intentions. This is especially significant because intentions and subplans can change in response to developments exogenous to the shared activity. For example, we could be painting a house together, and I feel what I take to be drops of rain. So I stop painting and begin to collect the brushes and paint. It turns out that what I felt was an errant sprinkler from next door. As a result, you keep painting while I am cleaning up (because you did not feel the errant sprinkler's spray). The systematic interconnection between our subplans and intentions has been broken. This can be addressed if you ask me what I am doing and why I am doing it and then I sincerely answer you. This would allow us to achieve epistemic agreement again. But it requires a commitment on both our parts to do so. An alternative way to keep me painting would be for you to threaten to beat me up unless I start painting again, but this would no longer be a shared intention (even if it might get the house painted).

Finally, it is true that in many cases epistemic agreement may be easy to achieve and that sustaining it may not be very difficult. In the painting case, as well as in the other small-scale cases Bratman considers, it is almost costless to ask someone a question and for that person to answer sincerely. But I argue below both that epistemic agreement is difficult to achieve in some large-scale contexts and that the commitment to epistemic agreement is difficult to sustain in large-scale contexts.

The fifth feature of Bratman's view is *strong practical commitment* to the shared activity, namely a commitment by each party to engage in the activity with the other parties and (if a shared cooperative activity) to being mutually supportive in the activity. It is not enough merely to have shared *beliefs* about each other's intentions and subplans; parties must also be practically committed to the shared activity and the subplans. Jon might believe that

---

57. *Shared Intention, in id.* at 117.

Phil intends to make a pizza with Jon, and Phil might believe that Jon intends to make a pizza with Phil. Furthermore, they might both intend that their subplans mesh so that they can make pizza together. Phil, though, might decide, just as they are about to begin the pizza-making, that he could be doing something better alone, for example, playing the guitar, and so announces to Jon (thereby maintaining epistemic agreement) that he intends to abandon the shared pizza-making endeavor. So Phil needs to have a strong practical commitment to making pizza together with Jon—strong enough that it will not dissipate when opportunities for other desirable activities come up.[58]

The requirement for strong practical commitment might seem extraneous. But that is because in small-scale coordinated activities of brief duration, such as making dinner together, driving to New York together (unless one is leaving from California), painting a house together, and playing a game together, practical commitment is cheap.[59] But in cases of longer-lasting forms of coordination, such practical commitment faces pressure from many sources. For example, people are usually committed to more than one shared activity at a time. It is not a stretch to imagine conflicts arising. In such instances, an agent must have a commitment to have all the subplans of different shared activities mesh and not just the subplans of a single shared activity mesh. Making the effort to do this can be costly—so costly that following through with the practical commitment to have the subplans of various shared activities mesh may make it impossible to complete one or more of the activities to which one is committed. That is one reason why very busy people often hire secretaries: the secretary does much of the work of meshing the subplans of all the different shared activities in which the busy person is engaged so that the busy person can do all that to which she is practically committed.

In sum, the five key features of Bratmanian shared activity are the following: conceptual agreement, commitment to conceptual agreement, epistemic agreement, commitment to epistemic agreement, and strong practical commitment. Bratmanian shared activity, then, is *hypercommittal*: parties must seek agreement and be committed to sustaining it. In the next section I argue that Bratmanian shared activities are too hypercommittal to be an adequate model of the social practices that constitute legal institutions. To

---

58. The source of this practical commitment cannot be coercion by the other agent involved in the cooperative activity. It remains an open question how much outside coercion can generate this practical commitment. For example, if Grant points a loaded pistol at Jon and Phil and says "Make a pizza together or die," could Jon and Phil form the relevant joint intention and then perform the SCA of making pizza together (they will be mutually supportive, lest Grant shoots each of them)? I am not certain where Bratman would stand on this issue.

59. Bratman writes, in *Shared Intention, in id.* at 114, that "the nonreconsideration of one's prior intentions will typically be the default." This is probably true in almost all short-term shared activities. But it is another matter altogether in long-term activities. In such cases, we can no longer *presume* that the nonreconsideration of prior intentions is the default. It becomes a matter of trust. *See* Matthew Noah Smith, Trust and Social Norms (in progress).

show that this is the case, I argue that each of the five characteristics outlined in this section is not likely to be realized in legal institutions.

V. ARE LEGAL INSTITUTIONS SHARED ACTIVITIES?

I begin first by reminding the reader that this section is not meant to be read as an attack on Bratman's theory of shared activity or shared intentions. I have no firm opinion about that theory. This section is, instead, the completion of an argument against the use of that theory as a framework for analyzing how the legal institutions at the foundations of law are social practices.

Second, let us recall an important feature of modern legal institutions. The agents whose activities constitute modern legal institutions are not only legislators and judges. In particular, modern legal institutions include many administrative agencies that have the authority to issue regulations that we have no reason not to take to be law (even if they are not legislation). The staffs of these agencies apply the regulations produced by these agencies, including settling questions of the content of the rules and settling disputes between parties about the application of the rules. There may be the option of appeal to the judiciary, but the existence of this option is not evidence that the administrative rules and the application of these rules should not be understood as law and the application of law, respectively. So officials in a modern legal institution are not only judges and legislators but also bureaucrats. Legal philosophers who wish to restrict legal institutions only to legislators producing legislation or judges applying legislation or judge-made common law bear the responsibility of argument here. It is worth noting, after all, that in *The Concept of Law* H.L.A. Hart never specifies *who* must adopt the internal point of view with respect to the rule of recognition, only that certain officials must if the rule of recognition is to exist in some population. So any theory of how legal institutions at the foundations of law are social practices must reckon with the fact that modern legal institutions are sprawling and involve individuals with heterogeneous educations and backgrounds. With this in mind, the problems facing an account of how legal institutions are hypercommittal social practices begin to emerge into something like stark relief. For such accounts presume that the officials of legal institutions at the foundations of law are hypercommitted to the activity of their respective institution. In this section, I show how this is implausible with respect to all five criteria of hypercommitment outlined above.

Turning first to conceptual agreement, we can note that in a legal institution, officials, together, are creating and/or applying *laws* governing private individuals. So the question is: Is there conceptual agreement among officials about the concept *law* and is there a commitment to conceptual agreement about the concept *law*?

Dworkin's criticisms of Hart in "Model of Rules II" and his "semantic sting" argument are supposed to show that there is always a fair amount of conceptual disagreement within an individual legal institution about the concept *law*.[60] Even if we reject Dworkinian interpretivism, there are other arguments for the claim that disagreement is a ubiquitous phenomenon when it comes to political concepts. For example, Jeremy Waldron argues in chapter 2 of *The Right to Private Property* that the concept *private property* is, borrowing from W.B. Gallie, an "essentially contested concept."[61] An essentially contested concept is one the definition of which is necessarily the subject of contestation. That is, a conceptually necessary feature of the concept is that there is disagreement about its definition. For example, when Waldron argues that the concept *private property* is an essentially contested concept, he is arguing that this concept is necessarily subject to disputes about which "incidents" are essential to private property.[62] It remains an open question whether similar points can be made about concepts central to other institutions such as *liability* in the institution of tort law and *contract* in institution of contract law.[63]

There are some additional concerns. Recent work by Joshua Knobe has revealed what has become called the "Knobe effect."[64] Apparently, whether an action is perceived to be a right or wrong action can sometimes be sufficient to determine for many people whether that action is an intentional action. Knobe argues that this is evidence that our concept of intentional action should be understood as "a multi-purpose tool" and that the function it is serving determines how it should be understood. Others argue that we might, in fact, have two concepts of intention.[65] How widespread the Knobe effect is[66] and whether it is best understood as evidence of conceptual disagreement remains to be seen. But if it turns out that any of the concepts that play roles in parties' concepts of J-ing are subject to the Knobe effect,

---

60. *See* DWORKIN, *Model of Social Rules II*, *supra* note 4; and DWORKIN, LAW'S EMPIRE, *supra* note 4. Actually in *Model of Rules II* Dworkin argues that there is disagreement about the grounds of law and then in LAW'S EMPIRE he argues that there is disagreement about the concept *law* itself.

61. JEREMY WALDRON, THE RIGHT TO PRIVATE PROPERTY (1989), at 51–52. The Gallie article is W.B. Gallie, *Essentially Contested Concepts*, 56 PROC. ARISTOTELIAN SOC'Y 167 (1956).

62. On the incidents of private property, *see* A.M. Honoré, *Ownership*, *in* OXFORD ESSAYS IN JURISPRUDENCE (A.G. Guest ed., 1961), at 160.

63. The way that Waldron spells out essentially contested concepts allows him to retain agreement as a background to disagreement. He does this by mobilizing the well-worn concept/conception distinction. There is a concept of private property about which there is agreement; the disagreement is about which competing conception of property is best. *See* WALDRON, *supra* note 61. I believe Waldron's account of the concept and conception of private property is incoherent. But even if it is not, it remains unclear whether the concept/conception distinction can be deployed to resolve the problem faced by the concept of law.

64. For an overview, *see* Joshua Knobe, *The Concept of Intentional Action: A Case Study in the Uses of Folk Psychology*, PHIL. STUD. (forthcoming).

65. *See* Shaun Nichols & Joseph Ulatowski, *Intuitions and Individual Differences: The Knobe Effect Revisited*, MIND AND LANGUAGE (forthcoming).

66. Knobe suggests that it is rather widespread. *See* Knobe, *supra* note 64.

418 **Language, Law, and Social Meanings**

agery) as "involvement strategies" used to involve and keep the interest of audiences. Similarly, work in functional linguistics, especially that directed toward issues of language and power, often approaches language as a mechanism for reproducing and contesting social structures (see, e.g., Fairclough 1989). As one critic has noted, these models never allow for linguistic creativity independent of "preexisting socially determined enablements and constraints" (Huspek 1991:133).

Language is certainly used in instrumental fashion to effect social goals, and no integrative theory of language use could neglect consideration of this aspect of language function. However, purposive attempts to use language quite often run up against a resistance or unpredictability that is the result of language's social structuring—that quality of language that results from it being a system that has developed in complex ways over time, a system that is widely shared (in complicated and variable ways) by a community.

Thus linguist Kurylowicz (1945–49) compared language to gutters or channels through which rainwater pours; the falling rain, like many linguistic innovations whose origins are social, comes from outside the system but must move through the grooves already laid down. In the process, of course, many of the grooves and channels will be altered or remade. As some parts of the system of channels shift in response to external (social) stimuli, there may be other changes within the system. For example, the process of change that began as a shift in a pronoun form (perhaps in response to changing social circumstances) may have unanticipated consequences as this changing pronoun form influences other parts of the linguistic system (see Silverstein 1985). Even these apparently language-internal shifts have social dimensions, because the system of language itself is socially grounded. But to understand the relationship between language and society in all its complexity, it is important to allow for a moment of linguistic creativity, a moment when language is more than a transparent window or tool expressing preexisting social divisions. This is an approach that is emerging from current work in linguistic anthropology and semiotics.

If we ask, then, what difference it makes that we pay attention to language using reflectionist or instrumentalist models, the response is that language is a good diagnostic tool, a good window on social process. But there is an even more compelling answer. As Conley and O'Barr explain in *Rules versus Relationships*, "[m]any other social science research traditions . . . use language as a window through which other, presumably more important, things may be viewed. . . . Our premise has been that the window itself is often more interesting than what can be seen through it" (p. xi). And, as I have suggested, per-then it may not be possible to establish conceptual agreement without substantial cost.

It is not at all news that there is not univocality about the concept *law*.[67] But that there is such disagreement should raise alarm bells for those who wish to employ the Bratmanian framework in their analysis of legal institutions as shared practices. For the J that all the officials of a legal institution intend to perform together is the creation and application of laws. But their intentions cannot be interreferential in the Bratmanian fashion if there is not intensional equivalence of officials' concepts of law. And in a large-scale and long-term social practice such as a legal institution—one in which there are many and heterogeneous officials and there is also a nonnegligible amount of turnover—there is likely to be a wide spectrum of intensions of officials' concepts of law. If this is so, there will be at least some officials whose concepts fall on different ends of the spectrum, thereby ensuring that the intensions of the concepts of at least some officials are likely to be so different that interreferentiality fails for them. This would, in turn, prevent these officials from sharing the intention that they create or apply laws together and would therefore rule out the systematic unity that the social practice of a legal institution is supposed to have.

The problem becomes even worse if either Dworkin or Waldron is correct. For if *law* is an essentially contested concept, then one cannot appeal to an unintentionally adopted convention that fully fixes the content of the concept *law*. Rather, the convention is that this concept is essentially contested and so is not fully shared. And because it is an essentially contested concept, there will be a great deal of pressure—in the form of political contestation—pushing officials away from conceptual agreement. Overcoming this would require substantial shared commitment to conceptual agreement. This threatens a Bratmanian account with a regress of iterated shared activities seeking to secure conceptual agreement.

Could hierarchical structures resolve this problem? It is unlikely. Within a large-scale institution, hierarchical structures can ensure at best only local agreement (e.g., a police officer learns from his commander what is and is not law). This is because the "semantic guidance"[68] officials receive as to the content of the concept *law* will come primarily from immediate superiors. For there to be global agreement, there would have to be a continuous hierarchical chain of such semantic guidance, and such arrangements are highly unstable. It is more likely that there will be only localized sites of conceptual agreement. If a Bratmanian framework is employed to analyze how legal institutions are social practices, the (contingent but nonetheless highly likely) existence of discontinuities in conceptual agreement would have the disastrous analytic effect of fragmenting a large-scale legal

---

67. For more, *see* Coleman & Simchen, *supra* note 44.
68. Apologies to Scott Shapiro, whose concepts of motivational and epistemic guidance I have just bastardized. *See* Scott Shapiro, *On Hart's Way Out*, 4 LEGAL THEORY 469 (1998).

institution into several discrete legal institutions along the (probably fluctuating) boundaries of "semantic authority."

One might reject the conceptual semantics I have employed, or one might take the requirement of conceptual agreement to be too strong, or one might reject my argument that this strong requirement will not be met in a legal institution.[69] I can easily grant any of these points, because employing the Bratmanian framework to explain how legal institutions are social practices requires that legal institutions meet the other three requirements: epistemic agreement, commitment to epistemic agreement, and strong practical commitment.

Epistemic agreement, recall, is necessary because, in order for an agent to include the efficacy of another's intention and subplans in the content of her relevant intention, she needs to have a reasonably accurate belief about what the content of the other agent's intention and subplans is. Even if the other agent has not yet worked out his subplans and the two need to bargain over the subplans at a later date, at that later date each would still need to have reasonably accurate beliefs about the subplans the other is considering adopting.

In a large-scale legal institution, even if there is conceptual agreement among officials about the concept *law*, there may remain disagreement among officials about what it is that they are doing together. As I mention above, most large-scale legal institutions are composed of a large and heterogeneous group of officials. These officials may not have the same education, political commitments, and level of identification with the institution within which they work. Thus it is likely that there will be a nonnegligible diversity in the beliefs among officials about what it is that they are doing. Officials may disagree about what the J of the legal institution is, what everyone else takes that J to be, and what each other's subplans are. The possibility of this disagreement cannot be glibly ignored: any Bratmanian account of legal institutions must give us sense of the source of epistemic agreement.

There is an even more serious problem faced by a Bratmanian analysis of legal institutions. It is unlikely that all officials will know, much less have beliefs about, who all the other officials are. For example, suppose that unbeknownst to one group of officials, another group of participants, with whom the first group never directly works but whom the first group has met on several occasions, drops out of the legal institution (say that the group's department loses funding). The members of the first group of officials can *intend* that they J with those who dropped out but they cannot successfully J with them. (It does not matter what the members of the second group intend because they are no longer part of the institution.) Suppose officials in the first group never knew about the second group in the first place.

---

69. This last tactic is especially plausible if one restricts the members of the class of officials to only those with the appropriate degree from accredited American law schools, but I have already indicated how this tactic is multiply problematic.

The problem becomes even worse for the Bratmanian account. In this case the members of the two groups could not have even *intended* that they J together from the get-go, much less have actually shared an activity.[70] Because in modern legal institutions it is highly unlikely that all or even most officials know of one another, it is unlikely that officials can share intentions in the relevant fashion.

One way to get around this would be to specify the extension of the "we" in "we will J" by the definite description "the people who will be J-ing with me" or a name "the Justice Department." But this may be just the kind of question-begging Bratman wants to avoid by characterizing J-ing in a cooperatively neutral way. Additionally, some philosophers of language have argued that there would simply be a failure to intend to J with anyone in particular if one replaces the "we" in "we will J" with a reference-fixing definite description or a proper name.[71] At the very least, if one tries to give a Bratmanian account of a large-scale social practice such as a legal institution, one must explain how it is that replacing the "we" in "we will J" with a reference-fixing definite description works in the way that one needs it to work for the Bratmanian analysis to go through.

It is consistent with what I have argued so far that without sharing beliefs about the J of the institution, officials have shared beliefs both about some local shared activity and about each others' subplans for the completion of that activity. For example, lawyers in the Justice Department might share beliefs about each other's intentions to write a brief together and might share beliefs about each other's subplans. This will allow the lawyers to engage in the shared cooperative activity of writing a brief.[72] But it might be the case that the lawyers who are presidential appointees view the overall activity that is performed by institution of the Justice Department (the J of the Justice Department) as the implementation and defense of presidential policies whereas those who are career lawyers take the J of the Justice Department to be something more like application of federal law. The appointees and the careerists might be able to share the activity of writing a brief, but can they, in a Bratmanian fashion, share the overall activity of the Justice

---

70. This is surely one reason why Bratman insists on cases of shared intention with usually only two people.

71. *See, e.g.,* David Kaplan, *Quantifying In,* 19 SYNTHESE 178 (1968–1969), esp. at 201ff. Kaplan restricts the condition in which such substitution is legitimate to conditions in which the agent with the propositional attitude can supply a sufficiently *vivid* name:

> The notion of a vivid name is intended to go to the purely internal aspects of individuation. Consider typical cases in which we would be likely to say that Ralph is acquainted with X. Then look only at the conglomeration of images, names, and partial descriptions which Ralph employs to bring X before his mind. Such a conglomeration, when suitably arranged and regimented, is what I call a vivid name. (*Id.* at 201.)

72. *See also* Keith Donnellan, *The Contingent A Priori and Rigid Designators, in* CONTEMPORARY PERSPECTIVES IN THE PHILOSOPHY OF LANGUAGE (P. French, H. Uehling, & H. Wettstein eds., 1979). Or it could be a joint intentional action—it does not matter here because in a JIA the only things missing are the parties' commitments to mutual support.

Department? This does not seem possible if they have such divergent beliefs about what the overall activity of the Justice Department is.

The same problem that arose for the commitment to conceptual agreement arises for the commitment to epistemic agreement, namely the problem of separate and possibly dueling cantons of epistemic agreement with respect to the activity that constitutes the social practice of the institution. I will not recapitulate that discussion.

Finally, we can turn to the requirement for strong practical commitment to the shared activity that is characteristic of the institution.[73] In large-scale social practices, it is not uncommon for the practical commitment of an agent to be the product of either the threat of sanctions or the promise of wages. This is consistent with Bratman's theory if the threat of sanctions or the promise of wages generates a commitment to the overall institutional activity. But many people who are motivated only by threat of sanction or by promise of a wage are committed only to do the minimum necessary to avoid sanctions or earn the wage. In such instances, they will not have a practical commitment to the overall activity of the institution but instead will have a practical commitment only to the activity they must perform in order to avoid sanctions or receive a wage, *regardless of whether that activity contributes to the overall activity of the institution.* Insofar as there is any practical commitment at all to the joint activity of the institution, it is an entirely derivative commitment.[74] Let us call this condition in which an agent performs the tasks as if she were practically committed to the J (or, as it were, the sub-Js) of the institution without actually being so committed *alienation from the institution.*

It is important that alienation from the institution is not a matter of the reasons for action that alienated agents take themselves to have. For the issue here is not the reasons for which someone forms a practical commitment but instead what it is to which the agent has a practical commitment. For the practical commitment of an agent, and not the reasons the agent takes herself to have, determines whether she contributes to the shared activity. In most ordinary cases, the same set of reasons warrants commitment to many different activities.[75] That is, the reasons someone takes herself to have

---

73. The discussion in this paragraph is much indebted to Scott Shapiro's discussion of alienation in Shapiro, *supra* note 1.
74. This will be especially clear if we imagine a case in which an official of an institution is offered by another institution a job that has better wages. This official may immediately leave her current institution and take up employment at the better-paying one. Or consider a case in which a costless opportunity for failing to perform the required activity comes up. The official motivated only by threats of sanctions or promise of wages will take that opportunity and not act. I see no way in which one could correctly claim that in these cases there is a strong practical commitment to the J-ing of the institution.
75. What a set of reasons do is to *rule* out commitments. But only some reasons rule out all but one commitment (and usually these are cases of authoritative reasons, i.e., reasons that are both peremptory and content-independent).

underdetermine the objects of her commitments.[76] So whether someone is alienated from an institution is not entirely a matter of the reasons she takes herself to have; it is a matter of what it is to which the agent is practically committed.

It must be the case that many officials of a legal institution can suffer alienation without the legal institution ceasing to be a social practice. This seems especially the case because there can be many sources of this alienation, not least of which are beliefs that the institution is corrupt, beliefs that one is underappreciated, desires just to make it through until retirement, a desire to have the social capital that goes along with being an official of the legal institution, or just plain boredom. I suspect that alienation from legal institutions is far more common than its opposite, the happier *identification* with legal institutions. Any theory of how legal institutions are social practices that would fail to account for how legal institutions in which alienation is rampant are social practices is a weak theory.

In the section above, I identify five characteristic features of members of a significant class of theories of shared activity and claim that these requirements make these popular theories of shared activity *hypercommittal*. In this section, I argue that the activities of officials in modern legal institutions are likely not to display at least one, if not every one, of these five characteristics.[77] Bratman's analysis of shared activities therefore cannot be the sole conceptual framework employed to analyze how legal institutions are social practices (although it may be useful as a framework for explaining how a particularly small and homogeneous legal institution is a social practice).

---

76. Furthermore, there is psychological evidence that people do not commit themselves to actions for reasons that prior to commitment they take themselves to have. Instead, they generate reasons *post hoc* to justify their commitment. *See, e.g.,* Jonathan Haidt, *The Emotional Dog and Its Rational Tail* 108 PSYCHOL. REV. 814 (2001). If shared activity is possible only in cases of explicit deliberative agency in which the agent reflects on all her reasons and then, based upon a careful consideration of all of them, identifies what it is to which the reasons recommend she ought to be committed, and she so commits herself, then shared activity will be quite a rare phenomenon. For a nice list of several forms of agency, from deliberative agency to automatistic agency, along with brief discussions about how rare fully deliberative agency is and the significance for responsibility attribution, *see* Neil Levy & Tim Bayne, *Doing without Deliberation: Automatism, Automaticity and Moral Accountability,* 16 INT'L REV. PSYCHIATRY (2004), at 209–215.

77. A natural objection to this argument is that I am not giving a charitable reading of the Bratmanian position by taking it to require such high levels of conceptual univocality and such explicit beliefs and intentions. I grant that there may be an alternative reading of the Bratmanian position that does not require the tokening of explicit beliefs or intentions. On this reading, one takes Bratman's view to be purely dispositional. This would help, because dispositions are not propositional attitudes in the way that intentions are and so are not subject to the problems I highlight in this section. But I fail to see any reason to read Bratman as defending such a dispositionalist position. Bratman explicitly argues that systematicity of shared activity consists in the way in which propositional attitudes refer to one another and corefer to joint actions. It seems to me that to retreat to a dispositionalist reading of Bratman, Gilbert, Lewis, and the others of their ilk would amount to abandoning their positions without good reason. Hypercommittal shared activity is a real phenomenon, and Bratman and company have provided an analysis of it. Why junk their stated views because they do not successfully model large-scale, temporally extended social practices such as legal institutions?

Another model of social practices—a model that is not hypercommittal in the way that the Bratmanian model is—is needed in order to explain how legal institutions are social practices.

VI. CONCLUSION

I argue that there are some distinctive constraints on explaining how the foundations of law are social practices. In particular, I argue that legal positivists ought not to represent the foundations of law as constituted by hypercommittal social practices. This constraint on theorizing about the foundations of law is not a conceptual truth about law but is instead based upon unobjectionable observations about law in contemporary society. Furthermore, my criticisms are not based upon any conceptual claims about law that are at odds with the conceptual claims to which leading positivist theories of law are committed. So my criticisms are consistent with leading positivist accounts of the law, and my conclusions therefore apply to positivist accounts of law and legal authority.

My arguments, because they focus on disagreement, might appear to be in line with Dworkinian attacks on positivism. But, unlike Dworkin, I do not believe that we should abandon legal positivism. For the mysteries of how the law is a social practice are no different from the mysteries of how anything in our world is a social practice. In this sense, the problems I claim are faced by positivists are not unique; they are difficulties faced by all, from philosophers to sociologists, who seek to explain how marriage, etiquette, language, racism, major league baseball, the state, and so on are, to some extent, social practices. So my arguments should be no more than cold comfort for the critic of positivism.

Part III
Common Objects: Modes of Explanation of Legal Phenomena

[13]

LAW AS TRADITION*

MARTIN KRYGIER

ABSTRACT. This essay argues that to understand much that is most central to and characteristic of the nature and behaviour of law, one needs to supplement the 'time-free' conceptual staples of modern jurisprudence with an understanding of the nature and behaviour of traditions in social life. The article is concerned with three elements of such an understanding. First, it suggests that traditionality is to be found in almost all legal systems, not as a peripheral but as a central feature of them. Second, it questions the post-Enlightenment antinomy between tradition and change. Third, it argues that in at least two important senses of 'tradition', the traditionality of law is inescapable.

Legal philosophers disagree about many things, few more than the nature of law. Notwithstanding these differences, there are significant family resemblances among contemporary approaches to this question. I am struck by three. First, it is common for law to be conceived as a species of some other more pervasive social phenomenon: commands, norms, rules, rules-and-principles, rules, principles and policies, and so on. Though this runs

---

* This article is part of a project on law and tradition, research for which has been aided by a grant from the Australian Research Grants Committee. It was written while I was a visitor at the Centre for the Study of Law and Society, University of California, Berkeley, and revised while I visited the Centre for Criminology and the Social and Philosophical Study of Law, University of Edinburgh. I am grateful to the members of both centres for generously providing me with extremely congenial and stimulating conditions for work. Versions of the paper were presented to seminars at these centres, to the 12th World Congress on Philosophy of Law and Social Philosophy, held in Athens in August, 1985, and to seminars at the universities of Warsaw, Lodz and Glasgow. I am grateful to participants in these seminars, especially Neil MacCormick, Philip Selznick, Wojciech Lamentowicz, Daniel Sinclair and Jerzy Szacki, and to Edward Shils for useful discussion and criticism.

the risk of explaining the obscure in terms of the more obscure, there are compensating benefits. Important among these is the opportunity of bringing to light central aspects of the complex set of phenomena known compendiously as 'law', which are encompassed by the concept(s) one favours but not by those of which one is critical. Thus Hart on rules versus habits, and on power-conferring laws versus command theories of law. Thus too, Dworkin on the importance of principles rather than rules alone, in hard cases. The aim is not merely to replace one word with another, but to draw attention to important legal phenomena not adequately grasped, or even likely to be much considered, in terms other than those one proposes.

Secondly, legal philosophy typically makes such progress as it does, without making discoveries. When Hart sought to show the significance of rules, or Dworkin of principles, for an understanding of law, they relied (and stressed that they relied) on extremely familiar elements of contemporary legal systems. Their aim, and I believe their achievement, was not to unearth hitherto unknown truths about law, but to focus attention on what was already familiar; frequently so familiar as to escape notice altogether. This is no small contribution, for as Wittgenstein observed, 'The aspects of things that are most important for us are hidden because of their simplicity and familiarity. (One is unable to notice something — because it is always before one's eyes)'.[1]

I have no quarrel with these characteristic moves in legal philosophy; on the contrary, I endorse and wish to continue them. One thinks differently, and more, about the character of law when one considers the ways in which it is like, and unlike, rules and principles — let alone habits, commands, obligations, rights, goals, policies.

However there is a third characteristic of modern legal philosophy which I would not wish to emulate. At least since Hobbes, theories of the nature of law have, as it were, lived in an ever-

---

[1] Ludwig Wittgenstein, *Philosophical Investigations*, 3rd edition (Oxford: Blackwells, 1967), para. 129, p. 50.

present world of sovereigns, commands, sanctions, more recently norms, rules, principles, policies and (for critically inclined theorists) interests, domination and power.² Similarly, modern social theories, full though they are of references to roles, interests, power, authority, structures, systems and 'socially constructed' realities, have few concepts which address the *traditionality* of law and life. Yet in law as in life traditionality is so pervasive that it is truly 'always before one's eyes' in fact, if not in theory. Others have drawn attention to the unsung importance of traditions in life,³ and elsewhere I have also.⁴ I will content myself here with law.

Law is a profoundly traditional social practice, and it must be. This is not merely to say that particular legal systems embody traditions, which of course no one would deny. To understand much that is most central to and characteristic of the nature and behaviour of law, the 'time-free' staples of modern jurisprudence are not enough. One needs to understand the nature and behaviour of traditions in social life. That is a large project. Here I will only discuss three elements of such an understanding. First, I suggest that traditionality is to be found in almost all legal systems, and not as a peripheral, but as a central feature of them. Second, I question the pervasive post-Enlightenment antinomy between tradition and change: whatever else is responsible for change in law, law's traditionality makes it inevitable. Third, I argue that in at least two important senses of 'tradition', and for at least two

---

² For an interesting criticism of, and partial exception to, this general trend, see A. W. B. Simpson, 'The Common Law and Legal Theory' in Simpson (ed.), *Oxford Essays in Jurisprudence*, Second Series, (Oxford: Clarendon Press, 1973), pp. 77–99. See also Harold J. Berman, *Law and Revolution: The Formation of the Western Legal Tradition* (Cambridge, MA., Harvard University Press, 1983).
³ See especially Edward Shils, *Tradition* (Chicago: Chicago University Press, 1981); Jerzy Szacki, *Tradycja* (Warsaw: Panstwowe Wydawnictwo Naukowe, 1971).
⁴ 'Tipologia della Tradizione', *Intersezioni. Rivista di storia delle idee* 5 (1985): 221–49.

reasons, tradition is inescapable in law, whether or not that is a good thing. Frequently, however, it is a good thing.

1. LAW AS TRADITION

I have argued elsewhere,[5] and only have room to assert here, that every tradition has three characteristics or elements. First is pastness: the contents of every tradition have or are believed by its participants to have, originated some considerable time in the past. Second is authoritative presence: though derived from a real or believed-to-be real past, a traditional practice, doctrine or belief has not, as it were, stayed there. Its traditionality consists in its *present* authority and significance for the lives, thoughts or activities of participants in the tradition. Third, a tradition is not merely the past made present. It must have been, or be thought to have been, passed down over intervening generations, deliberately or otherwise; not merely unearthed from a past discontinuous with the present. A necessary consequence of this third element is that traditions are social. Habits, even customs, can be born, live and die solely in the behaviour of one individual. Traditions, as a simple matter of definition, cannot. Like every tradition, law shares these elements. More than many traditions, law is organized to preserve, maintain and draw systematically and constantly upon them.

(i) *Pastness*

Every tradition is composed of elements drawn from the real or an imagined past. This is central to what it means for something to be a tradition. It is not central, or even necessary, to what it means for something to be an act, rule or principle. One can act, lay down a rule, enunciate a principle, and say imme-

---

[5] For a more extended discussion, see 'Tipologia della Tradizione'. Note, however, that I have modified my view on the second element of tradition. I had thought that it was enough that the past be present. I now believe that the past must be authoritatively present.

diately that that is what one is doing and has done. One cannot openly make a tradition all at once. Though of course one may *originate* a tradition, whether one has done so can only be decided after some time, and not on the basis of the originating act alone or even primarily. And while rules can openly be made retrospective (though they are hard acts to follow) traditions cannot.

In every established legal system, the legal past is central to the legal present. Like all complex traditions, law records and preserves a composite of (frequently inconsistent) beliefs, opinions, values, decisions, myths, rituals, deposited over generations. The stuff of legal doctrine — statutes, judgments, interpretations, rules, principles, conventions, customs — has been so deposited, in and by legal institutions where doctrine has been proclaimed, applied, recorded and passed down by officials specifically entrusted with these functions. Even if legal systems did not institutionalize the recording, preservation and transmission of so much of the legal past, residues of this past would still mould what can be done, indeed thought, in the present. This is evident in less institutionalized traditions such as those of art, literature and morals, as it is in the vast cultural inheritance embodied in the 'social facts'[6] which set much of the agenda of everyday living.

In law, however, past-maintenance *is* institutionalized: certain kinds of writings are recorded, some among them are defined as 'authoritative', others as persuasive; the decisions, opinions and judgments of certain kinds of readers, writers and officials are similarly distinguished. If not sacralized, they are at least ranked in orders of authoritative status, in ways familiar to initiates, though sometimes mystifying to rationalist outsiders. Successive participants in legal traditions are required to justify their arguments in terms of acceptable interpretations of these authoritative materials.

---

[6] See Emile Durkheim, *The Rules of Sociological Method* (New York: The Free Press, 1966), pp. 1–2; *The Elementary Forms of the Religious Life* (New York: The Free Press, 1965), p. 29.

Such practices give the past-in-the-present power over those who think and act in the present. Of course this power is not absolute. For one thing, even in constantly vetted traditions such as law, the past speaks with many voices. This is inevitable precisely because of the traditionality of law. For in every complex written tradition, any particular 'present' is a slice through a continuously changing diachronic quarry of deposits made by generations of people with different, often inconsistent and competing values, beliefs, and views of the world. This assorted stock forms the constantly changing present of the tradition, to which each generation of participants contributes in turn. Unless social and legal values, doctrines and beliefs are static, and few are ever completely static, tensions and inconsistencies between those embedded in legal doctrine at any time are bound to occur. This allows, indeed makes necessary, choice in particular legal applications. (This should be borne in mind by those, 'critical' lawyers and others, who take incoherence in doctrine as evidence of deep crisis. For it remains an important question in social and legal theory, insufficiently considered: when does incoherence within a tradition, which always occurs, amount to crisis, which only occurs sometimes?)

So, the past is not univocal in complex traditions. Even if it were, what is to be made of it is, in a very full sense of the word, a matter of interpretation. Many interpretations are available. Only some are authoritative, but as most lawyers and all students of hermeneutics are aware, there is always room to move. Such important legal concepts as the 'intention of the legislature' or the *ratio* of a case, for example, make decisive reference to past phenomena which may have been otherwise interpreted, may have been otherwise, or may simply not have been. Moreover, as we shall see, the very fact that texts and their interpreters are embedded in a broader complex tradition, ensures that meanings attributed to texts will change.

The interpretation of traditional texts is a complex subject which has engrossed hermeneutic theorists for centuries. It is not a specifically legal problem, though lawyers do it for particular practical purposes and within distinctive traditions. What lawyers recognise as ambiguities and gaps in the law are found, of course, in many other texts; so is the fact that texts written in certain periods have different significance to readers in different periods. What in literary hermeneutics is known as an 'aesthetic of reception',[7] which insists on the importance of the *audience* as an ingredient in the meaning of texts, has its parallels in, for example, the continuing debates over how the American Supreme Court should interpret the Constitution.[8] There, as elsewhere,

> It might be the intention of the recipient to adhere 'strictly' to the stipulation of what he has received but 'strictness' itself opens questions which are not already answered and which must be answered. If it is a moral or a legal code, or a philosophical system, the very attempt by a powerful mind to understand it better will entail the discernment of hitherto unseen problems which will require new formulations; these will entail varying degrees of modification. Attempts to make them applicable to particular cases will also enforce modification. Such modifications of the received occur even when the tradition is regarded as sacrosanct and the innovator might in good conscience insist that he is adhering to the traditions as received.[9]

However, if the hold of the past over the present in traditions such as law should not be exaggerated, it would be deep folly to dismiss it. Law is frequently conceived of as an instrument wielded for good or ill by lawmakers, lawyers and others to pursue their autonomous, freely chosen purposes, or at least purposes determined independently of the legal instruments they use. This instrumental view of law is indeed encouraged by conceptions of law-as-commands, rules, and so on, which are given, made, obeyed,

---

[7] See Hans Robert Jauss, *Toward an Aesthetic of Reception* (Minneapolis: University of Minnesota Press, 1982), especially chapter 1, 'Literary History as a Challenge to Literary Theory'.

[8] See for example, 'Symposium: Constitutional Adjudication and Democratic Theory' *New York University Law Review* 56 (1981), 259–582.

[9] Edward Shils, *Tradition*, p. 45.

applied, broken or ignored. Thinking of the character of traditions in general, of what it means to participate in them, and of legal traditions in particular, suggests that such instrumentalist conceptions are and must be, at the very least, seriously inadequate. Legal traditions provide substance, models, exemplars and a *language* in which to speak within and about law. Participation in such a tradition involves sharing a way of speaking about the world which, like language though more precisely and restrictively than natural language, shapes, forms and in part envelops the thought of those who speak it and think through it. For better or worse (almost certainly for better *and* worse) it is difficult for insiders to step outside it or for outsiders to enter and participate in it untutored. It moulds the thinking of insiders even where, perhaps especially where, they least realise, and evades the grasp of outsiders determined to pin it down. Of course where legal traditions are weak, or where the traditions of law are overwhelmed by the imperatives of power, particularly dictatorial power, 'law' — if it should be so called — may simply be a malleable instrument of power-wielders; another truncheon or water cannon. To this extent imperativist and instrumental conceptions are vindicated. It is odd that these conceptions should cope best with systems where law is least important and worst where it does its most distinctive work.

Moreover, apart from the ways in which the past is present in law as in every tradition, law and its practice involve highly organized and complex systems of past-reference, the consequences of which should not be minimized. Lawyers dwell on the words of past statutes and on glosses on them by past 'authorities' (a concept of central importance to many institutionalized traditions, as well as law). In court, and in the lengthy preparations for and attempts to avoid appearances there, lawyers seek to marshall a past more favourable to their clients' interests than to those of their opponents. All of this takes place in a context, often real, often hypothetical, where genealogical support for every argument is required and closely examined. That many legal genealogies seem contrived would not surprise students of lineage systems in 'traditional' societies. That they might fail to persuade the audience for which they are intended — or at least the canny realists in it — in no way diminishes the significance of the attempt. Moreover, judging, that activity so favoured with jurisprudential attention and writings, is an archetypally traditional and tradition-referring practice. For however innovative judges are, their modes of justifying decisions, and therefore the sorts of arguments which must be addressed to them, in fact or hypothetically, differ systematically from those of other decision-makers such as, say, engineers or entrepreneurs, or workers in less self-consciously authority-filled traditions, such as novelists, artists or scientists, who themselves are in no way free from the traditions of their calling. Judging is a specific and characteristic mode of making and justifying practical decisions: a judicial decision is one which is justified publicly by reference to authorized institutional tradition. In those hard cases that lawyers and legal theorists so enjoy to contemplate, the need publicly to justify one's decision in terms of interpretations of the legal past which seem plausible to experts, remains important long after simple rule-application has ceased to be possible. Doing this involves neither application of a clear unequivocal rule, as in the perhaps mythical easy cases, nor invention *ex nihilo*, but inescapably (though not only) interpretation of authorized institutional tradition.

(ii) Authoritative Presence

Law is not highly traditional merely because it has a past; so, after all, does everything over an instant old. However, the past of law, as of every tradition, is not simply part of its history; it is an authoritative significant part of its present. Without such authoritative presence, the past is not part of a living tradition or at least not a living part of such a tradition. Much of the past enters into no tradition. It simply disappears without trace, or leaves traces which survive without present consequence for anyone. Conversely, not everything from the past which has consequences in the present, such as an economically wise (or unwise) governmental decision, enters a tradition linking the past and the present.[10] To the extent, however, that the real or imagined past plays a present normative or authoritative role in one's values or beliefs, this second element of traditionality is satisfied.

The authoritative presence of the past in traditions is frequently unnoticed by participants. Indeed, the past is often most powerfully and pervasively present when it is not known to be past or present. It is simply 'obvious' or 'natural', an unremarked piece of the furniture of the world. This is true of many moral, religious and political beliefs, ideologies, legal traditions, scientific procedures, and the vast cultural inheritances they embody. On the other hand, the pastness of elements of one's present can be recognised and appropriated in a specifically traditional way, when what is known or thought to be the past of one's race, vocation, institution etc., is considered to be of continuing significance.

In law the past has profound present significance in both these senses. Simple reflection on what is involved in knowing the law of a single jurisdiction suggests the importance of the unnoticed present-past in law. For as everyone knows but jurists sometimes forget, 'to know a legal system is not just to have learned its rules but to understand how the rules are put together, how the system is structured, how the rules are interpreted'.[11] Such understanding is important not merely, or even especially, for the historian or theorist of law who seeks to account for these things. It is in fact an unsung precondition of practical lawyering; the 'tacit' knowledge[12] which underlies competence within any legal or indeed any social practice. Mastery of such underlying knowl-

---

[10] I am grateful to Philip Selznick for bringing home this (now obvious) truth to me.

[11] Alan Watson, *The Making of the Civil Law* (Cambridge, MA.: Harvard University Press, 1981), p. 14.

[12] See Michael Polanyi, *Personal Knowledge* (Chicago: University of Chicago Press, 1962); *The Tacit Dimension* (London: Routledge and Kegan Paul, 1967).

edge depends on tradition, both oral and written. As inexperienced lawyers learn quickly, knowledge of the rules is no substitute for this tacit knowledge. As experienced lawyers often demonstrate, such knowledge can frequently serve as a substitute for knowing the rules. What Bernard Rudden observes of judges is true of almost all legal professionals:

> ...not only is the individual judge conditioned by his background, but ... the decades, or even centuries, of a traditional training, of particular methods of recruitment, even of the physical characteristics of the place where the job is done, create a corpus of professional habits and assumptions which affects judicial method and, through it, the legal order, and does so all the more strongly for being so rarely made articulate.[13]

Like the expert cook or scientist discussed by Michael Oakeshott, a reflective lawyer:

> would observe that, in pursuing his particular project, his actions were being determined not solely by his premeditated end, but by what may be called the traditions of the activity to which his project belonged. It is because he knows how to tackle problems of this sort that he is able to tackle this particular problem.[14]

This should not be surprising, for to know and understand a system of law is in many ways similar to knowing and understanding a language. Indeed, as I have suggested, law contains a language of some density and complexity, and it is not only lawyers who speak it. We all do, and even the least legally expert of us arrange and transact some of the most and least significant of our everyday affairs in terms of our understanding of it. Moreover, like law:

> a language is not a fixed stock of possible utterances, but a fund of considerations drawn upon and used in inventing utterances; a fund which may

---

[13] 'Courts and Codes in England, France and Soviet Russia' *Tulane Law Review* 48 (1974): 1010–28 at 1014.
[14] 'Rational Conduct', in *Rationalism in Politics* (London: Routledge and Kegan Paul, 1962), p. 99.

be used only in virtue of having been learned, which is learned only in being used, and which is continuously reconstituted in use.[15]

Like language-speakers, lawyers and all who use law inhabit and manipulate traditions whose general intellectual structures, underlying conventions, canons of authority, and standards, change glacially and in ways that individuals rarely have power to affect radically. They may innovate within these traditional idioms, and of course in law, unlike ordinary language, it is possible to decree or legislate important elements of novelty, including rules, less often principles, and even new lawmaking or interpreting institutions, such as new tribunals. But at the level of underlying assumptions and presuppositions, change within legal systems is a more complicated, supra-individual and usually supra-generational affair. At this level, revolutions are rare in law, and more rarely still are they total. This of course is true of many traditions outside the law, none of which is best understood in terms of the 'time-free' concepts prevalent in modern legal and social theory.

The traditionality of law is reflected not merely in the pastness of its present, the extent to which current law is the presently visible residue of generations of deposits. It is equally reflected in the presence of the past, the extent to which only the presently authoritative past is treated as significant and only to the extent of this present authority. The lawyer preparing a brief, the judge justifying a decision, the layman trying to understand and predict the effects of law on his activities, are not engaged in disinterested forays into legal history, though they may be deeply concerned with the legal past. On the contrary, this past is treated as though it were a vast storehouse to be searched for solutions to present problems. One characteristic complaint by legal historians is revealing in this regard. In seeking to explain 'Why the History of English Law is not Written', Maitland suggested that one reason was the lawyer's peculiar attitude to the legal past:

---

[15] Michael Oakeshott, *On Human Conduct* (Oxford: Clarendon Press, 1975), p. 120.

what is really required of the practising lawyer is not, save in the rarest cases, a knowledge of medieval law as it was in the middle ages, but rather a knowledge of medieval law as interpreted by modern courts to suit modern facts.[16]

Applied to legal history itself, this attitude to the legal past has frequently led to history-as-genealogy or, as the American historian Daniel Boorstin has written, the considerations of legal history as 'an alchemy for distilling legal principles':

> So obviously has it seemed necessary to adopt the categories of the modern 'developed' legal system that much of legal history has become a sort of legal embryology — the search for the rudimentary forms of the 'full-grown' legal system. The present becomes the culmination of all the past, and the present forms of institutions seem to be their inevitable forms. The imagination is thus closed to the infinite possibilities of history.[17]

A similar complaint has recently been made by Douglas Hay. When it comes to thinking about the past, one characteristic of 'thinking like a lawyer', Hay argues, is what historians call 'presentism'; 'the fallacy of working from present concerns to past origins, is anathema to historians, but necessarily half the lawyer's method'.[18] What appears to historians as bad history is simply typical of the behaviour of participants within a tradition. Whig interpretations may be unsuccessful history, but they are often very successful law.

When participants in a recorded tradition consult its records, they are rarely concerned to reconstruct the past *wie es eigentlich gewesen ist*. All developed legal systems, for example, produce rules of statutory interpretation which prescribe and circumscribe the resources on which a lawyer may draw to interpret statutory provisions. A point little remarked upon by lawyers is that these are not rules for which an historian seeking to analyze the origins

---

[16] *The Collected Papers of Frederic William Maitland*, ed. H. A. L. Fisher (Cambridge: Cambridge University Press), vol. 1, p. 491.
[17] 'Tradition and Method in Legal History', *Harvard Law Review* 54 (1941): 424–36 at 428–29.
[18] 'The Criminal Prosecution in England and its Historians' *Modern Law Review* 47 (1984): 1–29 at 18–19.

and purposes of a statute would have much use. Even if he could make sense of the notion of the 'intention of the legislature', for example, no historian seeking it (or them) on a particular matter would feel bound to limit himself to the sources or kinds of inference allowed to a judge by whatever rules of statutory interpretation prevail in a particular jurisdiction. Nor should he believe he had found the intentions he was looking for if he did so. An historian, *qua* historian, is an outsider to the internally authoritative traditions of law, even though he may need to be an empathic outsider. A lawyer is bound to invoke legal rules of interpretation, not because he is an inferior historian, but because, *qua* lawyer, he is not an historian at all. He is a participant in a legal tradition, for whom statutes are primarily important not as sources of clues to events in the otherwise hidden past, but as authoritative materials from which meanings must be extracted by authorized means, to enable responses to *present* problems to be fashioned; or at least to be publicly justified to other cognoscenti of the tradition.

(iii) *Transmission*

Traditions do not exist automatically wherever the past has authoritative presence. There is, as a matter of etymological necessity, a third element in every tradition: transmission, a handing-over. A 'primitive' African mask, an ancient Japanese painting, which serve as models for French painters, are not, simply because they involve the normative presence of the past, elements in any tradition linking the past with the present. Traditions depend on real or imagined *continuities* between past and present. These continuities may be formalized and institutionalized as they are in the institutions of law and religion, though they need not be. Whatever the mode of transmission used in a particular tradition will affect directly and profoundly what passes from generation to generation, what is added, what subtracted, and how the transmitted past enters and is received into the present. As we have seen, in drawing on their store of present-past, contemporary legal systems depend upon sophisticated and complex means of recording, preserving, editing and transmitting a legally authorized past for present and future use. Such practices give this authorized past special importance for the present in institutionalized record-keeping traditions, with rules about and hierarchies of authority. They also give strategic importance to those entrusted with such tasks of transmission. Record-keeping allows more of the past to speak to the present and can help lend a sense of inter-generational continuity and coherence to traditions. Coherence of preoccupations over time, often quite self-conscious coherence, can be established. Also where records are kept, those who fashion and/or implement the criteria for selecting what to record have a means to edit the past and control the future.

In societies which have developed institutions of sacred and/or secular authority, castes of experts — kings, priests, judges, scholars — are frequently granted an official monopoly in the authorized interpretation of recorded texts. Where their authority is unappealable or ultimate, their interpretations of such texts become what their tradition is officially taken to mean. This gives, to these interpreters also, power over the past and the future. Such power, however, is rarely absolute, but must conform to canons of coherence and plausibility known to and accepted by participants in the tradition.

2. TRADITION AND CHANGE IN LAW

Central to the practices of law, then, are forms of tradition, transmitted components from a real or believed-to-be real past which are authoritatively present. This is not to deny the possibility, or the fact, of change in law. On the contrary, the familiar post-Enlightenment antinomies — tradition and change; tradition and progress; tradition and modernity — rest on a deep misunderstanding of the nature and behaviour of traditions. For whatever else leads to change in law, and there are, of course, many sources both internal and external, the very traditionality of law ensures that it *must* change. Although authoritative interpreters might police the present to see that it does not stray too far from their interpretation of the past, it is impossible for traditions to survive unchanged. Many traditions allow for deliberate change by, for example, revelation or legislation, or recourse to extra-doctrinal considerations. The changes thus made are then incorporated into the tradition and come to be interpreted in the traditional ways. Thus even radical legislation enters a continuing tradition which probably affected the way in which it was drafted and certainly will affect the ways in which it is read and applied.

However, quite apart from deliberate changes and even in traditions which permit no such change,[19] it occurs, always and inevitably. In oral traditions, the only available evidence of the tradition is what is conveyed to any generation by the existing members of earlier generations, what they recall and what they choose to transmit. What is forgotten is lost, what is currently inconvenient can be forgotten, in the process described by the anthropologist J. A. Barnes as 'structural amnesia'.[20] And just as inconvenient pasts can sink without trace, so more convenient ones can rise without independent evidence.

In written traditions, all who can read can examine evidence from and of the past. The past becomes more available for controversy, and notwithstanding the existence of written (after print, fixed) texts, the past-in-the-present remains unstable. Written traditions are continually subject to modification. Their transmission necessarily involves interpretation of writings. This ensures change. As lawyers know, natural languages are full of ineradicable open texture, ambiguity and vagueness. Legal texts, as Julius Stone has shown, are productively full of 'categories of illusory reference'.[21] Interpretation of such texts, even by contemporaries, is bound to yield different readings.

---

[19] Cf. A. R. Blackshield ed., *Legal Change: Essays in Honour of Julius Stone* (Sydney: Butterworths, 1983), especially chapters by Cohn and Perelman.

[20] 'The Collection of Genealogies', *Rhodes-Livingston Journal: Human Problems in British Central Africa* 5 (1947): 52.

[21] *Legal System and Lawyers' Reasonings*, (Sydney: Maitland, 1964), chapter 7; *Precedent and Law. Dynamics of Common Law Growth* (Sydney: Butterworths, 1985), *passim*.

Law as Tradition

Apart from ambiguities already present in texts,

...over time words change their meaning and values shift ... expectations as to form evolve. All of this is bound to have an effect on the reading of the text ... There is a sense in which *The Merchant of Venice* is for us unreadable, so different is the meaning of 'Jew' to Shakespeare and to us. And think how recently one's own use of the word 'gay' has been made problematic.[22]

Moreover, it is not just a question of the vagaries of texts. Texts do not stand on their own in a tradition. If they are taken to be part of it, they must be interpreted in ways that are consistent and coherent with it and thus the meaning of any traditional text will be affected by the nature of, and changes within, the tradition itself. Such changes will occur continuously over time as, independent of any particular text, new elements are added to the tradition and must be taken into account by subsequent participants. Gadamer makes the point well:

Every age has to understand a transmitted text in its own way, for the text is part of the whole of the tradition in which the age takes an objective interest and in which it seeks to understand itself. The real meaning of a text, as it speaks to the interpreter, does not depend on the contingencies of the author and whom he originally wrote for. It certainly is not identical with them, for it is always partly determined also by the historical situation of the interpreter and hence by the totality of the objective course of history.... Not occasionally only, but always, the meaning of a text goes beyond its author. That is why understanding is not merely a reproductive, but always a productive attitude as well.[23]

Thus the interpreter is confronted by far more than a text to interpret; he must interpret it in terms of the tradition to which both he and it belong.

This is as true of the interpretation of statutes, where a canonical form of words might seem to limit room for subsequent

---

[22] James Boyd White, 'Law as Language: Reading Law and Reading Literature', *Texas Law Review* 60 (1982): 415–45 at 427.
[23] Hans-Georg Gadamer, *Truth and Method*, 2nd edition (London: Sheed and Ward, 1979), pp. 263–64.

manoeuvre, as it is of case law. Indeed, given the impossibility of univocal interpretation of most complex texts, there is a sense in which legislation forces interpreters to rely more rather than less heavily on tradition than does the common law. For a relevant statute, still more a code, forces itself on an interpreter. Its words cannot be sloughed aside as *dicta* or dissent; they *have* to be interpreted. Since their meanings often will be plural, and since later lawyers nevertheless have to give meaning to them, they are bound to repair to interpretations which have become settled and accepted and/or to canons of statutory interpretation which, as we have seen, are highly traditional.

Finally, the interpreter is not a passive recipient of meanings. He is active in seeking to understand *them* in terms of what *he* knows, values, understands, and seeks to do with them. New questions render prior understandings problematic and yield new answers. Change, then, is never independent of the traditions in which it occurs. It is also without end.

3. CONCLUSIONS: THE INESCAPABILITY OF LEGAL TRADITION

The umbrella-concept tradition shelters many different types of phenomena with different characteristics. Any complex tradition, such as law, itself is likely to be made up of different sorts of traditions: traditions of claims about the world; 'second-order' traditions about such 'first-order' traditions and how one should respond to them;[24] real traditions which wreak their effects unnoticed; historically spurious traditions in which people believe and to which they are deeply attached. Adequate analysis of traditions needs to be able to encompass this complexity without denying or blurring it, as so much discussion of tradition does, in

---

[24] For the distinction between first-order and second-order traditions, see Karl R. Popper, 'Toward a Rational Theory of Tradition', *Conjectures and Refutations*, 3rd edn., revised (London: Routledge and Kegan Paul, 1969), pp. 126–27, and see Krygier, 'Tipologia della Tradizione', 234–35.

vague undiscriminating praise or blame. Yet the many different types of tradition do have some common features — the authoritative presence of transmitted past — and use of the concept of tradition allows one to speak of this. When one does, however, one must do more than speak of tradition-in-general. If one wishes to understand law or any other complex tradition, it is important first to appreciate their traditionality and then to make distinctions.[25]

One useful distinction between what, following Rawls and Dworkin, might be called three different conceptions of tradition, has been made by the Polish historian of social thought, Jerzy Szacki. Szacki distinguishes between three major foci of attention of writers on tradition, which are rarely distinguished; three different 'ways of approaching the problem of links between present and past.'[26] The first focuses on the *process* or activity of communication between generations, of transmission of elements of culture from one generation to another. It is what is referred to when we speak of things being passed on *by* tradition, and is much concerned with the means of such transmission. The second, which Szacki calls the *objective* conception of tradition, is concerned with traditions as historical deposits, as actual inheritances from the past; 'the dead hand of the past', 'the wisdom of ages'. The third, *subjective*, conception of tradition has to do with the evaluative commitment of a given generation to, or in opposition to, the past, 'that specific kind of value, whose defence (or criticism) involves on calling on its descent from the past'.[27] Weber's conception of traditional authority clearly has to do with tradition in this third sense.

For those speaking from within a tradition, the objective conception of tradition has priority over the others. Subjective traditions are parasitic upon the assertion of objective ones — participants in a tradition are always committed to allege, if often

---

[25] For one attempt to do this, see Krygier 'Tipologia della Tradizione', pp. 233–47.
[26] *Tradycja*, p. 97.
[27] *Tradycja*, p. 155.

falsely, that objective traditions lie behind their attachments — and without objective traditions there would be nothing for mechanisms of transmission to transmit.

For those wishing to analyze traditions, however, it is not clear that one should choose any one conception over the others; though it is useful to distinguish them. A priori, traditions in the second and third senses need have little to do with each other; objective traditions to which no one attends, subjective attachment to nonexistent pasts. In practice, the interrelationships between inheritance and subjective traditionality are complicated, often inextricable, frequently controversial among scholars, and in need of investigation in particular cases. Most complex traditions, such as the Judaeo-Christian tradition or the common law tradition, combine characteristic objective and subjective forms of traditionality, and ways of passing them on, in distinctive ways. What at any present of such a tradition is 'objective' is an amalgam of layers of past as it has been witnessed, recorded, interpreted, imagined, and assimilated. What is 'subjective' tradition may have little to do with the historical past of which it speaks, but it is rarely uninfluenced by the consciously and unconsciously transmitted past. Traditions are rarely either simply given *or* socially constructed, if only because what is given in one generation includes what had earlier been socially constructed, and social constructions are profoundly affected by whatever happens to be given when they occur. Important traditions are a combination of inheritance and (often creative) reception and transmission.

Law, in any event, rests upon mountains of inherited tradition, preserved, referred and deferred to by highly developed institutions and practices of tradition-maintenance; that is to say, it is highly traditional in at least the first two of Szacki's senses. This would remain true even if such traditionality were unaccompanied by any subjective traditionality on the part of contemporaries, as Max Weber believed was increasingly the case in the modern world. I do not believe that Weber was wholly right, particularly about law, as consideration of the central role of 'authority' in legal systems would reveal. However I will not pursue that here.

Traditionality in these first two senses is indispensable in social life generally and in law specifically. Its contributions are both cognitive and normative. The major cognitive contribution of transmitted inherited tradition is, as it were, to have done our thinking for us and to have done it ahead of time. Even when we do consciously reflect, the point Popper makes about tradition in science can be generalized: 'If we start afresh, then, when we die, we shall be about as far as Adam and Eve were when they died (or, if you prefer, as far as Neanderthal man)'.[28] Much of the time though, we do not have time, skill, imagination enough to solve each of our problems afresh. Traditions, particularly recorded traditions, provide us with storehouses of possibly relevant analogies to our present problems, ways of thinking about such problems, and successful and unsuccessful attempts to solve them. It makes sense to try to imitate the successful attempts and avoid those which with hindsight appear unsuccessful. Whether or not it makes sense, it is easier. David Armstrong makes the point well:

Conscious thought, choice and decision are difficult matters. They occupy no very extensive part of a human being's life.... Whitehead said that *thought* was the cavalry charge of the intellect. His point was that cavalry charges, though vitally important, could form no very extensive part of battles. Conscious deliberation followed by decision might be said to be the cavalry charge of the will. Now suppose that one is free to adopt a wide variety of courses of action, but no particular course is obviously superior. It will be an important volitional economy simply to do what one remembers that some conspecifics did.[29]

The relevance of this to law is obvious. Law deals with myriad practical problems which individuals who use it have not, indeed could not, alone foresee or forestall. Durkheim noted this when he

---

[28] Popper, 'Toward a Rational Theory of Tradition', p. 129.
[29] D. M. Armstrong, 'The Nature of Tradition', *The Nature of Mind and other Essays*, (Brisbane: University of Queensland Press, 1981), pp. 89–103 at 98.

insisted on the importance in every legal contract of the vast store of noncontracted elements which the law implies:

> ... contract law is that which determines the juridical consequences of our acts that we have not determined. ... A resume of numerous, varied experiences, what we cannot forsee individually is there provided for, what we cannot regulate is there regulated, and this regulation imposes itself upon us, although it may not be our handiwork, but that of society and tradition.[30]

Durkheim's observation applies generally, beyond contracts and in the everyday law-affected lives of everyone.

A related point can be made specifically about the activities of legal professionals. Charles Fried has argued that neither moral philosophy nor economics, which it is so fashionable to use to assess law, can provide solutions which are sufficiently *determinate* to solve the practical problems which face lawyers and judges and on which judges *must* pronounce. Fried asks:

> So what is it that lawyers and judges know that philosophers and economists do not? The answer is simple: the law. There really is a distinct and special subject matter for our profession. And there is a distinct method.... It is the method of analogy and precedent.... The discipline of analogy fills in the gaps left by more general theory, gaps which must be filled because choices must be made and actions taken.[31]

It is the traditionality of law in the two senses mentioned above which makes this 'distinct method' possible.

The presence of recorded past is also important to several normative functions that law performs, and in any large society must perform. In particular, many laws, and the very existence of bodies of authoritative legal propositions, solve what game-theorists call coordination problems between people. There are many social situations where our decisions are strategically interdependent, that is, where 'the best choice for each depends upon

---

[30] *The Division of Labor in Society*, (New York: The Free Press, 1964) p. 214.
[31] Charles Fried, 'The Artificial Reason of the Law or: What Lawyers Know', *Texas Law Review* 60 (1982): 35–58 at 57.

what he expects the others to do, knowing that each of the others is trying to guess what *he* is likely to do'.[32] Coordination problems are a subset of problems of strategic interaction: those where parties have reason to cooperate, have mutually conditional preferences (I will drive on the left if you will; you will if I will; each needs to know that the other will and knows that his counterpart will, etc.) and at least two alternatives to choose from. Edna Ullmann-Margalit has shown that in such situations, *norms* will be generated which provide 'some *anchorage*; some preeminently conspicuous indication as to what action is likely to be taken by (most of) the others, or at least what action is likely to be expected by everyone to be taken by (most of) the others.'[33]

Social life is full of recurring coordination problems and no society can exist without solutions to many of them. In a 'society' with nothing but unsolved coordination problems, life would be not merely nasty, horrible, brutish and short, as it is in many societies, but also impossibly and endlessly confusing. No one would know what anyone else would do, in any situation where coordination was necessary for interdependent decisions. Whatever else it was, such a solipsistic aggregation would not be a society. A large, populous and complex society full of anonymous (inter-)actors is likely to have institutionalized solutions to many pervasive and important problems of coordination, particularly among strangers. Legal systems contain rules of the road, in both the literal and metaphorical sense, as one way of institutionalizing solutions to such problems and of stabilizing and focussing the relevant expectations.

Legal systems vary in the degree to which they contribute usefully, or even positively, to the solution of life's coordination problems. Much that goes on in any legal system is concerned with other problems. Some legal systems contribute little to solving, or even compound, problems of coordination. Kafka

---

[32] Edna Ullmann-Margalit, *The Emergence of Norms* (Oxford: Clarendon Press, 1977), p. 78.
[33] *The Emergence of Norms*, p. 109.

insisted upon this and Stalin — some of whose instruments of random mass terror were in at least a formal sense legal — demonstrated it in ghastly fashion. So at its weakest my argument becomes that, *to the extent that* legal systems contribute to the solution of coordination problems, tradition in the two senses referred to is necessary. A normative implication is that, since rule without reference to the present legal past, for example rule by unpredictable *ad hoc* decree, fails to contribute to the solution of such problems, it is objectionable from this point of view, as it is from many others.

Even at its weakest, the argument amounts to more than might appear. Many legal systems contribute a great deal to the solution of coordination problems, by providing a matrix of commonly understood signals which masses of strangers can decode in familiar and similar ways. While systems differ significantly in their reliance on coordination-aiding traditionality, in no society will *all* law be up for grabs, or for decree, all the time. In matters of political indifference, even dictatorial rulers are likely to let law solve recurring problems of coordination. Even in contemporary Poland, after all, where decrees are rather thick, fast and confusing, everyone knows on which side of the road cars drive. Moreover, even legal systems poor at aiding coordination in extra-legal matters, by their very existence and activities create coordination problems which they themselves must resolve. For as Postema has argued, once a legal system exists, its own operations require it to generate mutually concordant expectations about the law, not only among citizens but between citizens and law-applying officials and among law-applying officials themselves;[34] 'co-ordination is fundamental to law and ... no legal *system* is conceivable without substantial coordination elements at its foundations'.[35]

---

[34] I owe the specification of these three co-ordination situations to Gerald J. Postema, 'Co-ordination and Convention at the Foundations of Law', *Journal of Legal Studies* 11 (1982): 165–202, especially at 182ff.

[35] Postema, 'Co-ordination and Convention of the Foundations of Law', p. 194.

Law as Tradition

What is necessary, and what the transmitted present-past of legal authority, precedents, conventions, practices, rules, common understandings of the way the system works and doesn't work, go some way to provide, are relatively identifiable and reliable 'anchorages' for the mutually interdependent expectations which arise about and through the law.

To the extent that the traditionality of law in Szacki's first two senses aids in the solution of coordination problems, this is an argument for, or at least a presumption in favour of, subjective traditionality. However, as Marxists and others have emphasized, solving coordination problems is not all that legal or other institutions do. And, as Weber's gloom about bureaucracy showed, not everything that is indispensable is in every respect good or to be welcomed. As it happens, I believe that many traditions, like many bureaucracies,[36] are much maligned and in need of defenders. But many traditions, like many bureaucracies, are vile and pernicious; all the more so because they are so hard to shift. Apartheid, anti-semitism, racism of all sorts are, after all, highly traditional practices in all three of the senses I have mentioned. It is, moreover, no accident that beneficiaries of entrenched advantages of wealth, power and status are often also supported by strong normative traditions. Such traditions render acceptable even hallowed and apparently 'natural' to those who believe in them, what might be, frequently should be, seen to be unjust, exploitative, tyrannical, and highly contingent once unmasked. The hold of such traditions on social life has not been negligible in human history, nor have the advantages accruing to the groups benefiting from them.

Social theory should not find it insuperable to accommodate the different functions that traditions perform; though scores of 'consensus theorists' on one side and 'conflict theorists' on the other appear to have found it difficult. And social theory is no substitute for moral argument. While it is always important to con-

---

[36] See Eugene Kamenka and Martin Krygier, eds., *Bureaucracy. The Career of a Concept* (London: Edward Arnold, 1979).

sider, it is never a sufficient argument for a practice that it has existed for 'time out of mind'. On the other hand, that is even less satisfactory as an argument against it.

Faculty of Law,
University of New South Wales,
Kensington, Sydney,
Australia.

[14]

Language, Law, and Social Meanings: Linguistic/Anthropological Contributions to the Study of Law

Elizabeth Mertz

Scholars who study the social constitution of law have increasingly come to appreciate the importance of language in legal processes. Talk of discourse and language has become prominent in the writings of sociolegal scholars and legal theorists alike.[1] This review essay considers the question, What dif-

---

I would like to thank Joseph Sanders for his careful editorial assistance and Bette Sikes for her expert editorial work.

[1] As Merry (p. 110) and Conley and O'Barr (p. 2) note, the term "discourse" has been used in different ways by different disciplinary traditions. Social theorists, anthropologists, and linguists use the term to refer to both spoken and written language and speak of "types" of discourse that vary in their structure. Thus discourses are stretches of language that can be viewed as structured or coherent; often analysts also examine the ways in which some stretches of language differ in principled ways from other kinds of language. Some discourse analysts from these traditions also pay particular attention to speech context. As Merry (p. 9) notes, a growing number of scholars, from Michel Foucault to Martha Fineman, have been concerned with understanding the social constitution and contexts of discourses. This kind of approach views discourses as always ideologically laden, as embedded in power relations in nonrandom ways.

From this vantage, then, kinds of "talk" are kinds of discourse. However, to the extent that we embrace Merry's somewhat Foucauldian vision of "discourses," discourse analysis would involve in-depth study of the social context of speech. It would be possible to analyze kinds of talk in terms of linguistic differences without much attention to the relevant communities and social history, but this would not be "discourse" analysis in Merry's sense. (It would, however, meet the definition of "discourse" analysis used by Conley and O'Barr—and by most linguists.) While at several points in this essay I use the distinction between "talk" and "discourse" to signal this kind of difference in approach, it is not my intent to assert any canonical usage of the terms. (Indeed, my own practice in general is to use the term "discourse" broadly.) Here the distinction is meant to signal a difference between Conley and O'Barr's more in-depth treatment of the language itself, as opposed to Merry's more in-depth analysis of the social/economic/political contexts of the language she studied.

ference does this attention to language make? I discuss a number of ways of approaching language, suggesting that some are more useful than others for social and legal analysis. In particular, I focus on the contribution of anthropological approaches and on two recent entries in the University of Chicago Press series "Language and Legal Discourse": *Getting Justice and Getting Even: Legal Consciousness among Working-Class Americans*, by Sally Engle Merry, and *Rules versus Relationships: The Ethnography of Legal Discourse*, by John M. Conley and William M. O'Barr.

The first section of the essay gives an overview of anthropological and linguistic approaches to language, from fundamental concepts in the work of Saussure and Peirce, through reflectionist and instrumentalist approaches used by sociolinguists and others, to the new anthropological vision of socially grounded linguistic creativity. The second section focuses on the study of language and law. It begins with a brief review of relevant past work on legal language, giving special attention to studies that focus on the contextual or social character of language. The section concludes with a discussion and comparison of the volumes by Merry and by Conley and O'Barr.

I. Ways of Thinking about Language

There have been many different conceptualizations of language in the linguistic and anthropological literature. Some have focused on formal properties of language as an abstract system with its own dynamics. Other approaches have concentrated on language as an instrument effecting social ends. And a number of linguistic anthropologists and sociolinguists have worked to formulate a theory encompassing both formal and functional aspects of language (see, e.g., Gumperz 1964, 1972; Hymes 1974; Labov 1964, 1966; Silverstein 1976, 1987). As this work has proceeded, a new focus has emerged: beyond formal grammatical structure or instrumentalist functions, language also embodies social creativity. We have just begun to explore the ways in which language functions not merely to express preexisting social categories but to forge, renew, shift, and break social bonds (see, e.g., Baumann & Briggs 1990; Brenneis 1984, 1988; Briggs 1986; Gumperz 1982; Hanks 1990; Irvine 1989; Lucy 1992; Mertz 1988a; Mertz & Parmentier 1985; Silverstein 1976, 1992; Woolard 1989).[2] This creativity is particularly obvious in legal arenas, where so much of the social "work" being accomplished is a powerful act of translation in which social ends are effected through the imposition of legal (and of course at the same time linguistic) cate-

---

[2] Although in this view language is an important structuring influence, the theory does not devolve into linguistic determinism because it conceptualizes language as itself shaped in crucial ways by social context.

gories.³ To appreciate what linguistic anthropology can offer the study of law, we need to explore a number of basic linguistic concepts and consider some alternative approaches to studying language.

A. Fundamental Linguistic Concepts

A key formulation of the division between language as an abstract system and language as a medium for social exchange can be found in the work of Ferdinand de Saussure (1959).⁴ Saussure made a distinction between *langue*—the abstract linguistic system that speakers of a language share (perhaps most easily understood as the system of "grammar") and *parole*—the "execution" of that system in use by individual speakers. The socially shared system of signs that comprise *langue*, described by Saussure as a union of sound-images (signifiers) and meanings (signifieds), is the crucial backdrop against which individual speech takes place:

> The signifier, though to all appearances freely chosen with respect to the idea that it represents, is fixed, not free, with respect to the linguistic community that uses it. . . . We say to language, "Choose!" but we add: "It must be this sign and no other." No individual, even if he willed it, could modify in any way at all the choice that has been made. (Saussure 1959:71)

The primary focus of Saussure's work was on the way in which language-internal structure generated meaning. The well-known Saussurean "proportion" posits a systematic relation between changes in the sound system of language and changes in meaning. (The actual social structuring of *langue* as it was realized in *parole* is not well explored in Saussure's work.) Subsequent work by Chomsky and other linguists continues the focus on abstract systematicity in language. As a result, a great deal of work on language structure has proceeded with a blind eye to the social grounding of language. This kind of decontextual approach by itself is of very limited value in understanding the social character of legal language.

Charles Sanders Peirce, the founder of the field of inquiry known as "semiotics,"⁵ pointed the way toward a more social

---

³ See, e.g., Edward Levi's (1949) classic study of the way in which classifying items as "inherently dangerous" was an essential part of tort law's response to social and industrial change.

⁴ Although in this essay I focus on linguistic theory, it is important to note that Saussure's work was broader, dealing not only with language but with "signs" and "signification" more generally. Linguistic signs are only one way of communicating, and so an inclusive theory of communication needs to encompass nonlinguistic signaling as well. Saussure was the founder of "semiology," a broad inquiry into the nature of communication that includes the study of language.

⁵ Peirce's "semiotics" and Saussure's "semiology" are obviously closely related endeavors, and much current work published in journals such as *Semiotica* draws on both traditions.

vision of language. Like Saussure, Peirce views the sign as composed of a sign vehicle (Saussure's sound-image or signifier) and a mental representation (Saussure's signified) (Peirce 1974:2.228).[6] However, Peirce also adds a third component—the *object* that the sign stands for.[7] As part of his analysis of sign meaning, Peirce characterizes signs according to the relations between sign vehicles and the "objects" they represent (ibid. 2.247–2.249).[8] He distinguishes three kinds of signs: (1) the *icon*, which represents its object by virtue of a perceived isomorphism between characteristics of the sign vehicle and of the object (e.g., a diagram), (2) the *symbol*, which represents its object "by virtue of a law, usually an association of general ideas" (e.g., the word "rose"), and (3) the *index*, which represents its object through an actual existential connection (e.g., a pointing finger and the object it points to, or the word "I" used by a particular speaker) (ibid.).

The index is of particular interest to those who study the social foundation of meaning, because indexes derive their meaning from the particular contexts in which they are used. This kind of context-based indexical meaning is also referred to as *pragmatic* meaning. Symbolic (or *semantic*) meaning, by contrast, is "general," obtaining apart from specific contexts. The word "rose," for example, acquires its meaning through a general rule or law—a cultural convention that tells us that this word ("rose") means this idea or concept ("kind of flower").

Linguistic signs usually function in multiple ways at the same time; thus a given stretch of language may at once index its context and convey symbolic meaning. Imagine, for example, that I tell you that "This rose is yellow." I index our speech context in the word "this," which relies on the details of where we are standing in relation to the rose to pick out (or index) that particular flower. The word "is" also indexes the current context (as opposed to a past or future tense verb) and thus depends on knowledge of the particular setting of our speech for part of its meaning.[9] The words "rose" and "yellow" rely

---

[6] I here employ the standard notation used by Peirce scholars; the number before the period is the volume number in Peirce's *Collected Papers* (1974); the numbers following the period indicate the passage number.

[7] As will become apparent from the examples below, the "object" need not be a concrete thing.

[8] Peirce introduced three trichotomies, each of which characterized signs according to different criteria; he then adduced ten classes of signs by combining some of these criteria. Here I focus on the second trichotomy and on the contextual character of the index.

[9] Even the words "this" and "is" rely on residual semantic meaning as well. For example, we know apart from any given context that "this" refers to things that are close rather than far away. Similarly, the words "rose" and "yellow" incorporate pragmatic meaning when they are used in speech to refer to particular instances of the categories. Our assessment that particular words rely more heavily on indexical or symbolic meaning is not meant to deny their multifunctionality.

more on our decontextualized understandings of their symbolic meanings. A number of long-standing traditions in linguistics and sociolinguistics have attempted to explicate how linguistic forms function pragmatically to index social context.

B. Reflectionist and Instrumentalist Views of Language Pragmatics

For some scholars, attention to language is important because language reflects social contexts. Alternately, language can be viewed as a way of effecting social ends. In either case, language itself is important only because it provides a window on social process; language is understood to be a straightforward expression of its social context. Much of the early (and some current) work in the field of sociolinguistics provides powerful examples of these aspects of language function. This work has been an important corrective to a prevailing focus on language as an abstract (grammatical) system for conveying decontextual (semantic) meaning.

Thus, for example, William Labov (1964, 1966) found that linguistic variation corresponds with class divisions. In a famous study of New Yorkers' speech, Labov demonstrated that a number of subtle linguistic distinctions (e.g., pronunciation of the terminal "r" sound in phrases like "fourth floor") mirror divisions in class identity. Labov used a sociological index combining occupation, education, and family income to designate four class groupings (lower class, working class, lower middle class, upper middle class). His study revealed that subtle variations in speech correlated with these class divisions. Sociolinguists also found that aspects of language structure mirror divisions of race and gender, as well as other divisions within and between social communities (see, e.g., Brown 1980; Eidheim 1969; Lakoff 1975; Quay, Mathews, & Schwarzmuller 1977; Van der Broeck 1977; West & Zimmerman 1975). This reflectionist view of language as a mirror of social reality has been characterized as a metaphorical approach (Silverstein 1992), for here variation in language forms is analyzed as a more or less straightforward expression of social variation. The social function of language is highlighted, but language does not have an independent role in shaping social results.

A similarly straightforward image of the language-society relation is at the heart of an instrumentalist theory of language. According to this theory, people use language transparently to achieve social goals. When we say language is "transparent," we mean that there is no distinctive effect imputed to language; linguistic forms operate as tools through which actors achieve certain social results. Thus, for example, Deborah Tannen (1989) views certain linguistic devices (tropes, repetition, im-

haps it is not a transparent window but one that refracts and changes what is seen in systematic and important ways. Merry makes this point in *Getting Justice and Getting Even*, as she explicates her view of conflict as "a form of communication, a kind of extended conversation" in which messages are exchanged that "are not simple or straightforward" but rather are "encoded communications, subject to interpretation" in structured sociocultural ways (p. 93; see also Merry 1990).

We look to language because the details of how something is said—the shape of a particular verbal exchange or written communication—matters. When attorneys submit briefs and argue to appellate courts, for example, how they write and speak (as well as how they are received) may well to some degree reflect class or gender identities. Attorneys in these settings are almost certainly attempting to use their language in a conscious attempt to effectuate social results. But what happens in the interaction is not always a simple reflection of preexisting social divisions or a straightforward use of language as a tool. There is a rich and complex dynamic that includes those aspects of language use but also includes the shaping of the interaction by discourse forms (appellate briefs, oral arguments), the complicated speech context of the institutional setting in general (the court), the influence of the particular individuals involved in this instance (the judge, other court personnel, the attorneys, the litigants in this case), the *creation* of new meanings and relationships and contexts by ongoing oral and written communication, and so forth. This is an opportunity to move beyond determinisms that would view legal outcomes as foreordained reflexes of preexisting social structures while yet not pretending that legal interactions are somehow free of the strong constraints generated by distributions of power and wealth in societies. In the socially grounded study of linguistic creativity there is both a strong respect for these constraints and yet serious consideration given to the creative possibilities that inhere in every new interaction and utterance.

C. Socially Grounded Linguistic Creativity: An Integrative Approach

The integrative approach to language and social context emerging in anthropology offers a challenging alternative to the approaches described above. I begin with a very brief overview of the somewhat technical literature in linguistics (with the caveat that I am of necessity simplifying considerably).

Exciting recent work in anthropological linguistics, building from a number of traditions, reverses the usual assumption in the philosophy of language and other traditions that the dominant function of language is conveying semantic information (see Silverstein 1976, 1979, 1985, 1992; see also Briggs 1986; Crapanzano 1992). An emphasis on the semantic or "referential" aspect of language is understandable, for it may be what makes human language unique: "[L]anguages may be unique among natural semiotic systems in their capacity to transmit descriptive [referential, semantic], as well as social and expressive, information" (Lyons 1977:174; see also Mertz 1985:8). However, under the newer approach developed by anthropological linguist Michael Silverstein (1976, 1985, 1992) and others, it is precisely the social and expressive function of language that orders and grounds its ability to convey semantic information.[10]

For language to be actually used[11]—for the abstract system of language to be translated into speech—there is a necessary move to the indexical or social contextual realm. Because it is in use that the system of language is created, the backbone of language structure is that part which is responsive to social contexts (see also Kurylowicz 1972). From this vantage, language-in-use is always functioning indexically, and conveying semantic information is but one of the things it does when that is happening (it can also express emotion, maintain social distance, etc.). Semantics thus becomes a subset, a special case of pragmatics (Silverstein 1992). The socially shared system of language is constantly being renewed and shaped as it is used by speakers in social contexts; thus, while it may add some twists and turns of its own (because it is a system with its own special dynamics), language is always responsive to social forces.

One of the key structuring pragmatic principles of language rests upon its capacity to refer to and represent itself (the "meta" level of language) (Silverstein 1992).[12] Recent anthropological work has focused on indexical or contextual structuring and its typification at "meta" levels (see Brenneis 1984; Briggs 1986; Errington 1988; Hanks 1990; Lucy 1992; Mertz n.d.; Parmentier 1987, 1992; Silverstein 1985, 1987).[13] One

---

[10] This formulation builds on work by a group of linguists known as the Prague School and on later work by Roman Jakobson, who began to unearth the ways in which indexical (or contextual) structuring plays a vital role in linguistic systems. Work by sociolinguists and ethnographers of speaking similarly forefronted the role of indexical meaning, but as noted above, earlier studies often treated indexicality as a more or less straightforward reflex of social context.

[11] We can translate this in Saussurean terms: for langue (the system of language) to be translated into parole (actual speech.)

[12] For example, when a speaker says "I'm asking you for information," she is naming and characterizing the act she is performing as she performs it. Such coincidence of reference and indexicality makes this kind of language particularly interesting to speech act theorists, for the unit of pragmatic meaning corresponds to the unit of semantic meaning.

[13] Work on political language, for example, has revealed that political oratory often embodies a model of social relations in the very structure of the discourse (Parmentier 1992; Silverstein 1979; see also Keenan 1975; Mertz n.d.). The linguistic struc-

aspect of linguistic creativity, then, is language's capacity to refer to itself, so that seemingly identical stretches of speech can be typified as different by the metalinguistic structure. If, for example, I read portions of the Bill of Rights to you in a questioning tone of voice, making questions of sentences that are written declaratively, I create a new metalinguistic structure, telling you through the pragmatics of how I am speaking that these words are not "a declaration of rights" but rather "a skeptical questioning"—an entirely different "type" of discourse. Creative use of this typification affords speakers an opportunity to create new understandings of what language is doing (and thus to use it differently) in given situations.

Two other key structuring principles contribute to linguistic creativity (Silverstein 1979, 1992). First, any particular event of speaking functions against a backdrop of "presupposed" social knowledge that can be specified ahead of time. For example, established norms may tell us that using first names or endearing terms rather than titles usually indicates social or emotional intimacy. Note, however, that in any given instance speakers may creatively manipulate these norms, using endearing terms to people they hardly know or formal titles with intimate family members. When this happens, the "same" linguistic form conveys a vastly different meaning (for example, an apparently endearing term takes on insulting meaning, as in the case of someone calling a stranger "dear," or an apparently formal term becomes humorous and affectionate, as in the case of parents referring to their infant son as "Mr."). In each of these cases, the new meaning is generated in part by a violation of presupposed linguistic norms. Indeed, linguistic creativity itself relies on the presupposing function of language as a background to work with and against.

At the same time, language also creates new meanings through its use in social context. Thus, in the example above, it is not just the presupposable norms that generate meaning but also the creative use of language in a particular time and place (Silverstein 1976, 1979). Let us look at two examples of language pointing to (indexing) its context of use. If I tell you that "that chair is broken but this chair is not," you will need to know something about the context to decipher my statement. If there is no chair in the vicinity, the statement becomes difficult to understand. If there are two chairs that are different dis-

---

ture acts as a commentary on the ongoing speech, a meta-level typification that contributes to speakers' feeling that a particular structure is "natural" or "right." White (1990) has advanced a similar argument about the structure of certain Supreme Court opinions in which judges' rhetoric mirrors their approach to constitutional interpretation. Thus Taft's "authoritarian" rhetorical structure matches his "plain meaning" approach to constitutional interpretation, while Brandeis's processual and democratic theory of interpretation is voiced in an "open" rhetoric embedded in the vernacular or "common" language.

tances from the speaker, you will be able to pick out the chair farther from me as the one that is broken. Decoding my use of the word "that" depends on your knowledge of aspects of the speech context that exist independent of my act of speaking; in conveying meaning here, I am relying on presupposable aspects of the context to a greater extent than I am creating new context.[14] On the other hand, the use of a formal title rather than a nickname to indicate formality may create a social reality that did not exist prior to the act of speaking. That is, if a close friend suddenly uses a more formal style of address, she is not pointing to an aspect of the context that was knowable ahead of time. Rather, she is pointing to and simultaneously creating a change in relationship between the speakers (part of the social context of speaking), indicating and creating a new distance between the speakers. Of course, there are also presupposing aspects of even this very creative use (knowledge of the norms for use of nicknames, knowledge of the previous relationship between the speakers, knowledge of the current speech situation). But this would be an example of language functioning at the more creative end of the scale.

As these examples suggest, if we only focus on the content (semantics) rather than the form (pragmatics) of speech, we miss a great deal about the creative function of language.[15] White (1990:x–xi) has eloquently critiqued this kind of static focus:

> The habit of mind I am describing assumes that our most important uses of language are fundamentally propositional in character, indeed that any meaningful piece of discourse asserts (or denies) that such and such is the case. . . . Once our auditors perceive the objects we are naming in the real or conceptual world, language has done its job and can—and should—disappear.

White proposes an alternative vision that focuses on what I have been calling linguistic creativity (see also Mertz 1988a, 1989, 1992a): "But we have another way of thinking about language. . . . This is a way of imagining language not as a set of propositions, but as a repertoire of forms of action and of life. . . . Our purposes, like our observations, have no prelingual reality, but are constituted in language" (White 1990:xi). This vision of language as constitutive focuses our attention on the creative role of language use.[16]

---

[14] This is, of course, a relative judgment, as all utterances change the context to some extent, contributing in some way to ongoing interaction among people, or to self-expression of some kind.

[15] Silverstein (1979, 1981) explains this skewing as a predictable outcome of the way language itself works (see also Weissbourd & Mertz 1985; Mertz 1992).

[16] In a similar vein, Sally Merry stresses the uncertainty and the contingent and potentially powerful character of language use as a conflict unfolds; while a "retrospective" analysis might make it seem as if a certain interpretation and concomitant legal

The framework I have outlined, then, provides a compelling reason for paying attention to the language of the law, for language *is* the process whereby cultural understandings are enacted, created, and transformed in interaction with social structure. At the same time, language is structured in crucial ways by its social context, and social power is implicated at every level of contextual influence on language (sometimes all the more powerfully at the subtle levels of pragmatic structuring that are not easily accessible to conscious awareness).[17] Legal language affords a particularly good opportunity to examine both the constraining influences of social context and the potentially creative power of linguistic interaction.

II. Socially Grounded Linguistic Creativity and the Law

The legal arena affords students of language an exciting locus for examining the connection between language and social power. Nowhere is an act of linguistic translation more obviously laden with socially powerful consequences than in judicial opinions, where, for example, the decision to call a certain verbal exchange an "offer and acceptance" carries with it direct social results. The socially grounded and creative character of language is everywhere evident in the law, and language functioning in this fashion is no small part of the way that the law achieves its results. A number of previous studies have provided accounts of linguistic creativity in the law and its social consequences.

A. Some Past Studies of Language and Law

Here I focus on a few previous studies that set the scene for the two books I discuss in more detail below.[18] I begin with studies focusing on the powerful effects that very slight linguistic differences can have on legal outcomes and then move to studies that have examined more broadly the ways in which legal language can affect relationships and social structures.

---

result was inevitable, from the perspective of a person in the process of an ongoing linguistic exchange, all manner of meanings could potentially result from their choices in speaking (p. 94). Conley and O'Barr also stress the contingent character of linguistic exchanges in the courtrooms they studied, demonstrating that results do not flow automatically from presupposable aspects of the context but flow rather from the creative use of language by litigants and judges.

[17] This approach to discourse merges a Foucauldian emphasis on social power (Foucault 1980; see also Bourdieu 1977) with a sociolinguistic concern for the social context of speech.

[18] I again begin with the caution that this is by no means an exhaustive literature review. There are a number of excellent sources for such a review of the language and law literature; see Brenneis 1988; Danet 1980; Levi 1982, 1986; O'Barr 1981.

424 **Language, Law, and Social Meanings**

Effects of Language Pragmatics on Legal Outcomes

A view of language as more than a system for conveying propositional or semantic meaning also emerged in earlier work on language and law. This work demonstrated that language functioning contextually is effectual in certain ways. For example, psycholinguists have demonstrated that language affects assessments of eyewitness reliability (Loftus 1975, 1979) and juries' comprehension of instructions (Charrow & Charrow 1979; Sales, Elwork, & Alfini 1977). Certain styles of speech in the courtroom may damage a truthful witness' credibility. In particular, Conley, O'Barr, and Lind (1978) found that use of a speech style that was characteristic of "powerless" people (women as opposed to men, lower-class as opposed to upper-class people, etc.) undermined a witness's chance of being believed (see also O'Barr 1982). In all this work, there is clear acknowledgment that language structure and the meaning it conveys play a potentially vital role in legal outcomes.

Another common thread in these works is that they focus on subtle—often pragmatic—aspects of language that are in danger of being ignored by the court in favor of more semantic readings. This danger arises when language is taken at face value, viewed as a medium for conveying abstract information rather than as a socially embedded system conveying meaning in multiple ways. Indeed, pragmatic cues are often subtle, because the pragmatic structure of language is often less accessible to awareness than semantic, "surface" meaning (see Silverstein 1981). For example, Elizabeth Loftus (1979:96) conducted an experiment in which witnesses were shown a film and then asked whether they had seen something that was not shown in the film. She found that they were much more likely to report seeing the nonexistent object if asked, "Did you see *the* broken headlight?" than if asked, "Did you see *a* broken headlight?" If we analyze Loftus's insights in linguistic terms, we see that the difference between "the" and "a" involves a shift in presupposable aspects of contextual structuring: the word "the" generally is used to point to (index) an object that has been previously introduced, whereas the word "a" does not presuppose previous introduction.[19]

Other studies have focused broadly on the way legal language affects the very constitution of ongoing negotiated relationships and of wider cultures and social structures.

Constituting Relationships, Social Structures, and Cultures in the Language of the Law

Other work on the language of the law has explored the

---

[19] On the different ways in which previous referents are introduced and accompanying presuppositions in children's speech, see Hickmann 1980.

possibility of still stronger formative effects of legal language on social outcomes and structures. I focus on two varieties of social results: immediate effects on the relationships of speaking parties and more global effects on whole cultures and societies.

Work in the "process-oriented"[20] tradition concentrates on the way in which the use of language in legal arenas structures the relationships of interacting parties. Combining the ethnomethodologist's focus on shared commonsense understandings (Cicourel 1974; Garfinkel 1967) with the conversational analyst's attention to linguistic detail (Sacks, Schegloff, & Jefferson 1974), scholars in this tradition view linguistic exchanges in courtrooms and law offices as part of an ongoing process in which participants negotiate and create social reality (see Atkinson & Drew 1979; Danet et al. 1980; Maynard 1984; Pomerantz 1978; see also Goodwin 1980). Atkinson and Drew (1979), for example, analyze the way speakers take turns talking, tracing the way in which different forms of questioning or response accomplish underlying social or psychological goals (blaming, denying, etc.). Here the organization of talk is viewed as a key to the ongoing interaction through which people together produce social structure. Language does more than reflect preexisting structures. However, this understanding of the effect of language on social interaction is limited by its focus on the immediate speech context.

A broader view emerges from work that examines the effects of semantic and discourse-level phenomena on the constitution of cultures and societies more generally. However, these studies vary in the degree to which they take pragmatic aspects of language seriously—and in the way in which they take account of the wider sociocultural surround.

In their study of the language of the lawyer's office, Sarat and Felstiner (1988) are concerned with how legally circumscribed linguistic interaction frustrates participant's goals:

> [M]ost of the time lawyers remain silent in the face of client attacks on their spouses. . . . When they do interpret behavior they limit themselves to conduct that is directly relevant to the legal process of divorce, and they stress circumstances and situations that produce common responses, rather than intentions or dispositions unique to particular individuals. In this way they deflect what is, for many clients, a strong desire to achieve some moral vindication, even in a no-fault world.
> (Ibid., p. 764)

This work employs a careful semantic-level analysis of linguistic interaction to explain the way in which lawyers use language to reinforce their own authority and their clients' dependence, re-

---

[20] See Maynard 1984:5; see also Brenneis 1988 for a review of this approach and an enlightening discussion of how it differs from ethnography of speaking approaches.

maining deaf to what clients view as the most salient parts of their stories, while fostering a negative view of the legal system (see also Sarat & Felstiner 1986, 1990). Here linguistic interaction creates and reinforces power relationships, validating only some stories, hearing only some voices. This vision of legal language has much in common with that of Conley and O'Barr and of Merry (see below).

In an interesting study of the "transformation of disputes," Mather and Yngvesson (1980–81:780) focus on

> the differing abilities of litigants to argue their cases; the role of lawyers in shaping the way disputes are defined and presented; the influence of various publics or audiences with an interest in the definition and outcome of a particular case; and the complex relationships and informal norms which develop among groups of persons who cooperate in processing cases.

Their conclusion links legal language and forms of reasoning with transformations of dispute in different kinds of societies, transformations that effectuate change in the social order and distribution of power in society. Thus, the effectiveness of different "rephrasings" of a dispute through "narrowing" or "expansion" depends on the structure of particular social contexts.[21]

The structure of particular societies is precisely the concern of a number of anthropologists who similarly view legal disputes as culturally specific and culturally laden ways of managing social conflict (see Brenneis 1987, 1988; Brenneis & Myers 1984; Duranti 1984; Goldman 1983; Hutchins 1980, 1981; Myers 1986; see especially Brenneis 1988:19–21).[22] Thus Brenneis and Myers examine the way in which various kinds of speech may function to exert political constraint differentially in egalitarian as opposed to hierarchical societies (see also Bloch 1975; Brenneis 1987; Irvine 1979; Myers 1986). Rosen (1989a, 1989b) views speech in legal settings as continuous with speech in other settings in Moroccan society, all of it constantly reasserting and creating a world in which webs of relationship provide the frame for cultural understandings and social interaction (see also Greenhouse 1986, 1992).

An appreciation for the formative effect of legal language emerges also from recent work by feminist, critical race theory, and critical legal studies theorists in the legal academy (see, e.g., Delgado 1989, 1990; Matsuda 1987, 1989; Minow 1990; Williams 1991). For example, Fineman's (1991) most recent

---

[21] Merry criticizes work on dispute transformation for its assumption that disputes "change along a unidirectional path" and for its omission of a description of contested interpretations (p. 92).

[22] Brenneis (1988:19–21) distinguishes three sorts of constitutive roles for legal language: socially constitutive, constitutive of knowledge, and constitutive of rules.

work analyzes legal and political language dealing with poverty and uncovers an ideological vision that attempts to attribute responsibility for poverty to the "pathology" of single motherhood. This discourse shapes and reinvigorates patriarchal culture and society, directing attention away from structural contributions to inequity for which it would be harder to disown responsibility. Crenshaw (1988:1372–76) examines the polarized categories central to a language subordinating blacks to whites. Matsuda (1987:334–36) describes the power of black women's poetry and of Douglass's and King's rereadings of the Constitution as sources of resistance to social and legal oppression. Anthropologists are similarly turning attention to the power of discourse in legal struggles over racial and gender inequalities (see Coombe 1991a, 1991b; Hirsch 1989; see also Frohmann 1991).

Each of the studies discussed in this section shares a view of language and discourse as formative in some way. In some studies it is the word meaning, the semantics of language, that does the crucial shaping. In others it is both the semantics and the structure of the discourse itself that create strong formative effects. In a sense, these studies have begun the work suggested by current developments in anthropological linguistics because they begin to explore the role of linguistic creativity in the law.

Two recent studies in particular continue this tradition. Taken together, they combine attention to details of the contextual structuring of language with a broader social vision of the role of language. The increased understanding of legal process that flows from this combination demonstrates the value of the integrative approach proposed at the beginning of this essay and suggests that we should proceed still further in analyzing the social foundations of linguistic creativity in the law.

B. Conley and O'Barr's Legal Talk, Merry's Social/Legal Discourses

Both of these studies are concerned with the social grounding of discourse as well as with careful analysis of the actual language of interactions. I use the designations "talk" and "discourse" only heuristically to highlight an apparent difference in approach between the two books (see note 1). After an initial discussion of the books, I focus first on the linguistic diversity Conley and O'Barr described and then on how that language might be embedded in the complex social picture Merry paints.

Merry and Conley and O'Barr begin with very similar problematics:

> This is a study of the ways in which ordinary people relate to the American legal system. (Conley & O'Barr, p. ix)
>
> The book talks about the ways people who bring personal problems to the courts think about and understand law and the ways people who work in the courts deal with their problems. (Merry, p. ix)

Both studies deal with the understandings and discourse of "ordinary people"—in Merry's case, specifically, of working-class people—who are approaching the legal system as nonexpert participants. In both cases the basic unit or organizing principle is the pattern emerging from a litigant's encounter with the legal system rather than a community, case, or legal institution: "My organizing principle is a pattern of court use" (Merry, p. 4); "our unit of analysis is the encounter of the litigant with the legal system" (Conley & O'Barr, p. 29).

However, the two studies employ quite distinct methodologies in attempting to analyze citizens' commonsense understandings of the legal system. Conley and O'Barr look at the language litigants and judges used in small claims courts, focusing on 14 courtrooms in six cities. By expanding their sample beyond one or two judges or communities, they are able to give us a feeling for broader patterns that emerge in different settings. Merry, on the other hand, examines intensively cases that reached three mediation programs (and sometimes the courts) located in two New England towns—Salem and Cambridge. She supplements observation of mediation sessions and court hearings with a number of other techniques: (1) she conducts ethnographic studies and surveys in several neighborhoods—one lower-middle-class and two working-class neighborhoods in Salem, and one affluent suburb; (2) she performs in-depth interviews with court personnel and participants in the struggles (as well as studies of comparable populations that wound up in court but either were not referred to mediation or failed to participate after being referred), and (3) she carries out quantitative analysis of two of the mediation programs' caseloads. Thus her discussion of the discourses in which problems are discussed in court and mediation sessions is grounded in a social contextual analysis of the particular courts and communities in question.

By combining the insights of these two studies, we begin to approach the kind of integrative vision suggested by the many-layered linguistic model outlined at the outset of this essay.[23]

---

[23] Thus the challenge of integrative work may also be integrative in another way, bringing together a community of scholars to contribute parts of the picture. This echoes White's (1990:20) more moving plea for intellectual integration:

> [My] dissatisfaction is especially acute with specialized professional or academic discourses, but it is not confined to those. More generally it is with a bureaucratized culture, one that reduces human actors to very narrow roles, human speakers to very thin speech. For me the best response is what I have

From Merry we get an in-depth vision of the way that legal discourse is grounded in social divisions and needs—a crucial part of any theory of language that takes social context seriously. From Conley and O'Barr we get a broader view of the varieties of speech in which litigants and judges construct legal processes and outcomes; at the same time, we also see a more detailed linguistic picture of the details of courtroom exchanges. Thus we can see linguistic creativity at work in the subtleties of courtroom exchanges and in struggles over power within and between communities. I do not suggest that the findings of the two studies are fully compatible; in fact, the two studies differ on the relation of particular ideologies and speech styles to class divisions. My question is not whether we can merge the findings of the two studies to create a "complete" picture but rather whether we can bring the perspectives of the studies to bear on one another to generate a more complex understanding of legal language. We begin with the more detailed linguistic study and then move to Merry's more contexualized approach to legal discourse.

Conley and O'Barr's study centers on 14 judges who varied in their qualifications and duties and whose courts varied in the amount of pretrial assistance given to litigants. Conley and O'Barr interviewed 101 plaintiffs before trial, taped trials in 466 cases, and performed follow-up interviews with 29 litigants—both plaintiffs and defendants. They transcribed 156 trials, choosing those that were "especially rich in dialogue."[24] From their analysis of those transcripts, Conley and O'Barr develop typologies of litigants' and judges' speech and then discuss what happens when different styles of litigant and judge speech mix or clash.

A fundamental distinction for Conley and O'Barr is one between "rule-oriented" and "relational" discourses:

> *relational* litigants focus heavily on status and social relationships. They believe that the law is empowered to assign rewards and punishments according to broad notions of social need and entitlement. . . . By contrast, *rule-oriented* litigants interpret disputes in terms of rules and principles that apply irrespective of social status. (P. 58)

Relational accounts of disputants' troubles focus on the social

---

called integration and transformation, the attempt to put together parts of our culture, and corresponding parts of ourselves, in ways that will make new languages, voices, and forms of discourse possible.

[24] As Conley and O'Barr admit, this biases their sample in favor of cases in which the defendants present an active defense (p. 32). Given their interest in litigant speech, this makes perfect sense. But just in case there are distinct linguistic processes at work in these cases, it might be useful to also develop a sketch of the quick, smaller cases, in order to discover continuities and differences between the two kinds of cases. This would also permit us to see if there is a relationship between the language of those cases and the social "work" they are doing.

relationships and histories of the people involved rather than presenting a focused theory of causality, contractual responsibility, or any of the other issues that might be central to a legal framing of the problem. Rule-oriented accounts center on facts that are relevant to the legal categories and rules at issue, often leaving us with very little feeling for the context or social relationships involved in the dispute.

In one landlord-tenant example, Conley and O'Barr contrast the relational account of plaintiffs (who eventually lose) with the more rule-oriented account of the defendant landlords. The plaintiffs rented a "fixer-upper" house from the defendants, thinking that they could repair the home and buy it. They now seek a return of their deposit and $1,000 to compensate them for repair work done, claiming that the defendants misrepresented the extent of the work needed on the home. In court the plaintiffs' accounts center on their needs and predicament (e.g., "But when we moved into the house, we were in a predicament at the time. We had formerly been renting a house in the country . . . . we were in a bind. We had only one month to find another house"; p. 158). The landlords, by contrast, in an effort to show that the plaintiffs had full knowledge of the condition of the house, focus their account on the crucial legal issue of the inspection done before the plaintiffs moved in.

One obvious question is whether these differing orientations correspond with social distinctions in any way. Although they "suspect a greater tendency" on the part of women litigants to emphasize relationships over rules, Conley and O'Barr do not see a straightforward link between the orientations they have isolated and any single social category such as gender (pp. 79–80). Rather, they describe a complex relationship in which gender, race, and social class all play a role in the shape of courtroom language. Conley and O'Barr defend their decision not to quantify convincingly (pp. 181–85), for it is apparent after a few well-chosen examples that forcing complex speech into simplistic categories for purposes of quantification would have yielded little of value. I would, however, have liked more discussion of comments such as "We suspect a greater tendency among women to emphasize social relations" (p. 79) or "We suspect that judges offer advice more often and in more detail to parties with whom they have some common social and cultural background" (p. 84). As Conley and O'Barr note, "[i]f one is interested in how litigants perceive [a certain judge], 'our impression' is a highly relevant datum" (p. 204), and so I would have liked more information on how these suspicions and impressions were formed and founded. This would of course not necessarily require quantification but would simply call for further explication and presentation of the kind of interpretive evidence that the authors so ably handle in other parts of the book.

In Conley and O'Barr's account, the language of the rule-oriented litigant appears to be generally more effectual in courtroom settings and is more typically used by business people, landlords, and professionals (p. 80). While "typical" women's socialization might foster a more relational style of speech, women who become part of the business and professional world often use rule-oriented discourse. However, Conley and O'Barr (pp. 80–81) find

> a convergence of the tendencies toward the powerless speech style and the relational orientation, and a complementary convergence of rule-orientation and the absence of powerless stylistic features. Thus, it may be that the burden of stylistic powerlessness, which falls most heavily on women, minorities, the poor, and the uneducated, is compounded on the discourse level by the tendency among the same groups to organize their legal arguments around concerns that the courts are likely to treat as irrelevant.

In previous studies, Conley, O'Barr, and their collaborator Allan Lind examined the relative impact of two distinct speech styles on potential jurors in experimental situations (O'Barr 1982; Conley et al. 1978). They found that the style that had been viewed as typical of women actually was typical of men and women occupying relatively powerless social positions and that people using this style were less likely to be viewed as authoritative or credible. Powerless speech contains marked use of features such as hedges ("I think," "kinda," "sort of") and hesitation forms ("um," "well"), while powerful speech does not.

Thus Conley and O'Barr posit a complex picture in which a discourse-level "orientation" and corresponding speech style can contribute to legal results that reinforce social inequities—but not in any necessary or reflexive way, for there is no neat correspondence between the language and any particular social category. Rather there are "tendencies," opportunities for negotiation of differing realities, and varieties of language that interact with legal logics in different ways.

Conley and O'Barr further distinguish five orientations typifying the approaches of the 14 judges in the study: (1) the *strict adherent* to the law (who views her/himself as "at times . . . an unwilling conduit for the nondiscretionary application of the abstract rules and principles that constitute the law"—p. 85); (2) the *lawmaker* (distinguished by "unabashed willingness to manipulate rules of law in pursuit of goals that they value more highly than respect for legal precedent"—p. 87); (3) the *mediator* (pursuing "justice primarily through the manipulation of procedure"—p. 90); (4) the *authoritative decisionmaker* (who stresses his "personal responsibility" (and power) in making decisions—p. 96); and (5) the *proceduralist* (who puts "high priority on maintaining procedural regularity"—p. 101).

Conley and O'Barr note that the judges who do more mediating tend to be women, while the proceduralists are all legally trained men (pp. 110–11). However, there appears to be a still starker contrast; all the white men were either authoritative decisionmakers, proceduralists, or unclassified. (Indeed, all the authoritative decisionmakers and proceduralists were white men.) All the women, black and white, were either strict adherents, lawmakers, or mediators. The one black male judge was a strict adherent. Of course, the sample is too small to permit much generalization, but it seems striking that there is so little overlap in predominant orientation between the white male judges and the other judges (see p. 205).

Conley and O'Barr relate these distinctions to their fundamental division between rule-oriented and relational approaches. For example, authoritative decisionmakers and strict adherents both stress legal rules rather than social relationships. However, strict adherents do so with a sense of powerlessness; they point to the rules as constraining them in ways they are powerless to overcome. By contrast, the authoritative judges "imply that the law, while no less binding, takes on life only through their intervention," with the result that they "appear as willing and active collaborators in the dominance of rules, not victims of it" (p. 108). This is particularly interesting given the gender and race distinctions noted above. Mediators obviously fall closer to the "relational" end of the continuum, given their interest in negotiating the relationships involved in the case. Conley and O'Barr describe the lawmaking judges as "an interesting blend of relational and rule-oriented tendencies" because they appear to ignore the content of legal rules while laying great stress on the formal, rule-dominated quality of their own judgments (p. 108). Similarly, the proceduralists pay a great deal of attention to rules of procedure yet "convey an impression of largely unfettered judicial discretion when announcing their judgments" (p. 109).

Conley and O'Barr then consider what happens when litigants and judges with similar and with different approaches come together in courtrooms. The most usual case of concordance is between rule-oriented judges and rule-oriented litigants (often experienced business people; p. 123). Discord is, however, more common than harmony (p. 126), and Conley and O'Barr describe a number of ways in which a rule-oriented and limiting legal system[25] disappoints litigants with relational

---

[25] I would note that there are points at which Conley and O'Barr's typification of the legal system's discourse as predominantly rule-oriented seems to overstate the role of formalist views in law school and in legal practice (see, e.g., pp. 52, 59, 60). In both

agendas who had viewed the legal system as potentially enabling.[26] Surprisingly, these litigants may yet maintain faith in the "legal system," approaching the system as an abstraction that can be differentiated from their own unsatisfying experience in court.

In terms of the model of language with which this essay began, Conley and O'Barr span a number of levels. The bulk of their analysis focuses on semantic themes in the language of litigants and judges, themes that emerge as framing orientations for the interacting parties. These themes (rules-relationships) are grounded in the social context of courtroom interaction and so are not neutral in institutional terms. Conley and O'Barr furthermore attempt to connect these semantic themes with pragmatic structure in several ways.

First, they correlate the speech styles analyzed in their previous study (powerful-powerless) with the discourse themes here (rules-relationships), so that there is at least a possible connection between the details of language structure ("powerless" speech making heavy use of features such as hedging and intensifiers) and broader semantic themes (rules/relationships). Given the important role of indexical structuring (see sec. I), however, it would seem that there is a great deal more that could be done to explore the ways language structure contributes to the creative linguistic process Conley and O'Barr found in the courtroom.[27]

Second, Conley and O'Barr stress the creativity involved in the production of "stories" in court contexts: "A 'story' does not exist fully developed on its own, but only emerges through a collaboration between the teller and a particular audience" (p. 171). Thus a litigant may have carefully rehearsed the story she will tell in court, but the story actually told emerges from the interplay of the litigant's attempt to tell her tale and the judge's attempts to elicit a story deemed appropriate for this arena. Interruptions, questions, encouraging or hostile background murmuring, and other sorts of reactions are all ways in which the audience of a story contribute to the shape of its telling (see Brenneis 1987).

Here Conley and O'Barr are insisting that the structure of

---

settings it is quite common for the role of social relations and equity to be considered as important components of "the law." However, as a significant part of Conley and O'Barr's discussion of judges deals with judges who vary from the rule-oriented model in one way or another, their discussion demonstrates, at one level, that they are aware of this.

[26] For example, relational litigants may want emotional needs to be met through the court (pp. 127–31).

[27] Some current work has attempted to develop the connection between details of indexical structuring and the creative role of language in legal struggles over social change—particularly as regards gender and race (see Hirsch 1989; Mertz 1988a, 1988b, n.d.).

discourse cannot be presupposed or dealt with abstractly but must be analyzed with full appreciation for the way it is created in social contexts. Litigants' accounts alone do not give the full picture, for they are often structured by or responding to judges' speech. And judges' speech is quite different in form and content from everyday speech,[28] so that the clash of two kinds of speech in court is another creative moment where language and institutional context/structure come together in a potentially formative but nondeterminative way. Thus Conley and O'Barr, in delineating the way in which differences in discourse styles can affect legal interactions and outcomes, demonstrate the role of linguistic creativity.

Sally Merry's book *Getting Justice and Getting Even* moves yet further in analyzing the role of context. As I have noted, her study focuses intensively on mediation programs and courts in two communities, combining attention to the discourse in legal settings with in-depth ethnographic and historical work on the social contexts involved. The result is an unusually rich combination of sensitivity to legal language with the nitty-gritty feeling for context that comes from good ethnography.

Merry begins with an investigation of the social histories of the two towns in question. She concludes that the people who use the lower courts in an attempt to solve "personal problems" are disproportionately from that segment of the working class in New England that lost a secure economic base when major industries (such as textile and leather) closed down (p. 29). At the time of Merry's study, the area was undergoing economic revitalization, with a boom in high technology industries and a shift on the part of major urban centers to financial, management, and service industries. However, the litigants with whom Merry worked were largely left out of this revitalization because they were unable to make the investment in education required for high technology jobs. Thus they were left with insecure, low-paid service jobs as their only option at the same time that low-cost housing became scarce: "As the working class is squeezed out of jobs, it is also squeezed out of housing" (p. 28). Thus Merry's (p. 27) informants

> are neither the poorest and the most recently arrived nor the educated and affluent; they are working-class individuals living in dilapidated and dangerous housing in neighborhoods experiencing the influx of new residents, people surviving without two wage earners in the family and coping with relatively low incomes. They also tend to be people who have lived for one or more generations in the United States.

---

[28] In addition to their typology of themes in judges' speech, Conley and O'Barr describe a structure of discourse common to most of the judges, beginning with "notice of the impending judgment" (p. 83), moving to an announcement of the decision, then an explanation of "the factual and legal reasoning underlying the judgment" (p. 84), and then sometimes concluding with advice (usually to the losing party).

Unlike recent immigrants, these people feel they are entitled to certain rights, including use of the courts for redress of wrongs.

Merry then moves to an analysis of the kinds of problems that are brought to courts and mediation programs.[29] A refreshing aspect of her approach is her use of litigants' cultural categories rather than legal categories to organize the analysis. Thus, she begins with neighborhood, marital, boyfriend/girlfriend, and family problems rather than sorting the problems by the legal categories (assault, harassment) or even the kind of court (juvenile, lower criminal, small claims) involved.

Like many of the plaintiffs in Conley and O'Barr's study, Merry's plaintiffs think in terms of relationships and rights: "These plaintiffs do not think in terms of specific doctrines or rules but instead think in terms of fundamental rights of property, autonomy, and parental authority. These rights are embedded in relationships with spouses, children, and neighbors" (p. 38). And the relationships are embedded in wider cultural constructions of self and society and in social contexts. At every turn, we find connections between the social history with which Merry began and the disputes she analyzes. For example, neighborhood problems center on issues of "shared space" and become more intense where parties cannot avoid one another, either because they lack financial resources to leave or because the space itself is in short supply (or both): "more intense and more frequent neighborhood fights came from working-class and poor neighborhoods than came from widely spaced suburbs" (p. 39). Neighborhood problems also often reflect tension between older inhabitants and newer immigrant populations. Marital problems also more often become severe enough to move parties to seek legal relief under economically difficult circumstances: "Marital disputes often emerge when a couple feels trapped in the relationship, money is short, the house is small.... These problems become most intense when marital disintegration is thwarted, when the couple lacks the resources to separate" (p. 48). Many problems between parents and children "are clearly related to crowded houses, long hours of work, and limited incomes" (p. 57).

Merry distinguishes the groups of plaintiffs bringing neighborhood and parent/child problems, who tend to be "settled-living" working-class people with middle-class aspirations, from those bringing marital and boyfriend/girlfriend problems, who correspond more to the "hard-living" category of poor families who have given up the fight for upward mobility and often suffer the pain of violence, desertion, and substance abuse at close

---

[29] Previous work by Susan Silbey and Merry had revealed continuities between mediation programs and normal court processing of disputes, so that mediation was not "sharply divergent in its modes of operation or ways of talking" from courts (p. 29; see also Silbey & Merry 1986; Merry & Silbey 1984).

quarters (pp. 60–61). For example, neighborhood disputes often occur among people who are homeowners, a common marker of "settled living." In one case, Merry details a dispute between a plaintiff who is a newcomer to the neighborhood and an older defendant whose son is accused of harassing and damaging the property of the newcomer. In counting the cases filed or referred to mediation that had originated in the middle-class Salem neighborhood she studied (in 1980–81), Merry finds that five out of the six cases were neighborhood problems, a much larger proportion than was found in the two working-class neighborhoods (p. 66). In another case, Merry describes for us the conflict between a young woman and her former boyfriend; both parties fall into Merry's "hard-living" category. The woman is seeking protection from continued harassment following her decision to end their relationship; she feels endangered by his actions, which include attacking her, pulling her hair, and continually calling her at work.

Merry's ethnographic and interview work reveals that use of the court for family and marital problems has itself become identified as embarrassing, a mark of lower-class origins, among the more upwardly mobile, "settled-living" people. For "hard-living" people use of the courts for such problems is "a more refined alternative to violence . . . the symbol of the way educated, professional people deal with differences" (p. 83). Yet, ironically, Merry shows us that the "escape from community" characterizing the flight of "settled-living" people to more suburban communities also leaves them more dependent on the courts, for as they escape the watchful eyes of the local authorities in their old neighborhoods (local parishes, ward bosses, etc.), they also leave behind them alternative sources for the solution of problems.

In addition to these class-based distinctions, Merry also notes that women are more likely to bring cases to court, partly because they are at a physical and economic disadvantage outside of a legal forum and partly because they are attracted to nonviolent solutions to their problems. This differential use by women highlights the role law can play in challenging hierarchies of authority, but Merry reminds us that court is also used by "previously dominant groups whose control is challenged: parents with rebellious teenage children or older people whose neighborhoods are changing" (p. 86). In either case, Merry tells us, it is the plaintiff whose position tends to be most strengthened by invocation of this symbolic power of the court—but often at some cost. The most important cost is a loss of control as the unpredictable power of the state intrudes on their lives and relationships.

Against this backdrop Merry explicates the way the legal process works for and against these plaintiffs. Her account (p.

110) of legal processing of conflicts is one of creative linguistic channeling of social interaction:

> Discourses are aspects of culture, interconnected vocabularies and systems of meaning located in the social world. A discourse is not individual and idiosyncratic but part of a shared cultural world. Discourses are rooted in particular institutions and embody their culture. Actors operate within a structure of available discourses. However, within that structure there is space for creativity as actors define and frame their problems within one or another discourse.

Merry distinguishes three kinds of discourses in the courts and mediation programs she observed: legal, moral, and therapeutic. She acknowledges an apparent similarity between her categories of legal and moral discourse and Conley and O'Barr's categories of rule-oriented and relational discourse, adding that their approach differs because "they see these two forms of account as characteristic of different kinds of people rather than as part of an available repertoire to be used from time to time by all litigants" (p. 205 n.11). However, she would seem to agree with their strong correlation of rule-oriented discourse with the legal arena; her discussion of the legal reframing of "problems" as "legal cases" describes precisely a shift from complex, ongoing emotion-laden relational problems to finite, dispassionate legal cases with simple legal labels (pp. 105–7).

Merry describes this labeling process as "crystalliz[ing] a few issues out of the wider matrix of the problem" (p. 108). When the judges she describes reach legal decisions, we see a similar boiling down of complex relational problems to legal results through imposition of legal categories and rules. Thus one judge, after urging the parties to handle the difficulty as a "social problem" to no avail, finally announces that he must reach a "legal decision" (p. 107). The result then depended on several simply stated legal "rules": a letter one party wished to use as evidence was inadmissible because it was not notarized, and the complaints of one party about the condition of her apartment were not relevant because she was not technically a tenant (but a former lover of the other party).

I am not concerned with reconciling the difference between Merry and Conley and O'Barr in the substance of their descriptions, as my goal here is to learn what can be gained by combining their approaches to legal language and its social constitution. But I would note several points that might clarify the issue. First, like Merry, Conley and O'Barr speak of litigants as using both kinds of discourse; however, unlike Merry, they focus on the relative distribution of these discourses in different litigants' and judges' speech. Second, a close reading of their examples seems to indicate that Conley and O'Barr are using somewhat different criteria than Merry; use of "legal" categories in an ineffectual way in accounts that otherwise center on nonlegal considerations does not count as "rule-oriented" discourse for them. In other words, there is a notion of legal effectiveness linked to their identification of rule-oriented discourse that does not seem to appear in Merry's approach. This might lead Merry to view the speech of a litigant whom Conley and O'Barr would classify as "relational" as more rule-oriented. Third, Merry is focusing on people who bring personal problems to court, often in cases likely to wind up in mediation. This might select against the kind of cases resulting from "arm's-length" business transactions that show up in Conley and O'Barr's account as the most heavily "rule-oriented" in terms of litigant speech. Merry's litigants do not typically seem to be business people of the sort that Conley and O'Barr find using more heavily rule-oriented discourse. Thus she might not have many examples of their more "rule-oriented" litigants in her study. This may explain some of the differences between the two studies.

Nonetheless, as I have noted above, it would be useful if Conley and O'Barr could give us a richer feeling for the basis of the class distribution they posit (as well as for race and gender dimensions). It would be interesting as well to hear from Merry whether the relative distributions of legal and moral discourse varied by kind of plaintiff and defendant. I was also curious about the differing styles of the mediators and judges in Merry's study, who in the excerpts we were given in the book seem to vary somewhat from each other in discourse styles.

Like the large proportion of Conley and O'Barr's litigants who are frustrated by the apparent unwillingness of the court to let them tell their stories, Merry's litigants are often unhappy with their treatment in court: "Many plaintiffs complain that the court is rushed, that the judge is bored, that their individuality is lost. They find the experience in court to be frustrating and humiliating and that their cases are handled in a hurried and impersonal way" (p. 134). This does not necessarily pose a contradiction to the findings of Lind et al. (1990) painting a brighter picture of litigant satisfaction, for both Merry and Conley and O'Barr describe processes whereby parties can be simultaneously unhappy and satisfied with their experience in courts and mediation programs:

> [W]e see a subtle process whereby litigants rationalize their experiences by separating the ideal of the law from the reality of its implementation. Their future legal behavior may be coopted by the ideology of limitation, but they retain a belief in the law as an instrument of enablement. The more sophisticated become competent players in the game of law and business, achieving enough satisfaction in small victories to dis-

tract them from the larger issues that originally brought them to the legal system. (Conley & O'Barr, p. 165)

These encounters with the legal system shift plaintiffs' consciousness of law. The people involved come to think of the courts as ineffective, unwilling to help in these personal crises, and indifferent to the ordinary person's problem. They discover that one need not fear the court; one need not even appear. Areas of resistance to the authority of the court open up.... One can insist on retaining legal discourse and block the shift to moral or therapeutic discourse. The court turns out to be different, in some ways, than what it seemed from the outside; but the reward of experience is greater skill in wresting help from the court. (Merry, p. 170)

This suggests that qualitative studies such as these two may be able to contribute a deeper cultural understanding of what the quantitative findings about litigant satisfaction mean.

The contrast between the two quotations above also suggests an apparent difference in attitude about linguistic creativity and resistance, although I believe that the difference is largely one of emphasis. Merry views the linguistic exchanges in courts and mediation sessions as truly creative encounters in which plaintiffs can resist and contest the hegemonic power of legal institutions, struggling through the creative power of their own language to gain control of the discourse.[30] Conley and O'Barr at times stress that the apparent openness of such moments is underlain by a deep conservatism on the part of the institutional structure itself; the promise of openness is but a mask for the courts' general failure to admit and hear new voices. However, Merry clearly acknowledges the power and the deceptive character of legal institutions. At the same time, Conley and O'Barr see creative possibilities arising in the interactions of different discourses and people, emphasizing that how both litigants and judges talk can be crucial to the outcomes of linguistic encounters in legal arenas. In both studies we see that linguistic interaction in legal settings can be creative, forging new and unpredictable understandings. The difference appears to be one of emphasis, with Merry leaning toward a more optimistic view of the creative power of plaintiffs' discourse, and Conley and O'Barr stressing the way even apparently creative language can function to reproduce existing structures.[31]

Merry concludes with the warning that even when plaintiffs believe that their stories were taken seriously, they face a fur-

---

[30] Here Merry joins a number of anthropologists and other scholars who are concerned with taking seriously the role of resistance (see, e.g., Comaroff 1985; Comaroff & Comaroff 1991; Lazarus-Black 1991).

[31] Their assessment of the power of discourse to affect individual outcomes, however, seems more optimistic than their assessment of its power to effect broader institutional and social change.

ther difficulty, for they in effect surrender control of their problem to the state when they go to court (p. 181). In powerful linguistic acts of naming (labeling) their problems (p. 132), whereby framing forms of discourse are forced on litigants (for example, refusing to permit a legal frame and forcing a "therapeutic" frame onto the case), the state acts through the law to take the power of interpretation away from plaintiffs. This is what Merry calls the "paradox of legal entitlement"—that attempting to use the courts for empowerment entails a disempowerment (pp. 181–82). She adds, however, that there are forms of resistance: plaintiffs return, "learning to use legal categories with more sophistication, mastering legal discourse" (p. 180). Here Merry's account elegantly illustrates the connection between creative uses of language and struggles over legal power, showing us the larger social structure at stake in seemingly mundane, face-to-face legal encounters.

III. Conclusion

In conclusion, we can see that together Conley and O'Barr and Merry give us an exciting view of the way that legal language makes a difference in socially powerful processes. Moving from the details of speech styles in interaction with one another to wider issues of discourse frames and labels, we see that imposition of legal language can still dissenting voices and reinforce socially powerful interests. And yet, at the same time, there is room for resistance, for struggles over language, for creative acts of translation and interpretation that shift the social ground as well. Here we can see clearly the power of linguistic creativity. Judges who come from historically excluded groups may also shift the ground as they operate in new kinds of language from the bench. In these two studies, careful attention to the language of litigants and judges has resulted in a more precise and sophisticated explication of the process whereby law participates in social transformation and reproduction. Here, then, is an anthropological response to the question, What difference does language make?

References

Atkinson, J. Maxwell, & Paul Drew (1979) *Order in Court: The Organization of Verbal Interaction in Judicial Settings*. Atlantic Highlands, NJ: Humanities Press.

Bauman, Richard, & Charles L. Briggs (1990) "Poetics and Performance as Critical Perspectives on Language and Social Life," 19 *Annual Rev. of Anthropology* 59.

Bloch, Maurice (1975) "Introduction," in M. Bloch, ed., *Political Language and Oratory in Traditional Society*. New York: Academic Press.

Bourdieu, Pierre (1977) *Outline of a Theory of Practice*. Cambridge: Cambridge Univ. Press.
Brenneis, Donald (1984) "Grog and Gossip in Bhatgaon: Style and Substance in Fiji Indian Conversation," 11 *American Ethnologist* 487.
——— (1987) "Performing Passions: Aesthetics and Politics in an Occasionally Egalitarian Community," 14 *American Ethnologist* 236.
——— (1988) "Language and Disputing," 17 *Annual Rev. of Anthropology* 221.
Brenneis, Donald Lawrence, & Fred R. Myers, eds. (1984) *Dangerous Words: Language and Politics in the Pacific*. New York: New York Univ. Press.
Briggs, Charles L. (1986) *Learning How to Ask: A Sociolinguistic Appraisal of the Role of the Interview in Social Science Research*. Cambridge: Cambridge Univ. Press.
Brown, Penelope (1980) "Why and How Women Are More Polite: Some Evidence from a Mayan Community," in S. McConnell-Ginet, R. Borker, & N. Furman, eds., *Women and Language in Literature and Society*. New York: Praeger.
Charrow, Robert P., & Veda R. Charrow (1979) "Making Legal Language Understandable: A Psycholinguistic Study of Jury Instructions," 79 *Columbia Law Rev.* 1306.
Cicourel, Aaron V. (1974) *Cognitive Sociology: Language and Meaning in Social Interaction*. New York: Free Press.
Comaroff, Jean (1985) *Body of Power, Spirit of Resistance: The Culture and History of a South African People*. Chicago: Univ. of Chicago Press.
Comaroff, Jean, & John Comaroff (1991) *Of Revelation and Revolution: Christianity, Colonialism, and Consciousness in South Africa*, Vol. 1. Chicago: Univ. of Chicago Press.
Conley, John M., William M. O'Barr, & E. Allan Lind (1978) "The Power of Language: Presentational Style in the Courtroom," 1978 *Duke Law J.* 1375.
Coombe, Rosemary (1991a) "Contesting the Self: Negotiating Subjectivities in Nineteenth Century Ontario Defamation Trials," 11 *Studies in Law, Politics & Society* 3.
——— (1991b) "Objects of Property and Subjects of Politics: Intellectual Property Laws and Democratic Dialogue," 69 *Texas Law Rev.* 1853.
Crapanzano, Vincent (1992) *Hermes' Dilemma and Hamlet's Desire: On the Epistemology of Interpretation*. Cambridge, MA: Harvard Univ. Press.
Crenshaw, Kimberle (1988) "Race, Reform, and Retrenchment: Transformation and Legitimation in Antidiscrimination Law," 101 *Harvard Law Rev.* 1331.
Danet, Brenda (1980) "Language in the Legal Process," 14 *Law & Society Rev.* 445.
Danet, Brenda, Kenneth B. Hoffman, Nicole C. Kermish, H. Jeffry Rafn, & Deborah G. Stayman (1980) "An Ethnography of Questioning in the Courtroom," in R. Shuy & A. Shnukal, eds., *Language Use and the Uses of Language*. Washington, DC: Georgetown Univ. Press.
Delgado, Richard (1989) "Storytelling for Oppositionists and Others: A Plea for Narrative," 87 *Michigan Law Rev.* 2411.
——— (1990) "Mindset and Metaphor," 103 *Harvard Law Rev.* 1872.
Duranti, Alessandro (1984) "Lāuga and Talanoaga: Two Speech Genres in a Samoan Political Event," in D. Brenneis & F. R. Myers, eds., *Dangerous Words: Language and Politics in the Pacific*. New York: New York Univ. Press.
Eidheim, Harold (1969) "When Ethnic Identity Is a Social Stigma," in F. Barth, ed., *Ethnic Groups and Boundaries*. Boston: Little, Brown & Co.
Errington, James Joseph (1988) *Structure and Style in Javanese: A Semiotic View of Linguistic Etiquette*. Philadelphia: Univ. of Pennsylvania Press.
Fairclough, Norman (1989) *Language and Power*. London: Longman.

Fineman, Martha L. (1991) "Images of Mothers in Poverty Discourses," 1991 *Duke Law J.* 274.
Foucault, Michel (1980) *Power/Knowledge: Selected Interviews and Other Writings 1972–1977*, ed. Colin Gordon. New York: Pantheon.
Frohmann, Lisa (1991) "Discrediting Victims' Allegations of Sexual Assault," 38 *Social Problems* 213.
Garfinkel, Harold (1967) *Studies in Ethnomethodology*. Englewood Cliffs, NJ: Prentice-Hall.
Goldman, Laurence (1983) *Talk Never Dies: The Language of Huli Disputes*. London: Tavistock.
Goodwin, Marjorie (1980) " 'He Said–She Said': Formal Cultural Procedures for the Construction of a Gossip Dispute Activity," 7 *American Ethnologist* 674.
Gumperz, John J. (1964) "Linguistic and Social Interaction in Two Communities," 66 (No. 6, pt. 2) *American Anthropologist* 137.
——— (1982) *Discourse Strategies*. Cambridge: Cambridge Univ. Press.
Gumperz, John J., & Dell Hymes, eds. (1972) *Directions in Sociolinguistics: The Ethnography of Communication*. New York: Holt, Rinehart & Winston.
Hanks, William F. (1990) *Referential Practice: Language and Lived Space among the Maya*. Chicago: Univ. of Chicago Press.
Hickmann, Maya (1980) "Creating Referents in Discourse: A Developmental Analysis of Discourse Cohesion," in *Papers from the Sixteenth Regional Meeting of the Chicago Linguistic Society: Parasession on Anaphora*. Chicago: Chicago Linguistic Society.
Hirsch, Susan F. (1989) "Asserting Male Authority, Recreating Female Experience: Gendered Discourse in Coastal Kenyan Muslim Courts." American Bar Foundation Working Paper Series 1, No. 8906. Chicago: American Bar Foundation.
Huspek, Michael (1991) "Review of *Language and Power* (N. Fairclough)," 20 *Language in Society* 131.
Hutchins, Edwin (1980) *Culture and Inference: A Trobriand Case Study*. Cambrdige, MA: Harvard Univ. Press.
——— (1981) "Reasoning in Trobriand Discourse (1979)," in R. W. Casson, ed., *Language, Culture, and Cognition: Anthropological Perspectives*. New York: Macmillan
Hymes, Dell H. (1974) *Foundations in Sociolinguistics*. Philadelphia: Univ. of Pennsylvania Press.
Irvine, Judith T. (1979) "Formality and Informality in Communicative Events," 81 *American Anthropologist* 773.
——— (1989) "When Talk Isn't Cheap: Language and Political Economy," 16 *American Ethnologist* 248.
Keenan, Elinor (Ochs-) (1975) "A Sliding Sense of Obligatoriness: The Polystructure of Malagasy Oratory," in M. Bloch, ed., *Political Language and Oratory in Traditional Society*. New York: Academic Press.
Kurylowicz, Jerzy (1945–49) "La nature des procés dits 'analogiques,' " 5 *Acta Linguistica* 15.
——— (1972) "The Role of Deictic Elements in Linguistic Evolution," 5 *Semiotica* 174.
Labov, William (1964) "Phonological Correlates of Social Stratification," 66 (No. 6, pt. 2) *American Anthropologist* 164.
——— (1966) *The Social Stratification of English in New York City*. Washington, DC: Center for Applied Linguistics.
Lakoff, Robin (1975) *Language and Woman's Place*. New York: Harper & Row.
Lazarus-Black, Mindie (1991) "Slaves, Masters, and Magistrates: Law and the Politics of Resistance in the English Speaking Caribbean, 1736–1834," American Bar Foundation Working Papers Series 1, No. 9124. Chicago: American Bar Foundation.

Levi, Edward H. (1949) *An Introduction to Legal Reasoning.* Chicago: Univ. of Chicago Press.
Levi, Judith N. (1982) *Linguistics, Language and Law: A Topical Bibliography.* Bloomington: Indiana Univ. Linguistics Club.
—— (1986) "Applications of Linguistics to the Language of Legal Interactions," in P. C. Bjarkman & V. Raskin, eds., *The Real-World Linguist: Linguistic Applications in the 1980's.* Norwood, NJ: ABLEX.
Lind, E. Allan, Robert J. MacCoun, Patricia A. Ebener, William L. F. Felstiner, Deborah R. Hensler, Judith Resnik, & Tom R. Tyler (1990) "In the Eye of the Beholder: Tort Litigants' Evaluations of Their Experiences in the Civil Justice System," 24 *Law & Society Rev.* 953.
Loftus, Elizabeth F. (1975) "Leading Questions and the Eyewitness Report," 7 *Cognitive Psychology* 560.
—— (1979) *Eyewitness Testimony.* Cambridge MA: Harvard Univ. Press.
Lucy, John A. (1992) *Grammatical Categories and Cognition: A Case Study of the Linguistic Relativity Hypothesis.* Cambridge: Cambridge Univ. Press.
Lyons, John (1977) *Semantics,* Vol. 1. New York: Cambridge Univ. Press.
Mather, Lynn, & Barbara Yngvesson (1980–81) "Language, Audience, and the Transformation of Disputes," 15 *Law & Society Rev.* 775.
Matsuda, Mari J. (1987) "Looking to the Bottom: Critical Legal Studies and Reparations," 22 *Harvard Civil-Rights Civil Liberties Law Rev.* 323.
—— (1989) "Public Response to Racist Speech: Considering the Victim's Story," 87 *Michigan Law Rev.* 2320.
Maynard, Douglas W. (1984) *Inside Plea Bargaining: The Language of Negotiation.* New York: Plenum.
Merry, Sally Engle (1990) "The Discourses of Mediation and the Power of Naming," 2 *Yale J. of Law & the Humanities* 1 (1990).
Merry, Sally E., & Susan S. Silbey (1984) "What Do Plaintiffs Want? Reexamining the Concept of Dispute," 9 *Justice System J.* 151.
Mertz, Elizabeth (1985) "Beyond Symbolic Anthropology: Introducing Semiotic Mediation," in E. Mertz & R. J. Parmentier, *Semiotic Mediation: Sociocultural and Psychological Perspectives.* Orlando, FL: Academic Press.
—— (1988a) "The Uses of History: Language, Ideology and Law in the United States and South Africa," 22 *Law & Society Rev.* 661.
—— (1988b) "Consensus and Dissent in U.S. Legal Opinions: Narrative Structure and Social Voices," 30 *Anthropological Linguistics* 369.
—— (1989) "Sociolinguistic Creativity," in N. Dorian, ed., *Investigating Obsolescence: Studies in Language Contraction and Death.* Cambridge: Cambridge Univ. Press.
—— (1992a) "Creative Acts of Translation: James Boyd White's Intellectual Integration," 4 *Yale J. of Law & the Humanities* 165.
—— (1992b) "Learning What to Ask: Metapragmatic Factors and Methodological Reification," in J. Lucy, ed., *Reflexive Language.* Cambridge: Cambridge Univ. Press.
—— (n.d.) "Recontextualization as Socialization: Text and Pragmatics in the Law School Classroom," in M. Silverstein & G. Urban, eds., *DeCentered Discourse.* (in preparation)
Mertz, Elizabeth, & Richard J. Parmentier, eds. (1985) *Semiotic Mediation: Sociocultural and Psychological Perspectives.* Orlando, FL: Academic Press.
Minow, Martha (1990) *Making All the Difference: Inclusion, Exclusion, and American Law.* Ithaca, NY: Cornell Univ. Press.
Myers, Fred R. (1986) "Reflections on a Meeting: Structure, Language, and the Polity in a Small-Scale Society," 13 *American Ethnologist* 430.
O'Barr, William M. (1981) "The Language of the Law," in C. Ferguson & S. B. Heath, eds., *Language in the USA.* Cambridge: Cambridge Univ. Press.
—— (1982) *Linguistic Evidence: Language, Power, and Strategy in the Courtroom.* New York: Academic Press.

444 Language, Law, and Social Meanings

Parmentier, Richard J. (1987) *The Sacred Remains: Myth, History and Polity in Belau.* Chicago: Univ. of Chicago Press.

——— (1992) "The Political Function of Reported Speech: A Belauan Example," in J. A. Lucy, ed., *Reflexive Language.* Cambridge: Cambridge Univ. Press.

Peirce, Charles Sanders (1974) *Collected Papers of Charles Sanders Peirce*, Vol. 2. Cambridge, MA: Harvard Univ. Press.

Pomerantz, Anita (1978) "Attributions of Responsibility: Blamings," 12 *Sociology* 115.

Quay, Lorene C., Marilyn Mathews, & Beth Schwarzmueller (1977) "Communication Encoding and Decoding in Children from Different Socioeconomic and Racial Groups," 13 *Developmental Psychology* 415.

Rosen, Lawrence (1989a) "Responsibility and Compensatory Justice in Arab Culture and Law," in B. Lee & G. Urban, eds., *Semiotics, Self and Society.* Berlin: Mouton de Gruyter.

——— (1989b) *The Anthropology of Justice: Law as Culture in Islamic Society.* New York: Cambridge Univ. Press.

Sacks, Harvey, Emanuel A. Schegloff, & Gail Jefferson (1974) "A Simplest Systematics for the Organization of Turn-taking for Conversation," 50 *Language* 696.

Saussure, Ferdinand de (1959) *Course in General Linguistics.* New York: McGraw-Hill.

Sales, Bruce Dennis, Amiran Elwork, & James J. Alfini (1977) "Improving Comprehension for Jury Instructions," in B. Sales, ed., *Perspectives in Law and Psychology*, Vol. 1: *The Criminal Justice System.* New York: Plenum.

Sarat, Austin, & William Felstiner L. F. (1986) "Law and Strategy in the Divorce Lawyer's Office," 20 *Law & Society Rev.* 93.

——— (1990) "Legal Realism in Lawyer-Client Communications," in J. N. Levi & A. G. Walker, eds., *Language in the Judicial Process.* New York: Plenum.

——— (1988) "Law and Social Relations: Vocabularies of Motive in Lawyer/Client Interaction," 22 *Law & Society Rev.* 737.

Silbey, Susan S., & Sally E. Merry (1986) "Mediator Settlement Strategies," 8 *Law & Policy* 7.

Silverstein, Michael (1976) "Shifters, Linguistic Categories, and Cultural Description," in K. H. Basso & H. A. Selby, eds., *Meaning in Anthropology.* Albuquerque: Univ. of New Mexico Press.

——— (1979) "Language Structure and Linguistic Ideology," in P. R. Clyne, W. F. Hanks, & C. L. Hofbauer, eds., *The Elements: A Parasession on Linguistic Units and Levels.* Chicago: Chicago Linguistic Society.

——— (1981) "The Limits of Awareness," *Working Papers in Sociolinguistics*, No. 84. Austin: Southwest Educational Development Laboratory.

——— (1985) "Language and the Culture of Gender: At the Intersection of Structure, Usage and Ideology," in E. Mertz & R. J. Parmentier, eds., *Semiotic Mediation: Sociocultural and Psychological Perspectives.* Orlando, FL: Academic Press.

——— (1987) "The Three Faces of 'Function' ": Preliminaries to a Psychology of Language," in M. Hickmann, ed., *Social and Functional Approaches to Language and Thought.* Orlando, FL: Academic Press.

——— (1992) "Metapragmatic Discourse and Metapragmatic Function," in J. A. Lucy, ed., *Reflexive Language.* Cambridge: Cambridge Univ. Press.

Tannen, Deborah (1989) *Talking Voices: Repetition, Dialogue and Imagery in Conversational Discourse.* Cambridge: Cambridge Univ. Press.

Van den Broeck, Jef (1977) "Class Differences in Syntactic Complexity in the Flemish Town of Maaseik," 6 *Language in Society* 149.

Weissbourd, Bernard, & Elizabeth Mertz (1985) "Rule Centrism versus

Legal Creativity: The Skewing of Legal Ideology through Language," 19 *Law & Society Rev.* 623.

West, Candace, & Don Zimmerman (1975) "Sex Roles, Interruptions, and Silences in Conversation," in B. Thorne & N. Henley, eds., *Language and Sex*. Rowley, MA: Newbury House.

White, James Boyd (1990) *Justice as Translation: An Essay in Cultural and Legal Criticism*. Chicago: Univ. of Chicago Press.

Williams, Patricia J. (1991) *The Alchemy of Race and Rights*. Cambridge, MA: Harvard Univ. Press.

Woolard, Kathryn A. (1989) *Double Talk: Bilingualism and the Politics of Ethnicity in Catalonia*. Stanford, CA: Stanford Univ. Press.

[15]

Mute Law

RODOLFO SACCO

Legal history deals with the past of the law. But how past is it? Conventional legal history covers Roman Law, sometimes Greek law, Germanic law, early common law, medieval law and the codifications. Throughout this history the great blocks of the law have remained the same: family, property, succession, torts, contracts, crimes, government, and courts.

Legal anthropology covers a much wider realm. But legal anthropology is usually beyond the scope of lawyers. Lawyers accept legal history and normally ignore legal anthropology.

I believe that a historical perspective needs to be macro-historic: it has to trace the origins of the basic structures of law far beyond the recent past covered by conventional legal history.

Let's start with a well-established notion: the "lawgiver" is a recent innovation, in the actual meaning of a central authority entrusted with overall legislative powers. It is a premise of modern legal theory that there is such an authority empowered to create whichever legislation it deems appropriate; that such authority is "The" legislative power. Different agencies or institutions may have veto power to oppose, but nobody, except "The" legislative power is permitted to artificially create equivalent legislation, with equal discretion. Civil lawyers formulate this picture in terms even more decisive and dogmatic than common lawyers.

This has not always been the case. The function of creating law was left, in times too recent to be ignored, to God (shari'a, in Muslim Law). In other legal traditions, the rules of social interaction were thought to mirror a cosmic order (chi'ing, li, lii, in Chinese Law; a variation of which is found in the giri, in the Japanese legal tradition). More often law preceded any individual design (mores mark the origins of Roman Law and customs those of the Common Law). Human power intervenes to regulate and improve the rules (as in the case of assemblies and praetors in Rome, and judges, chancellors and the Parliament in England), or to reduce all existing laws to a unitary body of written law (as in the case of Hammurabi in Babylonian Law). This power of marginal intervention should not be confused

---

RODOLFO SACCO is Professor of Law, University of Turin, Italy. Translated by Fabio Marino.

with the power of destroying an existing body of law and replacing it with a new one. In this regard, Justinian in Roman Law played a dual role. While in his time he simply organized and reduced to written form the body of existing laws, during the Middle Ages he was seen as though entrusted with a divine mandate to give law to Christianity.[1]

The idea of an overall legislative power is asserted only after the French Revolution (even though movement in that direction can be seen during the period of Absolutism). Such superpower was created within a peculiar context: in France absolute legislative power outlasted the liberal ideal. Legal positivism reached its apex in totalitarian countries, especially where the Communist Party refused to recognize any limits to its legislative authority.

The point is that "the Lawgiver" is a recent entry into the domain of Law and that law may live, and lived, even without a lawgiver.

Before the end of the 18th century, law lived without a lawgiver. Law was taught in Law Schools where students learned a technical lexicon, linked with a sophisticated framework. The legal process was directly tied to the existence of professional lawyers entrusted with the resolution of social conflicts. The Common law tradition, the Roman world, the Islamic world all had their own jurists, legal terms, and law schools. The rise of a technical language was tied to this learned tradition.

I doubt that Gaelics or Basques would have terms suitable to a sophisticated legal experience. Certainly neither the Corsicans nor the Venetians have developed appropriate terms to express legal concepts. Only scholarly languages provide such a lexicon of technical and exoteric nature.

Legal terms, jurists and law schools sprang up in Rome.[2] This was the great contribution of the Roman experience. Neither the Chinese, nor the Pre-Columbian civilizations, nor the Germanic and Slavic populations had any "jurist". Before the Roman era, the resolution of legal issues was entrusted to religious or administrative authorities (with the possible exception of Mesopotamia).

But the law can certainly exist and evolve without lawyers. Up until 2,000 years ago, the law existed and operated efficiently in the absence of either lawgivers or lawyers.

Anthropologists draw a distinction, in the context of oral cultures, between societies with centralized power and societies with distributed power.[3] In drawing a broad sketch of the history of the

---

1. See Rodolfo Sacco, *Introduzione al diritto comparato* 204 et seq. (1992).
2. Sacco, supra n. 1, at 209.
3. Refer to the seminal work of Fortes & Evans-Pritchard, *African Political Systems* (1940). See, also Sacco, supra n. 2, at 192 et seq.

law, this distinction is fundamental in illustrating a basic division in the classification of legal experiences.

Societies with courts, public officials and fiscal systems attest to the existence of a social power overwhelming individuals and minorities. All populations sharing our culture experienced a centralized sovereign power. And even some populations with a more traditional culture had the experience of some embryonic form of a centralized structure of sovereign power (kings, oligarchies, assemblies). However, these structures do not exist everywhere, nor—more importantly—have they always existed everywhere. And even where they do exist, they can influence the life of society to greater or lesser extent. In some cases they are only called upon in special circumstances, e.g., in case of war. In other cases, they can intervene also to solve inner conflicts.

When power is distributed each individual belongs to a small group (in its simplest form, a family, a clan or a tribe) which, in case of conflict, provides self-help. In case the reader were unfamiliar with the functioning of the mechanisms of self-help, let's just point out that until the end of the 19th century, self-help was the only way to enforce international law. Countries involved in a conflict could either wage war against each other or negotiate towards a pacific resolution; the war would either result in the elimination of one of the contenders or in a peace settlement. These events would take place by means of ritual acts dictated by the norms of international law (declaration of war, duty to wear uniforms, prohibition against the use of certain weapons, etc.) A variety of politico-legal devices (alliances, binding arbitrations, non-aggression treaties, protectorates) served to limit the risks caused by the lack of sovereign power.

The sovereign power—which, where it is found, is stable and operates through specialized and technically competent agencies—is the State. The State has not always existed. It was created when the sovereign power started to be exercised over society in a coherent and systemic way.

The origins of the State are in a way linked with the origins of the "Bronze Societies."

The State did not always come with the production of bronze, nor with the birth of the political structures contemporary with the age of bronze; and the State has also arisen not in connection with the age of bronze; however the peculiar characteristics of the bronze age can be persuasively traced back to the advantages of derived from a centralized power structure. The production of bronze takes away from the production of food important categories of people, whose sustenance thus weighs on farmers and cattlemen. Hence the need for a fiscal system which in turn requires a system of land registration and writing was entrusted to a group of specialists, whose sustenance in turn weighs on the class of food producers. The subdivision of agricultural and cattle products amongst producers and consumers implies the resolution of non-consensual relations, which brings about the painful need for a group of professional fighters. The society I am describing cannot operate simply by virtue of free exchange of goods and services, and is destined to dissolve without the establishment of a centralized power, observed by all. Obedience requires some sort of insurance to induce citizens to compliance by means of appropriate persuasion: magicians—who quickly become experts in this field—are called upon to substantiate, through the intervention of supernatural forces, the legitimacy of the authority.[4]

The aforementioned situation can be found in Egypt at the time of the Pharaohs or in the Middle East in the period immediately following the Sumers. However, it can also be found, without any contribution on the part of the production of bronze, in the Mayan and Inca empires. Also along these lines fall (this time in conjunction with the production of bronze) also the Indian and Chinese empires.

With the empires flourishing on the old continent in the bronze age the State was born and, for the first time a constitutional law appeared; and a complex and well managed administration gave rise to administrative law. A public criminal law and a judicial power were created operating in conformity with procedural rules.[5]

Centralized power spread from Mesopotamia and Persia to Greece and from there to Rome. A long series of confrontations, lasting over 1500 years, finally served to integrate the Roman system with the Germanic system, whose institutions had come into conflict with the Roman world long before being eradicated by the sweeping introduction of centralized power.

In short, prior to 3500 B.C. there was no centralized power and yet there was—and flourished—law.

During my tenure at the National University of Somalia, I had the opportunity to witness the remaining traces of traditional Somali law—the xeer—and thus I came into contact with an efficient and flourishing legal system, able to operate, as typical of any system of distributed power, in the absence of a lawgiver, a State or centralized power. Feuds and blood money are the building blocks of these legal systems—namely, the Somalian and the Berberic[6] as well as the Germanic in the age of the great migrations.

The law of the fifth millennium B.C. has not been the same as that in force 50,000 years earlier or 500,000 years earlier. A vital

---

4. The various elements at play in this context are superbly analyzed in V. Gordon Childe, *What Happened in History* (1939); See also, V. Gordon Childe, *The Prehistory of European Society* (1958).

5. Sacco, supra n. 1.

6. Sacco, "Di alcune singolari convergenze fra il diritto ancestrale dei Berberi e uello dei Sqomali" in *Scritti in onore di Angelo Falzea* 395 et. seq. (1991).

force of unprecedented vigor and able to produce radical innovations was undoubtedly the development of magic arts. Magic allows us to establish facts—ordeals and oaths were and still are the last in a long line of methods of proof with supernatural ties—, to identify the person against whom we must proceed, to find remedies to cure social illnesses. Magic rituals can be used to reinstate property, since magic spells can teach goods how to deter misappropriations. Curses can also be used to punish people who don't maintain their promises.

Anthropologists have collected an amazing quantity of documents on the dominant role of magic in social life. However, there have been no attempts at either synthesis or systemic approaches. Nobody has been able to establish the date of creation of magic, nor when it began to rule man's life. Can we assume that it started to play a larger role as man transitioned from Inferior Paleolithic to Superior Paleolithic? We do not know for certain, even though we know that man developed in that period skills that nowadays we consider artistic and that, at that time, served precisely to influence the fate of the people and things represented or through sounds obtain certain goals. Nonetheless law existed even before magic.

Law provides means to prevent and solve conflicts throughout society. Wherever we find a society we will find law. This holds true in human societies, as well as in advanced animal societies. Lions, wild dogs and many other carnivorous mammals "mark" their territory and obtain from their counterparts, i.e., from other members of their species, observance of their exclusive rights. Several varieties of birds live by the same rules, namely marking their aerial space by flying and screaming; observance of the rule is enforced by self-help. A complex interplay of glands and hormones greets the strength of the animal unjustly attacked. Rules observed by the animal itself protect the relationship between male and female, often preceded by courtship, and the duties incumbent on the parents with respect to their offspring.

When the Homo Habilis produced the first pebble tools his law could not be too different from that of the primates which immediately preceded him. Those pebble tools created issues of property, extending through time, of chattels: the weapon or the rock (flint stone, quartz, oxydian), valuable insofar as rare, to make the weapon. Possession probably solved the most common problems. The ceremony—marking of territory or courtship—was used to announce and qualify relationships. In cases where no ceremony was required, the relationship was inseparable from the act: possession constituted the exercise of legal power over the chattel, acquiescence implied recognition of the other's rights, performance implied obligation. The dichotomy between law and enforcement did not exist. The acts that were performed were legal, in other words, the right exercised was legal, the duty absolved was legal, the act acquiesced by others was legal. Trade was accomplished through an exchange of possessions. Improper acts immediately triggered self-help. Ceremonies and acts constituted legal acts. Adherence to the rule implied its existence and validity (manifested by the spontaneous conduct of the members of the group). The law was mute, except for the yelling accompanying ceremonies and self-help. Sources were mute. Acts were mute.

The biggest legal revolution took place when a descendent of the Homo Habilis began to use an articulated language. Until that time the Homo Erectus, who had taken the place of the Homo Habilis, had been practicing with great success a gestural language. It is difficult to assess the impact such gestural language had on the law, but I doubt that it was sufficient to destroy the pre-existing order.

Once the language had been developed it is not clear whether man began immediately to use it for purposes of the law. It would be fruitless to take a position on this issue. Rather, we must ask which new possibilities the articulation of language opened over time. The answer appears within reach of the careful scholar. Except for the two typical ceremonies, i.e., appropriation of land and courtship, unspoken acts and mute sources continue to operate today. We occupy, we own, we abandon. We do not enter private land. We do not pursue someone else's wife, nor do we feed someone else's child.

Language, however, introduces questions about the future, abstract questions about law not yet applied, principles unrelated, at least for the moment, to realities. "You will return that"; "This is my land, and it will always be, even if I leave. And I will be back"; "We are all going harvesting today but not tomorrow, we are all going hunting tomorrow, but not today".

Spoken law follows this primordial nutshell of law, i.e., the law that natura omnia animalia docuit. Spoken law controls all future developments, words support logic. At first, we are dealing with the elementary logic of participation, which permits the building of magic knowledge. Then with the logic that forms the basis for the magnificent, although oppressive, social and legal architecture of the bronze age. Later, with the logic which constitutes the basis for the conceptual and deductive legal reasoning of the (Roman and post-Roman) jurist. At the inception of the law that the omnipotent legislator is called to create from thin air, with pure rational law, intended to be the brightest point in the history of the law. In reality, the rationale law of the illuminists is not the brightest point: it is just an illusion born of good intentions; further developments, however, will follow.

Nothing however could be so diametrically opposed to rational law as natural law; nature has shown man a law that man, having achieved rational dominion of legal concepts, has thoroughly rejected.

The structural basis of a given legal system determines to a great extent its legal instruments. The non-speaking human society possessed a clear concept of subordination amongst individuals; exemplified by the child's reverence for the adult, in reason of the physical strength of the latter and the need for protection of the former. Several selection methods are available to determine which member of the group will enjoy greater power. Amongst several animal species, the prowess of those who aspire to the leadership role is tested in apposite competitions, and serves to legitimate their social position. Magic creates hierarchies of a supernatural nature, but has no reason to undermine the preexisting natural order. The agrarian and pastoral culture of the Neolithic allows the enjoyment of (slave) labor without any need to arm laborers or entrust them with possession of goods (the opposite was true of the Paleolithic society which lived on hunting and harvesting). This situation created the ideal conditions for the development of a subordination of an essentially economic nature (slavery or later forms of private servitude). The culture of the Bronze Age introduced the subordination of individuals to the sovereign and thus to the State. And the subordination to the State outlasted (in competition and only remotely contributing to their demise) the subordination due to descendance, physical prowess and prestige, religion and private servitude. The advent of legal science did not modify operative relationships, it simply improved the conceptual definition of the relationship between masters and dependents. The appearance of omnipotent lawmakers did not upset the preexisting structure even though in practice lawmakers will be inclined to deal primarily with the subordination of individuals to the State.

Subordination has as a corollary loyalty, in reason of which subordinates abstain from any intrusion upon the person and the property of their master. Loyalty is distinct from obedience. The person in power can verify whether or not there has been a lapse in the other's obedience. Disloyalty, however, takes place away from the eyes of the master. As a consequence, those who obey because they are convinced of their subordination normally remain loyal, while those who are forced into obedience are more likely to betray; by the same token, those who feel obliged up to a point, but not further, are likely to betray.

Loyalty means continuously acting against nature, against one's own interest, to obey the command or interest of the master. Any social structure creates loyalty ties amongst those who voluntarily accept their subordination. We can think of children who, in the early day of the Homo Erectus, did not steal the food set aside by their parents for "rainy days". We can think of devote young followers of a renowned wizard unwilling to steal from him and dutifully running his successful businesses (the receipt of a donation for each witchcraft performed). We are probably too far removed from the position of the slave to truly understand his mentality, but we can think of grateful servants (Joseph elevated to ministry by the Pharaoh) who choose to devote their lives to their masters.[7] We can think of associations, either voluntary or to which, in any case, followers are particularly attached, to which followers will offer any form of loyalty, by reason of profound identification with the group: friars, religious confraternities, religious or regional political clans either small enough for personal ties to be felt amongst the members or formed by people so dedicated as to feel bound to a large collection of people whom they have never met. We can picture all of these situations. Within all of these groups, loyalty appears spontaneous and entirely natural. But, outside of these contexts, unsolicited loyalty, based on the voluntary subordination of one's needs to the wills of a master or a group, is virtually unknown of.

Prior to the State, power was conferred in the exclusive economic interest of those who held it. It wasn't until the great cultures of the Bronze age that we see priests not stealing treasures from the temple or ministers (as emperor's slave) not taking advantage of his powers to defraud his subjects. Monks (including, I imagine, members of the military monastic orders) did not defraud the order nor did they defraud the subjects of the order (which doesn't mean, however, that they did not defraud their subjects in the interest of the order). Slowly ties developed outside family circles amongst neighbors interested in the common good; hence the origin of cities, and later, of States; loyalty towards the sovereign became loyalty towards the State; loyalty towards monastic orders became loyalty towards the (laic) community, permeated with ethical values. These were important, even if partial, advances; they make up the pages of an Atlas illustrating a reality only a few centuries or millennia old. At the basis of society at the "state of nature" loyalty does not extend outside the family circle. And since, by this time, the State is present everywhere, in a society ruled primarily by natural instincts, those put in power by the State, except for fear of criminal prosecution, do not administer it according to the law. Such practices are better known by their real name: corruption. A wealth of literature has been written on the central part corruption plays in the life of African societies.[8] It is unlikely that a society of centralized power, where feuds and vendettas are de facto still in existence, would have the sophisticated psychological structures required for the existence of the loyal-

---

7. Both Islamic and African histories are rich with examples of kings whose ministers were chosen primarily amongst slaves.

8. Resolution of legal controversies, registration of property, issuance of passports or licenses are typical examples of instances in which bribery is required. See, e.g., Pascon, "Les Seksawa depuis l'independance," in Berque, *Structures sociales du Haut Atlas* at 491 (1978).

ties required to protect society from corruption. Therefore every combination of loyalties and disloyalties is likely to be found in this society. Functionaries are thus loyal to political parties (that have taken the place of secret societies and monastic orders in society), but to serve the interests of the parties they defraud the people. They are loyal to the family and therefore disloyal to the community. Subjectively, they feel justified in betraying a loyalty in favor of an even stronger loyalty. They feel righteous. If caught, they feel like martyrs.

In several significant parts of today's world legal systems—or parts thereof—are in existence realities which date six thousand years back. According to several observers, the rules governing private matters in Japan and China are not legal in nature, but rather derived from philosophy, tradition and social interests, and are administered without courts, legal professionals, the intervention of the authorities or written rules.[9] We would probably be not too far from the truth in assuming that the rules governing private matter in Japan and China are indeed legal in nature, but outside the sphere of interest of centralized power. The State regulates public law (access to power, possible balancing powers, administration, i.e. administrative, constitutional and public criminal law). The rest is regulated by the lower strata of the social structure with rules well known by the people and capable of proving a solution to any conflict of interest as well as of forcing an unwilling litigant, through the fear of significant social sanctions, to comply with the decision.

According to the scheme I propose, traditional Chinese law would not regulate issues of either family or property law, while criminal Chinese law would punish family crimes and robberies. Under this set of assumptions, Chinese criminal law incorporates and codifies rules of family and property law derived from a separate system of sources, i.e., from that customary law that westerners mistakenly see as a form of philosophical ethics.

In other words, in the Far East, a variety of legal systems, or rather a variety of sections of a single legal system, have coexisted and continue to coexist on the same territory; amongst them the most ancient presumes a non-centralized power and dates all the way back to the Stone Age; the following is more modern and presumes a centralized power, even in the absence of lawmakers and lawyers; the most recent (of clear western origin) introduces lawmakers and lawyers. Thus, western-style lawmakers deal only with western-style law.

---

9. See in this context, R. David, *Les Grands systèmes de droit contemporains* 423 et. seq. (1992).

In 1980, at a symposium on African legal studies,[10] the legal life of the entire subsaharan African culture was declared imbued with sacral functions: heads of State are idolized; other heads of State have made political decisions based on their dreams, and so on. The same Supreme Court of Zambia issued a set of regulations overseeing actions involving the work of sorcerers or their effects.[11] To put it differently, European law introduced during the colonial era and law dealing with sorcery can coexist in subsaharan African countries.

These observations must be generalized.

Even legal systems that possess both lawmakers and legal professionals contain some elements residual of more primitive stages. Of course these elements may subsist as aberrations or simply lie outside of the legal order (the ritual Sardinian or Sicilian vendettas, typical of societies of distributed powers, fall outside the boundaries of the law in Italy). However, they can be incorporated into the official structure of the system.

The State tries to adjudicate all private conflict interests, however it puts into place several important deterrent measures to dissuade litigants from seeking access to the courts (expensiveness of stamped paper, burden of legal representation, poor quality of the legal system, etc.): isn't it here that the hidden governmental desire to keep out of private conflicts can really be felt? Or, at least, isn't it true that only a minimal part of private conflicts is indeed solved by governmental organs? And that in many cases a heavy social stigma is attached to the filing of a legal action? And in the legal field, is testimony considered a way of verifying a factual element (an efficient method since the witness, knows, remembers, and intends to serve the truth) or as a delegation to a third party of a factual determination, ruled purely by chance on either side and not capable of rational determination?

A combination of both spoken and mute elements can also be found at work. Our legal system is familiar with spoken sources (the written rules, of splendid form and content, produced by legislative assemblies) as well as with unspoken sources (commercial uses, determination of standards of conduct, construction, by an interpreter, of concepts such as fault, reasonableness, bad faith). It is familiar with acts carried out through words (contracts made by fax, deeds, wills) as well as acts carried out without words (deliveries, contracts made through devices that allow the buyer to pay and receive mer-

---

10. 4th Colloquium of the Centre d'etudes juridiques comparatives of the University of Paris I on the topic "Sacralite', pouvoir et droit en Afrique". Proceedings published by C.N.R.S. in 1978. See, also Sacco, "Di alcune convergenze", supra.

11. The memo of April 28, 1980 was drafted by the Office of the local Courts officer, signed by D.F. Zulu and circulated to all Court Clerks. I found a copy at the local Court in Kawambwa. The memo was issued in response to British instructions prohibiting actions against sorcerers.

chandise). Some categories include both spoken and unspoken acts: such are contracts that can be made by declarations, but also by material acts; such are confirmations; such are acceptances of inheritance, which can be expressed or implied.

But lawyers are primarily interested in spoken sources and acts and feel uneasy with mute sources and acts. To support this argument I will make four remarks:

1. If a category encompasses both spoken and unspoken acts, the definition of the category concentrates only on the spoken acts. Contracts are seen as joint declarations, bilateral legal acts, sequences of offer (given to the offeree) and acceptance (given to the offeror). Unspoken contracts is hurried and almost incidental. Unspoken contract is broken up (from a classificatory standpoint) so as not to appear too close to the center of attention: some hypothesis are presented as a result of construction, or as void contracts made valid by estoppel; civil lawyers speak of contrats de fait—faktisches Vertragsverhaltnis to guard themselves against their codes that forgot to regulate works actually performed and companies that have actually operated on the market.

2. When we refer to mute acts, we do it by analogy to spoken acts. We reason that the party wants to achieve a certain legal result and thus has to express the required intent and to this end, it might be sufficient to simply perform the act in question; thus performance serves as a (tacit) declaration. The party gives up a fruit from his own tree, i.e., he makes a donation. Spoken word jurists see this as a virtual declaration. A man acting silently directly performs a legal relationship. Spoken word jurists reconstruct this sequence in a more complex fashion. According to this classification, the silent party who intends to perform a relationship knows that in order to create the relationship, a legal act, i.e., a declaration, is required and that performance of the relationship is equivalent to a declaration and thus performs the relationship (but what does he really perform since, without a legal act, there is no executable duty arising from the act?).

Before men could speak, dynamics of the law were reduced (except for ceremonies) to performance of relationships (start, continuation, end of performance, substitution of parties during performance), nor is there any reason to view silent acts in more complex terms today than at that time.[12]

3. Planning is made towards performance. Of these two aspects, performance plays the pivotal role of which planning is simply a device (a dubious device at that: when the law drafts a plan it still remains to be seen whether citizens will comply). The purpose of

---

12. Some of these issues are discussed in Sacco, "Autonomia del diritto privato," *Dig 4a ed. civ. I* (1987).

property is the use and enjoyment of assets. A gift of property completely devoid of any possibility of use and enjoyment would be purely illusory. If my neighbor doesn't mind my use and enjoyment of his possessions, I would not complain of the absence of a deed granting me a lease held for a term of years. Law and legal acts are theoretical exercises. On the contrary, social discipline and performance have a practical dimension. However, jurists write thousands of pages on the intended program and only one page on its execution, i.e., the intent of its words. They don't like to admit that the intent of property is possession; that property is a structure created to ensure to parties (by means of imposing exclusionary obligations on others) their possessions; that those who claim the property invoke the logical medium that insures possession; that the focal point of law is possession, performance, observance of the law; and not the property, the contract, or the law.

4. An even greater abnormality is found on the logical level. The dynamics of the law are always presented as centered around fundamentally opposite plans so that historical events, belonging to the factual world, trigger legal reality (immaterial, made of thoughts). Writings of the sovereign, death of the sovereign, votes of the assembly, factual historical events trigger rules, succession to the crown, appointment of high dignitaries of State (thought creates these legal realities). Capture of fish gives origin to fishermen's property, contracts create obligations. Under this view the factual situation must necessarily predate the origin of the legal situation (ignoring the separate issue of retroactivity).

This scheme that sees facts preceding obligations is transferred by jurist to the field of mute acts and sources. Custom is created by long repetition of conforming behaviors; once created it is binding. Sellers complete their sales by shipping the goods. As soon as performance is made, the sale is complete and binds the parties. This scheme is inadequate, contradictory and even ridiculous. Consider the doctrine of custom. While conforming behaviors are being rendered, the parties are observing a rule not yet in existence, but since the rule is not yet in existence, it cannot yet legitimate the conforming behavior. Sellers shipping their goods, ordered by fax by buyers, would be performing an act not yet required (since at time of performance, no contract would yet be in existence), and incur double expenditure!

The truth is that with respect to unspoken law, the factual rules and the factual situation which create the duty do not precede the duty. Rule and relationship, as clear expressions of rights and duties, do not arise. Performance of a duty (exercise of rights, performance of an act, acquiescence, respect for another's individuality) is self-justifying and rises to the level of a duty (sometimes a duty of long duration). Observance of a rule, or the exercise of a right in conformity to a rule are self-justifying and justify the customary rule. A "natural" rule is sufficient to justify itself. It is justified by a complex of glands, hormones, and adrenalines infinitely stronger, as far as persuasive powers, than a collection of legal scholars added to a collection of legal precedents.

A linguistic remark could be added to these systemic remarks. The mute law could not give names to the legal institutions that already at that time sustained society and conditioned its survival. It could not give them names because it could not speak. But a lack of conceptualization followed the lack of verbalization, and the creation of language did not seek to give names to institutions that worked in the absence of speech. Clearly I don't know the first human language. But it is apparent, a long time after the inception of speech, that the legal institutions which date furthest back in history, those institutions "quae natura omnia animalia docuit", and that thus don't need to be defined by words in order to exist, have not been fully defined even in times when the legal lexicon has been fully developed. Ancient Romans did not define property because they found it to be self-evident; they did not define family authority for the same reason; they gave approximate and uncertain definitions to custom.

In the great scheme of history, the speaking man is conceptually and directly familiar with spoken law, which he created. He did not feel a need to look back to unspoken law that he found too obvious to require explanation. In cases where he felt a need to do so, he adapted categories belonging to the spoken law, which did not adequately suit the purpose.

Speaking jurists have given names to rules, subjective rights and legal duties. They were not so generous with behaviors conforming to rules, exercise of subjective rights and performance of duties. They define these concepts only in relation to the related ideas expressed by the spoken law. Against any natural linguistic logic, they used a key-word to define an instrumental, abstract, immaterial legal reality (rules, rights, duties) and then used compound derivative terms (behavior in conformity with the rule, behavior in violation of the rule, exercise of right, performance of duty) to indicate the real historical objects for which the instruments were intended.

[16]

Social Science and Diffusion of Law

WILLIAM TWINING*

The purpose of this paper is to point out a remarkable gap between the social science literature on diffusion and the legal literature on reception and transplantation and to explore the implications of this gap for research on diffusion of law.

INTRODUCTION

'[Comparative law's] failure to develop is evident in several regards ... [The] 'Country and Western tradition' with its main focus on nation state legal systems of Western capitalist societies, its obsession with the common law/civil law dichotomy, and its preoccupation with private law rules and doctrines, may have been adequate at the time but is in dire need of a major overhaul. Furthermore, despite many admonitions and obvious needs, comparative law has still not become interdisciplinary. To be sure, there is occasional interdisciplinary work, but it is a rare exception and has not set a broader trend. And despite many criticisms, comparative law has still not acquired a solid empirical base.'[1]

Modern sociological accounts of diffusion and modern legal discussions of reception and transplants are a rather clear example of two bodies of

---

* *University College London, 4 Endsleigh Gardens, London WC1H OEG, England*
wlt@wtwining.fsnet.co.uk

This article is a sequel to 'Diffusion of Law: A Global Perspective' ((2005) 49 *J. of Legal Pluralism* 1–45, hereafter Twining, 'Diffusion' (2005)). Much of the research for this paper was undertaken at the Center for Advanced Study in the Behavioral Sciences at Stanford in 1999–2000. I am grateful for the wonderful support of the staff of the Center and for advice on the historical and social science literature from Carol Gluck, Harvey Molotch, and David Snow. I am also grateful to Deirdre Dwyer, Trisha Greenhalgh, John Griffiths, David Nelken, Esin Örücü, and Gordon Woodman for helpful comments.

1 M. Reiman, 'The Progress and Failure of Comparative Law' (2002) 50 *Am. J. of Comparative Law* 671, at 685–6. On 'The Country and Western Tradition', see W. Twining, 'Comparative Law and Legal Theory: The Country and Western Tradition' in *Comparative Law in Global Perspective*, ed. I. Edge (2000a) ch. 2; see, also, W. Twining, *Globalisation and Legal Theory* (2000b) at 184–9.

literature seemingly addressed to similar phenomena that largely ignore each other.[2] Both are concerned with the spread of ideas. The purpose of this essay is to draw attention to this phenomenon and to explore its implications. It may be read as an introduction to these two bodies of literature or as a modest contribution to diffusion theory. It may be used to provide some general guidance to someone embarking on a study of some particular aspect of diffusion of law. It can be taken as an invitation to social scientists to pay more attention to law; and it may be interpreted as a further plea to social scientists, socio-legal scholars, and comparative lawyers to contribute to the cause of giving comparative law a more solid empirical base.

Leading comparative lawyers, including Sacco, Watson, Glenn, and Örücü, treat diffusion as central to comparative law as a sub-discipline.[3] In a companion paper I argue that we lack a systematic theory of diffusion of law and that from a number of widespread, though not universal, assumptions in the discourse about 'reception' and 'transplantation' of law, one can construct a 'naïve model of diffusion', consisting of twelve elements.[4] If one adopts a global perspective and a broad conception of law (including major examples of 'non-state law'), then each of the elements can be shown to be neither necessary nor even characteristic features of processes of legal diffusion. Instead of a single paradigm case one needs to construct a picture that emphasizes the complexity and variety of these processes.

In this paper I shall suggest that the heritage of studies of diffusion of law does not belong to a single research tradition. It has been generated by a variety of concerns – often diffusion has not been the primary focus – and it lacks a coherent framework, partly because of the complexity and variety of the phenomena involved. It contains some valuable case studies, some useful concepts and distinctions, and some unsatisfactory debates. Most of the leading studies have not deviated far from the 'Country and Western' tradition of comparative law and a naïve model of diffusion. On the other hand, there is a vast and varied social science literature on diffusion that has

---

2 Vol. 6 of *The International Encyclopedia of the Social and Behavioral Sciences* (2001) (hereafter *IESBS*) presents an overview of the historical development of diffusion studies in three separate articles, none of which even mentions law: R. Stade, 'Diffusion: Anthropological Aspects' (at 3673–76); L.A. Brown, 'Diffusion: Geographical Aspects' (at 3676–80), and N. Alter, 'Diffusion, Sociology of' (at 3680–84). This pattern is repeated in nearly all of the social scientific works considered below. On the variety of terms and metaphors (transplants, reception, importation, and so on) used to designate the field, see Twining, 'Diffusion' (2005). 'Diffusion of law' is here used as the generic term for the subject in order to point to the links with the social science literature.
3 A. Watson, *Legal Transplants* (2nd edn., 1993) ch. 1; E. Örücü, *Critical Comparative Law: Considering Paradoxes for Legal Systems in Transition* (1999); R. Sacco, 'Legal Formants: A Dynamic Approach to Comparative Law II' (1991) 39 *Am. J. of Comparative Law* 343; H.P. Glenn, *Legal Traditions of the World* (2nd edn., 2004).
4 Twining, 'Diffusion' (2005).

been largely ignored by legal scholars, who have in turn been ignored by the social scientists. This heritage of literature, much of it empirically grounded, can provide us with some basic tools for analysing particular examples of diffusion processes and a vast treasure house of concepts, hypotheses, findings, debates, concrete examples, and suggestive analogies that could help to guide, fertilize, and illuminate particular lines of research.

The naïve model postulates a paradigm case with the following characteristics:

> [A] *bipolar* relationship between *two countries* involving a *direct one-way* transfer of *legal rules or institutions* through the agency of *governments* involving *formal enactment or adoption* at a particular moment of time (*a reception date*) *without major change*. Although not explicitly stated in this example, it is commonly assumed that the standard case involves *transfer from an advanced (parent) civil or common law system to a less developed one*, in order to bring about *technological change* ('to modernize') by *filling in gaps or replacing* prior local law. There is also considerable vagueness about the criteria for 'success' of a reception – one common assumption seems to be that if it has survived for a significant period '*it works*'.[5]

While few writers on reception/transplantation have accepted this model in its entirety, all of the elements are still quite widespread in discourse and literature on the subject. The phenomena are too varied to be reduced to a single model.

Table I. A standard case and some variants

	Standard case	*Variants*
a. Source-destination	Bipolar: single exporter to single importer	Single exporter to multiple destinations Single importer from multiple sources Multiple sources to multiple destinations, etc.
b. Level	Municipal legal system-municipal legal system	Cross-level transfers Horizontal transfers at other levels (for example, regional, sub-state, non-state transnational)
c. Pathways	Direct one-way transfer	Complex paths Reciprocal influence Re-export

5 id., at p. 14.

Table I (continued)

	Standard case	*Variants*
d. Formal/ informal	Formal enactment or adoption	Informal, semi-formal or mixed
e. Objects	Legal rules and concepts Institutions	Any legal phenomena or ideas, including ideology, theories, personnel, 'mentality', methods, structures, practices (official, private practitioners', educational, and so on) literary genres, documentary forms, symbols, rituals, etc.
f. Agency	Government-government	Commercial and other non-governmental organizations Armies Individuals and groups: for example, colonists, missionaries, merchants, slaves, refugees, believers, and so on, who 'bring law with them' Writers, teachers, activists, lobbyists
g. Timing	One or more specific reception dates	Continuing, typically lengthy process
h. Power and prestige	Parent civil or common law >> less developed	
i. Change in object	Unchanged Minor adjustments	'No transportation without transformation'
j. Relation to pre-existing law	Blank slate Fill vacuum, gaps Replace entirely	Struggle resistance Layering Assimilation Surface law
k. Technical/ ideological/ cultural	Technical	Ideology, culture, and technology

Table I (continued)

	Standard case	Variants
l. Impact	'It works'	Performance measures Empirical research Enforcement

Each of these points is illustrated in the earlier paper. The next section of this paper examines some highlights of legal studies of reception/transplantation to illustrate how they have emerged from a variety of concerns and specialisms and how they are too fragmented and lack sufficient critical mass to constitute a single research tradition or to ground an over-arching theory. Some come out of the Country and Western tradition of comparative law – with its tendency to focus on the formal law of 'parent' or 'metropolitan' civil and common law state legal systems in the West and to ignore or marginalize other legal traditions and less formal kinds of law. Most of the studies deviate from the naïve model of diffusion in one or more respects; almost all treat diffusion as being concerned with one-way traffic between municipal law of two countries as part of a process of 'imposed' or 'voluntary' adoption by governments.

SOME LANDMARKS IN THE STUDY OF DIFFUSION OF LAW

Much of the discussion of diffusion of law in the literature is to be found in broader studies of colonial law or local legal history or law reform or structural adjustment. Study of diffusion on its own can be as sterile as the search for origins in history or of 'influence' in art or literature. However, for some purposes it makes sense to focus on diffusion as a process. When that has happened the underlying concerns, the perspectives and methods adopted, and the immediate historical context have been quite diverse. The literature on diffusion of law does not belong to a single research tradition,[6] but much of it fits within the paradigm of the Country and Western tradition.[7] This can be

---

6 Greenhalgh suggests that much of the social science literature on diffusion of innovations belongs to a single research tradition, which went through several phases, despite being located in different branches of sociology. 'Research tradition' is defined as 'a coherent body of theoretical knowledge and a linked set of primary studies in which successive studies are influenced by the findings of previous studies' T. Greenhalgh, G. Robert, F. Macfarlane, P. Bate, O. Kyriakidou, *'Diffusion of Innovations in Health Service Organizations: Systematic Review and Recommendations* (2004a) at 52 (hereafter, the Greenhalgh report) discussed below. For a useful summary, see T. Greenhalgh et al., 'Diffusion of innovations in service organizations: systematic review and recommendations' (2004b) 82(4) *Milbank Q.* 581.
7 See n. 1 above. As we shall see, by no means all leading accounts of diffusion of law belong to that tradition.

illustrated by briefly considering some landmarks in the study of legal diffusion as such.

1. Early diffusionism

The literature on transplantation or reception of law can be traced back to the work of Tarde, Maine, and Weber. To start with it had some connection with diffusion theory in cultural anthropology, but law soon faded into the background. Diffusionism represented a reaction against the prevailing nineteenth-century view that there were natural laws of evolution governing human progress. This theme was taken up mainly in cultural anthropology, in the early years concentrating on spatial distribution of culture traits more than on the processes of diffusion.[8] In time, strong forms of diffusion theory were discredited, and most anthropologists accepted that the history of nearly every society involves a mixture of indigenous factors and external influences. The development and functioning of institutions and practices rather than their spread thereafter tended to be the focal point of interest.[9] Nevertheless, in most social sciences there has been a steady stream of work in which diffusion has been the focus, the relative importance of local and external factors has had to be weighed, and their interaction considered.[10]

2. The reception of Roman law

The reception of Roman law in medieval Europe has long been a matter of interest to scholars of Roman law and legal history. After the Second World War, studies of 'reception' developed largely divorced from empirical studies of diffusion, especially the sociological literature on diffusion of innovations. The two classic studies by Koschaker[11] and Wieacker were

---

8 Strong diffusionists, notably Elliot Smith and W.J. Perry, emphasized humankind's hostility to change and the alleged lack of inventiveness of nearly all cultures; they argued that the origins of all 'higher' civilizations could be traced back to Egypt. Less extreme forms of diffusionist theory, such as the *Kulturkreis* school, allowed for multiple centres of invention, but nevertheless searched for origins and played down innovation.

9 For example, L. Mair, *An Introduction to Social Anthropology* (2nd edn., 1972) at 20, 40–52.

10 Stade, op. cit., n. 2, p. 3673, usefully tracks the main (overlapping) stages in studies of diffusion in anthropology in the twentieth century as focusing on cultural history, acculturation and culture contact studies, world system studies, and cultural imperialism, followed by transnational and globalization studies.

11 Paul Koschaker's best known thesis, taken up by many subsequent writers, was that the reception of Roman law in Central Europe and the spread of the Code Napoleon were more a matter of imperial power and prestige than of superior technical quality. P. Koschaker, *Europa und das römische Recht* (1946, 2nd edn. 1953) discussed by K. Zweigert and H. Kötz, *An Introduction to Comparative Law* (3rd edn., 1998, trans. T. Weir) at 100.

ambitious works of legal history, written on a grand scale, but essentially particularistic.

Franz Wieacker's *A History of Private Law in Europe*[12] has formed the starting-point of much European legal historiography since its publication. It has been described as a very wise book from a very harsh time.[13] Wieacker's aim, as Zimmerman puts it, was to provide a bridge between Roman law and contemporary legal science, while reasserting the values of personalism, legalism, and intellectualism.[14] Underlying his approach is the view that a systematic body of law based on a rigorous transnational legal science serves the values of consistency, justice, and the rule of law against the arbitrary power of the national state.

Wieacker's *magnum opus* is a learned, subtle, complex, magisterial history of the development of private law ideas in Europe over several centuries. It is a work of intellectual history hardly concerned with technical detail or the law in action. His is a strongly Weberian story of rationalization by legal *honoratiores*. The central thesis is that the history of modern private law in Europe starts with the rise of jurists trained in the Bolognese legal method of the *studium civile* who acquired key positions in the judicial and administrative branches of government.[15] Wieacker's is a story of a long-drawn out, complex process of diffusion over time and space of a particular approach to Justinian's *Institutes*, involving the steady intellectualization of law, especially in Germany, resulting in a particular form of 'legal science'.

---

12 F. Wieacker, *Privatrechtsgeschicte der Neuzeit* (1952, revised 1967), translated by T. Weir as *A History of Private Law in Europe, with particular reference to Germany* (1995); compare F. Wieacker, 'The Importance of Roman Law for Modern Western Civilization and Western Legal Thought' (1981) 4 *Boston College International and Comparative Law Rev.* 257; and his 'Foundations of European Legal Culture' (1990) 38 *Am. J. of Comparative Law* 1.

13 J. Whitman, 'Review of Wieacker (1995)' in (1999) 17 *Law and History Rev.* 400, at 402. In the 1930s, Wieacker (1908–1994) had been a member of the Nazi party and had worked to create a new nationalist law for the Third Reich. This had involved removing Roman law from the curriculum and substituting a Nazi version of European and German legal history. Later, Wieacker reacted strongly against Nazism and what he saw as the degeneration of positivism and the disintegration of private law. His superb work, first published in 1952, was explicitly a contribution to post-war reconstruction. His emphasis on Roman Law, *ius commune*, and legal science based on individual legal conscience represented a reaction against the nationalism and cynical positivism of the Nazi period.

14 R. Zimmerman, Introduction to Wieacker, op. cit. (1995), n. 12.

15 Wieacker, op. cit. (1995), n. 12, p. 7: 'Their dominance in public affairs ensured for ever the peculiarly legalistic character of Western society, its habit of seeing problems as legal and discussing them rationally, a habit which stamped society, the state, and the economy, even contemporary administrative technology, in such a way that life would be unimaginable without it. It distinguishes Western society from all other cultures known to us.'

3. Cross-cultural receptions: the case of Turkey

In the 1950s, the International Committee of Comparative Law allocated a leading place in their programme to the study of modern receptions of foreign systems of law by countries having a cultural background and tradition different from those in which they had developed.[16] This was the great period of decolonization which also saw the rise of the study of 'African law' and similar initiatives, most of which tend to get written out of stories of 'law and development'.[17] In 1955 a major conference on Reception of Foreign Law in Turkey marked the start of what is by far the richest literature on a single story of reception.[18] This is hardly surprising, for as Zweigert and Kötz wrote:

> Nowhere else in the world can one so well study how in the reception of a foreign law there is a mutual interaction between the interpretation of the foreign text and the actual traditions and usages of the country which adopted it, with the consequent gradual development of a new law of an independent nature.[19]

The story of the reception, or more accurately receptions, of foreign law in Turkey has stimulated much of the best detailed writing and, especially in the work of Esin Örücü, some of the most sophisticated theorizing about diffusion of law. I shall use the example of Turkey later to suggest that the best literature on legal diffusion runs in parallel with some of the literature on diffusion of innovations, but that it is still largely based on a simple model of the processes of diffusion.

4. Kahn-Freund and Watson: the 'transplants' debate

The nineteen-seventies saw a revival of sustained interest in diffusion under the label 'transplantation'. In his Chorley Lecture at the LSE in 1973, Professor Otto Kahn-Freund famously contrasted the transplantation of a human kidney from one human being to another with the transfer of a carburettor or a wheel from one car to another, arguing that:

---

16 Japan, Ethiopia and Turkey were viewed as especially interesting because they were interpreted as 'voluntary' receptions and therefore exceptional.

17 Histories of the 'Law and Development Movement' have tended to focus on American involvement, which began in the 1960s rather than with concerns about 'development', often under different labels, in the colonial period and particularly in the immediate pre- and post-Independence periods. See B. Tamanaha, 'The Lessons of Law-and-Development Studies' (1995) 89 *Am. J. of International Law* 470, J.P.W.B. McAuslan, *In the Beginning was the Law – An Intellectual Odyssey*, Paper 2 in Cornell Law School East Asian Law and Culture Conference Series (2004).

18 The proceedings of the Conference were reported in *Annales de la Faculté de Droit d'Istanbul*, no. 6 (1956) and UNESCO *International Social Science Bulletin* (1957) vol. IX. no. 1 For further references, see n. 69 below.

19 Zweigert and Kötz, op. cit., n. 11, at p. 178.

In the metaphorical language I am using, the kidney and the carburettor are the terminal points of a continuum and any given legal rule or institution may be found at a different point of it. ... there are degrees of transferability.[20]

Kahn-Freund was Professor of Comparative Law at Oxford and a leading exponent of 'law in context'. In this lecture he was addressing the uses and misuses of comparative law (and hence of foreign models) as a tool of law reform and making a plea for sensitivity to social and political context. His main point was that the difficulty of transfer depended largely on the closeness of the relationship between the transplant and the local power structure. Montesquieu argued that law was so much a creature of its environment that it is an extraordinary coincidence (*'un grand hazard'*) if the political and civil laws of one country can suit another. Recently commentators have tended to emphasize the importance of the cultural context, but Kahn-Freund laid more stress on political factors: the prevailing ideology, the political institutions, and the interests of the powerful are likely to be the greatest source of resistance to transplantation.[21] So the comparative lawyer engaging in law reform needs not only to have knowledge of foreign law but also to understand the social and political context of both the exporting and importing country.

In 1974 Alan Watson launched the first of a series of books on 'legal transplants'.[22] Adopting a deliberately polemical style, Watson argued that contextual differences are largely irrelevant to 'the success' of transplantation and so 'the recipient system does not require any real knowledge of the social, economic, geographical, and political context of the origin and growth of the original rule.'[23] The lines between the contextualists and the Watsonians were drawn in this first exchange, but the debate has continued ever since.

Like Wieacker, Watson came to diffusion from a background in Roman law and history. But his objectives, methods, and style were very different. Watson's first book, *Legal Transplants*, advanced the bold thesis that throughout history imitation has been the main engine of legal change.[24]

---

20 O. Kahn-Freund, 'On Uses and Misuses of Comparative Law' in *Selected Writings* (1978) at 298–9 (originally published in (1974) 37 *Modern Law Rev.* 1).
21 id., p. 300: 'But I submit – and this is my central thesis – that in these 200 years [since Montesquieu] the geographical, the economic and social, and the cultural elements have greatly lost, but that the political factors have equally greatly gained in importance'. A central theme of A. Chua, *World on Fire* (2003) is that often powerful elites or 'market-dominant minorities' have been instrumental in importing foreign law, thereby breeding resentment and racial conflict.
22 A. Watson, *Legal Transplants* (1974, revised edn., 1993); his most recent variations on the theme include *Law Out of Context* (2000a) and *Legal Transplants and European Private Law* (2000b), a reply to Legrand.
23 A. Watson, 'Legal Transplants and Law Reform' (1976) 92 *Law Q. Rev.* 79, at 81.
24 Watson has written so much on the theme, advancing here, retreating there, that he is difficult to pin down. However, he provided a useful summary of his position in his own words for the fifth edition of Rudolph Schlesinger's course book on

Initially, Watson seems to have been reacting against mainstream comparative law, especially the 'legal families' tradition, and sociological and 'contextual' approaches to law, such as that of Kahn-Freund, that emphasized the intimate relationship between law and society. In his more extreme statements, Watson seemed reminiscent of the early diffusionists, suggesting that innovation is almost unknown in law.

Watson's work provoked the worst kind of academic debate in which each side caricatured the other and rarely joined issue.[25] Watson attacked the belief that law 'mirrors' society (strong mirror theses) but it is difficult to find any serious scholar who holds a strong version of this thesis. Conversely, Watson's critics focused on some of his more extreme statements and accused him of claiming that legal change takes place largely independently of social conditions. Others, notably Pierre Legrand, have gone to the other extreme, arguing that 'transplants are impossible'.[26] When the protagonists adopt more moderate positions, they often get bogged down in a soggy middle.

This is not the place to consider Watson's work in detail. Isaiah Berlin reminds us that the fox knows many things, but the hedgehog knows one big thing. Watson is a juristic hedgehog. He has stuck persistently to the theme that there are enormous apparent similarities between legal systems around the world, that these similarities are a result of imitation, and that most law exists largely independently of local social, economic, and cultural conditions. He has done a great service as an agent provocateur, but one is left with the feeling that Watson's theory deals mainly with surface appearances. His generalizations are not backed by empirical evidence.

Comparative Law, eds. R. Schlesinger, H. Baade, M. Damaska, and P. Herzog (1988). For most purposes this can be taken as a representative text. The most accessible and useful interpretation of Watson's views is W. Ewald, 'Comparative Jurisprudence II: The Logic of Legal Transplants' (1995) 43 *Am. J. of Comparative Law* 489.

25 Ewald (id.) has usefully analysed the logical structure of Watson's theory, distinguishing two versions, one strong and ultimately self-destructive, the other weaker, but sufficient to achieve the main task. A similar approach can be taken with Watson's main critics, including L. Friedman, 'Borders: On the Emerging Sociology of Transnational Law' (1996) 32 *Stanford J. of International Law* 65, at 72, and P. Legrand, *Fragments on Law-as-Culture* (1999). A more balanced evaluation is by D. Nelken in *Comparative Legal Studies: Traditions and Transitions*, eds. P. Legrand and R. Munday (2003) ch. 12.

26 P. Legrand, 'The Impossibility of Legal Transplants' (1997) 4 *Maastricht J. of European and Comparative Law* 111. One commentator, William Evan, even suggested that the corpus of Watson's work may be interpreted as undermining the rationale for developing a theory of law and society (W. Evan, *Social Structure and Law* (1980) at 35). In fact, Watson explicitly claims to be advancing a theory about the distant nature of the relationship between law and society, one which emphasizes the relative autonomy of law. He follows Max Weber's thesis that a legal culture is given distinctiveness by the mentality of its legal elite (the legal *honoratiores*) who, according to Watson, are the main agents of transplantation, change, and inertia.

Watson treats law as a superficial gloss on society; perhaps his generalizations about law are similarly superficial.[27] One wonders how his thesis can be translated, refined, or adapted into a form that is capable of detailed empirical testing.

Watson's work fits the simple model of reception and he works squarely within 'the Country and Western tradition'. Much of the recent debate about convergence and harmonization in Europe has been framed in terms of Watson's thesis and its critics.[28] His thesis is largely confined to Roman law and modern Western municipal law;[29] he is mainly interested in private law; and his principal concern is the differences and relationships between civil and common law. So his central claims are limited in respect of subject matter and geography and, apart from his interest in classical Roman law, in respect of time.

6. *Esin Örücü: transposition and critical comparative law*

In the last ten years there has been a lively revival of critical theorizing about comparative law.[30] There is much of interest in that literature, but collectively it suffers from still being quite firmly rooted in 'the Country and Western tradition of comparative law', that is to say, an almost exclusive focus on municipal law of major – often 'parent' – legal systems, and an over-simple model of diffusion.[31] Some of the strengths and limitations of this secondary literature can be illustrated by the work of the Turkish comparatist Esin Örücü.

Örücü is only one voice among many, but I shall focus on her work for three reasons: it is intellectually ambitious; she places diffusion (what she calls transposition of law) at the centre of comparative law; and it is grounded in excellent detailed studies, especially about her native Turkey.

Örücü in her bold attempt to construct a comprehensive and coherent vision of what she terms 'Critical Comparative Law'[32] identified four

---

27 Compare Ewald's brilliant critique of the idea that a Roman law student from the age of Justinian would not be greatly astonished by the substance of a modern civil code ('The ignorance of Romulus' in W. Ewald 'Comparative Jurisprudence I: What was it Like to Try a Rat?' (1995) 143 *University of Pennsylvania Law Rev.* 1889, at 2095–104); compare W. Twining, 'A cosmopolitan discipline?' (2001) 1 *J. of Commonwealth Law and Legal Education* 13.
28 For example, J. Allison, *A Continental Distinction in the Common Law* (1996); Legrand, op. cit., n. 26; Legrand and Munday, op. cit., n. 25.
29 On Turkey, see Watson, op. cit. (2000a), n. 22.
30 Some of these are surveyed in Örücü, op. cit., n. 3. See, also, Edge, op. cit., n. 1; 'Symposium' in (1997) *Utah Law Rev*; Legrand and Munday, op. cit., n. 25; E. Örücü, *The Enigma of Comparative Law* (2004).
31 See, above, pp. 205–7.
32 In contrast to 'traditional' or 'conventional' comparative law; she insists that her choice of terminology should 'in no way be construed to mean that "Critical Comparative Law" is a branch of the Critical Legal Studies Movement.' (Örücü, op. cit., n. 3, at p. 7.)

distinct trends in comparative law scholarship since the mid-1970s:

(a) attempts to re-establish links between comparative law and legal theory, exemplified by the work of Geoffrey Samuel, William Ewald, and Örücü herself;

(b) comparative legal history, exemplified by Rudolfo Sacco and the Trento School, who maintain that comparison is an historical science which 'examines the way in which legal institutions are connected, diversified and transplanted from one country to another';[33]

(c) comparative law and culture, which has tended to emphasize the frequent mismatches between local (social and legal) cultures and legal transplants (for example, Pierre Legrand and David Nelken); and

(d) the extension of economic analysis of law to comparative law,[34] including the thesis that legal systems over time will choose the most efficient rules and institutions from a menu of 'solutions' developed by competing national systems – a sort of market, or perhaps garden centre, for legal transplants.

Örücü suggests that all four approaches treat diffusion of law as being at the core of the comparative legal enterprise and that:

> most of the current concerns of comparatists on convergence versus divergence, mismatch in borrowings, problems for the importers and exporters of legal ideas and institutions can be constructively approached under the name 'Critical Comparative Law'.[35]

She suggests that within the European Union the most prominent practical concerns understandably will be with inter-European relations, notably the movement for a new *ius commune*, the attempts to reconcile or harmonize civil and common law, the creation of European codes and comparative law as 'a tool of construction' in national and supra-national courts. One might add opposition to or scepticism about these ventures. There are similar trends in the common law world, but account also needs to be taken of some other tendencies, such as the perception that the United States of America is in competition with European countries as a legal exporter, the resistance of common lawyers to codification, and the development of comparative common law.

Örücü predicts that:

> The comparative law enterprise in the twenty-first century will be paying more attention to general, public, private and criminal comparative law as well as to comparative law in the EU, comparative law in the common law world,

---

33 R. Sacco, 'Legal Formants: A Dynamic Approach to Comparative Law II' (1991) 39 *Am. J. of Comparative Law* 343, at 388.

34 U. Mattei, *Comparative Law and Economics* (1997) and 'Efficiency in Legal Transplants' (1994) 14 *International Rev. of Law and Economics* 3, criticized by P. Legrand in Legrand and Munday. op. cit., n. 25, ch. 9.

35 Örücü, op. cit., n. 3, at p. 7.

comparative law in the Far East and reciprocal influences. The future of comparative law will be tied theoretically and practically to an enhanced legal science, convergence and integration as well as an appreciation of diversity, the use of foreign models in law reform and law and cultural studies. The trends we see developing will continue to centre round the role for comparative law as a means of theory testing; new approaches to harmonization; new receptions, mixed and mixing systems, and redesigning systems; a new European *ius commune*; redefining legal culture; and an emphasis on regional comparative law such as European, Central and Eastern European, common law, African, and Far Eastern.[36]

These indications of significant perspectives and lines of inquiry may sound daunting, especially if one is used to seeing comparative law as a lightly populated, rural sub-discipline involving a few specialists.[37] However, I suggest that from a global perspective this list is far from complete, even in respect of current activities, and that despite the breadth of her vision and the sophistication of her treatment of transposition, even Örücü is still partly rooted in 'the Country and Western tradition' of comparative law and a quite narrow concept of diffusion. Her focus is mainly on the municipal law of nation states, with a bias towards Europe and her native Turkey, and although she discusses the European Union, she does not deal systematically with cross-level interaction between legal orders or with non-state law.

7. Patrick Glenn

The approach of H. Patrick Glenn is very different from the works already considered here. His *Legal Traditions of the World* is written on a grand scale, setting law in the context of world history.[38] More clearly than the rest he has broken away from 'the Country and Western tradition' and substituted a historically based vision of complex major traditions in continuous and reciprocal interaction.

Glenn's picture of a tradition is of a continuous flow of ideas over time that contains a relatively stable core, but no precise boundaries. It emphasizes memory, communication, continuity, and selection. Glenn's work has major implications for the study of diffusion of law. First, diffusion is a pervasive, continuing phenomenon rather than a series of isolated,

---

36 id., at p. 8.
37 According to Becher 'rural' disciplines have a low people-to-problem ratio and typically cover broad stretches of intellectual territory in which the problems are not sharply defined. Within mainstream comparative law, probably only studies of the private law of 'parent' Western legal systems are highly populated enough to rank as 'urban'. T. Becher, *Academic Tribes and Territories* (1989). But on another view we are all comparatists now (Twining, op. cit. (2000b), n. 1, p. 255).
38 Glenn, op. cit., n. 3 and articles that develop some themes at greater length are discussed in Twining, 'Diffusion' (2005). See, also, the symposium on Glenn's book in the first issue of the *J. of Comparative Law* (forthcoming, 2005).

exceptional events. Second, there are no 'pure' traditions. Throughout history traditions have interacted, both influencing and resisting each other, in what is typically a reciprocal rather than a one-way process. Third, from this perspective, state law, legal positivism, and Western legal traditions lose their pre-eminence. They are just one part of a broader picture in which they appear as relatively recent phenomena that may already be in decline.[39]

The picture painted of law in the world in this essay is closer to Glenn's vision than any of the writings on diffusion discussed so far. He can be interpreted as distancing himself from the naïve model of diffusion. *Legal Traditions of the World* comes closer than any other work to providing a coherent alternative.

8. *Continuing diversity*

These landmarks of legal diffusion studies do not constitute a continuous research tradition. Rather the historical context of each belongs to the largely separate histories of loosely related academic specialisms: cultural anthropology (diffusionism); Roman law and legal history (Wieaker); comparative law (Kahn-Freund, Glenn, Örücü); recently major contributions have come via systems theory (Teubner[40]), sociology of law (Cotterrell and Nelken[41]), and law and development (Dezalay and Garth,[42] Pistor and Wellons[43]). In this context, Alan Watson seems like a wild card defying categorization.

In the last fifteen years, apart from the debates stimulated by Watson, there has been a very marked increase in explicit interest in diffusion of law both as a matter of scholarly attention and for practical reasons, especially in relation to law reform and harmonization as part of European integration, structural adjustment programmes in developing countries, reconstruction in 'countries in transition' in Eastern Europe, and post-conflict reconstruction.[44] This interest has arisen from a variety of concerns in a variety of contexts and again, in many instances, discussion of diffusion, transplants. and so on has been incidental to some broader issue.

Whereas the concerns of the early diffusionists and of legal scholars such as Wieacker, Watson, Glenn, and Örücü have been almost entirely academic,

---

39 See P. Glenn, 'The Nationalist Heritage' in Legrand and Munday, op. cit., n. 25, ch. 4.
40 G. Teubner, 'The Two Faces of Janus: Rethinking Legal Pluralism' (1992) 13 *Cardozo Law Rev.* 1443; G. Teubner, '"Global Bukinawa": Legal Pluralism in World Society' in G. Teubner (ed.), *Global Law Without the State* (1996).
41 D. Nelken and J. Feest (eds.), *Adapting Legal Cultures* (2001).
42 Y. Dezalay and B. Garth, *Dealing in Virtue* (1996); *The Internationalization of Palace Wars* (2002)
43 K. Pistor and P.A. Wellons, *The Role of Law and Legal Institutions in Asian Economic Development 1960–1995* (1999).
44 These developments are discussed in Twining, 'Diffusion' (2005).

some of these recent developments raise questions of immediate practicality: policy makers in international financial institutions want to know why 'transplants' have regularly been perceived to have failed and what are the conditions for and how to measure 'success' of reforms involving importation or imposition of foreign models; local reformers want to know what factors to take into account in choosing between alternative models (when they are given a choice); judges want guidance on when it is appropriate to treat foreign precedents and other sources as persuasive authority;[45] resisters want to learn about the most effective strategies and techniques for lessening the impact, or of subverting or transforming unwelcome foreign imports; legal educators need to decide how much they should focus on local law and context and how far they should go in treating law as a cosmopolitan discipline in an area of globalization; and so on.

These developments have put the assumptions in the naïve model under increasing strain. Not surprisingly, nearly all of the practical reform efforts focus on municipal law. There have recently been some valuable particular studies by socio-legal scholars.[46] Some of the more theoretical work of Teubner, Glenn, Chiba, and others ranges more widely. Individual assumptions have been challenged, but not in a systematic way. No alternative framework has emerged.

To sum up: The literature on diffusion of law does not belong to a single research tradition, but much of it fits within the paradigm of 'the Country and Western tradition of comparative law'. It contains some valuable studies and insights, but it is generally fragmented, unempirical, and unduly influenced by a simplistic model of processes of diffusion.

DIFFUSION IN THE SOCIAL SCIENCES

1. *Overviews: Rogers and Greenhalgh*

As we have seen, the legal and social scientific literatures have shared ancestors, especially in the work of Tarde, Maine, and Weber. Diffusionism went out of fashion in anthropology, but the subject continued to be a significant focus of attention in sociology, of which rural sociology was

---

45 A.-M. Slaughter, 'A Typology of Transjudicial Communication' (1994) 29 *University of Richmond Law Rev.* 991; D. Fontana, 'Refined Comparativism in Constitutional Law' (2001) 49 *UCLA Law Rev.* 539. On American state courts' tendency to 'exclusivity of local sources' see Glenn, op. cit., n. 3, at p. 249, fn. 86.

46 For example, A. Chayes and A. Chayes, *The New Sovereignty: Compliance with International Regulatory Agreements* (1995); Y. Dezalay and B. Garth, *The Internationalization of Palace Wars* (2002); E.T. Jensen and T.C. Heller, *Beyond Common Knowledge: Empirical Approaches to the Rule of Law* (2003); D. Galligan and M. Kurkchiyan (eds.), *Law and Informal Practices: The Post-Communist Experience* (2003).

perhaps the most important. Whereas the early anthropologists had concentrated on the large-scale spatial diffusion of cultural traits and a search for origins, differing among themselves about the extent of human inventiveness, the sociologists focused more on process and agency, with particular emphasis on the conditions of export and import of ideas and the channels of diffusion.

Diffusion research was spearheaded by studies focusing on innovations.[47] Pioneering studies dealt with such matters as the diffusion of hybrid corn in Iowa (Ryan and Gross),[48] of telephones, automobiles, and bovine tuberculosis tests in Sweden (Hagerstrand),[49] and medical innovation (Coleman et al.).[50] In addition to studying diffusion processes as such, many studies focused on particular aspects such as change agents, innovativeness, networks, or the role of the media. What might be called the classic tradition in sociology was ably synthesized by Everett Rogers in his *Diffusion of Innovations*, which we will consider below.

Over time the field expanded into different areas, some of which took on a life of their own. Within sociology, two areas that may be particularly suggestive for law are the study of social movements and the diffusion of innovations within and between organizations. Both of these moved beyond the emphasis on individual decision-making that had characterized a great deal of the early sociological research. However, the revival of interactionist perspectives in some sub-disciplines has again focused detailed attention on individual decisions and relations.[51] Distinct or only loosely related research traditions emerged over time in economics, anthropology, geography, and public health, to name but a few. As with law, a recurrent theme running through these loosely related bodies of research is that diffusion is often treated as an aspect of some broader topic such as social change, evolution, development, or globalization.

The social science literature is too vast and rich for it to be useful to try to identify all of the studies that might be directly relevant to diffusion of law – itself a quite diverse field. It is certainly beyond the ability of a single scholar.[52] Instead I shall focus on two works that taken together provide an

---

47 Everett Rogers's definition makes clear that this focus is not as narrow as it may sound: 'An innovation is an idea, practice, or object perceived as new by an individual or other unit of adoption.' E.M. Rogers, *Diffusion of Innovations* (1963, 4th edn., 1995) at 35. The early anthropological literature tended to contrast diffusion and innovation; Rogers combines the two, no doubt deliberately, by defining innovation from the standpoint of the recipient.
48 B. Ryan and N.C. Gross, 'The Diffusion of Hybrid Seed Corn in Two Iowa Communities'' (1943) 8 *Rural Sociology* 15.
49 T. Hagerstrand, *The Propagation of Innovation Waves* (1952); *Innovation of Diffusion as a Spatial Process*, (1953, American edn. 1968).
50 J.S. Coleman, E. Katz, and H. Menzel, *Medical Innovation: A Diffusion Study* (1966).
51 On interactionist perspectives, see below, pp. 236–7.
52 In addition to the works by Rogers, Greenhalgh, and the overviews in *IESBS*, op. cit., n. 2, I have found the following works to be especially useful: D. Snow and R.D. Benford, 'Alternative Types of Cross-national Diffusion in the Social Movement

accessible overview of a large part of the main social science literature in English: first, Everett Rogers, *Diffusion of Innovations*. This is still probably the best point of entry for an outsider canvassing the literature. Second, a recent systematic and broad literature survey by Greenhalgh and others, done on behalf of the Department of Health in the United Kingdom.[53] This built on and extended Rogers's synthesis for a particular purpose.

Between them, Rogers and Greenhalgh canvass and synthesize vast areas of mainstream diffusion research, but as we shall see there are other bodies of work that they do not cover, including language, religion, sport, music, political ideas, and, indeed, law. However, they do provide instructive histories of loosely related research traditions, some useful warnings about dead ends and false assumptions, a wealth of concrete examples, and some questions, concepts, and hypotheses that are potentially transferable. I shall explore some of the uses and limitations of this literature for legal studies of diffusion, first by considering the application of some of the orthodox sociological concepts to the story of the reception of foreign law in Turkey and then by highlighting some of the main biases and tendencies in social science diffusion research that need to be borne in mind by scholars interested in law.

(a) Everett Rogers's *Diffusion of Innovations*

Everett M. Rogers started his career in rural sociology, but over time he synthesized and generalized mainstream diffusion research. For nearly fifty years *Diffusion of Innovations* has been recognized as the basic handbook of the field. It is clearly written and illustrated with interesting examples drawn from many areas. In the fourth edition, the first part provides a basic theoretical framework (ch. 1), an historical overview of different research traditions of diffusion research in Europe and North America (ch. 2), and a critical assessment of the status of diffusion research in the early 1990s, including indications of some of the biases and controversies in the field (ch. 3). The ensuing chapters deal in more detail with different aspects of diffusion processes, including development of innovations, stages of decision, rates of adoption, adopter categories, networks, and change agents.

Arena' in *Social Movements in a Globalizing World*, eds. D. della Porta, H. Kriesi, and D. Rucht (1999); Hagerstrand, op. cit. (1953), n. 49; R. Heine-Geldern, T. Hagerstrand, and E Katz, 'Diffusion' in the *International Encyclopedia of the Social Sciences* 168–84 (1968); B.W. Arthur, 'Self-reinforcing Mechanisms in Economics' in *The Economy as an Evolving Complex System*, eds. P.W. Anderson, K.J. Arrow, and D. Pines (1988), and the economic literature on 'path dependency'. On specialized literature surveys see below, pp. 222–3.

53 The Greenalgh report, and Greenhalgh summary, both op. cit., n. 6; compare the related project involving a more specialized study of the social movement literature: P. Bate, H. Bevan, and G. Robert, *Towards a Million Change Agents: A Review of the Social Movements Literature: Implications for Large Scale Change in the NHS* (2004).

Most of the book focuses on relatively small-scale processes involving decisions by individuals, but the 1995 edition also deals with innovation in organizations and in third-world contexts. The final chapter on evaluation of consequences may be of a special interest to socio-legal scholars interested in the impact of attempted law reforms. Rogers does not cover all substantive streams of diffusion research and by the 1990s his book was beginning to appear rather old-fashioned. Nevertheless, it is still well worth reading as a solid historical survey, synthesis, and critical overview of mainstream social science research on diffusion.

Rogers states:

> [A]lthough diffusion research began as a series of scientific enclaves, it has emerged in recent years as a single, integrated body of concepts and generalizations, even though the investigations are conducted by researchers in different scientific disciplines.[54]

He lists ten different traditions of diffusion research in the social sciences, with rural sociology, marketing and management, and communication having the largest number of publications. Although he recognizes that even within sociology diffusion studies have different research traditions, he felt able to produce a synthesis of the major elements in the conceptual framework of modern diffusion theory.

Rogers further states that '[d]iffusion is a special type of communication concerned with the spread of messages that are perceived as new ideas.'[55] He continues:

> The main elements in the diffusion of new ideas are: (1) an *innovation* [in the eyes of the recipients] (2) which is *communicated* through certain *channels* (3) over *time*, (4) among members of a *social system*[56] ... Almost all of the new ideas discussed in this book are technological innovations ... The characteristics of an innovation, as perceived by the members of a social system, determine its rate of adoption. Five attributes of innovations are (1) relative advantage, (2) compatibility, (3) complexity, (4) trialability,[57] and (5) observability.[58]

Other key elements in Rogers' conceptual scheme are communication channels, innovation decisions, change agents, adoption, rejection, and consequences. The meaning of these is fairly obvious. The main jargon terms used by diffusion theorists refer to the extent to which change agents (exporters, importers, and other participants in the process) have shared characteristics

---

54 Rogers, op. cit., n. 47, at p. 94.
55 id., at p. 35. Compare Glenn, op. cit., n. 3, ch. 1. What links diffusion of law to most, but not quite all processes of diffusion is that it is concerned with the communication of ideas.
56 On transnational diffusion, see below, p. 235.
57 'Trialability is the degree to which an innovation may be experimented with on a limited basis [before adoption]' (Rogers, op. cit., n. 47, at p. 16). 'Observability is the degree to which the results of an innovation are visible to others' (id.).
58 id., at pp. 35–6.

(homophily) or different characteristics (heterophily).[59] Rogers' basic concepts at least give a flavour of one kind of approach that is quite transferable.[60]

At a very general level, one might codify the basic methodology as follows. In respect of any instance of diffusion one needs to ask a number of basic questions: What were the conditions of the process, and the occasion for its occurrence? What was diffused? Through what channel(s)?[61] Who were the main change agents? To what extent were the characteristics of the change agents and their contexts similar or different? When and for how long did the process occur? Why did it start at that particular time? What were the main obstacles to change? How much did the object of diffusion change in the process? What were the consequences of the process and what was the degree of implementation, acceptance and use of the diffused objects over time?[62]

(b) The Greenhalgh report

In 2002 my colleague, Trish Greenhalgh, and her associates undertook 'a systematic review of the literature on the spread and sustainability of innovations in health service delivery and organisation'.[63] This project was commissioned by the Department of Health as part of the modernization agenda set out in the NHS plan (2000). The report, which runs to over 350 pages, is remarkably ambitious: it develops a new methodology for

---

59 Rogers defines these terms in respect of individuals:
  Heterophily is the degree to which two or more individuals who interact are different in certain attributes, such as beliefs, education, social status and the like. The opposite of heterophily is homophily, the degree to which two or more individuals who interact are similar in certain attributes (id., p. 36).
  In so far as most reception decisions in law are to some extent collective, these terms apply to the contexts of the exporters and importers as well as the characteristics of the main change agents. On individualist biases in diffusion research, see below.

60 Other concepts that might be useful in legal diffusion studies include technology clusters (innovations are often interdependent); reinvention (id., p. 174), 'the empty vessels fallacy' (the assumption that inventions fill a vacuum, id., at pp. 240–2, discussed in Twining 'Diffusion' (2005)), and the distinction between optional innovation-decisions (individuals), collective innovation-decisions (consensual), and authority innovation decisions (taken by those with power, status, or technical expertise, id., pp. 36–37, 171–203, and see further below). A recent attempt at synthesis of the more abstract concepts is B. Wejnert, 'Integrating Models of Diffusion of Innovations: A Conceptual Framework' (2002) 28 *Annual Rev. of Sociology* 297.

61 One of the most promising perspectives is 'path analysis' borrowed from economics, see Arthur, op. cit., n. 52.

62 Further questions are suggested by the ideal type with variants set out in Table I (above) and by the Greenhalgh report, op. cit., n. 6. On the application of Rogers's basic conceptions to the reception of foreign law in Turkey, see below, pp. 223–8.

63 Greenhalgh report, id.

systematic literature reviews; its spread is very broad; it includes a review of more specialized reviews;[64] it goes beyond simple survey to synthesize the most significant data; it presents a unifying conceptual model and applies it to four cases studies relating to health services.[65] Although its main focus is on health, this remarkable report deserves the attention of any scholar interested in diffusion. Here, the only matter of regret is that it does not deal directly with law.

The Greenhalgh report is organized around the following questions:

1. Innovations: what features (attributes) of innovations influence the rate and extent of adoption?
2. Adopters and adoption: what is the nature of the adoption process – why do some people adopt innovations more readily than others?
3. Communication and influence: what is the nature of the diffusion process and, in particular, how does social influence promote the adoption of innovations?
4. The inner context: what elements of the inner (organizational) context influence the adoption and assimilation of innovations in organizations?
5. The outer context: what elements of the outer (environmental) context, including aspects of inter-organizational communication, influence the adoption and assimilation of innovations in organizations?
6. Implementation and sustainability: what are the features of effective strategies for implementing innovations in health service delivery and organization and ensuring that they are sustained until they reach genuine obsolescence? The report also presents a single model 'that can be used to explain (and to a limited extent) predict spread and sustainability of a particular innovation in a particular context'. It concludes with recommendations for practice, policy, and future research.

The Greenhalgh report builds on Rogers but goes beyond him. Apart from its focus on the health context, it diverges from Rogers in placing greater emphasis on internal and external organizational factors and on sustainability. In addition to being more recent, the analysis is more rigorous and the resulting conceptual model is more sophisticated. Like most of the

---

64 Useful specialized surveys outside the particular tradition of rural sociology include: R. Ference, 'Diffusion Theory and Drug Use' (2001) 96 *Addiction* 165; P.W. Meyers et al., 'Implementation of Industrial Process Innovations' (1999) 16 *J. of Product Innovation Management* 295; R. Pawson, 'Evidence-based policy: the promise of a realist synthesis' (2002) 8 *Evaluation* 340; D. Strang and S.A. Soule, 'Diffusion in Organizations and Social Movements: From Hybrid Corn to Poison Pills' (1998) 24 *Annual Rev. of Sociology* 265; Snow and Benford, op. cit., n. 52; A.H. Van de Ven, 'Central problems in the management of innovation' (1986) 32 *Management Science* 590; Wejnert, op. cit., n. 60; R. Wolfe, 'Organizational innovation: Review, critique and suggested research directions' (1994) 31 *J. Management Studies* 404. Most of these are discussed in the Greenhalgh report. See, also, *IESBS* entries, op. cit., n. 2.
65 On the concept of 'research tradition', see n. 6 above.

diffusion studies synthesized by Rogers, this survey focuses on small-scale innovations, largely from a practical exporter perspective.[66]

Read together, Rogers and Greenhalgh illustrate the vastness and diversity of the landscape of diffusion studies.[67] Rogers claims to have synthesized eleven kinds of research traditions in the study of diffusion of innovations, with a catch-all residuary category that included political science, agricultural economics, psychology, industrial engineering, and statistics.[68] The Greenhalgh report covers literature in nearly twenty disciplines or sub-disciplines; these are interpreted as belonging to thirteen distinct research traditions potentially relevant to diffusion of innovations in health service delivery and organization. Less than 25 per cent of these overlapped with Rogers. Yet law did not feature in either analysis; nor did language spread, sport, religion, or music. The *International Encyclopedia of the Social and Behavioral Sciences* has several articles on diffusion in anthropology, geography, and sociology with suggestive cross-references to a number of adjacent enclaves, including technology transfer, culture contact, innovation, sociology of fashion, and social influence. The question for any researcher will be: which of this vast heritage should be treated as relevant to my particular project on diffusion of law? No general answer can be given to this question; but some guidance can be given first by looking at the relation between the better legal literature and basic diffusion theory as exemplified by Rogers; and second, by identifying certain trends and biases in social science diffusion research that need to be borne in mind by those interested in diffusion of law.

2. Reception of foreign law in Turkey: a social science perspective

Although derived from small-scale diffusion of technological innovations, Rogers claims that his basic concepts are quite transferable. Let us consider how they apply to Turkey.[69]

---

66 Greenhalgh, op. cit. (2004b), n. 6 provides a useful summary, but is not a substitute for the full report.
67 When the first edition of *Diffusion of Innovations* was published Rogers found 405 publications on the topic; by 1971, this had increased to 1,500; the third edition noted 3,085; by the time of the fourth edition (1995) the number was approaching 4,000 (Rogers, op. cit., n. 47, preface). Greenhalgh's research team found over 6,000 titles from nearly twenty specialist areas. Of these, they analysed 1,200 articles and over 100 books that they thought might be potentially relevant to the study of the spread and sustainability of innovations in health service delivery and organization.
68 Rogers, id., presents a useful table at pp. 42–3.
69 This analysis of the literature is based on the following sources: 'Symposium on the Reception of Foreign Law in Turkey' (1956) 6 *Annales de la Faculté de Droit d'Istanbul*; 'Symposium' (1957) 9 *International Social Science B.*; P. Stirling, *Turkish Village* (1965); J. Starr and J. Pool, 'The Impact of a Legal Revolution in Rural Turkey' (1974) 8 *Law and Society Rev.* 533; J. Starr, *Dispute and Settlement in Rural Turkey: An Ethnography of Law* (1978); and *Law as Metaphor: From*

Ataturk's reforms of 1926 in Turkey are mainly famous because this is a perceived as a rather clear example of a large-scale 'voluntary' reception of secular Western law into a largely Muslim society. It included an attempt to use law to bring about radical social change in important areas of personal law – the converse of the 'mirror' idea. In fact the literature makes clear that Ataturk's reforms were but one large step in a process that began early in the nineteenth century and continues to this day. Örücü summarizes the incremental and eclectic nature of the formal process of importation:

> ... the early efforts of reform rested solely on import from the major continental jurisdictions as Turkey went through a process of total and global modernization, westernization, secularization, democratization, and constitutionalism. She thereby reshaped her private law, administrative law, the constitution, criminal law, civil and criminal procedures, commercial law, maritime law and the law of bankruptcy. Later, other laws such as labour law and social security law were passed, again based on foreign models. Later still, significant developments in the field of democracy and fundamental rights and freedoms and review of constitutionality found their way into Turkish law, the last by the 1961 Constitution. In the preparation of this Constitution wide use was made of the West German and Italian models, the provisions on economic development being inspired by the Indian model of 1949. The present Constitution, which greatly increased the powers of the President, was inspired by the 1958 French Constitution and the American Constitution. The impact of the early reforms of the Republic was not just on the legal system but also on the social system since they were accompanied and complemented by a series of social reform laws aimed at changing people. These laws are still protected by the 1982 Constitution. 'Modernity' was imported on a major scale.[70]

As Örücü makes clear, Turkey's interactions with foreign law do not form a unilinear story of adoption and implementation of Ataturk's reforms. Turkey has also acceded to a number of international conventions and in recent years a new phase of eclectic, incremental reception has continued in anticipation of accession to the EU and as a result of membership of WTO. Other steps were taken to develop a free market economy and to facilitate international trade.[71] These recent developments are best treated as part of another story.

Some of the recent measures have been a result of foreign pressure, but since they involved an element of choice between models, Örücü suggests that they represent a weak imposed reception.[72] Overall, the eclecticism of the Turkish approach has ensured that they are not beholden to or dominated

---

Islamic Courts to the Palace of Justice (1992); M. Zwalen, *La Divorce en Turquie* (1981); P.J. Magnarella, '*Kanun ve Aile*' [Law and Family] in *The World and I* (June 1988); E. Adal, *Fundamentals of Turkish Private Law* (1991); and. above all, the writings of Esin Örücü from 1987 to the present. Stirling, Starr, and Magnarella are social scientists.

70 E. Örücü, 'Turkey Facing the European Union – Old and New Harmonies' (2000) 25 *European Law Rev.* 57.
71 The changes made since 1963 are usefully surveyed in id. The extent is very striking.
72 Örücü, op. cit., n. 3, at p. 46.

by any single foreign 'parent' and that, for the most part, the reception of foreign law has been genuinely voluntary:

> Turkish law has been constructed through a succession of imposed receptions, voluntary receptions, imitations and adjustments, the elements of chance, choice, historical accident and the prestige of the competing legal models all playing important roles.[73]

My purpose here is not to give another account of the Turkish 'reception', but rather to see how far some available accounts fit the basics of Rogers' synthesis of sociological diffusion analysis. Although no account of this reception explicitly adopts this method of analysis, it is possible to piece together from standard sources a profile of the process that answers nearly all of the key questions, at least in general terms. In brief, *the occasion* for this reception was a steady movement towards modernization and secularization in an underdeveloped country the vast majority of whose population was Muslim. Ataturk's revolution represented the culmination of a long process of piecemeal reform; in turn the process continued and weathered resistance largely because the legal system was dominated by an elite that was committed to Ataturk's principles. The *conditions* for the reforms of 1926-9 included Ataturk's control of power, the existence of a small elite cadre of lawyers trained in civil, especially Swiss, law, and, most important, a lengthy prior process of piecemeal secularization of law and legal institutions dating back to 1829 (the *Tanzimat*). Most commentators agree that these were a necessary precondition for Ataturk's reforms, which were the most radical and substantial step in a long process that is still continuing. The *timing* of this phase is explained by Ataturk's accession to power (1923) and his programme of reform. The timing of developments since the 1960s is closely connected to Turkey's relations with the European Union and the international economy.

What was received? Standard accounts of Ataturk's reforms refer mainly to a series of codes borrowed eclectically from several European civil law countries with a minimum of formal change. But European, especially Swiss, legal culture was also imported by key personnel who had been trained in Europe and by the establishment of a new Law Faculty at Ankara, deliberately based on European models, to train judges and lawyers in the new law and its methodology. Almost as interesting is the fact that although the official language of the legal system is Turkish (the codes were translated into Turkish), unlike in some other receptions of civil law, there has been a conscious attempt by the superior courts and in legal education to maintain contact with the legal systems and literature of the exporting countries, especially in respect of Turkish-Swiss private law.[74]

The main *formal channel of initial reception* was, first, the legislature, which enacted the codes wholesale and the various officials who were

---

73 E. Örücü, 'Comparatists and extraordinary places' in Legrand and Munday, op. cit., n. 25, at p. 478.
74 Örücü, op. cit., n. 70, at pp. 93–94.

involved in their implementation. Similarly the main *change agents* at the start were a small legal elite of Ataturk's supporters led by the Minister of Justice Mahmout Es'ad Bey, who had studied law in Lausanne.[75]

After 1926–9 the range of *change agents* expanded. Many commentators emphasize the important role played by the courts (especially the High Court) in implementing and interpreting the codes in ways that harmonized the secular aspirations of the reforms with the realities of Turkish conditions and attitudes.[76] Others who played a key role in implementation included officials concerned with performing civil marriage ceremonies and registration of marriage (for example, as literacy spread, more and more headmen of villages in rural areas were authorized to perform the civil ceremony);[77] the professors of law who were the main agents for importing and disseminating civilian legal culture; some doctors, well aware of traditional sensibilities, helped the process of acceptance by issuing medical certificates for marriage after perfunctory or pro forma medical examinations;[78] no doubt, the most important agents of change in some fields were ordinary people.

Not surprisingly, family law has attracted much attention because the importation of the Swiss Civil Code was an extreme example of differences in culture and conditions between the exporters and the importers of personal law, that is, of *heterophily*. The story of the marriage laws is of a slow trend towards acceptance over more than half a century. Incentives to satisfy the requirements of civil marriage included income tax and social benefits; for example, during the Korean War, wives and widows of serving soldiers were only able to claim pensions and other benefits on the production of a valid marriage certificate. Not surprisingly, conformity with the marriage law developed more quickly in urban areas than in rural ones, and the extent of conformity correlated quite closely with levels of poverty, literacy, and remoteness from urban centres. The figures about conformity relate to such matters as how many people chose to go through a civil marriage ceremony in addition to or instead of a religious one; the incidence of bigamous (that is, polygynous) marriage; and the decline of abduction. More important still are less easily quantified changes in attitudes, for example, in regard to gender equality. Between 1933 and 1991 the Turkish parliament passed seven amnesty laws that enabled the legitimization of children of consensual unions that had not conformed to the requirements of the civil code.[79]

Starr's studies of Bodrum in the 1960s and her follow-up study in the 1980s confirm an overall picture of the gradual victory of this attempt to

---

75 For a rather clear example by the Minister presenting reception of codes as merely technological, see the statement cited in Starr, op. cit., n. 69, at p. 16.
76 See, especially, Zwalen, op. cit., n. 69, Starr, id., and Örücü, op. cit., n. 70.
77 Magnarella, op. cit., n. 69, at pp. 512–13.
78 id., at p. 513.
79 E. Örücü, 'Diverse issues, continuing debates' in *The International Survey of Family Law*, ed. A. Bainham (1994).

create a secular system in an unpromising environment. There was some adaptation and compromise, but overall we are presented with an unusual story of traditional practices, customs, and attitudes gradually falling into line with a relatively stable body of essentially alien law. This appears to have been achieved largely by rejecting overt legal pluralism for a centralized system that was legalistic, positivist, and 'top-down'. Similar patterns appear in the larger picture. It would require a very detailed study of the history of legal change in Turkey during the twentieth century to trace in what respects the imported laws and ideas changed in their new environment. What is striking to the outsider is the stability of the basic radical scheme backed by constitutional imperatives and political will over a long period of time.[80]

None of the accounts of the reception in Turkey that I have read conforms exactly to the basics of this kind of social science diffusion analysis. However, modern treatments of the famous 'reception' in Turkey and Wieacker's classic work suggest that there is quite close affinity between more sophisticated legal studies of reception and the mainstream sociological literature on diffusion of innovations.[81]

The reasonable fit between Rogers's framework and the Turkish story suggests that these particular concepts, developed mainly out of a synthesis of small-scale technical examples can be applied at a general level to a large-scale, ideologically driven reception involving a high degree of cultural

---

[80] The constitutionality of the principal reform measures still cannot be challenged:
 The Turkish ruling elite was interested in modernization and national integration. The aim was to become European legally, socially and culturally. To this end, eight principal reform laws established secular education and civil marriage, adopted international numerals, the Turkish alphabet and the new calendar, introduced the hat, closed the dervish convents, abolished certain titles and prohibited the wearing of certain garments. The goal, which also has symbolic value in Turkey, is still very much alive.
 (Örücü, op. cit., n. 70, at p. 70.)

[81] Wieacker deals with the what, why, when, who, and how of the process and of its impact, with sensitivity to the complexities. Provided that it is recognized that this is primarily a work of intellectual history that says little about either doctrinal detail or the law in action, his account could be translated without too much difficulty into the conceptual framework of sociological analysis. For example, he gives a clear account of the *occasion and conditions* for the reception, he identifies the main *change agents* and their characteristics, he emphasizes the importance of Bologna and later other centres of learning as vital *channels* of communication, he explains *why* the main events in the story occurred *when* they did, he indicates in what respects the received Roman law *changed* yet retained its basic *identity*, and he gives a clear, if rather abstract account, of the *impact* of Roman law on modern civil law systems. He does not give a very full account of the social and economic consequences of the reception in the short and medium term; that was not part of his aim. He avoids the pitfalls of the naive model of legal reception: ' "Prolific misunderstanding" is a typical, and perhaps a necessary feature in the process of appropriating another civilization.' (Wieacker, op. cit. (1981), n. 12.)

difference (that is, heterophily). In any study of diffusion processes it is useful to ask questions about occasions, motives, agents, recipients, pathways, obstacles, trialability, observability, impact, and so on.

This may be useful as a start, but can any more concrete guidance be given to researchers embarking on some particular study of diffusion of legal phenomena? My argument is that Rogers provides a broad framework of enquiry; that the picture of the variety and complexity of diffusion processes outlined in Table I sets a context in which to locate a particular enquiry; that the existing legal literature provides a number of usable concepts and distinctions; but that the social science literature represents a much more developed and extensive heritage of perspectives, concepts, hypotheses, methods, debates, and detailed case studies.

3. *Trends and biases in social science diffusion research*

What can students of diffusion of law learn from the social science literature? It would be a mistake to treat either kind of enquiry as monolithic. The stories told by Rogers and Greenhalgh depict a series of loosely related research traditions that involved differences in the objects studied, the scale in respect of space and time, the focus of attention, and the assumptions, objectives, and perspectives of the researchers. Similarly, the history of diffusion studies in law is of quite diverse enquiries in pursuit of varied concerns. In so far as there are uniformities, I have argued that many of these are based on a number of assumptions that taken together constitute a naïve and simplistic model of the process of diffusion of law. These assumptions are widespread, but not universal. Questioning each of them opens up a much more complex picture of the processes involved and many different potential lines of future research.

For these reasons, the question: 'What can legal scholars learn from this social science literature?' is too general. Socio-legal and other legal scholars will find different enclaves relevant to their particular interests. However, a striking feature of Rogers's and Greenhalgh's analyses is the unexpected connections, analogies, and generalizations that have emerged. Surprising leaps are taken from hybrid corn to poison pills; from hard tomatoes to modern maths; from family planning to transnational social movements. It is remarkable how Greenhalgh's team found research in nearly twenty different specialist fields to be potentially relevant to specific practical problems of disseminating ideas about medical practices in the National Health Service in England. Students of diffusion of law would will be well-advised to obtain a general acquaintance with the landscape of diffusion research and theory before reaching conclusions about what might or might not be relevant to their particular projects. The existence of a number of excellent literature surveys, in addition to those of Rogers and Greenhalgh, makes this quite manageable.[82]

---

82 See nn. 6 and 17 above.

Despite the dangers of generalizing across such a diverse landscape, it may be helpful to point to some tendencies and biases in the heritage of the mainstream social science literature that may be indicators of potential relevance and irrelevance. Rogers in his critical appraisal of past work gives some salutary warnings;[83] Greenhalgh provides a model for assessing broad sweeps of literature for a specific purpose; individual legal scholars will need to be selective in determining what might be relevant and useful for their purposes.

(a) Communication of ideas

What links the study of diffusion of law with the main body of social science literature is that they are both concerned with the spread and communication of ideas.[84] When we talk of hybrid corn or mobile phones or Coca Cola or wigs and gowns, we tend to think of material objects, but in fact the most important element for students of diffusion is the ideas behind them and their perceived meanings. Even in respect of migration of human beings it is not so much their bodies as the beliefs, attitudes, values, and skills that make up their cultures and traditions that are the main matters of interest to social scientists.[85] When we study diffusion of law we are also centrally concerned with communication of ideas. This applies not only to codes, legal concepts, theories, and controversies, but also to rituals, the design of buildings such as courts and law schools, training methods, and dispute settlement procedures. These may be visible, but it is the ideas behind them that give them meaning. Glenn interprets legal tradition as a process of communication of information.[86] Luhmann and Teubner interpret legal systems as systems of communication.[87] The elusive term 'legal culture' applies to beliefs, concepts, attitudes, and styles of thought.[88] It can also be applied to *practices*

---

83 Indeed, there is a note of disillusion in Rogers's latest edition (op. cit., n. 47, p. 39):
   This merger of diffusion researches has not been an unmixed blessing. Diffusion studies now display a bland sameness, as they pursue a number of research issues with rather stereotyped approaches.
   My canvassing of recent literature suggests that Rogers's criticism was overstated.
84 id., p. 35.
85 Of course, it would be unnecessarily reductionist to restrict the objects of diffusion to ideas: squirrels, weapons, drugs, unread law reports, and viruses have also been diffused. Even in the life sciences it is genetic codes rather than their visible embodiments that are the main concern of the scientists who study them.
86 Glenn, op. cit., n. 3, pp. 7–15.
87 For example, N. Luhmann, 'Operational Closure and Structural Coupling: The Differentiation of the Legal System' (1992) 13 *Cardozo Law Rev.* 1419.
88 For an excellent discussion of 'legal culture', see J. Bell, *French Legal Cultures* (2001). The coherence and utility of the concept has been disputed, see D. Nelken, R. Cotterrell, and L. Friedman in *Comparing Legal Cultures*, ed. D. Nelken (1997). This debate need not concern us here, except that Lawrence Friedman's distinction between external or lay legal cultures (the attitudes, and so on, to law of non-professionals) and internal legal cultures (the attitudes, and so on, of professionals or

that need to be interpreted from an internal point of view as the embodiment of ideas that give them meaning. This hermeneutic interpretation of practice is now generally accepted in legal theory. So, as in social science, the study of diffusion of law involves study of processes involving the communication of ideas.

(b) Empiricism

Almost all social science diffusion research has been empirical; most of the generalizations and theorizing of Rogers, Greenhalgh, and others has been based on a range of detailed empirical studies. By contrast, almost all writing about diffusion of law has been done in the library or the armchair rather than the field. Even Wieacker's classic work has been criticized for saying almost nothing about the law in action. Almost all of Alan Watson's generalizations relate to formal or surface law or else are speculative hypotheses. Glenn's magisterial overview of great legal traditions is based mainly on sources that are themselves largely library-bound. The same may be said of most comparative lawyers and legal theorists who have written about transplants/reception/diffusion of law. There are a few exceptions: some empirical research has been done on the impact of Ataturk's reforms, mainly by social scientists.[89] Some attempts to evaluate the actual effectiveness or 'success' or impact of foreign-funded legal reform programmes have been lambasted for their crudity.[90] Early attempts at statistical comparative law ended in disappointment.[91] The efforts of Dezalay and Garth[92] and Pistor and Wellons[93] are exceptions, but these too might be considered somewhat impressionistic by hard-nosed social scientists.[94] None of this is

---

regular participants in a legal system) is important in the study of diffusion of state law (L. Friedman, *Law and Society: An Introduction* (1977) ch. 7). A familiar theme in comparative law is that the 'mentality' of a legal elite – that is, aspects of the internal legal culture – is often a crucial part of what is diffused. It may often be the case that the exporting and importing internal legal cultures may be relatively similar (homophilous) but the external legal culture of the importers may be very different.

89 See n. 69 above.
90 For example, the controversy over the relationship between legal families and national economic growth/performance, see R. la Porta et al., 'The quality of government' (1999) 15 *J. of European Law and Economics* 222.
91 J.H. Merryman, D. Clark, and L. Friedman, *Law and Social Change in Mediterranean Europe and Latin America: A Handbook of Social Indicators for Comparative Study* (1979). For a post-mortem, see J.H. Merryman, 'Law and Development Memoirs II: SLADE' (2000) 48 *Am. J. of Comparative Law* 713.
92 Dezalay and Garth, op. cit., n. 42.
93 Pistor and Wellons, op. cit., n. 43.
94 Of course, there has been extensive socio-legal research on impact and compliance, especially in relation to regulation, human rights, and some aspects of international law. For example, Chayes and Chayes, op. cit., n. 46. Although most of this work has not been concerned with processes of diffusion, it is relevant to some of the issues concerning assessing impact.

surprising, because most traditions of legal scholarship are similarly unempirical.

Perhaps the most important general lesson to be learned from this foray into social science literature is that understanding the processes of diffusion is mainly a sociological enterprise, requiring detailed empirical research about the behaviour, ideas, attitudes, and interactions of human actors in particular contexts. Perhaps the best hope for advancing understanding diffusion of law is to persuade our colleagues in social science that this is a subject that deserves their attention.

(c) Innovation bias

The fact that much of the sociological tradition has attracted the label 'diffusion of innovations' is revealing. In order to build bridges between the legal and social science literature, I have deliberately followed social scientific usage in treating 'diffusion' as a generic term that includes such ideas as imitation, spread, transposition, adoption, and reception. But 'diffusion' implies emanation from a single centre or source and to that extent it has 'an export bias'. There is a similar tendency in Greenhalgh's distinction between 'let it happen' (diffusion) and 'make it happen' (dissemination).[95]

Rogers is careful to insist that 'innovation' refers to newness from the viewpoint of recipients. In that sense the term is broader than invention. But he also acknowledges that there was for a long time a tendency towards a pro-innovation bias within this tradition: the initiative tended to lie with the innovator-exporter; innovation was assumed to be desirable; resisters were labelled as 'laggards';[96] and 'the prevailing paradigm was gradually revealed as being couched in a powerful meta-narrative of growth, productivity, domination of the rural environment, and "new is better".'[97] The early rural research developed during a period of food shortage in the United States; later the emphasis changed when agricultural overproduction was perceived to be the main problem.[98]

Rogers acknowledges his own biases in his early research:

> Back in 1954, one of the Iowa farmers that I personally interviewed for my Ph.D. dissertation research rejected all of the chemical innovations that I was then studying: weed sprays, cattle and hog feeds, chemical fertilizers, and rodenticide. He insisted that his neighbors, who had adopted these chemicals, were killing their songbirds and the earthworms in the soil. I had selected the new farm ideas in my innovativeness scale on the advice of agricultural experts at Iowa State University; I was measuring the best recommended farming practice of that day. The organic farmer in my sample earned the

---

95 Greenhalgh report, op. cit., n. 6, p. 105.
96 Rogers, op. cit., n. 47, pp. 256–7.
97 Greenhalgh report, op. cit., n. 6, p. 66.
98 Rogers. op. cit., n. 47, pp. 60–1.

lowest score on my innovativeness scale, and was categorized as a laggard.
In the forty years or so since this interview, several of the farm chemicals that I studied have been banned because of their unhealthy effects on humans.[99]

This story could serve as a parable for enthusiastic exporters and reformers of law.

(d) Technological bias, top-down perspectives, and practical concerns

Closely connected to innovation bias is a technological bias. In my earlier essay I suggested that one needs to differentiate between technological, ideological, and expressive perspectives on law, although they are often inter-related.[100] One way of looking at laws is as problem-solving devices. In some contexts in relation to some legal phenomena this makes good sense. But to think of law solely or mainly as a form of technology is vulnerable to the well-developed criticisms of naïve instrumentalism and hyper-rationalism.[101] In my view, much of that criticism is well taken, but there is a danger of throwing the baby out with the bathwater if that leads to a refusal ever to think in terms of purposes, effects, or functions of law.[102] It is not necessary to enter into these well-worn controversies here. Suffice to say, as Rogers acknowledges, a great deal of the early diffusion research assumed that the objects of diffusion are technological improvements and that it exhibits a strong top-down, technocratic, sometimes evangelical bias.[103] This is, of course, not true of all diffusion research as is illustrated by studies of diffusion of epidemics, drugs, AIDS, and weaponry. The technological bias may help to explain why studies of language, diasporas, and religions are often not treated as part of the mainstream literature on diffusion.

Awareness of this bias may help to guard against two tendencies: first, the assumption that all examples of diffusion of law fit neatly into a means-end, problem-solving framework. Second, the assumption that all objects of diffusion are desirable, progressive or innovative. Analogies from epidemiology or language spread may be as apposite for particular legal studies as analogies from transfer of technologies.

---

99 id., at p. 425. The Greenhalgh report (at pp. 66–9) tells a closely analogous story in respect of the antibiotic tetracycline.
100 Twining, 'Diffusion' (2005) at pp. 25–9; I agree with David Nelken that it is a mistake to draw sharp distinctions between technocratic, organic, and normative perspectives: Nelken, 'Comparatists and Transferability' in Legrand and Munday, op. cit., n. 25, ch. 12.
101 W. Twining and D. Miers, *How To Do Things with Rules* (4th edn., 1999) at 153–5. For a recent general critique of instrumentalism, see J. Griffiths, 'The Social Working of Legal Rules' (2003) 48 *J. of Legal Pluralism* 1.
102 On 'thin functionalism', see W. Twining, ' A Post-Westphalian Conception of Law' (2003) 37 *Law and Society Rev.* 199, at 238–41.
103 Rogers, op. cit., n. 47, pp. 100–13. This is hardly surprising in respect of some areas such as market research and some kinds of medical and agricultural research.

The Greenhalgh report suggests that the pro-innovation bias is also linked to a bias towards studying the visible and 'measuring the measurable':

> This important bias means we know more about
> - Innovations that have spread successfully than those that have not;
> - Innovations that have spread rapidly than those that have spread more slowly;
> - Innovations that spread from the centre;
> - Adoption than non-adoption or rejection;
> - Continued use than discontinuation;
> - The fact of adoption than the reasons for it;
> - Adoption by individuals than by teams or organizations.[104]

So far as law is concerned, technocratic and exporter biases are to be found in the literature that treats diffusion of law as part of development, modernization, and convergence. However, there is a discernible strand in the legal literature that treats culture, tradition, local context, and resistance sympathetically.[105] One obvious reason for this is that so much of diffusion of state law is associated with colonialism and imperialism and neo-colonial forms of capitalism. Much of modern scholarship has been strongly anti-colonial and critical of ideas associated with development, modernization, and reform that are driven by various kinds of free-market ideology. Furthermore, James Whitman has commented on a 'neo-Romantic Turn' in comparative law, exemplified by critics of convergence and transplantation who stress the intimate relations between law and culture, tradition, or local context.[106] Obviously these ideological assumptions cut both ways. But it is the technocrats and the modernizers who claim to be more practical.

(e) Scale and geographical spread

Rogers defines diffusion in terms of communication between members of and within a social system.[107] Much of the sociological literature analysed by Rogers has been concerned with detailed examination of the pathways and processes of diffusion of quite limited particular products, techniques, or ideas.[108] Similarly Greenhalgh's survey mainly relates to relatively discrete innovations within a single country.[109] On the other hand, the bulk of the

---

104 Greenhalgh report, op. cit., n. 6, p. 73.
105 Resistance is, of course, a powerful theme in the historiography of colonialism. On law see, for example, M. Chanock, *Law, Custom and Social Order: The Colonial Experience in Malawi and Zambia* (1985) and L. Benton, *Law and Colonial Cultures: Legal Regimes in World History* (2002).
106 J. Whitman in Legrand and Munday, op. cit., n. 25, ch. 10.
107 Rogers, op. cit., n. 47, at pp. 5, 10, and 24. But he also emphasizes that '*One of the most distinctive problems in the diffusion of innovations is that the participants are usually quite heterophilous*' (p. 19, original italics).
108 id.
109 However, in a related NHS project, Bate et al., op. cit., n. 53, undertook a special survey of the literature about social movements because it 'offers a new perspective on *large-scale* systems change' (Executive Summary, p. 1, italics added).

legal literature has focused on relatively large-scale transnational receptions: the reception of Roman law in medieval Europe, 'the spread of the common law', the importation of a series of codes or at least of substantial fields of law such as insolvency or intellectual property.

It might be objected that to link Rogers and Greenhalgh's accounts to diffusion of law ignores the distinction between small-scale and large-scale diffusion. This might partly explain the lack of interdisciplinary contact. There is some force in this point, but its significance can be exaggerated, for several reasons.

First, we need to distinguish between extent of geographical spread and the scale of the objects that were diffused. Historically, early diffusionism in anthropology was concerned with global diffusion, but often with quite specific cultural traits. Studies of diasporas, language spread, and diffusion of sports and religion are well-documented transnational examples that vary in scale. Rogers himself deals with some examples of diffusion transnationally and in developing countries, both of discrete objects and of more extensive ones, such as epidemics.[110] Moreover, much transnational diffusion involves elites as change agents, such as doctors, engineers, lawyers, who could be said to belong to transnational sub-cultures.[111] Thus there are plenty of examples, besides law, that involve large-scale transnational diffusion.

Secondly, Rogers criticizes the neglect of 'technology clusters' in traditional diffusion studies:[112]

> Past diffusion research has generally investigated each innovation as if it was independent from other innovations. This is a dubious assumption, in that the adopter's experience with one innovation obviously influences that individual's perception of the next innovation to diffuse through the individual's system. In reality a set of innovations diffusing about the same time in a system are interdependent. It is much simpler for diffusion scholars to investigate the spread of each innovation as an independent event, but this is a distortion of reality.[113]

---

110 Rogers, op. cit., n. 47, pp. 125–9; the Greenhalgh report has a short section on the developing world (pp. 75–8). Other writers have placed more emphasis on this. For example:
> Seen as integral to economic development, diffusion of innovations in Third World settings has received much attention. Examples include improving agricultural production and living conditions; generating entrepreneurial activity and related employment; promoting family planning, and improving infrastructure ... More broadly, development itself has been treated as a diffusion process.

(Brown, op. cit., n. 2, at p. 3680.)

111 In Turkey, for example, the elite lawyers involved in Ataturk's reforms could be interpreted as homophilous importers from Europe, but heterophilous exporters of law to the country at large, especially rural areas.

112 'A *technology cluster* consists of one or more distinguishable elements of technology that are perceived as being closely interrelated' (Rogers, op. cit., n. 47, p. 15). Rogers emphasizes the importance of the adopter's perceptions and links this interestingly to positioning in marketing.

113 id.

Rogers regrets the absence of research in this area.[114] An important issue in law is how far individual concepts or mechanisms, such as the trust or the guilty plea, can be studied or imported as discrete items separated from the legal system or legal culture in which they are embedded.[115] The extent to which law can be conceived as 'systematic' is a recurrent issue in legal theory.[116] These are examples of topics in which the experience of law could be of particular interest to social scientists.

Third, even more important than the point about the interdependence of technology clusters or the elements of legal systems, is the fact that diffusion of law can be seen as part of some more general process: religious law spreads as part of the spread of religion; 'colonial law' has often just been a natural incident of colonialism; the spread and survival of common law has also been intimately linked with the spread and power of the English language; legal ideas are part of the baggage of colonists, émigrés and refugees.

Fourth, most social diffusion research focuses on processes within a single society or social system. In law, reception, transplantation, transposition are often assumed to be transnational – for understandable reasons. However, diffusion of law does take place within countries and social systems, although it is not often perceived as such. For example, the legal history of the United States is replete with examples of cross-cultural, inter-state, and nation-wide interaction and influence. In respect of municipal law, the citation of precedents from other states, the movement to harmonize state laws through the American Law Institute and the Commissioners for Uniform State Laws, and the story of the spread of the Langdell case method of teaching are familiar examples. Less obvious, perhaps, and often less visible are informal interactions and influences between non-state law and municipal law, or between different non-state legal orders and traditions within the American 'melting pot'.[117] As Alan Watson might have said, imitation is the main engine of legal change within the United States at all levels of ordering. Of course, many of these phenomena have been extensively studied, but rarely from a specifically diffusion perspective. If legal diffusion studies are to become more empirical, they will need to focus on actual behaviours on the ground. And one can study diffusion of law on one's own doorstep.

Finally, and perhaps most important, if one is interested in how diffusion works in practice, one is inevitably concerned with agency and the behaviour and perceptions of actual human beings. One of the most important

---

114 id., p. 235.
115 This is central theme of Allison, op. cit., n. 28.
116 A famous starting-point is Brian Simpson's statement that 'the common law is more a muddle than a system'. This challenges theories that conceive of law in terms of systems of rules (Hart), or of norms (Kelsen), or of communications (autopoiesis). A.W.B. Simpson, 'The Common Law and Legal Theory' in *Legal Theory and Common Law*, ed. W. Twining (1986) at 24. Compare C. Sampford, *The Disorder of Law* (1989).
117 For example, J. Walker, 'The diffusion of innovations among the American states' (1969) 63 *Am. Political Science Rev.* 880.

developments in diffusion research has been the growth in importance of interactionist perspectives, exemplified by the work of Goffman, Sachs, Molotch, and Latour.[118] This leads to a very detailed focus on the behaviour, beliefs and perceptions of individuals – maybe a few, maybe thousands – and their interactions in specific contexts at specific moments of time, even in respect of large-scale geographically dispersed diffusion.[119] This kind of perspective is so far largely absent from studies of legal diffusion.

(f) Individuals, organizations, social movements, governments and legal subjects

Early studies tended to focus on the dispersal of cultural traits or other relatively small-scale objects of diffusion. The classic research in rural sociology emphasized agency and tended to focus on individual actors, their characteristics, and their decisions. Although the focus of diffusion research spread out, especially to organizations and social movements, to some extent an individualist bias continued and has been the subject of regular criticism.[120]

Within the individualist tradition, Rogers differentiated between four types of innovation decisions:

> (1) *optional innovation-decisions*, choices made by an individual independent of the decisions of other members of the system to adopt or reject an innovation, (2) *collective innovation-decisions*, choices made by consensus among members of the system, and (3) *authority innovation-decisions*, choices made by relatively few individuals in a system who possess power, status, or technical expertise. A fourth category consists of a sequential combination of two or more of these types of innovation-decisions: *contingent innovation-decisions* are choices to adopt or reject that are made only after a prior innovation-decision.[121]

All of these treat the individual as the unit of analysis and stress decisions by potential adopters. This individualist bias came under criticism for not giving

---

118 Symbolic interactionism and ethnomethodology have had some influence on the sociology of law, though not in a sustained way in relation to diffusion (see R. Banaker and M. Travers (eds.), *An Introduction to Law and Social Theory* (2002) s. 4: Interpretive Approaches). Relevant works include E. Goffman, *Interaction Ritual: Essays on Face to Face Behavior* (1967); A.C. Kerckhoff and K.W. Back, *The June Bug: A Study in Hysterical Contagion* (1968); B. Latour, *Aramis* (1996); H. Molotch, *Where Stuff Comes From: How Toasters, Toilets, Cars, Computers and Many Other Things Come to be as They Are* (2003). On early conversation analysis, which was closely related to socio-legal studies, see the useful reader by R. Turner, *Ethnomethodology* (1974).
119 Significantly, Bate et al.'s report (op. cit., n. 53) was entitled *Towards a Million Change Agents*. The Greenhalgh report naturally deals with interaction (for example, at pp. 279–81), but has few references to symbolic interactionism or ethno-methodology.
120 Rogers, op. cit., n. 47, pp. 114–27.
121 id., p. 37.

sufficient emphasis to structure, context or collective action.[122] There was also a bias towards attributing success or failure of an innovation to individuals within a system rather than to failures of the system.[123] Connected with this 'individual-blame bias' was a tendency of the early models to adopt an exporter standpoint, focusing on the characteristics and attitudes of individual importers or resisters more than on the exporters themselves and blaming individual laggards and late adopters.[124]

At first sight, such individualist biases are not something that one would associate with classic studies of diffusion of law. Only a few individuals (mainly leaders and jurists) feature in the reception stories of Wieacker, Watson, and the Turkish reception(s). If anything, the biases are in other directions, reflecting mixtures of the assumptions underlying the naïve model of reception: the perspectives are macro, the focus is on the objects of reception (were they accepted, rejected, changed?), the emphasis is on formal change, the main agents are governments or international institutions (UN agencies, the EU, World Bank or IMF), and so on.[125] Perhaps the most striking aspect of the literature is that it very rarely tells us in any detail about actual impact on the ground.

Perhaps the most important lesson that students of diffusion of law can learn from the social science literature is that the processes of diffusion involve actual people perceiving, deciding, and acting. To understand these processes requires detailed empirical research based on the range of available frameworks and methods developed in sociology and anthropology. Of course, the behaviour of individual actors needs to be viewed in the context of broader structures, cultures, and so on. Of course, in some receptions the most important decisions may be taken by a few key individuals, such as judges, lawmakers or tycoons. But on a broad view of law and of its diffusion, very often both the operation of the processes and their consequences will turn on choices and actions of hundreds, thousands or even millions of actors, who may be consumers, victims, avoiders, evaders, or exploiters of law.[126] Legal scholarship has tended to neglect such 'bottom-up' perspectives.[127]

---

122 This is reminiscent of Marxian criticisms of symbolic interactionists that they assumed a liberal individualist picture of society and so ignored 'the structured inequalities in power and interest which underpin the processes whereby laws are created and enforced'. (I. Taylor, P. Walton, and J. Young, *The New Criminology* (1973) 168.)
123 id., p. 117.
124 id.
125 Again, Patrick Glenn (op. cit., n. 3) is an exception to these generalizations: his perspective is very broad, but he treats informal diffusion of law involving thousands or millions of individuals as historically more significant than formal 'receptions'.
126 Twining, op. cit., n. 102, pp. 246–8 and, more generally, Twining, op. cit (2000b), n. 1, ch. 5.
127 B. Tamanaha, *A General Jurisprudence of Law and Society* (2001) 236–40. A notable exception is John Griffiths' studies of the influence of 'the shop floor rules

It is perhaps ironic that in recent years it has been commercial law, broadly conceived, that has received the greatest attention in respect of diffusion. This has typically happened in the context of importing or imposing foreign or transnational law as part of structural adjustment or transition to a free-market economy. The impact of commercial law reform can hardly be assessed without reference to those who make more or less or no use of it, by forming companies, entering contracts, evading copyright, and so on. 'Top-down' accounts of commercial law reform can tell us little or nothing about the impact on the behaviour and situation of those whom it is meant to influence or serve.[128]

(g) Diffusion of diffusion studies: a health warning[129]

The social science diffusion literature seen from a distance may seem like a mass of individual studies in many quite different areas with a few oases of synthesis. One of the central issues of diffusion research is how far concepts, hypotheses and generalizations developed in one area of enquiry are transferable to other contexts. Can there be an overarching theory of diffusion?

Rogers' bold attempts at synthesis suggest that some of the basic concepts of diffusion theory are highly transferable. The reasonable fit between Rogers' framework and the Turkish story suggests that these particular concepts, developed mainly out of a synthesis of small-scale technical examples, can be applied at a general level to a large scale, ideologically-driven transnational reception involving a high degree of cultural difference. Moreover, as we have seen, the literature on diffusion is full of unexpected analogies and juxtapositions. The slow adoption of hybrid corn in Iowa in the 1940s may seem a far cry from the 'modernization' of commercial law in Uganda in the 1990s or the implementation of Swiss marriage law in Turkey over many years. But up to a point even these analogies are suggestive: a top-down perspective, modernizing enthusiasm, a technological attitude, denigration of resistance ('laggards', 'traditionalists'), and a general pro-innovation bias. Again, the main link is communication of ideas.

Suggestive analogies are one thing; a grand synthesizing theory is another. The Greenhalgh report quite rightly warns against a bias in favour of transferability and concludes with the following warning:

> It is important to be aware that the ubiquitously cited 'landmark' studies of diffusion of innovations [Tarde, Ryan and Gross, Coleman et al.], though outstanding in their own context were the product of particular social and

that doctors follow' on the development of national policies and legislation on euthanasia and decisions affecting the terminally ill in the Netherlands: Griffiths, op. cit., n. 101, at pp. 38–55 and his 'Self-regulation by the Dutch medical profession of medical behavior that potentially shortens life' in *Regulating Morality*, eds. H. Krabbenbaum and H. M. ten Napel (2000).

128 Twining, op. cit., n. 27, pp. 26–8.
129 On other biases, see Greenhalgh report, op. cit., n. 6, at pp. 73–5.

intellectual trends. Because they focused exclusively on individuals and relatively fixed innovations, and because they were characterized by an extraordinary low level of complexity, their findings have limited transferability to the spread of innovations in a 21st century health service. Hence, while they set the stage for this review, they inform our own conclusions to a limited extent.[130]

Obviously similar considerations apply in legal contexts. After considering a further range of research traditions, Greenhalgh usefully suggests a framework for evaluating 'transferability of innovations' based on the work of Gomm, Pawson, and Tilley on 'realistic evaluation'.[131] The applicability of this template to different kinds of legal 'innovation' also requires cautious appraisal.

CONCLUSIONS

1. Legal and social scientific studies of diffusion grew out of shared beginnings in cultural anthropology, but they have largely lost touch with each other. Leading accounts of 'reception' or 'transplantation' of law make scarcely any reference to social science literature on diffusion, which in turn has largely ignored law. The purpose of this essay is to explore the implications of this remarkable gap.
2. Diffusion of law refers to the processes by which legal orders and traditions are influenced by other legal orders and traditions. It is a pervasive aspect of interlegality at all levels of law and legal ordering. It is considered by some leading scholars to be a central aspect of comparative law.
3. For many purposes, diffusion is not a natural or a useful organizing category or focus of attention. Diffusion of law is often studied as an aspect of some other subject such as colonization, imperial rule, law and development, transition to a capitalist economy, or a detailed history of local law. There are, however, occasions when it makes sense to focus on processes of diffusion as such.
4. The literature on diffusion of law does not belong to a single research tradition, but much of it fits within the paradigm of 'the Country and Western tradition of comparative law'. It contains some valuable studies and insights, but it is generally fragmented, unempirical, and unduly influenced by a simplistic model of processes of diffusion.
5. There is a vast and varied literature on diffusion in the social sciences,

---

130 id., pp. 74–5; compare Wejnert, op. cit., n. 60 who concludes that future diffusion research needs to 'incorporate more fully (a) the interactive character of diffusion variables; (b) the gating function of diffusion variables, and (c) effects of an actor's characteristics on the temporal rate of diffusion.'
131 See R. Pawson and N. Tilley, *Realistic Evaluation* (1997), Pawson, op. cit., n. 64, and R. Gomm (ed.), *Using evidence in health and social care* (2000) at 171–91.

representing several loosely related research traditions, each with its own intellectual history and biases with occasional pockets of synthesis. This heritage of literature can provide us with some basic tools for analysing particular examples of diffusion processes and a vast treasure house of concepts, hypotheses, debates, concrete examples, and suggestive, sometimes unexpected, analogies that could help to guide, fertilize, and illuminate particular lines of research.

6. What links these bodies of literature is that they are concerned with the spread and communication of ideas across space and time.

7. Law is not one thing. Processes of diffusion can vary in respect of originating sources, scale, levels, pathways, objects of diffusion, changes in the objects, agents, degrees of formality, timing, relation to pre-existing law, degree of penetration, and consequences. Diffusion of law refers to a vast and complex range of phenomena, which can be studied from a variety of standpoints for a variety of purposes. It is accordingly difficult to give general answers to such questions as: what can students of legal diffusion learn from the social science literature?

8. This essay considers in particular two attempts, by Rogers in 1995 and Greenhalgh et al. in 2004, to survey and to synthesize the literature on diffusion of innovations (viewed as ideas that are new to the recipients or adopters). There are certain trends and biases in this literature of which researchers need to be aware, such as innovation bias, technological orientation, individual bias, and variations in scale and geographical spread.

9. Important issues arise about the transferability of concepts, models, and hypotheses generated largely from small-scale studies of discrete objects to different contexts and phenomena (to what extent can ideas about diffusion appropriately be diffused?). Nevertheless, some of the more abstract concepts and issues are highly transferable as is illustrated by the application of Rogers's basic framework to the story of the reception of foreign law in Turkey as part of Ataturk's reforms and their impact.

10. In addition to macroscopic studies of large-scale receptions, there is a need for middle-order and microscopic analyses of particular examples of diffusion, involving detailed focus on interactions and perceptions of actors, for which interactionist perspectives may be more appropriate.

11. There are further bodies of literature on the spread of languages, sport, music, religion, political ideas, and so on that could also be relevant to research on diffusion of law, but which fall outside the scope of this essay.

12. Nearly all of the social science literature is based on detailed empirical research. Lack of a sustained empirical base is the Achilles heel of comparative law. Renewing this link between two bodies of literature offers the best hope of developing a better empirical base for our understanding of processes of diffusion of law and hence of comparative law.

[17]

Understanding Legal Pluralism: Past to Present, Local to Global[†]

BRIAN Z TAMANAHA[*]

Abstract

The notion of legal pluralism is gaining momentum across a range of law-related fields. Part I of this article will portray the rich history of legal pluralism, from the medieval period up to the present. Part II will explain why current theoretical efforts to formulate legal pluralism are plagued by the difficulty of defining "law." Finally, Part III will articulate an approach to contemporary legal pluralism that avoids the conceptual problems suffered by most current approaches, while framing the salient features of legal pluralism.

1. Introduction

Legal pluralism is everywhere. There is, in every social arena one examines, a seeming multiplicity of legal orders, from the lowest local level to the most expansive global level. There are village, town, or municipal laws of various types; there are state, district or regional laws of various types; there are national, transnational and international laws of various types. In addition to these familiar bodies of law, in many societies there are more exotic forms of law, like customary law, indigenous law, religious law, or law connected to distinct ethnic or cultural groups within a society. There is also an evident increase in quasi-legal activities, from private policing and judging, to privately run prisons, to the ongoing creation of the new *lex mercatoria*, a body of transnational commercial law that is almost entirely the product of private law-making activities.

What makes this pluralism noteworthy is not merely the fact that there are multiple uncoordinated, coexisting or overlapping bodies of law, but that there is diversity amongst them. They may make competing claims of authority; they may impose conflicting demands or norms; they may have different styles and orientations. This potential conflict can generate uncertainty or jeopardy for individuals and groups in society who cannot be sure in advance which legal regime will be applied to their situation. This state of conflict also creates opportunities for individuals and groups within society, who can opportunistically select from among coexisting legal authorities to advance their aims. This state of conflict, moreover, poses a challenge to the legal authorities themselves, for it means that they have rivals. Law characteristically claims to rule whatever it addresses, but the fact of legal pluralism challenges this claim.

[†] The Julius Stone Institute of Jurisprudence, Faculty of Law, University of Sydney, The Julius Stone Address 2007, Thursday, 5 July 2007.

[*] Chief Judge Benjamin N Cardozo Professor of Law, St John's University, New York. The author thanks Neil Walker, Paul Schiff Berman, and an anonymous reader from the *Sydney Law Review* for very helpful critical comments on an earlier draft of this article.

There is another sense in which legal pluralism is everywhere. In the past two decades, the notion of legal pluralism has become a major topic in legal anthropology, legal sociology, comparative law, international law, and socio-legal studies, and it appears to be gaining popularity. As anyone who has engaged in multidisciplinary work knows, each academic discipline has its own paradigms and knowledge base, so it is unusual to see a single notion penetrate so many different disciplines.

This article will lay out a framework to help us examine and understand the pluralistic form that law takes today. The first part of the article will place modern legal pluralism in historical context, for the only way to grasp where we are and where we are headed is to have a sense of how we arrived at the present. Legal pluralism, it turns out, is a common historical condition. The long dominant view that law is a unified and uniform system administered by the state has erased our consciousness of the extended history of legal pluralism. To resurrect this awareness, the first part of this article will portray the rich legal pluralism that characterised the medieval period, and it will describe how this pluralism was reduced in the course of the consolidation of state power. It will then elaborate on the new forms of legal pluralism that were produced through colonisation, when Western European colonisers transplanted legal regimes abroad. These historical contexts will set the stage for contemporary legal pluralism, which combines the legacy of this past with more recent developments connected to the processes of globalisation.

The next part of the article will shift to the academic discussion of legal pluralism. Although the notion of legal pluralism is gaining popularity across a range of academic disciplines, from its very inception it has been plagued by a fundamental conceptual problem — the difficulty of defining 'law' for the purposes of legal pluralism. This issue lies at the very core of 'legal pluralism'. Debates surrounding this conceptual problem have continued unabated for three decades, often in unusually acerbic exchanges. Recent theoretical developments have taken a remarkable turn. Just as the notion of legal pluralism began to take off, the theorist who contributed the most to its promotion announced that, owing to its insoluble conceptual problem, legal pluralism should be discarded. This part will lay out a brief account of the conceptual problem that plagues legal pluralism and will indicate why it cannot be resolved. Scholars who invoke legal pluralism without an awareness of this conceptual problem and its implications will risk building upon an incoherent and unstable foundation.

The final part will articulate an approach to contemporary legal pluralism that avoids the conceptual problems suffered by most current approaches, while framing the important features of legal pluralism. It is drawn from and combines the insights produced in legal anthropology, comparative law, international law, and globalisation studies, in the hope that the framework can provide common ground for a cross-disciplinary focus on legal pluralism.

2. Legal Pluralism Past and Present

A. Legal Pluralism in the Medieval Period

By general convention, the medieval period covers about 1000 years, commencing with the 5th century collapse of the Roman Empire and coming to a close with the 15th century Renaissance. The earlier centuries of this period have the forbidding appellation, the Dark Ages, when the once great Roman Empire that extended from North Africa and the Middle East to Western Europe was overrun by successive waves of Germanic tribes, and later suffered incursions by Huns, Moslems, Norsemen, Magyars, and other fearsome external invaders. European society closed in upon itself, commerce slowed, feudalism developed, local dukes or barons were more powerful than distant kings or princes, and learning was limited, carried on mainly in the Roman Catholic Church. The 12th and 13th centuries, marked by the rediscovery of the works of Aristotle and the Justinian Code, and by the establishment of universities, was the first stage in the awakening of Europe from this long period of slumber.

The mid-to-late medieval period was characterised by a remarkable jumble of different sorts of law and institutions, occupying the same space, sometimes conflicting, sometimes complementary, and typically lacking any overarching hierarchy or organisation. These forms of law included local customs (often in several versions, usually unwritten); general Germanic customary law (in code form); feudal law (mostly unwritten); the law merchant or *lex mercatoria* — commercial law and customs followed by merchants; canon law of the Roman Catholic Church; and the revived Roman law developed in the universities.[1] Various types of courts or judicial forums coexisted: manorial courts; municipal courts; merchant courts; guild courts; church courts and royal courts. Serving as judges in these courts were, respectively, barons or lords of the manor, burghers (leading city residents), merchants, guild members, bishops (and in certain cases the pope), and kings or their appointees. Jurisdictional rules for each court, and the laws to be applied, related to the persons involved — their status, descent, citizenship, occupation or religion — as well as to the subject matter at issue.

'[T]he demarcation disputes between these laws and courts were numerous.'[2] Conflicts arose regularly with Church courts in particular, which claimed authority over matters dealing with marriage, property inheritance, and anything involving church personnel; '[m]any offences could in principle be tried either in a secular or in an ecclesiastical court.'[3] Not only did separate legal systems and bodies of legal norms coexist, a single system or judge could apply distinct bodies of law. In the 8th through 11th centuries, for example, under the 'personality principle,'[4] the

---

1 A detailed account of the different laws and institutions can be found in Olivia Robinson, Thomas Fergus & William Gordon, *European Legal History* (2000).
2 See Raoul van Caenegem, *Legal History: A European Perspective* (1991) at 119.
3 Gillian Evans, *Law and Theology in the Middle Ages* (2002) at 1.
4 An informative description of this principle and the legal pluralism that resulted from it is contained in Frederick Maitland, 'A Prologue to the History of English Law' (1898) 14 *Law Quarterly Review* 13.

same judges applied different laws depending upon whether one was Frankish, Burgundian, Alamannic, or a descendent of Roman Gaul.[5] Things were even more complicated in cities with Jewish populations or on the Iberian Peninsula following the Muslim invasion, for Jews and Muslims had their own comprehensive bodies of law, yet they interacted with one another and with Christians.

The mid through late Middle Ages thus exhibited legal pluralism along at least three major axes: coexisting, overlapping bodies of law with different geographical reaches; coexisting institutionalised systems; and conflicting legal norms within a system. In terms of the first axis — bodies of law — the *ius commune*, the *lex mercatoria*, and ecclesiastical law spanned separate kingdoms across a large swath of Europe; this transnational law (loosely described as such, for nations were not yet fully formed) coexisted with codified Germanic customary law on a national level, and with feudal law, municipal law and unwritten local customary laws on the local level.[6] In terms of the second axis — coexisting institutionalised systems — in the words of medieval scholar Raoul van Caenegem, 'there were also vertical dividing lines between legal systems: those which separated townsmen from countrymen, churchmen and students from laymen, members of guilds and crafts from those not so affiliated. The great (and the smaller) *ordines* of society lived according to distinct sets of rules, administered by distinct networks of law courts, for it was understood that everyone should be tried by his peers.'[7] In addition, royal courts could hear cases in the first instance or on appeal from other courts. In terms of the third axis — conflicting legal norms — within a single system and social arena there could be different bodies of legal norms, especially of customary law. 'It was common to find many different codes of customary law in force in the same kingdom, town or village, even in the same house, if the ninth century bishop Agobard of Lyons is to be believed when he says, "It often happened that five men were present or sitting together, and not one of them had the same law as another."'[8]

Medievalist Walter Ullmann summarised the legal situation in late Middle Ages in the following terms:

> The medieval system of positive law cannot be conceived as a homogenous and unified body of legal rules. Three distinct systems of statutory enactments can be discerned: Roman law, as transmitted through Justinian's compilation and modified subsequently by additional legislation of the Emperors; canon law, as represented in various collections; and thirdly, the Germanic Lombard law. To these must be added the numerous statutes of the municipalities and independent States, around which enactments there cluster many customary formations of law, mostly of a supplementary and interpretive character. This complex mosaic of

---

5 See van Caenegem, above n2 at 117–18. See also Patrick Geary, *The Myth of Nations: The Medieval Origins of Europe* (2002) at 152–154.
6 See Harold Berman, *Law and Revolution: The Formation of the Western Legal Tradition* (1983); Walter Ullmann, *The Medieval Idea of Law* (1969).
7 van Caenegem, above n2 at 118.
8 John Morrall, *Political Thought in Medieval Times* (1980) at 17.

legal systems naturally presented many difficulties to the application of abstract legal rule to the given set of concrete circumstances.[9]

To modern ears this multifarious legal situation sounds unusual, but historians have shown that the coexistence of more than one body of legal norms and systems was the normal state of affairs for at least 2000 years of European history, certainly since the heyday of the Roman Empire (which allowed locals laws to remain in force), and especially so after its collapse.

The fact that we have tended to view law as a monopoly of the state is a testimony to the success of the state-building project and the ideological views which supported it, a project which got underway in the late medieval period. For almost the entirety of the medieval period, the state system we are now familiar with was not in place in Western Europe. England had a relatively centralised system from the 12th century on, following the Norman conquest, but the continent was divided among various competing major and minor kings and princes, who had scant effective control of much of the landscape. Wars during this period were not fought between states as such, but rather were efforts by kings and princes to add territory to their personal holdings. There was no public/private separation of offices or assets. The primary sources of income for kings were their feudal lands, special customs they collected and fees from royal courts. Leading officials who handled their affairs were members of their personal staffs.

It took centuries to move from this situation to the establishment of states run by government bureaucracies, a story which cannot be told in detail here. Kings and princes first had to bring the nobility and the cities under their control.[10] A common strategy toward this end was to place members of the higher nobility on their payroll, while forming strategic alliances with leading burghers of the cities against the lower barons. It was also essential for sovereigns to establish their autonomy from the Church. This was facilitated by the Reformation, which broke the hegemony of the Roman Catholic Church and enabled sovereigns in Protestant regions to seize Church assets. Two famous treaties serve as early markers of the state building process. The Treaty of Augsburg in 1555 established the principle that sovereigns could decide the religion of citizens within their territory.[11] The Treaty of Westphalia of 1648 divided Europe into separate, secular territories under the authority of sovereigns. The treaty recognised that heads of state control internal affairs and have the right to defend territorial boundaries.[12] Although various forms of political organisation thrived prior to this time (including city states and urban leagues),[13] thereafter, territorial states would become the central political and legal unit of Western Europe.

---

9 Ullmann, above n6 at 71.
10 A superb exploration of the development of the state can be found in Martin van Creveld, *The Rise and Decline of the State* (1999) Chapter 2.
11 Hendrik Spruyt, *The Sovereign State and its Competitors: An Analysis of Systems of Change* (1994) at 191.
12 van Creveld, above n10 at 68.
13 Spruyt, above n11.

Consolidation of law in the hands of the state was an essential aspect of the state-building process. Central to this process was the implementation of an administrative apparatus that oversaw tax collection, law enforcement, and judging — different roles that were often exercised by the same individuals in a given location. The various heterogeneous forms of law described earlier were gradually absorbed or eliminated. As medievalist Marc Bloch observed, 'The consolidation of societies into great states or principalities favoured not only the revival of legislation but also the extension of a unifying jurisprudence over vast territories.'[14] Sovereigns and city merchants shared an affinity for the revived Roman law, which envisioned a powerful law-making role for rulers and was more amenable to the needs of commerce than canon law and the uncertain mix of customary law.[15]

During the slow course of the construction of the state legal system with its monopoly over law, customary law, which was a substantial bulk of the law during the medieval period, underwent a subtle but fateful transition that had begun much earlier. In the process of being incorporated within the state legal system, customary law was taken over by legal professionals. Historian Donald Kelley explained the significance of this takeover:

> With the advent of written forms... even with the proviso of popular "approval" and "tacit consent," custom lost its primary ties with its social base and came under the control of legal and political authorities. The classical formula designating *consuetudo* as the "best interpreter of the law" was intended by jurists to enhance their own power, as suggested by the gloss of Azo, who defined custom as the founder and abrogator as well as the interpreter of law.... Another, less authoritative maxim... suggests the true significance of the transition from "custom" to "customary law," which is that once again the legal experts have begun to take over. This indeed is the import of the twelfth-century revival of "legal science," in which custom joins civil and canon law in the arsenal of the "language of power" which jurists come in large part to monopolize.[16]

Kelley emphasises in this passage that, once legal professionals control the pronouncement and development of customary law, what is called 'customary law' by legal officials does not necessarily correspond to actual customs. Officially recognised 'customary law' develops in accordance with the modes, mechanisms, requirements, and interests of legal officials and the legal system (and those it serves), whereas social customs and norms are produced through a variety of processes and mechanisms apart from the official legal system.

In the 17th and 18th centuries, a sharper distinction emerged between the public and private realms.[17] State law became the pre-eminent form of law; international

---

14 Marc Bloch, 'The Feudal World' in Norman Cantor & Michael Wertham (eds), *Medieval Society: 400–1500* (1967) at 43.
15 See Spruyt, above n11 at 102–05.
16 Donald Kelley, *The Human Measure: Social Thought in the Western Legal Tradition* (1990) at 106.
17 In earlier periods the public/private distinction was not sharply drawn. See van Creveld, above n10 at 23–24.

law and natural law were also recognised, but mainly in virtue of and on the terms set by state law. Customary norms and religious law were, in effect, banished to the private realm. They did not disappear, but a transformation in their status came about. Some of these norms and institutions continued to obtain recognition and sanction from state legal systems; other norms continued to be observed and enforced in strictly social or religious contexts. The key characteristic they lost over time was their former, equal standing and autonomous *legal* status. Once considered independently applicable bodies of *law*, owing to the takeover of state law they rather became *norms*, still socially influential, but now carrying a different status from that of official state law. Customary and religious norms, it must be emphasised, often were more efficacious than state law in governing every day social affairs, but the loss of legal status had significant implications that would bear fruit over time.

An equally important development that followed the establishment of the state system was a shift in views of the role of the government and of law — in effect altering the dominant character and orientation of law. No longer was law thought to merely reflect an enduring order of custom or natural principle. Government and law instead came to be seen and utilised as instruments to achieve social objectives. This is an altogether different role and function, one based upon the capacity legal systems have as institutionalised apparatuses of power. With this change, the bulk of the law became less about enforcing social norms than about achieving collective purposes, and about structuring and ordering the government and its affairs.

The monopolisation of law by states in Western Europe reduced legal pluralism at home just as a new wave of legal pluralism was being produced elsewhere through colonisation. Before moving to that discussion, it is pertinent to note that, while the focus herein has been on legal pluralism within medieval Europe, the phenomena just described were by no means limited to that context. Wherever there were movements of people, wherever there were empires, wherever religions spanned different language and cultural groups, wherever there was trade between different groups, or different groups lived side by side, it was inevitable that different bodies of law would operate or overlap within the same social field. Since these were common conditions, the kinds of legal pluralism that existed in medieval Europe no doubt existed elsewhere.

B. *Colonisation and the Resultant Legal Pluralism*

European colonisation of the non-western world commenced in the late 15th century, peaked in the late 19th century, and for the most part ended by the 1970s. The shape and form of colonisation and its consequences depended upon the period in which the colonisation took place, the circumstances of the areas colonised, and the motivations of the colonising powers. For example, when initially encountered, North America and Australia were large land masses with relatively sparse and politically decentralised populations; this was different from the more centralised and populous societies that existed in Central America, parts of Africa, and Asia; and different from densely populated heterogeneous India under the Mughal rule, with its complex mixture of Muslim and Hindu laws and institutions; and different from the Cape of Africa, where two colonising powers, the Dutch and British, encountered one another as well as a large native population.

These contrasting situations and purposes led to variations in legal approach. Spanish colonisation of the Americas, for example, took place relatively early when the authority of the Catholic Church in Spain was still strong. The Spanish mission was not just to extract raw material using native and slave labour, but also to gain converts to Christianity, which led to intrusive involvement with the indigenous population. By contrast, British and Dutch colonisation of densely populated India and Indonesia, respectively, was organised initially through royally chartered private corporations, their East India companies, which exercised the power to establish laws and courts. Their aim was economic rather than territorial or religious expansion, which dictated a minimal legal presence, focused mainly on protecting their economic interests and governing the expatriate populations in the coastal trading cities.

'On the whole there was a striking reluctance to accept jurisdiction over subject people. Up to the late eighteenth century there was no serious European endeavour to develop jurisdiction over an indigenous population according to their own law. Nor were there attempts on a large scale to extend European law to the subject population.'[18] In most cases it was not necessary for colonial interests, nor practicable, nor economically efficient to extend legal rule over indigenous populations. 'Accordingly, indigenous legal institutions were mostly left alone, unless they directly affected the status of the European traders, missionaries, settlers, or officials.'[19] Jurisdiction was determined mainly by the personal principle, under which indigenous law was applied to indigenous people and colonial law to the colonisers (and to mixed cases).

When colonising powers began to exert greater legal authority, as occurred in various areas from the late 18th century through the late 19th century, it was typically accomplished through 'indirect rule', which relied upon pre-existing sources of political authority — using indigenous leaders — or involved the creation of so-called 'native courts' that enforced customary or religious laws. The result was, as in medieval Europe, a hodgepodge of coexisting legal institutions and norms operating side by side, with various points of overlap, conflict and mutual influence. In her superb historical account of the role law in colonisation, Lauren Benton describes one doomed British attempt to organise the unruly situation in India:

> The relationship of indigenous and British forums, and indigenous and British legal practitioners, was specified in the 1772 reforms. A plan drawn up by Warren Hastings created two courts for each of the districts. One court, the Diwani

---

18 Jörg Fisch, 'Law as a Means to an End: Some Remarks on the Function of European Law and Non-European Law in the Process of European Expansion' in Wolfgang Mommsen & Jaap de Moor (eds), *European Expansion and Law: the Encounter of European and Indigenous Law in 19th and 20th Century Africa and Asia* (1992) at 23.

19 Wolfgang Mommsen, 'Introduction' in Mommsen & Moor, above n18 at 4.

Adalat, was to handle civil cases, while a second court, the Foujdari Adalat, was to oversee trials for crimes and misdemeanors. The revenue collectors of each district were to preside over the civil courts, thus consolidating in British hands control over revenue and property disputes. The civil courts would apply Muslim law to Muslims, and Hindu law to Hindus. The criminal courts would apply Muslim law universally. An appellate structure was also created, with one of two courts at Calcutta to hear appeals from inferior civil courts.... Though British (Company) officials would preside in civil courts, the system built in formal and informal roles for Mughal officials. In a move that was purely pragmatic, zamindars were allowed to maintain jurisdiction over local, petty disputes. They had no formal rights to such jurisdiction, but the system simply would not function effectively without their playing a role they had assumed in the Mughal system. The criminal country courts continued to be operated entirely by Mughal officers, and in the civil courts, Muslim and Hindu legal experts were given monthly salaries as Company employees for their work in advising on local and religious law.[20]

This arrangement allowed matters of interest to the East India Company to be controlled by legal rules issued by the Company, with Muslim and Hindu law to govern local populations in their own affairs. Later, following concern in Britain about the unseemly way in which a private, profit-oriented company was allowed to control the legal arrangements governing a subject population, the British government created its own independent court with authority over British subjects and company employees, overlapping with the authority of other courts.

It is not possible to summarise here all the various shapes and forms that law took in the context of colonisation.[21] Instead, I will merely highlight a few common approaches and their consequences, especially in the relationship between transplanted colonial law and local customary law. The initial approach, as indicated above, was to leave indigenous institutions to function as they would, especially in the hinterlands, where colonisers had limited interests and little power. When colonising powers undertook to expand the reach of law, three basic strategies were applied to incorporate customary or religious law: the codification of customary or religious law; the application by state courts of unwritten customary or religious law in a fashion analogous to the common law; and the creation or recognitions of informal or 'customary' courts run by local leaders.[22] The customary law officially recognised by the system was often limited to family law issues, minor crimes, issues unique to the customary or religious law, and minor disputes. Often repugnancy or supremacy clauses were enacted that

---

20 Lauren Benton, *Law and Colonial Cultures: Legal Regimes in World History, 1400-1900* (2002) at 134.
21 An extraordinary book that covers a range of colonial contexts is Lauren Benton, id; another excellent source is Mommsen & de Moor (eds), above n18. This account draws heavily from both.
22 See summary in Brian Z Tamanaha, 'A Proposal For the Development of a System of Indigenous Jurisprudence in the Federated States of Micronesia' (1989–1990) 13 *Hastings International and Comparative Law Review* 71 at 102–107.

invalidated particularly offensive (by the coloniser's standard) local laws or practices; and often the official state court often would have final authority over indigenous courts.

All of these strategies suffered from various defects, and none were entirely successful in replicating customary or religious law.[23] The basic problem is that local norms and processes could not be removed from their original medium without losing their integrity. In many indigenous contexts, rules were not treated as binding dictates, but rather as flexible rules that could be negotiated in the course of resolving disputes. 'The essence of the customary systems may be said to have lain in their processes, but these were displaced, and the flexible principles which had guided them were now fed into a rule-honing and using machine operating in new political circumstances.'[24]

Recent scholarship, moreover, has shown that some of what was identified as customary law was not in fact customary or traditional at all, but instead were inventions or selective interpretations by colonial powers or sophisticated indigenous elites who created customary law to advance their interests or agendas.[25] A more innocent explanation applicable to many situations is that colonisers began to affirmatively incorporate customary law into the state legal system after a lengthy period of contact, by which time customary law and practices had been transformed or forgotten. The essential point is that, despite the label 'customary law,' it should not be assumed that the laws faithfully matched prevailing customs or social norms (as also indicated in the earlier discussion of the medieval period).

In many locations, what resulted was a dual legal system with various complex mixtures and combinations, and mutual influences. Coexisting within the ambit of an overarching legal system were state court processes and norms instituted by the colonising power that applied mainly to economic activities and government affairs, while officially recognised customary or religious institutions enforced local norms. Jurisdictional rules (often based on the personal principle) and conflicts of law rules addressed the relations between these systems. Although less formal by design, customary and religious courts sometimes adopted the forms and styles of state courts. Both sides of this dual system influenced one another in various ways, including exchanging or recognising the other's norms. Often the official law was markedly distant from the local law, set forth in the language of the coloniser which many indigenous people did not speak, its effective reach limited to urban areas where the institutionalised presence of the state legal system was strongest.

---

23 An overview of the problems can be found in Sally Engle Merry, 'Law and Colonialism' (1991) 25 *Law & Society Review* 889.
24 See Martin Chanock, *Law, Custom, and Social Order: the Colonial Experience in Malawi and Zambia* (1985) at 62.
25 Martin Chanock, 'The Law Market: The Legal Encounter in British East and Central Asia' in Mommsen & de Moor (eds), above n18; Francis Snyder, 'Colonialism and Legal Form: The Creation of "Customary Law" in Senegal' (1981) 19 *Journal of Legal Pluralism and Unofficial Law* 49.

Following decolonisation, in many locations customary law enjoyed an official boost in status, and in many Muslim countries the Sharia was given greater official recognition; in some instances customary law or Sharia were accorded a position of supremacy within and above official state law. But in most situations not much changed. A large bulk of the law was controlled by legal professionals, had transplanted origins, and covered economic or government affairs or other instrumental uses of law. As before, customary and religious law controlled selected areas, usually marriage, inheritance, familial property rights, and customary or religious offences.

It is essential to recognise that the priority officially accorded to state law in these situations says nothing about the power of law in social life. In many locations during and after colonisation, state legal institutions were relatively weak by comparison to other normative systems; they were poorly developed, under-funded and under-staffed, and their presence was limited to the larger towns or cities. Since the bulk of state legal norms were transplanted from elsewhere, they almost inevitably did not match the norms that prevailed in social life.[26] Thus, while the transplanted law held the upper hand on its own turf within the context of the legal system, matters were reversed in social life, where the state legal system frequently was unable to dictate its terms.

To offer additional generalisations about these extraordinarily varied situations would be hazardous, but one further observation can be made, as it as turns up repeatedly in close studies of these situations. Although it is correct to say that colonisers used law to establish their rule and advance their interests, this is not the whole story. As Benton detailed, indigenous people demonstrated a remarkable awareness of the differences in norms and processes between the various coexisting legal systems and showed a strategic understanding of how to exploit these differences, invoking whichever system serves their particular purposes, pitting one system against the other when the need arose. From the standpoint of a legal authority trying to consolidate its rule, legal pluralism is a flaw to be rectified. From the standpoint of individuals or groups subject to legal pluralism, it can be a source of uncertainty, but it also creates the possibility of resort to alternative legal regimes.

By the outset of the 20th century, the project of state-building using law extended around the world with mixed and varied results. In Western Europe, the pre-existing legal pluralism of the Middle Ages had been subsumed within a unified legal system, though cultural and religious plurality continued to exist outside the ambit of the legal system, usually without official legal status or sanction. Beyond Europe, especially in colonial and post-colonial situations, an overarching legal system was in place which internalised and explicitly recognised a plurality of norms and institutions. Old multinational empires, like the Ottoman, Hapsburg, Russian, and Chinese, also had unified systems that recognised internal plurality. Although states routinely claimed a monopoly over law and the enforcement of social order, the capacity of states to live up to this claim varied widely. In many

---

26 See Brian Z Tamanaha, *A General Jurisprudence of Law and Society* (2001) Chapter 5.

areas of the world, ranging from pockets in densely populated urban areas, to rural areas or dense jungle, state law was impotent, capable only of episodic or specific interventions. In all situations, norms and institutions that rivalled the state in controlling and influencing the behaviour of people continued to thrive.

C.   Late 20th Century Legal Pluralism

At the close of the 20th century, the various modes and manifestations of what has been labelled 'globalisation' have given rise to yet another wave of legal pluralism.[27] Globalisation refers to a cluster of characteristics that reflect an increasingly interconnected world:[28] the migration of people across national borders; the creation of global networks of communication (mass media and the internet), global transportation systems, and global financial markets; the building of global or transnational political organisations or regulatory regimes (European Union ('EU'), World Trade Organization ('WTO'), North American Free Trade Agreement ('NAFTA'), Association of Southeast Asian Nations ('ASEAN')); the consolidation of a global commercial system comprised of transnational corporations with production and sales networks that span countries around the world; the presence of non-governmental organisations that carry on activities around the world; the infliction of global or transnational environmental damage (damage to the ozone, global warming, Chernobyl nuclear fallout, depletion of fish stocks, acid rain and chemical pollution of rivers that cross several countries, etc), and terrorism with a global reach.

Connected to globalisation, observers have noted that states are losing power in various ways.[29] As in the example of the EU, states have given up some of their sovereign power to control their own affairs in certain economic, political and legal respects, subjecting themselves to a higher authority. States also have broken up internally into smaller units more closely tied to communities of shared identity, as occurred with the former Soviet Union and Yugoslavia; a similar process short of complete separation can be seen in the movements for greater autonomy in Scotland, Quebec, Kurdistan, the Basque regions of France and Spain, and other places. In addition to these political developments, states have lost their capacities to guide or protect their economies, as virtually every state is now deeply enmeshed in and subject to the vagaries of hyper-competitive, free-wheeling global markets.

Furthermore, and more immediately relevant, there are evident signs of a diminishment of the state's traditional legal functions. Private security forces now patrol and maintain order in gated communities, universities, places of public entertainment (theme parks, concerts, sporting events), public facilities (libraries,

---

27 The most extensive and sophisticated writings on the subject are by Paul Schiff Berman. See Paul Schiff Berman, 'Global Legal Pluralism' (2006–2007) *Southern California Law Review* 1155.

28 For an exploration of the jurisprudential aspects of this, see Catherine Dauvergne (ed), *Jurisprudence for an Interconnected Globe* (2003).

29 See Jürgen Habermas, *The Postnational Constellation: Political Essays* (2001) Chapter 4; van Creveld, above n10 at Chapter 6.

schools), shopping malls, corporate headquarters, many small businesses, and even public streets (neighbourhood watch). Privately owned and run (for profit) penitentiaries are handling an increasing number of prisoners. Many private organisations and institutions promulgate rules that apply to their own activities and to others within their purview. In situations of dispute, many parties choose (or are required) to bypass state court systems seen as inefficient, unreliable, too costly or too public, resorting instead to arbitration or private courts. Many of the massive slums that are ubiquitous in large cities around the world function with little or no official legal presence, beyond the purview of law and courts, often without legally recognised rights; order is maintained and intercourse conducted in these areas through other social norms, institutions or mechanisms.

Observers have identified or described legal aspects of these developments in terms of legal pluralism. One theme, called 'International Legal Pluralism,' is that the international legal system is internally pluralistic, with a sprawling multitude of separate tribunals (over 125 by one count) and functionally distinct bodies of legal norms tied to specific areas of regulation (for example, trade, human rights, intellectual property, law of the sea, crimes against humanity, pollution) that are not coordinated with one another and can overlap or conflict.[30] A dispute over whether a country can make available for its population generic drugs for the treatment of Acquired Immune Deficiency Syndrome, for example, simultaneously raises issues that fall with the jurisdiction of the WTO and under the purview of the World Health Organization, each of which has different norms and purposes.[31] Not only is the international system fragmented, additional complications arise because domestic or national courts incorporate international law in different ways and to different extents. The same kind of fragmentation and lack of coordination also takes place on the regional level. Within the EU, for example, the legal regimes of member states vary in certain respects from one another, and also come into conflict with overarching EU laws and institutions.

A second theme prominent in the literature highlights the invocation of human rights norms, often by non-governmental organisations ('NGOs'), to challenge state laws or actions or customary laws or cultural practices.[32] Suits are being brought in supranational human rights courts, like the European Court of Human Rights or the Inter-American Court of Human Rights, by citizens seeking redress against their own state. In these situations the norms and institutions of one legal system are being pitted against another.

A third theme of the global legal pluralist literature is the growth of 'self-creating', 'private', or 'unofficial' legal orders. A leading theorist, Gunther Teubner, suggests that functionally differentiated systems have developed with a

---

30 William W Burke-White, 'International Legal Pluralism' (2003-2004) 25 *Michigan Journal of International Law* 963.

31 See Andreas Fischer-Lescano & Gunther Teubner, 'Regime Collisions: The Vain Search for Legal Unity in the Fragmentation of Global Law' (2003-2004) 25 *Michigan Journal of International Law* 999.

32 See Sally Engle Merry, 'Global Human Rights and Local Social Movements in a Legally Plural World' (1997) 12 *Canadian Journal of Law and Society* 247.

global or transnational reach — commercial transactions, the internet, and sports organisations, for example — generating their own legal orders. What observers have dubbed the new *lex mercatoria* is the example most often mentioned.[33] Transnational commercial transactions are increasingly conducted in connection with a body of rules and institutions that are not entirely tethered to the international legal system or to any particular nation state. Binding rules derive from several international conventions on commercial contracts, from standard terms utilised in model contracts, and from business customs or usages. Disputes between contracting parties are resolved through private arbitration. What makes the *lex mercatoria* noteworthy is that its norms, practices, and institutions are self-generated by the parties and their lawyers, although it intersects at various points with international law norms and national courts (when parties seek recourse from arbitration decisions). A different version of privately created rules in the economic sphere focuses on the efforts of NGOs to pressure corporations to adopt better practices, for example, by adopting corporate codes of conduct that address labour conditions for employees.[34] The primary actors in these contexts are transnational corporations, NGOs (Amnesty International, Greenpeace, etc), trade associations, various subject-based international agencies, and lawyers who serve them; their collective activities are creating a multiplicity of regulatory orders with global reach.[35]

A fourth theme relates to the creation of 'trans-governmental networks' that have regulatory powers and implications. 'For example, the 1990s saw the creation of the Financial Stability Forum, a network composed of three trans-governmental organisations — The Basel Committee on Banking Supervision, the International Organization of Securities Commissions, and the International Association of Insurance Supervisors — along with other national and international officials responsible for financial stability around the world.'[36] Active networks have also been created among judges, NGOs, and development organisations, among others. The multiplication of these networks beyond the direct control of any national or international agency, according to observers, constitutes another form of legal pluralism.

A fifth theme relates to the global movement of people. Within nations, people are moving in droves from the countryside to burgeoning cities in search of jobs and a better life. People are also moving in large numbers from one nation to another for the same reasons, often settling in immigrant communities in the new land. They bring their own cultural and religious norms, which may conflict with the official legal rules of the new land. A study of Muslims in England, for

---

33 Tamanaha, above n26 at 125–127.
34 See Adelle Blackett, 'Global Governance, Legal Pluralism and the Decentered State: A Labor Law Critique of Codes of Corporate Conduct' (2000-2001) 8 *Indiana Journal of Global Legal Studies* 401.
35 See Francis Snyder, 'Governing Economic Globalisation: Global Legal Pluralism and European Law' (1999) 5 *European Law Journal* 334.
36 Paul Schiff Berman, 'From International Law to Law and Globalization' (2004-2005) 43 *Columbia Journal of Transnational Law* 485 at 502.

example, showed that many Muslims continue to practice polygamy, consistent with their religious law but contrary to English law. The author observed that 'Muslim law is still superior and dominant over English law in the Muslim mind and in the eyes of the Muslim community'.[37]

A final observation about global legal pluralism will help introduce the next part. Although the phenomena just described are real, the focus on global legal pluralism as such is not solely the product of changes in the world, but is also the consequence of two particular changes in the way the situation is perceived. Two shifts in perspective have, in a sense, 'created' global legal pluralism.

The first alteration involves positing the global or transnational level as the starting point of the analysis, then concentrating attention on internal divergences or conflicts. This shift in frame of reference and orientation immediately 'produces' legal pluralism. If one envisions matters from the standpoint of a global or transnational legal system, that legal system is immediately pluralistic because it contains and interacts with a multitude of coexisting, competing and overlapping legal systems at many levels and in many contexts. Or to put the point another way, all of the phenomena just identified as characteristic of globalisation also were present 50 years ago, albeit in less intensified forms; several of them, including international law, have been present since the Middle Ages. Conflicts of law regimes and jurisdictional rules have existed for centuries to deal with these situations. Forum shopping is a familiar legal phenomenon. Until recently, however, no one thought to describe these ubiquitous situations as a matter of legal pluralism.

As an illustration of this point, consider the EU. When the overarching union came into existence through a series of agreements and institutional manifestations, it was legally plural in the double sense that the member nations had their own legal systems, and these systems interacted with the broader EU legal system and norms. Note, however, that such combinations or federations with internal diversity and conflict with the national level are common, yet heretofore the term 'legal pluralism' has rarely been applied. Even hierarchically organised and unified legal systems — the United States, for example — have internal conflicts between different bodies of law or institutions that must be rationalised (from the 50 states to quasi-sovereign American Indian tribes), but few people think of this as a matter of legal pluralism. Rather, they were seen as complicated arrangements to be solved or managed, but not a dominant characteristic of the system. Legal pluralists, in contrast, construe them as fundamental, ineradicable, and important characteristics central to the operation and functioning of these systems. The very label 'legal pluralism' connotes this different orientation. Global legal pluralism, when viewed in this light, in a sense is 'produced' when one takes seriously the global or transnational legal order, while keeping an eye on the evident and inevitable divergences and conflicts.

---

37 Ihsan Yilmaz, 'The Challenge of Post-Modern Legality and Muslim Legal Pluralism in England' (2002) 28 *Journal of Ethnic and Migration Studies* 343 at 343.

The second alteration in perspective relates to what one considers 'law' for the purposes of legal pluralism. As indicated, discussions of legal pluralism on the global level routinely include various forms of private regulation, private dispute resolution bodies, and the activities of private entities like NGOs or trade associations.[38] This is considered legal pluralism because it counts as 'law' a range of private norms and regulatory institutions. Adherents of this approach, for example, assert that an international sports league and the internet give rise to their own 'legal' orders. Scholars who take this approach tend to be social scientists interested in law as a social phenomenon,[39] although a few international lawyers do so as well.[40] The mere fact of framing law in these inclusive terms 'produces' a profusion of legal orders, and hence produces legal pluralism, as will be explored in greater detail in the following part.

3. The Troubled Concept of Legal Pluralism

Legal pluralism first began to garner attention within academia in legal anthropology in the 1970s through studies of law in colonial and post-colonial situations. The label 'legal pluralism' in that context referred primarily to the incorporation or recognition of customary law norms or institutions within state law,[41] or to the independent coexistence of indigenous norms and institutions alongside state law (whether or not officially recognised).[42] In the late 1980s, legal pluralism moved to centre stage in socio-legal studies, when prominent scholars labelled it 'a central theme in the re-conceptualisation of the law/society relation,'[43] and the 'key concept in a post-modern view of law.'[44] Since then, its popularity has steadily spread, penetrating comparative law, political science, international law, and legal philosophy (in a limited way).[45]

Despite this apparent success, the notion of legal pluralism has been marked by deep conceptual confusion and unusually heated disagreement. One factor that contributes to the continuing disagreement is that participants come from several disciplines bring different concepts and orientations to the subject. An international lawyer who invokes legal pluralism has something very different in

---

38 See Blackett, above n34; Oren Perez, 'Normative Creativity and Global Legal Pluralism: Reflections on the Democratic Critique of Transnational Law' (2003) 10(2) *Indiana Journal of Global Legal Studies* 25; Merry, above n32.
39 See, for example, Gunther Teubner, 'The Two Faces of Janus: Rethinking Legal Pluralism' (1991-1992) 13 *Cardozo Law Review* 1443; Boaventura de Sousa Santos, *Toward a New Common Sense: Law, Science, and Politics in Paradigmatic Transition* (1995).
40 Paul Schiff Berman is an international lawyer who draws from the social scientific approach in his work. See Paul Schiff Berman, 'The Globalization of Jurisdiction' (2002-2003) 151 *University of Pennsylvania Law Review* 311.
41 See MB Hooker, *Legal Pluralism: An Introduction to Colonial and Neo-Colonial Laws* (1979).
42 See Leopold Pospisil, *The Anthropology of Law: A Comparative Theory* (1971).
43 Sally Engle Merry, 'Legal Pluralism' (1988) 22 *Law & Society Review* 869 at 869.
44 Boaventura de Sousa Santos, 'Law: A Map of Misreading. Toward a Postmodern Conception of Law' (1987) 14 *Journal of Law and Society* 279.
45 See Margaret Davies, 'The Ethos of Pluralism' (2005) 27 *Sydney Law Review* 87; Emmanuel Melissaris, 'The More the Merrier? A New Take on Legal Pluralism' (2004) 13 *Social & Legal Studies* 57.

mind from a legal anthropologist who talks about legal pluralism. People using the concept also have different motivations and purposes. Some are socio-legal theorists interested in developing a sophisticated analytical approach to contemporary legal forms, some are avowed social scientists dedicated to working out a social scientific approach to law, some are critical theorists who invoke the notion as a means to delegitimise or decentre state law, and some are seeking a useful way of framing complicated situations for their own political purposes. The literature invoking the notion of legal pluralism covers a broad spectrum, from postmodernism, to autopoiesis, to human rights, to feminist approaches to customary law, to international trade, and much more. Under these circumstances, miscommunication and confusion over the notion is inevitable.

No purpose would be served by rehashing the full debate over legal pluralism,[46] which has been written about elsewhere in detail.[47] Instead I will summarily identify the core problem it suffers from. Social scientists who tout the concept of legal pluralism emphatically proclaim that law is not limited to official state legal institutions. To the contrary, they insist, law is found in the ordering of social groups of all kinds. Taking this position necessarily requires that legal pluralists provide some basis by which to determine or delimit what is and what isn't law. The question 'what is law?', however, has never been resolved, despite innumerable efforts by legal theorists and social scientists.

Attempts to define law for social scientific purposes fall into two basic categories.[48] One approach defines law in terms of the maintenance of normative order within a social group. Since every social group has normative regulation, every social group has 'law', in this understanding, regardless of the presence or absence of state legal institutions. The pioneer of this approach was Bronislaw Malinowski, whose *Crime and Custom in Savage Society* is a classic of anthropology. Law among the Trobriand of Melanesia, according to Malinowski, was not to be found in 'central authority, codes, courts, and constables,'[49] but rather in social relations. As he put it, 'The binding forces of Melanesian civil law are to be found in the concatenation of the obligations, in the fact that they are

---

46 An excellent overview of the debate can be found in Gordon R Woodman, 'Ideological Combat and Social Observation: Recent Debate About Legal Pluralism' (1998) 42 *Journal of Legal Pluralism* 21.

47 Brian Z Tamanaha, 'An Non-Essentialist Version of Legal Pluralism' (2000) 27 *Journal of Law and Society* 296; Brian Z Tamanaha, 'The Folly of the 'Social Scientific' Concept of Legal Pluralism' (1993) 20 *Journal of Law and Society* 192. A few readers have suggested that my second article repudiates the analysis of the first article. That is not correct, as the second article makes clear. They have different targets and differing emphases, but the analysis is consistent. The early article criticised a specific position as misconceived: that there is (or can be) a single, objective social scientific understanding of law, upon which to build legal pluralism. The later article incorporates this conclusion to develop a different approach to legal pluralism that does not resort to any single concept of law. There is one clear difference between the articles, however. The initial article had a regrettably strident tone that was not conducive to a sober academic discussion of the issues. For this I apologise.

48 See Brian Z Tamanaha, 'An Analytical Map of Social Scientific Approaches to the Concept of Law' (1995) 15 *Oxford Journal of Legal Studies* 501.

49 Bronislaw Malinowski, *Crime and Custom in Savage Society* (1926) at 14.

arranged into chains of mutual services, a give and take extending over long periods of time and covering wide aspects of interests and activity.'[50] The problem with this approach was noted by legal anthropologist Sally Falk Moore: 'the conception of law that Malinowski propounded was so broad that it was virtually indistinguishable from the study of the obligatory aspect of all social relationships.'[51]

A second approach, found in the work of Max Weber and Adamson Hoebel, defines law in terms of public institutionalised enforcement of norms.[52] Perhaps the most widely invoked version of this approach is legal theorist H L A Hart's notion of law as the combination of primary and secondary rules (a primary set of rules that apply to conduct, and a secondary set of rules that determine which primary rules are valid, and how rules are created and applied).[53] Although this approach is not explicitly tied to state law, it was derived by Weber, Hoebel and Hart by stripping the state law model to its core elements. There are two basic problems with this approach. First, many institutions enforce norms, and there is no uncontroversial way to distinguish which are 'public' and which are not, which runs the danger of swallowing all forms of institutionalised norm enforcement under the label law. Second, some societies, at least historically, lacked institutionalised norm enforcement. According to this definition, such societies do not have law — as Hart asserted about primitive societies[54] — which is unacceptable to scholars who insist that all societies have law.

Although each approach has adherents, each also has flaws that lead some to reject it. Thus legal pluralists cannot agree on the fundamental issue: 'What is law?' This issue, is should be noted, has never been resolved in legal philosophy, and there are compelling reasons to think that it is incapable of resolution,[55] so legal pluralists cannot be blamed for this failure. Nonetheless, having this unresolved issue at its very core places the notion of legal pluralism on a tenuous footing. The problem is not just that there is a plurality of legal pluralisms because accounts of legal pluralism adopt different definitions of law; a further difficulty is that the definitions adopted in legal pluralist studies almost uniformly suffer from the same problem Malinowski did — they are unable to distinguish 'law' from other forms of normative order.

John Griffiths, whose 1986 article 'What is Legal Pluralism?' is *the* seminal piece in the field, set forth the concept of law that is adopted by most legal pluralists (at least among anthropologists and sociologists). After considering and dismissing several alternatives as inadequate, Griffiths argued that Sally Falk Moore's concept of the 'semi-autonomous social field' — social fields that have

---

50 Id at 76.
51 Sally Falk Moore, *Law as Process: an Anthropological Approach* (1978) at 220.
52 See Tamanaha, above n48 at 506–508 (describing Weber's and Hoebel's approaches).
53 H L A Hart, *The Concept of Law* (1961) at 89–96.
54 Id at 89–91.
55 For and explanation of why this issue cannot be resolved, see Brian Z Tamanaha, 'Law' in Stanley Katz, (ed), *Oxford International Encyclopedia of Legal History* (forthcoming, 2008); Tamanaha, above n48.

the capacity to produce and enforce rules[56] — is the best way to identify and delimit law for the purposes of legal pluralism.[57] There are many rule generating fields in society, hence there are many legal orders in society, including the family, corporations, factories, sports leagues, and indeed just about any social arena with social regulation. In another important and often cited early theoretical exploration of legal pluralism, published in 1983, Marc Galanter asserted: 'By indigenous law I refer not to some diffuse folk consciousness, but to concrete patterns of social ordering to be found in a variety of institutional settings — in universities, sports leagues, housing developments, hospitals.'[58]

The problem with this approach, as Sally Engle Merry noted almost 20 years ago, is that 'calling all forms of ordering that are not state law by the term law confounds the analysis.'[59] Merry asked: 'Where do we stop speaking of law and find ourselves simply describing social life?'[60] Galanter was aware of this difficulty at the very outset: 'Social life is full of regulation. Indeed it is a vast web of overlapping and reinforcing regulation. How then can we distinguish "indigenous law" from social life generally?'[61] Legal pluralists have struggled valiantly but unsuccessfully to overcome this problem. In an article canvassing almost 20 years of debate over the conceptual underpinnings of legal pluralism, Gordon Woodman, the long time co-editor of the *Journal of Legal Pluralism*, conceded that legal pluralists are unable to identify a clear line to separate legal from non-legal normative orders. 'The conclusion,' Woodman observed, 'must be that law covers a continuum which runs from the clearest form of state law through to the vaguest forms of informal social control.'[62] Similarly, Johns Griffiths asserted that 'all social control is *more* or *less* legal.'[63] Consistent with this view, a recent theorist on legal pluralism suggested that law can be found in 'day-to-day human encounters such as interacting with strangers on a public street, waiting in lines, and communicating with subordinates or superiors.'[64]

Nothing prohibits legal pluralists from viewing law in this extraordinarily expansive, idiosyncratic way, although common sense protests against it. When understood in these terms, just about every form of norm governed social interaction is law. Hence, we are swimming, or drowning, in legal pluralism.

One might argue against this approach to legal pluralism that law is just one type of normative or regulatory ordering, whereas this approach reverses the relationship to hold that all normative or regulatory orders are types of 'law.'[65]

---

56 Sally Falk Moore, 'Law and Social Change: The Semi-Autonomous Social Field as an Appropriate Subject of Study' (1973) 7 *Law & Society Review* 719.
57 John Griffiths, 'What is Legal Pluralism?' (1986) 24 *Journal of Legal Pluralism and Unofficial Law* 1 at 38.
58 Marc Galanter, 'Justice in Many Rooms: Courts, Private Ordering, and Indigenous Law' (1981) 19 *Journal of Legal Pluralism* 1 at 17–18.
59 Merry, above n43 at 878.
60 Ibid.
61 Galanter, above n58 at 18.
62 Woodman, above n46 at 45.
63 Griffiths, above n57 at 39 (emphasis in original).
64 Berman, above n40 at 505.

This observation raises the suspicion that the recent discovery of 'legal pluralism' mainly involves putting a new label on the old idea that society is filled with a multiplicity of normative orders or regulatory orders. Indeed, why should we call this *legal* pluralism rather than, what seems to be more fitting, *normative* pluralism or *regulatory* pluralism? Prominent legal pluralist Boaventura de Sousa Santos posed this question, then bluntly and without further elaboration responded: 'Why not?'[66] The short answer is that to view law in this manner is confusing, counter-intuitive, and hinders a more acute analysis of the many different forms of social regulation involved.

Although there are additional complexities to the concept of legal pluralism, those are the fundamental issues, and they have been known for decades. Rather than continue with the debate, I will briefly return to John Griffiths, for his intellectual progress over the years is instructive. A sophisticated theorist, Griffiths was for more than two decades the most strident champion of legal pluralism. In 'What is Legal Pluralism?', the most frequently cited article in legal pluralist literature, Griffiths flatly declared that 'Legal pluralism is the fact.' '"Legal pluralism" is the name of a social state of affairs and it is a characteristic which can be predicated of a social group. It is not the name of a doctrine or a theory or an ideology.'[67]

Yet from the very outset Griffiths was faced with an inconvenient thorn in the heart of his theory. Sally Falk Moore, who created the notion of the semi-autonomous social field ('SASF') that Griffiths adopted to identify law,[68] refused to apply the label 'law' to her own concept. Instead she proposed the unwieldy term 'reglementation', which, understandably, did not catch on. In a 2001 essay reflecting upon the past 'Fifty Turbulent Years' in legal anthropology, Moore laid out Griffiths's account of legal pluralism without mentioning that he adopted her influential idea at the core of his approach. She then issued this criticism:

> Following Griffiths, some writers now take legal pluralism to refer to the whole aggregate of governmental and non-governmental norms of social control, without any distinction drawn as to their source. However, for many purposes this agglomeration has to be disaggregated. For reasons of both analysis and policy, distinctions must be made that identify the provenance of rules and controls (Moore 1973, 1978, 1998, 1999, 2000).[69]

This criticism matches Moore's objection to Malinowski's conception of law, quoted earlier, for failing to distinguish among different forms of social regulation.

---

65 See Tamanaha, 'The Folly of Social Scientific Approaches to the Concept of Legal Pluralism', above n47.
66 de Sousa Santos, above n39 at 115.
67 Griffiths, above n57 at 4 and 12.
68 Id at 38 ('The self-regulation of a semi-autonomous social field can be regarded as more or less "legal" according to the degree to which it is differentiated... But differentiated or not, 'law' is present in every "semi-autonomous social field," and since *every* society contains many such fields, legal pluralism is a universal feature of social organization').
69 Sally Falk Moore, 'Certainties Undone: Fifty Turbulent Years of Legal Anthropology, 1949–1999' in Sally Falk Moore (ed), *Law and Anthropology: A Reader* (2005) at 357 (this chapter was reprinted from an article of the same name published in 2001).

Ironically, Griffiths invoked her SASF in legal pluralism in a manner that led to the same problematic result.

In support of her criticism of Griffiths's approach to legal pluralism, the first publication (1973) Moore cites is the very article that sets out her SASF,[70] and the second publication (1978) she cites is her important book, *Law as Process*,[71] which elaborates on and applies the SASF in various contexts (and which contains her criticism of Malinowski). Although politely and obliquely delivered, her implicit message repudiating Griffiths's use of her concept to identify 'law' is unmistakable. In case anyone missed the point, in the next paragraph Moore identified several social phenomena highlighted by legal pluralism, including this: 'the way in which the state is interdigitated (internally and externally) with non-governmental, semi-autonomous social fields which generate their own (*non-legal*) obligatory norms to which they can induce or coerce compliance'.[72] Recall that under Griffiths's account, the norms of the semi-autonomous social field *are law*. By pointedly injecting the qualifier 'non-legal' in this passage, Moore firmly demurs.

The story of the troubled concept of legal pluralism does not end there. In a 2005 article discussing legal pluralism, John Griffiths made a stunning series of assertions:

> In the intervening years, further reflection on the concept of law has led me to the conclusion that the word 'law' could better be abandoned altogether for purposes of theory formation in sociology of law.... It also follows from the above considerations that the expression "legal pluralism" can and should be reconceptualized as "normative pluralism" or "pluralism in social control."[73]

What makes these statements stunning is Griffiths's pre-eminent role in developing and promoting the concept of legal pluralism, often with an air of absolute confidence. In an article 10 years ago, for example, Griffiths wrote that law everywhere 'is fundamentally pluralist in character,' and 'anyone who does not [accept this] is simply out of date and can safely be ignored.'[74] Today Griffiths admits — to his credit as an intellectual — that his conception of legal pluralism was a mistake. He finally became convinced that it is impossible to adequately conceptualise law for social scientific purposes.[75] Griffiths now agrees with critics that what he previously identified as 'legal pluralism' is better conceptualised as 'normative pluralism'.

---

70 Moore, above n56.
71 Moore, above n51.
72 Moore, above n69 at 358 (emphasis added). Moore follows this statement with a footnote that makes an oblique reference to Griffiths's use of her concept.
73 John Griffiths, 'The Idea of Sociology of Law and its Relation to Law and to Sociology' (2005) 8 *Current Legal Issues* 49 at 63–64.
74 John Griffiths, 'Legal Pluralism and the Theory of Legislation — With Special Reference to the Regulation of Euthanasia' in Hanne Petersen & Henrik Zahle, *Legal Polycentricity: Consequences of Pluralism in Law* (1995) at 201.
75 For helping him come to this conclusion, Griffiths cites an article written in Dutch by G van den Bergh, and two of my articles, 'An Analytical Map of Social Scientific Approaches to the Concept of Law', above n48, and 'The Folly of the Social Scientific Concept of Legal Pluralism', above n47.

In light of these developments, the concept of legal pluralism stands in a peculiar state. The originator of the concept most widely adopted by legal pluralists to identify law, Sally Falk Moore, rejects this application of her idea. The most ardent promoter of the concept of legal pluralism for more than two decades, John Griffiths, now renounces legal pluralism. Nonetheless, the notion of legal pluralism continues to spread. Legal pluralist scholars continue to incorporate Moore's SASF to identify law, and continue to rely upon Griffiths's analysis, notwithstanding their explicit objections.

What makes the notion of legal pluralism so irresistible, despite its irresolvable conceptual problems, is the fact that diverse, competing and overlapping legal orders in different types and forms appear to be everywhere and multiplying. Griffiths was right that legal pluralism is a fact. Where Griffiths went wrong, he now recognises,[76] was in thinking that law could be formulated as a scientific category. Law is a 'folk concept', that is, law is what people within social groups have come to see and label as 'law'.[77] It could not be formulated in terms of a single scientific category because over time and in different places people have seen law in different terms. State law is currently the paradigm example of law, but at various times and places, including today, people have considered as law: international law; customary law; versions of religious law; the *lex mercatoria*; the *ius commune*; natural law and more.[78] These various manifestations of law do not all share the same basic characteristics — beyond the claim to represent legitimate normative authority — which means they cannot be reduced to a single set of elements for social scientific purposes.

Fortunately, it is not necessary to construct a social scientific conception of law in order to frame and study legal pluralism. As proof of this point, notice that the first part of this paper extensively elaborated on situations of legal pluralism in the medieval period and during colonisation without positing a definition of law. The exploration in the first part avoided the conceptual problem by accepting as 'legal' whatever was identified as legal by the social actors, as just described. Legal pluralism exists whenever social actors identify more than one source of 'law' within a social arena. The final part of this paper will demonstrate the utility of this simple approach by laying out a framework that highlights many of the important and interesting features of situations of contemporary legal pluralism while avoiding the aforementioned conceptual problems.

4. *A Framework for Legal Pluralism*

Six systems of normative ordering will be sketched, followed by comments on a series of issues relating to these systems and their interaction. The discussion will focus on matters highlighted in legal pluralist studies.

---

76 Griffiths, above n73 at 62.
77 This idea is extensively developed in Tamanaha, above n26.
78 For a more developed argument to this effect, see Tamanaha, above n47.

A. Six Systems of Normative Ordering in Social Arenas[79]

When the notion of legal pluralism is invoked, it is almost invariably the case that the social arena at issue has multiple active sources of normative ordering. The forms of normative ordering commonly discussed in studies of legal pluralism can be roughly separated in the following six categories: (i) official legal systems; (ii) customary/cultural normative systems; (iii) religious/cultural normative systems; (iv) economic/capitalist normative systems; (v) functional normative systems; (vi) community/cultural normative systems.

Official or positive legal systems characteristically are linked to an institutionalised legal apparatus of some kind; they are manifested in legislatures, enforcement agencies, tribunals; they give rise to powers, rights, agreements, criminal sanctions, and remedies. This category encompasses the entire panoply of whatever is typically regarded as law-related or legal, ranging from traffic laws to human rights. The modern period is marked by a vast expansion, proliferation, penetration, and multiplication of official legal systems, which social theorists (prominently Jürgen Habermas) have labelled the 'juridification' of the life world. Official legal systems can coexist in an uncoordinated fashion in a given social arena with different sources and institutions that can conflict with one another. Citizens in the EU, for example, are subject to laws and regulations generated locally (municipality or township), at district or state levels, at national levels, at the level of the EU, and internationally. These versions of official law are not completely reconciled with one another, and many are based upon separate institutional structures with potentially conflicting jurisdictions and norms.

The other five categories — customary/cultural, religious/cultural, economic/capitalist, functional, and community/cultural — are systems of normative ordering that are distinct from the official legal systems.

Customary normative systems include shared social rules and customs, as well a social institutions and mechanisms, from reciprocity, to dispute resolution tribunals, to councils of traditional leaders. In some locations the terms 'indigenous law' or 'traditional law' are also utilised. These terms (and their local translations) are labels usually invoked in post-colonial societies, and have limited application to other contexts. The very notions of 'customary' or 'traditional' or 'indigenous' were creations of and reactions to colonisation and post-colonisation, in which the norms and institutions of indigenous societies were marked (for various purposes) as distinct from the transplanted norms and systems of the colonisers. In my use of the terms, these are *not sociological notions*, but rather constructed labels and categories created for specific purposes in the circumstances of colonisation and its aftermath. Once created, these labels have been carried over and continue to the present in some form of coexistence with (or within) official legal systems.

---

79 I use a deliberately bland term 'social arena' for the purpose of identifying a given area of study. It is an empty framing device that can be defined in any way, according to any criteria, that a particular researcher desires. An entire nation can constitute a social arena, as can a local community, or a transnational network of business people.

Religious normative systems are in some societies an aspect of and inseparable from customary normative systems, and both can be considered aspects of culture (hence they share the term 'cultural'); yet religion merits separate mention for the reason that it is often seen by people within a social arena as a special and distinct aspect of their existence. Religions typically are oriented toward the metaphysical realm, and religious precepts usually carry great weight and significance for believers within a social arena. Certain bodies of norms are seen as specifically religious in origin and orientation, often set out in written texts (Bible, Koran, Torah), commentaries, and edicts; formal religious institutions as well as informal mechanisms exist with norm enforcing (as well as other) functions.

Although customary and religious sources of normative ordering are usually seen in terms distinct from and broader than official legal systems, they also can contain a subset of norms that have specifically 'legal' status, in two different senses: (1) through recognition by the official legal system; or (2) on their own terms. In the first sense, many official legal systems explicitly recognise and incorporate customary norms and institutions, and religious norms and institutions. Many post-colonial state legal systems, for example, acknowledge and enforce customary rules and practices in connection with marriage, divorce, inheritance, and other family related issues. A number of countries create or recognise the jurisdiction of Islamic Courts on various subjects, and a number officially recognise the Sharia as binding law. At the extreme, in full blown theocracies the official legal system will be inseparable from religious law (they are one and the same system in many respects). In the second sense, viewed as 'legal' on their own terms, certain customary systems have bodies of what the members consider 'customary law,' entirely apart from whether the norms and institutions so identified are recognised as such by the official legal order. Similarly, certain religious norms and institutions are recognised by believers as having independent 'legal' status. 'Natural law principles' in the Catholic tradition are an example.

Economic/capitalist normative systems consist of the range of norms and institutions that constitute and relate to capitalist production and market transactions within social arenas. This ranges from informal norms that govern continuing relations in business communities (including reciprocity, and norms that discourage resort to official legal institutions in situations of dispute), to norms governing instrumental relations, to standard contractual norms and practices, to private law-making in the form of codes of conduct, shared transnational commercial norms, arbitration institutions, and so forth, including shared beliefs about capitalism (like 'market imperatives'). Contemporary processes of economic globalisation carry along, and are carried by, these normative systems. Similar to customary and religious normative systems, many of these norms are not seen as 'legal' norms; a subset of these economic/capitalist norms and institutions are recognised and incorporated by official legal systems; while others are independently recognised as having 'legal' status. The so-called 'new *lex mercatoria*' — the body of law and institutions relating to transnational commercial transactions — is an example of this category.

Functional normative systems are organised and arranged in connection with the pursuit of a particular function, purpose or activity that goes beyond purely commercial pursuits. Universities, school systems, hospitals, museums, sports leagues, and the internet (as a network) are examples of functionally oriented normative systems, some operating locally, some nationally, and some transnational in reach. All possess some degree of autonomy and self-governance aimed at achieving the purpose for which they are constituted, all have regulatory capacities, all have internal ordering mechanisms, and all interact with official legal systems at various junctures. Often they have commercial aspects, and they can give rise to communities, but their particular functional orientation makes them distinctive and shapes their nature.

Community/cultural normative systems is the vaguest category of the five specified here. In general terms, it is an imagined identification by a group of a common way of life, usually tied to a common language and history and contained within geographical boundaries of some kind, but there can be 'communities' of interaction which exist purely on the internet comprised of people from around the world. At the local level, communities consist of thick, shared norms of interaction that constitute and characterise a way of life — including customs, habits, mores, and so forth — but at the broader level of the nation (or beyond) the bonds that constitute a community can be much thinner and mainly defined by a perceived identity. In its thinnest manifestation (which can nonetheless exert a powerful influence), the norms that bind and define the community may not be definite or reiterated enough to be considered a 'system' in the same sense that that applies to the other categories. Although the processes of globalisation have erased former boundaries in many ways, the very same globalising factors — by stimulating angst in populations about imminent threats to identity, self-governance, and economic opportunities — have also heightened the strength of group and individual identifications with communities. For example, the encroachment of regulations and rulings by the EU — the bureaucracy in Brussels and elsewhere — and the presence of large immigrant communities and populations within the cities with their own religions, languages, customs, moral views, lifestyles and food, have given new salience to local or national identities, to being English or Scottish, or French, or German or Dutch. The typical claim of community is to have some special connection (descriptive and prescriptive) to or entitlement to support by official state legal systems. Moreover, under certain circumstances communities can coincide with and be defined in religious or customary terms (or a combination of all three).

In many studies, the term 'legal pluralism' is used to characterise the interaction between competing and conflicting official legal systems or between an official legal system and one or more of the other normative systems. The interplay is complex and multisided. Once again, to forestall confusion and objections, it must be emphasised that these six groupings are rough labels used to mark off subjects and situations that repeatedly arise works about legal pluralism. No fundamental sociological or theoretical assertions are made about any of these categories. They overlap, there are borderline cases, different lines could have been drawn, and different categories could have been created. The value of this framework depends upon whether it offers a useful way to approach, study, and understand situations of legal pluralism. That is what the following will attempt to demonstrate.

B. Clashes among Normative Systems, and What Fuels Them

The six sources of normative ordering identified above typically make one or more of the following claims: they possess binding authority; they are legitimate; they have normative supremacy; and they have (or should have) control over matters within their scope. Owing to the dominant tenor of their claims to authority, these coexisting sources of normative ordering are poised to clash, particularly when their underlying norms and processes are inconsistent. These clashes can be magnified because people are often genuinely committed to the norms, purposes, or identity of the system. Such clashes are among the most dynamic aspects of legal pluralism. Some of these systems anticipate that they potentially interact with other systems, and sometimes try to account for this with provisions like conflict rules or choice of law rules; but also often they are silent about interaction with other normative systems.

Clashes can exist *within* competing versions of each type of normative ordering — as when recognised human rights norms (one body of official law) are inconsistent with the norms of the state law system (another body of official law); and clashes can exist *between* coexisting normative systems — as when the norms of the official legal system conflict with customary or religious or community norms (whether labelled 'legal' or not). Various mechanisms exist to manage these clashes, which will be taken up shortly, but clashes often remain unresolved, manifested as latent or overt sources of conflict within the social arena.

These conflicts are commonly fuelled from two different sources. Groups or actors who benefit from, have a stake in, represent, or give rise to, the institutional structures of competing normative systems (ie state officials and legal professionals, tribal leaders, clergy, business people) will defend and exert the power of their particular system in situations of a clash, not only because of their genuine commitment to and belief in the system, but also because their interests, identities, status, and livelihoods are linked to it. Efforts to defend the power and integrity of each system *vis-a-vis* the others provide one source of conflict.

Individuals and groups within a social arena also drive conflict by strategic resort to sources of normative ordering in an effort to advance their individual or collective goals or vision. For example, women (and supportive NGOs) have sought redress or protection from official legal norms as a way to escape or combat oppressive customary normative systems (ie female circumcision, bride burning). Business people create or resort to their own dispute resolution institutions (private arbitration) when they view the official legal institutions as untrustworthy, too slow, too adversarial, or too expensive for their purposes.

Many people within these social arenas are aware of three essential aspects that drive the dynamic: they are aware that the coexisting normative systems make competing claims to authority; they are aware that each has some capacity to exert power within a social arena; and they are aware of the inconsistency of their respective substantive norms and processes. These factors provide reasons for social actors to actively exploit situations of legal pluralism in the furtherance of group and individual aims. People who are truly committed to one set of norms or institutions, moreover, may undertake to defend or expand their system against others. In these ways, the presence of legal pluralism can promote or generate clashes over and through law.

Given the above factors, a useful way to observe clashes and their implications is to maintain a dual focus: on the systems themselves (including institutional actors), observing how they interact with one another in situations of plurality; and on strategic actors in social arenas characterised by plurality, observing how they invoke and respond to the presence of multiple normative systems.

C. Power Differentials between Normative Systems

Situations involving a clash between normative systems bring to the surface the fact that they have different capacities to exert influence that vary depending upon subject matters, regions, and situations. In the absence of such clashes, limited efficacy or power can be concealed or pass unnoticed. Official state legal systems, for example, typically *claim* to possess a monopoly of legitimate coercion within the territory of the state. Only when the edicts of this system are ignored or openly defied by actors following an alternative normative system is the limited power of the state legal system exposed. In some instances this can break out into actual combat, as when the Islamic Courts in Mogadishu mounted an armed challenge (and initially routed) the official governmental system. More common are situations in which official legal norms that are contrary to prevailing customary or community norms remain dead letters without effect. In the absence of a sustained effort by official legal systems, which may lack the resources necessary to accomplish the desired change, the lived norms will continue to govern social action.

A broad generalisation can be made about the relative power of the official state legal systems in developed and developing countries. In developed countries, the official state legal system is highly differentiated (legislatures, police, prosecutors, judges), with entrenched legal institutions supported by a well-trained legal profession and a long-standing legal tradition. Moreover, a legal culture exists in which government officials and the public feel some obligation — out of normative commitment, or owing to a fear of sanction — to abide by the dictates of the official state legal system. These factors enhance the power of official legal systems to achieve their objectives. The official state legal systems in many developing countries, by contrast, are less differentiated, with less entrenched legal institutions and a less well-trained legal profession and a shallower official legal tradition. The populace can be wary of the official legal system, often transplanted from elsewhere through colonisation (often kept in the coloniser's language), or voluntarily borrowed, and sometimes identified with the elite or with a particular subgroup in society. The power of the official legal system is commensurably weaker. In these latter situations, customary, religious and community systems may be more entrenched, have deeper roots, and have a greater role in day-to-day social life.

Power differentials also exist amongst official legal systems, for example, as between state legal institutions and international or transnational legal institutions. Their relative strengths depend upon the circumstances. International legal dictates can be resisted or ignored by well developed state legal systems as well as by less developed state legal systems, although the latter might be more susceptible to coercive attempts to achieve compliance. A more powerful nation would be less concerned about the imposition of economic or other sanctions than would a less powerful nation, for example.

Whatever the particular mix, official legal institutions seldom are able to dictate their terms or entirely have their way in a clash with other systems. Customary norms, religious norms, functional norms, and community norms can be powerful and resilient to change. And competing normative systems can align with others (combining their respective powers) in situations of conflict. Coexisting normative systems form a part of one another's environment, which must be taken account of, anticipated, responded to, and dealt with.

D. Two Basic Forms of Socio-Political Heterogeneity (Group and Individual)

Social-political heterogeneity, which usually accompanies legal pluralism, takes two basic forms: group based and individual based. A *group-based* heterogeneity occurs when a social arena consists of a number of discrete groups, often differentiated by language, religion, ethnicity, and culture, or sometimes by clans, factors which can exist in various combinations. Often these groups make up distinct communities (as identified by members and outsiders). Sometimes there is a majority group and one or more minority groups; sometimes a number of groups coexist with no single group having a majority. Often they are physically segregated (occupying distinct regions or distinct neighbourhoods in urban areas); sometimes they are also segregated by occupation. A major source of this is the movement of people within nations and across borders, a constant of human history, though accelerating in the raw number of people involved in recent decades (especially in the movement from rural to urban areas).

A crucial factor in situations of group-based heterogeneity is whether one (or more) group disproportionately controls or influences the government and/or the official legal systems within a given social arena. Groups may have differential opportunities to occupy positions in government and in official legal systems. Where this is the case, there will be differences among the various groups and their members in their resort to and identification with the government and the official state law. In these situations, the government and official law can be seen not as the law of everyone, but as co-opted by and representing the interests of whichever group(s) controls it.

An *individual based* heterogeneity exists in social arenas that contain individuals oriented to Western liberal norms coexisting with individuals oriented to non-Western customary or religious normative systems. This combination is typical of large urban areas both in the West and in non-Western countries.

Many social arenas combine both kinds of heterogeneity, with rural areas having group-based heterogeneity, and urban areas having one or both types. In Western cities with large immigrant populations, immigrants tend to live in segregated neighbourhoods; within these communities, some hold on to the language, values and religions of their land of origin, while others prefer the Western values of the surrounding society. In large non-Western cities, there are immigrants from the West who live scattered about or in expatriate enclaves (creating a group), as well as locals who have been exposed to and prefer Western ways, and there are large groups that maintain their customary or religious or community norms and orientations.

The spread of capitalist economic normative systems and imperatives, as will be indicated in greater detail shortly, is reshaping broad swaths of the world, particularly urban areas. Its effect is to (on different axes) increase, and simultaneously lessen, heterogeneity. The increase in heterogeneity is the result of work opportunities that prompt people to emigrate abroad or to migrate internally to cities in ever larger numbers, where they settle with familiar groups and bring along their cultural and religious norms, which differ from those of neighbouring groups or communities. The decrease in heterogeneity takes place because engaging in these economic activities, and living in large cities, exposes immigrants and migrants to a new set of workplace (capitalist) norms and living arrangements that they must conform to. These new situations disrupt former family and community ties and norms, often completely altering the rhythm and organisation of social life (both for the new migrants and for the places left behind). Immigrants and migrants living in large urban centres are also directly exposed to and bombarded with Western norms carried by the media and commercial enterprises. They are also exposed to the ways of life of other immigrant communities who live in adjoining communities or in the broader society.

Both kinds of heterogeneity play out in various ways in legal pluralism (they are sources of pluralism), which require attention. It is also important to recognise another dominant characteristic of these areas: the *hybridity* and *fluidity* of groups and individuals. In a manner of speaking, they absorb aspects of their environment into their respective identities. The fact that groups and individuals interact in heterogeneous environments inevitably affects both the groups and the individuals, building something new in group and individual identities even as the old identities remain recognisable. Although it is useful to distinguish forms of heterogeneity, group and individual identities are not static or discrete wholes, but are internally diverse and in a constant state of change.

E. *Relations and Strategies between and among Systems in Situations of Clash*

In each situation of legal pluralism, tensions arise among coexisting normative systems that create the potential for uneasy coexistence, supportive alignments or clashes. The main focus here will be on clashes in connection with the official state legal system. A common arrangement, when coexisting communities exist, is for the official state legal system to assume a stance (or posture) of neutrality with respect to the various communities (and religions), allowing a degree of autonomy to each. This is typical in liberal societies. Another common alignment (including in liberal societies) is for there to be an identity of some kind between the dominant community and the state legal system. Working from these baselines, clashes and accommodations are made between and among other competing normative systems. Sometimes state legal systems are oblivious to or purposely ignore the competing normative systems — and are taken by surprise when legal initiatives fail. When they are aware of the clash and aim to deal with it in some way, official state legal systems utilise a number of strategies, ranging from permissive to prohibitive.

It is not unusual for a state legal system to explicitly condemn or disallow a contrary customary or religious or community norm or institution, but take no action to repress it. This may be because the legal officials recognise that they lack the power to combat it, or because they are sympathetic to it, yet are pressured by some group inside or outside the social arena to officially (or symbolically) condemn it. In the latter case, the officials will make a show of support while subtly resisting efforts to invoke the state legal system against it (foot dragging by officials, or erecting barriers to actors who wish to invoke the official legal apparatus against the conflicting system). A similarly ambivalent strategy, coming from the opposite direction, is for the official legal system to formally 'endorse' the competing system (for political reasons), yet do nothing to support it, or even affirmatively (though not openly) work to undermine it.

Another common strategy is for the state legal system to absorb competing systems in some way. A common method is to explicitly incorporate or recognise customary, religious, economic or community norms, or to explicitly recognise and lend some support (financial or coercive) to existing customary, religious, economic or community institutions. An example of this in the economic context is when legal systems recognise the validity of private arbitration decisions, or even encourage (or compel) parties to resort to private arbitration. Official legal systems recognise or absorb other norms and systems for a variety of reasons. The private alternative may provide a useful function or service, legal officials may genuinely believe in the validity and legitimacy of the alternative norms and institutions, or political benefits may follow from embracing it, or it may simply be too powerful for the official legal system to supplant. Absorbing the competing system is also a way to control or neutralise or influence its activities — by paying the participants, providing them incentives to conform, or by situating the absorbed institution in a hierarchy that accords the official legal system final say.

A third alternative in situations of clash is for the state legal system is to make aggressive efforts to suppress the contrary norms and institutions — declaring the latter to be illegal, then working to eliminate them. These situations raise a direct test of the relative power of the competing systems. When the competing system is longstanding or deeply entrenched, the state legal system is confronted with a formidable task, which it often falls short of achieving. The barriers against success by the state legal system are also heightened when financial incentives and consequences are tied to the conflicting system, as occurs with economic normative systems.

A clash between or among coexisting official legal systems within a given social arena can also take place, as indicated earlier, and plays out in a variety of ways. An increasingly common example of this kind of conflict is when individuals or groups file complaints in a human rights court in an effort to invalidate or alter state law norms or practices. Official conflict of law rules can be utilised to mediate these clashes. Clashes can be resolved through political compromises arranged by their respective institutional authorities. In some situations the competing official legal authorities will ignore one another, or explicitly refuse to honour their determinations (as when states refuse to honour rulings of the World Court). One official legal system may acknowledge the contrary official legal system and accept its findings (begrudgingly or enthusiastically). Sometimes they will face off in a direct clash which continues unresolved. Sometimes the more powerful official legal system simply imposes its will on the other through superior raw economic or military or political power.

Although the primary focus of this discussion has been on clashes between state legal systems and other normative systems or between competing official legal systems, clashes also take place between and among coexisting, conflicting customary systems, religious systems, functional systems, economic systems, or community systems. There can be, in a given social field, more than one official legal system, more than one customary system, more than one religious system, more than one economic system, more than one functional system, and more than one community system, all of which can overlap, coincide and clash, as the case may be. Moreover, market imperatives — economic/capitalist normative systems — may penetrate the social arena along a variety of axes, consistent with or contrary to the norms of customary, religious, functional, and community systems. The potential combinations, mixes and matches, are limitless.

To avoid a misunderstanding, a corrective reminder must be injected at this point. The above discussion emphasises potential *clashes* owing to the presence of overlapping inconsistent norms and processes. As several of the points made above indicate, however, inconsistency does not necessarily lead to a clash. In some situations the inconsistent legal and/or normative systems may exist side-by-side without overt conflict; people within the systems and the social arena may be aware of the inconsistencies but prefer to avoid or suppress potential conflicts. In some situations, despite potential inconsistencies, the coexisting systems may actually support or bolster one another. The private arbitration tribunals of the *lex mercatoria*, for example, constitute an avoidance of state legal systems, yet state legal systems bolster this putative rival every time judges pay deference to or enforce arbitration decisions. Despite their many differences in norms and orientation, to offer another example, customary law regimes receive essential support from state legal systems that recognise them, and the state legal systems that do so in turn benefit by enhancing their legitimacy in the eyes of the populace as well as by demonstrating their superior power through the very act of granting recognition to customary law. Thus, while the emphasis in this discussion focuses on clashes, what results may also be a complementary coexistence, both from the standpoint of the coexisting systems and from the standpoint of strategic actors within situations of legal pluralism.

Owing to the complexity and variety of these situations, few generalisations beyond the above statements can be offered about interactions and strategies that arise in clashes between coexisting normative systems. Four tentative assertions will be offered, the first one relating to the interaction among the systems, and the final three relating to the choices made by strategic actors to invoke the systems.

The first assertion is that, riding on the tidal wave of economic globalisation, the most powerful contemporary impetus, momentum, and penetration of new norms is taking place through the economic/capitalist normative system. Capitalism and markets — in conjunction with the massive transfers of population worldwide from non-Western countries to Western countries and from rural to urban areas — are remaking broad areas of social life, often with the support of official legal systems (state and others).

The second assertion is that when a clash between normative systems takes place, strategic actors within that arena will seek to enlist the endorsement or support of existing *official legal systems*, to, if possible, lend legitimacy, resources, and coercion to their cause. In many situations, official legal systems possess enhanced institutionalised support and symbolic authority. Where there are coexisting official legal systems, those engaged in the conflict will resort to the official legal system that aligns with their cause. Women's rights advocacy groups may, for example, invoke human rights claims against customary or religious norms; in response, customary or religious advocates will invoke official legal norms that recognise the validity or worth of customary or religious norms. The main exception to this generalisation is that parties might not resort to a particular official legal system when they protest against its claim to authority in that arena; situations of this sort range from traditional leaders who dispute the authority of state law over certain matters, to organised separatist movements that are fighting the state politically and militarily.

The third assertion is that important factors that affect individuals and groups in the strategic choices they make in situations of legal pluralism are the 'distance' (geographical and cultural) and other barriers (information, expense and delay) that exist in connection with each system. To invoke official legal systems often requires information and access to legal professionals; possible barriers include high cost, lengthy delay, great distance from the official legal apparatus (requiring travel), and other forms of inaccessibility. Sometimes these can be overcome with the aid of other interested parties (supportive NGOs), but without this aid or intervention one may be effectively denied the ability to invoke an official legal system. Even individuals and groups who possess the necessary resources may nonetheless choose to bypass the official legal system (opting for private arbitration or informal resolution, for example) because the official legal system is too costly, unreliable, or unfair (inefficient, corrupt, or biased). Strategic choices are also influenced by the social or cultural proximity (or distance) of a given system: the more alien or inscrutable a legal or normative system appears, the less understandable and predictable it is, the less supportive it might appear, and consequently the less likely an individual or group is to invoke it. When the advantages offered by a particular system create a sufficient incentive to strategic actors, they may forge ahead notwithstanding the barriers.

The final assertion is that one must not assume that strategic actors pursuing their aims in situations of legal pluralism will consistently invoke or support the same official legal system or normative system over time. Long-term and short-term calculations are involved, especially for repeat players (like NGOs). Depending on the circumstances, for example: the same party may in one situation support customs in a contest with state law, while in another situation invoke state law against customs; a business entity may routinely utilise private arbitration to handle disputes, but after a painful arbitration loss it may seek recourse to a state legal system, contesting the legitimacy of that particular decision or the entire arbitration system. Repeat players often choose not to challenge adverse decisions, however. Purely strategic actors will be consistent in legally and normatively plural situations only when behaving in that fashion advances their overall interests, otherwise the course of action in each instance is decided based upon that particular configuration.

In closing, to correct against a misimpression created by the above emphasis, it must be reiterated that many actors in these situations are not driven only by strategic calculations. Considerations of loyalty, principle, familiarity, consistency, institution building, identity, tradition and other such factors also influence the decisions and conduct of individuals and groups in situations of legal pluralism.

F. *Common Types of Fundamental Orientation Clashes*

The preceding section addressed clashes between coexisting legal and normative systems, and the conduct of actors within these situations. This section elaborates on clashes at a higher level of abstraction: on clashes in fundamental normative or value orientation, rather than as specific systems. Only four major orientation clashes will be identified (not an exhaustive list).

(i) *Liberal (Individualist) versus Non-Liberal (Non-Individualist) Cultural Norms*

This is one of the most fecund sources of legal pluralist clashes around the world. Many official legal systems, especially those derived through transplantation from the West, enact liberal norms that protect individual autonomy, privacy, conscience, bodily integrity, liberty, formal equality, legal protections against state power and so forth. Most human rights norms fall into this category (though not all are exclusively liberal). Cultural and religious norms and practices that have non-liberal orientations are, almost by definition, different from liberal norms. While difference does not necessarily mean they conflict, often a clash exists. The most commonly cited clashes surround the position and treatment of women, family related issues, and caste related issues — including child marriages, arranged marriages, divorce rights, inheritance rights, property rights, treatment of low caste and religious imposed punishments. A clash also shows up in the criminal law context: official legal systems with liberal orientations affix criminal responsibility (in determinations of guilt, as well as imposing punishment) on individuals, whereas many customary systems do so in more collective terms, taking into consideration broader contexts when evaluating actions, as well as family ties and responsibility. Broadly speaking, in liberal terms an individual commits a crime against society, whereas in non-liberal terms the wrongful action is sometimes seen as a disruption of relations within the community or between families or clans.

(ii) Capitalist/Market Norms and Requirements versus Customary, Religious, or Community Norms

Economic norms relating to contract, property and credit can be inconsistent with prevailing customary and religious norms. A well-known conflict of this sort arises from religious prohibitions against usury, which is inconsistent with modern banking practices of charging interests, although this has largely been reconciled through creative structuring of transactions (as occurs in Islamic societies to comply with the Sharia). Another problematic situation occurs in connection with property ownership. Many customary normative systems characterise property in collective terms (not held by a single person or set of people), they divide up rights over property in a variety of ways (use of the resources, rather than ownership of the land itself), and they do not buy and sell land; in many places, moreover, the identity of families, clans, and villages is integrally tied to the land. Capitalist economic practices, in contrast, require the ability to buy and sell real property, which is a valuable economic asset, especially for the purpose of serving as collateral for loans. Western banking requirements often do not readily recognise collective ownership or community use rights. In the course of economic development, owing to the clash between these two normative systems, cultural normative systems are increasingly giving way to economic requirements, with a multitude of direct and indirect social consequences.

(iii) Systems That Recognise or Draw a Sharp Separation between Public and Private Realms versus Those that Do Not

This difference is as an aspect of liberal systems, but it bears separate mention owing to its significance. Government and law in liberal societies are constructed upon sharp differentiations between the public and private realms. The government and law are, in some sense (at least in theory and aspiration), neutral presences within society which work for and represent the good of the whole. Occupants of government or legal positions recognise that public power is to be held and exercised for public purposes, and that public purposes are distinct from the private purposes and the interests of government officials and their particular families or groups, as well as distinct from specific customary or religious purposes. One may not, for example, exercise public power for private gain (solicit bribes, favour family and friends, advance private interests). Societies in which the government and law are seen as instruments of power available for personal or groups uses, or as an extension of the community, or are seen in terms inseparable from religion (as in theocracies), do not recognise a sharp public/private divide. The consequences of this difference in orientation are myriad.

(iv) Rule-Based Systems with Winners and Losers versus Consensual Systems Oriented toward Satisfactory Resolution

Both types of approaches involve the application of norms in situations or disruption or dispute — and they exist on a continuum rather than as antinomies — but the overarching orientation of each is different. This contrast typically arises between official legal systems and local customary systems, but it also shows up between official legal systems and business communities with repeat players who wish to maintain good relations. Official legal systems may also differ amongst themselves in the degree to which they are oriented toward applying rules in a manner that leads to winners or losers, versus finding a consensual resolution.

The orientation clashes identified in this section largely have their origins in the contrast between Western and traditional non-Western societies, which has been the focus of the legal pluralist literature produced by legal anthropologists. However, as indicated earlier, capitalism driven globalisation and a massive shift around the world of population from non-Western countries to Western countries and from rural to urban areas are remaking contemporary societies and cultures in innumerable ways. These changes will affect the frequency, significance, and reach of the clashes identified above. The consensual dispute resolution systems studied by legal anthropologists, for example, have often come from small communities with face to face interaction (though parallels exist in modern business networks); similarly, customary normative systems continue to exert the strongest influence in places (steadily diminishing in number) that have undergone limited penetration from modern economic systems, mass media, government institutions, and public education. The massive urban areas that serve as magnets to population around world, with populations in the millions, have pockets with survivals of customary normative systems, but increasingly the dominant normative organisation is economic and modern (though not necessarily liberal). Heterogeneity and hybridity, described earlier, are becoming normal. As these developments continue, the frequency, mix, and relative proportion of the above clashes will change, and new kinds of clashes may well emerge. Nothing is standing still.

5. *Closing Observations*

The longstanding vision of a uniform and monopolistic law that governs a community is plainly obsolete. The situations of normative and legal pluralism described in this article are not passing phenomena. The expansion of capitalism and the movement of people and ideas — within countries and between countries — is accelerating, increasing heterogeneity along multiple axes (while bringing homogeneity in the spheres of capitalist development). Barring an unforeseen calamity, the further spread and penetration of capitalism seems inexorable, bringing many transformative consequences for law, society, politics, and culture in its wake. Existing normative systems — the people who believe in them, the people who hold positions in them, and the interests that benefit from them — will fight to maintain their power and positions. People and groups in social arenas with coexisting, conflicting normative systems will, in the pursuit of their objectives, play these competing systems against one another. Sometimes these clashes can be reconciled. Sometimes they can be ignored. Sometimes they operate in a complementary fashion. But very often they will remain in conflict, with serious social and political ramifications. To acquire a complex understanding of these situations, one must always keep an eye on two foci: on the normative systems themselves (including the people who staff them) and how they exist and interact with one another, and on how strategic actors relate to, deal with, or respond to legally plural situations. That was the underlying approach followed in this article.

As in the medieval period, today there are coexisting, discrete legal orders that can overlap and clash, ranging from various official legal orders to the *lex mercatoria* and the Sharia. As in the colonial period, some legal orders within states are internally plural and diverse with complex combinations of transplanted and indigenous norms and systems. And globalisation is bringing another layer of supranational and international legal regimes, with the potential for directly affecting people no matter where they live.

When placed in historical context, it is apparent that the texture of legal pluralism is intimately connected to the activities and fate of state legal systems. Legal pluralism was a normal condition during the medieval period; after law was consolidated within state structures, legal pluralism was reduced in Western Europe just as it was being increased elsewhere through colonisation; now legal pluralism is multiplying once again as certain powers held by states are devolving on to other entities or morphing into different political or legal configurations.

Seeing contemporary legal pluralism in historical context, moreover, offers the potential to produce general insights about the growth over time of official legal systems (of various types) in terms of social and institutional differentiation and expansion; to produce insights about how these official legal systems interact with other normative systems circulating within society; and to produce insights about how strategic actors negotiate these complexes of coexisting normative systems. A point of general significance, for example, is suggested by the fact that scholars of the medieval period and scholars of law and colonisation independently made the same observation: that 'customary law' recognised by official legal systems does not necessarily match actual lived customs. To offer another example, in colonial Latin American people concerned about the treatment of native Indians invoked Catholic norms and institutions to challenge their treatment by local government in the much same way that advocates for women's rights today invoke human rights norms to challenge the legal rights of women in post-colonial countries. Patterns that emerge from such disparate contexts (in time and circumstances) promise to shed light on fundamental issues with respect to coexisting regulatory systems.

For those that study legal pluralism as a social phenomenon, a useful caution is in order. One must avoid falling into either of two opposite errors: the first error is to think that state law matters above all else (as legal scholars sometimes assume); the second error is to think that other legal or normative systems are parallel to state law (as sociologists and anthropologists sometimes assume). In each social arena, particular official legal systems and normative systems must be examined on their own terms to see what their relations with other normative systems are, to observe their respective capacities to exert power, and to see how they are being utilised or responded to by individuals and groups. Sometimes state law is very powerful, sometimes it is weak, but rarely is it completely irrelevant or lacking in features that distinguish it from other competing official legal or normative systems. State law is in a unique symbolic and institutional position that derives from the fact that it is *state* law — the state holds a unique (domestic and international) position in the contemporary political order. Furthermore, official state legal systems, at least those that function effectively, have a distinctive instrumental capacity that enables them to be utilised to engage in a broad (potentially unlimited) range of possible activities, and to pursue a broad range of possible goals or projects, which extends far beyond normative regulation.

The forgoing framework brings on the same canvass much of what is discussed by scholars interested in legal pluralism, including legal anthropologists and sociologists, legal comparativists, socio-legal theorists, and international lawyers. It accomplishes this without stumbling over the conceptual problems that have incessantly plagued the subject. The conceptual debates that have marked legal pluralism for decades have been structured around issues that could not be resolved, especially the issue 'What is law?' The primary theoretical lesson of this article is that it is unnecessary to resolve these debates to come to grips with legal pluralism. For those interested in studying law and society, what matters most is framing situations in ways that facilitate the observation and analysis of what appears to be interesting and important.

Name Index

Abrams, K. 44
Adams, Michael 221
Akerlof, George 271
Albert, Hans 226
Alchian, Armen A. 227
Alexy, Robert 211
Alfini, James J. 372
Amstutz, M. xxv
Ansaldi, M. 32
Apel, Karl-Otto 211
Arbib, Michael A. 215, 221, 228
Aristotle 121, 211
Armstrong, David 355
Armstrong, Karen 192, 194
Ashe, M. 44
Ataturk, Mustafa Kemal 430–2
Atkinson, J. Maxwell 373
Aubert, Vilhelm 33, 209, 221, 227
Austin, John L. 4, 8, 40, 115, 116, 127, 131, 134, 135, 305

Badura, Peter 229
Baigent, Nicholas 274
Baker, L.A. 47
Balbus, I.D. 33
Balkin, Jack M. 43, 96–7, 98–9
Barnes, Barry 208, 221
Barnes, J.A. 350
Bartlett, K. 38
Barwise, Jon 212
Basu, Kaushik 269
Baudrillard, Jean 220
Baumann, Richard 362
Becher, T. 164
Becker, Gary 34
Bell, D. 40, 44, 161
Bell, J. xxix
Bender, L. 38
Benforado, A. xxii
Benhabib, Seyla xxxi
Bennett, L.W. 44
Bentham, Jeremy 127, 298
Bergel, J.-L. 198

Berger, Peter L. 208
Berlin, Isaiah 418
Berlusconi, Silvio 300, 303
Berman, H.J. xix
Berthelot, Jean-Michel xx, 170–2, 173, 176–8, 180, 183, 184, 186, 195, 199, 201
Bernstein, Lisa 257
Bey, Mahmout Es'ad 432
Bicchieria, Cristina 271, 272
Birks, Peter 191, 193
Black, C. 42
Black, Donald 33, 62, 63, 71, 86
Blackenberg, Ehrhard 288, 296
Blackstone, William 136
Blanché, Robert 190, 196
Bloch, Marc 452
Bloch, Maurice 374
Bloor, David 208, 221
Bobbitt, Philip 249
Bodenheimer, Edgar 9–10, 116
Bohannan, Paul 59, 77, 81
Böhler, Dietrich 211
Boorstin, Daniel 347
Bourdieu, Pierre xxiv, 33, 44–5, 220
Boyle, J. 45
Brandom, Robert xxvii
Bratman, Michael xxvii, 305, 306, 307, 308, 309, 312–15 *passim,* 316, 317, 318–9, 321–3, 325, 329, 330, 331
Brenneis, Donald 362, 368, 374, 381
Brennan, William 42
Brest, P. 42
Briggs, Charles L. 362, 368
Brigham, J. 46
Brint, M. 46
Brown, Penelope 365
Bruner, J. 43
Buchanan, J. 34, 35
Bumiller, K. 46

Cain, M. 31
Calabresi, Guido 35, 249
Calhoun, C. 33

Cardozo, B.N. 59
Carr, D. 43
Carroll, Lewis 205
Chambliss, W. 33
Charrow, Robert P. 372
Charrow, Veda R. 372
Chatterton, Thomas 205
Chiba, M. 423
Chomsky, Noam 363
Cicourel, Aaron V. 373
Clark, Robert C. 227
Coase, Ronald 34, 35, 156, 157, 160
Cohen, Felix 32, 57, 68, 221
Coleman, Jules xxvii, 33, 34, 35, 316–8, 424, 444
Colker, R. 39
Collier, R. 162
Collins, Harry 31, 208
Colson, E. 24–5
Conley, John M. 44, 362, 366, 372, 374, 375–82 *passim*, 383, 385–7, 388
Constable, M. 45
Coombe, Rosemary 45, 375
Cooter, Robert D. xxv, 35, 257, 263–4, 265
Cornell, D. 43
Cotterrell, Roger xvi, xvii, xxxii, 89–110, 126, 221, 225, 285, 422
Cover, Robert 43
Cownie, Fiona 162, 191, 194
Crapanzano, Vincent 368
Crenshaw, Kimberle 36, 39, 41, 375
Crozier, Michel 209
Cujas, Jacques 190

Dalton, C. 37, 38
Dan-Cohen, Meir 207
Danet, Brenda 373
Darwin, Charles 199
Davis, N.Z. 44
Davis, P. 38, 40
Deech, Ruth 158
Deggau, Hans-Georg 220
Delgado, Richard 40, 41, 44, 374
Del Mar, M. xxiii
Demsetz, H. 227
Derrida, J. 41, 43
Descartes, René 239
Devlin, Patrick 6, 118
Dezalay, Y. 422, 436
Di Paolo E. xxii
Dicey, A.V. 244

Domat, Jean 190
Douglass, Frederick 375
Douglas, Mary 217
Drew, Paul 373
Dreyfus, Hubert L. 213
Dudziak, Mary 166
Duguit, Leon 207
Duranti, Alessandro 374
Durkheim, Emile xi, 6, 18, 30, 31, 33, 67, 90, 103, 117, 118, 217, 355–6
Duxbury, N. 157
Dworkin, Ronald xxv, 6, 12–13, 38, 42, 112, 120–2, 124, 128, 139, 190, 192, 306, 308, 326, 332, 336, 353

Easterbrook, Frank 227
Eekelaar, J. 154
Ehrlich, Eugen xxvi, 33, 55-9, 60, 64, 66, 68, 69, 72, 73, 77, 79, 90
Eidheim, Harold 365
Eisenstein, Z. 43
Elkins, J. 44
Ellickson, Robert xxv–xxvi, 160
Elster, Jon 34, 209, 216
Elwork, Amiran 372
Ely, J.H. 42
Endicott, T. xxv
Errington, James Joseph 368
Eskridge, W.N. 36
Estrich, S. 38
Etchemendy, John 212
Etzioni, Amitai xxv, 216
Evan, W. 33
Evans-Pritchard, E.E. 22
Ewald, William 420
Ewick, P. 46

Fairclough, Norman 366
Fallers, Lloyd 21
Fama, Eugen F. 227
Farber, D.A. 35, 44, 47
Febbrajo, Alberto 209, 218
Feeley, M. xx
Feldman, Marta L. 44
Felstiner, William 33, 46, 373–4
Ferejohn, J. 36
Fineman, M.A. 38, 374
Finnis, John xxv, 119, 120, 121
Fish, S. 41, 42
Fiss, O. 42

Fitzpatrick, Peter 94
Fleck, Ludwig 217
Floud, Jean 117
Fodor, J.A. 218
Ford, John 192,
Förster, Heinz von 214, 215, 218
Fortes, M. 22
Foucault, Michel xxiv, 33, 44, 45, 207, 209, 210, 212–3, 214, 215, 216, 217, 220
Francis, C. 45
Frank, Jerome 32, 244
Frankenberg, Günter 219
Fried, Charles 356
Freud, Sigmund 27, 112
Frey, Reiner 211, 229
Frickey, P.P. 35
Friedberg, Erhard 209
Friedman, Lawrence 33, 285–6, 294, 297
Frohman, Lisa 375
Frug, M.J. 38
Fuller, Lon xxvi, 10
Fuller, Steve 208

Gadamer, Hans-Georg 351
Galanter, Marc xiv, 58, 69, 465
Gallie, W.B. 326
Garfinkel, Harold 373
Garland, D. 45
Garth, B. 422, 436
Geertz, C. 43
Geny, François 225
Giddens, Anthony 44–5, 209
Gierke, O.F. 31
Gilbert, Margaret xxvii, 319
Gilbert, Nigel 208
Ginsburg, R.B. 38
Ginzburg, C. 44
Giudice, M. xxv
Glasersfeld, Ernst von 215
Glenn H. Patrick 410, 421–2, 423, 435, 436
Goffman, Erving 442
Goldman, Laurence 374
Goldstein, L. 38
Gomm, R. 445
Goodhart, C.A.E. 164
Goodwin, Marjorie 373
Gordon, Robert 37, 160, 209, 210
Grace, C. 31
Granger, Gaston 173
Green, Edward J. 271

Greenhalgh, Trish 423–5, 427–9, 434–5, 436, 437, 439–40, 444, 445, 446
Greenhouse, C.J. 374
Grey, T.C. 46
Griffiths, John 464, 465–8
Gross, N.C. 424, 444
Grossberg, L. 36
Grünberger, Hans 219
Grzegorczyk, Christophe 219, 220
Guha, R. 44
Gumperz, John J. 362
Günther, Klaus 211, 459
Gur, N. xxiii
Gurvitch, G. 33

Habermas, Jürgen xxiv, 83, 84, 207, 210–12, 213, 214, 215, 216, 217, 469
Hagerstrand, T. 424
Hall, J. 33
Hamnett, Ian 58
Hanks, William F. 362, 368
Hanson, J. xxii
Harrington, C. 46
Harris, A.P. 36, 39
Harris, C. 40
Harris, J.W. 32
Hart, H.L.A. xi–xii, xviii, xxii, 3, 4, 5–7, 8, 9–10, 11–14, 15–28 *passim,* 53, 59–60, 76, 112–30 *passim,* 132–5 *passim,* 136–7, 138, 139, 141, 142–4, 146, 147–8, 152–3, 154, 161, 177, 257, 258–9, 263, 305, 306, 311, 325, 326, 336, 464
Hastie, R. 44
Hay, Douglas 347
Hayek, Friedrich von xxiv–xxv, 209, 237–450 *passim*
Heiner, Ronald 269
Heller, Thomas 220
Hertogh, Marc xxvi
Herzog, D. 37
Hesse, Mary B. 215, 221, 228
Himma, K. xiv
Hirsch, Susan F. 375
Hitchcock, Alfred 192
Hobbes, Thomas 27, 65, 71, 336
Hoebel, E. Adamson xv, 12, 22, 58–9, 64, 77, 81, 464
Hohfeld, W.N. 59, 127
Holmes, Oliver Wendell 32, 59, 64, 68, 111, 122, 127, 258

Homans, George C. 209
Honneth, Axel 213
Honoré, Tony 112, 126, 129–30, 132–5 *passim*, 136, 153
Horwitz, Morton 207
Hume, David 27
Humphreys, S.C. 43
Hunt, Alan 31, 32, 43, 45, 83–4
Huspek, Michael 366
Hutchins, Edwin 374
Hutchinson, A. 36
Hutter, Michael 206
Hymes, Dell H. 362

Ibbetson, David 150, 152
Irvine, Judith T. 362, 374

Jackson, Bernard xxix
Janowitz, Morris 71
Jefferson, Gail 373
Jennings, Ivor 244
Jensen, Michael 227
Jhering, Rudolf von 221, 225
Joerges, Christian 211
Johnson, A.M. 36, 40
Joseph, H.W.B. 114
Jutras D. xxvi

Kafka, Franz 357
Kahan, Marcel xxv, 264
Kahn-Freund, Otto 416–9 *passim*, 422
Kairys, D. 37
Kant, Immanuel 211
Kearns, T.R. 43
Kelley, Donald R. 29, 31, 173, 178, 180, 183, 189, 197, 452
Kelman, M. 37
Kelsen, Hans 4, 9, 91, 115, 116, 125, 127, 146, 177, 207, 244
Kennedy, Duncan 36, 37, 209
Kennedy, R. 38, 41
Kerchove, Michel van de 209, 218
Keynes, Lord John Maynard 8
King, Martin Luther 375
Kitschelt, Herbert 225
Klare, K. 36, 37
Knobe, Joshua 326
Knorr-Cetina, Karin 208
Knyphausen, Dodo zu 206
Kornhauser, Lewis A. xxv, 35, 112, 141, 255–77

Koschaker, Paul 414
Kötz, Hein 416
Krippendorff, Klaus 212
Kronman, A.T. 31
Krygier, Martin xi–xii, xv–xvi, xxvii–xxviii, xxix, 3–28, 335–60
Kübler, Friedrich 229
Kuhn, Thomas 172, 184
Kurylowicz, Jerzy 366, 368

Labov, William 362, 365
Lacey, Nicola xviii, xix, 111–48
Ladeur, Karl-Heinz 206, 211, 220, 225, 226
Lakoff, Robin 365
Lane, K.L. xxii
Langbein, John 137
Lasswell, Harold 97
Latour, Bruno 208, 442
Law, S. 38
Lawrence, C. 40
Leff, Arthur A. 35, 98
Legrand, Pierrre 172–3, 187, 188–9, 418, 420
Lempert, R.O. 33
Lerner, A. xx
Lessig, Lawrence xxv
Levinson, S. 41, 42
Lewis, David xxvii, 305, 306, 308, 312
Lind, E. Allan 372, 379, 386
Littleton, C. 38
Llewellyn, Karl 12, 22, 32, 59
Loftus, Elizabeth F. 372
Lopez, G. 40, 44
Lübbe-Wolff, Gertrude 226
Luckmann, Thomas 208
Lucy, John A. 362, 368
Luhmann, Niklas xvii, xxiv, 33, 44, 46, 65, 67, 70, 72–4, 82, 83, 84, 85, 98, 125, 160, 205, 206, 207, 210, 212, 214–6, 217, 220, 221, 224, 226, 435
Lukes, S. 31
Lyons, John 368

McAdams, Richard H. xxv, 257
McBarnet, Doreen 165
MacCormick, Neil 15, 23, 190
McCrudden, Christopher xix, xx, 149–68, 191, 193, 194
McDougal, Myres 97
Mackie, J.L. 27
MacKinnon, Catherine A. 38, 39

Maclean, M. 154
Maguire, Mike 289
Mahoney, M. 38, 44
Maine, H.S. 31, 414, 423
Maitland, Frederic William 346
Majone, Giandomenico 227, 229
Maleville, Jacques 198
Malinowski, Bronislaw 19, 55–9, 60, 64, 66, 67, 68, 69, 72, 73, 463–4, 466, 467
Marmor, Andrei xxvii
Marshall, Chief Justice John 219
Marx, Karl xi, 30, 31, 33, 37, 184
Mather, Lynn 46, 374
Mathews, Marilyn 365
Matsuda, Mari J. 39, 40–1, 44, 374, 375
Maturana, Huberto R. 214, 215
Maynard, Douglas W. 373
Mayntz, Renate 219
Meese, Edwin 42
Melamed, A.D. 35
Mengoni, Luigi 220, 223
Menkel-Meadow, C. 36, 38, 39
Merry, Sally E. 33, 46, 58, 362, 367, 374, 375–7 *passim*, 382–8 *passim*, 465
Merton, Robert K. 205
Mertz, Elizabeth xxi, xxix, 33, 361–93
Miller, J.C. 33
Minow, Martha 38, 39, 46, 374
Mnookin, R. 35
Molotch, Harvey L. 442
Montesquieu, C. 31, 417
Moore, Michael 143
Moore, Sally Falk 57, 58, 79, 464, 466–7, 468
Mulkay, Michael 208
Murphy, W.T. 153
Myers, Fred R. 374

Nader, Laura 11, 14
Nedelsky, J. 39
Nelken, David xvii, xx, xxvi, 92, 95, 97, 100, 106, 279–303, 420, 422
Nelson, Alan 209
Nerhot, Patrick 220
North, Douglass 159
Nozick, R. 243

Oakeshott, Michael 345
O'Barr, William M. 44, 362, 366, 372, 374, 375–82 *passim*, 383, 385–7, 388
Ogus, A.I. xxiv–xxv, 237–53

Olsen, F. 38
Onazi, O. xxiii
Opp, Karl-Dieter 222
Örücü, Esin 410, 416, 419–21 *passim*, 422, 430
Ost, François 209, 218, 219

Parmentier, Richard J. 362, 368,
Parsons, Talcott 3, 32, 67, 118
Pashukanis, E. 33
Patterson, D. 43
Pawson, R. 445
Peirce, Charles Sanders 362, 363–4
Peller, G. 40, 43, 45
Pennington, N. 44
Peters, E.L. 22
Petrazycki, Leon 90
Piaget, Jean 215
Pistor, K. 422, 436
Pizzorno, Alessandro 207, 219
Podak, Klaus 219
Polinsky, A.M. 35
Pomerantz, Anita 373
Popper, Karl 175, 209, 355
Porter, Robert H. 271
Posner, E. xxv, 257
Posner, Richard A. 34, 158
Post, R.C. 33
Postema, Gerald J. xii, xxvii, 358
Pothier, Robert Joseph 190
Poulantzas, Nicos 83
Pound, Dean Roscoe 32, 62, 64, 68, 154, 225
Preuss, Ulrich K. 211
Prins, H. 227

Quay, Lorene C. 365
Quine, Willard V. 212

Rabinow, Paul 213
Radin, M.J. 47
Rasmusen, Eric 269
Ratnapala, S. xxv
Rawls, John 353
Raz, Joseph xxii, xxiii, 6, 14, 121, 123, 147, 257, 259–61, 263, 264, 270, 307, 308, 310
Reagan, Ronald 42
Resnais, Alain 192
Revesz, Richard L. 268
Rhode, D. 36
Riesman, David 11
Riles, Annelise 172

Roberts, Simon xvi, xxxii, 61, 125
Robson, R. 38, 39
Robson, W.A. 244
Rodogno, R. xxii
Rogers, Everett 423–7, 428–9, 431, 433–5, 436, 437, 439–41, 442, 444, 446
Roos, Carl Martin 207, 227
Rose-Ackerman, S. 35
Rosen, Lawrence 374
Ross, Hamish 125
Roth, Gerhard 215
Rottleuthner, Hubert 219, 221, 227
Rubin, E. 36, 158
Rudden, Bernard 345
Rumble, W.E. 32
Ryan, B. 424, 444

Sacco, Rodolfo xxx, 395–407, 410, 420
Sachs, Jessica Snyder 442
Sacks, Harvey 373
Sales, Bruce Dennis 372
Samek, Robert 93
Samuel, Geoffrey xx, 169–202, 420
Samuelson, Paul 164
Sanders, J. 33
Santos, Boaventura de Sousa xxxi, 43
Sarat, Austin 33, 43, 46, 373–4
Saussure, Ferdinand de 362, 363–4
Savigny, F.K. 31, 77, 190
Scales, A.C. 39
Scales-Trent, J. 40, 44
Schanck, P.C. 43
Schane, Sanford A. 207
Schanze, Erich 227
Schauer, F. xvi, 42
Schegloff, Emanuel A. 373
Scheppele, Kim Lane xiii–xiv, 29–52
Schimank, Uwe 219
Schlag, P. 43
Schmidt, Siegfried 215
Schultz, V. 38
Schwartz, R.D. 33
Schwarzmueller, Beth 365
Schwindel, Hermann von 205
Scott, Robert 205
Scull, A. 31
Searle, John xxvii
Seidman, R. 33
Selznick, Philip xxi, xxxii, 33, 62, 217
Shakespeare, William 351

Shapiro, Scott xxvii, 305
Shavell, S. 35
Sherry, S. 44
Sherwin, R. 44
Shils, Edward xxiv
Siegel, R. 38
Silbey, S. 33, 46
Silverstein, Michael 362, 365, 366, 368, 369, 372
Simmel, Georg 33
Simon, J. 33, 45
Simoson, O.J. 85
Singer, J. 37
Sirk, Douglas 192
Skinner, Quentin 205
Smith, Matthew Noah xxvi–xxvii, 305–332
Smith, S.D. 47
Soskice, David 161
Spellman, E.V. 39, 46
Stalin, Joseph 26, 358
Starr, June 432
Stefancic, J. 41
Stephen, J.F. 136
Stone, Julius 350
Sunstein, C.R. xxv, 42
Supiot, A. xxxi
Susskind, Richard 190
Sutherland, Edwin H. 141–2
Szacki, Jerzy 353, 354, 359

Tamanaha, Brian Z. xiii, xiv, xv–xvi, xxvi, xxx, xxxii, 53–87, 115, 125, 447–83
Tannen, Deborah 365
Tarde, Gabriel 414, 423, 444
Tarski, Alfred 211
Teubner, Gunther xxiv, 46, 125, 160, 205–35, 422, 423, 435, 459
Thomas, K. 43
Thomas, Yan 185
Thompson, E.P. 33
Tilley, N. 445
Timasheff, N.S. 33
Torres, G. 36
Tronto, J. 31
Trubek, D. 36
Tullock, G. 34, 35
Tuomela, Raimo 319
Tushnet, M. 37, 41, 44
Twining, William xxxi, 4–5, 125, 191, 409–46

Ulen, T. 35

Ullman, Walter 178, 450
Ullmann-Margalit, Edna 357
Unger, Roberto M. 36, 123

Van den Broeck, Jef 365
van Zandt, D. 33
Vardaro, Gaetano 206
Varela, Francisco J. 214, 215, 218
Veitch, Scott xxi–xxii

Wacquant, L. 45
Waldron, Jeremy 326
Watson, Alan 187, 188, 410, 416–9 *passim*, 422, 436, 441, 443
Weaver, W. 46
Weber, Max xiii, 19, 30, 31, 32, 37, 58–9, 84, 90, 104, 117, 184, 206, 209, 211, 296, 354, 359, 414, 423, 464
Wechsler, H. 42, 129
Weinberg, Alvin M. 227
Weingast, B. 36
Weintraub, E. Roy 209
Weisberg, D.K. 38
West, Candace 365
West, R. 39, 44
Wellons, P.A. 422, 436
White, James Boyd 43, 370
White, L. 38, 44
Whitehead, Alfred North 355

Whitman, James Q. 30, 439
Whittington, Harry 320
Wieacker, F. 414–5, 417, 422, 433, 436, 443
Wiethölter, Rudolf 211, 229
Wigmore, John Henry 172
Wilkinson, P. 31
Williams, Glanville 136
Williams, Patricia J. 44, 374
Williams, W. 39, 40, 41
Williamson, Oliver 35, 159, 227
Willock, I.D. 4
Windscheid, Bernhard 222
Winter, Gert 225, 228
Wittgenstein, Ludwig 131, 134, 135, 336
Wolf, Rainer 225
Woodman, Gordon 465
Woolard, Kathryn A. 362
Woolgar, Steve 208
Wormell, C.P. 212

Yngvesson, Barbara 33, 46, 374

Zimmerman, Don 365
Zimmerman, R. 415
Zweigert, Konrad 416

Agobard of Lyons 450
Azo of Bologna 452
William of Ockham 184